Office

by PAUL WILLIAMSON, M.D.

Procedures

W. B. SAUNDERS COMPANY   PHILADELPHIA — LONDON

PREFACE

We doctors are often assumed to know how to do all minor office procedures but we frequently find that these assumptions are wrong. In my own practice I have a constant need for a reference encompassing instructions on this office work. Over a period of years I have compiled a series of notes freely lifted from other authors and from the experience of brother physicians as well as from my own work. It is from these notes that this book stems.

Only the most frequently used procedures are included. Frequency has been determined by a survey of our own clinical records and the records of two colleagues.

You will notice a profusion of references to hairpins, paper clips and other such instruments throughout these pages. It is, of course, better to use the instruments designed for a specific job rather than homemade equipment, but so very many times the particular instrument is not available at the moment needed. On this assumption I have described the use of material at hand to do the job. This is not a plea for frugality in equipping an office. It is a description of practical usage of readily available objects to complete an examination and treatment.

The illustrations were conceived to be as simple and explicit as possible, actually becoming a part of the text. I wish to express my appreciation for the cooperative efforts of the artists who made the drawings: Elinor Bodian, Robert Demarest, Edna Hill, Alice Mansueti, Patricia O'Neill, William Osburn, and Robert Smith.

For the sake of directness I have listed the drugs I use by their trade name. This does not necessarily constitute a recommendation to the exclusion of others, for there are many good drugs.

I wish to express my appreciation to the J. B. Lippincott Company, publishers of The *American Practitioner and Digest of Treatment,* for permission to use some of the material on cancer of the cervix which first appeared in that journal.

It is my sincere wish that you will find this volume helpful in day-to-day practice.

PAUL WILLIAMSON, M.D.

CONTENTS

Section I

EAR, NOSE AND THROAT

The Ear

EXAMINATION

Inspection through the otoscope serves to give much information about the ear and its pathology. There are only a few accessory tests that are useful to the practitioner. They are:

Test for Mobility of the Drum with the Siegle Pneumatic Otoscope

This instrument is used to alter pneumatic pressure within the external canal while visualizing the drum. The comfort of the patient is enhanced by slipping a short (⅜-inch) piece of rubber tubing over the barrel like this:

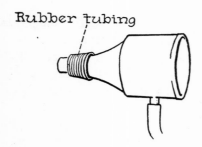

Rubber tubing

The scope is then inserted and the bulb alternately squeezed and released while watching the drum. The test is little used but occasionally is of value.

Hearing Tests

In the absence of an audiometer, only a crude estimate of hearing may be obtained. Seated about a yard from the patient, the examiner checks voice perception.

The following chart may be applied:

Voice heard	Hearing loss not over:	
Faint whisper	30 decibels	
Low voice	45 decibels	moderate
Normal voice	60 decibels	deafness
Loud voice	75 decibels	severe
Shout	90 decibels	deafness

The practitioner should use care not to confuse the "garbling" of sounds and consequent misunderstanding with inability to hear sounds. Loss of interpretative acuity with only minor loss of whole sound perception may occur in diseases that alter function of the movable structures of the ear. Just because a patient can hear sounds does not mean adequate aural function. If any doubt exists, audiometric studies are in order. There is no other way to get an accurate test.

Determining Type of Deafness

Both the Weber and the Rinne test are only partially accurate. They do, however, give enough information to be a part of the practitioner's armamentarium. The only instrument needed is a tuning fork.

Rinne's Test. The tuning fork is struck sharply and the base pressed firmly against the mastoid bone, like this:

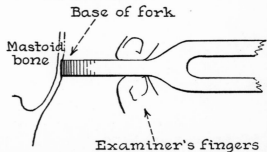

Base of fork

Mastoid bone

Examiner's fingers

When the patient no longer hears it the fork is removed and the tines placed close to the external auditory meatus. If there is question, the procedure is reversed, air conduction being first tested and then bone conduction. If the tone be heard longest through bone, this is evidence of conduction deafness. When both bone and air conduction are shortened, either perception deafness or mixed deafness is probably present. Normally, air conduction is more acute.

Weber's Test. The fork is struck a sharp blow and placed firmly against the vertex or forehead. In unilateral conduction deafness the tone will be heard best in the diseased ear. With unilateral perception deafness the sound is heard in the good ear. Unfortunately not all deafness is conveniently unilateral.

The labyrinthine tests are seldom performed by the practitioner.

OTHEMATOMA

The only danger from the hematoma is infection with consequent cartilaginous degeneration and permanent deformity. Asepsis must be exacting. A skin wheal is made with 1 per cent procaine over the most prominent part of the swelling. Then a large-bore needle is inserted, bevel down, into the hematoma, and aspiration is performed. The procedure may need to be repeated several times. One must avoid trauma to the cartilage by the needle. Bandage like this:

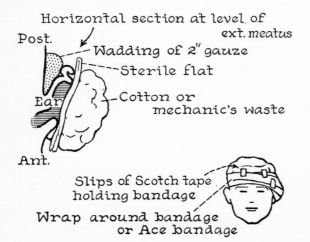

FURUNCLE OF THE EXTERNAL CANAL

The first office procedure is packing the canal with a ½-inch strip of gauze which has been soaked in alcohol. Avoid touching the swelling with the forceps if at all possible. When the furuncle has pointed give the patient a few whiffs of trichloroethylene through the Duke inhaler (or another general anesthetic) and nick the yellow area with a sharp scalpel, like this:

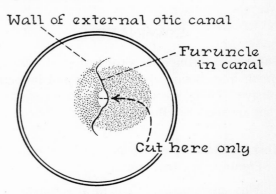

Remove the drainage with suction and repack the canal.

OTOMYCOSIS

There are several useful diagnostic procedures. Gently remove some of the material in the canal and place it on a glass slide without crushing. Look at it through the loupe or hand lens. The "dense forest" appearance of fungus elements is characteristic. Then spread a small portion of the material in a drop of 10 per cent potassium hydroxide and examine under the low-power lens of the microscope. This is a typical field:

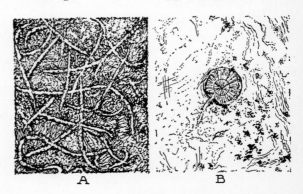

Now secure more debris from the canal and smear it on a culture plate of Sabouraud's medium. Incubation is not necessary. The fungus should grow out well in 6 to 8 days at room temperature.

IMPACTED CERUMEN

If movable this may be easily removed with a small ring curet which may be purchased or made from material at hand. If not movable, resort should be had to syringing. In cases where an opening exists between the cerumen and the canal wall, direct the stream from the irrigating instrument toward (or through) the opening, like this:

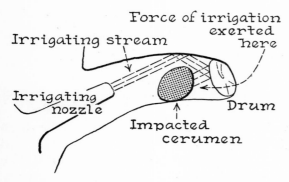

If no opening exists, attack the periphery of the mass by directing a forceful stream of water at 95° to 100° F. against it. Persistent syringing will remove most cerumen. Stubborn masses may be broken up by use of the ring curet. When this is impossible without causing the patient pain, instill several drops of hydrogen peroxide and try again in 15 minutes.

It is occasionally wise to order instillations to soften the mass and wait several days before final removal.

FOREIGN BODIES

Bugs are frequent foreign bodies which may cause exquisite pain by their motion against the drum. They should be killed by filling the canal with mineral oil, olive oil or Cresatin.

Dry bodies that absorb water swell and completely occlude the canal. Often they must be attacked with the knife for removal. This usually necessitates general anesthesia.

Most foreign bodies may be removed by syringing. Direct the stream of solution (at body temperature) over the extraneous mass so that it is pushed out from behind, as shown above in syringing of impacted cerumen. An ear hook may be made from a bit of wire and used to pull the foreign body out, like this:

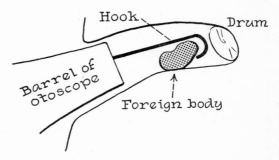

In manipulating within the canal, be sure not to touch the drum.

EUSTACHIAN SALPINGITIS

Catheterization of the auditory tube is the only important office procedure in this disease. Do it like this: Anesthetize the inferior meatus by spraying and by packing with cotton pledgets soaked in Pontocaine-ephedrine solution. Wait 10 minutes. Remove the pledgets and pass a cotton-tipped applicator soaked in anesthetic back to the eustachian orifice. Then insert the catheter with the beak pointing downward and sliding along the floor of the nose, like this:

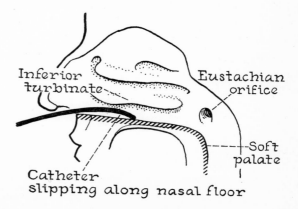

You will feel the beak slide downward over the surface of the soft palate, like this:

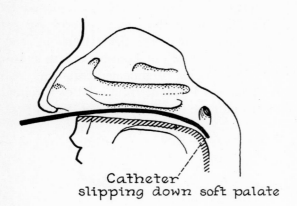

Catheter
slipping down soft palate

Now rotate the catheter laterally until the beak points outward and a little upward. At this time it will probably be just behind the eustachian orifice. Gently pull it out until you feel the beak slip over a little ridge into a pit. This is the eustachian orifice. Now make gentle pressure through the catheter with a hand bulb. If the tube is properly located the patient will verify the entrance of air into the ear.

OTITIS MEDIA

In spite of the antibiotics, myringotomy is still frequently performed. It is a simple operation if the physician keeps in mind certain principles. Proceed like this:

Only in a rare case can adequate myringotomy be done under local anesthesia. A short general anesthetic is always the surest way of allowing adequate work time and proper immobilization.

Clean the external canal with alcohol and cotton and visualize the landmarks on the drum, which looks like this:

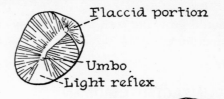

Flaccid portion
Umbo
Light reflex

Normal drum

Handle
of malleus
poorly seen
No
light reflex
Bulging drum

Begin the incision in the lower portion of the anterior inferior quadrant, here:

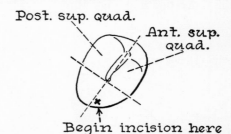

Post. sup. quad.
Ant. sup. quad.

Begin incision here

and carry it around the margin of the drum through the posterior inferior quadrant and just into the posterior superior quadrant, like this:

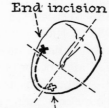

End incision

Start incision

Use only the tip of the knife, for deep insertion may be disastrous. Remember the slope of the drum is more pronounced in children. The normal drum faces slightly downward and forward.

Nose and Sinuses

EXAMINATION

The instruments and solutions needed for this procedure are:

1. Head mirror
2. Nasal speculum
3. Bayonet forceps
4. Atomizer with 2 per cent Pontocaine in 2 per cent ephedrine solution
5. Cotton dispenser
6. Flexible probe
7. Pontocaine solution, 2 per cent
8. Ephedrine solution, 3 per cent
9. Trichloracetic acid solution, 50 per cent (for treatment)
10. Suction pump (a pump to attach to a water faucet may be purchased for about $2.50)
11. Suction tip with finger-hole control
12. If much nasal work is done, a nasopharyngoscope is useful. A chair with head-rest is helpful, as are an operator's stool and a gooseneck floor lamp.

Begin the examination by inspection and, if needful, palpation of the external nose. Any pathologic condition will be apparent. Then focus a spot of light from the head mirror onto the tip of the nose. Insert the closed nasal speculum with the body of the instrument held along a horizontal axis in your left hand. The closed blades should enter the nose like this:

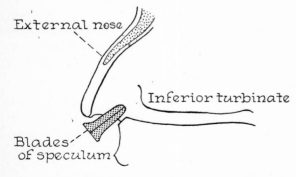

Open the blades gently and observe the floor of the nose, like this:

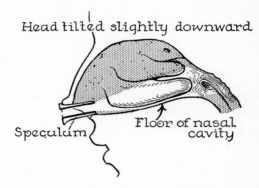

By having the patient tilt his head backward, examine the mid-portion and then the anterior portions of the nose, like this:

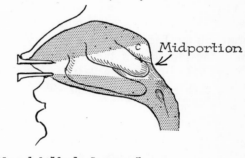

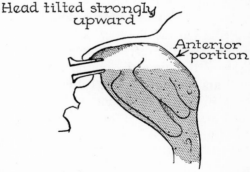

In the use of the speculum allow the blades to close when the patient changes position and be sure not to stretch the nostril when the blades are opened. This is painful. Proper use of the speculum should be entirely without discomfort.

When the mucous membrane evinces edema, you will be able to see only a short way into the nose with the technique illustrated. In this case, spray the nose with Pontocaine-ephedrine solution and wait several minutes. If you still cannot see, take a strip of cotton about this size,

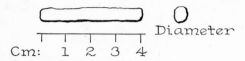

moisten it with 2 per cent ephedrine and place it against the edematous area, using the bayonet forceps. Grasp the moist cotton thus,

and push it *gently* into place. Leave it there for 4 to 5 minutes.

After adequate vision is established, examine the mucosa thoroughly. Palpate with the blunt probe where necessary. Be sure to visualize Kiesselbach's area, which lies on the septum about 1 cm. above and very slightly behind the junction of the septum membrane with the skin of the face. It is occasionally necessary to rotate the patient slightly to see this area clearly.

To use the nasopharyngoscope, it is necessary to anesthetize and shrink the mucosa of the floor and lower walls of the cavity. This can be done by moistening a double-size cotton pledget in the Pontocaine-ephedrine solution and inserting for 5 minutes. At the conclusion of this time the cotton should be removed and the instrument (after having been dipped in water at about 110° F.) gently slipped along the nasal floor.

Next turn to posterior rhinoscopy, using a 1 cm. mirror which has been dipped in hot water (to prevent fogging) and dried. Ask the patient to open his mouth but to continue breathing through his nose. Now gently depress the tongue and insert the mirror into the oropharynx to one side of the uvula. Prop the handle of the mirror on the tongue depressor to aid in keeping it steady and be sure not to touch the palate or pharyngeal wall. Then repeat the maneuver on the other side of the uvula. Pay particular attention to the eustachian orifices and surrounding tissue.

Careful attention to this examination routine will result in demonstration of about 95 per cent of the pathologic conditions encountered in the nasal cavities. Below are described the most commonly used procedures for additional diagnosis and treatment.

FRACTURE

Recent nasal fractures are simply diagnosed by palpation. When edema and hemorrhage have obscured the external anatomy proceed as follows: First, remember that most nasal fractures are compound into the nasal cavity. Avoid introducing more contamination.

Remove the clots by suction and stop bleeding by placing cotton strips dipped in 1:10,000 epinephrine. (For an approximate solution put 6 drops of 1:1000 epinephrine in 4 cc. of normal saline.) Leave these packs in place 10 minutes or longer. Remove and replace with packs moistened in Pontocaine-ephedrine solution. Leave these in place 15 minutes. This will render the membrane anesthetic and materially aid reduction.

Now break from a tongue blade a strip about ¼ inch wide and slip over it a piece of rubber tubing, like this:

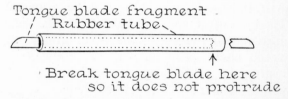

If no tubing is available, wrap the fragment of tongue blade with adhesive tape and dip in antiseptic solution. Push the fragments into apposition by inserting the lever into the nasal cavity and pressing the bones into position, aided by counterpressure from the fingers on the outside of the nose.

Occasionally it is necessary to use two such levers, one in each nasal cavity. *Be sure* to straighten the septum when it has been thrown out of alignment.

Pack the anterior area immediately around the fracture with petrolatum gauze and leave over night. Splints of any kind are rarely necessary except in excessively comminuted fractures. Even in these, adequate intranasal packing will serve for control in most instances.

See these patients daily and remove excessive crusting or discharge with suction or forceps. Do not leave a pack in place over 48 hours—24 is preferable.

FISSURE OF THE NASAL VESTIBULE

If this persists after a cold or infection, anesthetize by packing with Pontocaine and cauterize with a very weak coagulating current.

FURUNCLE

This is mentioned only to warn against mechanical procedures. If the lesion has "come to a head" the yellow area *ONLY* may be nicked with a scalpel. The best practice is to use hot packs, antibiotics, and *let it alone*.

CHRONIC RHINITIS

Much relief can be obtained by shrinking the mucosa of the inferior turbinate with cautery. Trichloracetic acid is a satisfactory chemical. Do it this way:

Put a teaspoonful of sodium bicarbonate in a medicine glass and add ½ ounce of water. Place several cotton applicators in this solution. Then anesthetize the mucosa by insertion of cotton strips moistened in Pontocaine solution. Leave these in place for 15 minutes.

Remove the pledgets and dry the turbinate by insertion of dry cotton plugs. When these have been removed, dip an applicator stick without cotton in 50 per cent trichloracetic acid and draw two white lines on the inferior turbinate, like this:

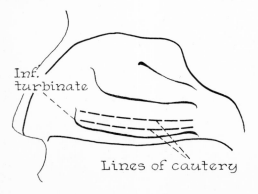

It will be necessary to dip the stick several times to complete the lines. Excessive action of the chemical can be stopped by applying the sodium bicarbonate solution.

NASAL POLYPS

Removal of one or two polyps is a simple procedure but when there are a great many the case is best referred. Polyps are insensitive and do not bleed easily upon being touched by the probe. Morrison has offered the best description, saying they look like the pulp of a skinned white grape.

To remove, anesthetize the pedicle by inserting a cotton pledget which has been moistened with Pontocaine-ephedrine solution. Place the open end of the nasal snare against the free end of the polyp, like this:

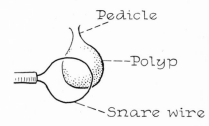

Now, seize the polyp with forceps through the circle of the snare, like this:

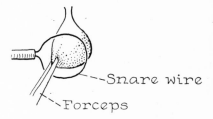

While holding the polyp with the forceps, work the snare upward toward the pedicle as far as possible. If you wish to try to prevent bleeding, tighten the snare without cutting and hold for a few moments. (I question whether there is any great advantage.) Then, close the snare to snip off the polyp and remove it by traction on the forceps.

Polyps frequently recur unless the nasal allergy which usually accompanies them can be controlled.

FOREIGN BODIES

These are seen most frequently in children and are diagnosed by direct vision after suspicion has been aroused by unilateral, foul discharge, usually bloody.

After ascertaining the position of the foreign body, fashion a hook from a paper clip, like this:

Make the hook end to fit the size of the foreign body. Now try to dislodge it with pulling and gentle pressure. If not successful, it may be necessary to give a short general anesthetic in small children.

When the patient is anesthetized slip a previously prepared postnasal plug in place to prevent aspiration and try again to remove the extraneous material. If still not successful, it is usually necessary to bisect the foreign body with scissors and remove half at a time. If cutting is unsuccessful, try crushing with heavy forceps.

Tissue in contact with the foreign body becomes edematous. Removal often may be facilitated by placing a drop or two of 2 per cent ephedrine solution in the nostril and by packing the "removal tract" with a cotton pledget soaked in 2 per cent ephedrine. This should be left in place for at least 5 minutes.

Only rarely is a foreign body so tenacious that referral is necessary.

EPISTAXIS

Most nosebleeds are trivial in extent. Rarely we see an exsanguinating hemorrhage from the nose. There must be cases which cannot be controlled by the practitioner but I have been fortunate enough never to have seen one. Begin treatment by cleansing clots from the nose by suction and, if necessary, irrigation with a small rubber ear and ulcer syringe.

Look first for bleeding from Kiesselbach's area, which is on the septum about here:

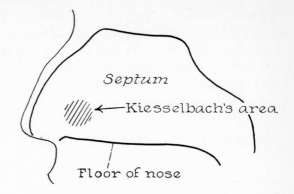

If the bleeding point is not here, examine the ends of the inferior and middle turbinates. If the area still is not seen, shrink the entire nasal cavity with a spray and pledgets soaked in Pontocaine-ephedrine solution and look again.

When the bleeding point is seen, place a Pontocaine-ephedrine pledget firmly against it and hold for several minutes. Then dry the area and cauterize with 50 per cent trichloracetic acid. If the bleeding is anterior a piece of fat salt pork may be cut to fit the cavity and inserted. It will absorb moisture and swell to press on the bleeding point. Commercial intranasal tampons do not work as well as pork but are less expensive and more dignified.

If the bleeding point is not readily accessible, the nasal cavity may be packed with oxidized cellulose (Hemopak). Properly packing a nose is more trying than difficult. Do it this way:

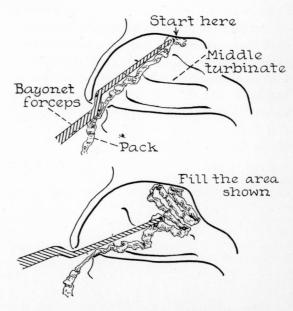

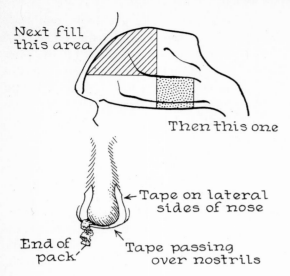

Next fill this area

Then this one

Tape on lateral sides of nose

End of pack

Tape passing over nostrils

If the pack shows a tendency to come out either put a cork of proper size in the nostril or affix a piece of cellophane tape as shown. Do not use tape unless both nostrils are otherwise occluded.

Should bleeding still continue, both anterior and posterior packs may be used but hemorrhage severe enough to demand this is more properly dealt with in the hospital.

SINUS DISEASE

Approach the patient who says he has "sinus trouble" with sincere doubt. Tension headaches can well mimic the pain which the average man believes typical of sinus disease. Confronted with such a case, proceed as follows:

1. Attempt to discern by history which of the three common types of sinus disease is present. These types, in order of frequency (as seen in a rural practice) are: (a) "Air lock" sinus pain.* Here the swollen mucous membrane simply blocks the sinus opening and pressure changes cause pain; (b) infectious sinusitis; (c) allergic sinusitis.

* The concept of aerosinusitis is not new but the condition has often been thought to be peculiar to aviators or to those subjected to frequent change in atmospheric pressure. This seems to be not necessarily true. Any irritation of nasal membranes may cause edema with resultant closure of sinus ostia and absorption of contained air. This is a frequent happening.

2. If there is any history of allergy, take a nasal smear and stain with Wright's or Giemsa's stain (Wright's is quicker, Giemsa's more versatile and more likely to give a good stain). Examine for eosinophils. If more than an occasional such cell is seen, further exploration of the possibility of allergy is in order.

3. Now, clear excess secretion from the nose with suction and spray with Pontocaine-ephedrine solution.

4. While waiting for shrinkage, transilluminate the maxillary and frontal sinuses like this:

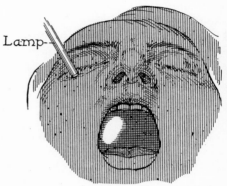

Lamp

Transillumination of the maxillary sinus. The slender lamp is inserted over margin of inferior opening of orbit in its outer third and pointing inward and slightly backward.

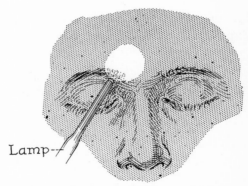

Lamp

Transillumination of the frontal sinuses. The lamp is applied against floor of frontal sinus well within site of supra-orbital notch and pointed upward, inward and backward.

5. With infectious sinusitis there tends to be some increased pressure extending to nerve canals running in the walls of the sinuses. These nerves will be tender to mild digital pressure where they emerge from the bone.

Press here:

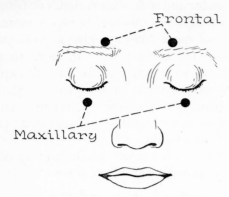

Pressure may be made on the anterior ethmoid cells by putting a finger on either side of the bridge of the nose and exerting force backward and inward. The floor of the frontal sinus may be palpated here:

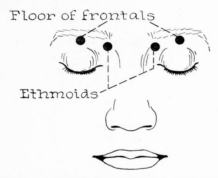

and will be exquisitely tender in acute disease. The antral wall may be palpated here:

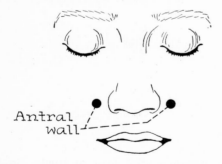

6. Now re-examine the nasal cavities, which should show maximal shrinking of the membranes. Remove any secretion and watch for its reappearance. If pus appears above the middle turbinate, the posterior ethmoid cells or the sphenoidal sinus is infected. If below the turbinate, the anterior ethmoids, frontals, or maxillaries are infected.

7. If necessary—and it seldom will be—take an x-ray of the sinuses. The P-A (posteroanterior) view is easiest for the practitioner to read. This is taken straight P-A with the nose and chin touching the cassette. This diagram from Morrison, *Diseases of the Nose, Throat and Ear,* is helpful in interpretation:

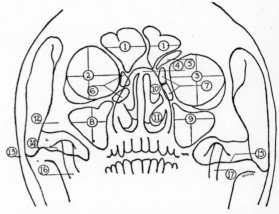

Structures seen in the radiograph of the sinuses in the Waters Position.
(1) Outlines of right and left frontal sinuses.
(2) Outline of right orbital cavity.
(3) Outline of left orbital cavity.
(4) Roof of nose.
(5) Supra-orbital ethmoid cell on left side.
(6) Right ethmoid cells.
(7) Left ethmoid cells.
(8) Outline of right maxillary sinus.
(9) Outline of left maxillary sinus.
(10) Left middle turbinate.
(11) Left inferior turbinate.
(12) Right malar bone.
(13) Outline of outer table of skull.
(14) Upper surface of petrous portion of right temporal bone.
(15) Upper surface of petrous portions of left temporal bone.
(16) Right ramus of mandible.
(17) Left ramus of mandible.
(Morrison: Diseases of the Nose, Throat and Ear).

Most disease of the nasal accessory sinuses can be diagnosed by following meticulously these procedures and extending them when necessary. Specific disease and the office procedures most frequently useful are listed below.

Acute Sinus Infection

The acute sinus infection offers pain of maddening intensity and persistence. There are five basic procedures in treatment of acute sinusitis which should be in the armamentarium of every practitioner.

Shrinkage of the Mucous Membrane. This is achieved by the insertion of cotton pledgets moistened in 3 per cent ephedrine. Frequently the Pontocaine-ephedrine solution can be used effectively. One must be certain of an adequate knowledge of the anatomy involved before good results can be predicted. The frontal and ethmoid openings are on the lateral wall of the nose underneath the middle turbinate. With the turbinates in place, the lateral wall looks like this:

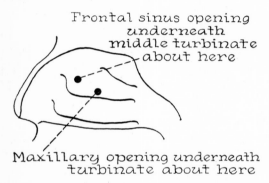

When the middle turbinate is removed, the openings are like this:

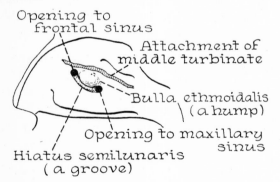

Unless the pledgets are inserted in the immediate area of these openings, little will be gained. It may be impossible to reach the proper place with the first application. An occasional case will require repeated insertion of fresh pledgets for as much as an hour to be effective. Moderately free drainage of pus, frequently admixed with blood, is the criterion of success.

Suction Drainage. This is of definite benefit unless too strong suction is applied. Too much negative pressure is the most frequent error and results in increased congestion of membranes with worsening of symptoms. The procedure can be done with the water suction apparatus mentioned in the section on examination. A glass nasal tip is attached to the apparatus.

A rough estimation of the negative pressure may be gained by holding the suction tip firmly against the operator's cheek. If a definite sensation of "pinching" occurs the suction is too great and the water should be turned down.

When proper adjustment is gained the glass tip is inserted in one nostril and the other nostril is held shut by the fingers of the operator. No suction can be applied until the posterior nasopharynx is shut. This is achieved by asking the patient to say the letter "K" several times.

Negative pressure techniques should not be used for protracted periods. Sinus drainage may usually be accomplished with four or five applications of suction, and solutions will enter the sinuses with four or five more.

Medication may be made to enter the sinus cavities by positioning the head so that the medicated solution will pool about the sinus openings and then applying gentle suction (see next section). Suction should not be applied more often than twice daily, and for only a few seconds at a time.

Proetz and Parkinson Techniques. These are best illustrated in simple drawings. The following are from Morrison, *Diseases of the Nose, Throat and Ear*.

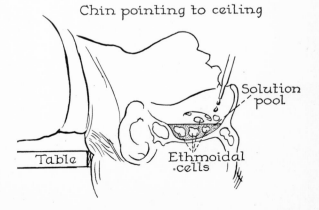

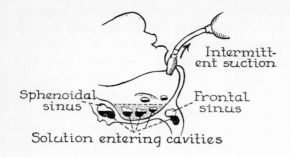

Head-low-and-lateral position
(Parkinson technic)

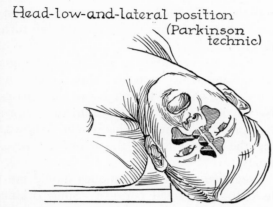

Solution in nasal sinuses and cells
following intermittent suction

Proetz technique is best for posterior ethmoid and sphenoid sinuses; the Parkinson method for frontal and maxillary disease.

One pitfall trips half the patients who try the technique on their own, and a surprisingly large number of physicians as well. It is in the instillation, which often misses entirely the area which it is designed to attack owing to use of too small an amount and poor placement.

With the nose inverted, drops are often instilled like this:

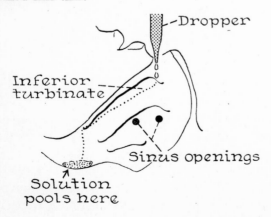

The solution strikes the inferior turbinate and is guided backward by it. A surprisingly large amount of solution can be trapped by this turbinate and never reach the area where it can be effective. Do it like this:

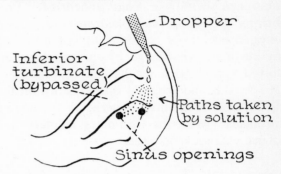

Maxillary Irrigation. This should be done through the natural opening if at all possible. Try it first by anesthetizing with Pontocaine-ephedrine solution the area under the middle turbinate. Let the pledget stay in place at least 15 minutes, and preferably longer.

Slip the cannula under the middle turbinate with its tip pointing outward and slightly downward. The hiatus semilunaris is easily traced, for the point of the cannula is held in the groove by its walls unless excess pressure is exerted. The normal maxillary opening is at the very posterior end of the hiatus, like this:

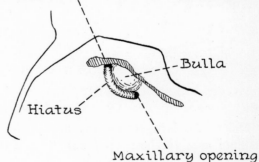

The tip of the cannula can be felt to enter the orifice and should be gently forced further in by pressing the tip outward and downward. Irrigation fluid should be warm normal saline.

Cannulization of the other sinuses is difficult and seldom within the range of the practitioner. Fortunately such procedures are rarely needed. Antral puncture is relatively easy but seldom used since the advent of the antibiotics.

Diathermy. Gratifying relief can be obtained from application of diathermy. There are no special techniques of note and the physician should follow instructions for sinus application which are furnished with each machine. Several companies make special sinus applicators and I have found these useful though by no means indispensable.

Chronic Sinusitis

Office diagnosis and treatment of this annoying disease offers excellent hope of relief and a good percentage of cures. Nasal obstruction and postnasal drips are important symptoms. Diagnostic procedure is not different from that in the acute disease with the exception that the smear should be studied for lymphocytes (which will be found to make up from 25 to 50 per cent of the recognizable cells) as well as for eosinophils.

An x-ray should be taken routinely. Notice (*a*) size of sinuses, (*b*) degree of opacity, (*c*) outlines of the mucous membrane, if visible, and (*d*) changes in the bony walls.

Office treatments should be given frequently and should consist of the following steps:

1. Shrink the mucous membranes and put a pledget of cotton dipped in ephedrine solution as nearly in apposition to the sinus openings as possible.

2. Use gentle suction to aid in removing secretion.

3. Instill some ephedrine solution into the sinuses using Proetz and/or Parkinson techniques.

4. If allergy is suspected, follow the instructions given in the section on allergy.

Mouth and Throat

EXAMINATION

Material necessary for adequate examination of the pharynx is as follows:

1. Head mirror
2. Tongue blades
3. Laryngeal mirror
4. Glove or finger cot
5. Slides and cotton-tipped applicators
6. Paper clips
7. Pontocaine solution, 2 per cent.

Begin by having the patient extend his tongue for examination. Much information about systemic disease can be gained from this inspection. Next, notice the gum margins and take a smear if any infectious process seems present. Pull the cheek aside with a tongue blade and inspect the molars and posterior gums.

If you suspect an active dental abscess, use the handle of the laryngeal mirror to tap sharply the top of the questioned teeth. The patient will tell you clearly which is involved.

Now, inspect the openings of the salivary ducts. When the possibility of obstruction has to be considered, wipe away the secretion from the mouth of the duct with a cotton-tipped applicator and watch carefully for its reappearance. This should take only a few seconds. If the question of obstruction still exists, palpate the offending duct with the tip of a finger. Before engaging in any work that requires insertion of your finger into the oral cavity, tape two tongue blades firmly together and insert them between the teeth, like this:

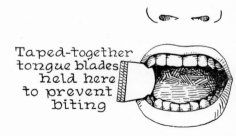

Taped-together tongue blades held here to prevent biting

Next examine the visible area of the oropharynx, using the head mirror and tongue blade. The procedure is very probably the one most often poorly done by physicians. It is not necessary to gag the patient. Even 3 and 4 year old children can be shown how to cooperate in a matter of seconds. Here is how I have been taught to do it:

First, tell the patient that you will teach him how to have his throat examined without gagging. Have him open his mouth and touch his lower incisors with his tongue. Keep the tongue blade out of sight at this stage and, in younger patients, show where to put the tongue by indicating or touching the lower incisors with your finger. When this position is attained tell the adult to relax his tongue or the child to "let his tongue go floppy." Demonstrate what you mean by pushing on the *anterior* surface of the tongue with the depressor and repeatedly cautioning the patient *not* to push back. He will soon learn what you want. Now, place the depressor about halfway back on the tongue, like this:

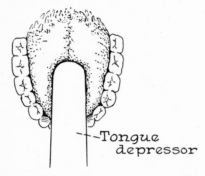

Push very gently downward and the pharynx will come into view. Too forceful action will only engender resistance by the patient and ruin all preceding efforts.

Now depress the lateral sides of the tongue and examine the tonsillar area. If a pillar retractor is not available make one from a paper clip by bending it like this:

A second tongue depressor may sometimes be made to do as well.

Occasionally you may want to examine or determine the quantity of the secretion in the tonsillar crypts. If a tonsillar suction cup is available it may be used or a small amount of secretion may be lifted out with a probe or with the end of a straightened paper clip.

If the adenoidal area needs examination, this may be done with the small mirror as described in the section on the nose. In addi-

tion, the area may be directly visualized in many cases and palpated in all. Direct visualization may be done as follows:

Anesthetize the posterior pharyngeal wall and soft palate with a spray of Pontocaine solution every 3 minutes for three or four applications. Have the patient throw his head back and extend his tongue. Use the pillar retractor, a tongue blade, or a homemade device to lift the palate upward and forward, like this:

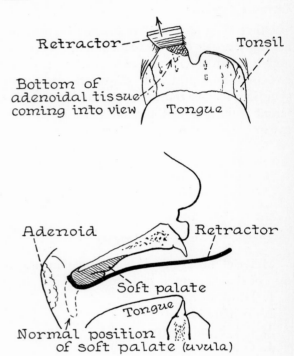

To palpate the adenoids, anesthetize with a spray as above, fix a tongue depressor between the teeth and push one finger gently into the nasopharynx. Be careful not to touch the posterior pharyngeal wall more than is essential. Palpation should be gentle and, above all, quickly done.

Inspection of the larynx may be carried out by use of the laryngeal mirror or directly by use of the laryngoscope. The practitioner should be able to do both but will find more use for the indirect method because of its simplicity. Material needed is the head mirror, laryngeal mirror, and a 4 by 4 inch flat or square of clean cloth.

Ask the patient to tilt his head slightly backward and to breathe quietly through the mouth. Then have him grasp the anterior end of his tongue with the folded flat and pull it forward out of the mouth as far as possible without causing pain. Dip the laryngeal mirror in a glass of hot water and shake off the drops that cling. Now insert the mirror without touching the tongue until the back is gently pressed against the soft palate and uvula. Push these backward until they touch the pharyngeal wall, like this:

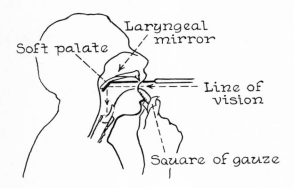

An occasional patient will gag. This necessitates removing the mirror and spraying the pharyngeal wall with a local anesthetic.

Direct examination through the laryngoscope will seldom be used by the practitioner but, when necessary, the need is great. Emergency clearing of the airway is the most frequent procedure demanded.

If necessary the throat may be sprayed with local anesthetic solution. (This should not be done in small children or those who are dyspneic if possible to avoid it.) After this has become effective the patient is moved so that his body is off the examining table from the mid-portion of his scapulae upward, like this:

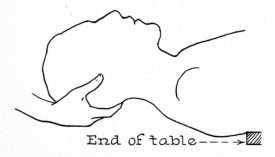

End of table----→

The head is supported by an assistant—or the operator's knees if no assistant is available—about 4 inches above (forward) from its usual level and is maximally extended, like this:

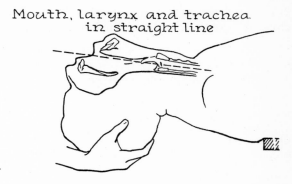

Mouth, larynx and trachea in straight line

Remember that the object of the position is to get the mouth, throat and trachea in as nearly a straight line as is possible, and the position will be simple to achieve. Now, the operator should *recheck personally* the fact that all removable dental work has been taken from the mouth.

Insert the laryngoscope over the dorsum of the tongue to visualize the epiglottis. Now put your finger between the patient's upper lip and teeth and the barrel of the laryngoscope to avoid bruising the lip or breaking teeth. Pass beyond the epiglottis with the beak of the instrument and on down toward the trachea, meanwhile lifting the whole instrument upward as if to pick up the patient with it. An absolute essential is to lift the whole instrument—*NOT* to rock it on the upper teeth as a fulcrum. When inserted, the laryngoscope should be in this position:

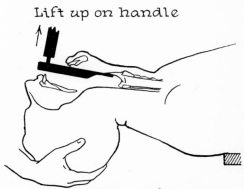

Lift up on handle

Note clearance of teeth from scope

During the examination, a folded square of gauze should be slipped between the upper teeth and the 'scope. A tip for those who own a nasopharyngoscope: It makes an excellent laryngoscope with no bother at all. Simply put it far back in the mouth, have the patient close his lips on it, and turn the lens downward.

FOREIGN BODIES

The most common place for the lodgement of small, sharp foreign bodies is in the tonsil. Occasionally they may lodge in the lateral pharyngeal wall, seldom in the posterior wall. Larger fragments should be searched for in the valleculae, pyriform recess and lingual tonsils. Look for them here:

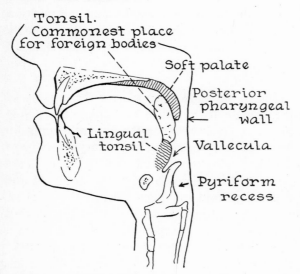

Tonsil. Commonest place for foreign bodies

Soft palate

Posterior pharyngeal wall

Lingual tonsil

Vallecula

Pyriform recess

Those foreign bodies that can be seen without instruments should be plucked out with the forceps under direct vision. Those lodged deeper require direct laryngoscopy.

PERITONSILLAR ABSCESS

Quinsy seems progressively more rare as the antibiotics find wider and earlier use. Instead of 20 or 30, the average practitioner now sees only 3 or 4 cases each year.

The "dont's" are just as important as the "do's" in office treatment. Perhaps most important is *don't* incise the abscess until you are reasonably sure that suppuration is present. This is indicated by softening, yellow discoloration of the mucous membrane and a feeling of fluctuation to the finger or probe.

Anesthesia is unsatisfactory. A surface anesthetic (perhaps the new Cyclaine in 5 per cent concentration) applied several times at intervals of 5 minutes helps somewhat. Do not use general or infiltration anesthesia.

The abscess usually points about 1 cm. above and internal to the lower molars. In preparing to incise, the knife blade should be wrapped with tape so that it cannot penetrate more than 1 cm. It should be stabbed into the upper part of the wound and jerked out, cutting downward at least 1 cm. or more.

If no pus extrudes, insert a blunt hemostat into the cavity about 2 cm. and open the blades. If there is still no pus, quit and use antibiotics.

POST-TONSILLECTOMY BLEEDING

Seat the patient and prepare for examination with the head mirror. Have on hand a pillar retractor, local anesthetic in a syringe, clamps, needle holder, needle and fine gut.

First remove the clots with gentle suction, trying to keep the suction tip out of contact with the tonsillar bed if possible. Now moisten a small sponge with 1:1000 epinephrine and exert gentle pressure on the bleeding area for 5 minutes. While doing this remove excess secretion from the mouth and throat with suction. This has no utility but makes the patient much more comfortable since excess secretion increases his urge to swallow.

If bleeding is still present when you remove the sponge you will be able to see the site clearly. Since tonsillar vessels tend to retract beneath the level of the bed it is often difficult to pick them up without taking large bites of tissue. A stitch is probably preferable to a tie for these annoying vessels.

Anesthetize the area by injecting a few drops of local anesthetic and wait a few minutes, all the while applying a sponge firmly against the bleeding point. Then seize the area at the bleeding point and lift it slightly, like this:

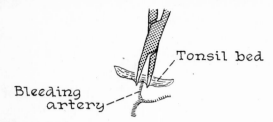

Put the suture in like this:

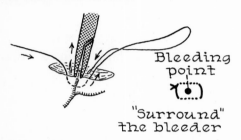

Always remember that there is no bleeding from tonsillar vessels that pressure will not control. Only in the event of an aberrant vessel or altered hemostatic mechanism is there cause for alarm.

If the bleeding comes from the adenoidal area proceed like this: Have the patient lie down and gently remove the clots with suction. Anesthetize the pharynx with a spray and wait several minutes. Now use the pillar retractor to lift up the soft palate, suck out accumulated blood and visualize the bleeding area. Apply pressure with a sponge moistened with epinephrine for 5 minutes.

The small arteries that supply the lower portions of the adenoidal tissue course up the posterior pharyngeal wall about ¾ cm. from the midline, like this:

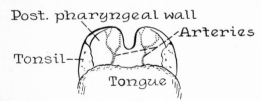

They may be palpated, and bleeding can often be stopped by exerting firm pressure on them for several minutes.

Suture of the bleeding point is very difficult in this area. If electrocautery is available the vessel may be touched with the cautery after application of a sponge wet with 2 per cent Pontocaine with ephedrine solution for several minutes. If there is still bleeding, insert a postnasal plug. Material needed is (1) a small catheter, (2) heavy surgical silk, and (3) a rolled gauze flat to make a cylinder ¾ inch in diameter and 2 inches long. Tie two pieces of heavy surgical silk about the center of the roll, like this:

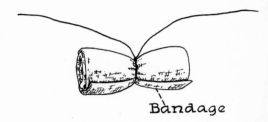

Insert the catheter through the nose until its tip is visible in the nasopharynx. Grasp this tip with forceps and pull it out through the mouth so the catheter is in this position:

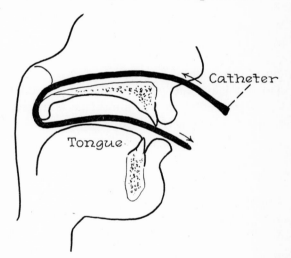

Tie the end of one of the pieces of suture that is fixed to the bandage roll to the end of the catheter. Now pull the catheter back out through the nose, carrying the suture through the mouth, nasopharynx and out through the nose. Repeat, bringing the other suture through the opposite nostril. Tie still another suture onto the bandage roll and let it dangle.

Test the posterior pharyngeal wall to see if it is anesthetized properly. If not, respray. When maximal anesthesia has been obtained, take the strings that exit through the nares in one hand and the gauze roll in the other.

Place the roll in the posterior oropharynx and push it up into place with one finger, like this:

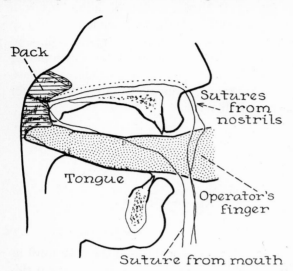

Use the sutures coming out through the nares only to help jockey the plug into proper position. Do not pull it into place with these sutures. Then tie them *loosely* together so that no pressure is made on the columella. Tape the remaining suture that exits from the mouth to the side of the cheek.

Do not leave the pack in place more than 24 hours. Infection will almost certainly supervene if this limit is exceeded.

TRACHEOTOMY

Only the emergency tracheotomy should ever need be performed by the practitioner outside the hospital. The technique given here is not the best one for tracheotomy. It is the quickest one (except the stab technique) for reestablishment of the airway.

Put a pillow beneath the patient's shoulders and extend the head as far as possible. If time permits and the patient is alert enough to need it, inject the line of incision with 1 per cent procaine. This line should extend from 1 cm. above the suprasternal notch to 1 cm. below the border of the cricoid cartilage, exactly in the midline. At the top and bottom of this proposed incision infiltrate deeply around the trachea so that the anesthesia is here:

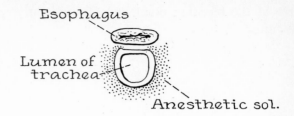

Put a finger on the notch in the superior border of the thyroid cartilage to mark the midline and make the incision. Go deeper until the white fascia of the infrahyoid muscles is seen. Then, if time permits, stop and carefully establish hemostasis. Now cut the exposed fascia with blunt-pointed scissors, exposing the trachea.

If you can, simply push the isthmus of the thyroid gland out of the way; if not, put two ligatures on it and cut between them. Now, stick a needle through the space above the first tracheal ring and inject forcefully into the cavity of the trachea a few drops of surface anesthetic (Pontocaine).

Divide the second, third and fourth cartilaginous rings in the midline. Put a stay suture around the second ring, like this:

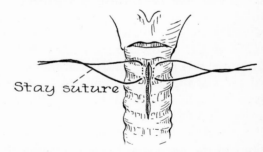

Now insert the tracheal tube under direct vision, using the stay sutures as retractors. There are only two important safety principles: (1) *stay* in the midline; (2) be meticulous in hemostasis.

If death by strangulation seems imminent forgo the above. Make a quick midline incision. Put your finger in the wound and feel a tracheal ring. Push the knife into the trachea alongside your finger. Bend a hairpin or paper clip into a retractor and hold the wound open with it. Turn the patient on his abdomen so that blood will not run into the trachea. When the airway is established turn to hemostasis.

Section II

THE EYE

THE EYE

EXAMINATION

Simple examination with equipment available to every practitioner will reveal over 90 per cent of the pathology to which the eye is subject. Material necessary is as follows:

1. Ophthalmoscope.
2. Applicator stick.
3. Paper clips.
4. Binocular loupe (a small hand lens can be made to serve as well).
5. Pontocaine hydrochloride solution, ½ per cent.
6. Homatropine hydrobromide, 2 per cent.
7. Pilocarpine hydrochloride, 1 per cent.
8. Fluorescein, 2 per cent. This should be dissolved in a 3 per cent solution of sodium bicarbonate.

General inspection will reveal evidences of swelling, inflammation, and excessive discharges. After inspection have the patient look down and, with the tip of one finger, press gently inward on the upper lid toward the optic nerve head. Increased tension will be apparent. If in doubt, compare with your own eye.

Then have the patient look up and evert the lower lid, like this:

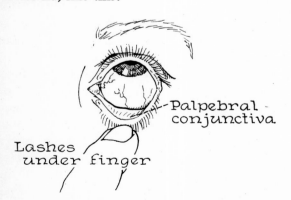

Examine the lid margin, palpebral and bulbar conjunctiva, and lacrimal punctum, using the hand lens when necessary. If indicated, attempt to express secretion from the punctum by placing one finger on the lateral surface of the bridge of the nose and rolling it toward the eye.

Now evert the upper lid like this: Tell the patient to look down. Grasp the eyelashes in the middle of the upper lid and pull *gently* down and out from the globe. Place an applicator stick like this:

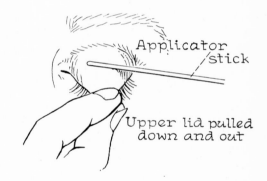

Press gently backward with the stick and pull upward on the lashes to do this:

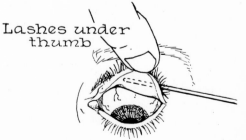

Position of applicator stick behind lid

The object is to flip over the tarsal cartilage which is firm and cannot (or at least should not) be bent.   The cartilage occupies approximately this position in the upper lid.

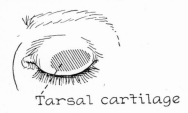

Tarsal cartilage

With the upper lid everted you still cannot see the inner corner of the palpebral conjunctiva.   This can be exposed—while keeping the upper lid everted—by putting the tip of one finger on the lower lid immediately below the unseen area and pushing firmly inward and upward.

After completing the examination of the lids, turn next to the globe itself.   When necessary to use lid retractors, make them from paper clips.   Bend the clips like this:

Be sure to anesthetize the eye by instilling a few drops of ½ per cent Pontocaine and *waiting* 5 to 10 minutes before using these retractors.   Examine the bulbar conjunctiva and cornea, using the binocular loupe or a hand lens.   In the event of a suspected corneal abrasion or other interference with corneal continuity, anesthetize the eye and instill 1 drop of fluorescein solution.   Then flush the eye copiously with normal saline or sterile water.   The dye will cling to the abraded spot, leaving a dirty greenish yellow smudge. Proper diagnosis is certain and easy through use of flourescein.

Use oblique light from the ophthalmoscope to examine the iris and anterior transparent media.   Then turn to examination of the fundus.

Examination in a darkened room with the ophthalmoscope about 15 inches away is proper first procedure.   Use a plus 5 lens. The normal eye will give a homogeneous orange light reflex.   If the vessels of the fundus are seen—no matter how indistinctly—a refractive error is probably present.   When these vessels are seen the examiner next watches the reflex while moving his head from side to side.   If the vessels seem to move in the opposite direction the eye is myopic; if in the same direction, hyperopic.

Opacities in the media will appear as black spots.   Their position can be estimated by the examiner's moving his head from side to side. When the opacity moves in the opposite direction it is in front of the iris; when in the same direction, behind.

Now ask the patient to stare at an object at least 10 feet away (I use the gold seal on a diploma across the room).   Try to relax your own accommodation as much as possible and examine the fundus with the ophthalmoscope immediately in front of the eye.   Follow a definite routine in covering visible areas.   The routine followed is of little importance so long as no part of the examination is omitted. Check disk, macula, horizontal and vertical peripheries in order, and then re-examine the circulatory apparatus.

There is one difficulty that must be overcome.   Occasionally it is impossible to get good visualization without dilating the pupil. Use 2 drops of homatrophine solution instilled 5 minutes apart.   Wait approximately 20 minutes.   Increased intra-ocular tension is an absolute contraindiction of use of "drops" for examination.   Upon completion a drop or two of pilocarpine should be instilled, particularly in old people.

Occasionally it may be necessary to check the visual fields.   An estimation may be obtained by seating the patient facing you and asking that he stare at your nose without allowing his eyes to move.   Take a bright object in your hand (a package of cigarettes) and rotate it through an arc from behind the patient's visual fields toward the front until he sees it—like this when looking down on patient and doctor:

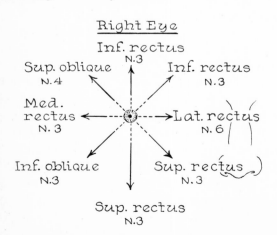

Do this in at least four areas of the visual circle, With an intelligent patient one can even map scotomata by this method.

Color vision can be checked with the excellent charts available but an adequate estimation can be done with hanks of yarn available at any variety store. Cut strands about 6 inches long; two each of red, green, blue, yellow and black. Throw them on your desk at random and ask the patient to pick out the red *one* and the green *one*. If he looks at you indignantly and hands you both red ones and both green ones, he has adequate color distinction for red and green.

Extra-ocular movements should be checked to determine imbalance and paralyses. The following chart may be used:

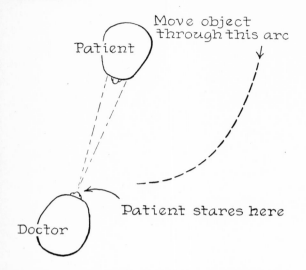

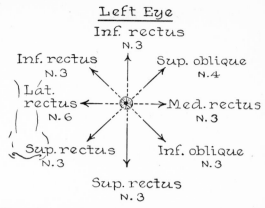

When the pupil deviates in the direction shown in the chart, the labelled muscle is probably weak (---) or paralyzed (——). This does not take into account muscle shortening. Combinations are common.

By no means should the practitioner attempt to treat complicated ocular diseases, for their treatment lies strictly in the province of the ophthalmologist. On the other hand, about 8 of 10 cases involving the eye can be handled adequately by any conscientious physician who will take the time to inform himself and to examine carefully.

There are many good textbooks on diseases of the eye; each year excellent postgraduate courses are given and many medical centers are happy to welcome the practitioner to their ophthalmology departments for a brief stay. All these are excellent sources of information on diseases of the eye.

In the following pages the most common office procedures are summarized.

TRICHIASIS

By common usage this term has come to mean inversion of the lashes so that they touch the cornea. In actuality the practitioner is more often consulted about inverted lashes near the inner canthus that irritate the conjunctiva. These hairs are fine, short, usually pale blond in color, and are most difficult to see. Look for them in oblique light. They may be epilated with simple forceps but the procedure will probably have to be repeated every month or six weeks.

Electrocoagulation with the diathermy is the most satisfactory means of removal and is practically painless. Before the procedure a local anesthetic should be infiltrated into the lid margin (I use 1 per cent procaine), like this:

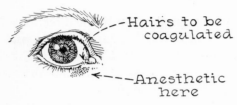

The diathermy should be set at the lowest possible setting for coagulating current and a very fine needle (an ordinary household sewing needle) placed in the active electrode holder. The needle should be inserted along the base of the hair like this:

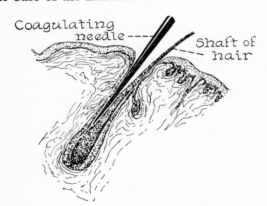

The current should be turned on for only a brief interval. A barely perceptible change in skin coloration around the follicle is acceptable; a definite white area indicates too much current. We sometimes use a small tongue blade lubricated with petroleum jelly to hold the lid up and away from the globe.

Before beginning on the lid check the current by coagulating a hair follicle on the arm.

BLEPHARITIS

There are two office procedures to be used in treating blepharitis. First is careful cleaning of the lid margin with a cotton-tipped applicator. Usually this is done by first dipping the applicator in boric acid solution and then rubbing firmly along the margins, taking care to dislodge scales and plaques.

The second is expression of infected fluid from the meibomian glands. Do it like this: evert the lid over a tongue blade held along the skin side. Use a foreign body spud or the rounded end of a paper clip to express the secretion, thus:

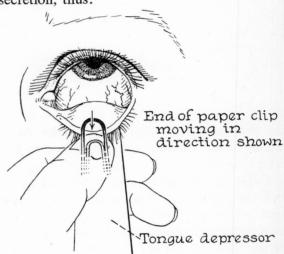

STYE

A stye should be evacuated when a yellow "head" appears. In most instances no anesthesia is needed if the job is done rapidly. When necessary a breath or two of trichloroethylene through the Duke inhaler is valuable. A small *horizontal* incision should be made through the yellow portion but not beyond the margins of the suppuration.

CHALAZION

Differential diagnosis of this lesion may be made by noting its attachment to the tarsus and not to the lid.

For operative removal, evert the lid over a tongue blade for stability. Anesthetize the conjunctiva with a solution made up of 1 minim of 1:1000 epinephrine added to 1 cc. of 1 per cent procaine.

After waiting a few moments make a vertical incision in the palpebral conjunctiva extending into the cavity for its entire length and wipe out the cheesy contents with a moistened applicator. (To save solution preparation and to help control oozing, squirt the left-over anesthetic solution on two or three sterile applicators.) If you have a small curet, use it on the walls of the cavity; if not, scrape them well with the knife blade. Any remaining bleeding can be controlled with gentle pressure.

Do not suture the gap that is left. If a clot forms and, therefore, swelling remains for a few days, assure the patient that there is no cause for alarm. Gentle massage beginning the second day will speed absorption.

CORNEAL ULCER

With modern treatment few office procedures are necessary to control corneal ulcer. Occasionally it will be necessary to remove debris from the degenerated area. This can be done by first anesthetizing the eye and then gently scraping the ulcer crater with a foreign body spud (or with the *back* of a standard knife blade). Warnings to the contrary notwithstanding, it is almost impossible to perforate the cornea with careful operative technique.

If perforation by the ulcer seems imminent the patient should be referred to an ophthalmologist if possible. If referral is not possible, drain the anterior chamber by inserting a pointed knife at the inferior border of the cornea, like this:

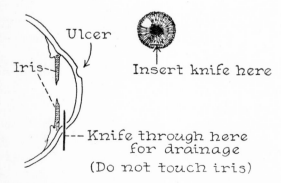

This procedure should be almost non-existent in the average practice but may have to be done by isolated physicians.

TRAUMA

Most trauma to the eye is of relatively simple nature because of the excellent protection of this organ and the lid-closing reflexes. There are four very common types of injury seen in the practitioner's office.

Lacerations of the Lids

These should be cleaned adequately (with normal saline) and closed at once with very fine cotton sutures. (See the section on surgery.) *Never*, when working on the upper lid, include the tarsal cartilage in the tissue sutured. It is seldom if ever necessary to put sutures in the conjunctiva. If the skin be adequately closed the conjunctiva will fall in place of its own accord.

Vertical lacerations which extend into the orbicularis gape; others seldom do. If the wound does not involve the lid margin and does not gape, don't put in more than one or two sutures. Gaping wounds should have a suture or two in the fibers of the orbicularis or other subcutaneous structures exposed. These may be of fine cotton or gut. Try to avoid a suture in the lid margin that may occlude a meibomian duct.

Lacerations of the Bulbar Conjunctiva

The important thing to do here is nothing. Not one in a hundred of these lacerations requires suturing. Flush the eye copiously with normal saline. Stop minor bleeding by gentle pressure for several minutes (don't look every 30 seconds to see if it has stopped), and bandage the eye.

Subconjunctival Hemorrhage

Again, do nothing. This trivial condition is alarming to patients and we are importuned to take some drastic action. In the event that there is enough blood to cause a definite swelling, aspiration may be permissible but is certainly rarely necessary. I bandage these eyes —so that the patient can't see them—and do my best to think up some innocuous procedure that can be done frequently by the patient or his relatives.

Lacerations of the Cornea

This is an entirely different situation. Any perforation of the cornea is potentially highly dangerous and the case should be referred to a competent ophthalmologist if one is available. If immediate referral is possible do nothing but bandage the eye. If referral must be delayed cleanse the eye (not the wound) gently with cotton-tipped applicators which have been sterilized. Be wary of irrigating the eye copiously lest you drive foreign material through the laceration into the anterior chamber.

Rarely a foreign body will remain in the wound or in the anterior chamber. When the case is to be seen by an ophthalmologist within a few hours, these are best left in place. They may have to be removed if delay is to be encountered. Foreign matter which has been pulled by gravity to the dependent portion of the chamber may be removed through an incision in the lowermost portion, as shown on page 27. Manipulation *must* be held to a minimum. Actually, it is best to avoid this procedure if possible to do so without impairing the final result.

If the iris protrudes, sterilize a large household needle and push it back into place, using the eye end of the needle. A small crochet hook will do as well. Then pick up the bulbar conjunctiva about 1 mm. from the edge of the cornea and snip a hole in it, like this:

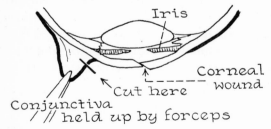

Notice the direction of the cut. Then free the conjunctiva about halfway around the cornea, thus:

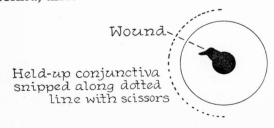

Draw the flap across the cornea and stitch it like this:

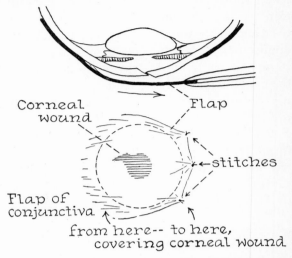

Begin immediately using the antibiotics systemically and 1 per cent atropine ointment locally. Get the patient to an ophthalmologist as quickly as possible.

FOREIGN BODIES

This is the most common eye condition seen by the physician other than refractive error. An overwhelming number of these foreign bodies are corneal, for conjunctival ones are frequently removed by the patient.

The man with a corneal foreign body will be willing to swear that it is under the upper lid about the middle, for it is here that the scratchy sensation is referred. There is usually some spasm of the eyelids and some photophobia. The first problem with such a foreign body is to find it. Use oblique illumination, the hand lens or loupe, and, if necessary, a drop of fluorescein.

Anesthetize the eye and warn the patient to look fixedly at a certain object. Remove the offending substance using either a spud or the *back* of a standard detachable knife blade. Foreign bodies can be tenacious, and if it is necessary to work longer than 30 to 45 seconds, stop and let the patient move his eyes about for a moment. It is almost impossible to hold one's eyes steady for a long time.

Adherent foreign bodies may be lifted from the cornea with the point of the knife. The only important caution is to be careful not to push the foreign body on through the cornea by too vigorous effort.

At the conclusion of the removal the eye will have an ulcer where the extraneous substance was located. Debris should be curetted out with the back of the knife or the spud and the eye should be bandaged.

Conjunctival foreign bodies are only minor insults, although they may disturb the patient greatly. Removal under local anesthesia is simple in the extreme if adequate exposure is gained. This may be achieved by using the principles enumerated in the section on examination of the eye.

DRESSING THE EYE

Take a piece of standard roll cotton about 1½ inches square and moisten it with normal saline or boric acid solution. Place this firmly against the *closed* eye. Then insert two layers of such cotton, unmoistened, between the leaves of a 2 by 2 inch gauze flat like this:

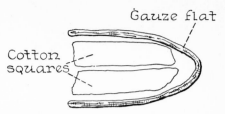

If you have no 2 by 2 inch flats, make one from a 2 inch roller bandage. Put this on the eye over the wet sponge, fitting it firmly around the bridge of the nose. Have on hand a small piece of thin, sterile plastic sheeting (I use plastic popcorn bags for a basic supply) and cut a square 2½ by 2½ inches to seal the dressing. Hold it in place with strips of adhesive tape applied like this:

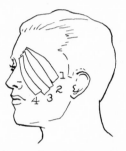

Such dressings should be changed at least every other day, and preferably daily.

Section III

MUSCULOSKELETAL SYSTEM

MUSCULOSKELETAL SYSTEM

MYOFASCIAL DISEASE

If superficial contusions be excepted, myofascial disruption is the most common form of injury to which we are susceptible. There are no statistics available—and little possibility of getting any—but I would estimate the incidence of such injuries at approximately a 10,000 to 1 ratio in relation to fractures. It is an interesting commentary on the logic of our thought processes that so very little work has been done to clarify and establish a means of treatment for these simple injuries.

Since there are no authorities in the field this represents only what I think after reading the material available, consulting various colleagues, and treating many patients. The information is subject to change as knowledge increases. Incidentally, this is one of the most profitable fields of research which can be carried out by the practitioner in his own office.

To begin with, a consideration of anatomy as applied to the superficial tissues is essential. Particularly is it important to know areas replete with nerve endings. Important details are these :

Notice particularly the relative number of nerve endings in each type of tissue and the relative speed of healing. A thorough understanding of this diagram will serve as an excellent basis for diagnosis and treatment of simple myofascial injuries. There are several pathologic pictures which may be represented. This is the picture of a simple bruise:

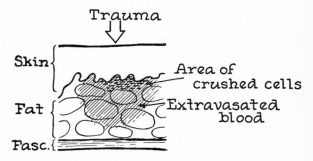

A simple bruise is an extravasation of blood from ruptured vessels in the subcutaneous tissues and a crush injury to cells. Extravascular blood and dead cells function as chemical irritants. Here the irritation is spent on fatty tissues which have few nerve endings. Hence, the simple bruise in this area is not very painful. This is a deeper contusion:

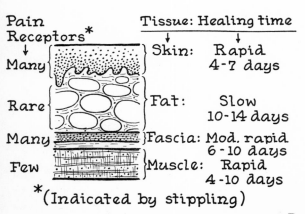

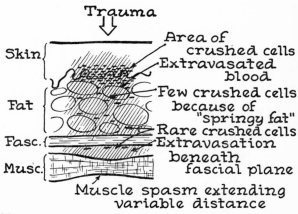

There is direct pain from torn fascia and chemical irritation from extravasated blood and cellular degeneration products in both muscle tissue and surrounding fascial layers. It is this chemical irritation that is responsible for the muscle spasm that accompanies such injuries. Palpation will occasionally indicate areas of major pooling of blood, but this is unusual. More usual is palpatory evidence of muscle spasm.

Diagnosis is quite simple. Sharp pain will result when you gently extend the involved muscle, like this:

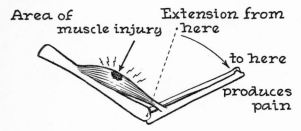

A more serious myofascial injury with tearing of muscle and fascia looks like this:

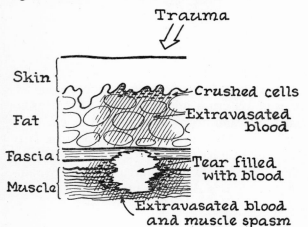

In general, such an injury results in severe pain and marked muscle spasm.

A special type of injury seen frequently is the fascial tear. It may be represented like this:

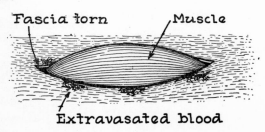

Acute pain usually appears at the time of injury. This is frequently aching in character and nauseating in intensity. It is relieved somewhat upon relaxation of the fascia involved unless there is hemorrhage and consequent chemical irritation with muscle spasm. These injuries are treacherous because many patients will not cooperate to allow full repair.

Fascia heals well and firmly if given a chance. The layers, however, must be held in apposition. A typical example is the laparotomy incision and its closure. In the majority of fascial injuries the edges of the torn tissue lie closely enough together to heal quickly unless wrenched apart by circumstances similar to those that created the original disruption. To rephrase, fascial lacerations heal well unless the patient tears the wound apart by some sudden or unpropitious movement.

When unsatisfactory results are obtained the picture is usually something like this: The injury is sustained and the patient reports to his physician. Proper treatment is given and, within a day or two, the patient feels much better. He is warned that not enough time has elapsed to insure healing but he ignores the warning and goes about his business in the usual way. A sudden movement or a misstep pulls on the fascia and the healing edges tear apart, recreating the original injury. This routine can go on for months if not interrupted by explanation and firm direction from the physician.

Not infrequently a bit of fat or a bit of muscle may herniate through a fascial tear, giving a picture like this:

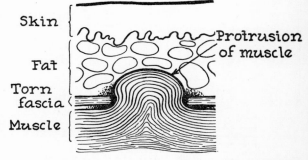

Usually these protrusions can be felt and are slightly tender to the touch. Spontaneous reduction and healing are usual in areas where

the fascia can relax to a sufficient degree so that the herniated material may slip back into place. Many of these cases, however, herniate again on the slightest strain. The torn edges may not be allowed to heal together, leaving a permanent rent in the fascia and resulting in periodic formation of a small hernia.

Treatment in General

When you see the patient immediately after injury, try to reduce internal bleeding by gentle pressure and by application of cold packs. This should be continued for several hours. Immobilization of the involved area is one of the best treatments available and is too seldom used. Cardboard splints, elastic bandages, and web belt supports are very helpful. After all likelihood of internal bleeding has ceased, heat will speed absorption of extravasated blood and aid healing.

If pain is acute and tends to be of long duration, injection with a local anesthetic is of value. Longer-acting anesthetics, such as Intracaine in oil, or Efocaine, are the most helpful. Do it this way:

First, make a wheal on the skin using 1 per cent procaine in water or saline solution. Do *not* use anesthetics dissolved in oil to inject the skin. Now insert the needle bearing the long-acting anesthetic until the point lies just below the fascia, like this:

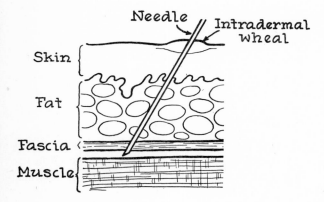

It is easy to ascertain this location by feel. The fascia has a definite resistance to penetration and the patient often notes a twinge of pain when it is penetrated. Spread a small amount of anesthetic just below the fascial layer. Be sure to aspirate before injecting any oily solution.

Wait several minutes and then check the area for pain, using gentle pressure. If pain is still present reinsert the needle and spread a small amount of solution in the muscle tissue around the site of the injury, like this:

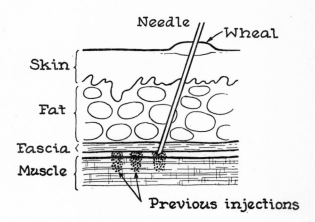

Again check for the presence of pain. When gentle pressure fails to elicit discomfort, move the involved area so that the injured tissue is put on the stretch. If this produces no pain, chances for complete relief are excellent. Be sure to tell the patient that the injection itself will cause a certain residual soreness for a day or two.

It is of paramount importance to know when not to inject these injuries. Remember that the simple contusion is not a good candidate for injection. It is only when there is disruption of tissue that injection tends to be successful. For that reason it is best to use conservative treatment for 24 to 48 hours. Then, if there is no resolution, inject.

Small herniations of fat or muscle through torn fascia are not infrequent. The procedure used varies, depending on size and type of tissue herniated. Small protrusions of fat can often be reduced permanently after needling. Herniated muscle requires surgical reduction.

Diagnosis is made by history and physical examination. The important office procedure in diagnosis is palpation. Notice the level of mass and its loose "attachment" to the fascia, like this:

Muscle hernias are more easily felt when the involved muscle is gently (not forcibly) contracted. In actual usage a thorough knowledge of the anatomy of the involved part is the best means of differentiating fat and muscle hernias.

To needle a fat hernia, anesthetize the area by injecting a small amount of procaine into the base of the herniated area, like this:

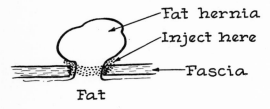

If too much is injected palpatory landmarks will be obscured. Some physicians advocate injection into the mass with the thought of aiding breakup of the fat. I have not usually done this.

Now insert a large bore needle (18 gauge) into the mass and move it sharply about, like this:

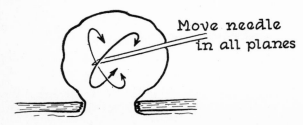

The object is to break up the fine connective tissue bands which are present in all normal fat. This, in most instances, will result in spontaneous reduction.

When you and the patient agree that the procedure is necessary, reduction may be accomplished by surgery. After anesthesia cut down to the fascia just to one side of the hernia, like this:

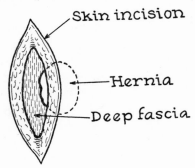

Pick up one edge of the fascial opening to accomplish reduction, like this:

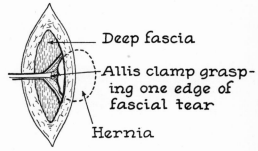

Use very fine suture material to close the fascial rent (I use white cotton sewing thread). Close the skin and put on a light dressing. A word of warning: Don't be too enthusiastic about this procedure. It is excellent if your diagnosis is accurate, but there are many causes of "tender bumps" other than these hernias.

Muscle Tears and Ruptures

Soreness due to extravasated blood after minute tears of muscle fibers is quite common. Differential diagnosis between these lesions and fascial tears comes under the classification of minutiae, for the treatment is the same and, in most cases, both are present.

The best procedure for partial rupture of a muscle is to splint the involved part and let it alone. Firm healing is not a quick process. One should leave the splint on for 10 days or more and then caution the patient about use of the muscle for another two weeks. *Be sure* both to demonstrate the actions you are interdicting and to be certain that the patient understands clearly.

Complete rupture should be treated by suture. Since this usually involves deep dissection it is seldom within the range of the ordinary office.

Low Back Pain

Every back that hurts is not a ruptured disk. In this discussion we will confine attention to the office procedures useful in diagnosis and treatment of other back lesions involving principally ligaments, muscle, and fascia. These, of course, are by far the most common. For purposes of planning treatment they can be divided into five classes involving areas rather than specific tissues. These are:

1. Lumbosacral, in which tissues immediately surrounding the lumbosacral joint are involved.

2. Sacro-iliac.

3. Lumbar, involving tissues about the interlumbar joints.

4. Gluteal, involving these muscles and their attachments.

5. Tilt of pelvis, involving any or all tissues because of mechanical imbalance.

Diagnostic Tests. The testing procedures required to diagnose these lesions require an examining table, an operating stool, a foot stool, and a tape measure. It is necessary to know these tests in their entirety in order to make proper diagnosis. We will refer to them later in discussing specific lesions.

One should remember that examination of the back is a confusing procedure at best. Out of the myriad of possible procedures one must select and become adept at a small group. This is the group I use but many others are available.

TEST I. With the patient standing "at attention," look at the posterior superior iliac spines. If they do not seem on the same level, take a sheet of 8½ by 11 inch stationery and

place it so the long edge touches the spines, like this:

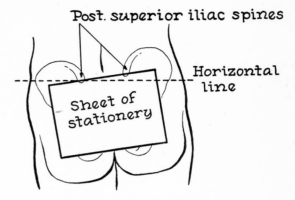

Any tilting of the pelvis will be noticed immediately. Verify it by measuring from the *anterior* superior spine on each side to the floor. Variations of ¼ inch are normal, much more is suspicious.

TEST II. Have the patient stand on one foot and then the other. Note whether there is pain, and which foot is raised when it occurs.

TEST III. Ask the patient to bend forward and touch the floor. Particularly notice how he returns to the erect posture. Make a note of these things:

1. Whether the lumbar spine flexes or tends to remain rigid.

2. Whether there is pain and *when*.

3. Whether there is increased prominence of the right or left erector spinae group.

Now apply pressure on the crests of the ilia, like this:

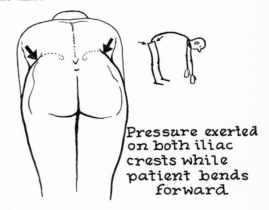

Pressure exerted on both iliac crests while patient bends forward

and have the patient repeat the test. Note whether pain is partially relieved.

TEST IV. Have the patient walk across the

room.   Notice whether he extends the hip and knee joints freely.

TEST V.   Have the patient sit down on the stool in as comfortable a position as circumstances permit but so that his feet are flat on the floor.   Palpate both erector spinae groups for spasm.   Then apply pressure in the midline on the ligaments between the spinous processes.   Note any tenderness.   Now apply pressure about 1 inch medial and 1 inch lateral to the sacro-iliac joint, like this:

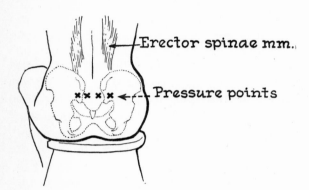

Make a note if pain occurs in any of the four spots.   There are other "trigger areas" which give pain on palpation but these are by far the most frequent.   One may also palpate the area of the lumbosacral joint.

TEST VI.   Have the patient put both hands behind his head.   Grasp him by the shoulders and rotate his body.   If there is pain on rotation, note it.

TEST VII.   Ask the patient to get on the examining table by using the footstool.   Notice which foot he places on the footstool first and whether he uses his hands to help raise the foot and leg.   The patient may get on the table by bending at the hips so that he first puts his head and chest on the table, like this:

then he will bring his legs up and roll over. If this is done, make a note of it.

TEST VIII.   With the patient in the supine position, put your hands on the iliac crests, here:

First pull apart as if trying to separate the crests, then push them together.   Note any pain.

TEST IX.   Grasp one leg by the ankle.   Put your other hand on the thigh in order to hold the knee joint in extension.   Now raise the leg slowly, keeping the knee extended until pain occurs either in the back or in the muscles of the leg itself.   How high you may go before pain occurs in the leg muscles depends, of course, on the age and general "flexibility" of the patient.   Notice if back pain occurs and upon which side.

Now raise both legs, keeping them extended.   If pain occurs it will probably be present before you approach the 45 degree angle.

There are many other ways to apply the same general forces used in this test.   All are entirely acceptable but certainly only one is needed for confirmation.   The one I use is Laguer's sign.   Have the patient flex the hip and knee joints by locking the fingers of both hands together and pulling the leg into position, like this:

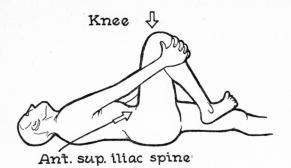

Knee ⇩

Ant. sup. iliac spine

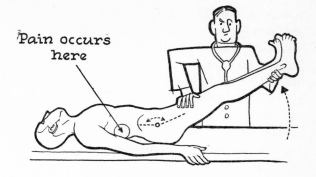

Pain occurs here

Now apply pressure on the knee and the anterior superior spine, as shown. Note the presence of any pain.

TEST X. Have the patient lie on his side with the leg nearest the examining table extended. Now flex the other leg at hip and knee. Put one hand on the shoulder and grasp the ilium with the other. Now, rotate the trunk sharply in each direction successively, alternating the direction of the force applied to shoulder and ilium, and make a note of pain.

These ten tests by no means represent a complete orthopedic examination of the back but their use on each patient with low back pain will help to bring order out of chaos. When you use them you must make note of findings as the tests are done. There is far too much information to remember it all.

Findings in Common Areas of Pathology.
LUMBOSACRAL DISEASE. In test II the patient will complain of pain when he tries to stand on the leg opposite the lesion. In test III he will attempt to perform the movements without using the lower lumbar joints. Pain will be present when the test is repeated while pressure is applied on the iliac crests. In test V some erector spinae spasm will probably be apparent in the lumbosacral area. In test VI there will be pain when the patient is rotated away from the side of the lesion. If this pain seems quite severe, take an x-ray.

In test VII the patient will probably use his hands to lift the involved leg to the footstool. There will be no pain in test VIII. Test IX will give extreme pain when both legs are raised. The pain starts early, usually at about this angle:

There will be some pain when each leg is raised independently but not nearly so much as when both are raised. Laguer's sign will be negative. In test X rotation away from the side on which the lesion is located will cause acute pain (and it sometimes stops the pain—why I don't know).

SACRO-ILIAC DISEASE. In test II the patient will usually have pain when he lifts the foot opposite the lesion. In test III the lumbar spine will move quite freely at first but may be somewhat limited as strain comes on the sacro-iliac joint. The maneuver may be pain-free when pressure is made on the iliac crests. Test IV often shows a peculiar "walking on eggs" gait, with knees and hips not fully extended at any time.

Test V will show no spasm of the erector spinae. There will be pain upon pressure medial to the affected joint. Rotational pain will be present but not excessive. Have the patient stand and repeat the rotational test (test VI). Pain will be less in the erect position. Test VII will show that the patient does not use the foot on the involved side to mount the footstool. Test VIII will produce pain on the involved side.

Test IX will show acute pain on the involved side when the leg is raised to about 45 degrees. There will be little pain from raising the opposite leg and practically none when both legs are raised. Laguer's test will produce acute pain. Test X is somewhat inconclusive.

LUMBAR DISEASE. In test II the patient can stand on either leg with only mild aggravation of pain. In test III the lumbar spine is held rigid and stiff, with loss of normal curvature of the back. Spasm of the erector spinae group is usually very apparent if the patient can bend over. Test IV will show normal but cautious walking with the back held rigid. Spasm and tenderness of the erector spinae will be apparent in test V.

Test VI will show acute pain when the rotation is away from the lesion. In test VII the patient usually gets on the table without using the lumbar area, as shown on page 38. Test VIII will be negative. The tenth test will show acute pain upon rotation away from the side on which the lesion is located.

GLUTEAL DISEASE. The ten tests are not needed. Flexing the hip joint usually causes pain and pressure over the involved area is uncomfortable. Gluteal trauma is not rare and occasionally these cases can be difficult to differentiate from sacro-iliac disease. Particularly is this true when gluteal attachments to the ilium near the sacro-iliac joints are pulled free.

Tilting of the pelvis may be responsible for any of the other groups except gluteal disease. The first test is the only one of importance.

I have memorized the ten tests by frequent usage. All that any of the tests do is push on or stretch involved structures. Reflection on anatomy will allow exact prediction of the outcome when a test is applied.

Treatment. Procedures in treatment are essentially those of any such lesion. Splinting by means of webbing, belts, etc., is excellent. Tape should be applied as a last resort when no other support is available.

Injection into involved areas is done exactly as it is for any musculofascial area (see page 35), with one exception. The sacro-iliac area can only be reached by an angular approach because the ilium "overhangs" the area where pain is produced, like this:

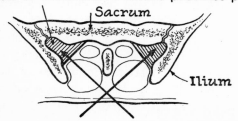

Area of structures which produce pain

Manipulation is not bad treatment, particularly in those cases when the patient heard a "snapping sound" at the time of injury. An obvious word of warning: fractures should not be manipulated. If there is any question, use the x-ray first. Two maneuvers are helpful.

1. Hyperextension. Grasp the patient as shown and lift him from the floor by bending forward, like this:

2. Have the patient lie on his side with the leg closest to the table extended and the uppermost leg flexed. By grasping hip and shoulders, sharply rotate his body, like this:

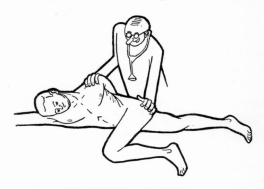

TENDON INJURIES

In spite of bitter warnings to the contrary, simple tendon repair is within the reach of the well equipped minor surgery. After cleansing the wound thoroughly use small rake retractors to afford complete visualization and to estimate the degree of damage. If severed tendons can be rejoined without grafting and if you estimate the repair will take only a few minutes, I believe it can well be done in the office when proper equipment is available.

Some tissues heal so well that one need achieve only a rough approximation to get a good result. Tendons are *not* in this category. To begin with, a thorough knowledge of the anatomy of the tendon and its sheath is necessary. The blood supply of a tendon, which is relatively very minute, is furnished like this:

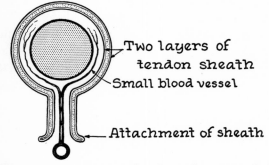

Two layers of
tendon sheath
Small blood vessel

Attachment of sheath

There are no nerves in the substance of the tendon itself and few in the sheath. Relative insensitivity to pain is a helpful factor in repair.

Normally there is some stretch force on tendons, owing to muscle tone. When division is accomplished the end attached to the muscle usually retracts and cannot be found in the wound. Three procedures are valuable in locating the proximal stump.

Before mentioning these three methods there is one thing that anyone who does any surgery should reflect upon. I believe that surgical results in equivalent cases will be in direct proportion to the gentleness exhibited. This point cannot be overstressed.

If you will pardon a personal example in a textbook I would like to tell you a true story about surgical gentleness. Some years ago while in practice, I was doing appendices as I had been taught, with results generally similar to those of other doctors in the area. One night while staring into the fireplace, my wife and I and our associate fell to reflecting about the appendectomy. After all, routine amputation of the appendix is about as simple a procedure as one can think of in terms of surgery, yet these patients did not feel well for several days.

Two possible reasons suggested themselves at once: (1) the anesthetic and medication, and (2) trauma imposed by me in removing the appendix. Just as a matter of curiosity we wrote out a routine for appendectomy and followed it to the letter in the next few operations. This is the routine:

Preoperative medication will be limited to sedation with barbiturates and to a dose of atropine if required. The skin will be cleansed with soap and water followed by alcohol and ether if desired. No strong antiseptic will be applied. Local anesthesia will be used until the peritoneum is reached, but only minimal quantities will be injected.

After the skin incision is made, individual bleeders beneath the skin will be caught with forceps *but* the forceps will not be so tightly closed as to crush tissue. We found that old forceps which had grown somewhat stiff would stay in position if handled carefully. Ties are not used unless the vessel continues to bleed after being held for three to four minutes. Then 4-0 plain is single-tied and the ends clipped short.

As dissection is continued there is *absolutely no crushing* and tearing with knife handle or finger covered with gauze. Particularly is this enforced in the upper and lower ends of the wound. Very slow, sharp dissection is used to separate fat from the anterior rectus sheath for about ⅜ inch laterally from the proposed incision in the sheath. After further injection of anesthetic the rectus sheath is incised in the direction of its fibers without regard to paralleling the skin incision. It is *incised,* not ripped away from the muscle and torn with a pair of scissors.

Using only the gentlest of pressure the rectus is freed from its sheath, cutting, not tearing away, any attachments to the sheath. The fingers are not inserted beside the muscle and forceably parted. It is usually possible to avoid the horizontal tendinous insertions (inscriptiones tendineae) in the rectus and this must be done if feasible. At this time administration of nitrous oxide and oxygen is begun. Sometimes it is profitable to use a few whiffs of cyclopropane to speed general anesthesia. The peritoneum is opened in the usual way with one exception. It is usually possible to avoid handling by peeking underneath and snipping with the scissors as one goes.

At no time is more pressure used for retraction than approximately that necessary to slide a textbook across a desk top. Try it and you will see the amount of pressure needed. It seemed as though it took an hour and a half to enter the peritoneal cavity on the first abdomen I opened this way. Actually, it took about twenty minutes.

After having the peritoneal cavity exposed, STOP. Don't plunge your hand in among the intestines and start fishing for the appendix. By gently moving the incision about (curare may be used) one can avoid much handling of peritoneal content. Be patient and *look* for a minute and you can reach down and pick up the cecum. It is held *gently* in rubber jawed forceps while the appendix is amputated.

On the way out, pin-point approximation is necessary. First, the peritoneum is replete with nerve endings. To "bunch it up" with the posterior rectus sheath in a heavy suture would seem to be asking for trouble. In most cases the peritoneum and sheath are partially separated. Finish the separation and tack the peritoneum together with tension using 4-0 plain. Use the smallest number of sutures possible. Use 2-0 chromic to suture the posterior sheath somewhat loosely. Don't jerk it together so tightly that all possibility of blood supply to the suture line is removed. Of course, the suture line must be free of gaps. The anterior sheath is closed with interrupted cotton sutures tied gently—again, not jerked together. The skin is closed with a subcutaneous plastic suture for cosmetic reasons.

If the anesthetic has been properly given the patient is usually waking but drowsy at this time. The head and feet are elevated slightly in the bed to take pressure off the rectus. No narcotic is given unless requested. Dosage, when requested, is usually limited to 50 mg. Demerol.

The first appendectomy we did this way nearly drove me wild. It seemed to take at least three days. Actual time was an hour and twenty minutes. The patient was a 21 year old girl with a swollen, pus-filled appendix. By evening she was sitting in a chair demanding food (she didn't get it), and the next morning she was in the hospital lobby talking a mile a minute when I arrived. On the fourth postoperative day she refused to stay

longer and returned to her job as a theatre usher. On the seventh day she went horseback riding.

During the first week I was more ill than she was. I could just see her viscera spilling out over the theatre floor, or the development of a fine fecal fistula. Nothing happened. Since then, we have used this maddening gentleness routine in many procedures. It takes planning and it takes almost superhuman patience in execution, but it works. Try it and see.

Recovery of Retracted Tendon

The three useful ways to recover a retracted tendon are:

1. Compressing the muscle to which the retracted end is attached. Using the tendons at the wrist as an example, do it like this:

Obtain a piece of rubber tubing ½ inch or smaller in diameter. In a situation where tubing is not available a belt or a necktie can be made to serve. Starting near the origin of the muscle, wrap the tube tightly around the arm, like this:

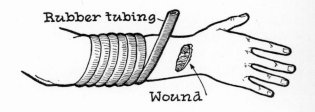

2. If the first method does not suffice, inject 1 per cent procaine into the muscle belly, being sure to spread the solution widely throughout the muscle. Wait 10 minutes and reapply the rubber tube.

3. If there are still no results, make a transverse incision in the course of the tendon about 2 inches above the original laceration, like this:

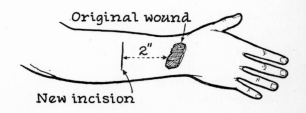

Gently pull the tendon down until the severed end appears in the original wound. Tendon suture is best accomplished like this: Thread two small straight needles on a piece of size 34 stainless steel wire. Grasp the very ends of the tendon to be sutured with Allis forceps, and take the first stitch in the proximal end of the tendon, like this:

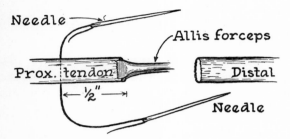

Using both needles, take the second stitch and with the sharpest scissors you have, or with a razor blade, cut off the tendon next to the Allis forceps, like this:

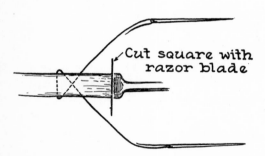

Take a final stitch like this:

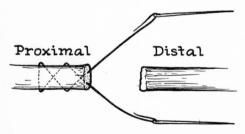

Unless the tendon be severed squarely to begin with, square the distal end by use of a razor blade (or scissors) and an Allis clamp. Then finish the suturing, like this:

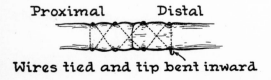

A common error is failure in approximation of the ends. As sutures are taken in the distal portion, the tendon ends should be *gently* worked together.

After tendon repair be sure to splint the part so that the tendons are held in such position that muscle tone will exert minimum force. A good rule of thumb is to bend any joint over which the injured tendon passes toward the injured tendon. For example, if the tendons at the volar surface of the wrist are involved, fix the hand with wrist and fingers flexed.

Specific tendon injuries occur most often about the fingers. The most important of such injuries are:

Baseball Finger

In this injury the extensor is literally jerked away from the distal phalanx, often pulling with it a small piece of bone, like this:

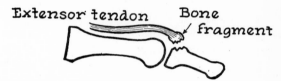

Maximal relaxation to speed healing may be obtained by splinting the finger in this position:

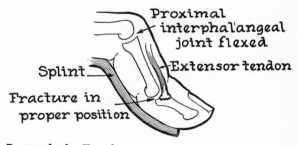

Buttonhole Tendon

Occasionally the extensors will rip longitudinally, giving a picture like this:

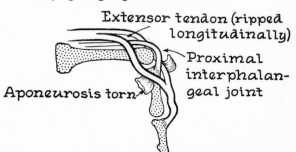

The finger should be incised and the rip repaired, taking stitches like this:

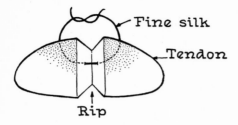

Use very small silk. Do not hold out hope of excellent results, for there is usually some minor limitation of motion.

Rupture of the Supraspinatus

The repair in this lesion is frequently surgical and should seldom be attempted outside the hospital.   One procedure is useful in diagnosis.

It is frequently most difficult to differentiate between supraspinatus rupture and reflex inhibition of movement from acute bursitis.   To make the differentiation, inject about 10 cc. of 1 per cent procaine into the bursa, aiming the needle at the greater trochanter or just above, like this:

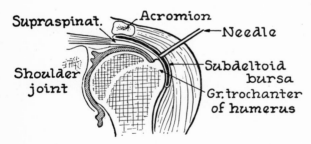

Wait 15 minutes and then ask the patient to elevate his arm.   In most cases of bursitis the elevation can now be accomplished, whereas in cases of ruptured supraspinatus tendon no difference in motion will be observed after procaine.

BURSAL INJURIES

Certain basic considerations must be brought forward before discussing office procedures used in treatment of bursae.   There is much confusion about the pathology in-

volved and about available treatment methods. To begin with it is important to note that, with the advent of cortisone, indications for mechanical treatment have been reduced approximately 50 per cent, but by no means is mechanical treatment rendered useless by the drug.

Bursae form, for the most part after birth, at points of friction between bone and skin and between muscles and bone.   By the time adult status is reached there are several hundred bursae in the body.   It is fortunate for us that only a half dozen are troublemakers.   Those involved with sufficient frequency to make discussion worth while are (1) the subdeltoid, (2) the olecranon, and (3) the prepatellar.

Bursae are potential cavities lined with membrane in all respects similar to the synovial membranes of joints.   The reaction of this membrane to injury is similar to the synovial reaction.   Particularly important from the standpoint of minor surgical procedures is the fact that the attachment of bursae to the "fixed point" of their periphery is among the most firm in the human body.   For example, the subdeltoid bursa is attached to the capsule of the shoulder joint by a dense matrix of connective tissue through which many vessels course to make up the profuse blood supply to the bursal membrane.

Pathology and Principles of Treatment

No procedure can be planned for bursae without a knowledge of the pathology.   There are three types of bursal injury commonly seen. They are:

1. *Suppurative Bursitis*.   This is the least frequent type.   Because it is a purulent infection, the treatment is incision.

2. *Acute Traumatic Bursitis*.   This is, in actuality, a tearing or disruption of the lining membrane.   It is followed by an outpouring of serosanguineous fluid which fills the bursal cavity and frequently causes pain by distention.   This fluid is reabsorbed in the healing process but the bursal wall is usually somewhat thickened, and granulations may form where areas of the lining membrane have been de-

stroyed. Not infrequently, adhesions form between the opposing surfaces that have been denuded.

When fluid continues to form in spite of repeated aspiration, it is usually because of friction between denuded surfaces. The two procedures of use in acute traumatic bursitis are repeated aspiration and firm bandaging, including splinting and pressure dressing.

3. *Chronic Bursitis.* In the presence of repeated mild irritation the characteristic fibrous overgrowth which we call chronic bursitis appears. Bulbous protrusions of villae spring up from the lining membrane and the capsule becomes greatly thickened—so much so that it becomes palpable as a doughy or rubbery mass. Calcium is occasionally deposited in areas of this fibrous tissue. Treatment for this type of bursa is excision or obliteration of the cavity.

A good means of obliteration that has been somewhat neglected is the injection of sodium morrhuate into the cavity. Begin by irrigating the bursal cavity with 1 per cent procaine for several minutes. Wait another 5 minutes but do not remove the needle through which the irrigation was performed. Then inject 2 cc. of 5 per cent sodium morrhuate. Apply a pressure bandage. This procedure may be repeated in 10 days if desired.

The Subdeltoid Bursa

This seems to be the most frequently involved bursa seen by the practitioner. Its anatomic relations are shown below. Notice how the bursa can be squeezed between the head of the humerus and the acromion when force is applied up the arm. It can easily be traumatized also by force applied over the deltoid muscle. Note, too, that the tendon of the supraspinatus runs along the floor of the bursa. There are those who claim that calcified lesions in this area are cysts of the tendon sheath filled with calcareous material.

Acute traumatic bursitis of the subdeltoid bursa is relatively common. The best office procedure is aspiration and irrigation. After making a skin wheal, insert an 18 gauge needle. Inject some 1 per cent procaine into

the area of the bursal wall before penetrating it, like this:

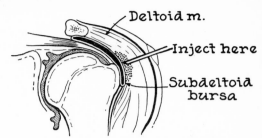

Wait a minute or two and then insert the needle into the bursa. If the needle point goes through the bursa and touches bone, withdraw it about ¼ inch. Irrigate with the 1 per cent procaine solution remaining in the syringe. Then use normal saline to flush the bursa copiously.

After this procedure immobilize the arm for several days. A sling is sufficient for reliable patients. For others I use two strips of muslin sheeting about 4 inches wide. Put a folded surgical dressing pad (abdominal pad) in the axilla. Then apply the first strip of muslin like this:

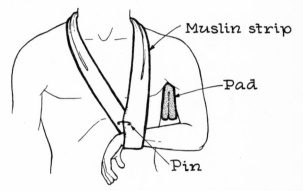

And the second like this, using pins to hold the dressing in place:

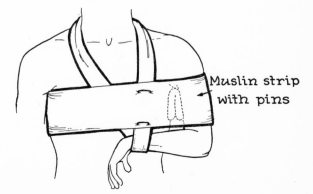

Chronic subdeltoid bursitis is a far more difficult problem. X-ray is valuable as a guide to treatment. A straight A-P of the shoulder will indicate the presence of calcification in tissues surrounding the bursae. In the absence of calcified areas, conservative treatment (infiltration, diathermy) will give good results. Occasionally it will be necessary to break up adhesions. This is best done under general anesthesia. Put the arm forceably through its full range of motion. *Be careful,* for there is a resorption and thinning of bone in many cases of long standing, and fractures may be caused. *Be sure* to insist that the patient begin active exercise immediately and continue.

This manipulative procedure works for adhesions but I don't like it. To begin with, active exercise after manipulation is devilishly painful and the actual manipulation is a perfect example of applying force blindly. Nonetheless, it is a procedure of occasional value.

Chemical obliteration of the subdeltoid bursa works but is dangerous owing to the proximity of the shoulder joint. The best office procedures for non-calcified chronic bursitis are conservative ones with occasional use of manipulation.

In the presence of calcified deposits, needling the area has real therapeutic value. Do it this way:

Prepare a tray with two 2½ inch 18 gauge needles, a 2 cc. syringe containing 1 per cent procaine and tipped with a 24 gauge needle. Have two sterile medicine glasses, one filled with 1 per cent procaine and the other with normal saline solution. Make a skin wheal about 1 inch lateral to the acromion and infiltrate the tissues down to the bursa, like this:

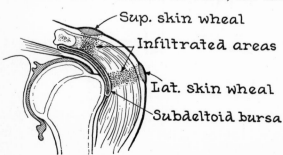

Sup. skin wheal
Infiltrated areas
Lat. skin wheal
Subdeltoid bursa

After waiting a few minutes, insert one of the 18 gauge needles into the calcified area. I have found the fluoroscope a real help in placing the needle in the proper position. When proper placement is secured it is usually possible to aspirate a gelatinous, milky material. When this is achieved, irrigate through the needle with 1 per cent procaine followed by normal saline until the irrigating fluid returns relatively clear. Do not limit motion after this procedure.

In cases with moderately severe symptoms, minor surgery is probably the best treatment. Draw a line about 3 inches straight down the arm from the acromion. Anesthetize the skin and subcutaneous tissues along this line. After waiting 10 minutes make your incision like this:

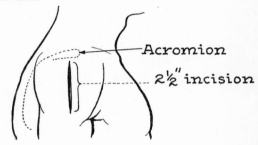

Acromion
2½" incision

Dissect down to the deep fascia and split it in the direction of its fibers. Inject procaine through the area of the deltoid which you intend to invade. Now, using the utmost gentleness, separate the fibers of the deltoid. Insert a clamp and spread it or use your knife handle, like this:

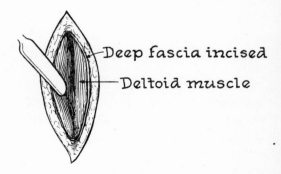

Deep fascia incised
Deltoid muscle

Dissect down to the bursa but make no move to open it until the incision and dissection are sufficiently progressed that you can see at least an inch of the bursal capsule, like this:

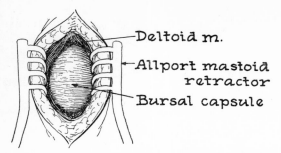

Deltoid m.
Allport mastoid retractor
Bursal capsule

Anesthetize the bursa and open it. I find it helpful to take a stitch with heavy silk sutures on either side for retraction, like this:

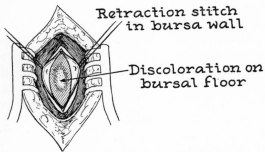

Retraction stitch in bursa wall

Discoloration on bursal floor

Now have your office girl grasp the patient's lower arm and slowly rotate the shoulder joint so that you can see the whole floor of the bursa. Usually about the middle of the bursal floor you will see a yellowish discoloration surrounded by a zone of hyperemia. Make a very shallow incision into the yellow area that parallels the fibers of the supraspinatus. Pasty yellow-white material will exude from the incision. Irrigate with normal saline to remove the major portion of this material.

In closing, take no stitches in the bursa. Use 3-0 plain catgut to approximate *loosely* the muscle. Try to take no more than two such stitches. I usually close the deep fascia with interrupted cotton and the skin with Scotch tape (more of this later). Have the patient start active motion as soon as possible.

The Olecranon Bursa

Diseases of the olecranon bursa are quite common and very easy to treat. Acute traumatic bursitis can usually be cured by aspiration and an elastic bandage. Chronic bursitis should be treated by excision of the bursa. Do it this way:

Have the patient place his arm across his chest. I usually place a drape across the chest

and ask the patient to take hold of his belt just above the pocket on the opposite side. In planning the incision, remember to see to it that no part of the incision is in the skin immediately over the olecranon. Perhaps the best approach is an ellipse with the convexity toward the radial side, like this:

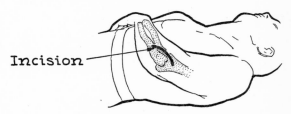

Incision

The olecranon bursa is a surgeon's trap. The incision gives beautiful exposure, hemostasis is easy and the bursa practically dissects itself free. Within a minute or so everything is done except freeing the bursa from its attachment to the olecranon. It is this last step that can cause trouble.

Tugging at the bursa gives one the impression that it is either nailed or welded to the olecranon. If one continues snipping with the scissors in a blind field one soon begins to wonder how many pieces of periosteum and how many bone chips are going to be attached to the specimen. Do it this way: Grasp the bursal wall with two Allis clamps near the attachment. Now take a sharp knife and cut the attachment, meanwhile rolling the bursa upward, like this:

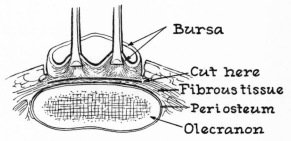

Bursa

Cut here
Fibrous tissue
Periosteum
Olecranon

Pay attention to the olecranon, not to the bursal wall. The tendency of most of us is to get too close to (or under) the periosteum. When the bursa is out, a hot wet pack will help to control the oozing. If complete hemostasis is not possible, by all means drain the wound with a small rubber drain (rubber band) for 24 hours.

The Prepatellar Bursa

The prepatellar bursa is easily treated and simple to excise. In acute bursitis simply aspirate at the most dependent portion, thus:

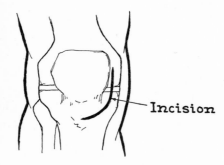

- Patella
- Pre-patellar bursa
- Aspirate here

To excise, avoid making an incision that will leave a scar over the knee. Turn a flap, like this:

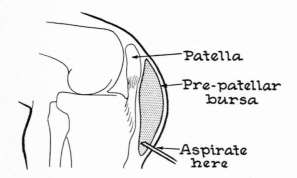

- Incision

Pressure after closure is easily maintained by dressing with gauze, covering with a ten cent plastic bath sponge and wrapping with an elastic bandage.

In most cases it is wise to apply a posterior splint and leave it in place for a few days. Usually sufficient healing will take place within four days to make removal of the splint possible. After stitches are removed, use plastic tape or adhesive "butterflies" to hold wound edges coapted.

JOINT INJURIES

The Temporomandibulbar Joint

This joint is unique in structure and in function and is frequently involved in dislocations and disruptions within the joint itself. The important points of anatomy are:

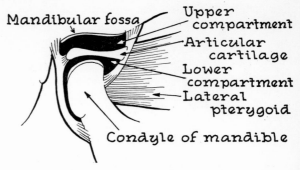

- Mandibular fossa
- Upper compartment
- Articular cartilage
- Lower compartment
- Lateral pterygoid
- Condyle of mandible

Notice that the joint is divided into an upper and lower compartment by the articular cartilage and also that the mandibular condyle can ride forward and backward and from side to side, as well as rotating about a horizontal axis when the mouth is opened.

Dislocation without fracture is not infrequent. Reduction may usually be accomplished this way: Wrap both of your thumbs with heavy gauze or devise some other way of protecting them. (On occasion I have worn lead-lined x-ray gloves.) Then insert both thumbs in the patient's mouth and apply pressure downward on the posterior molars with the thumbs while lifting the point of the jaw upward with the fingers, like this:

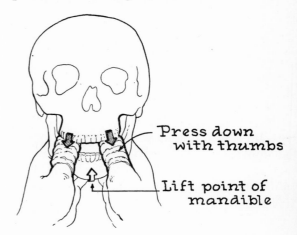

- Press down with thumbs
- Lift point of mandible

Reduction may usually be accomplished by this method without the use of anesthesia. If the procedure fails it should be repeated under anesthesia. If results are still not satisfactory, hospitalization is indicated.

Occasionally, as a result of trauma or during a particularly intense yawn, cough or sneeze, the articular cartilage is ruptured. Pain is usually intense and there is an audible click when the jaws are opened or closed. When seen in the acute stage, 1 per cent procaine may be infiltrated into the joint for pain relief. Do it like this:

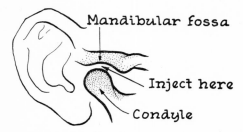

The mandibular condyle can be felt when the patient wiggles his jaw from side to side. Then have the patient open his mouth and exert firm forward pressure behind the angle of the jaw, like this:

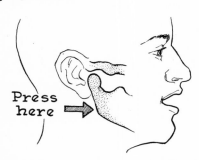

In cases of chronic clicking after rupture of the cartilage a reasonably good result may be obtained by injecting a sclerosant into the joint cavity. Best results have been obtained by injecting 0.25 to 0.5 cc. of Searle's sodium psylliate weekly for 3 to 6 weeks. These injections are, unfortunately, uncomfortable.

The Acromioclavicular Joint

Dislocation is the common lesion seen in this joint. The anatomic factors involved are these:

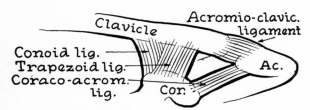

The acromioclavicular ligament is usually ruptured. The trapezoid and conoid ligaments may be ruptured also. Notice that the extent

of dislocation may be determined by whether or not the trapezoid and conoid ligaments remain intact. One point of prime importance is illustrated in the following diagram. Upon first glance it appears that the clavicle has sprung upward and that pushing it down into place will produce anatomic approximation. This is *not* true. Actually, the shoulder and arm have "fallen away" from their normal attachment, like this:

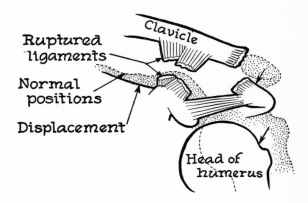

In reduction one must plan to lift the arm into its proper position as well as to push downward on the clavicle. Conservative treatment will give good results in the majority of cases. Taping and bandaging have been unreliable and torturesome methods for me, but seem to work occasionally. I prefer a modified shoulder spica.

To apply one, first assemble the following material in addition to plaster:

1. Stockinet of various sizes, and sheet wadding.

2. A roll of regular army web belting and two buckles. (Other belting and fasteners are just as good but are more expensive.)

3. A yucca board.

4. Several pieces of orthopedic foam rubber.

5. A roll of cellophane tape ½ inch wide.

Begin by washing the area to be covered with soap and water and drying thoroughly. Next sponge with alcohol. Then make a jacket from tube stockinet, and wrap roll stockinet from the wrist to the shoulder of the affected arm. Make an axillary pad out of ten layers of sheet wadding and a layer of ½ inch foam rubber and use the cellophane tape to hold it in place, like this:

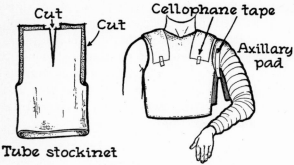

Tube stockinet

Wrap the elbow with sheet wadding and a layer of ¼ inch foam rubber and tape the wrapping in place. Now take rolls of sheet wadding and cover with two layers the entire area to be incorporated in the cast.

Have your assistant or the patient hold the involved shoulder upward and backward and see to it that it stays there. Make a six layer splint of 4 inch plaster and place it like this:

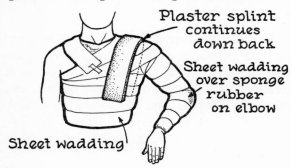

Then use 6 inch rolls of plaster to go around the body until the body portion of the cast is four or five layers. Take four straps of webbing and incorporate them in the next several layers so that they exit several inches below the shoulder on each side, and so that they droop about 4 inches below the bottom of the cast, like this:

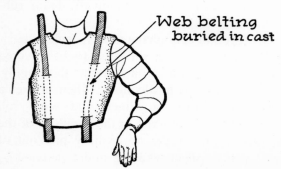

Now, fold the lower ends of the straps up and incorporate them in the cast. Using 3 inch plaster make a ten layer splint and place it like this:

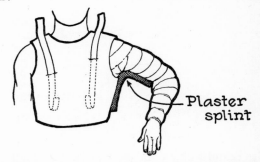

Make a six layer splint of 3 inch plaster and place it like this:

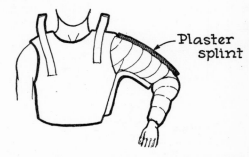

Now wrap the arm and shoulder with plaster and cut the yucca board to proper length and width and place it like this:

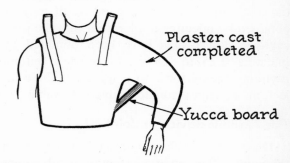

Now cut away the shoulder area so that the cast looks like this:

Finishing the cast edges is important from both practical and esthetic standpoints. In areas where skin pressure is not likely to occur, do it this way:

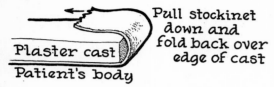

Fold 4 inch plaster lengthwise to make a two layer, 2 inch strip. Apply to hold stockinet in place. Where the edge is likely to press into the skin, use this method:

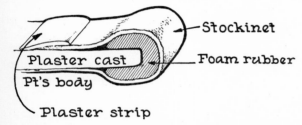

Areas that should be protected by rubber are marked "✕" below.

The belt buckle is attached (in back where the patient can't reach it) to one strap, a foam rubber pad is applied over the distal end of the involved clavicle and the belt is tightened sufficiently to maintain reduction. By adjusting the opposite shoulder strap, twisting or canting of the cast may be avoided.

Reduction should be maintained for 6 to 8 weeks. If proper healing does not occur, hospitalization and surgery are the methods of choice in further treatment.

The Shoulder

The shoulder is the most complex movement system in the human body but, in spite of this, there are only two common lesions and these two are very simple to repair when seen in their usual uncomplicated state. The lesions are subcoracoid and subglenoid dislocation.

There are four simple office procedures that are useful in diagnosis of dislocation or fracture. First, ask the patient to place his hand on the opposite shoulder. Normally, his elbow can be brought into apposition with the anterior abdominal wall, like this:

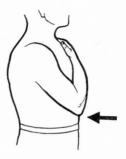

If the shoulder is dislocated this cannot be done.

Second, compare on each side the triangle formed by the tip of the acromion, the coracoid process, and the greater tuberosity of the humerus. Normally the triangle is nearly equilateral, like this:

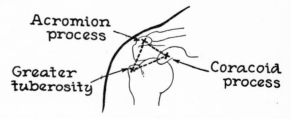

Difference in the two sides will be apparent.

If the patient is fat, run a tape measure through the axilla and over the acromion. The measurement will be greater on the injured side. One should remember that there may be a normal difference of one-half to one inch in any adult.

The last test is simplest and probably best of all. Place a ruler along the lateral side of the arm so that it touches the lateral epicondyle of the humerus and passes to the acromion, like this:

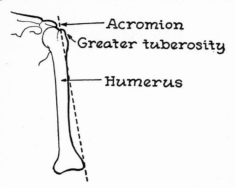

If the ruler touches the acromion and lateral epicondyle without bending, the head of the humerus is not in its proper position for it would interfere with the straight line.

Both types of dislocation may usually be repaired under local anesthesia. To accomplish this, inject 15 cc. of 1 per cent procaine into the joint space and 8 to 10 cc. around the dislocated head of the humerus. While waiting 10 minutes for the anesthetic to become effective it is wise to check for nerve damage insofar as possible. Be sure to note on your record if any damage seems present. Some attorneys have learned the impossibility of proving whether damage occurred at reduction or before. Unfortunately we seem to face an increase in such claims.

The subcoracoid dislocation is usually easy to reduce using Kocher's method. Do it like this:

Grasp the patient by the elbow and wrist. Hold his elbow close to his body and achieve maximal external rotation by moving the wrist slowly outward, like this:

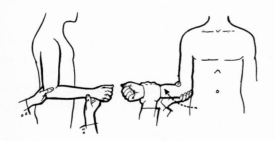

Now bring the elbow slowly to the midline (*A*, below) and roll the arm from external to internal rotation by slowly placing the patient's hand on his opposite shoulder (*B*):

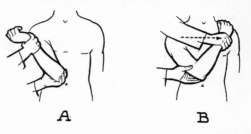

A   B

In subglenoid dislocation, remove your shoe and place your foot in the involved axilla. Grasp the arm firmly and pull, gradually increasing the amount of force used. Do NOT jerk—pull. This is the better method of reduction for all subglenoid dislocations and may often be applied equally well to subcoracoid dislocations. If done carefully, it is less traumatic than the Kocher method.

The Elbow

The elbow joint occasionally is dislocated posteriorly. If seen early before severe muscle spasm intervenes, gentle traction will usually effect prompt reduction. Most cases, however, are not seen until after onset of muscle spasm. These should probably be reduced under a brief general anesthesia. The Duke inhaler or a minimal dose of Pentothal may be useful. The examiner grasps the upper arm with one hand and holds while an assistant exerts mild traction on the wrist. Slight downward pressure over the muscles of the forearm usually effects reduction, like this:

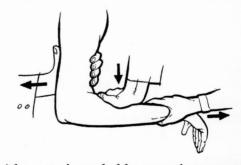

Aftercare is probably more important than actual reduction. This dislocation tends to cause severe damage to the soft tissue of the antecubital fossa and should be immobilized for 3 or 4 weeks. A plaster cast with the arm bent at a little more than a right angle is very useful. Vigorous physiotherapy with active and passive movement should NOT be started immediately after removing the cast.

The Digital Joints

Digital joints are frequently dislocated, but these dislocations are usually so simple to reduce as to be scarcely worth mention. Anesthesia is only rarely needed. Simply pull gently and, if necessary, increase the force of the pull very slightly. The important thing to do is to insist on immobilization for 2 or 3 weeks in order that joint capsules may have ample time to heal.

In rare cases the joint capsule will fold into the joint at the time of reduction so that the deformity immediately recurs as soon as traction is released. Repeated attempts at reduction when this occurs merely waste time. Anesthetize the finger by injection of 1 per cent procaine into the digital nerves at the base, like this:

After waiting 10 minutes make a **Z** incision on the dorsum if the rent in the joint capsule is dorsal and here if the rent is ventral:

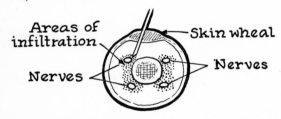

Dissect carefully down to the joint, retracting, not severing, nerves and vessels. Slow, gentle, sharp dissection will pay with good results. The pathology usually looks like this:

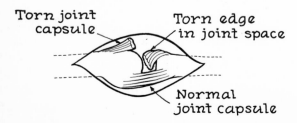

Gently release the incarcerated joint membrane and reduce the dislocation. Close the joint capsule with interrupted sutures of fine cotton, and quit. In lieu of skin sutures I usually wrap the finger with Scotch tape and drill small holes in the tape along the wound line for escape of secretions. The skin may be *loosely* sutured with cotton.

To secure a good result, two things are of utmost importance. First, avoid trauma. Jerking tissue about, forceful retraction, too tight suturing all cause trouble. Second, place the skin incision so that it does not cross a skin crease. That, of course, is the reason for the **Z**. Another important factor is to incise the skin perpendicularly to the skin surface, not obliquely.

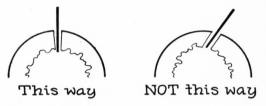

This way   NOT this way

The Knee Joint

The knee joint is just another cross we must bear. Injuries are legion, diagnosis is difficult, and treatment only moderately successful. There are five types of pathologic condition which are seen with sufficient frequency to make consideration important. They are:

1. Effusion.
2. Injury to the medial semilunar cartilage.
3. Injury to the medial ligament.
4. Injury to the cruciate ligaments.
5. "Wear and tear."

Effusion. Anteriorly the knee joint extends upward above either side of the patella, like this:

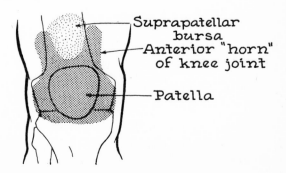

Palpation of the limbs of the **U** will often reveal relatively small amounts of fluid. As the amount of fluid increases, the patella "floats." Diagnosis with this much fluid is easy. Simply push the patella backward. You can feel and hear it hit the femur after a short travel.

Aspiration of the knee is a simple and rewarding procedure. Make a wheal with 1 per cent procaine, then, using the same needle, inject the area of the joint capsule, like this:

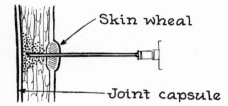

There are two sites where aspiration may be easily accomplished. They are these:

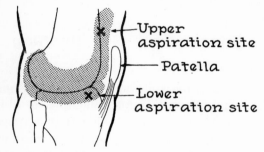

After aspiration, cut two pads of foam rubber to fit the area and place them like this:

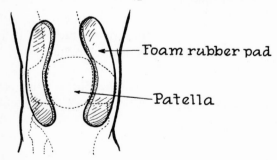

Then wrap with an elastic bandage.

Injury to the Medial Semilunar Cartilage. This is the most frequent internal derangement of the knee joint. Since the cartilaginous tissue has no blood supply and is exposed to the frequent compression and release in the course of even minimal standing and walking, healing is frequently delayed or does

not occur. Common types of lesions and repair are: (1) crack, which does not heal or fills with connective tissue; (2) "bucket handle" fracture, which neither heals nor fills with connective tissue; (3) rupture of anterior attachment which often heals; (4) avulsed fragment, which moves free in the joint.

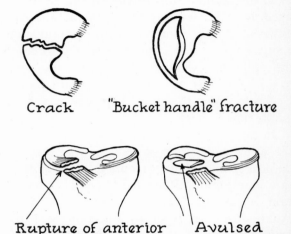

Crack   "Bucket handle" fracture

Rupture of anterior   Avulsed
attachment   fragment

Acute trauma followed by inability to perform complete extension is the history in most acute cases. Usually reduction of the misplaced cartilage has been accomplished before the patient is seen. To reduce, first aspirate any effusion that is present, then, if you feel it is necessary, anesthetize by infiltrating the tender areas with procaine, like this:

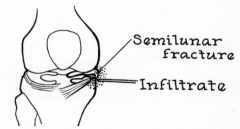

After anesthesia is effected have the patient sit on a table with his legs dangling over the side. Make strong traction on the ankle, externally rotate it and then extend the leg rapidly. Reduction is usually accompanied by an audible click and full extension returns immediately.

If displacement has been reduced before you see the patient or if the case is one of long standing, the only procedures of use in making a diagnosis are taking an accurate history and noting tenderness here:

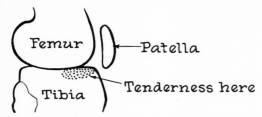

By no means are we justified in assuming that this procedure is specific for ruptured semilunar cartilage. In the presence of negative x-rays and negative findings as far as ligamentous damage is concerned, one may assume that the semilunar cartilage is at fault.

Treatment procedure in the acute case is aspiration of the knee and application of a firm posterior splint. A ⅛ inch wedge is applied to the inner side of the heel and the patient is allowed to walk. One month is the minimum time for such immobilization if healing is to be complete.

Injury to the Medial Ligament. This is the most frequent injury to a ligamentous structure about the knee. Unfortunately, the medial ligament overlies the semilunar cartilage and we may have difficulty differentiating injury of the two structures.

After aspirating the joint, which usually is filled with sanguineous exudate, the area which remains painful to the touch is injected with 1 per cent procaine. After waiting a few minutes, the joint is tested for flexion and extension. If the ligament is injured and the cartilage intact, full extension is possible and no audible click is heard upon extension.

Next the joint is tested for abnormal motility. If the medial ligament is torn there will be abnormal lateral motion.

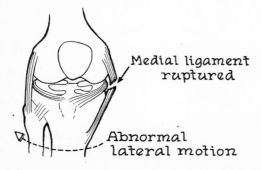

Treatment is application of a posterior splint, which should be applied snugly. In the presence of actual rupture of the ligament, fixation should be maintained for at least 60 days. Sprains, of course, need be fixed for only a week or two.

Injury to Cruciate Ligaments. The cruciate ligaments run like this:

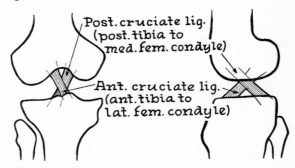

They are seldom injured separately but may be involved in other knee injuries quite frequently. Their integrity may be tested by seating the patient on an examining stool with both his feet flat on the floor. Grasp the leg by the calf and try to pull the tibia forward on the knee joint. If there is a distinct increase in range of motion you may postulate rupture of the anterior cruciate. Backward motion indicates posterior cruciate disruption. Treatment is limited to prolonged immobilization.

"Worn-out Knees." Actually we can find numerous syndromes of painful knees ascribed to everything from estrogen levels to weather changes due to the atomic bomb. As nearly as I can coordinate the usual clinical picture and the multiplicity of theories, the facts are these:

Symptoms usually appear in women and occur soon after they have added weight, but not ordinarily until about the time of the menopause. No one knows whether the actual change in estrogen level has any effect. There appears to be a definite weakening of supporting musculature. Arches drop, there is slight inward rotation of the lower leg. As a result there is slight shortening of the inner hamstrings, which finally becomes permanent and limits full extension at the knee.

These women are seldom athletes and the changes noted are of little significance except for one fact: they increase the amount of weight borne by the medial semilunar cartilage. This results, first, in tenderness over the cartilage after long standing or walking. Insult to the cartilage is poorly repaired and symptoms usually get worse until mild inflammatory reaction and fibrosis are present throughout the knee.

The principal diagnostic procedure is to notice the changes in structure and function mentioned. Take an A-P x-ray and notice the bony lipping that occurs and the "sharpening" of the tibial spines.

Treatment procedures begin with procainization of the tender areas, which should be repeated as indicated. A program of weight reduction is begun and the patient fitted with proper arch supports. Now an Unna paste boot is applied with the heel rotated slightly inward and the fore part of the foot level. At times it may be wise to elevate the inner surface of the heel ⅛ inch by placing proper heel pads in the shoes. Actually, the whole object of treatment is to force weight bearing on the outer surface of the heel and, by overcorrecting, remedy the deformity. These procedures, if carefully done, give excellent results. Pain usually disappears in a very few weeks but treatment should be continued at least 3 or 4 weeks after the patient is comfortable.

Since the Unna paste makes such an excellent immobilizing dressing for a multitude of lesions, suppose we stop right here and discuss manufacture and use. The formula is:

Gelatin	200 gm.
Zinc oxide powder	100 gm.
Glycerin	400 cc.
Water	375 cc.

Heat the water to boiling and dissolve the gelatin in it. Mix the zinc oxide with the glycerin until smooth and add to the gelatin-water mixture. Cook for ½ hour. This will make enough paste for about four leg dressings. If you like the dressing and plan to use it often, much more can be made up at one time. When cool, it forms a rubbery mass which can be cut into chunks and stored. I keep mine in the refrigerator.

A hot plate and a double boiler are all that you need to melt the paste. To apply, wrap the part to be covered with a single layer of gauze, dip a 2 inch paint brush in the liquefied paste and paint a layer over the gauze. Apply another layer of gauze and another layer of paste, etc. An adequate dressing may require from two to eight layers. Removal is easy—simply cut with bandage scissors and lift off.

I would urge the average practitioner not to forget the advantages of this dressing. If you do not have an adequate assistant it is a nuisance, for preparation and application do take time. On the other hand, a bright helper can apply these dressings under your supervision and results will justify the time he spends.

The Ankle Joint

Sprains of the ankle are very common, but, unfortunately, so are disruptions of the ligaments in this area. A moment to consider the pathology of the two lesions will make the reason for different treatment procedures quite clear.

The ligaments and other periarticular tissues are richly supplied with nerve endings. Sudden stretching of a ligament may do mechanical damage to any number of these nerve endings. In addition, extravasated blood from ruptured small vessels may act as an irritant. The strain will get well in a few days with or without immobilization.

A sudden stretch may snap a ligament, leaving an actual laceration which will heal poorly if constant motion is allowed. These cases must be immobilized for 4 to 6 weeks.

There is no definitive test for ligamentous rupture. Several procedures are useful, but first notice the anatomy of the medial and lateral deep ligaments:

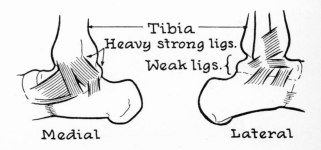

Medial   Lateral

and the anatomy of superficial ligamentous structures:

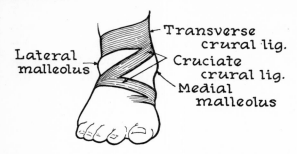

Notice, in the illustration of deep ligaments, that the lateral ligaments are much smaller and, therefore, weaker than the medial. For this reason, sprains of the lateral ligaments are much more common.

The most reliable guide to possible rupture of a ligament is the apparent severity of the injury. A test for functional integrity of the lateral ligaments may be made by injecting the tender area with procaine and attempting to elicit increased motion in the ankle. First rotate the normal ankle to its maximal non-painful degree. Then do the same with the injured ankle. In the presence of a ruptured ligament you may expect at least 10 degrees additional rotation.

One lesion that is frequently missed is tearing of the superficial ligaments. These tears usually take place near the malleolar attachment, like this:

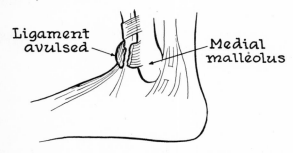

Superficial swelling and extreme tenderness are important points in diagnosis but I know of no way to be certain whether stretching or actual tearing has occurred except to base a guess on the relative intensity of the symptoms.

Adhesive strapping is a second-rate treatment for the damaged ankle. For sprains I believe the Unna paste boot (at times applied over a tight elastic bandage) is the best simple

treatment. Using as an example a sprain of the lateral ligaments, first inject the painful area with procaine or Efocaine. Have the patient elevate the foot and cold pack it for several hours and then return for dressing.

Reinject the area if necessary at this second visit. Place the foot in a position of inversion to secure maximal shortening of the involved ligaments and apply an Unna boot. Leave this in place for 4 to 6 days.

If you feel a ligament has been ruptured, rest and cold pack the extremity for 24 hours and apply a cast from calf to toes. Six to 8 weeks are required for healing.

FRACTURES

In this section we will consider only the most common fractures that are within the realm of office treatment. Where diagnostic procedures are useful in more complex fractures, they will be given but treatment procedures will be omitted.

I know that we face a real problem of decision in considering the office treatment of a fracture. The tendency is to hospitalize them all with no regard for simplicity. Many common fractures are so simple to treat that this seems only a way of increasing medical costs to the patient. I do not pretend to know the answer, but I treat many fractures in the office.

Malar Bone

These fractures are relatively frequent results of blows on the head. In my own practice the beer-bottle fight has been most productive in this respect. Orbital edema or hematoma with exophthalmos, subconjunctival hemorrhage, and frequently diplopia are the usual symptoms. To check for the fracture, stand behind the patient and *gently* run your fingers around the edge of both orbits. Defects will be readily felt if they extend to the orbital margin.

If there is the remotest doubt about the existence of a fracture, be sure to take an x-ray. The same position used for sinuses gives good delineation of the orbital areas. Place the patient with nose and forehead touching the table, like this:

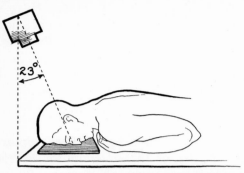

The view gives good delineation of the orbital margin. Here is a sketch of what is seen with a fracture on one side:

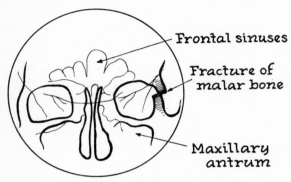

When the displacement is minimal (⅛ inch or less) and there is no interference with movements of mastication, reduction is not necessary. This is true even in the presence of diplopia. In such instances the double vision is a result of the edema following injury and is unlikely to last more than 3 or 4 days.

Greater displacements may be replaced in the office surgery if there is no involvement of air-bearing structures near the bone. Do it like this:

First, sterilize a small wood screw, a nail, a pair of pliers and a screwdriver. Orthopedic equipment is desirable but garden variety dime store tools can be made to work. After anesthesia with procaine, make a vertical incision about ¾ inch long, like this:

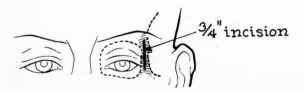

Using sharp dissection, expose the bone. If you have a drill, open a hole into the displaced bone somewhat smaller than the screw. The nail can be made to serve the same purpose. Put it in place and tap it (NOT hit it) with the pliers so as to drive a small hole through the cortex, which is not particularly heavy. Now insert the screw just enough to get a firm purchase on the bone. Remove and re-insert in the same threads so that it won't be stuck fast after you have replaced the bone. Now your operative field looks like this:

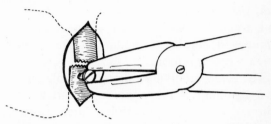

Grasp the head of the screw with the pliers and use the purchase secured by this along with external pressure to replace the fragment. Fixation is not necessary. Remove the screw, close the laceration and instruct the patient to rest for 12 to 24 hours and to avoid strenuous activity for at least 10 days.

During the process of reduction be very careful not to slip or jerk the fragment. Proximity to orbital contents should be remembered at all times.

Zygoma

This bone, too, is usually fractured in the barroom brawl. A few cases are seen as a result of automobile accidents. If there is little or no displacement, and mastication is functionally adequate, the fracture is trivial and may be ignored. *Be sure* to explain to the patient that a fracture is present but that it will heal without treatment.

The best x-ray technique for examination of the zygomatic processes is this:

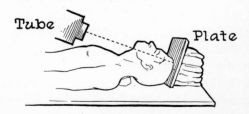

In the presence of a depressed fracture, mechanical elevation is necessary and fixation for a few days to a week may be desirable. Place a tongue blade over the zygomatic process and mark the edges of the tongue blade, like this:

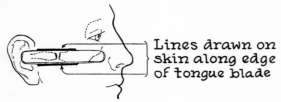

Lines drawn on skin along edge of tongue blade

Make stab wounds in the skin on both sides of the bone just inside the two lines you have drawn. Using a full curve cutting needle threaded with tantalum wire of heavy gauge, enter through the upper incision, pass behind the bone and out through the lower incision. (In this area the skin is mobile enough to allow manipulation to the needle point.) The tantalum wire should be inserted on a curved needle passing through the stab wounds in the skin and behind the zygoma like this:

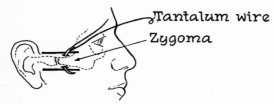

Tantalum wire
Zygoma

Traction on the ends of the wire will usually bring prompt reduction. If position is not maintained, cut a tongue blade to half its normal length, place it between the exits of the wires and twist them together over it, like this:

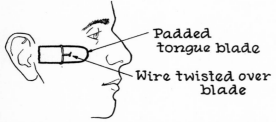

Padded tongue blade
Wire twisted over blade

Usually 10 to 15 days' fixation by this method is ample.

Clavicle

A brief summary of function will serve to explain causation and treatment of clavicular fracture. The acromioclavicular articulation represents the only bony connection between the arm and the trunk. The clavicle not only serves as a point of attachment for the muscles that elevate the shoulder but also keeps the shoulder a fixed distance from the sternoclavicular articulation, like this:

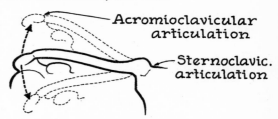

Acromioclavicular articulation
Sternoclavic. articulation

A sudden blow tending to push downward on the shoulder will fracture the bone at its weakest portion—the junction between middle and outer thirds. When this fracture occurs the shoulder drops, pulling the outer fragment downward, and the sternocleidomastoid tone tends to elevate the inner fragment, like this:

Sternocleido-mastoid m.

Since we can do little or nothing about the position of the inner fragment without major procedures, our job is to make the outer fragment conform to the inner. This is done by elevating the shoulder and pulling it backwards. Seen from the lateral aspect, reduction is accomplished by this movement:

If one uses gentle manipulation, no anesthesia will be needed for many of these cases. If obtundation of pain is necessary, inject 10 cc. of 1 per cent procaine into the hematoma at the fracture site. Attempt manual reduction by standing behind the patient and slowly elevating and pulling back both shoulders. If reduction is not achieved immediately, have an assistant maintain traction while you manipulate the bone by grasping each part between the fingers.

Should reduction be difficult or seem too traumatic, try this method: Have the patient lie on his back on a firm mattress with the injured shoulder at the edge of the bed and the arm hanging over the edge, like this:

If the patient wishes a pillow *be sure* it is placed under the head and not under the injured shoulder. Reduction usually occurs spontaneously in a matter of 1 to 2 hours. Have someone stay with the patient to be sure the position is maintained and to notice any signs of circulatory obstruction or nerve damage.

There have been several hundred methods proposed to immobilize or hold in position the clavicular fracture. None is very satisfactory, so you are faced with a choice of evils. The method I prefer is a homemade **T** splint constructed from 1 by 3 inch boards and web belting with three buckles. These splints may be made like this: Mortise the two boards together, fastening them with several ¾ inch flathead screws. Using similar screws, attach the belting to the splint like this:

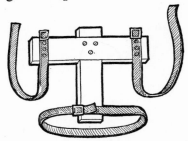

Notice that the buckles are all placed so they will not touch the patient. Cut two or four axillary pads of ½ inch foam rubber. They work better if shaped like this:

Top view   Side view

Place them in position and apply the splint (pad the bare wood with sheet wadding). Do not put it on tightly to begin with, for the patient must learn to tolerate it and some people do not accommodate readily to axillary pressure. Actually the patient will unconsciously "rear back" to avoid the pressure and will soon learn to hold himself in the proper position. See him each day and tighten the straps a little at each visit until proper position is attained.

Fixation should be maintained for 3 to 4 weeks but the patient should be encouraged to continue light activity during this period.

There are far more complications from overzealous treatment than from the fracture itself. Extensive manipulation is dangerous and unnecessary. These fractures heal well almost without regard to treatment. Nerve and blood vessel damage may occur if fixation involves too much axillary pressure. In older people there may be loss of joint function if fixation is maintained too long.

Humerus

To begin with, you must realize that many fractures of the humerus are hospital problems and ill-advised attempts at reduction merely make things harder for you to accomplish proper treatment in the hospital. In this discussion we will only mention those less complicated fractures that are candidates for office procedures.

Separation of the upper epiphysis of the humerus is a common lesion of adolescence. Two anatomic points are of some importance in preparing for reduction. First, the epiphysis sits on the shaft like a modified dunce cap with the inner part of the epiphyseal line inside the joint capsule and the lateral part outside the joint, like this:

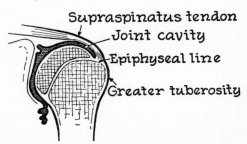

Supraspinatus tendon
Joint cavity
Epiphyseal line
Greater tuberosity

Second, in cases of complete separation, the muscles attached to the tubercles tend to pull the upper fragment into a position of abduction, external rotation, and slight flexion. To simplify, picture a man in the process of saluting with the hand about halfway between the beltline and the forehead. That is the position the upper fragment assumes.

Since there is little hope of changing the position of the upper fragment as just described, we must make the lower fragment conform. Reduction would be easy (or at least, easier) if it were not for the thick, tough periosteum of the upper humerus seen in this age group. It seldom tears free all around the circumference and, therefore, makes sufficient stretching of the arm difficult. This periosteum is so thick that it often tears off a fragment on the inner side of the shaft, like this:

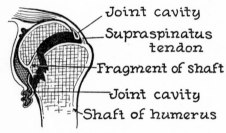

Joint cavity
Supraspinatus tendon
Fragment of shaft
Joint cavity
Shaft of humerus

Office procedures are seldom applicable to an injury of this nature.

Fortunately most epiphyseal separations merely represent a jerking free of the epiphysis without major displacement. It is important to remember that *the original x-ray may be negative* in these cases and that diagnosis must be made on an assumptive basis. Films taken three weeks after injury may show new bone formation where the periosteum has been stripped away from the upper shaft, like this:

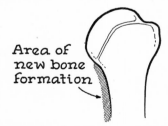

Area of new bone formation

When there is no displacement, the arm may be bound to the side with a muslin strip and the forearm carried in a sling. Usually

10 days of such fixation is enough if the youngster is cooperative enough to avoid strenuous exercise for an additional 2 weeks.

If moderate displacement is present without complicating factors, such as fracture of the shaft, reduction may be accomplished in the office if equipment for general anesthesia is at hand. Strong traction must be made for 10 minutes and then replacement accomplished by finger manipulation of the head and shaft. Fixation in the "half salute" position is usual. Should adequate reduction not be obtained immediately, these patients become problems for the orthopedist.

Fractures of the upper humerus are quite common and a substantial percentage show little or no displacement of the fragments. Procedures used in treatment are simple in the extreme. A muslin swathe dressing is sufficient in most instances. To apply one, first cut an axillary pad of ½ inch sponge rubber and apply it as shown below. Next make a wrist sling of folded muslin, like this:

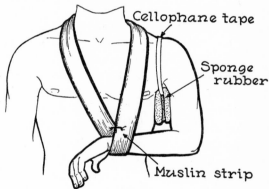

Cellophane tape
Sponge rubber
Muslin strip

Finally, apply a piece of muslin, like this:

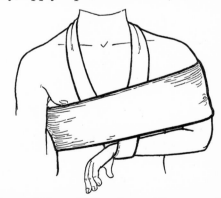

Time of immobilization will range from 1 to 3 weeks. This should be followed by a period of exercise gradually increasing in extent until the full range of motion at the shoulder is brought into play.

Impacted fractures may be treated this same way if range of passive motion is adequate and if shortening does not exceed ½ inch. The important thing is to test for full motion at the shoulder joint before assuming that the impaction need not be broken up. Particularly in old people is the impaction best left alone, even if there is slight decrease in normal range of motion.

Fractures through the surgical neck with displacement of moderate degree may often be treated as office problems. Such fractures often show slight abduction and external rotation of the proximal fragment, like this:

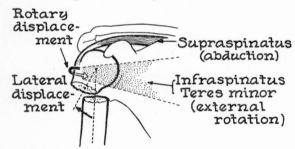

while the distal fragment is pulled internally by the pectorals, like this:

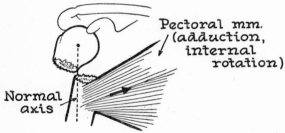

In considering office procedures for use in treatment, several anatomic points are of prime importance. The tendon of the long head of the biceps is firmly anchored in the bicipital groove between the tuberosities, like this:

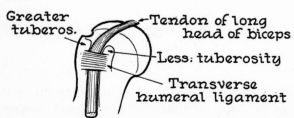

It tends to resist great displacement of the upper fragment and to serve as an excellent "splint" favoring retention of the fragments in place. Unless ruptured or torn from its bed, the tendon is one of our best allies.

In normal position the greater tuberosity and the lateral epicondyle are in the same plane. This furnishes the best guide we have for proper positioning in the rotary plane. The two landmarks should be palpated often during the course of the reduction.

Local anesthesia works excellently for reduction of such fractures when the injury is less than 24 hours old. Make two skin wheals and insert the needle into the hematoma through each wheal, like this:

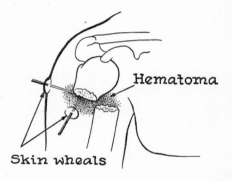

and inject 10 cc. of 1 per cent procaine. Wait 10 minutes for the anesthetic to reach full effectiveness. Have the patient lie comfortably on a table and "tie him down" with a muslin band around his waist. Place another muslin band around your waist and around the patient's flexed forearm, like this:

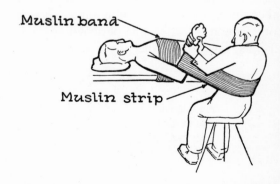

By leaning back, exert steady traction on the arm in about 45 degrees abduction for 5 to 10 minutes. When sufficient traction has been exerted to overcome the muscle pull, press the upper fragment into line, like this:

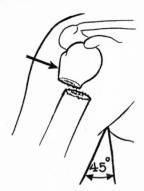

When proper apposition is obtained, release the traction gradually and bring the arm to the side. During this maneuver place one hand lightly over the fracture site. If there is any movement at the fracture site you will feel it. If position is well maintained and the fragments seem well engaged, the arm may be bound to the side by means of a swathe dressing as mentioned on page 45. In addition, a protective cap of cardboard is valuable. Cut a piece of cardboard in the shape of a "race track oval" and soak it in water for a few minutes. Put a layer of cotton over the shoulder and mold the wet cardboard over it. Bandage like this:

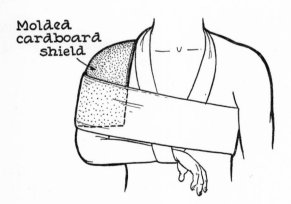

Molded cardboard shield

Should the fragments slip when the arm is brought to the side, or if you feel that engagement is insufficient to maintain proper reduction, repeat the entire procedure, including at least five minutes of traction, and put on a plaster spica to hold the arm in a "half salute" position. It is best for the physician to maintain reduction while an assistant applies the

cast. This is proper "half salute" positioning:

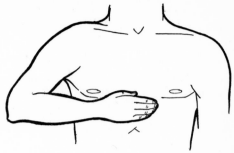

Speedy application of functional exercise is an absolute essential in the care of these fractures. Within a week the hand should be exercised. A good way to accomplish this is to have the patient buy a sponge-rubber ball and squeeze it regularly. Within 10 days the cast can be cut off at the wrist and within 2 weeks or a little longer the forearm portion may be bivalved and the upper half removed. Four to 6 weeks is ample in the average case.

Fractures of the humeral shaft in good position can be treated with a sugar-tong splint and sling. To apply the sugar-tong splint, measure from the greater tuberosity down the arm, around the elbow and back up the inner surface to the axilla. Using 4 inch bandage make a ten layer splint of this length. Cut a piece of ½ inch foam rubber 4 inches wide and 6 inches long. Fold the foam rubber over the end to be placed in the axilla and apply the splint like this:

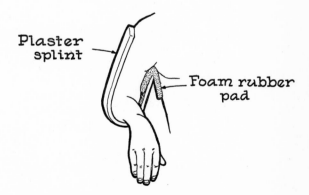

Plaster splint

Foam rubber pad

Over this apply the standard swathe dressing. Early motion is essential but you must remember the tendency for non-union in these fractures. A minimum fixation period of 8 weeks seems advisable even for those fractures in good position.

Major displacement is most common in fractures at the junction between the medial and upper thirds. The displacement is effected by the medial pull of the pectorals on the upper fragment and the lateral pull of the deltoid on the lower fragment, like this:

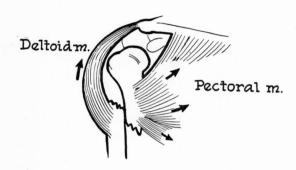

In addition, spasm of the biceps and triceps tends to produce overriding.

Most of these fractures can be reduced easily under local anesthesia produced by injecting 15 to 20 cc. of 1 per cent procaine into the hematoma. Occasionally, brachial plexus block may be of service. The technique is as follows:

Notice that the plexus runs back of and a little superior to the subclavian artery as it passes between the clavicle and first rib, like this:

The area to be injected lies just above the middle of the clavicle, where the plexus is most safely approached. For the solution you may use plain procaine or procaine to which hyaluronidase has been added. Have the patient lie down comfortably on his back without a pillow and ask him to turn his head away from the site to be injected. Be sure that both arms lie relaxed along the sides of the body; this serves to lower the shoulders.

Now make a skin wheal about ½ or ¾ inch above the middle of the clavicle, here:

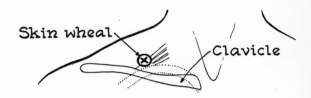

Using a 2 inch needle without attached syringe, enter through the center of the wheal and aim the needle point toward the fourth lumbar vertebra. The needle without syringe is used so that the operator may be immediately aware of the act if he should enter a blood vessel. Before making deep insertion, attempt to palpate the subclavian artery with a finger. In most people, it can be felt with ease and will serve as a valuable landmark. You want the needle to go past the artery in the direction mentioned, just "skimming by" the arterial wall.

Let me hasten to say that should the needle inadvertently enter the artery—which practically never happens—no great tragedy has occurred. Simply withdraw the needle and apply pressure for a few minutes.

After locating the artery by palpation, insert the needle slowly in the direction indicated. Paresthesias about the elbow and in the fingers commonly occur when the plexus is entered. Patients usually describe them as an electric sensation, and an indignant, "Hey, you shocked me!" is an indication of success. If paresthesias of some sort are not obtained it is worthwhile to withdraw the needle and reinsert it, for anesthesia is much more successful in those cases in which paresthesias are obtained.

When you are relatively certain of proper needle position, attach a syringe of 1 per cent procaine, aspirate to be certain a small vessel has not been entered, and inject 15 to 20 cc. It is not necessary to move the needle about while injecting.

When the operator uses reasonable caution, complications are exceedingly rare. Of course, punching about with the needle invites trouble. It is easier to be sure where one is going before one starts. Too deep insertion usually results only in contact with the first rib. Penetration of the pleura is theoretically possible but I have never seen it occur. A cough and a prompt complaint of regional pain should be indications for partial withdrawal of the needle.

Rather infrequently, seepage of the solution may cause transient phrenic paresis. The condition rarely lasts more than an hour or two and has no significance for the injured patient who is otherwise in good condition. When lung disease or marked shock is present the phrenic weakness may have grave consequences. Particularly in cases of shock is this a serious matter, and such cases are better treated under local anesthesia. Fortunately, few upper extremity fractures have severe shock.

One avoidable complication occurs with sufficient frequency to demand discussion. It is the brachial neuritis that follows trauma to the nerves. In theory this complication may be caused in two ways: First, by repeated trauma to the fibers from careless handling of the needle. This can be almost eliminated by careful planning to make necessary insertion of the needle only a minimal number of times and by being sure to withdraw the needle nearly to the skin before changing direction.

Second, it is possible (in conjecture, at least) to inject the solution into nerve sheaths under sufficient pressure to cause damage. It is probably wise not to force the procaine in rapidly under high pressure.

All this sounds rather like the grim warnings that are written about all procedures. As a matter of fact, the brachial plexus block is an easy thing to do, an excellent anesthesia producer, and far safer than any general anesthetic that I know of. By all means know and use this useful procedure.

Before this digression, we were talking about fracture of the humeral shaft. After proper anesthesia is secured, traction is applied, using a steadily increasing pull until muscle spasm is overcome. Bones are manipulated gently into position and the traction is slowly released. One great danger is that rough manipulation or too much pressure from the examiner's fingers may literally push soft tissue between the fragments, like this:

Impacted muscle

This, of course, is a potent cause of non-union and of imperfect reduction.

If you can secure ⅓ or more apposition of the fragments with solid engagement and the arm in correct functional position, the final result is likely to be good. If the bone is in proper position and stays that way when traction is released, splint with a sugar-tong splint and dress exactly as specified in the preceding paragraphs on fractures in good position.

Rarely, we have a case where the bones will remain in apposition while in abduction or the "half-salute" position, but will slip immediately upon the arm being placed at the side. The answer is obvious. Use a plaster shoulder spica and keep the arm in the most advantageous position.

Spiral and oblique fractures will not often be amenable to treatment without mechanical extension. They are, of course, usually hospital problems. Under unusual circumstances a hanging cast applied in the office will have to serve. To apply a hanging cast, first put a sugar-tong splint on exactly as specified in the preceding paragraphs. Then make another sugar-tong to run from the elbow to the metacarpophalangeal joints on both volar and dorsal surfaces. Apply it like this:

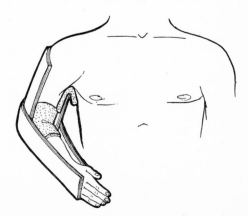

Now pad the antecubital fossa with foam rubber and use roller plaster to complete the cast. Incorporate a loop of webbing in the cast just proximal to the wrist joint so that the cast may be suspended from a sling. The final application should look like this:

Instruct the patient to sleep in a semi-erect position without any support to the cast. In 24 hours take an x-ray to see if reduction is complete. If angulation is present it may usually be corrected by shortening or lengthening the sling. If more weight is needed at the elbow, add plaster or tape metal weights under the elbow. Have the patient start movement at the shoulder within a week, or sooner, by bending forward and gently rotating the arm.

If the patient is followed carefully enough and proper adjustments are made in weight and angle of the cast, this is often a very satisfactory method of treatment. I cannot, however, emphasize too strongly that to throw a hanging cast on and forget it is to court disaster.

Fractures of the humeral shaft are particularly treacherous in two respects. There is a greater than normal tendency to non-union, which is due, I have been led to believe, more often to engagement of soft tissues between the bone ends than to poor blood supply. There is also a tendency toward injury of the radial nerve, which lies directly on the surface of the periosteum. It may be contused or lacerated at the time of fracture, caught in callus, or surrounded by scar tissue. These complications should be kept in mind.

Supracondylar fractures with posterior displacement of the distal fragment are common, particularly in children. The normal ana-

tomic features of the elbow joint which must be restored are these:

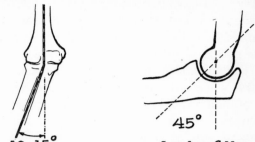

The "carrying angle" (ant. view)   Angle of the humeral articular surface

The fracture usually looks like this:

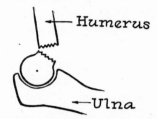

This is one of the few fractures we see with any frequency in which the soft tissues take precedence over the fracture itself. *Never forget for one moment* the likelihood of extensive and dangerous soft tissue injury. Interference with the brachial artery is all too common and we see too many cases in which this was ignored because of the dramatic appearance of the fracture in x-ray. Again let me say, it is better to have a patient with limited elbow function than a patient with no forearm.

When such a fracture is seen the first step is to evaluate the status of the circulation in the forearm. In the presence of a full radial pulse, treatment may be directed toward reduction of the fracture in a leisurely manner. If the pulse is absent or faint, follow these steps:

1. Do a brachial block both for anesthesia and to relax arteriospasm if present.

2. Make gentle but strong traction on the arm to release the artery if it be pinched between fragments. This is, of course, proper procedure for reduction. If you get a good reduction, fine; if not, release the artery anyway.

3. If there is extreme swelling, aspirate the area with a large-bore needle. Should prompt re-establishment of swelling lead you to believe the artery is severed, get the patient to a hospital at once, call a vascular surgeon and follow his directions. If you cannot do this, it may occasionally be better to ligate the brachial artery distal to the branching of the profunda than to face certain trouble later. This is by no means a rule, or even, usually, a good idea. It is something for consideration as a measure of desperation.

4. If there is great edema that is interfering with circulation, never hesitate to incise the skin and deep fascia widely to release pressure. This procedure is sometimes the most important of all. Do it in a hospital if possible; if not, do it at home or under whatever circumstances are necessary. Do it with good surgical tools if possible; do it with a razor blade or a dull pocket knife if not. But by all means, *do it immediately* if and when indicated.

Now that we have mentioned some of the horrible things that can happen, let me hasten to say that most of these fractures are simple, uncomplicated injuries. Reduction and maintenance of position can be deceptively easy. To accomplish this, begin by establishing anesthesia, preferrably by means of brachial block.

After obtundation of pain has reached maximum, begin reduction by exerting firm traction along the axis of the arm, by either of these methods:

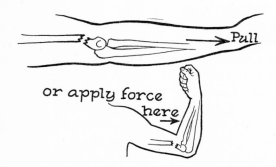

When you feel that muscle pull has been overcome, replace the fracture by grasping the distal fragment between the fingers and thumb of each hand and lining up the lateral epicondyle with the greater tuberosity. Check for lateral angulation by comparing the carrying angle on the good side with the carrying angle re-established on the fractured side.

When reduction is complete, flex the arm until the radial pulse is altered or fails. Gradually release the flexion until the pulse resumes its normal character. Then continue to extend for another 10 degrees. This 10 degree motion may be estimated by moving the hand downward about 5 inches as shown below.

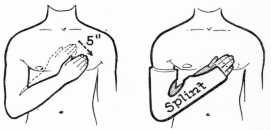

Place the hand in neutral position, i.e., halfway between pronation and supination. Now measure from the surgical neck of the humerus, around the elbow to the base of the fingers. Make a fifteen layer plaster splint this length and apply it to the skin, as shown above. While wet, trim the splint as shown by shaded areas above. Pad the antecubital fossa with ½ inch sponge rubber and bandage the splint in place. Have some member of the family check the radial pulse every hour for the first 6 hours and every 2 hours for the next 12 hours. *Be sure* to caution the patient about numbness, cyanosis and pain in the forearm and hand. Have him report immediately if any of these symptoms occur.

Should there be interference with circulation, remove the arm from the cast immediately, elevate it and use hot packs. Under no circumstances should anything be assumed about such a fracture or splint. *Always* check often and thoroughly.

Other fractures about the distal end of the humerus are only rarely treated as office procedures.

Radius and Ulna

Fractures of the olecranon are relatively common but many are surgical problems. If the fragments are in good position or if they are in apposition upon extending the arm, office treatment may be satisfactory. Simply put on a firm anterior or posterior splint, skin-tight, and fix it in place with gauze bandage, like this:

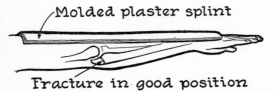

Have the patient begin active use of the arm immediately.

Fracture of the head of the radius is fairly common and, surprisingly enough, the fracture is not infrequently missed. The usual cause is a fall on the extended and pronated hand. Fortunately, the usual fracture is a splitting or chipping of the head that looks like this:

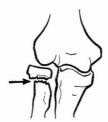

Angulation and extensive comminution are sometimes seen. Such fractures are problems to be handled in the hospital and should not be manipulated elsewhere.

Diagnosis may be suspected by rotating the head of the radius beneath the palpating finger, like this:

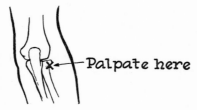

These fractures are not always readily visualized by x-ray and it may be necessary to take several oblique views before clear delineation is obtained.

When fragments are in good position, all that is necessary is a posterior skin-tight plaster splint with the elbow in flexion and the hand in neutral position, like this:

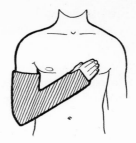

Early motion at the shoulder is imperative and fixation for 4 or 5 weeks is usually adequate.

When the radial head is found to be extensively comminuted but remains in relatively good position, some method is needed to prevent excessive roughness of the articular surface. One which seems to have had some success is repeated procainization of the fracture area with immediate active motion of the injured area. If such treatment is chosen, inject the fracture area. If the fracture extends to the joint surface, inject the joint capsule, otherwise inject this area:

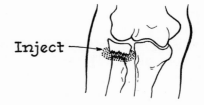

Have the patient carry his arm in a sling but do not interdict any motion except that involving heavy lifting. Encourage the patient to pronate and supinate the arm.

In treatment of other fractures of the radius and ulna, an understanding of the mechanics of the forearm is necessary. Force traveling up the arm is transmitted through the interosseous membrane, which is very tough and strong, like this:

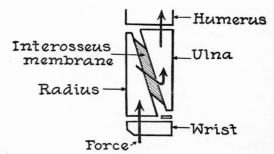

Both proper transmission of force and the movements of pronation and supination depend on maintenance of proper space between the radius and ulna. In replacement of fractures the proper preservation of the interosseous space and the membrane is more important than exact bony apposition. A good functional result may not be obtained unless this is kept in mind.

Fractures of the forearm can be exceedingly difficult. If there is comminution or obliquity of the fracture line or if there is soft tissue injury with great swelling, hospitalization is indicated. When no displacement is present or when there is only minor displacement with preservation of the interosseous space, application of anterior and posterior plaster splints held in place by gauze wrappings is sufficient treatment. After several days the splints may be wrapped with plaster to form a circular cast.

Children often sustain a greenstick fracture with bowing. Reduction is usually quite easy. While steady traction is applied on the wrist, the deformity is sharply overcorrected and released suddenly. The bones will usually spring back into proper position. One precaution is paramount. *Never* grasp the bones so that they are pressed together, obliterating or narrowing the interosseous space. A good way to avoid this is to grasp the arm with the fingers in the interosseous space on one side and the thumbs in the space on the opposite side.

When there is a fracture of one bone with displacement, reduction can occasionally be effected this way: Have an assistant apply firm traction at the wrist. Grasp the fractured bone and convert the deformity into a posterior bowing, like this:

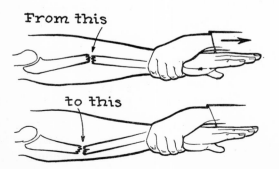

Now adjust the ends into proper apposition *while maintaining* the posterior bowing. Next, place your fingers in the interosseous space to maintain separation and align the bone (eliminating the posterior bowing) by a quick pull.

When both bones are fractured, reduction may be obtained the same way. After reduction, traction is maintained while anterior and posterior splints are applied from the base of the fingers to the axilla, with the elbow in 90 degree flexion. If the fracture is in the lower two-thirds of the forearm, keep the hand in neutral position. If in the upper third, supinate the hand.

After 3 days the splints may be converted into a circular cast by rolling with plaster. X-rays should be taken on the first, third and fifth days, for there is a great tendency for these fractures to slip. Fixation should be maintained for a minimum of 6 weeks.

We should never hesitate to seek skilled orthopedic consultation in such fractures. Open reduction is seldom necessary but improper closed reduction can be a tragic and crippling procedure. Once again, always remember the interosseous membrane.

Colles' fracture is not unduly difficult to treat if one keeps firmly in mind the anatomic principles concerned. Many poor results are due simply to lack of knowledge of anatomy in treating the fracture.

The normal relationship of the distal end of the radius and ulna may be represented like this:

Note particularly the normal angle formed by the bones at their junction with the carpals. The radius is essentially an upward continuation of the hand and wrist, while the ulna absorbs very little of the weight bearing at the wrist joint. The radius is longer than the ulna, by nearly ½ inch, and the two bones are quite close.

Viewed laterally, the normal wrist looks like this:

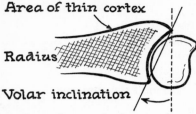

Notice that the articular surface of the radius inclines volarward. The thinner cortex on the dorsal surface of the radius is about ¾ inch from the articular surface of the bone.

Most of the fractures without deformity are simply crushing injuries of the cortex in its thinnest area. These are much more frequent in children than in adults. To use the term "fracture without deformity" is misleading, for frequently the articular surface of the radius may lose some of its volar angulation in these fractures. The lateral x-ray should be examined most carefully in wrist injuries in children for this loss of angulation.

The diagnosis of a Colles' fracture *with* deformity is relatively easy. This is a picture of a typical fracture:

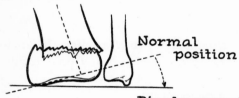

Notice that the radius has been impacted and shortened, allowing a radial deviation of the hand. This is the most important sign of Colles' fracture. Also, the radial and ulnar styloids are at approximately the same level. Comparison with the styloids of the opposite wrist will make the presence of fracture amply clear. Here is a lateral view of the same fracture:

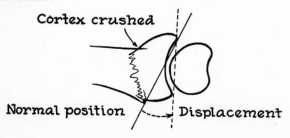

The dorsal inclination of the articular surface of the radius is exaggerated, indicating the reason for the typical "silver fork" deformity. Actually there is seldom this much angulation at the site of fracture. Emphasis on the "silver fork" deformity to the exclusion of some of the other more valuable signs is not good, for the "silver fork" deformity is perhaps the least important sign.

In repairing the Colles' fracture, there are three problems to overcome:

1. If the radius and ulna are separated, they must be brought back into apposition.

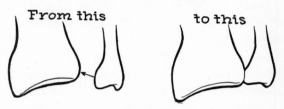

2. Shortening of the radius must be overcome.

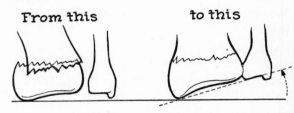

3. The volar inclination of the articular surface must be re-established.

Of the problems illustrated, the most important is shortening of the radius. In badly impacted fractures there may be necrosis of bone at the site of impaction, with an outcome of permanent shortening. This is seen in older people particularly and should be thought of when the fracture is reduced.

Anesthesia for reduction, except in badly comminuted fractures or extremely nervous people, is preferably 1 per cent procaine injected into the hematoma. This should consist of a single dorsal injection of approximately 10 cc. of the anesthetic. If it is thought necessary, an additional 2 to 5 cc. may be placed from the volar surface. In the event that the ulnar styloid has been pulled off, 2 cc. of procaine in this area will aid in reduction. Here is where the anesthetic solution should be placed:

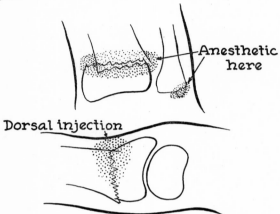

One should wait 10 to 15 minutes after injection of the anesthetic to allow a complete effect to take place before instituting reduction. There is no need to attempt reduction until the pain, which is the genesis of muscular spasm, has been eliminated.

Steady traction with mild ulnar deviation is the first step in reduction. It is done like this:

Next, the deformity is accentuated, like this:

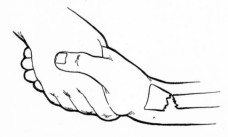

This serves, along with the steady pull, to break up the impaction. Next, the bones are brought back into normal apposition by manipulation, the proximal fragment being held between the thumb and first two fingers of one of the operator's hands, the distal fragment held by the other hand in the same grip, like this:

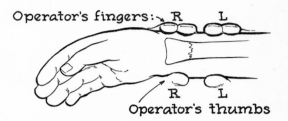

The correct position can frequently be maintained by a firm grip around the wrist. Three things should be checked to indicate completeness of reduction. If the reduction is satisfactory, (1) passive volar flexion of the hand should be easy and complete (compare with the opposite wrist), (2) the radial and ulnar styloids should be in their normal relationship, and (3) the radial deviation of the hand should be gone.

The fracture should be held in place by a dorsal and volar splint, secured in place by means of roller bandage. The volar splint should extend from just below the elbow to approximately the distal palmar crease. The dorsal splint should, likewise, extend from just below the elbow almost to the knuckles. There should be free movement of the metacarpophalangeal joints.

The patient should be cautioned to report any numbness or tingling of the fingers, swelling, or cyanosis, and should be encouraged to use the fingers and thumb as much as possible. Within 3 to 4 days the anterior and posterior splints can be changed into a cast simply by wrapping with a roll or two of plaster. This cast should remain on from 3 to 5 weeks.

One should not expect completely normal function of the wrist joint upon removing the cast. Intensive physiotherapy and mild exercise will do much to restore function. The patient should be told that the ultimate result depends upon his willingness to cooperate in re-establishing joint function.

Carpal Navicular

The carpal navicular is fractured with some frequency. It is probable that many of these fractures are dismissed as a sprained wrist. There are two types of disruption: (1) avulsion of the tuberosity, which is extra-articular and need not be immobilized more than 4 to 6 weeks, and (2) fracture of the body, which is intra-articular and requires a minimum of 8 weeks' immobilization. They appear like this:

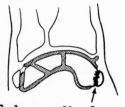 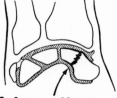

Extra-articular   Intra-articular

The x-ray is not always efficacious in demonstration of navicular fracture. Particularly is this true of the A-P and lateral views. It is wise always to take an oblique picture. If symptoms should continue in the presence of negative x-rays, treat the injury as a fracture and repeat the films in 2 weeks.

Diagnosis is relatively easy. To begin with, have the patient shake hands with you and ask him to grip your hand forcefully. He will experience pain if a fracture is present. Compare the anatomic snuff box on each side for swelling and tenderness. Next have the patient extend his thumb and push on it. Acute pain will result if there is a fracture.

Healing depends somewhat on adequacy of blood supply. In these injuries a portion or all of the minuscule arterial supply through the joint capsule and into the periosteum may be avulsed. The whole bone or a portion of it may die or undergo cystic degeneration (Kienböck's disease).

Fractures with displacement are hospital problems. Those in good position may be treated by immobilization in a skin-tight cast from knuckles to elbow with the hand in neutral position and the thumb slightly extended. The plaster should cover the thumb as far distal as the interphalangeal joint.

Metacarpals

Metacarpal fractures are frequent. Fortunately, most of them tend to remain in good position with simple splinting. The usual displacement is flexion of the distal fragment with palmar bowing. Diagnosis is usually made by palpation, noticing three factors: (1) bowing with undue prominence of the metacarpal head in the palm; (2) asymmetry between the knuckles of both fists; the deformity is apparent at first glance; (3) extreme tenderness at the site of fracture, and crepitation (but it is sheer cruelty to elicit this sign).

In questionable cases, gentle percussion is an excellent sign. Have the patient flex his fingers at the first interphalangeal joint, like this:

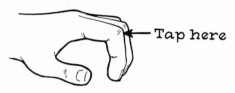

Tap here

With your finger, tap the flexed joints gently. Pain will be felt when force is transmitted to the involved metacarpal. Most of these fractures may be reduced without anesthesia by means of a forceful, quick tug at the base of the phalanx just distal to the fractured bone. They should be splinted in extension using a skin-tight plaster cast that extends from the middle third of the forearm past the first interphalangeal joint.

Rarely, there will be a fracture that requires traction to maintain reduction. Bend a coat hanger wire like this:

and incorporate it in the cast as specified below for thumb traction. Metacarpal fractures should be immobilized for from 4 to 6 weeks.

Bennett's fracture of the first metacarpal is, in reality, a fracture-dislocation. This is the usual position of the fragments:

Volar surface of hand

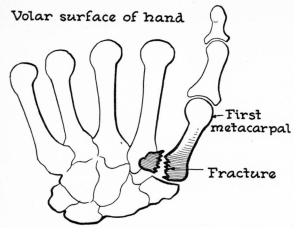

First metacarpal

Fracture

These injuries can cause major functional disability and must be treated with care. To begin with, there is little use of attempting reduction if extreme swelling is present. When this is the case, pad a tongue blade and tape it to the dorsum of the thumb, like this:

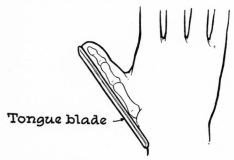

Tongue blade

Have the patient elevate the hand on two pillows at night and carry the arm in a sling during the day. Ice packs will help reduce the swelling. Within 24 to 36 hours the fracture will usually be ready for reduction.

Begin by injecting 4 to 6 cc. of 1 per cent procaine about the fracture site. After anesthesia is established apply firm traction on the extended thumb for 6 to 10 minutes. While maintaining traction use the fingers of your opposite hand to press the displaced fragment into place, like this:

Traction

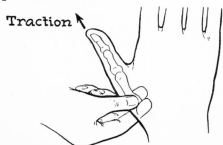

While still maintaining traction, have your nurse make two splints 8 inches long from 4 inch plaster. While still wet, have her cut both splints like this:

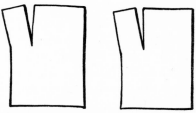

Now apply to both surfaces of the hand:

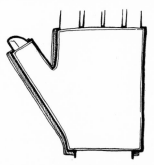

Use 2 inch rolls of plaster to finish the cast, then trim it so that the final result looks like this:

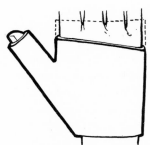

Take another x-ray after the cast has been applied, and again in 24 hours. If reduction is maintained, leave the cast in place for 5 to 6 weeks.

Severely comminuted fractures which may be replaced while traction is exerted but which immediately spring out of position when traction is abandoned may be treated by incorporating skeletal traction with the above plan of treatment. Begin by assembling the following material:

1. A wire coat hanger.
2. An eye screw 1½ inches long, and a wing nut.

3. A 20 gauge needle and a 4 inch piece of tantalum or stainless steel wire that will pass through the bore of the needle, both sterile.

4. A syringe with 1 per cent procaine and a 26 gauge needle.

5. A tongue blade.

6. Material for application of cast.

7. Two pairs of pliers and a wire cutter.

First anesthetize each side of the distal phalanx of the thumb. Be sure to deposit anesthetic in both the skin and periosteum. Push the 20 gauge needle through the bone, like this:

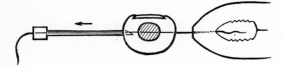

Now thread the wire through the bore of the needle until the tip of the wire emerges from the needle point. Grasp the wire with pliers and hold it while withdrawing the needle, like this:

Next cut a piece of the coat hanger and shape it like this:

Start application of the cast while maintaining firm traction on the thumb and incorporate the wire from the coat hanger, like this:

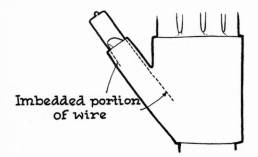

Imbedded portion of wire

Now thread the wire through the eye screw and hold the eye screw in position, like this:

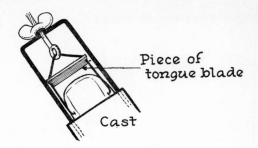

Piece of tongue blade

Cast

Notice the piece of tongue blade used as a spreader. Adjust for proper traction by tightening the wing nut.

Phalanges

Displacement in phalangeal fractures depends upon location. These are the usual types:

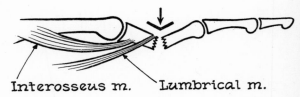

Interosseus m.   Lumbrical m.

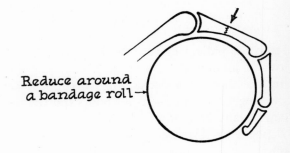

Reduce around a bandage roll →

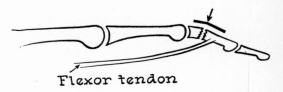

Flexor tendon

Simple rule :
⌣ immobilize around bandage roll
⌢ immobilize straight

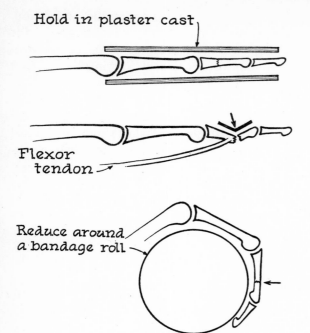

Hold in plaster cast

Flexor tendon

Reduce around a bandage roll

Simple rule :
∨ immobilize around bandage roll
∧ immobilize straight

Plaster is still the best immobilizing agent for these fractures and should be used often. Reduction is usually simple and often may be accomplished without anesthesia. If possible, fixation in extension at the metacarpophalangeal joint should be avoided. Slight flexion here is better.

The cast should extend from the lower third of the forearm to pass the joint distal to the fracture site. It should be applied tightly without padding and should be cut away to allow maximum use of uninvolved joints. An example of proper casting is this:

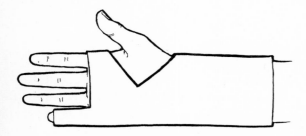

In a few cases, constant traction will need to be applied. Use the same method shown under fractures of the metacarpals. When these fractures are in traction it is essential to take x-rays frequently to ascertain position. Perhaps the most frequent mistake is to fail to remember this fact. Steady traction gradually overcomes muscle tone and, unless frequent adjustments are made, the fracture ends may be gradually pulled apart.

Ribs

Fractures of the ribs are among the worst-treated injuries we see. In the absence of injury to the lung, relief of pain is the primary problem in the usual fracture, and partial immobilization is more important from this aspect than from the standpoint of aiding healing.

First of all, we are inclined to place far too much emphasis on x-ray in the diagnosis of rib fracture. Any roentgenologist will tell you that demonstration of a fractured rib can be a difficult and trying task. A simple physical test has been, in my experience, much more reliable. Place one hand about the middle of the thoracic spine and the other over the sternum, like this:

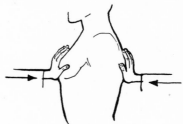

Gently compress the chest. The patient will tell you if a fracture is present and exactly where it is. If there is any doubt, ask the patient to take a quick, deep breath. This he cannot do if a rib is fractured through.

In slender individuals it is possible to palpate the lower ribs throughout their course. A useful procedure is to slide your thumbnail along the edge of the rib, using firm but not hard pressure.

After these tests have been found positive, use the x-ray to resolve any doubt or to make a record for medicolegal purposes. Before performing any other procedure, check the chest carefully for evidence of damage to lungs or pleura. When you are satisfied of the minor nature of the injury, proceed to the next step, which is pain relief, not taping.

Inject the intercostal nerves with procaine or 5 per cent Intracaine in oil. This injection should be performed about 2 to 4 inches proximal to the fracture site. Do it like this:

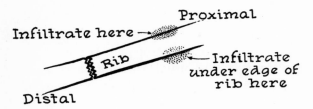

Pain relief should be complete. There are three good methods of producing relative immobilization. They are:

1. The rib belt. This is a cheap commercial device built on the order of the Sam Browne belt. It works well and I have found it advantageous to keep a supply of various sizes in my office. It looks like this:

2. The muslin bandage. Tear a strip of muslin about 8 to 10 inches wide and 3 to 4 yards long. You hold one end and have the patient hold the other end over the fracture site, like this:

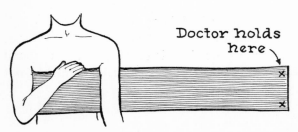

Now have the patient twist round and round, winding the muslin around the chest like putting on a cummerbund. You can control the amount of tension by varying the amount of pull on your end of the bandage.

3. If tape is the only thing available, have the patient, male or female, put on an old cotton undershirt (not a T-shirt) and cut several strips of tape about 8 inches longer than necessary to go *completely around* the patient. Apply this "full circle" taping over the undershirt.

Do not hesitate to reinject if pain recurs.

Lumbar Vertebrae

Fractures of transverse processes of the lumbar vertebrae are not rare. Until recently these were looked upon as somewhat serious injuries that required long periods of immobilization. Apparently this is not necessarily so, for ambulant treatment has given consistently good results.

I have my patients get a lumbar support— not an expensive brace but an elastic webbing support. Inject the area of the fracture with procaine, Efocaine, or Intracaine in oil, like this:

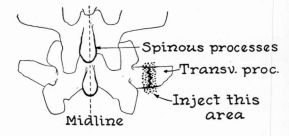

During the first 2 or 3 days the patient usually remarks about minor discomfort, but he is urged to stay ambulatory. The injection is repeated if it is thought necessary, and within a week the patient is allowed full activity.

Tibial Tuberosities

Fractures of the tibial tuberosities with displacement are hospital problems, but we see a few such fractures with the fragments in good position. In these cases, immediate application of a cast is good procedure if swelling is minimal. If there is effusion into the knee joint—and there usually will be—begin by aspirating.

Next, the proper size stockinet is rolled onto the leg from toes to groin. Two strips of ½ inch thick orthopedic felt are cut to 1½ by 3 inch size. These are applied over the tuberosities and held in place with Scotch tape, like this:

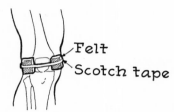

Now cut a strip of ½ inch foam rubber 3 inches wide and long enough to reach around the upper leg in this position:

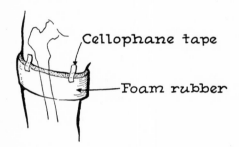

Tape it in place with tabs of Scotch tape. Now measure a posterior splint to extend from midway on the foam rubber to just beyond the toes. This should be of 4 or 6 inch plaster and fifteen to twenty layers thick. Now make thinner lateral splints for each side and apply them.

From an old tire cut a 4 inch portion and trim it like this:

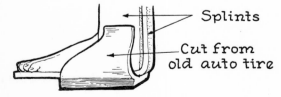

Put it in place on the foot and use roller bandages to wrap the entire cast, leaving the tire tread exposed on the bottom. At the top, roll the sponge rubber over the outside of the cast to form a cuff, like this:

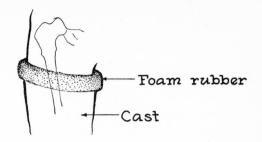

If the patient is well muscled or very active it is wise to reinforce the popliteal area by cutting two 10 inch wires from coat hangers and embedding them longitudinally in the cast about 1 inch apart between the posterior splint and the roller bandage, here:

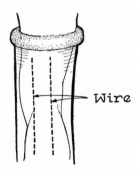

There is only one complication that occurs with any frequency, and it is usually not serious. Traumatic paralysis of the peroneal nerve should be checked for in all such injuries. There will be paralysis of muscles of the anterior fascial compartment (deep peroneal nerve) which dorsiflex the foot; hence, there will be foot drop. The superficial peroneal nerve supplies muscles of the lateral fascial compartment. Loss of active eversion is the most readily seen effect of paralysis. These traumatic paralyses of the common peroneal nerve tend to get well spontaneously in 4 to 6 weeks. The condition should be checked for and noted on the record, if present.

Tibia and Fibula

Fractures of the shaft of the tibia or fibula (but not of both) which are in good position are amenable to office procedures. There is one exception to this statement. Fractures of the tibia at the junction between middle and lower thirds are among the most treacherous bone lesions we see. Because of the possibility of deficient blood supply to the fracture site, the incidence of non-union is high. Because of this—not because of any difficulty in immobilization—these fractures should be hospitalized for treatment.

Should much swelling be present it is a good idea to have the patient prop the leg up on pillows at home and apply an ice pack to the area. A posterior splint of molded plaster held in place by an elastic bandage should be applied as a temporary expedient while this is done. After the swelling is reduced, lateral splints are added and roller bandages applied to make a cast. Bowing, if present, can usually be corrected at this time. To do this, it is often necessary to remove the posterior splint and reapply after bowing is eliminated.

After 48 hours a piece of an old tire is cut to fit and glued into place, like this:

Immobilization should be continued for at least 6 weeks and often longer. After the cast is removed, an Unna paste boot may be applied to give some support. The prescription of mild therapeutic exercise may be of marked benefit in these cases.

When the fibula alone is fractured there is seldom much displacement. Simply inject the area with procaine if there is much pain, apply an Unna paste boot and send the patient about his business. Only strenuous activity should be interdicted.

Fractures about the ankle joint are often amenable to ambulatory treatment, but the more complicated ones are hazardous and reduction should be effected in the hospital. Diagnosis is relatively simple. Suspect fracture in any painful ankle when the history of twisting injury is present.

Begin diagnostic procedures by compressing the tibia and fibula in midleg, like this:

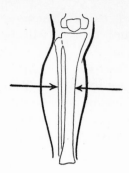

Pain will be felt at the fracture site. Next, grasp the heel and press it firmly upward in the axis of the leg. Be sure there is no rotation in this maneuver. There will be no pain with a simple sprain, but fractures usually are painful to such pressure.

Fortunately, pain is localized immediately over the fracture. Using only your fingertips and the gentlest of pressure, investigate the malleoli and the posterior, inferior border of the tibia. The patient will tell you where the fracture is.

Ligamentous structures about the ankle are exceedingly strong. Frequently it is more difficult to tear the ligaments than to fracture the bony structures surrounding a joint. One of the common types of fractures amenable to office treatment is:

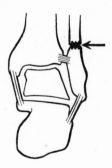

This is a simple fracture of the fibula without rupture of ligamentous structures. There is seldom much displacement, and treatment is simple. Begin by examining the upper fibula for fracture. While this is not the usual thing, it happens often enough to warrant careful examination in *all* cases of ankle fracture. If there is no displacement, inject the painful area with procaine, apply an Unna paste boot and instruct the patient to engage in minimal activities for a few days. *Be sure* to warn him to take off the boot if swelling makes it become painfully tight.

If there is displacement, inject the hematoma with procaine and manipulate the fragment into position. This is very easy and requires no special method. Put the foot in a position of inversion (a ¼ inch felt pad under the outer side of the heel) and slight dorsiflexion. As preliminary fixation, a 3 inch posterior plaster splint may be applied and held in place by an elastic bandage.

After 2 or 3 days (when swelling has been reduced by elevation and ice packs) lateral splints may be applied, and roller bandages used to make a cast. This cast should begin just below the knee and extend out to make a platform for the toes, like this:

When x-ray examination shows adequate reduction, the cast may be prepared for walking by use of a tire fragment built up inside by an extra portion of the tread, like this:

Other methods are cementing a sole to the cast or finding a shoe or firm-soled house slipper large enough to go on over the cast. Weight bearing should be encouraged and immobilization continued for 6 to 8 weeks.

This is a typical bi-malleolar fracture without ligamentous rupture:

Displacement of some degree is usual. Treatment differs from the fracture above only in the non-use of inversion. Here the foot is kept in neutral position.

These are other types of fracture about the ankle that are amenable to office therapy:

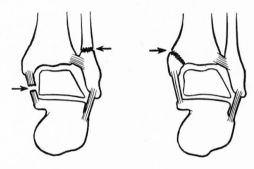

Treatment will be apparent. These are fractures that should be hospitalized for treatment:

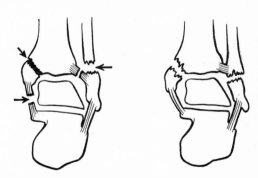

The practitioner must be cautious about such fractures. No effort should be made to do any kind of office manipulation.

There is a simple rule of thumb to determine whether an ankle fracture is likely to cause trouble and, therefore, should be hospitalized. To begin with, any posterior disruption is a potential cause of difficulty. They should all be repaired in the hospital. Other than the posterior, there are three main areas of support to the ankle joint:

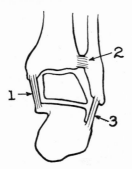

Loss of only one of these means office repair is almost certain of success. Loss of two without displacement *usually* can be fixed in the office. Loss of two with severe displacement or loss of all three means hospitalization.

Calcaneus

Simple fractures of the calcaneus require only immobilization. On the x-ray, check for presence of this angle:

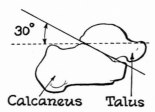

If it is diminished to less than 20 or 25 degrees, hospitalization is indicated.

Metatarsals and Phalangeals

A well-fitting shoe is the best splint for metatarsal and phalangeal injuries of the foot that show only minor displacement. Only one point is paramount. *Be sure* to support both the longitudinal and transverse arches during the healing period. Commercial supports are cheap and generally obtainable, but their fit *must* be checked by the physician.

SOME GENERAL DISCUSSION

There are a number of fallacies about the locomotor system that seem quite prevalent in the medical profession. I would like to take a few paragraphs to discuss them.

To me the most important is the seeming contempt with which we treat the soft tissues. Ligamentous and cartilaginous injuries can be many times more serious than fractures but they don't show on the x-ray, so we ignore them. Take a few examples:

Disability from fracture of the femur only rarely lasts more than a few months, but a crack in a tiny semilunar cartilage can cripple for life—even, at times, in spite of the very best surgery.

You can pop the tip off the external malleolus with monotonous regularity and get along fine if properly treated. But tear the internal ligaments of the ankle and let the physician say, "You've just got a sprain. Put this Ace bandage on and wear it a few days," and you have an excellent chance of being hindered for life by a "weak ankle."

I know fractures are more dramatic, but this is a plea: *please watch out for the soft tissues.* There is just as much, if not more, chronic morbidity from soft tissue injury as there is from fractures.

Next on my list is the theory, "It's either fractured or it isn't." Some of us seem to believe that if there isn't a ragged gap in bone continuity at least half an inch wide, nothing is wrong. It is possible to bruise and crush periosteum, to dent bone, to cause microscopic dehiscences, and in other ways to disarrange bone structure by force of a blow without causing a major fracture. These are injuries and deserve treatment, although, of course, they are not so important as the fracture. Keep in mind that, just because you can't see something on x-ray, it doesn't necessarily follow that damage is absent.

The last item is financial. Most of our health insurance companies have so organized their fee schedule that a patient cannot collect for a fracture unless it is treated in a hospital. This has led to one of the most ridiculous wastes of money that the medical profession has ever had the misfortune to see. Of 10,-000 fractures selected at random, 5000 to 8000 will be amenable to office treatment. It is much less expensive to treat a fracture on an ambulatory basis but, in order to collect, hospitalization is necessary. In the final analysis the patient pays the bill.

Section IV

GYNECOLOGY

GYNECOLOGY

THE EXAMINATION

Adequate and complete gynecologic examination is the first and most important office procedure in this field. More lesions are missed because of a careless examining routine than because of the physician's lack of knowledge. As a matter of curiosity, I have had my office nurse time with a stop watch the duration of both a careless and a good gynecologic survey. The complete examination averages about 50 seconds longer than the one carelessly done. Material needed is:

1. Sponge forceps with cotton or gauze sponges.

2. Tenaculum, preferably the four-toothed variety.

3. Speculum. It is best to have both regular and large sizes on hand. These should be cleaned with green soap and water and boiled for a minimum of 3 minutes before each use.

4. Two hairpins. Use the old-fashioned bent-wire pins—not bobby pins.

5. A wide-mouthed bottle containing Caroid powder.

6. A sterile uterine sound.

Some doctors find a head mirror useful. It does afford better light than the gooseneck lamp placed at the physician's shoulder. This is a matter of individual preference but it is certainly worth trying. The proper position for use is this one:

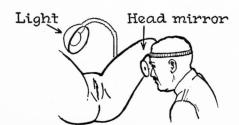

Light   Head mirror

Begin by inspecting the external genitalia and the surrounding area. Next, separate the labia with the fingers of one hand and take a moment to examine intralabial structures. Palpate deep in the labia for Bartholin's glands. If there is no abnormality they cannot be felt.

Next look at the urethral meatus and strip the distal ½ inch of the urethra to make apparent any discharge. If discharge appears or if the patient complains of tenderness, make retractors from the hairpins by bending them as shown, and use them to visualize the duct openings, like this:

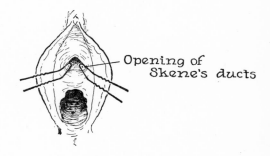

Opening of Skene's ducts

Next ask the patient to strain down and notice the status of bladder supports, rectal supports and whether or not the uterus descends.

Check to see if discharge presents at the meatus and notice its characteristics. Is it white or yellow? Is it tinged with blood? Does it present in quantity or is there only a small amount? Remember that a scanty mucoid discharge is usually normal. Particularly notice whether there is inflammatory reaction of the skin which the discharge covers.

Lubricate the gloved fingers and insert them into the vagina. It is at this moment that the patient's cooperation is assured or completely foregone. Gentleness is imperative. Remember that any pain is likely to be caused by the actual penetration of the fingers into the vaginal opening. Here is why:

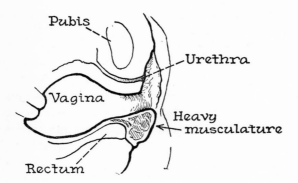

Pain will be elicited by pressure on the urethra or heavy musculature, but not by pressure on the highly distensible vagina. Remember, too, that pressure posteriorly toward the coccyx is not particularly painful unless the patient is holding her muscles in spasm. If she is doing this, take a moment to reassure her and to illustrate, if necessary, the fact that relaxation of the muscles makes adequate examination possible. Never allow your fingers to make pressure anteriorly so that there is impingement on the urethra or contact with the clitoral area.

Having made proper insertion of the fingers, locate the cervix and palpate it gently for irregularities (lacerations) and nodules. This is one of the most important procedures in the gynecologic examination, although it is often omitted. A better idea of the condition of the cervix may frequently be gained by palpation than by visualization. Next move the cervix firmly back and forth. If there is a pelvic inflammatory process the patient will complain of pain. Be sure to warn the patient of the possible occurrence of pain before accomplishing this examination. While performing further palpation, remember always that a gentle pelvic examination will furnish much more information than a rough one.

Now outline the uterus between the abdominal and vaginal fingers, taking time to cover the lateral border on each side and to "go over" from front to back. You will get more information if you will hold one hand still and push the part to be examined gently against it with the other hand.

After outlining the uterus, feel the parametrial tissues just lateral to the upper portion of the cervix, here:

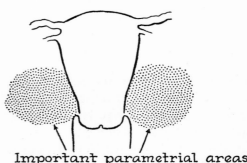

Important parametrial areas

Then, beginning palpation about 1 inch lateral to the uterine edge, gently "sift" the contents between your fingers and attempt to palpate the adnexa. Remember that many women have pain and nausea if you squeeze the ovary between the fingers. After identifying the structures immediately to each side of the uterus and examining the tubes and ovaries, if they are palpable, sweep the examining finger far laterally toward the pelvic wall.

Now insert one finger in the rectum, leaving the index finger in place in the vagina. Again palpate the areas lateral to the uterus, and the adnexal structures, from this particular position. This rectal-vaginal examination is of the utmost importance in illustrating many gynecologic diseases. Never omit it.

Now visualize the cervix by inserting and opening the Graves vaginal speculum. Begin the insertion with the speculum in this position:

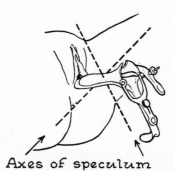

Axes of speculum

Press the bill of the speculum firmly backwards, like this:

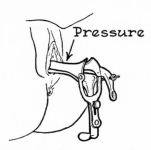

so that any force is applied to perineal musculature rather than to anterior structures. Now slip the speculum in place gradually, bringing it to this position:

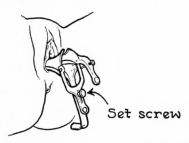

Now loosen the set screw on the base of the instrument and push the base of the speculum open, using very little force so as not to cause pain. Tighten the set screw when the proper position is attained and then open the bill of the instrument to visualize the cervix and fornices, like this:

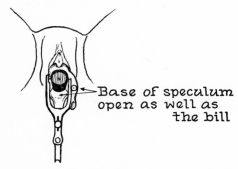

Now dip a dry cotton sponge in the Caroid powder and place it firmly up against the cervix so that the powder comes in contact with the cervical mucus. Hold this position for 2 or 3 seconds. When you bring the sponge away, you will notice that the Caroid powder has liquefied the mucus and that the cervix is clearly visualized.

Unless the cervical canal is quite obviously patent, it is sometimes wise to test it with the uterine sound. To do this, grasp the cervix with the tenaculum in order to stabilize it. Make no effort to pull the cervix downward. From your previous palpation of the uterus you will have an idea of the curvature of the cervical canal. Bend the sound to approximate this curvature and insert it gently into the canal. Use no pressure to force it on into the uterine cavity—rather, work it gently from side to side and from front to back as it slips through the canal. A common error is to diagnose as an obstruction what is actually a simple diverting of the point of the sound, like this:

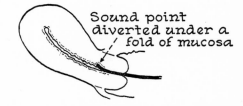

When you meet what you think is an obstruction, back up ½ inch and try again to insert the sound in a little different direction.

A common error is seen repeatedly in the use of the tenaculum. A review of this procedure may be useful at this point. Distribution of sensory nerves in the cervix varies from person to person, but in the average group the sensitive and insensitive areas of the cervix are about like this:

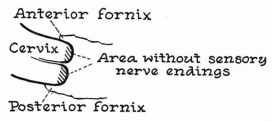

In using the tenaculum, it is, of course, necessary to grasp the cervix in the insensitive area. The best way to do this is to put the tenaculum in place and to start closure very slowly, asking the patient if there is any pain. After the teeth have penetrated the mucous membrane, and if there is no complaint of pain, you may close the tenaculum with complete assurance.

Another unfortunate error in the use of the

tenaculum is all too prevalent. This instrument was not designed as a means of making extreme traction on the cervix in order to pull it to the vaginal opening. It should *never* be used for this purpose. The tenaculum will stabilize the cervix and move it approximately 1 inch in any direction with safety, but this is the full range of its utility. May I repeat, *it should never be used to make forceful traction on the cervix.*

There are three examinations that need not be done with every patient but that are occasionally very useful. These procedures are:

1. *Palpation of the Ureters.* The ureters extend from the base of the bladder about ¾ inch lateral to the cervix. By careful palpation through the fornix they may be felt and they most certainly will make their presence known in case of any inflammatory reaction of the urinary tract. Palpate for them here:

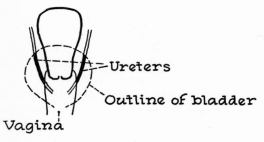

2. *Examination of the Clitoris.* Since relative frigidity is such a major problem among American women, you will frequently be asked to determine whether or not the clitoris is normal. Fortunately, abnormalities are tremendously rare. To check the structure, separate the sheath and visualize the clitoris by pulling downward on the tissue immediately below it, like this:

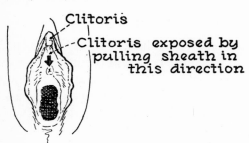

I have never seen an abnormality of the clitoris or of the surrounding structures except in bi-

sexual individuals. I have talked to many physicians with a great deal more experience than I have had who say the same thing.

3. *Examination of the Standing Patient.* In occasional cases where there is question about the adequacy of the uterine, perineal or bladder supports, it will be advantageous to examine the patient in a standing position. Have the patient separate the labia and strain down. Notice the presence of cystocele or rectocele, or the presentation of the cervix at the vaginal opening.

ANATOMY AND PHYSIOLOGY

Before we consider further the various office procedures of use in gynecology, a brief review of basic anatomic and physiologic facts is definitely in order.

The Clitoris. There are perhaps more misconceptions about this part of the female genitalia than about any other. The organ is in every respect the complete analogue of the male penis. Anatomic variations are not great and clitoral pathology is exceedingly rare. The organ has been proven to be the major seat of normal feminine sexual enjoyment. There are many specialized nerve endings in the clitoris and a number of similar nerve endings in the labia minora in the clitoral area. While there are unquestionably feelings in other portions of the genitalia, it seems well established that stimulation leading to orgasm is centered in the clitoris and the surrounding area. Many doctors make an unfortunate mistake in telling patients otherwise.

Skene's glands are a series of mucus-secreting glands lying to either side of the urethra, with openings just inside the urethral meatus, like this:

Their main importance is in connection with certain infectious processes.

Bartholin's glands lie deep in the labia majora, about here:

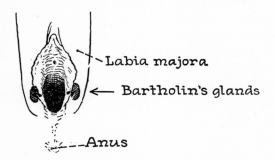

They are not palpable in the normal subject but are important in certain infections. We must remember that they lie deep in the labia majora, beneath the superficial fascia.

The Vagina. The important anatomic feature to keep in mind about the vagina is the fact that the body of the structure has the capability to balloon out to relatively enormous size, while the perineal opening is guarded by musculature, like this:

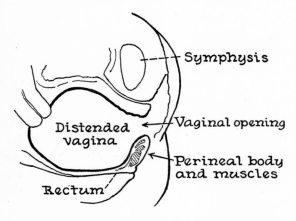

If manipulation in the vaginal area is painful, the discomfort is largely due to impingement of structures near the narrowed opening.

The size and relative strength of muscles in the pelvic sling vary greatly from person to person. These muscles may be small and weak, firm or flabby or thick and heavy. No diagnostic picture of the pelvis is complete without an estimate of their condition.

The cervix and cervical canal may be represented diagrammatically in this fashion:

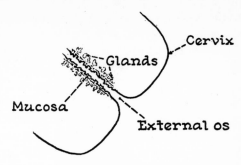

Because of the frequency of infection in the glandular diverticula, it is important that the **physician remember this general picture**. There is a junction in type of membrane at the external cervical os. The normal cornified epithelium of the vaginal wall gives rise to the columnar epithelium of the uterine lining at a rather sharp line of demarcation about here:

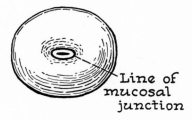

The supports of the uterus may be represented diagrammatically in this fashion:

A study of uterine motility showing normal range of motion permitted by each pair of ligaments

Round ligaments seen from above

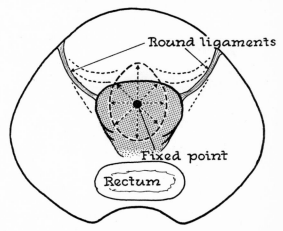

Notice that the fixed point ● may appear anywhere in the ellipse

Round ligament seen from the lateral aspect

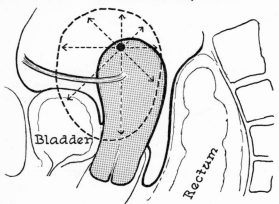

Normal round ligaments will permit fixed point ● to move as shown

Cardinal ligaments seen from the anterior aspect

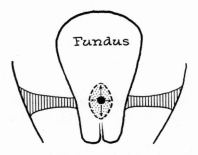

Notice restricted movement of ●, which is at level of internal os

Cardinal ligaments seen from above

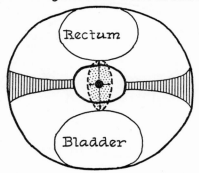

Uterosacral ligaments seen from above

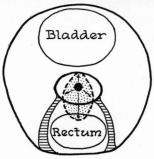

Axis of motion is most accurately located near internal os

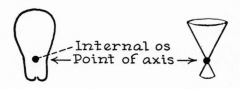

The whole cone may move like this

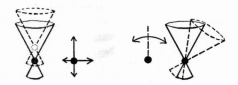

Or may tip, like this

Notice that the uterosacral ligaments tend to anchor at the lower part of the uterus against forward motion and that the round ligaments tend to pull the body of the uterus forward and prevent extreme retroversion. Notice, too, the relatively heavy connective tissue at the base of the broad ligament, which, while it does not hold the lower portion of the cervix fixed in position, does tend to fix that portion of the uterus at about the internal os, thus allowing rotatory movement of the cervix below this point and rotatory movement of the uterine corpus above. Because of this the uterus is actually one of the most freely mobile organs in the peritoneal cavity.

The bladder is held in position anterior to the uterus and forward of the vagina by the pubocervical connective tissue, which forms a sling about like this:

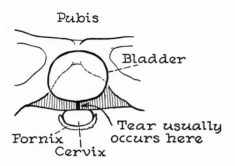

When vaginal walls and surrounding connective tissue are distended and the pubocervical tissue is torn, the sling support of the bladder is gone and it herniates toward the anterior vaginal wall, which is incapable of retaining it in proper position. The process occurs like this:

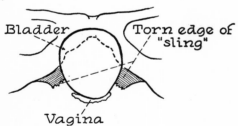

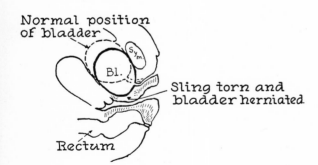

Rectovaginal Relationships. Fibers of the pubococcygeus and the urogenital diaphragm separate the rectum from the posterior vaginal wall. When these fibers are lacerated (usually in childbirth) the support maintaining the rigidity of the posterior vaginal wall is gone

and the bowel wall may protrude into the vagina like this:

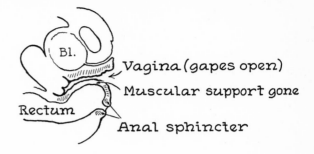

GONORRHEA

During the 1940's, we physicians were very optimistic about this disease for it appeared that there was every chance for complete eradication. Now, in spite of our good efforts, there is some indication that the disease is reestablishing itself. Perhaps we have become a bit careless in treatment, and almost certainly we have allowed ourselves to underestimate the damage done by the humble gonococcus. It is true that we do not see women who are childless and who are chronic pelvic cripples as a result of gonorrheal infection as frequently as we once did, but such cases are by no means rare. I see cases that must have originated in the 1940's when we were so certain that the disease was going out of existence. For this reason, I would counsel caution and extreme thoroughness in all office procedures dealing with gonorrhea.

Identification of the gonococcus is usually relatively simple. The thick, heavy, purulent discharge from the cervix and the urethral meatus is almost characteristic. After smear, it may be fixed in a flame and stained with simple methylene blue. The gonococcus usually looks like this:

Two findings that we have been taught to regard as uniform in this procedure are not invariably present: (1) Quite often leukocytes ingest large numbers of the organisms and the gonococcus is therefore found intracellularly. This is a useful point to keep in mind but by no means an absolute criterion of diagnosis. (2) Gonococci are relatively constant in their shape and staining, but not absolutely so.

If any question exists about the diagnosis after examination of methylene blue smears, and confirmation, if needed, by Gram's stain, then by all means culture. Since the organism grows well only under slight carbon dioxide tension the procedure is usually not within the range of the average office.

To prepare a stain from the cervix, proceed as follows: Expose the cervix with a speculum and wipe away excess discharge. If necessary, dip a cotton sponge in Caroid powder and hold it against the cervix for a moment to liquefy discharges. Now take a cotton applicator and procure some discharge from just inside the cervical os, here:

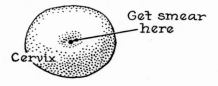

Smear it on a slide.

In examining discharge from the urethra, first ask the patient whether or not she has urinated within the past 2 hours. If she has, have her come back 2 hours later and instruct her not to urinate in the meantime. Upon her return, strip the distal ¾ inch of the urethra with your finger. Be gentle, for this can be extremely painful to the patient. When a bead of discharge appears at the urethral opening, pick it up with a cotton-tipped applicator and spread it on a slide.

Invasion of the bladder with moderately intense trigonitis is not a rare complication of acute gonococcal disease. To test for it, use this procedure: With one finger in the vagina, apply gentle upward pressure. With the abdominal hand situated immediately superior to the pubis, apply gentle downward pressure so that the trigone is pressed against the vaginal finger, like this:

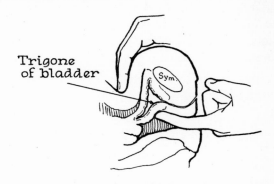

If done carefully, this procedure will not cause pain in infected fallopian tubes. In the presence of trigonitis, it will be painful.

Abscesses of Skene's glands or ducts can usually be palpated if the finger moves gently along either side of the urethra, here:

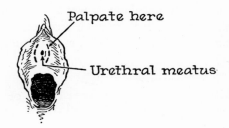

Rectal gonorrhea is not unknown although it is relatively rare. In the presence of rectal pain and irritation with purulent discharge, make a routine Gram's stain of the purulent material.

A most valuable office procedure in the treatment of gonorrhea of any type is to lock the instrument cabinet at once and show the patient a masterly neglect as far as any manipulation is concerned. With our present drugs there is seldom, if ever, any indication for the use of office procedures.

Ordinarily, gonorrhea is a self-limited disease. In a matter of 30 to 60 days there are few or no viable organisms left and the patient is non-infectious *with one rather frequent exception.* For some reason that we are unable to explain, chronic gonorrheal abscesses of Skene's glands or Skene's ducts are not excessively rare. There have been frequent reports of recovery of viable organisms 4 to 6 months after original infection. When there is chronic tenderness in the area of these glands and when the thickened ducts can be palpated, minor surgery is the procedure of choice.

Using a hairpin as a retractor, expose the opening of the ducts of the urethra and thread a duct on a surgical needle, like this:

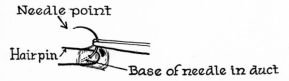

Now take a knife and incise down to the needle. In the event an abscess tract extends up toward or through the urogenital diaphragm, the procedure should not be attempted in the office.

Make no attempt to close the incision or to apply a dressing to the wound. A surgical sponge tucked up between the labia majora is convenient for the patient and some women will prefer it to the usual sanitary napkin.

It is a mistake to drain a Bartholin abscess unless nonresponse to antibiotic therapy has been amply proven. If in your judgment such drainage is absolutely necessary, do it like this: Anesthetize the skin area by injecting with procaine. Dissect down to the gland wall, which will usually be 5 to 10 mm. below the surface; then inject under the fascia which covers and restrains the gland in the depth of the incision, like this:

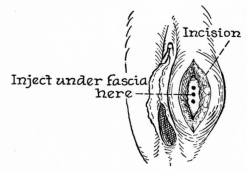

Now make a wide incision into the most prominent part of the abscess and insert a tissue drain. The common vulvar pad or sanitary napkin makes an excellent dressing.

In general, it is a much better procedure to wait until these glands have recovered from the acute inflammatory stage and then excise the entire gland. If the physician will be exacting in following a satisfactory procedure, this can be done in the office surgery. If there is deviation from this standard procedure, every chance exists for a bloody mess. This is not an overstatement. Bleeding can be of serious amount.

Anesthetize the skin immediately over the gland and expose it by sharp dissection. Incise the gland widely, exactly as was described in opening the Bartholin abscess. After evacuating the contents, pick up the gland wall like this:

and dissect down to the base of the gland like this:

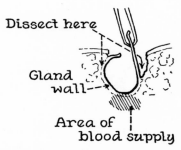

When you have freed all but the very superior attachment (the bottom of the gland as you look in the incision), place two clamps on the inner surface, here:

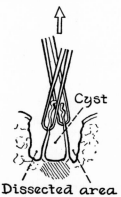

Pull the gland upward and clamp the tissue by which it is attached with a curved Kelly forceps, like this:

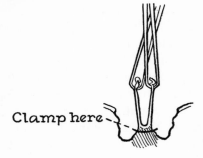

Clamp here

With a sharp knife cut along the top of the Kelly forceps and remove the gland, leaving a wound that looks like this:

Now with a piece of 3-0 chromic catgut, go round and round the Kelly forceps loosely like this:

Remove the clamp, pull the suture tight and tie it, securing hemostasis like this:

Some operators try to obliterate the cavity left by approximating the sides loosely with 3-0 plain catgut. I agree with this procedure only in the event that the sutures are very loosely inserted. Tight sutures may result in a deformity of the labia about which most women are quite sensitive. Once again, the vulvar pad makes an excellent dressing.

After the acute phase of gonorrhea is past, if the patient still complains of bladder symptoms due to an unhealed trigonitis, daily instillations of silver nitrate may provide some relief. Begin with 0.5 per cent solution, instilling 50 cc. in the bladder and instructing the patient to void in approximately 5 minutes. Use the same strength solution the second day; the third day increase to 1 per cent and use this strength on three succeeding days. Results are usually excellent.

In summary, the most important single phase in consideration of office procedures in treatment of gonorrhea is to remember that *no office treatment is indicated* during the acute stage. Needless instrumentations, vaginal irrigations and other such procedures have probably caused as many complications as the gonococci themselves have initiated.

PELVIC CELLULITIS

This title embraces a multitude of sins. Heretofore the three principal causes of pelvic cellulitis have been listed as instrumentation, childbirth and pessaries. With regard to office procedures several points about these causes are of utmost importance. First, regarding instrumentation, a prominent gynecologist has claimed for many years that the uterus may be invaded *once* with impunity. He has stated that a second invasion hard upon the heels of the original one usually is the offender. Here is the reasoning behind that statement:

The uterus, like other structures of the human body, has tremendous defensive capabilities. In invading the first time, one may introduce bacteria, but, in the vast majority of cases, the uterus will be able to overcome this original invasion. If, during this process of the body's inactivating bacteria from the original invasion, there is a secondary attack due to further instrumentation, then the mathematical chance of spontaneous recovery by uterine tissues is greatly lowered. I have only the evidence of a clinical impression to back me up but I am in complete agreement with these statements. If you need to invade a uterus or a cervical canal in the office, by all means do so, but never, except as a matter of life and death, make a second invasion within 48 hours.

The matter of pelvic infection following childbirth also has come up for a great deal of discussion. The usual acute invasion by the hemolytic streptococcus is not a matter for discussion in a book on office procedures. However, there is good evidence to support the idea that occasional invasion may be made by bacteria of relatively low virulence which are present in the generative tract or which appear a very few days after childbirth. The diagnosis and treatment of these cases are frequently found in the realm of office procedures.

That cervical stem pessaries can be gross offenders is so well proven that further discussion is needless. The first and most logical procedure, when one of your patients shows up wearing a cervical stem pessary, is to remove the pessary and throw it away. By no means does this statement apply to pessaries which do not enter or occlude the cervical os.

The most important office procedures when a case of acute cellulitis presents are immediate smear and culture of discharge and an order for hospitalization. The smears should be stained with both methylene blue and Gram's stain and culture materials should be streaked on plain agar and chocolate agar plates. The morphology of the organism as seen in smear will give at least a starting place for antibiotic therapy, and culture will verify diagnosis.

Returning now to the patient who has a chronic pelvic cellulitis of relatively low virulence, we must consider office procedures in diagnosis and treatment. In my own practice I see approximately a hundred such cases to every one of acute cellulitis, if gonorrhea be excepted. These are the chronic pelvic cripples who go from doctor to doctor looking for some miraculous relief from more or less constant discomfort.

Procedures of the examination are identical with those of the general gynecologic examination as mentioned in the first of this section. There is one particular area that should be palpated with extreme care. The broad ligaments just lateral to the internal os are frequently indurated and thickened and give one the impression of feeling foam rubber. Unfortunately, there are no tests that can be applied. Since discharge is not usual, smear and culture procedures are not applicable. As a result, diagnosis rests on a painstakingly accurate history and upon assumptional procedure by the physician.

Many times the procedure used by a physician is to label these women neurotics and send them out of the office as quickly as possible. As near as I can tell, I believe in psychoneurosis about ten times as deeply as the average physician, but these chronic pelvic cellulitis cases seem by no means of neurotic origin.

Other than medication, the application of pelvic heat is of great benefit to approximately 40 or 50 per cent of these women. Diathermy, which is discussed in the section on physiotherapy, should be considered in every such case. Other procedures, in or out of the hospital, are not usually indicated.

THE VULVA

Warts

The common wart is seen frequently in the vulvar area. It is often found when there is irritative vaginal discharge. The first office procedure is to examine the vagina and vaginal flora for common irritating organisms such as trichomonads or streptococci. Look particularly for lesions, such as cervicitis, which predispose to a rather heavy discharge. Incidentally, when you see these warts, be on the lookout for gonorrheal infection either past or present.

The warts themselves, if small, may be destroyed with the cautery needle. Anesthesia is usually not necessary but it is well to test the sensitivity of the structure and to inject a small amount of procaine at the base if necessary. Destroy the tissue like this:

Char superficial layer
Remove with forceps

Devitalize second layer
Remove

Cauterize base until white

If the wart mass is at all large, it may be removed in toto with the cutting current. Use a wire loop with the cutting current to under-cut the mass, like this:

Vulvar Eczema

Vulvar eczema may usually be relieved by medical therapy. Occasionally it will be necessary to gain temporary relief by using nerve block. Inject 1 per cent procaine into the pudendal and cutaneous nerves like this:

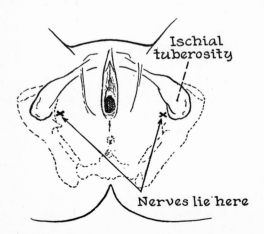

Ischial
tuberosity

Nerves lie here

The injection should be made with a spinal needle inserted so that the point lies just medial to the ischial tuberosities. Then do this:

Insert needle at •
and inject along dotted tracts

Fungus Infection

Fungus infection of the vulva is usually associated with a similar infection on the feet. To make the diagnosis, scrape the *edge* of the lesion with the side of a knife blade, like this:

Skin   lesion
surface

Put the scrapings on a slide and add a drop of 10 per cent potassium hydroxide and a cover glass. The branching mycelia usually look like this under the microscope:

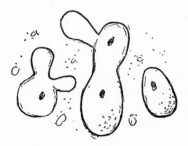

Be certain to inquire whether the patient's husband has similar difficulty. If he has, no treatment is likely to be of avail until he, too, is using proper medication.

Follicular Vulvitis

Follicular vulvitis is a common inflammation about hair follicles, usually caused by the staphylococcus. The only procedure of value is to clip or, preferably, shave the hair before active treatment is instituted.

Pruritus Vulvae

Pruritus vulvae has many causes, the most common of which seems to be fungus infection. Scrapings from the affected area should be examined after being mounted in 10 per cent potassium hydroxide. Fungus elements will be apparent in this preparation if present.

Pinworms are a frequent cause of pruritus and, if question exists, an NIH swab should be taken as described on page 286.

Leukorrhea is also a common cause, particularly the leukorrhea of Trichomonas infection. A wet slide preparation for trichomonads should be made in every case.

Allergic reactions seem to play a part in the cause of pruritus vulvae. Particularly frequent as allergens are medicated douches, contraceptive preparations, fingernail polishes, soaps, and wool or silk underclothing. Skin tests may be made for these substances if it seems necessary.

In addition to medications, only two useful procedures for treatment are commonly employed. Have the patient procure a gooseneck lamp and show her how to take two 20 minute light treatments daily. This can well be done at home with preparation of this nature:

Straight chairs with pillow over back for knees

Bed edge

Gooseneck lamp

Subcutaneous injection of 95 per cent alcohol will give good relief but is somewhat dangerous because of the possibility of slough.

In severe cases, results are good enough to warrant use of this therapy. Make a series of procaine skin wheals approximately 1 cm. apart, like this:

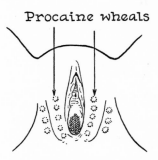

Procaine wheals

Insert a small gauge needle perpendicular to the skin surface just into the subcutaneous tissue like this:

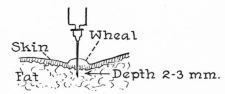

Skin   Wheal
Fat   Depth 2-3 mm.

Be sure to go all the way through the skin but only 2 or 3 mm. deep. Inject 3 drops of 95 per cent alcohol through each skin wheal.

Urethral Caruncle

Urethral caruncle is a small sometimes polypoid growth that usually appears in the posterior edge of the urethral meatus. It is extremely sensitive to touch and frequently bleeds on slightest manipulation. Deep electrocautery is the best treatment, although recurrences are all too common. The most common error is not to cauterize deeply enough. As a simple rule of thumb, go just twice as deep as would seem necessary from the appearance of the lesion.

Anesthetize the area by injecting procaine around the distal urethra, like this:

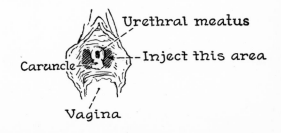

Urethral meatus
Inject this area
Caruncle
Vagina

With the desiccating current, cauterize deeply the area of the caruncle, like this:

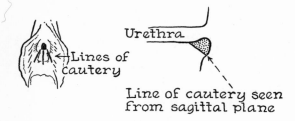

Persistent minor bleeding may be encountered but pressure will usually stop this. Occasionally it is necessary to take a stitch with very fine catgut. The stitch should be removed within 24 to 36 hours.

Varicose Veins

Varicose veins of the vulva are not uncommon. Their rupture may cause a large hematoma or serious external hemorrhage. Since these veins are usually found in the presence of pregnancy or pelvic tumor which obstructs venous return, treatment of the primary lesion assumes greatest importance.

Occasionally, however, the veins remain after the primary lesion has been properly treated. Ligation and excision are relatively simple procedures and may be done in the well equipped office surgery. Begin by anesthetizing the skin, like this:

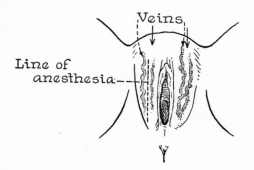

Make a longitudinal incision extending the full length of the vulva, but remember that the veins are subcutaneous and therefore subject to perforation at the time of the incision. When exposure of the veins is adequate, pass a suture underneath the anterior and posterior end of each vein, like this:

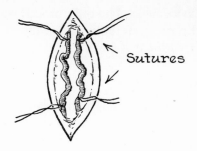

Tie the sutures, leaving the ends long, and excise the vein with a cuff remaining approximately ⅜ inch long beyond each suture. Now take one of the ends of the tied suture and thread it through the cuff as a safety stitch, like this:

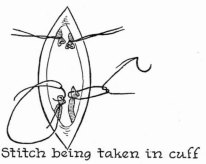

Stitch being taken in cuff

Tie the ends and turn your attention to another vein.

THE VAGINA

Maintenance of the normal vaginal flora is almost solely dependent upon the proper hydrogen ion concentration of the vaginal secretion. The pH of various areas of the vagina is approximately this:

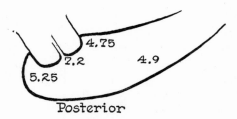

The increased alkalinity of the posterior fornix is probably due to the fact that alkaline cervical secretions pool in this area. One of the most valuable procedures in gynecologic examination is the determination of the vaginal *p*H by means of nitrazine paper. Simply place a bit of nitrazine paper in forceps and touch it to the vaginal wall well inside the introitus. Compare the paper with the color chart furnished and you get a reasonably accurate estimation of *p*H.

This determination is a great deal more important than some physicians seem to believe. Diagnosis of the various common vaginal invaders can often be made by careful inspection and *p*H determination with accuracy approaching that of laboratory procedures. As a measure of successful therapy, the *p*H determination has no peer. When vaginal hydrogen ion concentration returns to normal there is little chance that infection can be present. Determination of vaginal *p*H should be a part of every pelvic examination.

The normal *average* *p*H for the vagina ranges about 4.5. Doederlein bacilli, which, when present, are a criterion of normal flora, grow best at *p*H 3.8 to 4.5. None of the common pathologic organisms grow well in this *p*H range.

Trichomonads usually appear from *p*H 5 to 6, monilia from *p*H 5.5 to 6.5, staphylococci and streptococci from *p*H 6 to *p*H 7.5, and gonococci from *p*H 7 to 8.5. In many instances this simple procedure of testing the vaginal *p*H will give an excellent clue to the etiology of any infection that is present.

To prove that the vaginal milieu is normal, first determine the *p*H as instructed above; then pick up a bit of secretion, fix it and stain with methylene blue. If Doederlein bacilli are present in this stained specimen you may be relatively certain that the vagina is normal. These are literally huge, blunt-ended rods that take the stain heavily. They look like this:

An important fact too seldom appreciated is that the vagina tends to reestablish the normal milieu spontaneously. The principal object of both medication and office procedures in vaginal disease is to give an opportunity for this reestablishment. By no means do we seek to eliminate bacterial contamination, nor do we seek complete eradication of pathogenic organisms solely by our own treatment. Once again, our objective should be to produce conditions that allow and aid the reestablishment of the normal vaginal flora.

Infections

Leukorrhea from vaginal infection is the most common form of discharge we see. Various lesions of the cervix which cause discharge will be considered later on. This particular section will deal only with the vaginal infections, of which there are three general types.

Trichomoniasis. By far the most important vaginal infection is *Trichomonas vaginalis* vaginitis. Control of this infection in the past years has been exceedingly difficult and it is only recently that we have realized the meticulousness necessary for cure. Office procedures play an extremely important part and should be done with the greatest of care.

Diagnosis, fortunately, is quite simple. Do it this way: Before doing a bimanual examination, have your office assistant put approximately 1 cc. of normal saline solution in a test tube and heat it until it feels slightly warm to the touch. Then cork the tube and put it in your shirt pocket or the inside pocket of your coat where the body heat will keep it warm.

Upon insertion of the vaginal speculum use plain water rather than jelly as a lubricant and open the speculum so that the posterior fornix is well visualized. Uncork the tube and hold it in your hand while you pick up some liquid from the posterior fornix on a cotton applicator. Insert this applicator in the normal saline and twirl it around several times.

Since the trichomonads have a tendency to die rather quickly, it is a good idea to make immediate microscopic examination. Heat a penny in the Bunsen flame and put it on one

end of a glass slide.   In the center of the same
slide place a drop of the material from the test
tube and cover with a cover glass.   Examine
under low power of the microscope with the
condenser stopped down so that lighting is
minimal.   Trichomonads can be seen easily
because of their extremely active motion and
characteristic flagella.   Under low power they
look like this:

Ordinarily, when you observe organisms of
roughly this shape which are extremely motile
and have one or more flagella apparent, you
may assume that you are dealing with a
Trichomonas infection.

These organisms tend to live deep in the
vaginal folds, and in various lesions of the
cervix and the vaginal membrane and in moist
parts of the vulva.   The principal purpose of
office treatment is to try to eliminate those organisms not readily reached by the women in
home treatment.   To begin with, any cervical
lesions should be cared for as specified in the
next section.   Schedule office treatment approximately weekly and begin by swabbing the
entire vagina vigorously with tincture of green
soap diluted one-half with water.   Rinse the
vagina and dry thoroughly.   Next, use a solution of 3 to 5 per cent silver nitrate to paint the
entire vaginal mucosa, covering first the cervix
and the lateral vaginal walls, then moving the
speculum like this:

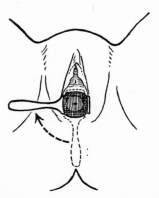

to cover anterior and posterior walls.   Make
a thorough search at this time for minute
lesions which might harbor the trichomonads.

Wait 3 or 4 minutes for silver nitrate to
reach maximum activity, then insufflate one of
the standard powders, such as Floraquin
powder, into the vagina, being certain to cover
the forniceal areas.   Be sure to instruct the
patient in proper methods of douching and
proper methods of preparing the douche.
These are discussed in the section on feminine
hygiene.

Not infrequently, trichomonads invade the
bladder, causing a moderate trigonitis.   As
the vaginal infection comes under control this
usually disappears spontaneously.   In the
event that it does not do so, daily instillations
of any of the common bladder antiseptics will
usually effect complete cure within a week.
It has been my practice to use half strength
antiseptic solutions for these instillations rather
than beginning with the full strength.

Trichomonads are frequently carried by the
male, and experience would seem to indicate
that the infestation is venereal in origin in a
great many cases.   Certainly, it is impossible
to offer cure to a woman who is recontaminated
by her husband.   The most frequent places
where these organisms are found in the male
are (1) in the secretions under the prepuce,
and (2) in prostatic secretions.   It has been
our practice to assume that the preputial secretions of the male will be contaminated when
his wife has trichomonads.   Medical treatment is prescribed for this area.   Fortunately,
prostatic contamination is less frequent.   This
may be checked by massaging the prostate to
expel a drop of secretion onto a warm slide,
and subjecting it to immediate examination as
mentioned before.

Only during the past few years has adequate
treatment for prostatic contamination become
available.   Some authors have recommended
prostatic massages as an adjunct to treatment
in the male.   While this is purely a clinical
impression not backed up by proper research,
I feel that this procedure is useless in the absence of concurrent infection with bacteria.

Moniliasis. Mycotic infections of the vagina are not as rare as we supposed at one time. *Candida albicans* is the principal offender. Through the speculum one sees irregular white patches about half the size of the end of a cigarette over both the cervix and the vaginal walls. Inflammatory reaction around these plaques is present but minimal.

A Gram's stain smear of monilial vaginal secretion looks like this:

In the past it has been customary to swab the vaginal wall with gentian violet as an office procedure, but it would seem that modern therapy has fairly well eliminated this procedure as one of any usefulness.

Other more persistent fungi are occasionally found contaminating the vagina but their diagnosis and treatment are too unusual to appear in this work. One procedure may be useful. If there is question about the fungus involved, inoculate Sabouraud's medium and let the fungus grow at room temperature for about a week. This may be sent to a laboratory for differential diagnosis if necessary.

Mixed bacterial infection of the vagina may be seen in all stages from the obviously acute inflammation, which is rare, to the low grade chronic inflammatory process, which is seen with some frequency. I have heard much about obtaining pure cultures from various vaginal invaders but in practical experience I have never seen a case in which several organisms were not involved. In these chronic cases one usually finds streptococci, staphylococci and gram-negative rods. No case can be considered adequately worked up until a Gram's stain smear is done.

It is usually wise in these cases to check for the presence of trichomonads, which will be found in a substantial number. Treatment is entirely medical and does not involve the use of office procedures.

Vaginismus

Vaginismus, or spasm of the muscles surrounding the vaginal orifice, is a relatively frequent complaint which sometimes is not discussed freely with the physician. The cause, of course, is psychogenic in an overwhelming number of cases, although painful lesions about the introitus may cause an occasional case.

After adequate examination, the first office procedure is to bend a sympathetic ear to the complaints of the patient and to attempt to explain certain functional aspects of sex. Unfortunately, not all physicians are well informed regarding the psychologic and emotional aspects of the sexual relationship. As the years go on it seems that we see an ever-increasing number of sexual problems, and it certainly behooves us at least to make an effort to attain some reasonably accurate psychologic information on this point.*

Gradual dilation of the vaginal orifice is of service in these cases and should be done as an office procedure. This, however, should not be undertaken until adequate explanation has been given to the patient. Treat the psychologic aspects first. During the procedure of dilation instruct the patient to make a conscious effort to relax perineal musculature. Begin by gentle stretching of the muscles with one finger, like this:

Stretch muscles gently in these directions

Then, if you wish, use various dilating bougies, although they are unnecessary, for the procedure can be done quite adequately with the fingers.

* I cannot stress too strongly the concept that sexual problems are at the root of many complaints. Many men and women live in a constant sexual storm. If the doctor does not understand this fact the result will be needless procedures and no help to patients.

Cystocele

This is a disruption of the sling of fascial tissue which supports the bladder like this:

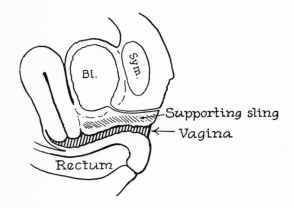

allowing it to assume this position:

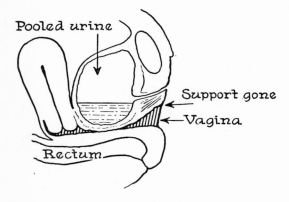

Office procedures are concerned only with diagnosis and with elimination of possible complications until surgical repair can be done.

Notice in the illustration above how urine tends to pool at the lower aspect of the cystocele. At times it becomes absolutely imperative to secure adequate urinary drainage in order to prevent infection of the stagnant urine in this area. Insertion of a pessary, which will be discussed later, is an excellent temporary procedure. It is, of course, not adequate for permanent treatment.

An excellent estimation of the extent of fascial disruption may be obtained by passing a metal sound into the bladder and by feeling the tip of the sound here:

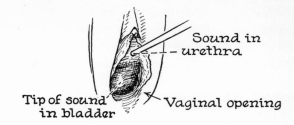

This will give some estimate as to the difficulty of repair and the extent of bladder support loss.

Rectocele

The rectocele represents a loss of the musculofascial septum which lies between the rectum and the vagina, here:

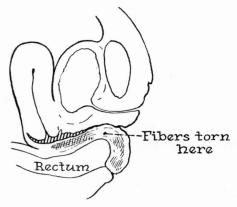

It allows protrusion of the rectum anteriorly into the vaginal area, and loss of vaginal support may let the vagina gap open like this:

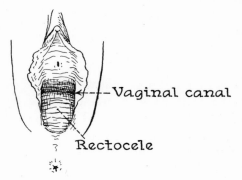

Surgery is the only treatment of any use. The extent of muscular damage may be best determined by placing a finger in the rectum and a finger of the opposite hand in the vagina to palpate the tissues lying between these two structures. An estimate of the severity of the damage and the extent of the surgical problem in correction can be obtained readily in this way.

Imperforate Hymen

The imperforate hymen is usually seen 4 to 16 months after the menarche and in many cases is susceptible to treatment in the office surgery. This is the general pathologic picture:

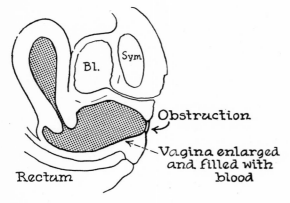

You may be sure where the obstruction lies and of the approximate thickness by palpating the mass of menstrual blood immediately behind the imperforate hymen, like this:

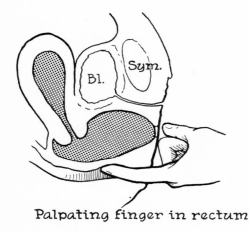

Palpating finger in rectum

Anesthetize the hymeneal area with procaine and gently force a needle into the tissue, keeping the long axis of the needle in the long axis of the vagina, like this:

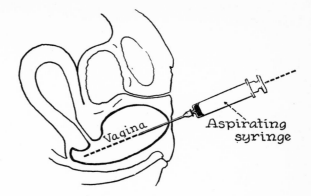

Aspirate as you go, and if you have not reached the incarcerated blood after penetrating ½ inch, abandon the attempt and carry on further treatment in the hospital. In most cases the septum will be ¼ inch or less in thickness.

When you have reached the mass of blood, use a knife to incise along the course of the needle, like this:

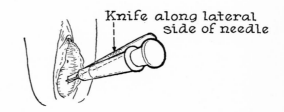

If you can get rid of the draining blood sufficiently well to see what you are doing, wide cruciate incision of the septum is a good procedure. By no means excise the septum, for this is very likely to cause a ring of scar tissue which will, depending on its size, make coitus very enjoyable or quite impossible for the future consort.

THE CERVIX

At some time or other nearly every pain known to womankind has been attributed to disease of the uterine cervix. Actually, symptoms other than purely local ones are quite rarely, if ever, due to cervical disease if we except cancer. Office procedures are mainly concerned with the treatment of chronic cervical processes, which may be separated conveniently into three types: (1) the laceration with eversion, (2) the chronic cervicitis with erosion, and (3) endocervicitis. There are other lesions which appear with some frequency and which will be discussed later.

In order to plan adequate office treatment one must be able to differentiate exactly between the three common lesions.

Laceration of the cervix with resultant eversion simply means that the cervix has been split and the lips are pushed out in "kissing" position. This allows the endocervical mucosa to be seen through the speculum and also presents this mucosa to the vaginal content for possible infection. The lesion usually looks like this:

Unless there is infection of this everted mucosa, discharge is not a common finding. Pain is usually absent unless the laceration extends laterally into the parametrial tissue and perhaps involves the plexus of Frankenhäuser.

The cervical erosion, on the other hand, is apparently exactly what the laity call it, "an ulcer of the mouth of the womb." Epithelium of the exocervix surrounding the surface of the cervical os sloughs off owing to infection or irritation. At times, columnar epithelium from the endocervix may partially overgrow this denuded area. A reddened, granulated, chronically infected surface presents.

Discharge containing mixed organisms is relatively common and quite annoying to the patient. There is no evidence that this lesion directly produces pain of any kind. The lesion usually looks like this:

Ropy, mucopurulent discharge

Endocervicitis is a diagnosis based on the appearance of the external os, on the discharge coming from the os, and on a healthy bit of assumption.

By careful use of a Kelly forceps the cervix can usually be opened sufficiently to present a view like this:

The glairy redness of chronic infection is immediately apparent. Discharge may be proved to originate in the endocervical canal like this: Cleanse the exocervix as described in the section on examination, using Caroid powder. Now dip a cotton-tipped applicator in Caroid powder and touch it to the mouth of the cervical canal. Sponge away excess secretions and gently separate the lips of the external os with a forceps. Purulent discharge will be seen up the cervical canal like this:

If palpation has indicated no higher lesion, the endocervix is at fault.

Cautery and Conization

Electrocautery has completely revised treatment procedures for the cervix. Instead of rather tedious operations performed in the hospital we now use the simplest of office procedures and get totally excellent results. The important procedures are: (1) thermocautery, (2) electrocautery with the wire loop, and (3) conization.

Thermocautery. This procedure is applicable mainly to the simple erosions and is excellent treatment. Prepare the patient by assuring her that there is practically no pain to the procedure and by pointing out that the cautery tip will never touch a sensitive structure. The procedure is best done approximately 5 days following cessation of the menses.

Insert the vaginal speculum and clean the cervix with Caroid powder. Use a gauze sponge to dry any excess secretion. If your hand is not perfectly steady, put a tongue blade in either lateral fornix, like this:

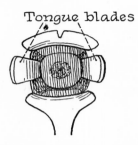

Tongue blades

This will avoid accidental touching of the lateral vaginal wall with results that are likely to cause a serious break in the doctor-patient relationship.

Linear deep cautery is neither necessary nor particularly wise. Heat the cautery point to a very dull red and move it rather rapidly over the cervical mucosa, like this:

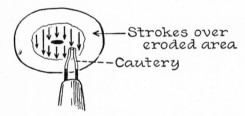

Strokes over eroded area
Cautery

until the entire eroded area assumes an off-white color. Under no circumstances let the cautery point touch the cervical canal. Stenosis is an almost certain complication of careless cautery in the edges of the cervical canal.

If proper depth of cautery has been achieved, sloughs should be minimal and there should be little danger of postoperative bleeding which sometimes follows deeper cautery. It is a good idea to examine the cervix 3 days after the procedure and again 10 days after the operation. Precautions to maintain the acidity of the vagina should be taken.

Use of the Electrosurgical Loop. This is serviceable in the deeper erosions and in some cases of laceration with eversion. Excess granulated tissue in the deeper erosions may be

literally amputated, using the cutting loop like this:

Cutting loop used to "skin" erosion

The only dangers are the possibility of going too deep and the possibility of carelessly cauterizing the cervical canal.

Prepare the patient exactly as for thermocautery and, using the cutting current, make several sweeps like this:

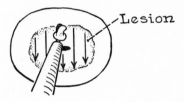

Lesion

Laceration with eversion may occasionally be treated by use of the electric cautery with some success. Before you attempt this procedure let me warn you that it is still in the experimental phase and may not turn out to be as good as it looks right now. I have used it less than twenty times, with reasonably good results.

Use the cutting loop to freshen the edges of the laceration like this:

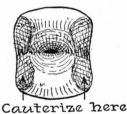

Cauterize here

Try to "skin off" the superficial mucosa without destroying any deeper tissue. Next, if the everted mucous membrane appears to be infected, cauterize it very lightly without actually removing pieces of membrane. It will usually be necessary to change the intensity of the current to accomplish this. Now take a rather heavy wire suture (why wire I do not know, except that we started by using it) and insert it like this:

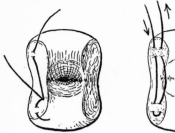
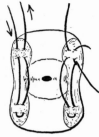

Twist the ends of the wire loosely together, cut them and bend the ends of the wire over like this:

Examine the operative field every 3 days and remove the wire sutures as soon as the lacerated edges have united.

Let me warn you again that this is a purely experimental procedure which, while it looks as if it may be satisfactory, has by no means been proven.

Now let's take a moment to discuss the problem of the invasive carcinoma and carcinoma *in situ* in regard to these procedures. Some recommend amputation of diseased cervices or even hysterectomy. We should not take a chance with any potentially malignant lesion, yet we are scarcely in economic position to abandon a highly successful and inexpensive procedure for the treatment of the uterine cervix in favor of tremendously expensive procedures such as complete hysterectomy or extensive and repeated biopsies of every diseased cervix.

A good compromise to this situation is to insist on the Papanicolaou smear from every cervix before any procedures are undertaken. This is a reasonably accurate method of case selection and is within economic reach.

The problem of carcinoma *in situ* to me seems one that is largely academic at the moment. If cells with malignant tendencies are not picked up on the Papanicolaou smear and if there exists a carcinoma *in situ* in spite

of this, it appears quite logical that what we are going to do is convert the lesion from carcinoma *in situ* to carcinoma *in absentia*, which, while not scientifically satisfying, does achieve the basic objective for the patient. Please do not take this as scoffing at a very serious lesion or as an attempt to negate the excellent work that has been done on these malignant changes. It simply seems to me that the work is not far enough advanced as yet to warrant extensive changes in our office procedures. There is every possibility that the next few years will see satisfactory changes in out methods which will better accommodate this problem of carcinoma *in situ*.

Conization. This procedure is applicable to deep erosions and to endocervicitis. Results are excellent and the technique quite easy. Necessary equipment is a series of conization electrodes which look like this:

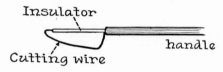

and an electrosurgical machine capable of supplying both cutting and coagulating current as may be indicated.

Unless one attempts a very deep conization, a procedure may be done without anesthesia and works well as an office technique. If you feel that some anesthesia may be needed you may inject the plexus of Frankenhäuser on either side of the cervix, like this:

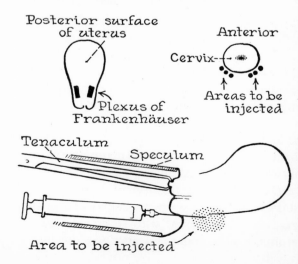

Prepare the patient exactly as for thermo-cautery. It is wise to have on hand material to pack the conized area should a rather large vessel be encountered, and suture material if vessels should have to be tied. Bleeding is by no means a regular complication to this procedure and your use for this material will be limited in the extreme. However, rarely one does sever a vessel large enough that control is somewhat difficult by coagulation. Packing under pressure for 5 to 8 minutes, followed by coagulation of the area, usually suffices to control all such bleeding.

If you have not used the conization loop before it is wise to practice a few times before applying it to the patient. Beef heart is an excellent imitation of the cervix, and fresh ones are relatively easy to obtain. Removal of half a dozen wedges of tissue will teach you the use of the cutting and coagulating current and will allow achievement of the hand-foot coordination usually needed.

When the patient is prepared, insert the electrode into the cervix like this:

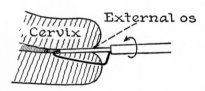

Do not attempt to move quickly. Take your time to adjust the current to the cutting level and perhaps to coagulate any bleeders before advancing further. Now turn on the cutting current and gently rotate the electrode like this:

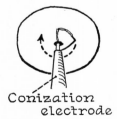

When you have made a full circle the plug of tissue will usually cling to the electrode and may be removed as the electrode is withdrawn. Save the tissue for pathologic examination and turn your attention again to the cervix.

Usually there will be several small bleeding points like this:

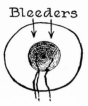

I usually change from the wire electrode to a pointed electrode and coagulate these bleeding points using a bare minimum of current. The tendency of most of us is to use far too heavy current and to delay healing thereby. This procedure is by no means complicated and should be part of the armamentarium of every practitioner who sees gynecologic cases.

Nabothian Cysts

Nabothian cysts of the cervix are simply occluded mucous glands that usually look like this:

They may be destroyed with the cautery tip or simply pricked with the knife to allow release of incarcerated secretion. These have no serious connotation whatsoever and you should remember always that patients confuse these nabothian cysts with the much more serious ovarian cysts. Be sure you explain to the patient that, while minor treatment is needed, the cysts have absolutely no serious aspect.

Cervical stenosis seems to be a rather common lesion, sometimes responsible for sterility and occasionally responsible for dysmenorrhea. The usual pathology is this:

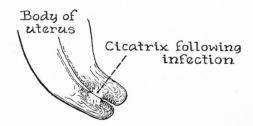

It may be checked for by using a sterile uterine sound. In case a stenotic cervix is found, be sure not to promise the patient too much from relief of the obstruction, but indicate that it is the first step in achieving the desired results. Dilation is quite simple. I use graduated Hegar dilators and have had one made a size smaller than is usually found in the standard set.

To perform the procedure the cervix is cleansed with green soap and water and the cervical canal is swabbed out with the same solution as far upwards as it is possible to reach with a cotton-tipped applicator. The applicators are, of course, sterile.

Grasp the cervix with a tenaculum and gently insert the dilator, like this:

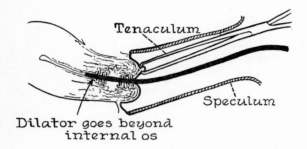

Gentleness is an absolute necessity, particularly with the smaller dilators. They can be made to penetrate the uterine or cervical wall with the greatest of ease and, while this is no tragedy as we have been urged to believe, it certainly does offer a point of entrance for virulent bacteria. The dilators need not be *forced* through the cervical canal but may be gently pushed through by taking a little time.

Ordinarily the procedure is done about every 4 to 6 days (never invading the uterus twice within 48 hours), and the dilatation is not carried past approximately lead pencil size.

Cervical Polyps

Cervical polyps are very common extrusions of the mucous membrane and occasionally cause mild symptoms and pinkish vaginal discharge. To remove one, put a wire loop nasal snare over the shank of an Allis forceps, like this:

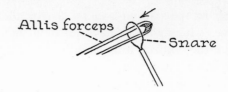

Now grasp the polyp as high up on its pedicle as is possible and clamp the forceps firmly together like this:

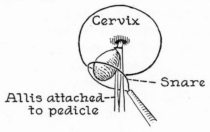

Run the snare down over the end of the forceps and snip off the polyp like this:

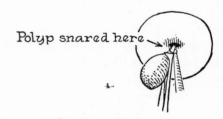

Malignant degeneration does occasionally occur and these polyps should be sent to the pathologist for examination. There are those who prefer to perform this procedure without the Allis forceps, simply slipping the snare wire over the polyp like this:

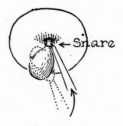

I use the Allis to avoid dropping the polyp.

Carcinoma of the Cervix

Carcinoma of the cervix is one of the most hellish lesions with which we physicians have to deal. It seems to be a constant threat to women between the ages of 35 and 60 and is a constant threat to us because of the difficulty in diagnosis and the tendency of the lesion to remain silent for a long period of time.

The only hope that many of us see for adequate treatment of these cancers is early and adequate diagnosis on the part of the family physician. We country doctors are the men who can lower mortality from cervical cancer. I think it behooves us to do so in a much more effective fashion than we have done in the past.

Begin by regarding every cervix much the same way that you would regard a coiled rattlesnake. Cervices may be attached to nice people but there is nothing even remotely nice about the deadly killing power of those cells presented so innocently to view through the speculum. Economics forces us to take some things for granted but never should anything else force us to refuse complete investigation of any suspicious cervix.

It has been my practice to discuss freely with my women patients the possibility of cervical malignancy and to suggest a yearly pelvic examination and a yearly Papanicolaou smear for all women over 37 or 38. Because this is somewhat expensive and may be an economic burden to some of the patients, I have done the pelvic examination free and the Papanicolaou smear at absolute cost for these people.

To take the Papanicolaou smear, have the patient take a plain water douche the night before the day of the examination. She is to use no vaginal preparation of any kind in the interim. Insert the speculum lubricated only with water and take a smear of the cervical secretion from the os, around the os, and the posterior lip. Spread these smears on clean glass slides and put them in a mixture of equal parts of alcohol and ether. They should be sent to the staining laboratory in this mixture.

In the routine yearly pelvic examination, first, of course, check with the naked eye. If there are questionable lesions, palpate them and then instill approximately 10 cc. of Gram's iodine solution (or Lugol's solution) into the vagina and leave it for a matter of a minute or two. Remove the solution by sponging gently and again look at the cervix. Any area in

which the cells are low in glycogen will look like this:

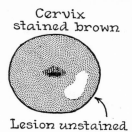

Biopsies from such lesions are frequently indicated and should be taken, including both normally stained and unstained cells, from this area:

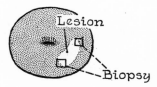

Various biopsy punches and forceps are on the market, all of which work excellently, and it is possible to get an adequate biopsy with the ordinary knife. When done with a knife, make four stab wounds outlining a square of tissue, like this:

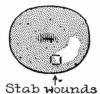

The wounds need be only ⅛ inch in depth. Now pick up the square of tissue between the forceps and use either scissors or the knife to undercut it, like this:

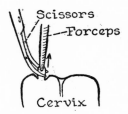

The biopsy tissue should be put in 10 per cent Formalin solution and sent immediately to a pathologic laboratory.

Now we come to the point where some judgment is indicated.   If every cervix in the world which has any sort of lesion on it were to be biopsied tomorrow there aren't enough pathologists to get the tissue read in the next year. Somebody is going to have to separate those cases that need biopsy badly and those cases than can wait.   I have no rules or suggestions as to how this should be done. If you are familiar with the patient and her history, if you know the appearance of her cervix and the various lesions to which it has been subject, you have a fair basis for determining the need of biopsy.   By no means do you have a 100 per cent accurate basis for making this determination.   About all that can be said is to suggest that it is better to biopsy fifty cases needlessly than to miss the one that counts.

The diagnosis of late cancer is simple in the extreme and need not be discussed here.   Another of our problems is the cervix with a lesion that appears benign.   There is no known test that can be performed at the office which is reliable in these cases.   Perhaps a reasonably good rule to follow is this one: If immediate biopsy is impossible and a Papanicolaou smear cannot be done, then treat the lesion in such fashion that malignant cells are not likely to be disseminated.   Cautery does not seem to be a potent means of disseminating such cells in spite of grim warnings to the contrary.   Certainly surface treatment seldom causes metastasis.   If the lesion seems to clear up, check it once monthly for 6 months before assuming that everything is all right.   If there seems a tendency to recur within a few weeks or months, biopsy no matter what excuse is presented.

Certain points are imperative in considering biopsy technique.   In the first place, the specimen must be adequate.   Second, if the lesion is at all large, biopsies should be taken from several points in its periphery.   Third, normal tissue should be included for comparative purposes if possible.

In all seriousness, many of us wish we could offer something really promising in the early diagnosis of cervical cancer.   As it is, hard work and a tremendous distrust of the cervix are the most important factors.   Let me repeat, it is the family physician who is the great hope in the early diagnosis of this lesion.

Relief of Pain.   In hopeless cases in which pain relief is a very real problem, the physician may do much to aid his patient.   Opiates are not a satisfactory means of granting relief, except in those cases that are actually terminal.

There are two excellent procedures for relief, depending on the origin of the pain. Diagnosis and treatment are as follows:

1. SOMATIC PAIN.   This is felt in the distribution of the spinal nerves.   Its principal characteristic, in addition to its distribution, is the extreme accuracy with which the patient localizes the sensation.   The pain is frequently described as stabbing in nature, and may have acute exacerbations after exercise or at night.   Occasionally, objective neurologic signs are present.

This type of pain is best treated by alcohol injections into the subarachnoid space.   No premedication is given, for this makes it difficult to evaluate the result of the injection. The field is set up exactly as for a spinal anesthetic, the patient lying on the unaffected side. The foot of the bed is raised slightly.

Notice the relative location of the sensory nerve roots in the illustration.

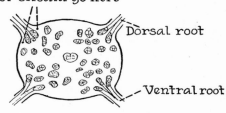

The patient should be placed in such a position that these sensory nerve roots are uppermost.   The solution of alcohol is, of course, hypobaric, and rises to the topmost layer of the spinal fluid.

The puncture is made with a standard spinal needle in the second lumbar interspace. (The first may also be used.)   When spinal fluid returns through the needle, a tuberculin syringe containing 0.5 cc. of 95 per cent ethyl alcohol is attached.   The injection is made slowly, drop by drop, as much as 5 minutes being taken for completion. The patient should not be allowed to move for at least an hour; then she may move about at will. Side effects usually pass quickly. In most cases, the injection will give relief for from 6 to 12 months, at the end of which time it may be repeated. In case of bilateral pain, at least a week should elapse between injections.

2. VISCERAL PAIN. This is diffuse and poorly localized. It is usually described as a deep sensation in the pelvis, is colicky and spasmodic, and is frequently noticed in conjunction with a demonstrable pelvic lesion. When a lesion is present, pain is often brought on by function of the affected organ.

Before measures are used for relief of visceral pain, an attempt should be made to find and eliminate the causative lesion. An abscess or secondary ulceration may be found and simple measures will suffice to cure the difficulty.

If this is not possible, one should give caudal anesthesia with one of the oil-soluble anesthetic agents. The technique is quite simple. After thorough cleansing, the caudal opening of the sacral canal is marked with a daub of iodine or mercurial antiseptic. A spinal needle is inserted at an angle of 45 degrees to the skin until the needle contacts bone. It is then withdrawn ¼ inch, the shank depressed, and insertion continued. There should be little resistance after the sacral canal is entered.

When the needle is in place and has been checked to ascertain that neither blood nor spinal fluid returns when the stylet is removed, injection of 10 cc. of 1 per cent aqueous procaine is made. If the needle is properly inserted, this injection is nearly effortless. One may check to see that the needle is in proper position by feeling over the sacrum for the pool of anesthetic which is deposited in case the needle lies posterior to the sacrum. The same precaution should be used for anterior position by inserting a palpating finger into the rectum.

If proper insertion is proven, one attaches a 10 cc. syringe full of anesthetic in oil (Intracaine). Very slow injection of 40 to 50 cc. of solution is made, checking the level of anesthesia with a pin every 2 minutes. When the pain is relieved, or when cutaneous anesthesia reaches the lower thoracic cage anteriorly, the injection is stopped. This procedure may have to be repeated each 2 to 3 months.

UTERINE DISPLACEMENTS

These are among the most common gynecologic lesions we see. There are two sharply differentiated types of displacements, one of which causes rather severe symptoms but is seldom discussed among the laity as a cause of difficulty, and the other which very seldom causes symptoms but which is blamed by many patients and not a few doctors for all sorts of aches and pains.

Retrodisplacement

The retrodisplacement of the uterus is, in most cases, innocuous. Occasionally, if the uterus is severely retroflexed, there may be dysmenorrhea and difficulty in maintaining pregnancy. Other than these cases, which are somewhat rare, the retrodisplacement is frequently innocent.

If it is felt that symptoms may be caused by this, the first office procedure is to attempt manual replacement of the uterus. With the vaginal fingers in the anterior fornix, push downward and with the abdominal hand attempt to get behind the corpus of the uterus and lift up like this:

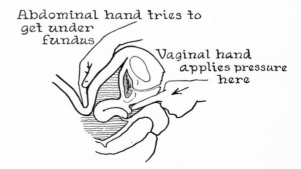

Abdominal hand tries to get under fundus

Vaginal hand applies pressure here

If it is impossible to get the abdominal hand under the body of the uterus, have the patient assume the knee-chest position and with the vaginal hand apply pressure in the cul de sac like this:

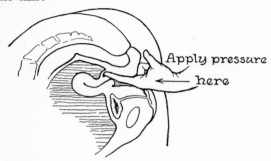

In the event that the uterus still stubbornly maintains its position you may reasonably assume the presence of firm adhesions. In this instance, office procedures are of little avail, although you should have the patient do knee-chest position for ½ hour a day for 30 days and make another attempt to replace the uterus.

If, on the other hand, the uterus assumes proper position with gentle manipulation, it is possible to make a therapeutic test regarding symptomatology. If the insertion of a pessary which holds the uterus up in proper position relieves symptoms after a week or two it is a reasonable inference that an operation will achieve relatively permanent relief in similar fashion. The Smith-Hodge pessary is an excellent device for holding the uterus in position, and a pessary called the Gynefold, of similar shape but hinged in the middle, like this:

is equally good as well as being somewhat easier to insert.

The proper size of the pessary may be estimated by a rough measurement of the dis-

tances from the posterior symphysis to the posterior fornix, like this:

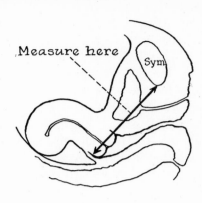

Width, of course, is determined by the size of the cervix. Use the following technique to insert the pessary:

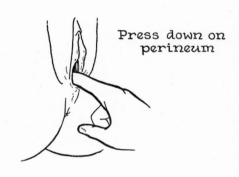

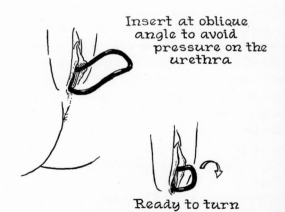

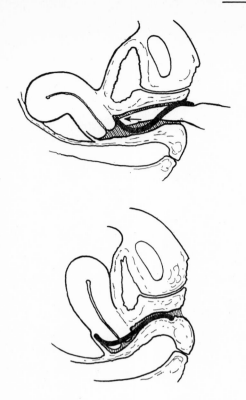

Most doctors consider it unwise to leave a pessary in place longer than 60 to 90 days at one time. While the pessary is in place the cervix should be examined by the physician every 30 days for signs of mucosal irritation or infection. The patient should be instructed to take regular douches with vinegar water. It should be emphasized that the pessary is by no means a cure, although it may give excellent temporary relief.

Prolapse

Prolapse of the uterus, which most often follows weakening of uterine supports during rigorous childbirth, is a much more serious disorder than the retrodisplacements. Normal vascular relations of the pelvis are destroyed, blood supply may be markedly cut down and, in an occasional case, a partial occlusion of the ureters exists and causes kidney complications. The only treatment that offers any reasonable hope of success is major surgery, and delay may occasionally result in serious damage. Special pessaries have been designed to hold the uterus up in place, and

they work with more or less success as measures for temporary relief. A common plastic bath sponge trimmed to proper size and inserted in the vagina each morning after douching will do the same job and do it equally well. This sponge should be removed at night.

UTERINE TUMORS

Cancer of the uterine corpus is another disease that is treacherous in the extreme. The symptoms of advanced cancer and procedures for detecting it are too well known to require delineation here. In early detection of this growth only two office procedures are of great value. The Papanicolaou smear of cervical discharges has some value but it is not 100 per cent accurate. If facilities are available it should be taken yearly on all patients in the cancer age group.

In the non-pregnant patient and the patient without necrotic myomas one frequently finds free bleeding upon gentle exploration of the uterine cavity with a sterile sound. While this test may be used as an office procedure I certainly feel that it should be abandoned because of the danger involved. One may easily perforate a necrotic uterine wall and the bleeding engendered may be difficult to control.

FUNCTIONAL UTERINE DISORDERS

Dysmenorrhea

Dysmenorrhea is one of the commonest gynecologic complaints seen by the practitioner. Literally thousands of articles have been written on this subject, many of which have been a real contribution to understanding. It is, however, necessary to have a simple basic concept of the subject in order to initiate proper office procedures and treatment. There are four types of dysmenorrhea which will encompass more than 95 per cent of the cases seen. They are:

1. *Psychogenic*. Girls are taught almost from birth that menstruation is a painful process. The very terms used in describing this cyclic bleeding have an emotional implication. For example, one of my patients never menstruates—she "has the curse." Back-yard gossip among women not otherwise occupied frequently takes the form of intimate discussion of menstrual periods and their horrors. Just as a matter of amusement, a beauty shop operator who was a friend of ours kept track of the number of women who mentioned their menstrual flow while becoming more beautiful. Her statement was that nearly 80 per cent of her regular customers were willing—nay, eager—to discuss their menstrual difficulties at some time while in the shop. One thing we physicians can do is to emphasize that children should be taught about menstruation as a normal process, not as the burden of womankind.

2. *Mechanical Obstruction to Flow*. Stenosis of the cervical canal is not a rare gynecologic problem. It is diagnosed at examination by the use of the uterine sound and usually may be relieved by dilation with Hegar dilators. Dilation should be done once weekly for several weeks, beginning with the smallest dilator that will fit snugly in the canal and, progressing through the sizes of dilators, double the size of the original one at each treatment. Force should never be used in the insertion of these instruments. A good "office trick" that I have found very useful is to grasp the dilator between the thumb and forefinger like this:

and to insert it using this same grip—never grasping firmly in the entire hand. This is just a simple way to make sure that you do not apply too much force.

Operative procedures are occasionally advised for the stenosed cervix but are useful only in the rare case. Office procedures will correct this problem in the vast majority of cases.

Other mechanical obstructions, such as sharp anteversion or retroversion of the uterus, seem more often present in the mind of the doctor than actually in the patient. Perhaps in the rarest of cases a cervical canal may be shut by a bend of the uterus like this:

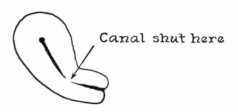

Canal shut here

But unless there is gross abnormality causing the malposition of the uterus, it is assumed that the canal can and will adapt itself to the normal or usual uterine position.

3. *Congestion of Tissues*. Preceding the menses by 5 to 8 days, there is a pelvic vascular dilatation with retention of fluids and increased succulence of all pelvic tissues. This can be well demonstrated on any patient who requires repeated pelvic examinations. There are two possibilities for causation of pain which may be attributed to this process. The first is stretching of tissues due to the increased fluid content. The second is mechanical, the increased weight of the movable organs causing position change.

If the first alternative be true (and we have no proof that it is), one would expect pain to be minor and nagging in character, without noticeable changes in intensity. If the pain is due to the second alternative (mechanical stretching), one would expect pain to be intermittent, depending on position, and to be relieved by rest with the hips elevated or by the knee-chest position after which the patient would assume the prone position.

We would expect either of these types to be relieved by administration of a diuretic, to be aggravated by the application of heat, and possibly to be helped by the use of mechanical devices that tend to support the organs involved. That such is the case has been amply proven and you may easily prove it in your own patients. To summarize, this type of dysmenorrhea is due to increased succulence of pelvic tissues with stretch of nerve-bearing structures. It may be relieved by the proper application of drugs and by a prescription of therapeutic exercise. Various office methods of applying heat, such as diathermy, are absolutely contraindicated.

4. *Uterine Ischemia.* There are pronounced changes in the uterine vessels at the time of menstruation. These vessels have been observed to contract and relax periodically. It would seem that occasionally this vascular contraction may be generalized throughout the uterine blood supply, with consequent relative ischemia of the uterine musculature and spasm of this musculature as a further consequence. If such be the case, pain would be expected to be typical of that caused by muscular ischemia. Since the vessels contract rhythmically, the pain would occur with rhythmic variations. The pain would be grinding, boring, pressure-like and of a relatively extreme intensity. This, of course, would vary with the amount of vascular spasm.

An excellent example of similar pain is the acute coronary spasm. Since discomfort from ischemia varies principally with the nerve supply, one would expect the pain of the coronary attack and the pain of uterine ischemia to vary in proportion to the relative number of nerve endings in cardiac and uterine muscles. That particular statement is theory. The statements about uterine ischemia are not.

It would follow that the exhibition of vasodilators and the application of heat would be excellent treatment for this difficulty. This works out to perfection. Two office procedures are extemely useful in this type of dysmenorrhea.

Application of the diathermy has in my experience given these patients almost complete relief for periods ranging from 6 hours to 2 days following the treatment. If the dysmenorrhea is properly classified and diagnosed, diathermy is one of the most valuable treatments we have. Injection of the ganglions of Frankenhäuser has been an established procedure in many European medical centers since the early 1930's. Injection with alcohol relieves menstrual discomfort in approximately 70 per cent of properly selected cases and has carried a very low morbidity. The actual injection is a simple procedure and, while alcohol has some degree of permanence, I much prefer to inject monthly if necessary with 1 per cent procaine. Relief is relatively quick and usually lasts for the duration of the period. I have had no cases in which relief lasted longer than one menstrual period.

In summary, remember the four basic causes of dysmenorrhea and be sure that any case is properly classified as to the cause. Office procedures will then give totally excellent results except in the very rare case. The four causes we have mentioned will encompass over 95 per cent of the cases of dysmenorrhea seen by the physician. The remaining 3 to 5 per cent are obscure gynecologic problems and remain strictly in the realm of the qualified specialist.

Uterine Hemorrhage

This brief paragraph will sound like rank heresy to many excellent gynecologists but I believe there are absolutely no office procedures of value for the investigation of functional uterine hemorrhage. The vaginal smear has been largely discarded and endometrial biopsy, while a fine research tool, does not usually afford information that is worth the cost to the patient. Hormonal assays, which indeed may be valuable, are completely out of the range of the average office. There are certain acceptable drug therapies which may be chosen on the basis of history and varied to suit the individual patient with good results. Undoubtedly, this unfortunate situation will change in the next decade or so and there will be devised excellent office procedures for diagnosis of various endocrine disorders which effect the menstrual function. I find myself believing that many of these problems are purely psychogenic and that hypermenorrhea as well as amenorrhea may arise from psychic tensions.

STERILITY

Sperm Tests

Most cases of sterility may be completely investigated in any well equipped office. Procedures should begin by checking adequacy of sperm and ejaculate from the husband. For complete accuracy, two specimens should be examined. For collection of the first specimen, have the man wear a condom during coitus. Instruct him to tie the neck of the condom in a knot and to hold the specimen in his hand to keep it warm or place the tied condom in a small jar of water at body temperature and bring it immediately to the office. First, a sperm count is made this way: In a regular 1:20 blood counting pipet, draw semen up to the 0.5 mark, then fill the pipet to the 11 mark with diluting fluid which is made up like this:

Sodium bicarbonate	5 gm.
1 per cent Formalin solution	100 cc.

Agitate the pipet and fill a standard counting chamber with the resultant solution. Count the number of sperms in each of four 1 square millimeter areas (the same area as used for a white count) and average the number. Multiply this average number of sperms per square millimeter by 200,000. This gives the number of sperms per cubic centimeter. Fewer than 75 million sperms per cubic centimeter indicates the possibility of sterility.

Next place 1 drop of the semen on a clean warm slide and cover the drop with a cover glass. Examine under a microscope using a minimal amount of light. A normal sperm looks like this:

and is very actively motile. Check 100 or 200 sperms at random for motility. If fewer than 30 per cent are motile you may predicate abnormality of these sperms as a possible cause of sterility. Now look at a number of sperms individually for evidence of various malformations. These are legion and cannot be listed as individual types. Simply check a number of single sperms, looking at head, neck and tail for signs of any structural defects. If more than 30 per cent of the sperms seem in some way deformed, make a stain smear like this:

1. Fix the smear with heat.
2. Use 0.5 per cent Chlorazene solution as a wash.
3. Next wash in tap water.
4. Immerse briefly (2 or 3 seconds) in 95 per cent alcohol and allow to air dry.
5. Stain 1 minute with a solution made up of carbofuchsin, 2 parts; bluish eosin, 1 part, and 95 per cent alcohol, 1 part.
6. Wash in tap water.
7. Counterstain 1 minute with methylene blue.
8. Wash and dry.

Abnormalities of sperm will be quite apparent after this staining technique. Since some technical knowledge is required to read this slide, if there is any doubt send it to the nearest pathologic laboratory for confirmation of your findings.

The next procedure is to have the wife report for examination within a few minutes after sexual congress. With a pipet, a few drops of semen are removed from the posterior vaginal fornix, one drop is placed on a clean warm slide, a cover glass added and check made for motility of the sperm. If more than 40 to 50 per cent of the sperms are not motile and if they appear to be dying rapidly as you watch, you may infer some characteristic of the female secretion as an active killing agent. The most important characteristic is, of course, pH, which will be discussed further below. It does, however, seem that there is an occasional incompatibility between the vaginal secretions of the wife and the semen of the male. We are unable to explain this at the present except to call attention to some rather unusual experiments in which women were immunized against pregnancy by subcutaneous injections of sperm. This is not advocated as an office procedure, although the thought of an active immunity to the male is a fascinating one.

Vaginal pH

Studies of female sterility should begin with determination of the vaginal pH using nitrazine paper. Extreme acidity of the vagina, which is rare, may be a cause for failure to conceive. To be in this range the pH should be 3.5 or less. Much more common is over-alkalinity of the vagina, which much more often is a cause for relative sterility.

Patency of Cervical Canal

If the vaginal pH is normal and there is no evidence of vaginal or cervical infection, next determine the patency of the cervical canal. This is done using the uterine sound as specified in earlier sections. Should there be narrowing or partial obliteration of the canal, a program of dilation is definitely in order.

Very rare cases of sterility may be caused by retrodisplacement of the uterus, which should be diagnosed and treated as previously noted.

Patency of Fallopian Tubes

Perhaps the most important technique in determining feminine causes of sterility is that of tubal insufflation. The most valuable apparatus and by far the easiest technique is instillation of Lipiodol, using the Jarcho apparatus. It looks like this:

Begin by cleansing the cervix with green soap and water. Then, using cotton-tipped applicators, cleanse the cervical canal insofar as is possible. Grasp the cervix with a tenaculum

and hold it firmly in place while inserting the Jarcho cannula like this:

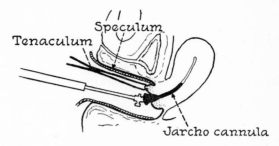

Use 15 to 20 cc. of Lipiodol in the syringe and inject by means of steady pressure, using only a minimal amount of force on the plunger of the syringe. In my own practice I have usually made the injection with the patient on the x-ray table and instructed the technician to expose a film as soon as 5 to 10 cc. of the Lipiodol had passed into the uterine cavity. Some leakage is inevitable around the cannula but this is unimportant and may be ignored.

If the tubes are patent the Lipiodol will outline their lumen and escape into the pelvic cavity, appearing in x-ray somewhat like this:

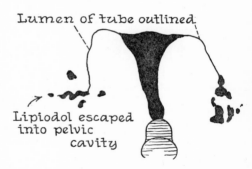

In the event of tubal obstruction the picture usually appears something like this:

There have been attempts to open the tubes by repeated instillations of Lipiodol under gradually increasing pressure. The technique has more often been performed using air insufflation rather than the drug. While I have tried it only a limited number of times, several of my friends who have made extensive attempts to use the procedure tell me that it is only rarely effective.

Determination of Ovulation by Biopsy

Failure of ovulation is a not infrequent cause of sterility. There is one technique which will give a great deal of information. It is the endometrial biopsy. Here, it is necessary to include a word further about this test so that I may not be accused of writing one thing on one page and a different thing on another. The endometrial biopsy is reasonably good proof of whether or not ovulatory cycles are occurring. We disagree with its use *only* as a routine in attempting to elicit information about cases of dysmenorrhea. For sterility study do it this way:

Grasp the cervix with a tenaculum and dilate it gently, using Hegar dilators. If carefully done this procedure usually causes very little pain and anesthesia is seldom necessary. Use the endometrial biopsy curet, to which is attached a 20 cc. syringe. Insert the biopsy curet, place it firmly up against the endometrium and draw it gently outwards, meanwhile making suction with the syringe like this:

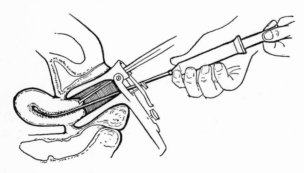

If it is possible to obtain specimens from several areas this will be most helpful to the pathologist. Occasionally this may be done without removing the curet from the uterus, but it may be necessary to remove it and expel the contents into a solution of 10 per cent Formalin before getting the next specimen.

After obtaining specimens from four differ-

ent areas, remove the curet and preserve the specimens as stated.

It is probably wise to exhibit one of the antibiotics for a day or two following this procedure, but morbidity of any kind is extremely rare if the cardinal principle of gentleness be kept in mind. For the best possible determination of ovulation, the specimen should be taken on the second day of menstruation.

Determination of Ovulation by Temperature Record

We see an occasional case in which failure to conceive is due purely to chance—insufficient sperm being present in the tube at the same time that the egg is available. This may be due to a patient's lack of knowledge about when she ovulates. The daily record of basal body temperature is extremely useful in these cases.

Have the patient secure a reliable thermometer and take her temperature (either rectally or orally) at the same time each day. The best and most reliable time for this temperature determination is upon arising. Have the patient plot these daily temperature readings on a graph, like this:

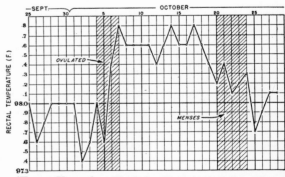

(From Karnaky, Karl J.: Practical Office Gynecology, Charles C Thomas, Publ., 1947.)

Be sure to caution her to get a normal night's sleep each night during the time she is plotting the graph. A night of riotous living will cause changes in the body temperature that make interpretation difficult.

At the time of ovulation there will usually be a minor drop in temperature followed by a sudden sharp rise of three-quarters of a degree or more. When the patient has established a relatively reliable schedule timing her ovulation, advise her to have coitus on the third day preceding her time of ovulation, the first day preceding, the day of ovulation, and one day and three days afterwards.

PREGNANCY TESTS

Tests for pregnancy are beyond the scope of the office. There are newer tests which seem reliable but which at this writing have not been demonstrated as adequate. One little procedure which may be done in any office gives a clue. Put a drop of Schiller's iodine solution on a clean slide. Now dry the lateral vaginal wall thoroughly with a sponge and use the sharp edge of a knife blade to scrape (not cut) off some epithelial cells. Put this cellular debris in the Schiller solution for 10 seconds. If it turns black one should suspect pregnancy. This little test is not as reliable as the Friedman or the Aschheim-Zondek but it is helpful.

INCOMPLETE ABORTION

Occasionally we see an incomplete abortion as an office emergency. There is only one procedure of use. It is to check the cervical canal for the presence of the fetus or a portion of the placenta, usually the placenta. If the fragment remains in the canal, bleeding will continue, so it must be removed.

Insert a sterile speculum into the vagina and examine the cervix. When placenta is incarcerated in the partially dilated cervix, it will look like this:

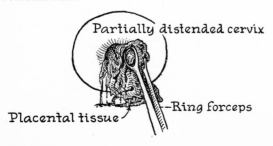

Grasp the placental fragment in a pair of sterile ring forceps as shown, and try to tease it out gently. Do not pull the fragment roughly away. In most cases, bleeding will cease immediately and the patient may be transferred to a hospital for proper care.

FEMININE HYGIENE

Proper feminine hygiene is a frequent subject of discussion with many patients and, although there are no office procedures involved, the doctor should be familiar with acceptable techniques and how the procedures may be used at home.

There are many women who regard a vaginal discharge as normal. The secretion of a very slight amount of mucus *is* normal, but this should seldom be secreted in sufficient quantity to stain underclothing. The normal secretion is not colored and has no appreciable odor if the parts are kept clean.

It is a standing joke in certain parts of our society that a woman smells like fish. The *clean* woman has no noticeable odor except in cases of extreme sexual excitement, and even then the odor is barely appreciable. Many women do not appreciate the value of vaginal cleanliness. It is, however, entirely possible to follow instructions from all the newspaper advertisements about "daintiness" and to achieve only a chronic vaginal irritation that tends to increase the offensive odor.

I know of only two preparations that are of particular usefulness in cleansing the female generative tract. The first, used principally for external cleansing, is soap and water. In spite of some years of effort, man has failed to invent a more satisfactory cleansing procedure than washing with soap. The second procedure is the acidifying vaginal douche.

Douches

A good method for douching is this: Use warm but not hot water and acidify it with 3 to 5 tablespoonfuls of vinegar per quart. The patient should, if possible, lie in a bath tub and should prepare for her douche by washing the external parts vigorously with soap and water. The douche tip should be removed from the hose and the rubber tube itself inserted into the vagina about 2 inches. The first bagful of water should be used to irrigate thoroughly, like this:

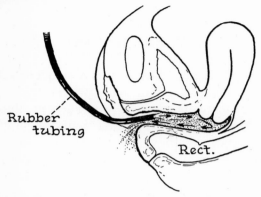

Rubber tubing

Rect.

Another bagful of acidified water should be prepared and the douche point inserted exactly as previously. This time, however, the labia should be firmly clamped together around the tubing, like this:

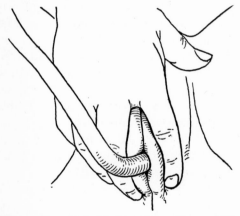

The water should be allowed to distend the vagina, like this:

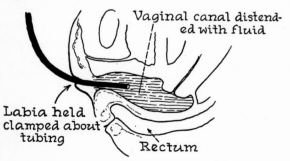

Vaginal canal distended with fluid

Labia held clamped about tubing

Rectum

After maximal distention, the douche tubing should be clamped with the fingers of one hand and the vaginal opening released suddenly to allow the escape of the accumulated fluid. This procedure should be repeated as many times as is possible with one bagful of water.

An important factor in the douche is thorough drying of the external genitalia. Have the patient stand up to secure adequate drainage from the vaginal canal. Then have her dry the genitalia thoroughly. This massage with the towel should not extend into the vaginal canal.

There are many commercial products on the market used for douching. I know of none superior to vinegar and water.

There are many superstitions prevalent about the douche. Actually there are few, if any, contraindications. Douches may well be taken during the menses and are frequently very gratifying to patients at this time. As far as I know the number of douches is limited only by the possibility of wearing a callus with the douche tube or completely water-logging the tissues, neither of which seems very likely. Douches may usually be taken with impunity during the first two trimesters of pregnancy and there are few proven cases where they have done any damage during the latter trimester, although it is probably wise to limit their use during this period.

Vaginal Tampons

Women frequently ask about the use of vaginal tampons for absorption of menstrual fluid. While opinions of all sorts are rampant, I know of no contraindication to their use if a woman prefers such sanitary protection. I have occasionally prescribed the use of intravaginal tampons in cases where vaginal discharge was excessively heavy. These tampons should not be retained in place for more than 3 or 4 hours, but they may serve a psychologic and practical use by protecting a woman against social difficulties between douches.

Section V

OBSTETRICS

DIAGNOSIS OF PREGNANCY

There are many secondary signs of pregnancy. They are useful in making the diagnosis. There are three important primary signs apparent in the uterus and one regarding the breasts that may be elicited by palpation. The procedure of checking these signs should never be slighted. I cannot frown too much on the careless and inaccurate diagnosis of pregnancy. These important examination procedures are:

1. *Softening of the Cervix.* By the fifth or sixth week of pregnancy the cervix transmits to the palpating finger a soft sensation somewhat akin to the feeling of foam rubber. The normal cervix, on the other hand, is quite firm.

2. By the sixth week the uterus usually shows unequal softening and enlargement in a portion of its substance, like this:

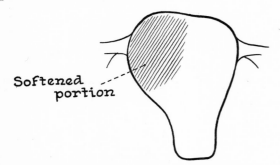

Softened portion

One should mention that this sign can occur in non-pregnant women and it must not be taken as a final and unequivocal diagnosis of pregnancy.

3. *Hegar's Sign.* The normal isthmus is firm and resists bending. In the pregnant uterus the isthmus becomes somewhat compressible and may be bent very freely, the cervix frequently doubling back almost to the body of the uterus like this:

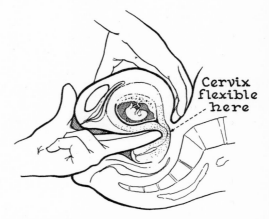

Cervix flexible here

4. By the same time, i.e., six weeks, a thin secretion looking like a mixture of water and milk may be expressed from the breasts of many pregnant women. This is more reliable in those women who have not previously been pregnant. The later signs, which depend upon more complete development of pregnancy, have been of little use in my clinic. After three months, the women tell me—I don't have to tell them whether or not they are pregnant. This is not meant sarcastically. In office practice it is a rarity to find a diagnosis of late pregnancy clouding the picture. This is, of course, not so in hospital practice, where differentiation between pregnancy and tumor in the menopausal woman may be exceedingly difficult.

The Aschheim-Zondek and Friedman tests for pregnancy are usually beyond the range of the small office and must be performed at a regional laboratory where facilities are available.

Pelvimetry

The measurement of the pelvic outlet is a rewarding procedure which takes only a moment or two. The measurements usually obtained, and their normal values, are as follows:

Interspinous, 25 cm.
Intercristal, 28 cm.
Intertrochanteric, 31 cm.
Right and left oblique, 22 cm.
External conjugate, 21 cm.
Diagonal conjugate, 12.5 cm.
Bi-ischial, 11 cm.

The interspinous measurement is taken between the outer surfaces of the anterior superior spines. The intercristal is measured from the outermost points of the iliac crest. The intertrochanteric is measured between the two greater trochanters. Oblique diameters are measured from the posterior superior spine on one side to the anterior superior spine on the other.

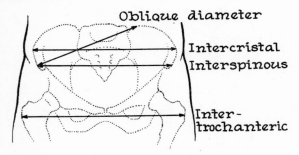

The external conjugate is measured from the depression beneath the last lumbar spine to the superior surface of the symphysis pubis, like this:

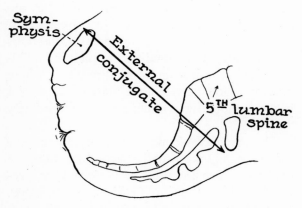

The diagonal conjugate is an internal measurement which gives an estimate of the distance between the promontory of the sacrum and the inferior margin of the symphysis pubis. With your hand in the vagina, feel the promontory of the sacrum and place a

finger of the opposite hand on your glove by the symphysis pubis, like this:

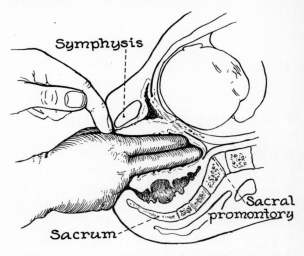

Measure the distance with the routine pelvimeter.

The bi-ischial diameter may be determined by first measuring the width of the obstetrician's closed fist, like this:

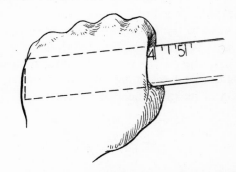

An attempt is made to insert the fist between the ischial tuberosities, like this:

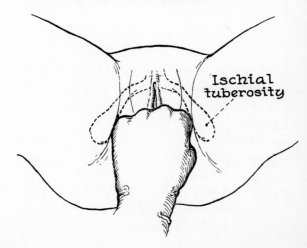

Knowing the width of the fist, one can estimate quite accurately the bi-ischial diameter.

ESSENTIAL PROCEDURES AT PERIODIC VISITS

Weighing

A great deal of information can be gained by charting the weight of the pregnant patient. Rather than use the office weights I prefer to give the patient a sheet of ordinary graph paper which my office nurse has marked off by days. Have the woman weigh herself on her own scales each morning and keep a chart on the graph paper. Any sudden upswing in the graph line is suggestive of edema formation. The graph is, of course, normally "jerky," showing a variation in weight of as much as 2 or 3 pounds each day, but a consistent and continuing rise for three or four days makes one somewhat suspicious.

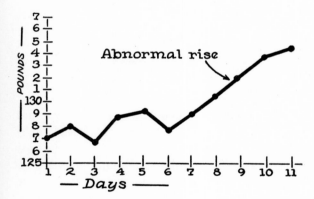

Incidentally, we have found a good thing to do is this: Prepare an ordinary 8½ by 11 inch file folder containing the records of the patient and give it to her. Many women will pore over them at length and will be inordinately proud of their part in the conduct of the pregnancy. Several graphs and charts showing the height of the uterus above the symphysis, the weight, blood pressure fluctuation, etc., not only give the young lady something with which to occupy herself but also make a quick summary of the case very easy for the physician.

One must be judicious in doing this and occasionally one wishes to keep a private note or so, but it is a good trick for maintaining a woman's interest in prenatal visits.

Urinalysis

The patient should bring a morning sample of urine at each visit. This should be checked for specific gravity and albumin and a microscopic examination should be done as a bare minimum. The complete urinalysis is, of course, better.

One warning: It is perfectly normal for a pregnant woman to show a trace of sugar occasionally. I don't know how many of these patients I have seen who have been scared to death because someone has mentioned diabetes. To repeat: *IT IS NORMAL FOR A PREGNANT WOMAN TO SHOW A TRACE OF SUGAR IN THE URINE OCCASIONALLY.* The presence of albumin in the urine, unless there are many pus cells, should lead to a very complete check. When many pus cells are present, the albumin may very well be derived from the degeneration of these cells and therefore be insignificant.

Pus cells may be from vaginal contamination or from actual infection of the urinary tract, which is common in pregnancy. Vaginal contamination may be avoided by instructing the woman to wash the parts carefully before collecting her specimen for urinalysis and then to hold the labia apart while urinating so that a stream of urine exits directly from the meatus to the receiving vessel.

We have found it advisable to give these women a regular urine specimen jar and cap to avoid the usual half ounce medicine bottle full of urine for a specimen.

Blood Pressure Determination

The regular determination of blood pressure, which may be charted on a graph, is a valuable adjunct to estimating the status of an obstetrical patient. In my own experience, I have found that a steadily climbing diastolic pressure is of more significance than a single high blood pressure reading. In the vast majority of cases a single high reading disappears by the next visit but the steadily climbing diastolic may suddenly shoot upward and remain high.

Low Blood Pressure. This is one of the most pernicious diagnoses in American medicine. Unquestionably, there are rare people who have a hypotension sufficient to cause symptoms. This is as true in pregnancy as in non-pregnant individuals. As a rough guess, I would say that about one person out of every 100,000 who is told he or she has low blood pressure actually has symptoms due to the hypotension. Many of the psychoneuroses show hypotension as a manifestation, but the hypotension is the result, not the cause, of the psychoneurosis.

People with blood pressure ranging in the 95 to 105 level have statistically a better outlook for a long, healthy life than those in the 140 to 150 pressure group. Such being the case, it would seem likely that most of the "hypotension of pregnancy" is a disease only in the mind of the physician and has no significance from the standpoint of the patient.

Abdominal Examination

Abdominal examination is the least informative of all the methods at our command. The fetal heart tones, development of the uterus and placental location may be elicited with fair reliability. When a patient complains of persistent pain, do not forget to palpate at the costovertebral angle for possible kidney involvement.

Eye Ground Examination

The ophthalmoscope is the most valuable tool you have for eliciting the general status of the vascular system. After one knows how to use the instrument, findings are much more reliable than those garnered from the other tests. I have been needlessly alarmed many times by a sudden rise in blood pressure or a urinalysis showing albumin, because other factors enter into these tests besides the vascular elements which we seek. The ophthalmoscope, on the other hand, gives a pure test, for one looks directly at the vessels. If a mistake is made, the examiner makes it—it is not

due to contamination of the test with extra-vascular variables. Such being the case, I feel that it behooves us practitioners to become experts with the ophthalmoscope.

The normal fundus and some of the various pathologic pictures important in obstetrics look like this:

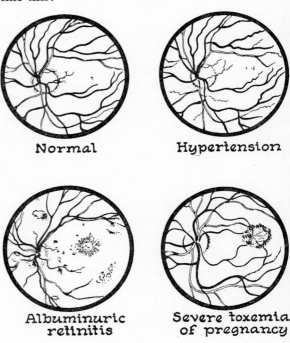

Normal   Hypertension

Albuminuric   Severe toxemia
retinitis   of pregnancy

MINOR COMPLICATIONS

Vaginal Discharge

The increased succulence of the vaginal tissues during pregnancy makes both infection and infestation with parasitic organisms more likely. Vaginal trichomonads are a common infesting organism and should be diagnosed and treated exactly as in the non-pregnant individual (see page 97). Monilial infections are often seen. This condition is characterized by white flaky plaques of irregular shape on the vaginal wall, like this:

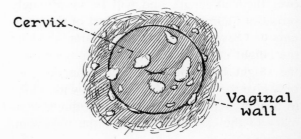

Cervix   Vaginal wall

To make a final diagnosis, pick up a piece of the whitish membrane, place it on a slide with a drop of 10 per cent potassium hydroxide and crush it with a cover glass. Under the microscope the field will look like this:

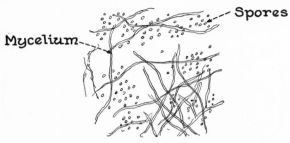

Monilia albicans

Drug treatment is entirely effective and may be done exactly as in the non-pregnant woman.

Cervicitis

Slight erosion or eversion occurs so often in the latter six months of pregnancy that it may become routine rather than exceptional. One should hesitate to apply the more rigorous office procedures. There are those who feel that cautery may be performed until the beginning of the last trimester. Statistics are impressive and are probably quite right, but I have always been too chicken-hearted to use the cautery on a pregnant uterus. Chemical cauterization, if discharge from the irritated area is profuse, will sometimes give temporary relief.

If the cervicitis is sufficient to cause a great deal of annoying discharge and does not respond readily to the most conservative treatment, I prefer the opinion of an expert gynecologist before undertaking any treatment.

Varicosities

Varicosities of the lower extremities and vulva are seen in approximately 5 to 10 per cent of pregnant women. Unless thrombophlebitis intervenes (and it seldom does) no treatment is necessary, for the majority of these veins will disappear after the period of gestation. By no means should treatment be undertaken until an opportunity for spontaneous restoration after pregnancy has been given.

Pyelitis

As the uterus enlarges in pregnancy, it tends to rotate slightly in a clockwise direction as seen from above. This rotation plus the increased succulence of pericervical tissues may be the factors that operate to cause a partial blockage of the ureters, more pronounced on the right, with occasional resulting infection of the urinary tract.

This pyelitis of pregnancy may be a severe, difficult-to-treat infection that does nothing but make trouble until delivery is accomplished. In severe cases, it is wise to perform cystoscopy and to catheterize the ureters, leaving the catheters in place for a day or two so that ample drainage may be established. Irrigation of the urinary tract with sterile normal saline solution containing an antibiotic suitable to the organism found in the urine will provide great relief.

OFFICE INSTRUCTION OF OBSTETRICAL PATIENTS

Would you mind reflecting with me for just a minute on the feeling of a woman who goes to the hospital to have a baby? She is the one who is having the baby, yet she is the one who is the most ignored from the standpoint of hospital routine. She is told to do this and told to do that with no explanations of why or wherefore. She sees people preparing various things for her about which she has no choice and no knowledge whatsoever.

The people she loves and depends upon are frequently excluded from her and the obstetrician is often so busy that he has time to do nothing but concentrate on her nether regions by performing a series of strange and terrifying rituals and issuing forth little grunts of approval or disapproval which may be interpreted in any of a hundred different ways.

If you think about this just a minute it may occur to you that even we big brave men might turn green with fright in a similar situation. Add to this all the old wives' tales which neighbor ladies have taken the greatest pleasure in telling about the horrors of childbirth, and you have a mental torture worthy of the inquisition. One time we decided to obviate this.

The procedure worked so very beautifully that I am going to pass along the general outline to you. We even had the impression that there was a statistically significant lowering in maternal morbidity. Let me make this clear —we never ran the figures to see. This is merely a clinical impression. If such a study could be conducted using adequate controls and submitting the results to statistical analysis, I suspect that the findings might provide impetus for some widespread changes.

A registered nurse met with the obstetrical patients approximately once a month. At the first meeting they were taken through the hospital and shown in great detail how everything worked. They were told what was done when they entered the hospital; they were told the purpose of the various procedures concerned with their care immediately preceding delivery and were taken into the delivery room where instruments were explained in general and where all questions were freely answered. Particular emphasis in the delivery room was given to safety factors, with repeated explanations of the common terms used by doctors and nurses in referring to the progress of delivery.

At the second meeting, an anatomic mannequin and charts were used to explain just what happens in the process of delivery, just what the doctor does and just what changes take place following delivery. The third meeting was used to explain the perineal musculature and the advantages to be gained when delivery is accomplished with relaxation of this musculature.

Still another meeting was devoted to the psychologic aspects of childbirth, with some lengthy discussions about the part that fear plays in causing pain. Other meetings were used to answer questions. No punches were pulled in these answers. Morbid questions were answered frankly with no hesitation and no stuttering. Obstetrical figures are so very good that one need not hesitate to discuss them freely with the patient.

The most important part, I believe, of this whole thing was the training given our subsidiary obstetrical personnel. Lest this sound like huge hospital material, our accessory obstetrical personnel consisted of two practical nurses, both over fifty, both weighing over two hundred pounds and both just about as nice as it is humanly possible to be. We made it a point to have these ladies, the RN on duty, the doctor, and delivery room RN treat the patient as if she were queen for a day instead of an outsider who happened to butt in on an obstetrical procedure. Her opinion was asked about practically everything that was done. Decisions were discussed freely with her and she was urged to put in her two cent's worth at any time she felt like it. Not only did many of these patients actually seem to enjoy the process but I must confess that we got a terrific amount of enjoyment out of it, too. I believe that many physicians would find their outlook on obstetrics changed completely if they used such a routine.

Again, stop and think just a moment. The only one of the whole obstetrical team that doesn't amount to anything, the only one that is not taken into full confidence about the procedures involved is the particular person who is doing all the work—the prospective mother. This may not violate the principles of medicine but it certainly violates the principles of common sense.

POSTPARTUM EXAMINATION

The postpartum examination is an easily neglected part of obstetrics. There is much to be learned and, as a preventive against future trouble, the postpartum check can be valuable.

The examination may be the typical routine

physical examination, abbreviated in some parts. The obstetrical chart should contain a record of blood pressure, temperature, pulse and respiration. The ocular fundi should be examined and any deviation from the normal recorded. Size of the heart and quality of heart sounds should be noted and, particularly if infection is suspected, the presence or absence of dullness or rales in the lungs. Nipples should be inspected for fissures and the quadrants of each breast palpated individually.

Presence of striae on the abdominal wall should be noticed and the rectus muscles examined for diastasis. The ureters should be checked for tenderness by making firm pressure about 2 inches lateral to the umbilicus and rolling the ureter against the spine. In examining the pelvis, the condition of the episiotomy, if one has been done, should be checked carefully. At six weeks there should be little, if any, tenderness of the episiotomy wound and firm pressure made along the internal limb of the incision should reveal no gaps in the repair of muscles. The presence of cystocele and rectocele should be checked for and, if either is found, the degree of relaxation should be noted.

The cervix should be firm and well contracted at six weeks. Many women show a degree of cervicitis but in most instances this will heal spontaneously.

There should be little if any pain on motion of the uterus. The parametrial area should show no bogginess, and tenderness should be absent. The corpus of the uterus remains slightly enlarged at six weeks in about 50 per cent of women. This is not to be taken as subinvolution of the uterus. At six weeks there will be normally some relaxation of uterine supports, with a minor degree of descensus. The relative amount of descent of the uterus should be recorded on the chart. The tubes are rarely palpable and the ovaries are usually normal, with one possible exception: The corpus luteum may remain palpable as an enlarged rounded body which gives the clinical feel of an ovarian cyst. It is most important that these not be considered ovarian cysts until checked further.

There is too much tendency to "slide over" this pelvic examination, which should be thorough, extensive and complete.

The legs should be inspected for signs of venous thrombosis and the general posture of the woman should be evaluated carefully. The evaluation of carriage and posture is most important and should not be neglected.

In our clinic we have seen many women whom we refer to as "obstetrical cripples." These are women in their forties and fifties who have had chronic pelvic disorders since childbirth. We have not had the facilities to make accurate scientific study of these women but have gained some distinct clinical impressions.

We feel that the trouble which these patients have is not due to poor obstetrics but rather to poor postpartum care, many times on the part of the woman herself. The common lesion we have found is a chronic parametritis with soft, boggy, parametrial tissues and chronic mild pelvic pain and resulting relatively constant minor discomfort. We believe this is due to invasion of these tissues by bacteria of low pathogenicity in the puerperal period. While our patients have been followed only a very few years, we believe that intensive treatment of these lesions when discovered at the six week examination will do much to relieve these women of future difficulty.

At the six week checkup the patient should have a urinalysis and a determination of hemoglobin, although a complete blood count is preferable. If there is suspicion of pelvic infection, smear and culture of the uterine discharge should be made. In those women who have hypertension during pregnancy, a cold pressor test should be performed as a matter of routine.

No attempt will be made in this brief paragraph to go into details of treatment. Rather, there follows a summary of the simple treatment of some common disorders of the puerperal period.

Cervicitis may be treated by one of the suppositories designed to correct vaginal pH. Vinegar douches will do the same thing. We do not recommend cautery of the average cervical lesion until three to four months post partum.

Many postpartum retroversions may be avoided by the insertion of a well fitted pessary at the six week examination. One should remember, however, that there is much controversy about the use of a pessary. Although many fine obstetricians recommend this procedure, it is well to watch for the future evaluation in current literature.

Section VI

UROLOGY

UROLOGY

Certain urologic instruments and their use come well within the purview of the average practitioner. Most urologic procedures may be done in the office and are simple of accomplishment. There is no reason for any physician not to become reasonably proficient at using them, at least as diagnostic instruments.

CYSTOSCOPY

The Brown-Buerger cystoscope is an instrument which will prove valuable and which every physician should know how to use. It looks like this:

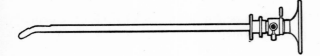

There are usually two telescopes with the instrument, one large one which is called the examining telescope and which has a relatively wide field of vision like this:

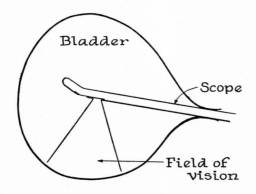

The second scope is much smaller and is used for ureteral catheterization. It has a field of vision approximately like this:

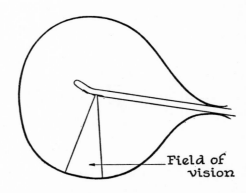

Notice that the field of vision is at right angles to the axis of the scope.

The next few pages are included on the assumption that the reader is not familiar with the cystoscope and its operation. There is given a step by step resume of assembly, checking, and operation of the scope. The inexperienced operator should assemble and disassemble the scope until he is entirely familiar with the operation of every part.

Be sure to know the common points of difficulty in operating the scope and the remedy available for each. This is imperative if petty annoyances are to be avoided.

Begin by assembling the scope and checking its component parts. First connect the water inflow to the right-hand spigot (if you are right-handed).

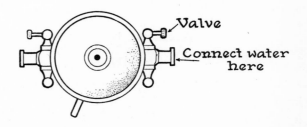

Open the valve to see if water runs through the cystoscope. Next, plug the light cord either into a battery box or into a transformer and connect it to the cystoscope like this:

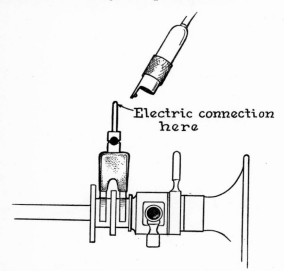

Electric connection here

Upon looking at the shank of the post to which the light cord is connected you will note two insulated spots like this:

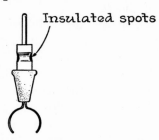

Insulated spots

By rotating the light cord so that the contact touches either the metal or the insulated spot you may turn the light on and off at the cystoscope. Now put the examining scope in place; notice that it fits and locks into grooves on the collar of the instrument here:

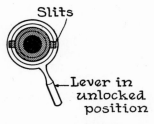

Slits

Lever in unlocked position

Now look through the scope toward the ceiling of the room. You should see the ceiling light clearly and should be able to make out details of the ceiling area. Turn on the cystoscope light and adjust the intensity, using the rheostat on the box of the transformer. One

warning: many transformers will overload this light if turned too high. It does not take a lot of light to visualize the inside of a bladder and bulb mortality will be tremendously high if you turn the transformer full on. Now remove the examining scope and put the small catheterizing scope in place. Notice the small metal partition which clamps on to the scope and which keeps the catheters separated as they pass through the tube.

Partition

Rotate the small round wheel near the eyepiece of the scope and notice the tiny operculum or flap that comes up on the end of the scope. This serves to move the catheters and to help you aim them when entering the ureters. A common error is to forget this operculum and to remove or try to remove the scope from the bladder with the operculum elevated. I know of no quicker way to make an enemy, for it is extremely painful. Now put the perforated rubber tips on the two lateral tubes that protrude near the eyepiece. Use a non-perforated (black) tip for the center tube like this:

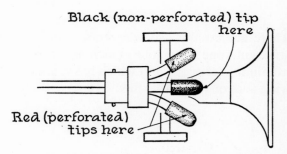

Black (non-perforated) tip here

Red (perforated) tips here

You can now pass catheters through the hole in the red rubber tips and into the body of the scope itself.

Turning now to the actual procedure of cystoscopy, if you go about it with the utmost of gentleness and with a heavy respect for both the scope and the patient, there is absolutely nothing difficult in the process. Cystoscopy is easy and by far the most accurate means we have of making some urologic diagnoses. There are, of course, certain contraindications to the procedure. The first would be an obvious obstruction to insertion of the scope. A mildly hypertrophied prostate is usually only an annoyance; a severe prostatic hypertrophy is a contraindication.

Since the procedure cannot help being somewhat irritating it should not be used in the presence of infection. Quite obviously this is a relative statement. Severe fulminating urinary infection is an absolute contraindication to cystoscopy. Chronic low-grade infections, difficult of diagnosis, are the prime indications for use of the cystoscope. Some place in between there is a dividing line which there is no exact way to define. Perhaps the best rule of thumb would go something like this: Cystoscopy in itself is slightly irritating. If the infection is acute enough that an additional irritation might turn it into a major problem, then cystoscopy is contraindicated. If, on the other hand, a slight irritation would make little or no difference in the course of infection, cystoscopy may be done.

In making this determination of judgment, lean always to the conservative side. Very few people have ever died because the cystoscope wasn't used today. Some people have died because it *was* used today.

After an exhaustive history and physical examination have indicated the necessity for cystoscopic work, then proceed with entering the bladder. I know that the average urologist will disagree with this statement, but anesthesia is practically never needed if you will be gentle enough in using the scope. Sedation and perhaps even morphine or Demerol are wise precursors. For some reason that I am not able to explain, some people who use the cystoscope routinely seem to lose their respect for the other fellow's urethra. They frequently center their attention on pursuing a lesion and forget that the patient has a hearty regard for the area which is being entered. From my point of view, it is better to be a gentle cystoscopist or not be one at all.

To enter the female bladder, put the obturator in the cystoscope and lubricate the scope, preferably with olive oil. Place the beak at the urethral opening, holding the long axis of the scope almost vertically, like this:

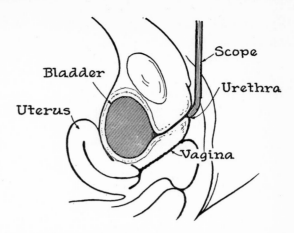

Now gently depress the base of the scope, allowing the beak of the scope to slide into the urethra like this:

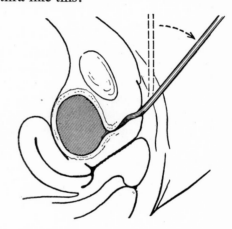

No force at all is needed. The weight of the scope itself merely guided by your fingers will allow it to slip into place. Now, holding the body of the scope at approximately a 45 degree angle, advance it gently for half an inch or so and then gradually lower the base as the beak slips into the bladder like this:

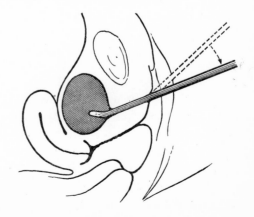

The female bladder generally lies approximately 1½ or 2 inches from the urethral meatus although upon occasion the distance may be more nearly 3 or 4 inches. When the scope actually enters the bladder it usually does so with a relatively sudden movement, the end toward you moving sharply downward and the scope slipping forward as much as an inch quite quickly.

Now remove the obturator and *gently* depress the base of the scope to drain urine from the bladder. Replace the obturator with the examining telescope and turn on the normal saline. There is no use trying to visualize anything in the bladder until you have allowed the saline to run at least 30 seconds to distend the organ.

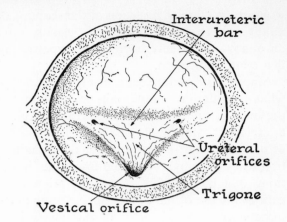

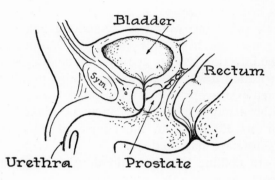

The first time one looks into a cystoscope after having accomplished the above procedure, he generally sees a field of solid red. This is usually true because the scope has spontaneously advanced until the beak is on the posterior superior bladder wall and the wall lies in direct apposition to the lens like this:

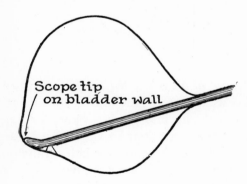

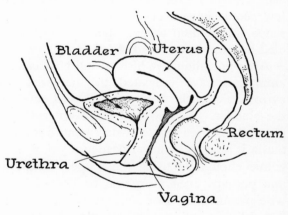

Pull the scope gently back toward you for better visualization. When the scope is in proper position the color seen by the eye will change from the bright red to a pale orange and the chances are you will still see nothing. This is usually due to a drop of water which seems invariably to get on the eyepiece. It should be wiped off with a gauze sponge, at which time the cystoscopist is now prepared to examine the interior of the bladder.

The normal interior anatomy of the bladder may be represented like this:

Most often the original field seen by the cystoscopist is approximately this:

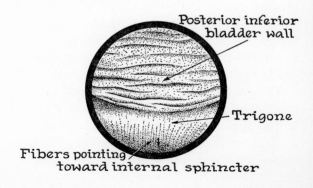

By rotating the scope and by moving it back and forth *gently* the ureteral openings may be examined along with the trigone and the periphery of the bladder.

While doing this examination be sure to ask the patient to tell you if her bladder feels over-distended. When she mentions this, shut off the inflow and let out approximately 25 cc. of water, which will usually make the patient comfortable and keep the bladder near maximum distention.

Occasionally the field of vision will become indistinct as the saline in the bladder becomes clouded with pus or blood. When this happens the cystoscope should be drawn toward the operator until the mid-trigone is seen. The scope is then removed, allowing drainage, and the bladder is refilled. Occasionally this must be done repeatedly to maintain an unobstructed field.

Entering the male bladder is somewhat more difficult but by no means extremely hard. Grasp the penis and hold it in the position of erection like this:

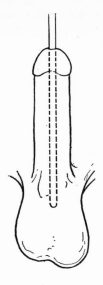

No force need be applied. When the scope ceases to advance gently, push it downward to see that the urethra is traversed to the maximum amount possible in this direction.

Now begin gently to lower the base of the scope, allowing the beak to pass through the area of the urogenital diaphragm, and approach the prostate like this:

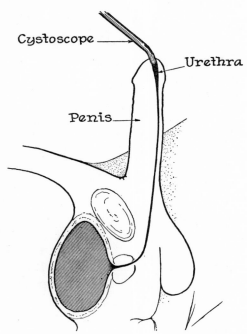

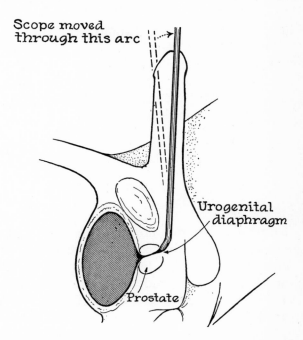

Slip the scope through the urethra with the long axis of the scope paralleling the long axis of the penis and the beak of the scope at 12 o'clock, like this:

A very slight, gentle side to side motion may aid the progress of the scope in this area. Continue with gentle depression at the base until the scope slips into the bladder exactly as mentioned in describing instrumentation of the female.   The procedure then differs in no way.

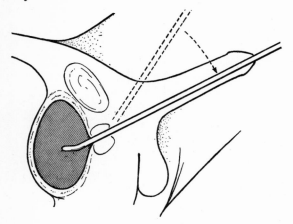

It is important to make a thorough examination of the bladder in each case and to have a routine to follow in doing so.   There is no particular routine better than any other and many doctors simply devise their own.   I examine the trigone first, then the opening of the ureters.   Then I divide the circumference of the bladder into four quadrants and by rotating the scope and moving it back and forth examine each of these four quadrants.

The most important thing is to be certain that no area of the bladder is missed or slighted in the examination.   Many cases have more than one finding present and will be partially misdiagnosed if one is not cautious.

URETERAL CATHETERIZATION

Catheterizing the ureters is a procedure which takes some practice but one which is quite easy once it has been done a few times. First, examine the bladder thoroughly with the examining telescope and locate the ureteral orifices.   Then put the catheters in the catheterizing scope and replace the examining scope with the catheterizing one.   Locate one ureteral opening and, while watching it, advance the catheter until the tip is visible through the scope like this:

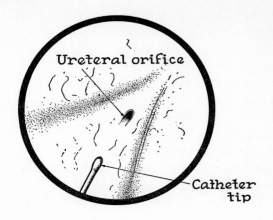

Now raise the operculum until the catheter points at the opening of the ureter.   This may take a bit of *gentle* jockeying around with the scope in order to get the catheter properly lined up.   One frequent error is to try to follow the catheter down to the ureteral opening with the scope lens.   Be sure to stay far enough away so that your view is adequate. Put the catheter in this position:

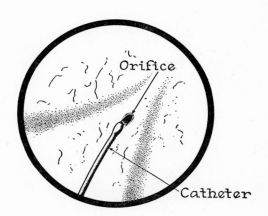

and advance it gently until it enters the ureter.

Now force it gently up the ureter for approximately 20 cm.   (You will notice the graduation on the catheter.)   Move your cystoscope away from the ureteral opening and turn it slightly so that some of the catheter will "double up" in the bladder and insert perhaps another 4 or 5 cm.   This is to give you some play in moving the cystoscope around without disturbing the position of the catheter in the ureter.   Now catheterize the other ureter in identical fashion.   When both ureters are catheterized put another 10 to 15 cm. of catheter into the bladder so that the catheters arch up into the dome of the bladder like this:

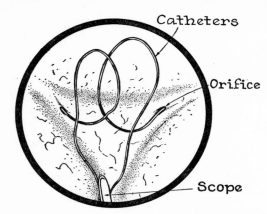

This is a means of giving slack so that you can get the cystoscope out of the bladder without pulling the catheters out of the ureters. Be sure the operculum is lowered and remove the cystoscope while feeding a bit more catheter into it. Once it emerges, pull out one catheter like this:

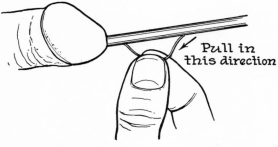

Have an assistant tape it to the leg of the same side as the ureter which it enters. Do the same with the opposite catheter and the job is finished.

I apologize for repeating something over and over again but one more caution: Accidents with the cystoscope are practically unheard of *if it is used without excessive force.*

URETHRAL INSTRUMENTATION

The technique of urethral instrumentation with sounds, catheters, filiforms and similar instruments has one criterion which must be observed. It is, of course, the avoidance of trauma. To use the urethral sounds properly, attempt the biggest size, not the smallest, which you think will pass the obstruction.

Grasp the penis in one hand and hold it in the position of erection while inserting the beak of the sound in the meatus. Gently lower the entire body of the sound so that the penis is literally threaded upon it like this:

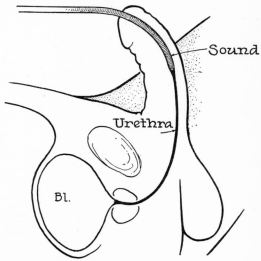

Now advance the point of the sound toward the perineum, being sure not to elevate the handle more than may be done with a bare minimum of pressure. When obstruction is reached, one may gently move the tip of the sound back and forth in an attempt to enter the orifice of the obstruction itself. This is the part of the procedure which frequently causes undue trauma. A false passage may be made quite easily by applying undue force like this:

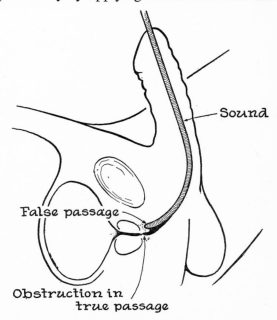

If the lumen of the obstruction is not entered with relative ease by the sound, it is best to use one size smaller without attempting force. It has been my policy to dilate a stricture not more than six or eight sound sizes above the sound which will enter the obstruction easily. For example, if an 18 will enter the obstruction easily, then dilation is usually not carried beyond size 24 to 26.

One should always remember that bacteria normally live in the anterior urethra and are almost inevitably carried up the urinary tract by the sound. Normal resistance will result in elimination of these bacteria if there be no trauma. In the presence of minor degrees of tissue insult these organisms may gain a foothold and provide a troublesome focus of infection.

If anesthesia is necessary for performing the procedure, instillation of 5 to 10 cc. of 1.5 per cent Metycaine by means of an Asepto syringe will provide nearly complete obtundation of pain. After instillation, the meatus should be held closed for at least a minute to allow the anesthetic to gain full effect before being drained away.

Sterilization of instruments for urethral invasion should be as nearly complete as possible under the circumstances. Olive oil makes an excellent lubricant.

INJURIES TO THE KIDNEY

Serious renal injuries are, of course, apparent and require immediate hospitalization. Minor kidney trauma, however, is somewhat more common than we tend to realize and may usually be readily diagnosed in the office. The first procedure is examination of voided urine. In more than 80 per cent of cases of mild to moderate kidney injury either microscopic or gross hematuria is discoverable at the first voiding following the accident. Catheterization is best avoided, since trauma from the catheter may rarely cause a few red blood cells and may confuse diagnosis of the minor cases.

Usually no more than gross and microscopic examination of the urine is needed to clarify diagnosis of the mild kidney contusion. An excellent indication of progress may be had from the following procedure: Have the patient void into a glass container each few hours during the day. Pour 5 cc. of the urine into a test tube and tape it near the head of his bed with the date and the hour of voiding written on the tape. One may then compare the sediment of red blood cells in each specimen of urine or the color due to hemolized cells and gain a reasonably accurate estimation of the degree of bleeding and of any increase or decrease in loss of blood.

SURGICAL INJURIES TO THE URETER

Pelvic operations on the female are a potent source of ureteral injury. Perhaps the most common is to include the ureter in a tie of the uterine artery. Most of these cases are diagnosed relatively quickly by the severe flank pain which occurs two or three days after operation and may be confirmed by excretory urography. However, we occasionally see such a case in the office several weeks or months after surgery and find that there has been a partial reestablishment of the ureteral lumen but not sufficient reestablishment to allow free drainage.

Immediate cystoscopy and gradual dilation of the strictured area by means of urethral catheters is the procedure of choice. There is nothing particularly difficult about it and such dilations may usually be done in the office unless it is necessary to leave a catheter in place for several days for establishment of proper drainage.

An excellent procedure when a difficult pelvic operation is to be done is to place catheters in both ureters immediately before the operation. These catheters may be felt in the pericervical area and serve as a warning of the location of the ureters.

CYSTITIS

Several facts are of importance in planning office procedures or diagnosis and treatment of acute cystitis. To begin with, a severe cystitis is an absolute contraindication to intravesical manipulation of any kind except the lifesaving variety.

One must realize, too, that vesical irritability and frequency of urination may be caused by a pathologic condition lying outside the bladder. As an example, an appropriately situated fibroid of the uterus may cause it. The practitioner should remember that cystitis is more usually a secondary manifestation of the urinary tract infection and seldom occurs as a chronic disease without the existence of a focus of infection elsewhere in the tract. Also, bladder irritability without pus in the urine may occur in cases of interstitial cystitis or chronic inflammation of the trigone.

One may occasionally cystoscope acute *regional* inflammations of the bladder. There are three places which are immediately suspect and which should be thoroughly examined. They are the two ureteral orifices and the trigone. The trigone is most frequently involved. It is more vascular than other regions of the bladder but in the absence of inflammatory process the tiny vessels may be clearly visualized like this:

With inflammation and edema, however, the vessels lose their identity and the trigone takes on a hazy red color about equivalent to the red on a Lucky Strike package. Details are not readily visible and the whole area looks "fuzzy." Occasionally there are areas of subcutaneous ecchymoses which present darker blurs or blobs in the smooth red picture.

This same thing may occur around the orifice of either ureter but the inflammatory reaction is ordinarily not so intense. There is some redness, some blurring and some obvious dilatation of small vessels but in most cases the vessels do retain their identity.

Interstitial Cystitis and Hunner's Ulcer

This is a relatively frequent chronic vesical irritation seen in women but rarely in men. Symptoms are so characteristic that diagnosis may often be made from history alone. Cystoscopic examination in these cases usually reveals minute mucosal ulcers situated either at the top or on the anterior wall of the bladder and disappearing and recurring with monotonous regularity from examination to examination.

Diagnosis may be confirmed by attempting gentle distention of the bladder after measuring bladder capacity by injecting normal saline through a catheter. A much restricted capacity, frequently as low as 60 to 90 cc., will be found and the patient will complain bitterly of a chronic aching pain upon any attempt to distend the bladder wall further.

If the ulcer is large or severe, the patient may be referred to a urologist for cauterization, which has an excellent effect. Twice weekly instillations of 1 per cent silver nitrate often afford relief. In preparing for and doing these instillations remember that chlorine precipitates the silver in the form of inactive silver chloride. The bladder should be emptied and rinsed out through the catheter with sterile water. One ounce of a 1 per cent solution of silver nitrate may then be injected through the catheter and kept in place for 1 or 2 minutes. At the conclusion of this time, inject 2 ounces of normal saline solution, which will completely inactivate the silver nitrate.

VARICOCELE AND HYDROCELE

The operation for hydrocele is found on page 188. Varicocele is a common lesion, being seen in as many as 15 to 20 per cent of young men and regressing spontaneously in most of these. It is thought to be related to ungratified sexual desire, but this has never been proven. If my observations of young men are reliable, there should be practically no varicocele in existence if the cause has been properly assigned.

Most cases will respond to a scrotal support and marriage or its equivalent. By no means should the physician advise a young man who has been relatively chaste to gratify his carnal desires in order to get rid of his varicocele. If symptoms persist, complete relief may usually be given by injection done in this manner:

Palpate the mass of veins here:

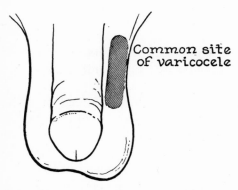

Common site of varicocele

Anesthetize the skin by making a wheal with 1 per cent procaine and wait 2 or 3 minutes. Then pick up the veins between thumb and finger and insert a small gauge needle into one of the veins near the superior pole like this:

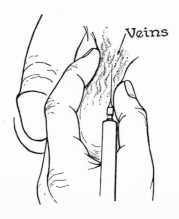

Veins

Be sure to aspirate and make certain that venous rather than arterial blood returns. Obliteration of the artery will result in testicular atrophy. When you are certain that the needle lies within the lumen of a vein, inject about 0.25 cc. of 5 per cent sodium morrhuate. It is usually advisable not to inject more than two veins at each treatment. Have the patient stand up but not move around for 5 or 6 minutes after the injection. Warn him that there will be some pain of minor nature within 12 hours and insist that he wear a scrotal support for at least 24 hours following the injection. Drugs are not usually necessary to relieve pain. As a precaution, however, I usually give the patient a codeine tablet.

Operation, when necessary, may be done under local anesthesia. After proper injection of the skin, make an incision about like this:

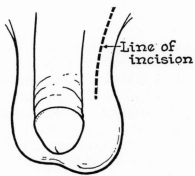

Line of incision

Dissect down to the spermatic cord and inject procaine around the cord sheath. Now open the sheath like this:

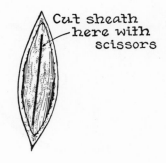

Cut sheath here with scissors

Be sure to isolate the artery and vas deferens from the group of distended veins. Then doubly ligate the veins, using a transfixion ligature as shown in this sketch.

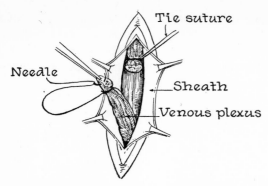

The groups of ligated veins may now be pulled into lateral apposition and firmly tied like this:

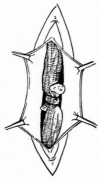

A scrotal suspensary should be worn for approximately seven days after the operation. There is no reason that the patient should not remain ambulatory throughout the whole treatment.

VASECTOMY

This is an excellent procedure to sterilize the male if one condones such operations. It is also frequently used as a preliminary to prostatic operations in order to prevent epididymitis. After cleansing and shaving an area of the scrotum here:

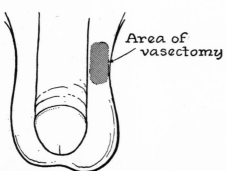

pick up the vas between thumb and fingers. It is easily identified by its much heavier consistency than any other structure in the area. Held through the skin of the scrotum it seems about the size of a wooden match and may be easily rolled around between thumb and fingers like this:

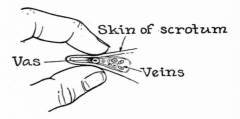

While holding the mass in position, anesthetize the skin to either side of it with 1 per cent procaine and pass a long straight needle underneath the skin and underneath the vas so that it is held in position like this:

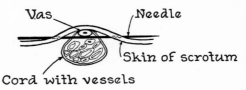

Now make a small slit in the skin parallel to the vas and expose it by sharp dissection, like this:

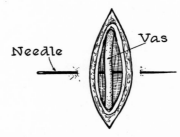

The vas may then be pulled out for approximately an inch and two ligatures of cotton thread tied about it leaving one tie long, like this:

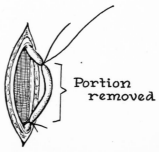

The central portion between the ligatures is then removed and the remaining pieces of vas are brought into lateral apposition and tied somewhat loosely like this:

A word of caution is apropos here. A tight suture holding the vas in lateral apposition may result in prompt reuniting, with forthcoming children and a major dent in the physician's reputation.

While I suppose it would not happen again in a hundred years, I shall never forget the man who was proven to have three vasa deferens and on whom I carefully ligated two. Fortunately, he was a good sport and named the boy after me.

PROSTATIC DISEASE

This is seldom amenable to office treatment but most of the necessary diagnostic procedures may be carried out in the office. The rectal examination is the first step and must be properly done. Best delineation of morbid anatomy will be obtained if the patient is placed in the modified knee-chest position like this:

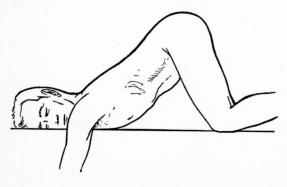

Unnecessary roughness will invalidate the findings of the examination to a very great extent. Begin by lubricating well the gloved finger to be used in the examination. Place the lubricated finger on the anus like this:

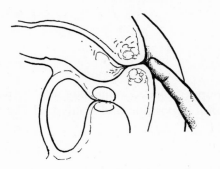

and push gently but firmly while raising the hand to a position like this:

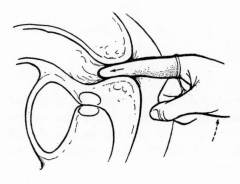

The patient should be cautioned not to hold his sphincter tense.

One should be extremely gentle in examining the prostate itself for these enlarged glands are not infrequently secondarily infected and very tender. The normal prostate seems practically flush with the rectal wall and may be clearly outlined by the palpating finger. As the prostate enlarges it bulges into the rectal cavity and tends to enlarge both laterally and upward out of reach of the examining finger.

Ordinarily, prostatic hyperplasia presents an elasticity somewhat similar to the feeling of the deflated bicycle tire. Inflammation may change the characteristics of the hypertrophied gland, making it somewhat harder and less resilient than the pure hypertrophy. A good example is to picture the same bicycle tire now inflated. Carcinoma has a rocky, unbending hardness which has always reminded me of a cover of a book. It is nodular, indurated and irregular in outline.

If it is possible to catheterize the patient, one should do so immediately after he has voided and make a note of the residual urine remaining in the bladder after the most complete voiding possible.

Cystoscopy is a valuable procedure in diagnosis of prostatic disease when it can be performed without injury or danger to the patient. Certainly in cases of marked and severe hypertrophy with acute retention of urine, cystoscopy is not a wise procedure in the hands of us family physicians. Neither should it be done if there exists gross urinary infection.

Usually upon the first visualization, the tremendous hypertrophy of muscular bundles in the bladder wall will be apparent immediately. It looks like this:

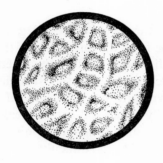

In addition to routine examination for other bladder pathology, one should particularly note the amount of this trabeculation or muscular thickening, the size and depth of the "pouch" immediately behind the prostate and the relation of the prostatic swelling to the bladder outlet. This information, considered *in toto,* will make accurate evaluation of bladder pathology possible.

Cystoscopy may also be valuable in demonstrating the so-called "median bar" obstruction which may occur in conjunction with prostatic hypertrophy or entirely independent of unusual enlargement of the prostate gland. The median bar is simply an elevated ridge of tissue here:

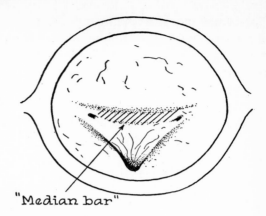

"Median bar"

It tends to foreshorten the trigone, thus:

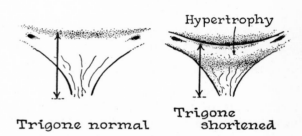

Trigone normal   Trigone shortened

and to offer obstruction to free egress of urine. The bar is usually readily visualized by the cystoscope and looks something like this:

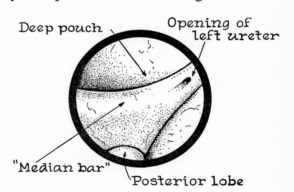

Deep pouch   Opening of left ureter

"Median bar"   Posterior lobe

Such cases should be evaluated by a urologist.

Prostatic Massage

This simple technique is frequently poorly done and for that reason will be reviewed here. Begin by realizing that the normal prostate is somewhat tender to extreme pressure. Furthermore, the patient is inclined to be apprehensive and a little dubious of the whole procedure and, therefore, to be a bit more sensitive to pain than usual.

Lubricate the gloved finger well, place it against the anus, and follow the procedure for insertion described and illustrated above. Touch the lateral lobes of the prostate and apply gentle pressure, questioning the patient as to the degree of tenderness.

Using the predetermined degree of pressure, massage the prostate from above downward, like this:

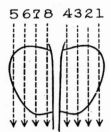

Note that the massage strokes go from above down and each stroke is more toward the medial part of the gland. Now repeat the technique on the other side of the midline and finally express prostatic secretion by gentle midline massage along the course of the urethra, which may be clearly felt here:

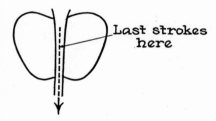

Once again, the old familiar caution: It is not necessary to apply great force to accomplish the desired results.

ACUTE RETENTION OF URINE

This is a common emergency in the practitioner's office and is usually easily disposed of by the insertion of a simple soft catheter. Occasionally, however, we see a case that requires increasingly complex procedures to insure adequate urinary drainage. If insertion of a plain catheter fails, one may make another attempt with the olive-tipped Coudé. If

gentle manipulation with this catheter also fails one may then attempt to enter the bladder with the woven catheter. Patience and avoidance of trauma are the only really important factors in the procedure. Should all attempts at catheterization fail, one may enter the bladder with a spinal needle through the space of Retzius like this:

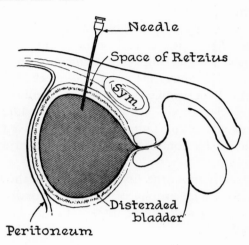

In spite of the appearance of gross danger there is none from this procedure if the bladder is widely distended and if the needle is inserted in the midline pointing straight back or slightly downward into the cavity of the bladder. Usually relief of intravesical pressure will result in diminution of sphincter spasm which has added to the difficulty of catheterization. When this spasm is relieved one may then insert a retention catheter such as the Foley for constant drainage until further steps can be taken. A Foley catheter that remains in place should be irrigated daily.

UROLITHIASIS

Stones in the urinary tract are among the very common diseases seen by the family physician. The history is entirely typical in the vast majority of cases. The diagnosis may be made from the history alone, once you keep in mind the typical distribution of pain from various areas of the urinary tract:

Pain from:
(1)
Kidney pelvis
& upper
tract

(2)
Middle
ureter

(3)
Lower
ureter

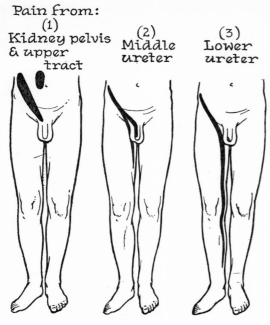

Two confirmatory procedures may be used to help one decide if a stone is present. First remember that the ureter may be rolled against the spine by pressure approximately 1 inch lateral to and just below the umbilicus as shown here:

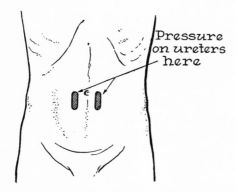

Pressure on ureters here

Acute pain at the time of this maneuver is indicative of spasm and inflammatory reaction of the ureter.

A voided specimen of the urine should be examined for the presence of red blood cells, which will almost invariably be present if a stone is traversing the tract. Use of the office x-ray in demonstrating such stones is discussed on page 401. There are few other diagnostic procedures of great interest which can be done in the office other than analysis of a stone, should it be discovered.

Begin by telling the patient to strain his urine through a gauze flat or through a handkerchief and to save all the particles that pass with the urine. Most of the stones I see are passed and are caught in this manner. The stone is then taken to the laboratory and treated like this:

Grind in a mortar and pestle until the stone is reduced to powder. Add to 5 cc. of distilled water, shake and let stand until the insoluble residue precipitates.

Place 1 cc. of the supernatant liquid into a test tube, add 1 cc. arseno-molybdic reagent, then add excess sodium carbonate solution. A deep blue color proves the presence of uric acid and urates.

Shake up the remaining material in the original test tube and place 1 cc. of it in another tube, then add 5 drops of 50 per cent sodium hydroxide. Bend a piece of red litmus paper and tape it across the top of the test tube, using a Scotch tape band around the top of the tube like this:

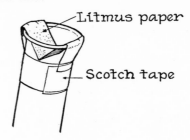

Litmus paper

Scotch tape

Bring the contents of the tube to boiling. The litmus paper will turn blue if ammonia is present.

To the rest of the ground stone in water solution in the original test tube, add 2 cc. of concentrated hydrochloric acid. Formation of many gas bubbles with marked evolution of gas indicates presence of carbonate. Boil for about 2 minutes to expel excess carbonates and divide into three parts.

To part one, add 2 cc. of a saturated potassium acetate solution. A white precipitate will form in the presence of calcium oxalate. If there is no precipitate, divide into two portions; to one add a few drops of calcium chloride. A white precipitate proves the presence of oxalate. To the second portion add a few drops of sodium oxalate. A white precipitate indicates the presence of calcium.

To part two, add excess ammonium hydroxide and drop in a slip of litmus paper. Then add, dropwise, nitric acid, until the litmus paper barely turns pink. Heat nearly to boiling and add several drops of ammonium molybdate reagent. A canary yellow precipitate proves the presence of phosphate.

To the last portion, add 1 drop of para-nitro-benzene-azo-resorcin, 0.5 per cent solution in 0.5 normal sodium hydroxide, then add excess 20 per cent sodium hydroxide solution. A blue color indicates magnesium.

Results may be interpreted as follows:

Ion Present	Indicates
Carbonate	Calcium carbonate, magnesium carbonate or both
Oxalate	Usually calcium oxalate
Phosphate	Calcium tri- or di-phosphate
Ammonia and phosphate	Ammonium phosphate (triple phosphate)
Uric acid and ammonia	Ammonium urate
Calcium	Calcium carbonate, calcium oxalate or calcium phosphate
Magnesium	Ammonium magnesium phosphate or magnesium carbonate
Ammonia	Ammonium urate or ammonium magnesium phosphate

Treatment of large renal calculi is usually operative in nature. If there is relatively severe infection of the kidney pelvis, weekly lavage by means of cystoscopy and ureteral catheterization may be of benefit. One should, of course, lavage with a solution containing an anti-bacterial substance suited to the particular bacteria found and of proper pH to exert maximal solubility influence on the stone. This may be calculated from information given in the section on Internal Medicine, the section on The Small Laboratory and the preceding information on analysis of stones. One should also prescribe either an acid- or alkaline-ash diet as may be indicated by the type of stone present.

When a ureteral calculus becomes impacted, one may occasionally remove it by this simple expedient: Insert a cystoscope into the bladder and catheterize the offending ureter, using a small (size 4 or 5) catheter. Working very gently, attempt to get the catheter past the stone. If it is possible to pass the obstruction, the catheter is advanced on up the ureter to the renal pelvis and left in place for 48 hours. This can be done with the patient at home, although it is frequently more satisfactory to hospitalize in such cases. When the catheter is removed, the stone frequently will either come with it or follow within a very few hours.

Small ureteral calculi may occasionally be removed by means of multiple ureteral catheters. If the stone can be visualized by x-ray, place the patient on the x-ray table, insert the cystoscope and attempt to pass a small (size 4 or 5) ureteral catheter past the stone. Visualize with the fluoroscope to see whether or not this is done. Having succeeded with one catheter, leave it in place and try again with another.

If this second catheter succeeds in passing the stone it may be possible to insert still another. Make certain that the beak of the scope is not near the bladder wall. Twist the catheters by rotating the cystoscope like this:

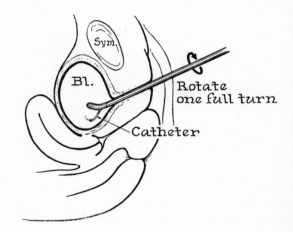

Now give the patient a bit of Pentothal Sodium in the vein or several deep whiffs of trichlorethylene through a Duke inhaler and withdraw the twisted catheters. In a certain number of cases the stone will come along with the catheters.

This procedure is not particularly dangerous but can be beastly painful. It is perhaps better for use in cases of stones in the lower third of the urinary tract and then only for small stones that seem not to be passing rapidly.

Bladder calculi may be easily visualized by the cystoscope and may be crushed with a special stone-crushing forceps which can be passed through the cystoscope, or with a special instrument which is usually not in the armamentarium of the family physician. Since the procedure is done under direct vision, there is nothing at all difficult about it.

TRAUMA TO THE GENITALS

Severe contusion to the penis or male perineum may rupture a sufficient number of vessels so that the resultant swelling occludes the urethra and causes acute retention of urine. If one is reasonably sure that the urethra has not been ruptured, a small catheter may be passed and the effusion treated with cold packs the first few hours, followed by heat and immobilization. Occasionally, incision and drainage is required. When this is done, one must incise only the superficial tissues and must be guided by frequent aspiration like this:

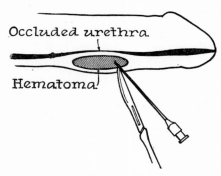

Hematocele following scrotal contusion should be aspirated from the dependent portion, like this:

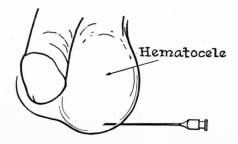

and a scrotal suspensory should be worn for several days. If the commercial suspensories are not available in local drug stores, one may be made like this:

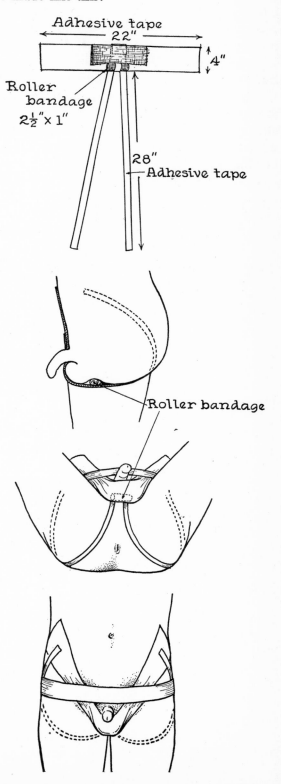

Wounds of the penis offer no peculiarity of treatment with one exception. Since the organ has a blood supply much greater than that of average tissue, hemostasis must be unusually careful. Erection after repair should, of course, be prevented by administration of proper drugs.

Acute epididymitis is still seen with relative frequency despite the antibiotics. When these cases become severely painful and tend to drag on for several days in spite of penicillin and proper adjunct therapy, incision and drainage is still an excellent method. Do it like this:

First anesthetize the skin over the epididymis from the posterior side of the scrotum about here:

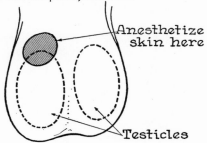

Open the scrotal sac and visualize the inflamed epididymis like this:

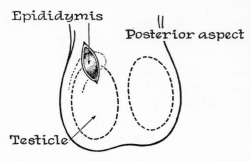

Now incise the epididymis, being careful not to incise the tunica albuginea of the testicle. Insert a small rubber drain (a rubber band), apply a large fluffy dressing to the area and provide proper support. The drain may usually be removed in 24 or 48 hours and there should be little or no pain if the drainage incision has been adequate.

Even after this procedure has been accomplished one should exhibit the antibiotics in high and prolonged dosage. In most cases it is also wise to give drugs for relief of pain.

Paraphimosis is covered in the section on Pediatrics. Its treatment in the adult differs in no way from its treatment in children.

Section VII

PROCTOLOGY

Anorectal disease is exceedingly common and it is a poorly equipped practitioner who is not prepared to deal with the vast majority of such difficulty that he sees. Fortunately, there is nothing particularly difficult about most anorectal disease; the procedures for diagnosis are simple and treatment is within the range of office surgery in a great number of cases.

Anatomy

Proper office procedures cannot be adequately understood without a brief review of the anatomy involved.

The External Sphincter Muscle. This muscle is made up of two groups of fibers, a superficial circular group which surrounds the anal canal like this:

and a deep layer of fibers which run longitudinally from the coccyx forward to surround the anus and insert in the median raphe like this:

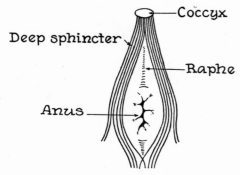

Seen in cross section the sphincter looks something like this:

The Anal Canal and Lower Rectum. Important points in the anal canal and lower rectum are these:

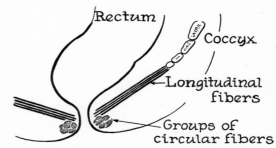

Notice particularly the crypts of Morgagni and their relationship to the anal papillae.

The rectal valves of Houston are usually three in number and situated like this:

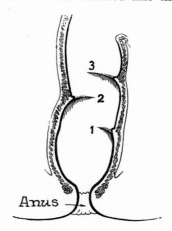

As one looks into the rectum, they look like this:

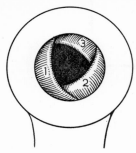

It is particularly important to remember that these valves are made up of more than simple folds of connective tissue. They contain blood vessels, muscular fibers and fibrous tissue.

The ischiorectal fossae are located on either side of the rectum, here:

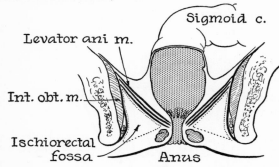

They are roughly pyramidal in shape, the base presented to the examiner and the apex pointing upward toward the abdominal contents. They are normally from 1½ to 2 inches deep.

It is important to remember that the lower part of the rectum and the anal canal are replete with sensory nerve endings. The upper part of the rectum, on the contrary, has few or none. The nerves to the sphincter enter bilaterally approximately here:

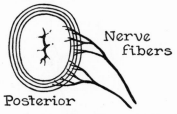

It is of great importance that this nerve supply be properly blocked in administering local anesthesia for rectal procedures.

EXAMINATION

The equipment needed for a thorough examination of the anal region and the lower bowel includes the following:

1. National Body-Cavity Set with source of current. There are other makes just as satisfactory as this particular one but I will refer to it because I have had one for years and am quite familiar with the set and its use. It looks like this:

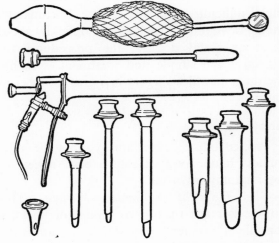

2. An improvised rectal table can easily be made from an old physiotherapy table, or a wooden rest for rectal work can be made like this:

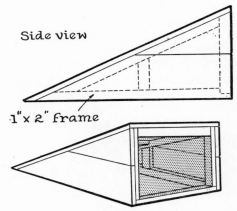

3. A rectal mirror approximately 1 cm. in diameter may be very useful. A laryngeal mirror with a wire extension welded on the handle will do very well.

4. A bendable silver probe is useful for examining crypts although a paper clip will do the job just as well if it is bent like this:

A routine of examination is necessary for proper diagnosis and treatment for this type of disease.   After eliciting a good history (which is the best single procedure in diagnosis), place the patient either in knee-chest position or in lateral position like this:

Pull the buttocks apart and make a thorough examination of external factors, noticing particularly any inflammations, discharges or abnormal protuberances.   Next insert the lubricated gloved finger into the rectum *gently* and palpate all areas of the anal canal and as high into the rectum as you can reach.   Upon removing the gloved finger, examine the fecal matter clinging to the sides of the glove, particularly noticing if any blood is admixed with the feces.

Now prepare the anoscope and lubricate it well.   Do not put a blob on the tip of it and assume that the scope is lubricated.   Take a moment to spread the lubricating jelly with your finger over the entire area of the scope to be inserted.   Place the tip of the obturator against the anal opening with the barrel of the scope aimed toward the umbilicus, like this:

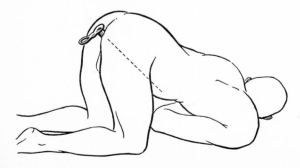

Make gentle and steady pressure on the axis of the scope.   Do not "jam it in."   You will be surprised how very little pressure is needed to insert an anoscope if a bit of patience is used.

Now remove the obturator and focus the light so that its principal beam shines in the area of the scope fenestra.   Check for the presence of hemorrhoidal excrescences and notice particularly any changes in and around the crypts.   Keep well in mind that the tiniest of lesions in this area can cause excruciating pain and be careful not to overlook a small, insignificant fissure or spot of inflammation which may be the key to the whole problem.

If there appears to be any inflammatory change in the crypts, explore them with a probe or a bent paper clip like this:

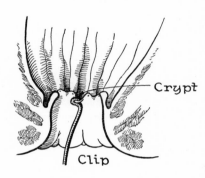

Crypt

Clip

After checking the entire circumference of the anal canal the scope may be withdrawn and a short proctoscope inserted for examination of the rectum itself.   The insertion of this instrument is in no way different from the insertion of the anoscope except that once it has entered the rectum the beak should be pointed more posteriorly before advancement is made, like this:

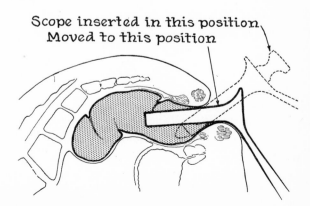

Scope inserted in this position.
Moved to this position

Once again, be painstaking in examination of the rectal wall and the valves of Houston. If there is any sign of reddening of the valves, use the mirror to gain a view of the far side, like this:

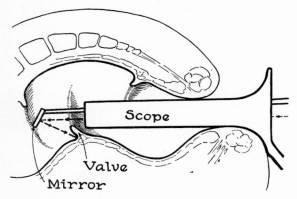

The sigmoidoscope is a valuable tool and should be in the armamentarium of all general physicians. Its use is simple and the information gained is well worth the trouble associated with the procedure.

Prepare the patient by having him take one of the stronger laxatives the night before. I use 2 teaspoonfuls of compound licorice powder or a dose of castor oil. The morning of the procedure, have him take repeated plain water enemas until the return is clear, and then report to the office. At this time we usually give ¾ grain of Nembutal or Seconal.

After waiting 30 to 40 minutes for the sedation to take effect, place the patient on the table and tape the buttocks apart like this:

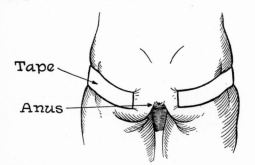

A preliminary examination with the anoscope will reveal hemorrhoidal masses and fissures which may cause the patient pain. If a fissure is present we anesthetize with 2 per cent Pontocaine by local application before inserting the sigmoidoscope.

Now lubricate the instrument along its whole length and place its beak or obturator against the anus with the axis of the scope pointing toward the umbilicus. Use steady, gentle pressure to make the insertion. When the scope has advanced approximately 1 inch depress the body of the instrument so that the axis now points approximately toward the chin and insert it about 1 more inch for a total of 2 inches.

Remove the obturator and look at the anal canal and rectum. Not infrequently you will see several pools of water stained with feces. These can be removed by long (12 inch) applicator sticks around the ends of which have been wrapped good-sized pledgets of cotton.

Now place the air lock in the end of the scope like this:

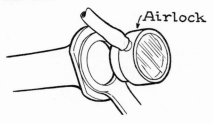

and gently inflate the rubber bag with air.

As one traverses up the bowel with the scope, a good safety principle to remember is always to see where the scope is going. Never force it blindly up the intestinal tract. You can distend the bowel with air sufficiently so that the entire course of the scope is visualized as it passes up the distended lumen. If one does this carefully there is *no* danger involved. The view through the scope as it passes up the bowel should look like this:

After the examination is completed remove all but the last inch or two of the scope and then detach the air lock to let excess air escape from the bowel and save the patient several embarrassing moments after the scope has been removed.

There are two additional techniques useful in office examination. In females a finger inserted in the vagina may often effectively be made to push the anterior rectal wall downward toward the sphincter, making examination of this area quite easy. It is done like this:

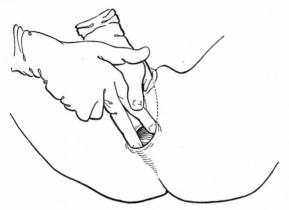

If there is question about hemorrhoids have the patient squat down on the table and strain downward while you examine the anus like this:

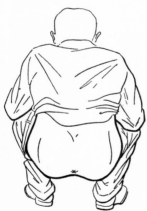

RECTAL PROLAPSE

Prolapse of the rectal mucous membrane is seen both in young children and in adults. Essentially what happens is this: The mucosa becomes "partially detached" from the muscular coats of the rectum like this:

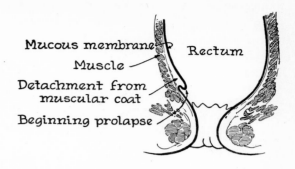

As it becomes more and more redundant it tends to be carried downward with each attempt at defecation until finally the membrane protrudes and looks like this:

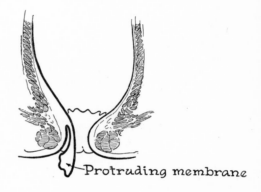

No particular diagnostic procedures are needed, for the appearance is entirely typical and diagnosis may be made by inspection.

If the prolapse is seen within an hour or so after it occurs, ice packs and gentle pressure will usually effect immediate and complete reduction. The ice packs should be allowed to remain in place for at least 30 minutes before any attempt at reduction is made. Often a longer time is helpful in reducing swelling.

In the more chronic cases where prolapse is frequent and persistent, there are two procedures of some use. The first is to pour the contents of one ampule of 1:1000 epinephrine solution over a cold pack just before it is laid on the mucous membrane. The resultant contraction of the vessels will sometimes allow quick and easy reduction. If this does not work, dilute the contents of an ampule of hyaluronidase with 20 cc. of water and inject a few drops into the base of the redundant mass. Wait 5 minutes, then reduce the prolapse one side at a time by pulling the buttocks apart with one hand while gently forcing the membrane in place, like this:

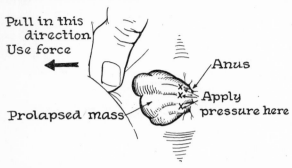

Most of these cases, if they are at all severe, belong in the realm of the trained proctologist; however, some are minor and may be treated by the injection of simple sclerosing agents. Have the patient prepare his rectum as for sigmoidoscopy and report to the office after the final enema; then have him assume the squatting position and strain so that the membrane protrudes like this:

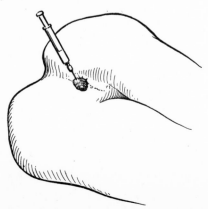

A few drops of local anesthetic may be injected at the site of the proposed sclerosing, although this is by no means always necessary. Now put the patient in Sims' position and insert a small gauge needle which is attached to a syringe containing 5 per cent sodium morrhuate, like this:

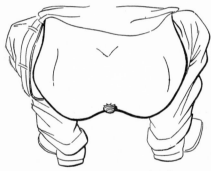

When the needle is in place and you have aspirated to be certain that it is not in a vessel, inject 4 or 5 minims of the sclerosing solution under the mucous membrane like this:

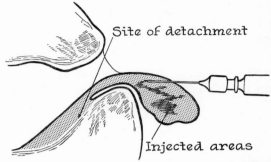

Repeat this procedure in several areas of the circumference of the bowel; then take a cotton pledget of good size, lubricated with petrolatum, and use it to push the prolapsed membrane back into the rectum. Leave the cotton in place to be passed with the next defecation.

One caution is necessary: The object of injecting sclerosants is to produce scar tissue. This will serve to hold the prolapsed membrane in place, but the scar tissue must be located at least ½ inch, and preferably as much as 1 inch, above the anorectal junction.

Occasionally you will see an infant who has persistent constipation and who produces only occasional shreds of mucous in spite of forceful straining at stool. Examination with the infant proctoscope for the possible presence of a concealed prolapse is most important. The concealed prolapse in cross section looks like this:

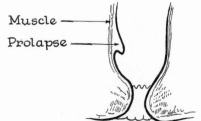

Seen through the proctoscope, it looks like this:

If an infant proctoscope is not at hand, a cystoscope may sometimes be made to do, or a nasopharyngoscope.

HEMORRHOIDS

Surprising as it may seem, this simple lesion is frequently misdiagnosed and grossly mishandled by the practitioner. Marginal doctors have made fortunes by applying (frequently correctly) the simple methods of treatment which are available to every physician but which all too often are scorned. I know it seems that this book sometimes is a series of warnings, but in order not to break our record, here is a warning about hemorrhoids. They are by no means the only or even the most frequent cause of rectal bleeding.

There are three symptoms which usually bring these patients to the physician, none of which are found exclusively in the presence of hemorrhoids. The first, of course, is rectal bleeding, which is more often present with a fissure. The second is pain, which is found in most rectal conditions, and the third is protrusion. Rectal polyps and other growths near the anus may protrude and be diagnosed as hemorrhoids unless a careful examination is made. Perhaps the most pernicious habit we physicians get into—and I confess with shame that I have done it too—is to make the diagnosis of hemorrhoids on the history of bleeding at stool and upon the basis of physical signs elicited by only a careless digital examination. Such a diagnosis is unreliable in the extreme.

External Hemorrhoids

The external thrombotic hemorrhoid is commonly seen in the office. It is an exquisitely tender, swollen, bluish mass usually located here:

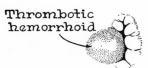

which comes on suddenly and which is usually covered by skin rather than by mucous membrane. Diagnosis may be made by inspection.

Treatment is incision and evacuation of the clot. Begin by spraying ethyl chloride over the external edge of the hemorrhoid. Now insert a needle through the "frozen" area and inject the smallest possible amount of 2 per cent procaine immediately under the skin and transitional area overlying the hemorrhoid, like this:

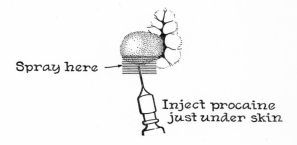

Wait at least 3 or 4 minutes and then plunge the knife into the mass with the blade in this position:

and jerk it out quickly, making a linear incision extending from the periphery toward the center of the anus.

Express the clot with gentle finger pressure and inspect the wound carefully for signs of bleeding. There will seldom be any, but should active hemorrhage occur, it can be controlled by gentle pressure. This pressure should be maintained for 5 to 10 minutes. After bleeding has ceased, tuck a sponge tightly into the sulcus between the buttocks and allow the patient to go his way.

Healing will be facilitated if the patient is instructed to take hot sitz baths several times daily.

There is very rarely any excuse for conservative treatment of a thrombotic external hemorrhoid.

Internal Hemorrhoids

Diagnosis of internal hemorrhoids should involve the systematic use of several procedures at our command. Begin by inspecting the anus, particularly noticing the presence of any discharges and their character. After this inspection it is wise to inject 2 or 3 cc. of one of the anesthetic rectal ointments and do nothing for several minutes. After anesthesia is complete, a gentle digital examination is made. Always remember well that the pressure of the finger may flatten the dilated veins and make hemorrhoidal masses exceptionally difficult to feel. This digital examination is more valuable in ruling out thrombosis and various inflammatory processes with consequent induration than it is in delineating hemorrhoids.

After conclusion of a satisfactory digital examination, insert the anoscope until the tip of the instrument is just beyond the sphincter. Now ask the patient to strain down as if he were having a bowel movement. This straining will usually cause the hemorrhoids to prolapse into the anoscope and will allow an excellent visualization of them. A word of warning is in order: During the process of straining, do not look into the anoscope; this warning comes from personal experience.

Diagnosis under direct vision is simple and needs no further delineation here.

Treatment by Injection. While frowned upon by many excellent surgeons, the injection of sclerosants, when properly done, may afford gratifying relief to many patients. There is no reason at all why this procedure should not be used when operation is not immediately feasible from the standpoint of either the physician or the patient. One should, however, remember that permanent cures from injection are somewhat rare. The average patient will gain good relief for several years, sometimes as many as 10 years from an adequate series of injections. But he will, in all probability, be back for further treatment.

Exuberant injection is dangerous and may produce many complications. Unfortunately, it is not unusual to see cases which have had far too much sclerosing solution in far too many places, and who have a mass of dense scar tissue surrounding the lower rectum and upper portion of the anus which requires dilation.

If you feel that injection treatment is the proper course, begin by instructing the patient to take a laxative the night before the proposed injection and a soap and water enema immediately before reporting to the office. An ordinary 2 cc. syringe and an angled tonsil needle are good equipment for making the injection. Begin by getting the hemorrhoid to be injected in the fenestra of the anoscope so that it is clearly visualized, like this:

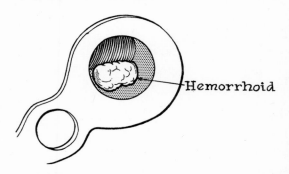

Most patients will be grateful if an anesthetic ointment is applied several minutes before inserting the anoscope or if a drop of local anesthetic is injected into the mucous membrane before passing the needle for sclerosant into the hemorrhoid itself. After adequate anesthesia has been secured, insert the tonsil needle into the base of the hemorrhoid, like this:

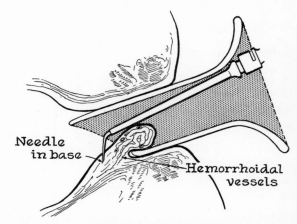

The point of the needle should be from 2 to 4 mm. from the surface of the mucous membrane and aspiration should be done to make certain that a vein has not been entered. Now inject 3 to 5 drops of 5 per cent sodium morrhuate into this area while moving the needle slowly back and forth so that the injection is somewhat "spread out," covering an area like this:

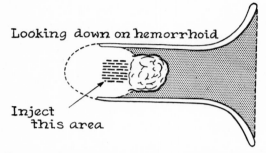

Looking down on hemorrhoid

Inject this area

It may be necessary to withdraw the needle partially and reinsert it so that adequate coverage is obtained.

Occasionally rather marked bleeding may occur at the point of puncture after the needle is withdrawn. Should this happen use a curved Kelly clamp to grasp the hermorrhoid at the point of puncture, like this:

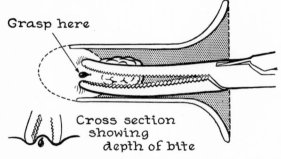

Grasp here

Cross section showing depth of bite

Crush it firmly and keep the clamp in place for 5 or 6 minutes. This will serve to control almost any bleeding engendered by needle puncture.

In my own practice I have not usually injected all three hemorrhoidal masses at one time although some physicians do so and get excellent results. Injections are usually made twice weekly until the base of each hemorrhoid has been injected twice. One then waits a week to 10 days and observes the results. In most cases there will be an area of lighter color around the injections at the base of the hemorrhoid and some signs of diminution in size of the mass itself. When this is present further injections are seldom needed.

A re-examination 30 days after the final injection should show at least a 60 per cent reduction in size of the hemorrhoidal masses, which seem to consist now of redundant surface membrane with little or no dilatation of veins. This is the criterion for a satisfactory result. If, at this 30 day examination, there remain grossly dilated veins one should not hesitate to repeat the course of injections. The most frequent error is to inject too much solution too close to the mucous membrane. This can be an embarrassing mistake for the membrane may slough and resultant scar tissue may cause a partial stricture.

Reduction of a hemorrhoidal protrusion sounds as if it should be a simple process but it may prove very difficult. If there is an irritative phenomenon when hemorrhoids protrude (and there usually is), the sphincter may enter partial spasm with resultant occlusion of venous return, increase in edema, and further sphincter spasm. Such a vicious circle may make it impossible to reduce a hemorrhoidal mass without active treatment.

Application of an ice pack may be all that is requi ed for proper reduction. A routine we have used on difficult cases is this:

1. If possible, insert a small rectal nozzle and inject 2 or 3 cc. of anesthetic ointment into the lower rectum. Next, paint the hemorrhoidal mass with 1:1000 epinephrine solution and apply a cold pack.

2. If this is not effective, anesthetize the sphincter by injecting 1 per cent procaine as shown on page 333. Now inject a solution of hyaluronidase into the hemorrhoidal mass at the point of constriction, here:

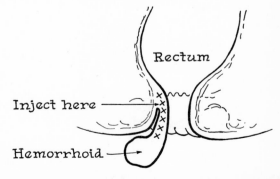

Rectum

Inject here

Hemorrhoid

Relaxation of the sphincter usually occurs in a few minutes from the effects of the anesthetic, making replacement of the mass easy. We believe the hyaluronidase acts to disperse rapidly any edema fluid and reduces chances of immediate re-extrusion and incarceration.

Control of Hemorrhage. Occasionally one may see hemorrhage of alarming extent from rupture of the hemorrhoidal veins. Control is easy when surgical implements are immediately available, but we do sometimes get caught with a case in such circumstances that we are unable to control hemorrhage surgically for several hours. A good country trick to remember in such a situation is this:

Take a 4 by 4 inch surgical sponge and unfold two flaps. In an emergency an ordinary piece of flannel may be cut to approximately the same size. Now take a piece of cotton thread several feet long and insert it doubled, like this:

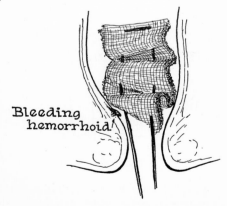

With a pair of forceps, your finger, a lead pencil, or any other long, straight object currently at hand, push this cloth as far up into the rectum as possible so that it appears like this:

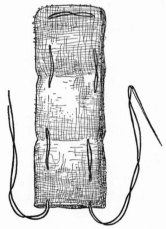

Bleeding hemorrhoid

Now roll a bit of cloth around a short lead pencil, a fountain pen cap, or a bit of paper and place it up against the anus so that one pair of threads exits on either side, like this:

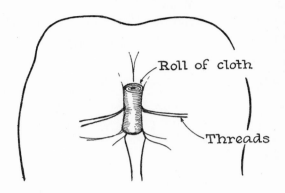

Roll of cloth

Threads

Pull the threads sharply downward until the pack is wadded and pressed against the bleeding hemorrhoid and tie the threads securely together over the external objects, like this:

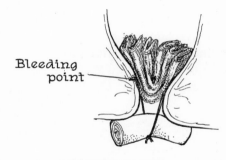

Bleeding point

In my experience this has been an excellent means of checking completely any hemorrhoidal bleeding until such time as surgical correction becomes available.

Shrinkage or removal of hemorrhoids by means of electrical current is a procedure of some promise. It will be discussed briefly in the section on physiotherapy. This does *not* mean electrocautery. I know of no arguments in favor of either thermo- or electrocautery for hemorrhoidectomy. Such procedures are pernicious and should be abandoned.

HYPERTROPHIED ANAL PAPILLAE

The anal papillae appear along the dentate line like this:

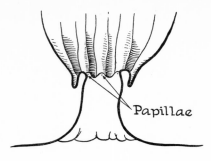

Papillae

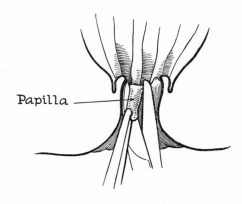

Papilla

They are the fortune of many irregular practitioners who have become benefactors both of mankind and of the Department of Internal Revenue by knowing a very few facts about the papillae and applying these facts with some discrimination. I would urge every practitioner to become cognizant of these tiny structures and the difficulties which they frequently cause.

The usual pathologic picture is something like this: The papillae may be forced downward by the passage of large, hard stools. With each such passage they are stretched a little more until they become both hypertrophied and irritated. Occasionally they become long enough to remain in the grasp of the external sphincter after the completion of a bowel movement, serving as a mechanical irritant to the sphincter and increasing the tone of its contraction until a more or less constant state of spasm is maintained. These papillae are more than amply supplied with nerve endings and may cause a dull, aching sensation while in the grip of the sphincter. Pruritus and a general irritated sensation of the rectal area follow.

Diagnosis is easy for when these papillae become irritated there is an increased deposition of fibrous tissue. They tend to become slightly reddened and remain more erect than usual. After hypertrophy has become fully established the papillae lose their bright red color and become a pale pink, being much lighter in color than the surrounding mucous membane.

These structures may be snipped away without difficulty. Begin by injecting 1 per cent procaine at the base of the papilla. Use a sufficient amount to distend it until the mucous

membrane is white. Using either a snare or a pair of scissors, snip the papilla off like this:

Bleeding is minimal and may be controlled by minor compression. When one of the papillae is removed, the accompanying crypt should be incised as mentioned in the next few paragraphs.

Again, one caution: This is a very common lesion and should be looked for in every rectal examination.

Cryptitis

This condition is frequently associated with and, indeed, may be the cause of many cases of hypertrophied papillae. The crypts of Morgagni look somewhat like this:

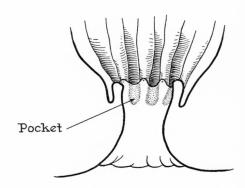

Pocket

As you can see, these crypts may occasionally retain particles of undigested food matter or other fecal contents in their pocket-like recesses, with consequent irritation of the crypt. The resulting inflammatory process frequently spreads either through contiguity of tissue or through overflow of the accumulated secretions so that a linear area of suppuration is present which looks like this:

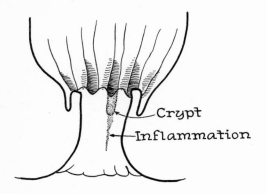

Resultant discharge may seep out of the anus and be a frequent cause of perianal irritation and sometimes of pruritus ani. Visual inspection will serve to make the diagnosis.

Procedures in treatment are well within the range of any minor surgery. Begin by removing hypertrophied papillae which may be present. Then insert a grooved director into the infected crypt, like this:

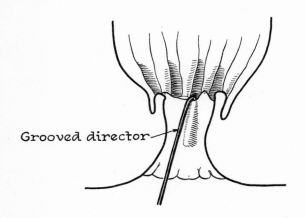

and incise it to the very bottom so that no pocket remains. If a probe or flexible grooved director is not available, one may use a bent paper clip to good advantage.

Occasionally a V-shaped incision is more adequate and this should be used without hesitation. Do it like this: Bend the grooved director and insert it into the crypt. Pick up the mucous membrane with the director and hold it away from the usual contours of the anus by the director. With scissors make a cut just under the grooved director, like this:

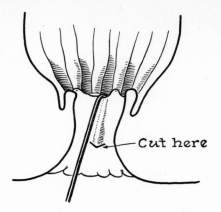

Now remove the director and pick up with toothed forceps the tiny flap you have created. Use a sharp knife to go from the edges of this flap to a central point about ½ inch upward from the flap, like this:

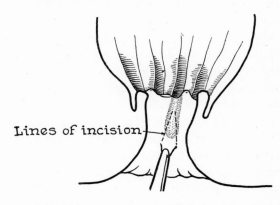

There is only one precaution: Be sure not to leave any cupping of tissue that may retain fecal matter. To avoid this, it may often be necessary to continue the incision outward to the perianal skin.

PROCTITIS

Inflammatory reactions of the rectal area are not so rare as one might suppose. Seen through the anoscope the rectal membrane resembles for all practical purposes a pharyngeal membrane that is undergoing an acute streptococcic infection. Particularly notice that blood vessels of the rectal wall are dilated and easily visualized and rarely may even be seen to pulsate synchronously with the heartbeat. When this condition is present, office treatment is of little avail unless one is equipped to give a warm saline enema, which may or may not contain some 2 per cent Pontocaine to gain the local anesthetic effect. Irrigations with mild silver protein may be beneficial and some authors recommend application of 1 per cent silver nitrate as an office procedure. I have not used this and therefore cannot speak of its efficacy.

Localized ulcers, when present, should be cauterized with 1 per cent silver nitrate.

A chronic form of proctitis known to the specialist as chronic atrophic proctitis is not rarely encountered by the practitioner. The patient complains of a feeling of warmth of the rectum and a feeling that the lower bowel has not been completely emptied by defecation. Sometimes there is mild to moderate pain preceding stool. The long-time use of irritant laxatives has been blamed for the condition, but this is by no means proven. Through the scope, the area appears dry and rough and gives one the impression of inelasticity. The condition may progress so far that there are small areas of whitened, membranous-appearing material that seem to be clinging to the surface of the gut but which upon attempt at removal turn out to be an atrophic surface of the membrane.

The anal canal itself shows a multitude of small cracks in the mucous membrane which extend barely through the mucosa and should not be confused with true fissures.

Ofter there are pinhead-sized ulcers, which may be treated with 10 to 20 per cent silver nitrate solution through the proctoscope. Bland, non-irritating irrigations are frequently of value and may be performed either in the office or in the home.

FISTULA IN ANO

Ordinarily this condition is not amenable to office surgery because of the extensive dissections that sometimes accompany proper excision. There is, however, one excellent office technique for diagnosis that is very simple and

should be performed on every case. Prepare the patient as for proctoscopy and have him report to the office after having taken his last cleansing enema. Using a blunt needle, inject the fistulous tract with any common radiopaque substance, such as water bismuth paste or Lipiodol, and x-ray the area to determine the extent of the tract.

Because of the frequent leakage of Lipiodol into the gut and resultant clouding of the x-ray picture, I prefer to use a somewhat watery solution of bismuth and to visualize and cleanse the anal canal and rectum immediately after the injection to remove excess bismuth seen in the lumen of the bowel. Study of the film will indicate immediately the general course and ramifications of the fistulous tract.

In a very rare case in which the tract is shallow and straight, incision under local anesthesia may be sufficient treatment. After routine preparation of the fissure, pass a blunt wire or probe through the fistulous tract and inject above, around and under the probe with local anesthetic solution. Wait at least 5 minutes for proper anesthesia to be effective and then incise down to the probe. If it is necessary to incise a few fibers of the sphincter muscle, be sure that these are cut transversely:

Actually, there are very few cases of fistula in ano simple enough to warrant this type of treatment. By far the greatest majority should be hospitalized and adequate or more than adequate dissection with excision of the tract done.

ANAL FISSURE

Anal fissure is probably the most common disease of the anus and rectum seen by the practitioner. It is literally a crack or tear in the anal mucous membrane extending down into the submucosa. It is kept from healing by the presence of chronic infections and repeated traumatic episodes at time of defecation. After having been present for some time, there is usually the formation of a tag of mucous membrane known as a "sentinel pile." The pathology at this time looks like this:

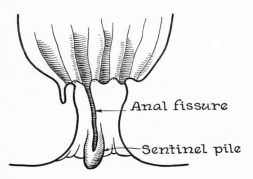

Anal fissure

Sentinel pile

Diagnosis usually may be made from history alone but is simple using direct visualization. Frequently when the buttocks are pulled apart the distal end of the fistula and the sentinel pile may be seen with the anoscope. It is wise to remember that the majority of fissures in males occur at or near the posterior commissure of the anus, while the same lesion in females is about equally divided between anterior and posterior commissure. Since the mucous membrane may be inflamed and exquisitely tender, with resultant sphincter spasm, one should use a local surface anesthetic before attempting visualization by means of one of the scopes.

Treatment of fissure, regardless of degree of severity, is in most instances purely an office procedure. For the simple lesions obviously just started where there is no sentinel pile and only minor evidence of inflammation, cautery with the electrocautery or with 100 per cent silver nitrate is frequently sufficient. One word of caution is necessary: Be sure to cauterize the entire length of the fissure under direct vision so that the upper angle is treated as well as the lower aspects of the wound.

Injection with an oil-soluble anesthetic, such as Intracaine in oil, or injection of the base with one of the sclerosing agents, such as 5 per cent sodium morrhuate, is a reliable office procedure. In either case, be sure that the ma-

terial is injected approximately ⅛ to ¼ inch below the mucous membrane and that it is spread underneath the entire surface of the lesion. Do it like this: Begin by making a skin wheal at the very edge of the anus:

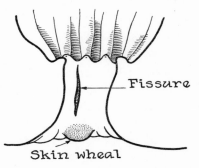

Fissure

Skin wheal

After inserting the scope into the canal, which has been anesthetized with a surface agent, visualize the entire length of the fissure like this:

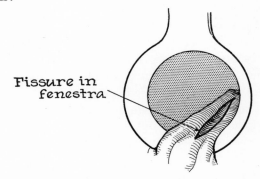

Fissure in fenestra

Now insert the needle which will carry the injectant until the point can be seen or felt under the topmost portion of the fissure, like this:

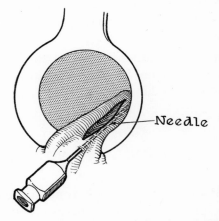

Needle

It may be necessary to inject small amounts of water-soluble local anesthetic as the needle is advanced into this position. Now attach a syringe bearing either the oil-soluble anesthetic or the sclerosing agent and inject a very small amount while the needle is being withdrawn. Particular caution should be observed in using the sclerosant to see to it that a minimal amount of the solution is used in this area. Large sloughs can and *have* occurred from the injection of too great quantity of either oil-soluble anesthetics or the sclerosants.

In all probability the best treatment is complete excision, which may be done under local anesthesia. In preparing for the procedure, be sure to anesthetize the sphincter and an area at least ½ inch on each side of the proposed excision. After waiting at least 10 minutes for the anesthetic to assume full effect, have an assistant place a retractor in the rectum opposite the lesion and, using his other hand, pull the anus open so that the lesion is visualized like this:

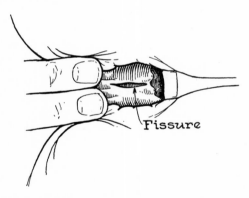

Be sure that you can see the dentate line before proceeding further. Begin by taking a moderately deep stitch (5 to 6 mm.) just above the dentate line, like this:

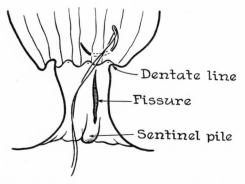

Tie it so as to occlude blood supply to the area operated. Now excise the fissure down to the deep fascia (one must frequently include a few fibers of the sphincter), like this:

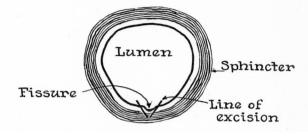

The excision extends well into the perianal skin, and the axis of the excision is radial to the anus. If hypertrophied papillae are present above the fissure and if a sentinel pile is present below, excise both of these as well as the fissure itself.

Wounds in this area heal rapidly and well. The common error is not to excise enough tissue. After-treatment consists of keeping stools soft and minimal by means of a low residue diet and insertion of a plug of petrolatum gauze into the anus for a day or two following surgery. There is no reason why the patient should not continue to be ambulatory at all times after the procedure.

Anal Ulcers

The anal ulcer seems in most instances to be an extension of the fissure process. The chronically inflamed edges of the ulcer seem to slough away leaving a raw granulated surface, most often approximately the size of a lead-pencil eraser. It is exquisitely tender and frequently bleeds at stool. Treatment is in no way different from that in fissure except that in my experience it has been easier to avoid abortive attempts at conservative treatment and perform the necessary surgery immediately when this condition is diagnosed.

ABSCESSES OF THE ANORECTAL AREA

There are several types of minor abscess which we find in this area and which are amenable to office treatment. However, perhaps we should begin this discussion by enumerating two types of abscess that should not be treated in the office. The first is deep ischiorectal abscess that cannot be accurately delimited by simple palpation. To say this a different way, the ischiorectal abscess should not be treated in the office unless one is sure of its exact limits and positive of the area which must be drained.

The second type of abscess which is somewhat too formidable for office treatment is the submucous rectal abscess, which is a collection of pus between the mucous membrane and the muscular coats of the rectum. Actual incision is easy but it is difficult to get accurate visualization for complete incision in the office. These two types of rectal abscess should usually be taken to the hospital and incised under caudal or spinal anesthesia with ample mechanical facilities for any procedure that may be necessary.

The "cutaneous perianal abscess" is a typical illustration of medical terminology as queer as a nine-dollar bill. This imposing term simply means a pimple on the bottom, and the disease may be treated in the office by using the principles of abscess surgery apropos for any area.

The marginal abscess, which usually occurs near the junction of normal skin with the transitional skin of the anus and which may frequently burrow into the sphincteric area, is quite another matter. It frequently looks something like this:

Marginal abscess

Drainage may be accomplished in the office under local anesthesia, but two or three important points should be borne in mind when this is attempted. To begin with, one is incising an area replete with nerve endings and certain precautions to save the patient pain are a necessary part of the technique. In applying local anesthesia, be sure not to enter the abscess cavity and distend it further by injecting it with anesthetic solution. This is one of the most painful errors a doctor can make and is almost certain to evoke some succinct comments from the patient.

Incision itself should be more extensive than that usually used for an abscess. After adequate incision, one should explore the cavity with the hemostatic forceps to break down any partitions which may occur in it and be certain that adequate channels for drainage in all parts of the cavity exist. Since healing tends to be relatively rapid, the insertion of a rubber drain is wise and it is an excellent idea to leave the drain in place for two or three days or even longer before considering removal.

When an ischiorectal abscess presents itself, the first procedure is to attempt exact delineation of its extent. Insert a palpating finger into the rectum and feel the abscess between the rectal finger and the thumb, which is palpating the fossa from outside like this:

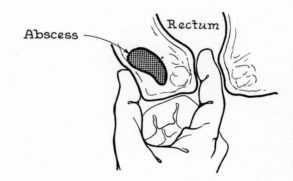

If you cannot feel absolutely certain of the extent, hospitalize the patient. On the other hand, if you are sure that the entire abscess has come within range of the palpating fingers and that it has not burrowed into higher fascial planes, then anesthetize the skin over the surface of the abscess and prepare to incise it. Remember that the nerves and blood vessels of the perianal tissues run bilaterally like this:

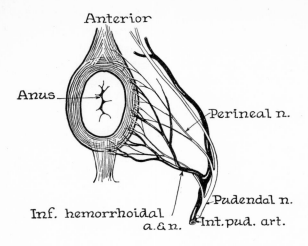

Anterior

Anus

Perineal n.

Inf. hemorrhoidal a.&n.

Int.pud. art.

Pudendal n.

Plan your incision to avoid them if possible or, if this seems impossible, to parallel their course. Dissect—don't stab—toward the abscess and attempt to pull essential structures out of the way. This is an absolute *MUST* in opening the ischiorectal abscess. Incontinence will result from severance of certain nerves, and severe bleeding may be encountered if an unsuspected artery is cut. After evacuation of pus, a drain should be inserted into the abscess cavity and should be left for at least 48 hours. An ordinary sanitary napkin makes an excellent dressing and the patient may usually be allowed to go his way after a recovery period of only a few minutes.

Some of these cases respond a great deal better if the abscess cavity is irrigated daily with normal saline solution.

FECAL IMPACTION

Fecal impactions are seen often in old folks, particularly those who are bedridden or nearly so. It is incumbent on the practitioner not to forget the possibility of a watery "irritation diarrhea" which sometimes occurs in the presence of impaction. Fortunately, most of these fecal concretions are located within a finger's length of the anus.

I shall never forget the pungent description one of my rural friends offered when he said something like this: "Granny ain't hardly been to the pot since we'uns got statehood." And as I remember, it rather seems that he was right, for Granny had a tremendous fecal impaction. When such a case shows up in the office, begin by injecting 2 ounces of mineral oil, allowing the patient to rest for half an hour or so and attempting to break up the impaction by means of a finger in the rectum.

If this does not work, we have been in the habit of trying what we refer to as a "dynamite enema." It consists of 2 ounces of green soap, 2 ounces of glycerin and 2 ounces of peroxide. After injecting this enema, it is a wise thing to leave the enema tube in position to allow the escape of the gas produced which otherwise may cause pain. After this enema has been in place for approximately 15 minutes, an effort is again made to break up the impaction by means of a finger. It will usually succeed. If not, it may be necessary to pass an 8 or 10 inch hemostatic forceps, such as a hysterectomy clamp, into the fecal mass and open the forceps like this:

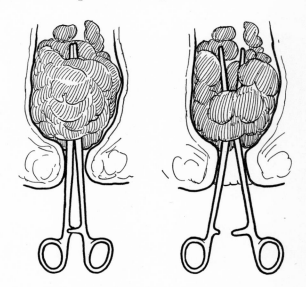

Since this is a blind procedure, it is not recommended except as a last measure and if it is done I would urge the utmost of gentleness and caution. I have not seen a fecal impaction that cannot be broken up by one of these three methods.

FOREIGN BODIES

Surprising enough, our practice has produced quite a few foreign bodies in the rectum. Most of them are very small, such as bristles, bits of bone, etc., which are undigested and become engaged in the rectal crypts. They are easily removed under direct vision. I cannot recall having removed a foreign body from an adult which was inserted into the rectum directly, though I presume such cases will occur.

Section VIII

PEDIATRICS

PEDIATRICS

THE NEWBORN

Normal Characteristics

Office examination of the newborn at the end of approximately the first seven days of life is a common procedure in some practices. It is necessary to keep in mind certain normal characteristics of the neonatal period if this examination is to be performed with successful results. Some of the important points, listed numerically, are:

1. *Hemoglobin and Erythrocyte Count.* Toward the latter part of the first week of life and most markedly in the second week of life, there is a rapid decrease in the amount of hemoglobin and a slower decrease in the erythrocyte count. This has been stated to be the cause of physiologic jaundice of the newborn, which occurs in approximately 65 per cent of infants and which begins on the third day, is in decline by the end of the first week and gone by the end of the second week. Actually, recent investigations have indicated that this decline in hemoglobin is not the direct cause of the jaundice.

2. *Weight loss* usually continues until the fifth day and seems to be mainly due to loss of fluids. During the first week urine is likely to contain albumin and frequently contains so much uric acid that the diapers are stained a bright pink. It is important not to confuse this pink with the redder stain of blood.

3. *Stools of a transitional character* usually appear at the end of the first week. These may be rather more moist than usual and somewhat green in color. They are sour, thin and foul and frequently contain undigested food particles. These characteristics are un-important unless associated with other pathologic conditions. If excess fat is fed there may be a soapy characteristic in the stools. This picture is often seen by mothers as a diarrhea. It is not significant.

4. *Breast hypertrophy* in both boys and girls, with some secretion of milk, is normal by the end of the first week. Girls may occasionally show a bloody vaginal discharge.

5. *Heart murmurs* are not rare during the neonatal period, owing to the extensive changes in the circulatory system. Many of these are purely functional. The electrocardiogram taken during this period shows a normal right ventricular preponderance. Evaluation of possible heart disease frequently has to wait until several weeks after birth.

6. *The digestive tract* normally takes several weeks to assume relatively adequate function. While extreme gastric disturbances in the neonate are usually pathologic, minor disturbances occur with such frequency that we may consider them normal or only minor deviations from normal. One point is of particular interest. By the end of the first week the newborn is digesting proteins and simple sugars well but his capacity to handle fats is still very limited and remains so for 60 to 90 days. Provision for this fat intolerance must be made in preparing feedings.

7. *The lungs* may not be completely expanded at the end of the first seven days. Careful examination will sometimes elicit evidence of this, which brings up the problem of differentiating incomplete expansion of the lung from active disease of the lung. Fortunately, pulmonary disease is quite rare in the young baby, which tends to simplify the problem somewhat. Occasionally x-ray is the only

possible means of active differentiation, although questionable pulmonary findings in a baby who is obviously well need not be taken with a great deal of seriousness.

Certain points in examination of the child at the end of this first week are important. Occluded sebaceous glands forming tiny white spots known as milia are quite common about the face and occasionally alarm mothers. There is no office procedure necessary in either diagnosis or treatment.

In examination of the head, one occasionally finds areas that may be depressed by pressure of the fingers and give the impression of approximately the same resiliency as a Ping-pong ball. The only procedure of importance is to x-ray these areas if they persist. There is no indication for immediate x-ray. While examining the mouth, it is common to notice a short frenulum and what seems to be evidence of tongue-tie. No procedure is indicated in this age group, and if the infant can protrude his tongue far enough to touch the vermillion border of the lips, as shown below, there is likely to be no indication for future operative interference.

In rare instances the child's tongue will be held down so sharply that it seems to interfere with nursing. If this be so, then the infant's head may be firmly held and the shortened frenulum observed for the location of vessels by shining a light through it like this:

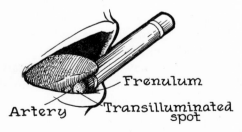

If the frenular artery is not in the distal fold (and it seldom is), then snip the frenulum with a pair of scissors while continuing to note the location of the artery by use of a light, like this:

These cases are exceedingly rare.

If we detect a heart murmur in the examination of the chest we may usually assume it to be functional if heard during the first two weeks of life and *if unaccompanied by other symptoms*. A note should be made of the murmur and various office procedures used for investigation at a later date if it persists.

When examining the abdomen the usual findings of importance are umbilical or inguinal hernia. These two entities will be discussed in a separate section on pages 178 and 180.

In performing the neurologic examination, one reflex is important and there is a definite procedure for both eliciting and interpreting it. The Moro reflex is a concussion reaction and should be elicited while the infant is lying at ease on his back. Strike the table sharply and observe carefully what the infant does. In the presence of a normal nervous system, the legs are drawn up and the arms are thrown out and then forward in the position of an embrace. A symmetric response of this nature indicates normalcy. Asymmetry may be caused by difficulty in the locomotor apparatus (such as a fracture) or by damage to the nervous system.

At the end of the first week the pupillary light reflex is usually present and can be elicited by throwing the beam of the otoscope into the infant's eyes. Contraction of the pupil is usually immediate; the reaction is seldom well sustained in the infant, a compensatory dilatation occurring within 1 or 2 seconds. This is normal.

Pathologic Conditions

Various types of pathologic conditions may be observed at the examination at the end of the first week, and most of these are amenable to treatment by office procedures.

Fractures in the newborn are not as uncommon as we might expect. The clavicle is often injured. This is usually noticed when the Moro reflex is elicited. In the presence of a fracture the infant will move all extremities except the affected one, like this:

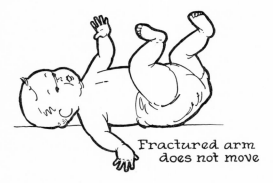

Fractured arm does not move

The simplest of immobilization will give excellent results. Frequently a simple bandage applied to raise the affected shoulder and to hold it well back will suffice. Here is the way to apply an adequate dressing:

Muslin bandage
Padded board

Most fractures of the humerus may be treated by applying a simple Velpeau bandage, like this:

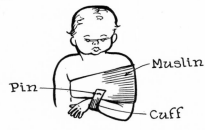

Muslin
Pin
Cuff

Fractures of the femur are well treated with Buck's extension, which may often be done quite satisfactorily in the home. To apply the extension, first wash the involved leg with alcohol and dry thoroughly. Then apply tincture of benzoin and place one long strip of 1 inch adhesive tape along each side of each

leg. Use a wooden spreader in the end of the extension with a hole for attaching traction.

Wooden spreader
Adhesive strips

Attach a piece of clothesline rope to the spreader on the fractured leg and suspend the child so that the buttocks are barely lifted from the bed, like this:

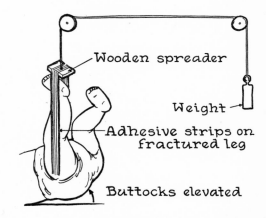

Wooden spreader
Weight
Adhesive strips on fractured leg
Buttocks elevated

Now lift the other leg with less traction, like this:

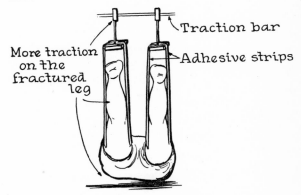

Traction bar
More traction on the fractured leg
Adhesive strips

Erb-Duchenne paralysis involving the fifth and sixth cervical roots of the brachial plexus is unfortunately all too prevalent. The infant will usually assume a position like this:

Treatment may often be initiated at home by simply tying the arm to the head of the crib, like this:

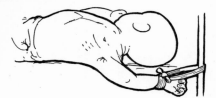

The muscles that are paralyzed normally pulled like this:

Treatment is designed simply to overcome antagonistic pull of non-paralyzed muscles. Physical therapy which can be performed in any well equipped office is a distinct aid in treatment.

Septicemia appearing in the first two weeks of life is not a rare disease. It should be suspected in all cases of illness in which the diagnosis is obscure, whether or not fever is present. The white count is slightly indicative but by no means a reliable procedure in making the diagnosis. Not until the second week of life does the normal infant show a predominance of lymphocytes, and this factor may be extremely confusing. Blood culture carefully done is a very important and reliable means of diagnosis usually within the range of any well equipped office laboratory.

OBTAINING BLOOD SPECIMENS. Blood is usually easiest obtained from the neck veins of infants of this age. Lay the infant firmly on the table and hold his head extended off the edge of the table, like this:

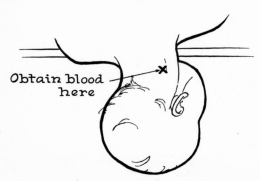

Obtain blood here

The normal infant is somewhat resentful of this position (but not nearly so much so as the normal mother) and will make his resentment known by crying lustily. This, of course, is falling right into our trap, for it distends the superficial veins of the neck. These veins are easily entered at the point where they cross the belly of the sternocleidomastoid muscle, and ample blood may be secured without great difficulty.

Another, somewhat more difficult, way to obtain blood is from the femoral vein. The relationship of vein, artery and nerve just below Poupart's ligament is this:

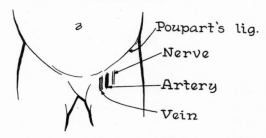

Poupart's lig.
Nerve
Artery
Vein

Palpation of the artery is quite simple. Insert a needle approximately ¼ inch medial to the pulsating artery and to approximately the same depth. There are no structures liable to severe damage by this procedure and a few attempts will allow one to become quite expert at performing it.

Meningeal infection, if suspected, is usually simple to identify at this age. The infant's spine may be tapped with impunity if strict asepsis is the goal of the basic technique. If you do not have a small spinal needle, an ordinary 2 inch, 21 gauge needle will usually do the job very well. Ordinarily, I have the nurse hold the infant wrapped around her middle like this:

After thorough cleansing of the skin with soap and water and alcohol, the needle is attached to a 2 cc. syringe (to aid maneuverability and to prevent egress of the spinal fluid should it be under pressure) and inserted just below the spine of the fourth lumbar vertebra. Important anatomic details to be considered in entering the spinal canal of the newborn are these:

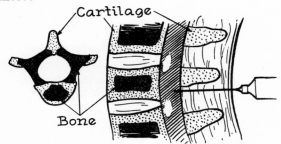

There is some tendency to penetrate too deeply and this should be guarded against by frequent aspiration. It is ordinarily a wise precaution not to withdraw more than 2 or 3 cc. of spinal fluid from the neonate.

Spontaneous pneumothorax is sometimes seen in these young children. If respiratory embarrassment is at all severe, aspiration of the intrathoracic air may be a wise procedure. To accomplish this, I use procaine anesthesia of the skin and pleura, on the somewhat unusual theory that pain is likely to make the child gasp and thereby increase chances that the original lesion will recur. The usual site of aspiration is the anterior axillary line at the level of the nipple:

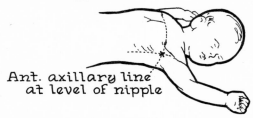

After anesthesia, attach a stopcock to an ordinary 2 inch, 21 gauge needle and attach the stopcock in turn to a 20 cc. syringe so that the final instrument looks like this:

Insert the needle gently toward the pleura halfway between adjacent ribs, like this:

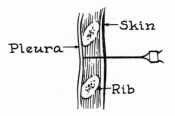

There is a definite feel of resistance when the deep fascia and pleura are penetrated and one may verify entrance into the pleura by opening the stopcock and aspirating to see if air is obtained.

Improvement in respiration is usually immediate. One should usually aspirate only that amount of air necessary to gain maximal immediate respiratory benefit. An attempt to exhaust the air completely in the pleural cavity is likely to result in the penetration of the lung by the needle which, while it is not particularly serious, is just as well not done.

Urinary Tract Infection. In the presence of obscure anorexic symptoms, failure to gain weight, and sometimes fever, one should never neglect the urinalysis and stained smear of urinary sediment. Infection of the urinary tract with colon bacilli (gram-negative rods) seems to be relatively common in the neonatal period and can only be diagnosed by adequate urinalysis and staining procedures.

Imperforate anus may, in rare cases, be first noticed at the office examination. The mother, of course, will remark on the fact that the baby has had no stools. Digital examination may be all that is necessary for demonstration of this anomaly, but occasionally x-ray is needed to get an accurate picture of the level of obstruction. Do it this way: Using the regular wall chest plate holder, grasp the child by the ankles and hold him in an inverted position for at least 2 minutes. (It is best to send the mother to the nearest drug store to have a coke while this is being done.) Now take a penny and place it at the anal opening, hold the child in front of the chest plate holder and snap a picture. The gas in the intestine will rise to maximum height and its relationship to the penny will provide an excellent illustration of the pathologic condition, like this:

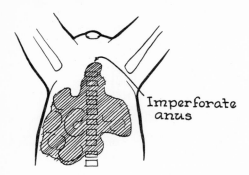

Imperforate anus

The foregoing has been a brief listing of the office procedures important in the treatment of the child approximately one week of age. There are many other more rare conditions, and many conditions which require immediate hospitalization. We must realize that disease in the neonatal period is difficult of diagnosis and treacherous in treatment. A good rule is: when in doubt, abandon office procedures and hospitalize.

EXAMINATION OF THE WELL CHILD

This is an office procedure which we all believe to be necessary but which many of us do cursorily if at all. Since it is essential to proper care of pediatric patients we will include here a typical routine for quick and reasonably thorough evaluation of the child. Begin by having the nurse record height, weight, age and other essential information.

As I observe children through an increasing number of years I find myself tending to attach less and less importance to weight. If the child is within proper height range for his age group and if he seems firm and well developed one can certainly assume a state of adequate health. Perhaps this is simply another way of saying the same thing that the weight charts do.

The nurse should next conduct the child and mother into an examining room and see that the child is completely undressed. In looking at the naked child, notice particularly evidence of skin disease or evidence of muscular atrophy or postural defects. If the child is old enough to walk, have him walk to his mother and notice any peculiarities in gait or bearing. If the child is still creeping and crawling, watch him creep across the examining table or the floor. Next examine the head and notice if the fontanels are closed or open. Normally they should be closed by the age of twelve to fourteen months.

Next inspect the ears with the otoscope, noticing the character of cerumen, if any, and the attitude and coloration of the drum. Hearing may usually be checked roughly by engaging the child in conversation interesting to him and gradually talking in a softer voice. If the child is too young to give vocal response, scratch the surface of the examining table a few inches to either side of the child's head. If he hears this sound he will turn his head toward it in at least one or two cases out of eight to ten tries.

Next look at the eyes and move your lighted otoscope in front of them, noticing whether or not the child follows the light adequately. Squint will be present to some degree in normal children under six months of age. Pupillary responses should be checked and, when the child is old enough to cooperate, an opthalmoscopic examination of the fundus should be done.

With the child's mouth closed occlude one side of the nose like this:

Then notice whether or not there appears to be obstruction to breathing. If either or both nostrils show obstruction, use the large ear speculum on your otoscope to look into the nose for anterior obstruction. Should none be apparent, hypertrophied adenoids are the usual remaining cause.

With a tongue blade and flashlight examine the tongue margin and the pharynx, paying close attention to the tonsils and the lymphoid tissue on the posterior pharyngeal wall, and being sure to ascertain whether or not there is a discharge coming down from the posterior nasopharynx. Then feel for enlargement of the glands in the posterior angle of the jaw.

Detailed examination of the thoracic content takes approximately 15 minutes and simply cannot be done with our present schedule. It is usually adequate to listen to the apices in front and the bases in back and to examine the apex and base of the heart.

The abdomen should be palpated for masses and the umbilical and inguinal regions examined for hernia.

Male genitalia should be checked for phimosis and degree of testicular descent; female genitalia should be examined for intralabial irritations and vaginal discharge.

No periodic examination of the well child is complete without visualization of the anus. Pull the buttocks sharply apart like this:

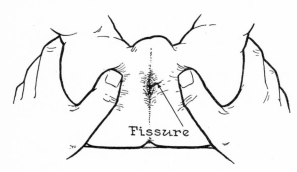

Fissure

Perianal irritations will be seen immediately and, if sufficient exposure of anal mucous membrane is obtained, bright red streaks of anal fissure will be apparent.

This procedure of periodic examination of the well child has frequently been carried to the point of absolute foolishness by parents and physicians. It is a valuable procedure and one which should not be neglected. It is, however, possible to make this a financial rather than a medical process and I would counsel some careful thought before deciding on the frequency of such examinations.

Certain diseases have peculiar features in children and, of course, certain other diseases are peculiar to children. In this brief section we will discuss some office procedures applicable in the diagnosis and treatment of these diseases.

POLIOMYELITIS

Not infrequently these cases are seen for the first time in the practitioner's office. Needless to say, in the presence of suspicious symptoms a spinal tap should be done. Unfortunately the findings are nearly identical in polio and in lymphocytic choriomeningitis, which seems to be a benign disease. The spinal fluid findings are an increased number of cells in the fluid. During the first 3 to 5 days of the disease these cells may be polymorphonuclears. Beginning about the third day and becoming fully apparent about the fifth, there is a change in cellular character, with lymphocytes predominating.

There is an elevation in spinal fluid protein but seldom any change in chlorides and sugars. Some prognostic significance may be attached to the cell count. In the usual case it ranges from 60 to 100 cells per cubic millimeter. If the cell count is extremely high, there is indication of an intense meningitic reaction and the probabilities of severe permanent paralysis are somewhat lessened. Needless to say, hospitalization is indicated.

HERPETIC STOMATITIS

These mouth lesions are frequently seen in conjunction with a Vincent's infection of the gum margin. While many local treatments have been advised, probably the best is daily applications of 3 to 5 per cent silver nitrate done by the physician in the office. The application should be made until the ulcers turn white. In general experience it has been found that parents do this job poorly and, while it is a simple task, it is usually best done as an office procedure.

VINCENT'S INFECTION

The swollen red gum edge of Vincent's infection is a familiar sight to any physician who takes care of children. Occasionally it is necessary to prove the presence of the infection by means of smear. Take a particularly succulent looking area of the gingivae and roll a cotton swab gently toward the gum margin, like this:

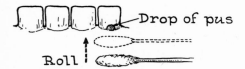

If a drop of pus exudes, discard the first swab and, using a clean cotton-tipped applicator, pick the drop of pus up and smear it on an ordinary slide. In the presence of Vincent's infection the smear will usually look like this:

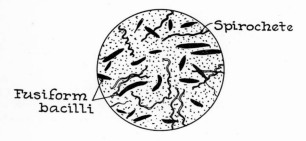

DIARRHEAL DISEASES

Confronted with a case of moderately severe diarrhea in a young child, begin by making a pH determination of the urine if a specimen is obtainable. Squibb nitrazine paper is reasonably accurate and will give you a good estimation. A low pH in the presence of obvious dehydration with persistent diarrhea and some vomiting is a danger signal that calls for immediate administration of fluid. In very young children the most satisfactory method for office administration of fluids is to combine the fluid with hyaluronidase and inject it subcutaneously into the soft tissues (see p. 196).

After acute fluid needs have been met it may then be wise to attempt differentiation. Gently insert a large lubricated ear speculum into the rectum, using a cotton-tipped applicator coated with petrolatum as an obturator. Remove the petrolatum-coated applicator and use a second applicator to clean off excess lubricant. Now take still another applicator, push it through the speculum and gently swab the rectal wall. Make a culture of this material and place it immediately in the incubator. While it occasionally may be valuable, one should remember that this procedure seldom offers any information until the diarrhea is over. Diagnosis in retrospect is important to the physician but may not be so to the patient.

As you know, diarrhea in children under two years of age is serious and occasionally fatal. If you see a severe diarrhea in such a youngster, it is best not to temporize. Give fluids on an emergency basis if they are required. Use what office procedures may be helpful in diagnosis and then hospitalize immediately.

INFECTIOUS HEPATITIS

Diagnosis of this disease may sometimes be made several days before appearance of clinical jaundice by using a very simple office test which will demonstrate bilirubin in the urine. Place 10 cc. of urine in a test tube and add 2 drops of Loeffler's methylene blue stain. If bilirubin is not present the solution will remain blue, but if it is present a bright green color results.

A direct van den Bergh reaction is seen during the first days of jaundice (p. 367). As recovery progresses, reaction usually becomes indirect only.

UMBILICAL HERNIA

Umbilical hernia is rather common in the newborn and will usually respond excellently to the simplest of treatment. I usually hold the hernia in place with tape, using a special technique of application which seems to give better reduction. Begin by cutting two pieces of 2 inch tape 8 inches long and sticking approximately 4 inches of each strip to the lateral abdominal wall like this:

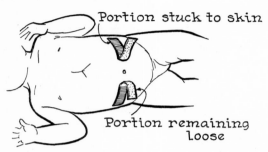

Now bring one piece of tape over the hernial opening and cut a slit in it where it passes over the hernia, like this:

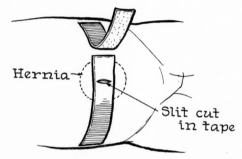

Fold a 4 by 4 inch gauze sponge and place it over the hernial ring, like this:

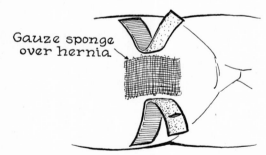

Now fold the piece of tape that has no slit in it so that the sticky side is out, like this:

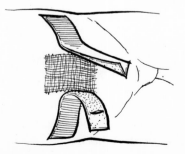

and insert it through the slit in the other piece of tape like this:

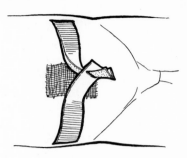

Pull the tapes tight experimentally and notice how much tension is required for firm reduction of the hernia. When the correct amount of tension is obtained, mark the point on the edges of the folded tape where it emerges from the slit in the opposite tape. Separate the tapes and make a cut through the folded tape about halfway to the center and unfold the tape. It now looks like this:

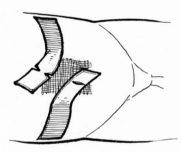

Now thread the perforation and pull the tapes taut and you have a dressing that looks like this:

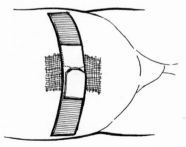

This method seems to give somewhat better stability than a simple piece of tape applied across the abdomen, and the average mother can learn to do it almost immediately. If after 4 to 6 months of reduction by this method the hernia still remains, it is then wise to consider surgical repair.

INGUINAL HERNIA

Inguinal hernia is also common in young boys. Cure is frequently accomplished by wearing a truss and it has been my experience that the homemade truss is often much superior to the purchased article.

Have the mother get a piece of rather heavy outing flannel and cut two triangles 2½ inches on each side. She should then sew two edges of the triangles together like this:

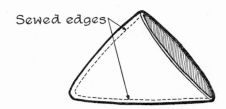

Sewed edges

Now turn this cloth pouch inside out, put in it a piece of ½ inch foam rubber cut to size, and stuff the area on both sides of the foam rubber with cotton like this:

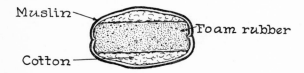

Muslin

Foam rubber

Cotton

Now sew up the open edge and sew three shirt collar buttons to each of the angles of the triangle so that the pad looks like this:

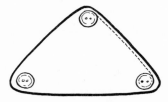

Next get a piece of pliable rubber taping like that used to hold an anesthetic mask in place, and make of it a lopsided rubber "T" like this:

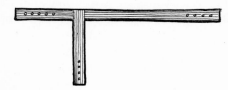

Apply the truss so that it fits like this:

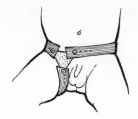

If there is not a noticeable diminution in size of the hernia after several months of such treatment one then should consider surgery.

PANCREATIC FIBROSIS

There is one simple office test that will save literally hundreds of dollars worth of diagnostic procedures in demonstrating this disease. If the pancreas is functioning properly there is an excess of pancreatic enzymes in the normal stool.

Mix a pea-sized portion of the child's stool with approximately five times its volume of water. Take an unexposed dental x-ray film from its package and put three drops of this stool and water specimen on the coated side of the film. Place the film out of the way and let it sit for 30 minutes, then wash in tap water. If adequate pancreatic function is present the stool and water specimen will have digested the coating off the x-ray film so that when held to the light one can see a clear area where the specimen was placed. In the presence of inadequate pancreatic function, there will be little, if any, change in the film.

ACUTE PHARYNGITIS

This, of course, is one of the most frequent diseases of children. There are only two office procedures to be considered: one which may rarely be most helpful, and one which never should be done. The first is culture from the offending membrane. This probably should be resorted to only in cases of persistent infection or in those cases which might conceivably be diphtheria.

The procedure which never should be done is "painting" the throat. It has been amply proven for years that the various mercurial antiseptics (and most of the other antiseptics, for that matter) do considerably more damage to the mucous membranes than they do to germs. The only thing one has to gain by this antiquated procedure is the obvious benefit of psychotherapy when it is done.

If pressure from the patient forces you to put something in or on the throat, use something relatively harmless like Cresatin or compound tincture of benzoin—or try a special preparation which we keep in our office to gratify such patients. It is made up of 1 drop of green food color to which is added 1 ounce of normal saline solution. Occasionally a drop of some aromatic substance is added to make the preparation seem very potent. We have used menthol or wintergreen.

CHRONIC COLDS

The child with chronic upper respiratory infection deserves a rather thorough office investigation, which he seldom gets. Begin by examining the nose through a speculum, looking for sources of chronic discharge from the anterior portion of the nasal chamber. These are quite rare, for the sinuses are only partially developed at birth and seldom become infected before eight to ten years of age. Check the inside of the mouth for sources of chronic irritation and in particular look at the posterior nasopharynx, here:

In my experience most of these children have had chronically infected adenoidal tissue which is hypertrophied and drains rather constantly, producing a mild throat irritation and bronchitis.

If after one or two examinations you can verify the existence of this chronic drainage, it is frequently a good idea to culture the material and to test the organism for sensitivity to various antibiotics.

Intranasal application of shrinking agents, along with appropriate antibiotic therapy, is an excellent way to cure these children. Show the mother how to make the instillation like this: Place a pillow under the child's shoulders and have him hold his head firmly back against the surface of the bed or examining table, like this:

Aim the dropper containing the shrinking solution straight through the inferior meatus and squirt the solution so that it comes directly in contact with the swollen adenoidal tissue, like this:

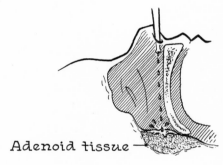

Adenoid tissue —

Remember that continued use of any of the solutions we have for shrinking the mucosa will finally result in chronic chemical irritation. Order the treatment done intermittently. A week's treatment followed by a week's rest, then by a week's treatment, etc., is an excellent schedule.

TONSILS AND ADENOIDS

The most frequent disease of the tonsils and adenoids still seems to be what has been referred to as acute remunerative tonsillitis. Actually, not a small portion of the public is thoroughly convinced that tonsils rank in the same category with income tax as a causer of problems. If you will stop and think about this just a minute, it becomes ridiculous beyond description. The whole nasopharynx is literally filled with lymphoid tissue which is constantly subject to invasion. (For that matter, lymphoid tissue over the rest of the body is rather consistently bombarded with infectious organisms, too.) The lingual tonsil unquestionably has as much opportunity for infection as the faucial tonsil. The other tissue of Waldeyer's ring is equally subject to infection. We have, however, picked the particular portion of this tissue that we can see and blamed it for everything from fallen arches to dysmenorrhea.

History is a much more accurate means of evaluating the tonsil than any office procedure. If you get a history of repeated tonsillar infection you may attempt by two simple techniques to verify this history. First, of course, feel the glands of the jaw. *They are palpable in most people.* Enlargement beyond the size of a pea and chronic tenderness are of some importance.

Occasionally it is thought useful to obtain material from the tonsillar crypts and make a Gram's stain for bacteria. This is a vaguely useful procedure but one should keep in mind that crypts are not openings into the tonsils but simply canyons in tonsillar tissue, and the bacteria obtained from them are actually obtained from outside the tonsils themselves, not inside.

To repeat, history is far more valuable than any office procedure in determining whether tonsils should be removed. I know of no particular characteristic appearance of tonsils that harbor chronic infection. Hypertrophy is not a good guide, for some children have big tonsils just as some children have big ears. Hypertrophy of sufficient degree to cause mechanical difficulty is, of course, an indication for removal.

Peritonsillar abscess, at least if it occurs more than once, is a definite indication for tonsillectomy.

Adenoids represent a different situation altogether. Hypertrophy of the adenoidal tissue can result in the occlusion of the eustachian tubes with consequent deafness and/or ear infection. Respiratory distress frequently results from adenoidal hypertrophy, and chronic adenoidal discharges may be responsible for "frequent colds." Diagnostic and therapeutic office procedures have already been mentioned.

It is wise to keep in mind that there is a gradual atrophy of both tonsillar and adenoidal tissue which becomes clinically apparent about the age of five. Then, too, the posterior nasopharyngeal air passages grow and literally "grow away from" the enlarged adenoids.

UPPER RESPIRATORY INFECTION

When one is presented with an acute upper respiratory infection one knows to begin with that chances of an accurate diagnosis are several hundred to one against. The one important point which every effort must be made to determine, however, is the differentiation between those respiratory processes caused by viruses and those by the streptococcus.

A simple methylene blue smear of the involved area will usually help make the differentiation. A white count or centrifugation of blood with measurement of the buffy layer will also help, but only in a few cases is the disease severe enough to warrant this procedure.

Systemic symptoms also provide a method of reasonably accurate discrimination between the two but are not to be considered in this volume.

CONGENITAL HEART DISEASE

These lesions, many of which are becoming surgically correctable, may often be diagnosed by application of simple office procedures. Once diagnosis becomes comparatively clear they are seldom problems for local treatment but rather should be sent to one of the major centers for further evaluation and possible surgical correction. There are, of course, literally hundreds of different types of congenital malformations; however, the principal ones seen by the family physician can be summarized in a very few categories.

Interventricular Septal Defects, or Roger's Disease

This is a relatively common form of congenital heart disease which usually produces no symptoms whatever. It is frequently picked up on routine examination by finding a harsh systolic murmur midway between base and apex about here:

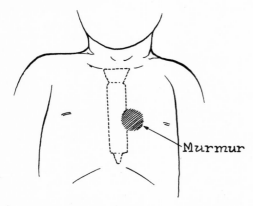

The murmur is characteristically not transmitted far in any direction and is frequently confused with a functional murmur. The Roger murmur, however, does not change with change in position and is relatively constant from one examination to the next.

There is no typical x-ray configuration of the heart, although occasionally slight ventricular enlargements may be seen. The EKG is normal unless the "hole" has interfered with conduction pathways, in which case the QRS complex is widened like this:

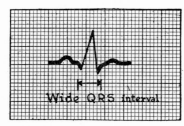

Unless the defect is literally huge the outlook is excellent. The only serious danger is that of infection, and office procedures should be geared to prevention of this tragic happening. By and large, these patients need not be

sent for expert evaluation unless symptoms are present.

Interatrial Septal Defects

These may be an entirely different situation. Typically, the child is malnourished and retarded in growth. Cyanosis is usually absent except in conditions wherein the pulmonary circulation is retarded. Examples would be a severe chest cold or pneumonia.

There is usually a loud systolic murmur extending along the left border of the sternum in about this location:

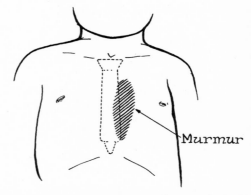

Fluoroscopy and x-ray are diagnostic helps in the more severe cases, illustrating enlargement of the right ventricle, the right atrium and occasionally the pulmonary artery. On fluoroscopy the marked pulsations of the pulmonary artery produce the so-called "hilar dance" which is quite characteristically found in serious lesions. Prolonged P waves, which may even be notched, like this:

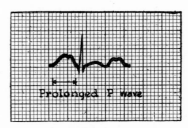

and right axis deviation are common findings in the electrocardiogram. It must be remembered, of course, that right axis deviation is quite normal in the infant for a period of several weeks after birth.

In the presence of these findings, the patient should be referred to a cardiac center immediately.

Patent Ductus Arteriosus

This is another rather common congenital lesion which may usually be diagnosed by application of only the simplest office procedures. Symptoms seem actually somewhat rare. Examination of the chest reveals the so-called "machinery" murmur to the left of the sternum near the base of the heart. This has always sounded to me like the muffled whine of high speed gears. Particularly characteristic is the rising and falling tone level and intensity of the murmur, like a siren synchronized with the heart beat.

When a hand is placed along the upper left border of the sternum a sharp thrill is usually felt which may be continuous or appreciable only during systole.

In such cases there are two additional office procedures which always should be done. First, take blood pressure in both the upper and lower extremities. An increased pulse pressure, usually 50 mm. of mercury or more, is a common finding. Next, place the stethoscope over the femoral artery just below Poupart's ligament, here:

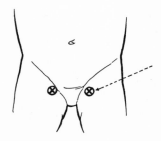

A popping murmur is common and is contributory evidence of the disease. Cases of patent ductus arteriosus should be referred to a cardiac center immediately for evaluation and possible corrective surgery.

Tetralogy of Fallot

The tetralogy of Fallot and various modifications of it are the commonest causes of cyanotic heart disease in children. Upon routine chest examination a harsh systolic murmur will be heard over the major portion of the left chest, like this:

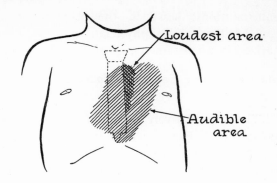

Usually the child is quite obviously ill and retarded development is common.

The chest x-ray shows a relative enlargement of the ventricular area with a striking concavity where the pulmonary artery is usually seen. The hilar areas of the lungs are much clearer than usual and show considerably less than normal movement with ventricular systole. The x-ray usually looks something like this:

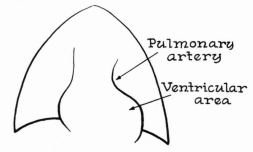

The electrocardiogram illustrates right axis deviation. High and peaked P waves like this are frequently seen:

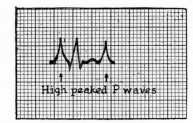

Red blood cell count is usually increased and hemoglobin is markedly elevated. These cases should be evaluated as soon as possible by the nearest cardiac center. For the first time in medical history something can be done to help these children. This is a great achievement.

RHEUMATIC FEVER

Many cases of this treacherous disease are first picked up in the office and not a few must be managed by utilizing home and office procedures.

First, some diagnostic points which may help elicit the characteristic signs: If pericarditis is suspected and the typical scratchy to and fro murmur is not heard upon the first examination, have the patient stand and bend over forward, assuming approximately this position:

Now listen along the left border of the sternum. Very mild exercise (but by no means vigorous exercise) may help demonstrate this murmur. My own thought is that the exercise procedure is not warranted, but some excellent physicians use it.

In carditis, gallop rhythm may frequently be elicited by listening at the apex and may be brought out by the mildest of exercise, such as walking across a room.

Certain little clinical tests are valuable in proving the presence or absence of a typical chorea. Begin by asking the child to count. Usually he will speak clearly for three or four numbers and then "get his tongue all tangled up" and be unable to go on without a second or two of enforced rest. Next ask the child to clasp his fingers together and hold the hands quiet for a few moments. He will usually be able to do so, but upon release of the fingers choreiform movements will be greatly increased. Next, ask the child to hold his hands out in front of him and watch for the usual jerky hyperextension of wrist and fingers which will occur in a very few seconds. Now play at shaking hands with the child and feel the jerky, at times, fibrillary, and totally unco-

ordinated movements of the fingers while you gently hold his hand.

Chorea is so typical that a few seconds of careful observation will serve to make an accurate diagnosis in the vast majority of cases.

Office laboratory procedures are excellent methods of following a case of rheumatic fever. They have, however, several unreliable aspects which must be emphasized lest the unwary physician rely too heavily upon them.

The erythrocyte sedimentation rate is an excellent indication of rheumatic activity. Of course it is by no means specific for rheumatic fever, but, in the absence of infectious process and in the presence of a proven diagnosis of rheumatic fever, it is a good guide to the status of activity. There is one peculiarity in the test that yawns as a major pit for the unwary. At the onset of congestive failure the sedimentation rate may return to normal in spite of rheumatic activity and then, when congestive failure is corrected, may suddenly become much increased. In the presence of a suddenly normal sedimentation rate, by all means first make a careful clinical appraisal of the patient for possible congestive heart failure.

The electrocardiograph is a valuable means of estimating *current* cardiac injury. It by no means gives a clue to permanent cardiac damage. Increase in the P-R interval, like this:

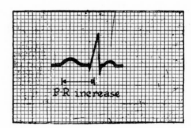

usually indicates that there is rheumatic involvement of the heart. Return to normal of this interval is significant of the recovery stage. However, we see an occasional patient in which the lengthened P-R interval becomes fixed and, for some reason which we cannot explain, remains so throughout life. The best guess at the moment is that scar tissue is formed in a portion of the conduction system and causes this fixation of the interval. When you suspect a recurrent attack of rheumatic fever, be on guard against the possibility of this fixed P-R interval.

INFECTIOUS MONONUCLEOSIS

The only office procedure of worth in this disease is a Wright's or Giemsa's stain for the presence of the typical foam cell. This is a mononuclear with an irregularly rounded nucleus and cytoplasm that looks foamy and is deeply basophilic. There is no way to sketch such a cell so it cannot be illustrated here. Look at the colored plates in a good hematology text. Once having seen it you will not miss it in the future.

IRON DEFICIENCY ANEMIA

Diagnosis and treatment of this condition in children is not particularly different than in adults except that there exists one trap for the unwary that may be somewhat confusing. Marked gastro-intestinal disturbances are not rare in these children and, upon testing, achlorhydria may be found. This appears to be functional and *is a part* of severe cases.

URINARY TRACT INFECTIONS

In children, infections of the urinary tract are frequently generalized rather than specifically located. For example, cystitis is rare without some infection in the ureter and kidney pelvis. These infections are particularly treacherous in that they tend to "dig in" and establish a chronic focus. If this be the case there are recurrent episodes of pyuria and symptoms which disappear under the most minor treatment but which recur with monotonous regularity.

When this situation arises, culture is indicated along with testing the organism for sensitivity to the antibiotics. Treatment should be pursued vigorously until at least three negative cultures taken at 1 week intervals have been obtained.

Recurrent infections make intravenous pyelography a necessity because of the obstructive malformations of the urinary tract which lie at the root of some of these problems. The procedure is in no way different from adult pyelography except that the amount of dye used is reduced proportionately to conform to the size of the child. If any malformation is noted on these films the child should be referred for complete urologic investigation, which is usually beyond the range of the average office.

During the course of active treatment, repeated (not occasional) urinalyses are indicated. One pitfall seems to cause a great deal of trouble: vaginal discharges are not particularly uncommon in little girls. The pus cells from the vagina will, of course, contaminate the voided urine specimen, and some children are treated for urinary infection when, as a matter of fact, a vaginal foreign body or a minor cervical lesion is causing the difficulty. If there is any question obtain a catheterized specimen from even the smallest child.

Acute Glomerulonephritis

Acute glomerulonephritis is a common disease of childhood and may be diagnosed with the simplest of office procedures. When the urine shows albumin, casts, and red blood cells a test should always be made for ketone bodies which, when present, indicate early acidosis and are a positive indication for immediate hospitalization.

Daily examinations of the urine for red blood cells will give a rough estimate of progress. An excellent unofficial record may be kept by measuring 5 cc. of the urine into a test tube before it has time to settle and taping the test tube to the wall beside the patient's bed. Mark on the tape the date and the time of specimen and notice from day to day the changes in the number of red blood cells in the bottoms of the various tubes.

The Addis count is of value in estimating the progress of the disease. Count the cells in sediment from 10 cc. of urine. Calculate total sediment in a 12 hour specimen.

Perhaps the best indication we have of the status of the disease is the sedimentation rate. It tends to remain increased in all cases which go on to chronicity. This is not necessarily true of the Addis count or of urinary findings. Most of these patients should be hospitalized, although this is not always possible.

If any sign of chronicity occurs, tests of renal function (p. 370) should be made and a determination of non-protein nitrogen (p. 366) is indicated.

ADHERENT PREPUCE

Occasionally this condition is allowed to persist for several months and a child will be seen with obvious irritation behind the corona where smegma has collected. An attempt should be made to retract the foreskin by using gentle pressure, like this:

If this is unsuccessful it may be necessary to insert a blunt probe and separate adhesions between the foreskin and the glans like this:

Sometimes the foreskin is so tight that a dorsal slit must be made to free it. Unless the full procedure of circumcision is to be carried out at the time, this dorsal slit should be made as small as feasible to accomplish exposure of the corona. It is possible to anesthetize the foreskin with a drop of procaine and use scissors to make the incision along the mid-dorsal line, like this:

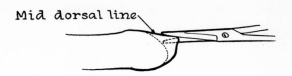

After gentle cleansing with soap and water, the foreskin should then be returned over the glans and the patient's mother instructed to retract it at least once (and preferably two or three times) each day.

PARAPHIMOSIS

This is very common in children. The foreskin is incarcerated while retracted behind the glans and, because of its tightness, partially occludes circulation, causing the glans to swell. The foreskin itself becomes edematous and proper repositioning seems all but impossible. Begin by lubricating the coronal area with petrolatum. Hold the penis as shown below and push gently with the thumb while pulling steadily with the fingers for a matter of at least a minute. Most cases can be reduced by this maneuver.

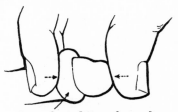

In the event that reduction still has not occurred, dilute a vial of hyaluronidase with 4 cc. of water and inject a few drops at one or two places around the constricting band. Edema will rapidly dissipate and reduction is usually spontaneous.

HYDROCELE

This collection of fluid in the tunica vaginalis is common in infancy. The main problem is to differentiate between hydrocele alone, hernia alone or hydrocele combined with hernia. Begin by transilluminating the swelling in a dark room. Light passes freely through the hydrocele but only very dimly through the hernia. Next, listen to the area with your stethoscope. Be patient and keep your stethoscope in place a full minute. A peristaltic rush through the bowel in the hernia will be very apparent. Now put the child's buttocks on a pillow and gently manipulate the swelling. There are very few non-reducible hernias in childhood, and any gut that is present will usually slip back into the peritoneal cavity.

The infantile hydrocele will usually be cured spontaneously. Treatment is not necessary. After the age of 4 to 6 months simple aspiration is usually all that is needed. Begin by locating the position of the testes, which will usually be high in the posterior medial aspect of the sac. Anesthetize the skin with a drop of procaine and insert the needle, bevel upward, into the sac like this:

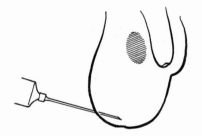

Notice that the needle itself points somewhat downward to avoid possible penetration of the testes as the sac is emptied. A tape support worn a few days will usually be all that is needed in the way of a dressing.

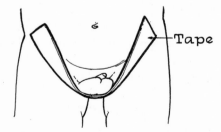

In still older children, operation may be done in the office surgery. Under local anesthesia expose the tunica vaginalis like this:

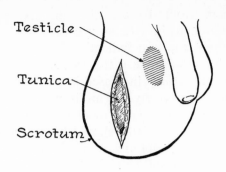

Now make a small incision in the tunica and extrude the testicle through it, using gentle pressure like this:

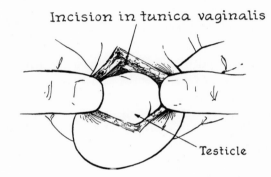

Free the excess tunica, which may be quite easily pulled away, and trim it off, leaving a cuff about 1 inch on all sides of the testicle like this:

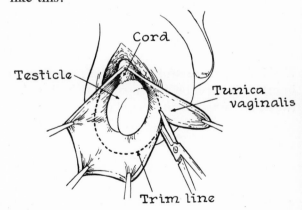

There should be little or no bleeding but, should a vessel ooze persistently, clamp it for a minute or two.

Now, using 3-0 or 4-0 plain catgut, sew the edges of the tunica together inside out so that it is kept everted, like this:

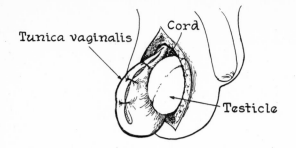

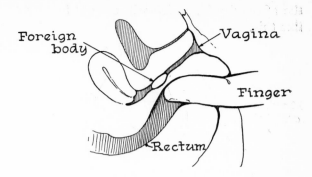

Following the operation, a simple suspension dressing is all that is needed.

GONORRHEAL VULVOVAGINITIS

Gonorrheal vulvovaginitis is still common in young girls. There is no particular office procedure involved in its treatment except that one should remember to be suspicious of vaginal discharges in children and to smear with methylene blue and Gram's stain unless the etiology is immediately apparent. Perhaps one suggestion to those physicians who have not seen a great deal of the disease will not be out of line. I know of no surer way to get in a fight with the average mother than to mention the term "gonorrhea" in discussing her daughter. Except with a highly intelligent patient, it is probably as well to discuss "infection."

A good policy, I believe, is to make a smear of all purulent discharges in young girls. The methylene blue stain is usually sufficient but in any case where there is question, Gram's stain must be used.

VAGINAL FOREIGN BODIES

During the process of their explorations of the body, young girls frequently insert foreign substances into the vagina. A purulent vaginal discharge and occasionally a serious infection may result.

The first office procedure when this is suspected is palpation through the rectum, like this:

If nothing is felt, vaginal examination occasionally can be made by using a large ear speculum with the otoscope as a source of light. This is not always satisfactory. A urethroscope may be used; occasionally, the nasopharyngoscope, or if you have none of these instruments, the cap of an old fountain pen with the clip taken off and the end removed makes an excellent tubular vaginal speculum.

When reasonably sure that a foreign body exists, examination and removal should be done under general anesthesia. This can be done in the office but is often more easily performed under hospital conditions. Alligator forceps or a hook made of a bent paper clip may be used.

CONGENITAL DISLOCATION OF THE HIP

Congenital dislocation of the hip is seen frequently enough to warrant examination of the young child for this congenital anomaly. To check for it, place the child face down on the table and hold the heels with the right hand. Notice the crease in the buttocks. On the affected side in the presence of shortening there will be a lifted gluteal fold and the knee crease of the afflicted leg will be somewhat above that of the other.

Now turn the child over and feel the area of the hip joint while attempting gentle abduction. Not infrequently increased muscle spasm can be palpated. Then try to abduct the legs widely and notice the limitation on the affected side, which will usually be about like this:

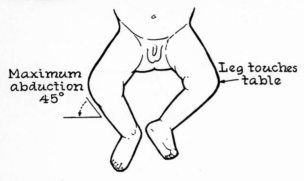

Lay the child on his back and notice the increased angle between an imaginary horizontal line running across the pubis and the inguinal crease on the affected side like this:

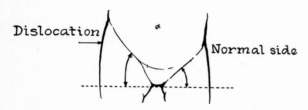

By 60 days of age, x-ray will usually demonstrate an abnormality, like this:

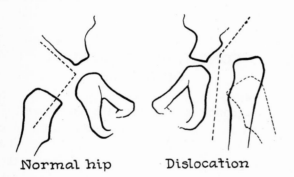

POISONING

Acute poisoning in children may be seen as an office emergency. Certain procedures are of value in the office before hospitalization. The important drugs, the chief symptoms and principal office procedures are:

Arsenic

Intense gastric pain with severe projectile vomiting of "rice water" material is the common initial finding. If the drug has been ingested for an hour or more, severe watery diarrhea, possibly bloody, may also be present.

Intensive lavage is the first and principal office treatment. The patient should be sedated and given some drug to alleviate pain. British anti-lewisite, 3 mg. per kilogram or 7 mg. per pound, should be given intramuscularly immediately and the patient sent to the nearest hospital.

In cases where the hospital is somewhat distant and time is to be consumed in transportation, start an intravenous infusion of 5 per cent glucose in water before dispatching the patient.

Atropine

Atropine and other belladonna derivatives are sometimes the cause of acute poisoning. Dryness of the mucous membranes, with extreme thirst but difficulty in swallowing, and wide dilatation of the pupils are immediately noticed. The temperature is usually increased; pulse is weak and rapid, and there is frequently restlessness and excitability.

Injection of 5 to 10 mg. of Mecholyl, if available, is indicated for both diagnosis and therapy. Lavage with tincture of iodine, 2 cc. to 1000 cc. of water, or with strong tea should be done immediately. If respiratory paralysis is present, artificial respiration should be begun and maintained. Pilocarpine may be given for its effect on mucous membranes and visual symptoms, but it apparently has no central effect at all. The patient should be taken to the nearest hospital as an acute emergency.

Barbiturates

There are three standbys in the treatment: lavage, a saline cathartic and stimulants. Picrotoxin given intravenously in small doses is helpful in the deeply comatose patient. The lavage solution may contain small amounts of potassium permanganate (1:5000, or a 3 grain tablet to 5 pints of water). This will be useful in Alurate and Dial poisoning. The patient should, of course, be taken to the hospital at once.

Hydrocarbons

The hydrocarbons are common poisoning agents, particularly in rural areas. Kerosene, gasoline, benzene derivatives, dry cleaning solvents, etc., are all members of this group.

The first symptoms are usually those of inebriation and, since the hydrocarbons are usually excreted partially through the lungs, the breath has a typical odor.

Unless very large amounts have been taken, the principal danger is that pulmonary excretion will result in a pneumonitis which may become serious. Lavage is probably not indicated unless the child has taken more than 20 cc. of the hydrocarbons. A saline laxative should be administered at once and, in the event that a relatively great amount has been ingested, the child should be sent to the hospital. When only a swallow or two has been taken, saline catharsis and careful observation for respiratory depression may be all that is indicated. By all means the child should be seen every day for several days and the chest examined most carefully.

Lye

The administration of an antidote for lye poisoning is useless unless done within the first 15 minutes. Since we seldom see the patient this quickly there will not often be an indication for an office antidote. Frequently the mothers of these patients call in immediately after the poisoning, and they should be told to stay at home a few minutes and to give the child at once a glass of water to which 1 tablespoonful of vinegar has been added, or a tablespoonful of lemon juice diluted with 2 tablespoonfuls of water and containing some sugar. The antidote should be administered as quickly as possible and the child should be encouraged to take as much of the antidote as he can tolerate. If this can be accomplished by the mother at home before bringing the child to the office, final results will be much better.

When seen in the office, administration of 1 or 2 tablespoonfuls of olive oil is indicated immediately, and the child should be sent to the hospital. Lavage is probably not only dangerous but a waste of time unless the child is seen within minutes after ingestion.

Phenol

The corrosive action of this drug brings on immediate and severe pain. Absorption is rapidly followed by shock and death. Immediate lavage with olive oil is the best possible treatment. The major factor in preventing death is quick action, and the procedure should be done as rapidly as possible.

Phenolphthalein

The various candy laxatives contain phenolphthalein as their principal active ingredient, and children frequently have the misfortune to eat one or several boxes of these laxative tablets thinking that they are candy.

Severe toxic reactions are fortunately rare. In the event the child has eaten large quantities of the material, gastric lavage is indicated and usually a sufficient amount of the material is recovered that no serious symptoms ensue. To put it mildly, copious bowel movements are usual in a very few hours. Since phenolphthalein is a chemical indicator, diagnosis of the poisoning may be made by alkalinizing the stomach contents and noting the bright purple color which results.

Salicylates

Acute salicylate poisoning is common in children and is frequently underrated as a potential cause of death. When large quantities of salicylates have been ingested—particularly salicylic acid and oil of wintergreen—mortality may be higher than 50 per cent. Immediate and copious lavage followed by a saline cathartic is the treatment of choice. If there is severe diarrhea and vomiting at the time the child is seen, an intravenous solution of isotonic saline should be started and the child dispatched to the nearest hospital.

Strychnine

The symptoms of strychnine poisoning are far too well known to be delineated here.

Treatment should begin by an exhibition of an intravenous barbiturate immediately. Pentothal Sodium and Sodium Amytal are the most satisfactory drugs. Caution in their administration is necessary because there is a rather narrow margin between the amount of drug required to stop the strychnine convulsions and the amount which will produce respiratory paralysis in the child.

As soon as satisfactory relaxation is obtained, the stomach should be lavaged with a solution of strong tea, or with 4 cc. of tincture of iodine to a quart of water, or with 2 per cent tannic acid solution.

Should the patient be brought to the office in a severe convulsion, chloroform or ether anesthesia must be administered immediately until a barbiturate can be prepared. This cannot be emphasized too strongly. It takes from 5 to 10 minutes in the ordinary office to prepare a solution of one of the barbiturates. This much time can be critical to the patient. Ether or chloroform may be given through a face mask if available, or through a wadded handkerchief which is saturated with the drug if formal equipment is not at hand.

THE CONSTIPATED BABY

There is one procedure which seems to be almost consistently neglected in diagnosis and treatment of the constipated infant. After a survey of the feeding problem *be sure* to do both a digital and a visual examination of the anus and rectum. These children often have a temporary episode of constipation lasting from 24 to 36 hours during which passage of a large stool initiates an anal fissure. Since it hurts for the child to have a bowel movement after this, he will avoid it as long as possible, then pass another hard stool which further irritates the anus. This is a vicious circle which is frequently seen in young babies and which can be broken by the simplest of medicinal treatment. *Be sure* to check the anus and rectum when presented with a case of constipation.

IMMUNIZATION

There is raging, at this writing, a tremendous tempest in a teapot about immunizations for children. One would think that the question of whether to immunize at 3 months or 6 months is soon to assume world-shaking proportions. As in most such furors, there is probably a deal of truth on both sides. I have been telling my mothers the principal arguments for both sides and then sneaking out of the controversy by saying essentially that it is six of one and half a dozen of the other. Why not split the difference and start immunizations between 4 and 5 months?

Diphtheria-Pertussis-Tetanus Immunization

Unquestionably, in areas where there is a high incidence of pertussis, early immunization is of great practical value. Injection of 0.5 cc. of the combined diphtheria and tetanus toxoids and pertussis vaccine into the subcutaneous tissues of arm or buttock is the first procedure. Then at monthly intervals additional injections should be done. There is some discussion as to whether 0.5 or 1 cc. is the best dose for the second and third injection. If there is any question, it is probably better to give the larger dose.

After these three preliminary injections, the child should be given 0.5 cc. booster doses at 1, 3 and 5 years of age. Following the injection at age 5, it is no longer necessary to include pertussis vaccine in the booster injections, but diphtheria and tetanus toxoids should be repeated at 3 to 5 year intervals as long as the patient remains under your care. Many adults are inclined to neglect their own tetanus injections. This, of course, can be a tragic error.

Poliomyelitis Vaccination

The report on the 1954 field trials of the trivalent, formalinized vaccine developed by Dr. Jonas Salk showed the vaccine to be 80 to 90 per cent effective against paralytic poliomyelitis. In this trial primary immunization was achieved by a three dose schedule in which the third dose was given only 5 weeks after the first.

Dr. Salk now (1955) recommends—and the Vaccine Advisory Committee of the National Foundation for Infantile Paralysis concurs—that the third dose be delayed for about 7 months. This schedule, he feels, can result in full immunization that will be effective for a much longer time. The reason is this: The first two inoculations produce a primary stimulation of antibody. A hyperreactive state develops over a period of months, during which time the antibody level may not be high. However, a booster dose at least 7 months later causes a rapid increase in the antibody level. Even more important, after the hyperreactive stage is reached a natural poliomyelitis infection will cause fast, high-level production of antibodies.

The 1955 dosage schedule for the vaccine, therefore, is two 1 cc. doses administered intramuscularly 2 to 4 weeks apart, and a third "booster" dose given no sooner than 7 months thereafter.

Smallpox Vaccination

One month after the combined toxoid-vaccine injections, vaccination for smallpox should be undertaken. This is often carelessly done and as a result immunity is poor. Some men wiser than I have mentioned the possibility of a widespread smallpox epidemic sometime in the next few decades unless vaccination techniques are improved. I think we should heed their warning and be most careful in doing this procedure.

To begin with, procurement and storage of the vaccine are of the utmost importance. The solution quickly becomes non-effective unless kept cold at all times. Smallpox vaccine should be shipped in containers cooled by dry ice, although this is seldom done. It should be stored in the freezing compartment of the office refrigerator and never removed from this compartment until immediately before use.

Alcohol inactivates the vaccine. It is perfectly acceptable to cleanse the area to be vaccinated with alcohol if ample time is allowed for complete drying to occur. Acetone is probably a better cleansing agent and if

acetone is not available there is certainly nothing wrong with a thorough scrubbing using soap and water. When a site for vaccination has been properly cleansed *and dried,* a drop of vaccine from the capillary tube is squeezed onto the skin. The needle point is held nearly parallel with the skin and the point pressed up and down on the skin like this:

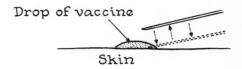

The object is for the needle not to penetrate but to scratch the "overlap" when it is lifted, like this:

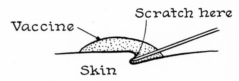

For the first vaccination, ten to fifteen pressures should be used, but for revaccination, thirty or thirty-five pressures are more satisfactory.

Care of the vaccination site to avoid dissemination and to produce maximum comfort for the patient is an important adjunct to this office procedure. After actual completion of the vaccination the needle may be rolled across the area of perforations a few times to "rub in" the vaccine. The solution should be allowed to stay in place on the skin for from 5 to 10 minutes but at the end of this time it may be wiped off gently with a dry cotton pledget. One error which I have seen several times is to use an alcohol sponge to remove excess vaccine; this, of course, merely serves the function of inactivating any living virus that is present.

No dressing of any kind should be applied to the vaccination site until the papule appears. At this time there may be itching and it may be necessary to protect the site from the child's fingers. An oversize gauze dressing held in place by tape placed far away from the vaccination site may be acceptable. You must remember that the tape itself, should it irritate the skin, might cause complications by allowing entrance of the virus into areas of tape-produced chafing. In removing the dressing it is wise to cut off the gauze portion near the tape but without removing the tape from the skin. To apply a new dressing put additional tape on over the original tape, which is left on the skin.

In many cases no dressing at all will be indicated, and this is unquestionably the best form of treatment.

Reactions to Smallpox Vaccination. There are three types of reaction with which the physician must be familiar, and a careful record of the type should be kept on each child vaccinated. The primary take or vaccinia reaction is the one which we see often when first inoculating a child. In this reaction nothing usually happens until the fourth or fifth day, when a small papule appears. During the next 48 hours it usually vesiculates. The vesicle enlarges in the next day or two and becomes covered with pearly gray membrane. This area is surrounded by a zone of erythema and edema. By the tenth day the reaction is at its height, usually showing gross swelling of the arm, an area of redness extending from 1 to 3 inches beyond the vesicle and enlargement of the regional lymph glands. At this stage, the patient is usually just plain sick. The temperature may be elevated, there is malaise, loss of appetite and general fussiness. Within a day or two the vesicle scabs over and the reaction begins to subside. At approximately the twentieth day the scab falls off spontaneously and there is left a small, white, puckered scar which may enlarge as the patient grows for several years.

The second reaction, which is not seen very often in babies, is the accelerated or vaccinoid reaction which apparently takes place in the partially immune person. Actually it is identical to the take but much milder and much quicker. There are all degrees of vaccinoid reaction, from those closely resembling a take and utilizing ten to fifteen days for the complete cycle to the extremely mild vaccinoid reaction in which, by the end of the first week or ten days, the process is nearly completed.

The negative or "immune" reaction shows a small area of erythema approximately the size of a cigarette cross-section at the area of vaccination, which fades in a few days without any of the characteristics of the vaccinia or vaccinoid reaction. It is important to realize that this is not a positive indication of immunity. It may, for example, indicate use of a non-potent vaccine.

Should an immune reaction occur, revaccination in 30 days is indicated in every case. The possible exceptions to this statement are those persons who are allergic to the type of vaccine used. Since there are now two types available, even this is not always a valid objection.

There is a popular fallacy that smallpox vaccination provides immunity for life. This must be true in some instances but they are exceptions. Average immunity is sufficient to protect against active exposure for about 5 years after vaccination. Revaccination should be done a minimum of every 10 years throughout life and, even better, every 5 years. It is not necessary more often than this.

Typhoid Immunization

After successful vaccination against smallpox, the next immunization should be against typhoid. The typhoid-paratyphoid multiple vaccine is usually furnished by the state health department and any physician may obtain it by writing to his state director of health.

Injections should be given weekly in dosage of 0.5 cc., 1 cc., and 1 cc. The vaccine should, of course, be injected into the subcutaneous tissues. Booster shots of 0.5 cc. should be given at 2 year intervals throughout life.

Rocky Mountain Spotted Fever Immunization

In certain areas immunization against Rocky Mountain spotted fever is definitely indicated. Three weekly injections of 1 cc. each should be given in the spring before ticks are prevalent. Yearly series must be given to maintain adequate immunity. Information about the two vaccines available and their use may be obtained from the state health department of any state in which the disease is seen.

Tetanus Re-immunization

There has been some confusion concerning re-immunization against tetanus at time of injury. Ordinarily if there has been a tetanus booster injection within the past 36 months, a 0.5 cc. subcutaneous injection of the *toxoid* will give adequate protection. This is only true in those people who have kept up their immunizations and who have had the original injections or a booster injection within 3 years.

Children who have not had proper immunizations against tetanus should be given the *antitoxin* at time of injury. A sensitivity test must be made by injecting 1 drop of the solution intradermally or placing 1 drop in the conjunctival sac and waiting 15 minutes for interpretation. In the event of a large skin wheal at the site of subcutaneous injection, or marked conjunctival irritation, the antitoxin should not be given without desensitization procedures. When tests are negative, 1500 units of the antitoxin should be given subcutaneously and will protect the child from all but overwhelming tetanus infections for 7 days.

MISCELLANEOUS PROCEDURES

There are several miscellaneous procedures and bits of information useful in the office practice of pediatrics which are grouped in this section.

Circumcision

Office circumcision is relatively rare but may be easily done. The use of the Gomco clamp and Ross rings has made the procedure so simple and effective that there is little or no indication for using the old "cut and tie" method. There are, of course, a number of older physicians who decry the use of any mechanical gadget as ruining all our young men. They are both right and wrong. They are right to the extent that we should know how to do procedures without the gadgets before getting mechanical help. They are wrong in suggesting that we do without mechanical help which can better our work.

The most satisfactory circumcision device I have ever used is the Gomco clamp, which looks like this:

Full instructions for its use come with the apparatus but, to summarize briefly, the bell is placed under the foreskin (it frequently requires a dorsal slit to do this) and the clamp tightened against the edge of the bell. It is left in place for 5 to 10 minutes, which efficiently occludes the vessels. The foreskin is trimmed off with a knife and the clamp removed. The method is simple and efficient.

The Ross ring is a grooved ring which fits under the foreskin. A suture is tied tightly around the ring, fitting in the groove, which gives hemostasis and supplies a guide to amputation of excess tissues.

Circumcision by the cut and tie method is done like this: First, use a blunt probe to separate any adhesions between the glans and foreskin as shown on page 187. Now use a sharp knife to make a dorsal slit in the skin over the grooved probe, like this:

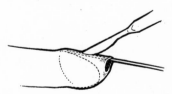

Amputate the foreskin about 5 to 10 mm. in front of the corona, like this:

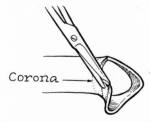

Corona —

Be careful not to engage the frenulum in the point of the scissors because of the danger of hemorrhage from the frenular artery. There are three relatively constant bleeders in the penile skin which, seen in cross section, are here:

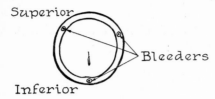

If readily seen they may either be clamped and tied or, better, included in the suture. When they are difficult to visualize, pull the skin back like this:

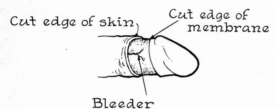

Now suture the skin and mucous membrane together loosely in several places. Some physicians leave the suture ends long and tie a rolled-up piece of petrolatum gauze in the suture.

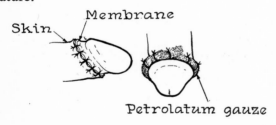

While it probably has little effect on the wound itself, the gauze may serve as a good "bumper" and offer some protection. In small children an excellent dressing may be made by unfolding a surgical flat and cutting a hole in it, like this:

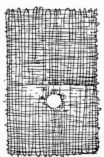

Then put a piece of half-inch tape at the fold, put the penis through the hole, and tape the dressing like this:

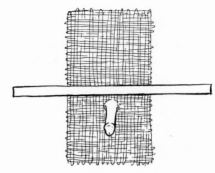

Allow the upper half of the surgical sponge to fall forward over the tape and you have anterior and posterior protection from a loose dressing that can be changed with ease.

Sutures ordinarily come out spontaneously within a few days but occasionally have to be removed. One precaution is absolutely necessary: There is a tendency to tie these sutures too tight. This *must* be avoided at all cost.

Administration of Subcutaneous Fluids

Sometimes it is necessary to administer subcutaneous fluids in the office. This is seldom necessary in older children but may be a matter of emergency in babies. Dissolve the contents of one ampule of hyaluronidase in 500 cc. of the fluid chosen. Two and a half per cent glucose may be used. Isotonic saline is usually far more satisfactory for emergency office use. Put 50 cc. of the chosen solution in a syringe and attach a 3 inch, 21 gauge needle to it. Pinch up a portion of the soft tissue of the back or legs. Insert the needle subcutaneously as far as it will go and start injecting the fluid like this:

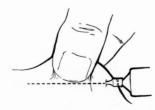

By moving the needle about you can usually get from 20 to 40 cc. in the area which the needle will reach. Inject the fluid while withdrawing the needle so that the subcutaneous tissues at the site of injection are widely distended.

Seldom will there be indication for office injection of more than 100 cc. of subcutaneous fluid for the infant. Fifty cc. will more often be adequate. This is not to say that 50 or 100 cc. represents an adequate fluid intake, but rather that most such procedures done in the office are merely preliminary to hospitalization where a more exact job of establishing fluid balance can be done.

Collection of Urine

A satisfactory urine specimen may be obtained from male babies by taping a loosely fitting test tube over the penis and allowing it to remain in place until the baby urinates. A specimen from girls may be procured by obtaining a small glass feeding trough as used in birdcages and taping it in place until urination occurs.

Determination of Osseous Development

It is sometimes useful to know the physiologic age of the child in order to compare it with the chronologic age. X-rays of the wrist are a reliable way of securing this information, for bony development follows a reasonably rigorous schedule in normal children. The time and order for appearance of the carpal bones are given in the following table and drawing. The table also includes data on other ossification centers.

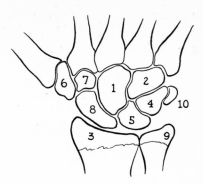

Age at Onset of Ossification

No. in Drawing	Bones Name	Boys Mean Yrs.	Boys Mean Mos.	Boys S.D.* Mos.	Girls Mean Yrs.	Girls Mean Mos.	Girls S.D.* Mos.
1	Capitate	0	2	2	0	2	2
2	Hamate	0	3	2	0	2	2
3	Distal epiphysis, radius	1	1	5	0	10	4
4	Triquetral	2	6	16	1	9	14
5	Lunate	3	6	19	2	10	13
6	Greater multangular	5	7	19	3	11	14
7	Lesser multangular	5	9	15	4	1	12
8	Navicular	5	6	15	4	3	12
9	Distal epiphysis, ulna	6	10	14	5	9	13
10	Pisiform	—	—	—	—	—	—
	Distal epiphysis, tibia	0	4	2	0	4	1
	Epiphysis of metacarpal II	1	6	5	1	0	3
	Proximal epiphysis, 5th finger	1	9	5	1	2	4
	Epiphysis of metacarpal V	2	2	7	1	4	5
	Distal epiphysis, 3d finger	2	4	6	1	6	4
	Proximal epiphysis, 1st finger	2	8	7	1	8	5
	Metatarsal II	2	10	7	2	0	5
	Middle epiphysis, 5th finger	3	3	10	1	10	7
	Distal epiphysis, metatarsal V	4	5	10	3	2	8

* Standard deviation, adjusted to nearest month. The range included between minus 1 and plus 1 standard deviation for any ossification center will usually include 68 per cent of a population of healthy children.

Adapted from Nelson, Waldo E.: Textbook of Pediatrics 6th ed. Philadelphia, W. B. Saunders Co., 1954.

Union of the epiphyses with the shaft of the bone offers a useful indication of developmental age during adolescence.

Age at Onset of Fusion of Epiphyses

	Boys	Girls
	Modal Skeletal Age, Years	Modal Skeletal Age, Years
Humerus, distal end	13.0–13.5	11.0–11.5
Great toe	14.0–14.5	12.5–13.0
Hand, distal phalanges	15.0–15.5	13.0–13.5
Tibial tuberosity	15.0–15.5	13.5–14.0
Greater trochanter of femur	15.5–16.0	14.0–14.5
Humerus, greater tuberosity	15.5–16.0	14.0–14.5

Adapted from Nelson, Waldo E.: Textbook of Pediatrics. 6th ed. Philadelphia, W. B. Saunders Co., 1954.

Written Instructions

After completing diagnosis and plans for therapy, one still has the problem of conveying the necessary instructions to the mother. We find that taking the time to write these instructions out down to the most minute detail, including dietary instructions, sick room care, etc., has done a great deal to bring satisfaction to our patients. The total time expended is less than two minutes except in the more complicated cases, and the achievement of better public relations as well as better medical care has been more than worth the trouble.

Section IX

MINOR SURGERY

Minor Surgery

Minor surgery is just that—minor. Every year we seem to make more and more of a production of surgical procedures. It is common sense to exercise in the operating room the utmost caution to protect the patient and to aid his convalescence, but the physician should probably have called to his attention rather frequently that surgery is a means to an end, not an end in itself. The object of both major and minor surgery is to insure and speed the convalescence of the patient. This end should never be forgotten. After accomplishment of this goal to the best of our ability, there enters the common-sense goal of economy of both time and money.

May I offer an example about "making a production"? Just the other day, I was reading in an old surgical text that had somehow slipped into my library. It was written about 1900 and, in talking about the hysterectomy, had essentially this to say: "The operation should be done most carefully, the surgeon locating principally the ureters. Next the organs to be removed are held up strongly and cut out with a pair of scissors, hemostasis being ignored until removal is complete because the vessels are small and easy to grasp with the fingers. After removal, arteries may be picked up and the hemostatic forceps applied. Ligatures are tied about those vessels which may conceivably bleed."

Isn't that amazing? I certainly wouldn't advocate such a procedure and I am glad that those of us today can do it a better way, but it does provide some interesting thinking and an excellent illustration of the subject which I would like to bring to your attention.

These old-time surgeons simply cut the uterine arteries, grasped them and tied them.

That is not very elegant, but have you ever seen a modern surgical team consisting of eight or ten people go into convulsions when a uterine artery is lost accidentally and make a major, heartrending emergency out of clamping it, instead of simply picking the tissue up in their fingers, exerting pressure to control bleeding and applying a tie? That is what I mean about making a production out of surgery.

In a modified way, the same thing is all too often done in the office minor surgery. Common sense is forgotten and the procedure itself becomes the goal to be accomplished according to priest-like ritual, with little consideration for the practical aspect of immediate and future results to the patient.

I cannot warn the practitioner too strongly against operating such a minor surgery in his office. I must apologize if I occasionally scoff at some of the minor surgery routines that have become ingrained in our art, and I hasten to say that it is entirely possible that I am wrong. The ideas and techniques described here are simply the ideas and techniques that have worked for me in my practice and that seem to work equally well for my colleagues.

PREPARATION FOR MINOR SURGERY

We doctors are great gadgeteers and many times our minor surgery setup is more elaborate than could ever conceivably be necessary. An entirely adequate minor surgery tray should consist of the following:

1. Knife and scissors.
2. Needle holder and needles.

3. Thumb forceps.
4. Three mosquito Kellys.
5. Three Allis clamps.
6. Several lengths of large size cotton thread or a better quality quilting thread for sutures.
7. For a retractor, I have found the Allport mastoid retractor, which is self-retaining, an excellent device.

There need be added only such special equipment that may be made necessary by the particular procedure to be undertaken.

The surgery itself should have facilities for local anesthesia and perhaps for minor inhalant anesthesia, such as the Duke inhaler for trichlorethylene, and an ether mask and ether. Oxygen should be available as well as certain drugs for revival, such as epinephrine and the ephedrine derivatives. Perhaps the most important feature of the minor surgery is adequate lighting. Two or three gooseneck lamps strategically placed will direct ample light into most incisions, but a word of caution is in order: Be sure not to try to work in the dark. Nothing is more difficult than to do adequate surgery without proper visualization.

The use of mild sedation in preparing the patient for operation is a wise precaution that is frequently overdone. One and a half grains of Nembutal or Seconal taken the night before operation and ¾ grain of the same drug given approximately 1 hour before the procedure starts will serve to allay anxiety and to provide a relaxed and cooperative patient. This preoperative sedation is particularly significant in children, who will cooperate much better if given a small dose of sedative 1 hour before the operation is scheduled. Excessive doses are not needed, and there is seldom reason for use of the opiates.

The actual field of operation should be shaved and scrubbed with green soap and water (or a detergent) for several minutes. It may then be rinsed with alcohol or ether. The application of mercurial antiseptics, iodine and other similar drugs serves no practical purpose that I can see except a psychological one of convincing the patient that he has been thoroughly prepared by dyeing the area of skin about the incision.

We have been preparing to discontinue entirely the current form of draping, which is both cumbersome and expensive and which probably does not protect the wound nearly as well as we should like to have it protected. In its stead, we plan to substitute plastic incise drapes. These are sterile sheets of polyethylene or similar plastic with a non-toxic glue covering one side of the center area of the sheet like this:

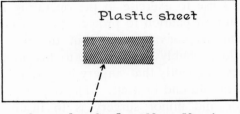

Area backed with adhesive

The adhesive area is placed over the site of the wound and fastened to the skin by pressing momentarily, and the rest of the drape is unfolded so as to cover the field entirely. Incision is then made through the drape, which is adherent to the sides of the wound and which offers as nearly perfect wound protection as we have been able to find.

Such a procedure is decidedly cheaper, quicker and more satisfactory than conventional drapes. I believe that this or something better will completely supplant cloth drapes within the next decade or so.

In most of our cases anesthesia is accomplished through use of local agents. We make wide use of field and regional blocks and have found such procedures to be far more widely useful than they are thought to be. For this reason I have included a section on anesthesia, which begins on page 323. I would certainly recommend the wider use of local agents and would suggest that a study of their uses is most important to the average practitioner.

Assistance is seldom needed in the performance of minor procedures but when necessary can usually be provided by any office employee. It is very seldom necessary to have an assistant scrubbed in with the surgeon, for most help required consists of simple retraction which may be done by reaching under the drapes and grasping the handle of an instrument, like this:

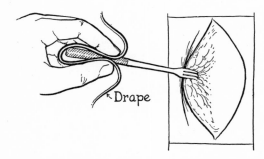

Drape

A series of three hooked weights which may be attached to the handle of any instrument is a very handy addition to the minor surgery and one that many of us are turning to for help. The recommended weights are 8 ounces, 1 pound, and 2 pounds. They look like this:

The preparation of the surgeon himself is a matter of some controversy. By all means a sterile or a recently laundered gown should be worn for these procedures. A mask is an essential part of the equipment and a cap probably should be worn.

As between a few bacteria and glove powder introduced into the wound, there is very little choice. Modern antibiotics have made some of our precautions against infection just a little bit ridiculous, although many surgeons have tended to become too careless since their introduction. Somewhere there exists a happy medium. While I know this would be frowned upon by some of my purist colleagues, by no means do I always use gloves for minor surgery. This depends somewhat on the part to be invaded. When the blood supply is good and the chances of infection seem rather remote, a thorough scrubbing of the hands may be all that is necessary. On the other hand,

in areas of slight blood supply where chances of infection are great, sterile precautions should be every bit as exacting as those used in the most complicated surgery.

To say this a different way, it is a little ridiculous to go through a tremendous ritual to open a superficial abscess when all one needs is a knife. But it is equally ridiculous to insert hundreds of bacteria deep in tissues that have poor blood supply and poor healing potentialities. This is a typical example of the profession forcing a ritual upon us all because a few ignorant physicians do not know when to take precautions and when not to. A good rule to follow is: when in doubt, use precise and exacting technique. Never break technique unless you are sure of yourself and the area that you propose to invade.

POSTOPERATIVE CARE

A great portion of the success any practitioner meets in his minor surgical cases depends upon the skill of the postoperative care offered. A good operation can be changed into a debacle by careless and inefficient treatment of the resulting wound. Once again, I feel that we have at times ritualized our postoperative care to the point of absolute foolishness.

Assuming an average wound, properly closed and properly dressed, certain principles are essential for adequate healing. The first and most important is to immobilize the wound as far as possible. This may be done by means of splints or by means of proper instruction to the patient about wound care. We make it a practice to see our patients' wounds the day following surgery and to cleanse them carefully with ordinary soap and water if the dressing is removed. Usually it is not.

In the interim between surgery and this first cleansing, the patient is supplied with a small amount of some drug to relieve the stinging sensation that usually follows such a wound. Ordinarily we prescribe four tablets containing aspirin, phenacetin and ¼ grain of codeine to be taken when necessary for pain. In addition, we give a teaspoonful of elixir of phenobarbital three or four times during the first 24 hours. A surprising number of people report that the tablets containing codeine are untouched when they return the first day.

In the case of wounds of an extremity, it is always wise to prescribe elevation of the involved extremity on a pillow or pillows to utilize the force of gravity for draining away any edema that may be present.

When the patient is seen 24 hours after the original surgery, we usually avoid removal of dressings and handling of the wound unless there is some specific reason to inspect it. If we feel that the wound should be seen, we remove the dressings and wash the incised area with soap and water. No other antiseptic of any kind is applied. If swelling is rather more than expected and sutures seem to be cutting, we remove them. To determine whether sutures are too tight, I insert the eye end of a needle underneath the suture and gently tug on it. There should be slack enough in the suture to allow slight pressure without disturbing the skin. In the event that the slightest movement of the suture causes movement of the whole wound with resultant pain, I feel that the sutures have been inserted too tightly and am prone to remove them. It is better to redo a suturing than to cause the patient inordinate pain and a severe scar by allowing sutures that are too tight to remain in place.

If there seems to be a large collection of fluid in the wound and if drainage is not entirely adequate, we insert a drain (a rubber band or strip of polyethylene) or loosen a suture at this first visit.

After the first day, dressings are kept as light as possible. In many places no dressing at all is needed and we vastly prefer this treatment if it seems feasible. The patient is encouraged to remove the dressing and wash away accumulated secretion with plain soap and water as often as the wound feels uncomfortable. He is warned against using any of the common antiseptics. This, of course, applies only to

relatively intelligent patients. There are some people who think that tobacco juice and cow dung are normal for a wound and who will not hesitate to apply them at every opportunity. When this type of person reports to our office with a need for minor surgery, we will do almost anything to keep him away from the wound, even going so far as to put it in a cast at times. This may sound facetious, but it is not. An intelligent person can use plain soap and water and clean dressings without the slightest danger. A stupid person who always knows better than the doctor is best kept as far away from his wound as possible.

If the wound is healing properly and presents no signs of complication at the first dressing, I usually instruct the patient to return in 3 days for another check. All but the most minor wounds are kept somewhat immobilized during this period. At the 3 day check, the wound is always visualized and in most cases the sutures are removed. Only in certain areas of the body is it necessary to leave sutures in 5 to 10 days. These areas will be discussed in the section on traumatic wounds. If there is a tendency for skin gaping after the sutures are removed, we use plastic tape to hold the edges together.

In a great many instances we have begun to do away with wound suturing altogether and to depend on pressure-sensitive polyethylene tape for closure. This seems to be the best method of closure we have tried. A word of warning: No commercial product is as yet available for this use. It is at present a research project. The technique is, however, too young to have been proven. It is mentioned here as a matter of interest and as an intriguing possibility which must be further explored before it is offered for general use.

Should the wound be progressing adequately on the second inspection, I usually write out instructions for its care and let the patient do the majority of his own after-care for the next week. We make a final inspection of the wound at about 10 days, at which time it is checked very carefully for any disturbances of regional function and arrangements are made to correct these disturbances if they are present.

Another word of warning: Adequacy of postoperative care is one of the most important parts of minor surgery. To neglect it is to invite a poor result.

Immobilization of Wounds

The immobilization of wounds has been previously mentioned. Here are some techniques which may be of assistance in achieving this. For wounds of the distal end of the fingers or thumb, use an old-fashioned hairpin covered on both sides and taped to the finger like this:

Cellophane tape

Hairpin covered with tape

For wounds of the base of the fingers or the hand or wrist an Unna paste dressing may be applied like this one, which is for a volar laceration at the base of the second finger:

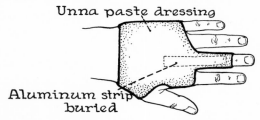

Unna paste dressing

Aluminum strip buried

If the wound involves the fleshy tissues of the lower or upper arm, adequate immobilization may usually be achieved by attaching the patient's wrist to his belt. A flannel cuff for the wrist may be made and pinned in place. The patient's belt is then inserted through a slit in the cuff or, in the case of a woman, pinned to the cuff, so that the arm is held like this:

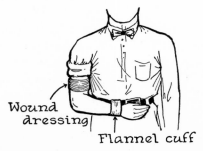

Wound dressing

Flannel cuff

A sling, of course, is just as adequate but some people object to the appearance and prefer the method that we have delineated.

Wounds of the shoulder region may be protected by means of a cardboard shoulder cap which is taped in place like this:

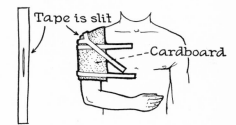

Tape is slit

Cardboard

The neck may be immobilized by a cardboard collar taped in place like this:

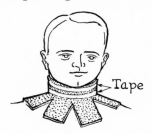

Tape

Since I am sure you will admit, as I have had to, that this contrivance looks rather silly, I would suggest that you cover it with bandage so that the patient looks horribly traumatized instead of simply nailed in a cardboard box. There is no medical reason for this but there is an ample social reason.

Wounds of the scalp do not need immobilizing and I have found it impossible thus far to immobilize wounds of the face adequately. Various methods, such as taping the area thoroughly and even incorporating applicator sticks in between layers of tape, seem to cause more annoyance than they do good. If anybody knows how to immobilize a facial wound on an outpatient basis I should like very much to hear of his method.

Wounds of the trunk seldom need extensive immobilization, which is a good thing, for this immobilization is difficult to maintain if the patient pursues his usual occupation. Severe wounds of the back will occasionally get well more quickly if a back brace is worn. The average patient is very resistant to this because of the expense involved, and I do not blame him.　Relative immobilization of the skin may be obtained like this: Lay two strips of tape on the table with the sticky side up and put three or four applicator sticks in this position:

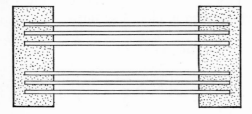

Now cover the ends of the applicator sticks with another strip of tape, sticky side down. Place this apparatus to either side of the wound and push it together so that the area of the wound is slightly bunched up or is given extra slack, like this:

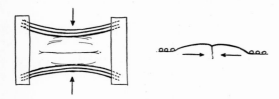

Now interweave tape over the applicator sticks and the dressing like this:

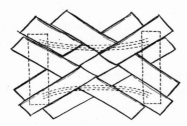

I do not think such a dressing is very valuable but at times it may help to gain immobilization for rapid healing.　It is certainly worth trying.

Wounds of the upper leg may be adequately splinted by fixing the knee with a simple posterior splint.　For some reason it is easy for a patient to remember not to make sudden movements that involve the hip joint but almost impossible for him to avoid flexion at the knee.

Boots will provide fairly good immobilization for wounds of the lower leg, and there is no better splint than a well fitting shoe for the foot.　If swelling is too great to allow the use of boots or a shoe, an Unna paste dressing will achieve the same thing.　The average office associate can learn rapidly the technique of applying Unna's paste.　It is a technique far too often neglected in the office of the average practitioner.

There are two complications seen in the postoperative period.　Both of them, fortunately, are getting increasingly rare.　The first, of course, is infection and the second is loss of tissue from inadequate blood supply.

Wound Infections

If good common sense is followed in the treatment of wounds, either surgical or traumatic, infection should seldom be seen.　An occasional case, however, seems inevitable until we have far more knowledge of wound contamination and wound healing than we have now.　The signs and symptoms of wound infection are far too well known to be delineated here but the treatment has changed so much in the past few years that we are perhaps justified in a review of the more common aspects.

To begin with, an excellent rule of thumb is: If in doubt, drain.　Unless done with exceeding care, wound drainage frequently adds to scarring, and many of us are justifiably loathe to drain unless it seems absolutely necessary.　This, of course, is good rather than bad, for it indicates our desire to protect the patient as much as possible and to avoid unsightly complications whenever we can.

Just recently, I have begun using small strips of polyethylene for drain material and I find it very satisfactory with a great deal less scarring than is usually caused by the more commonly used rubber drains.

There is no magic formula for when to insert a drain and when not to.　The practitioner must use the best judgment at his command and remember the dictum: *When in doubt, drain.*　This means at the operation, the first postoperative day, or the third or any other postoperative day.

There are four not uncommon types of wound infection, and the treatment of each differs somewhat from the other. The first and formerly the most dreaded is the acute streptococcic infection in which there is local redness and some tenderness of the wound, a tendency toward lymphangitis and frequently acute systemic manifestations. The wound discharge is usually thin, watery, and may be rather foul.

Fortunately, the streptococcus responds excellently well to the antibiotics and wound drainage seldom becomes a problem. If formation of pus seems heavy and if a tendency toward abscessing is indicated, then it is well to insert a drain. The practitioner should remember always that we see occasional cases of streptococcic infection that do not respond to antibiotic therapy. When this happens, wide incision done as soon as non-response is proven may be the best hope for the patient. Most of us have learned or will learn the hard way not to be too optimistic about the result from antibiotics alone.

Staphylococcic infections, which usually cause acute tenderness at the site of the wound with infrequent and mild systemic symptoms, do not respond as readily to exhibition of the antibiotics. The pus from such a wound is usually viscid, yellow material which may contain cheesy flakes. Immediate local drainage is by far the best treatment.

In certain areas the colon bacillus (*Escherichia coli*) may invade wounds with resultant copious discharge of foul-smelling pus and moderately acute local signs at the site of the wound. Systemic signs are not usually marked. While one may usually make an acute guess about the presence of colon bacilli from the area in which the infection occurs and from the general characteristics of the wound, the only sure differentiation between the colon bacillus and staphylococci is with the microscope. The colon bacillus responds moderately well to antibiotics but it has been my experience that drainage is usually the method of choice in treatment.

Pyocyaneus (*Pseudomonas aeruginosa*), the producer of green pus, is usually seen as a surface contaminant and fortunately seldom invades the deeper layers of wounds. I have never seen a case in which it could be proven that major systemic toxicity arose from invasion by pyocyanea. The micro-organism can, however, be as stubborn as a Missouri mule and hang on with a persistency quite unbelievable, delaying wound healing and annoying both doctor and patient by profuse production of pigment and discharge.

Pyocyaneus is quite sensitive to pH changes and does not live well in an acid medium. The old-fashioned vinegar water pack will serve to eliminate the organism in most cases. A tablespoonful of vinegar to a pint of water is quite adequate. A very much stronger solution applied to an abraded surface will probably serve not only to eliminate the germ but to eliminate return visits from the patient, for it is, of course, painful. Streptomycin and other antibiotics are also effective against pyocyaneus. I have not seen a case in which wound drainage seemed to be necessary to eliminate the organism.

The presence of wound infection makes proper immobilization doubly important. This should be done with great care and should be fully maintained until healing is progressing well.

Loss of Tissue

In certain wounds, particularly those caused by trauma, there is interference with the blood supply and consequent loss of tissue. This is usually apparent at the time the wound is seen, although in rare cases it may not make itself known until the first or second inspection of the wound. Débridement at the original visit will do much to eliminate this sloughing of tissue. When it occurs in spite of adequate preliminary débridement, certain precautions are necessary to avoid difficulty with the wound.

To begin with, the question of a secondary débridement always arises. Is it better to eliminate obviously dead tissue by performing a secondary minor surgical procedure, or should one be conservative until an absolute line of demarcation is present? One can find authorities in the field to argue both sides of the question. Purely as a personal opinion, I believe wounds like this get along better if left alone for a brief time and if adequate prophylaxis against infection is made a part of better routine care.

Dead tissue is, of course, a perfect culture medium for many kinds of bacteria and will most certainly become infected if not properly cared for. Exhibition of the antibiotics will frequently prevent spread of infection to viable tissue and careful cleansing of the wound area will often prevent infection of dead tissue. I believe that when tissue has become completely, obviously and finally non-viable, it may, in most cases, be removed.

There can be no hard and fast rule at present for determining the question of what to do with non-viable tissue. Remove it at the original operation if you can. If it turns up later, at least a short period of conservatism so that an exact line of demarcation may be established is not unwarranted.

DRESSINGS

The art of applying a nice-looking and effective dressing seems almost to be forgotten. Many times we practitioners simply throw a piece of gauze on and tape it in place. If for none other than aesthetic reasons one should attempt to apply a snug-fitting, well formed dressing that will serve the purpose for which it was intended.

For the average incised wound, the simplest of dressings will suffice. After the minor surgical procedure is finished, I usually wash the wound with soap and water and dry it, using sterile four by fours to absorb excess moisture and secretions. Then I cover the actual area of the wound with a sheet of plastic that has been sterilized by soaking it in alcohol and that is perforated over its entire surface to allow the escape of wound secretions. A sterile gauze bandage is placed on top of the plastic and the whole thing taped in place. The only value of polyethylene plastic is that it will allow the escape of wound secretions if perforated correctly and will make removal of the dressing a great deal easier on the patient. From a surgical standpoint, I can see no change in result whatsoever from its use. In hot weather, when there tends to be a great deal of sweating of the skin surfaces, I would not recommend the use of plastic dressings.

For the simple incised wound, this is usually all that is necessary. When the patient comes in for redressing of the wound, one removes the tape, lifts the bandage and snips with scissors any wound secretions that adhere between the plastic and the bandage. When this is done the sheet of plastic (we now use a polyethylene film) can usually be lifted off without pain to the patient and the wound cleansed with soap and water.

As I look back over several years' practice, I find that my dressings for simple incised wounds get progressively less and less elaborate. Unless located in such a place that contamination is almost inevitable, such as on a finger or wrist, I am more inclined to reduce the dressing to a bare minimum or occasionally to eliminate it altogether. It rather seems to me that facial wounds in particular do better if left open and if the patient is instructed to wash them regularly but gently with soap and water. This is a clinical impression and is backed up by no survey of any kind.

The rough wound with "dog ears," imperfect apposition of skin edges, and minute denuded areas may call for a more extensive dressing. The same technique is used but the wound is kept sealed off somewhat longer than the simple incised wound and may be protected for 24 hours or so with a single thickness of petrolatum gauze before a dry dressing is applied.

Removal of a dry dressing from an abrasion can be devilishly painful to the patient and I feel that if any dressing at all is used a *single thickness* of petrolatum gauze should be applied next to the abraded area and covered with a simple surgical gauze flat. Most abrasions seem to do just as well without dressings if adequately cleansed and if the patient is given instructions for care. To return to the same old story, frequent washing with soap and water seems about as good after-care as any agent or technique we have available at the present.

For areas from which the skin has been completely denuded the petrolatum gauze dressing should be used, covered by a sufficient number of surgical sponges (or sterile mechanic's waste) to allow pressure to be made on the surface of the wound. This pressure is achieved by application of elastic adhesive or a wrap-around elastic bandage.

Five per cent scarlet red ointment still seems a good stimulus to the growth of epithelium but it is messy almost beyond belief. The ointment stains clothing badly and will soak through the average bandage quite quickly. If it is used, it has been my practice to cover loosely the entire dressing with a sheet of cellophane held in place by strips of Scotch tape. This has no medical purpose at all but simply serves to protect the patient's clothing from the inroads of the ointment.

Profusely draining areas may require a dressing of maximum absorbency. One can easily be made by inserting a piece of cotton between two layers of gauze. The dressing probably should be applied directly to the wound surface without intervening petrolatum gauze or other such material. It may be removed by use of a peroxide solution to soften any adherent drainage.

Dressings for Specific Areas

The average scalp wound needs little or no dressing at all. A 4 by 4 inch gauze sponge cut down so that it is slightly bigger than the wound itself will usually stay in place if held firmly against the wound for a few minutes. If necessary, such a dressing may be held in place by an old stocking nightcap or the collegiate type skull cap which may be found at most ten-cent stores. Blood supply in the scalp is so profuse that healing takes place very quickly, so that dressings are needed only a short time.

Deep wounds that require a more extensive

dressing are usually best handled like this: Apply a simple gauze flat to the wound, then obtain a piece of surgical gauze approximately 20 inches square and drape it over the head like this:

With the gauze "drape" in place, put a roller bandage two turns around the head from forehead to occiput. Then on the third time around tuck the gauze upward under the roller bandage like this:

After several layers of gauze have been applied with the bandage constantly tucked up under, the dressing should look like this:

Now apply tape to hold the dressing in place, like this:

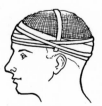

Dressings are seldom needed for the forehead and face. If they are applied, use the smallest dressing possible and stick it in place with adhesive or cellophane tape. Never attempt to put a dressing on the lower lip or chin. It merely serves as a receptacle to catch everything from soup to tobacco juice, and while some of these things may be salutary from the standpoint of wound healing, I am sure they are not all so. A saying of one of my professors has always intrigued me, and I should like to pass it along to you. It is this: "In certain areas of the face, cleanliness is next to godliness and sterility is next to impossible." Various elastic patch dressings are available and are vastly superior to anything that can be made in the office for dressing areas of the face and neck.

For profusely draining areas, particularly of the back of the neck, it may be necessary to apply a swathe dressing. The figure-of-eight is by far the most satisfactory. It looks like this:

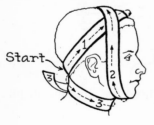

Occasionally one may need temporary compression of lesions of the lower face or jaw, in which case the Barton bandage is the best. It is applied like this:

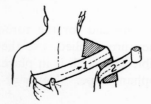

A dressing for the shoulder is best covered with a protective cardboard shoulder cap, which has been mentioned previously. The first layer of the spica bandage for the shoulder is applied like this:

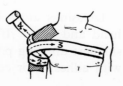

The axillary pad dressing is best made and applied like this:

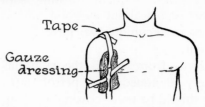

Dressings for conical areas such as the arms and legs are best done by first applying a gauze dressing held by adhesive in the conventional manner. Then apply a second layer of tape with the sticky side out, like this:

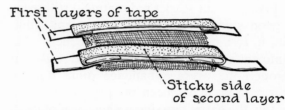

Now apply the roller bandage like this:

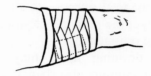

An elbow dressing is applied in this fashion:

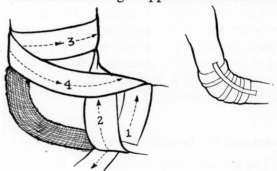

Dressings for the palmar or dorsal surfaces of the hand are applied like this:

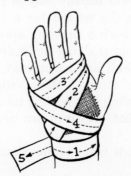

Finger-tip dressings may be made by cutting a 3 inch gauze compress as shown. The loose ends are then folded over each other on the finger tip.

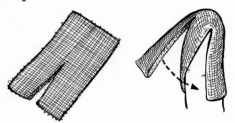

A gauze strip is used to make circular anchor turns around the base of the bandage and then folded back and forth over the finger tips:

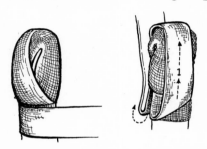

The bandage is then completed with additional circular turns and anchored with a longitudinal adhesive strip held in place by circular adhesive strips.

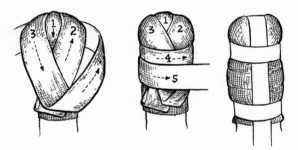

I have seen no breast dressing superior to a good brassiere under which gauze has been applied and held in place by strips of tape. A **U** of tape may be added to aid breast immobilization, like this:

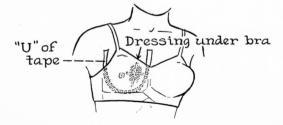

Dressings for the groin may be applied in figure-of-eight fashion, using elastic adhesive, like this:

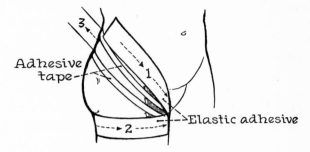

Knee dressings are done like this:

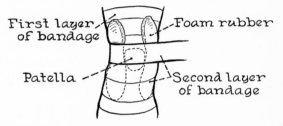

Dressings for the heel are made like this:

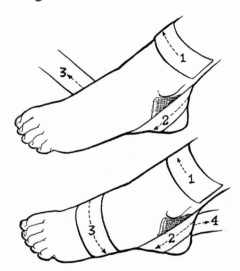

A loose shoe or elastic-sided house slipper will do more to keep a bulky dressing of the foot in proper position than any amount of taping that we have discovered.

For the perineal region, a vulvar pad may be applied, using the ordinary sanitary belt as a support. A **T** binder will, of course, do just as well to hold the dressing.

As a matter of prediction which may or may not be right, I would venture to say that plastics, both those now known and those as yet undiscovered, will begin to play a tremendous part in surgical dressings within the next few years. I look forward to a major change in many surgical techniques because of the advent of many new materials, and I am afraid that it is going to be a bit difficult for us physicians to keep up with the plastics and electronics engineers in the next few decades. I suppose it is plain nostalgia, but to think of the passing of our custom-shod minor surgery is a little painful, somewhat like the passing of the steam locomotives from the railroads. I should not be surprised, however, to see a change just as great as has been the change in the railroads.

THE GOOD RESULT

Now we come to a part of minor surgery that offers both theory and practical application. Most minor surgery we do gives very poor results. By the standards of 1890 we do well; in terms of the knowledge we have today, we do badly.

This is not to say that the prime object of minor surgery, which is to separate the patient from his disease, is not achieved, for it is. It is in the subsidiary fields of morbidity and functional impairment as well as cosmetic results that we fall down miserably. Sometimes I think we operate on the theory that, after all, the patient is going to get well, and if it takes him seven days instead of five, who is to say whether that is bad or good. The answer with regard to eradication of pathology is quite clear. Nobody is to say, for the pathology is eradicated.

From the standpoint of needless pain and needless scarring, I would make this challenge: The average physician can cut down on the morbidity of his minor surgery 50 per cent and can improve his cosmetic results 75 per cent by applying simple basic principles which are well known. Please let me make my point clear. I have not mentioned improving medical results. As far as eliminating pathology

is concerned, most of us do excellent minor surgery.

If you will bear with me, let's consider a typical wound and point out many of the places where our adherence to custom and our ignoring of simple principles add to morbidity and poor results functionally and cosmetically.

To begin with, it is almost impossible to kill a human being with the surgical tools at our command. Many times we draw the inference that because human tissues are difficult to kill, they are likewise difficult to injure. This, of course, is a fallacy. Gentleness in handling human tissue is the prime requisite of the physician who would do good surgery, either major or minor. There is little or no excuse to pull and tug on the tissue. A bigger incision will do far less damage than forceful retraction. If I may, I will give you a personal example. To retract the edges of small wounds I like to use an Allport mastoid retractor, which looks like this:

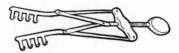

It is a fine little instrument that will open the wound edges widely and expose the tissue I wish to see without the necessity for an assistant. One day, however, one of my associates suggested to me that not only was I retracting wounds with the instrument but that I was literally tearing them open. I got a bit curious and decided to check the force used. I found that I could take two 32 pound cinder blocks sitting on the ground and push them aside by opening the Allport retractor between them.

I am no authority on mechanical forces, but common sense would certainly suggest that enough force to move 64 pounds of cinder block is too much force to be applied to any wound. We still use the retractor, for it is an excellent instrument, but it is used with a great deal more caution than formally.

It is the easiest thing in the world to get busy and start thinking about the pathology one is after and then suddenly wake up to the fact that one is pulling on the wound with all the force at his command, something that is inexcusable if a good result is desired.

To go on through our hypothetical wound, begin with the incision. Such a small thing as being sure that the skin incision is vertical is important. An angular skin incision disturbs the blood supply to the overhanging flap and also makes good opposition difficult:

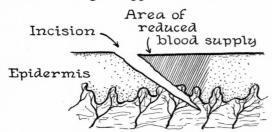

Dissection should be sharp wherever possible. Tearing tissues with a knife or a gauze-covered finger simply adds to the trauma and makes healing slower. It does not change the result from the standpoint of pathology but it may make a major change in morbidity and in functional and aesthetic results. An excellent example is the process of removing fat from fascia. The technique can be greatly speeded by use of the gauze-covered finger or by inserting the knife handle between the fat and the fascia and jerking it forcefully along the fascial planes, but functional results are much poorer. It has been known for many years that a clean cut heals more quickly than a torn, bruised surface.

The elimination of bleeding vessels is another point of contention. Catgut is, of course, a foreign substance and should be used in the smallest possible quantity. Also, the smallest size consistent with the strength desired should be utilized. I think you will agree with me that it seems somewhat ridiculous to see a tiny vessel half the size of a pencil lead tied with 0 catgut. To me this is somewhat analagous to hanging a mouse with a hawser.

Most such vessels may be caught in the point of a hemostatic forceps and held for a few minutes while the procedure goes forward. If this is done they will seldom need tying at all.

If the application of a tie should prove absolutely necessary, a single tie, i.e., "half a knot" of 4-0 or smaller plain catgut will suffice. As you know, catgut swells when it becomes moist and the single tie, except for large vessels, is usually entirely sufficient. I have used it for seven or eight years and cannot remember an instance of such a tie slipping.

Let me make the point clear—this is for small vessels. When dealing with larger arteries, all of us should be cautious in the extreme. A good point to remember is that a very fine suture doubled has just as much or more tensile strength as the larger suture and provides somewhat less foreign body reaction. To reiterate, the tying of small vessels is seldom, if ever, necessary. Larger vessels and those that bleed persistently may be tied with the finest of suture material.

Fatty tissue should be incised, not torn away, and annoying bits that get in the way may be removed with impunity. Fat re-forms rapidly and seldom, if ever, leaves a depression. This is not to say that an empty cavity may be left within the wound or that removal of large areas of fat is wise. I am talking about the tiny tags, smaller than a lead pencil eraser, that seem constantly to clutter up the field. Removal of two or three such tags has no consequence of note.

If the fascia must be penetrated it should be opened in the direction of its fibers regardless of the direction of the skin incision. Cross incision in fascia is not likely to heal as well and is much more difficult to close than longitudinal incision. Muscles should be separated at the fascial planes, if possible, and, if not, the fibers may be gently separated with the handle of the knife. If separation is not readily accomplished, it is better to incise than to traumatize.

Having achieved entrance into the tissue with a minimum of trauma and having accomplished the surgical purpose in the same manner, the problem of wound closure now becomes paramount. This is the most important of all minor surgical techniques aiming toward the good result.

Beginning with muscle tissue, this ordinarily need not have sutures if it has been separated or incised in the line of its fibers. Muscle sutures frequently do more harm than good and are best left out.

Closure of the fascia is often a point of error. This tissue is more or less replete with nerve endings and, in addition, it is a tissue that must heal properly if a good result is to be obtained. The common thing we do is to insert a suture and jerk the fascia together so that it is bunched up at the suture line. This not only provides pressure on the sensitive nerve endings, but if the suture is tied at all tightly it absolutely prohibits any blood supply to the line of healing in the immediate vicinity of the stitch. The purpose of a fascial suture is to hold the tissue gently in apposition, not to jerk it together.

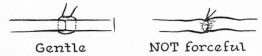

In many wounds, the fascia may be gently held by sutures and kept from moving out of place by proper immobilization of the wounded area. This is a tremendously important point in adequate wound healing and one which should be given consideration by all physicians.

In closing fatty tissues, no sutures are necessary but one wishes to be sure that no cavities are left within the wound. This is better accomplished by pressure from the outside than by foreign bodies on the inside.

Skin closure is a matter of great importance. Take a look at some of the scars resulting from minor surgical wounds. Look at them critically from the standpoint of appearance or from the standpoint of functional impairment following deposition of scar tissue. If this is not enough, look at the abdominal wounds of people who have had one or two major surgical operations. They almost appear to have been victims of a javelin thrust, rather than the skilled surgical scalpel. It would seem that the wound was nailed together rather than held together gently.

I will be the first to admit that such wounds are perfectly adequate from the standpoint of separating the patient from his pathology. I sometimes wonder, however, just what their aesthetic effect might be.

It is perfectly possible to close skin so that there is minimal scarring and marking. If this be done, there is not only aesthetic advantage but there is definite lowering of morbidity.

Most skin sutures turn out to be a means of bunching the incision together, which interferes with normal blood supply and normal apposition of tissues. A good substitute is careful application of the subcuticular suture with very fine plastic material such as dermalon. The actual method of use will be discussed in a later part of this section.

We have been exploring the use of pressure-sensitive polyethylene tapes for skin closure as a means of eliminating skin sutures and as a means of holding tissues in close apposition. This is by no means a technique ready for general use as yet, but it seems most promising.

Please look once more at the preceding pair of drawings, remembering that the fascial suture should merely hold the tissue in apposition, not jerk it together. How one does it is probably of no great importance as long as non-toxic material is used, but whether or not one does it can make the difference between a good and a poor result.

There is unquestionably a psychogenic element in our problems of minor surgery. A lot of us are prone to hate the word "psychogenic" because it seems only a polite way for others to explain our failures in terms of our own ignorance. I confess that I have been as short of patience as many other doctors. Nonetheless, whether we like it or not, certain truths are past intelligent question about the psychogenicity of many of the problems with which we deal. Without making any further effort to delve into the deeper aspects, we should perhaps discuss one or two of the simpler items regarding this. One of the most important is the question of pain. If the minor surgery patient begins his experience with painful stimuli, fear may dominate the whole procedure.

In other words, if the procedure starts with pain the patient has every right to fear that it will continue the same way and to build up a kind of inner resistance against the whole thing.

Probably one of the most important things that the successful practitioner of minor surgery does is to explain to his patients carefully exactly what he proposes to do and exactly what he expects to happen during the process of doing it. Pain should not come on without warning.

Another measure of great importance is the matter of adequate anesthesia. There is little or no reason to torture a patient in the performance of minor surgical procedures. In the section on anesthesia, there is a discussion of means and methods for providing complete obtundation of pain. This, in conjunction with explanation, will serve to put the majority of patients at ease. I have not enough training in psychiatry to explain why, but I know that a patient who is at ease seems to recover more quickly than one who is apprehensive and dreading every move the surgeon makes.

In summary, the good result depends on explanation and psychological preparation of the patient, adequate anesthesia, gentle handling of tissues, elimination of foreign bodies and dead spaces insofar as possible, and accurate apposition of tissues without undue pressure. Any of us can improve our minor surgery greatly by application of these general techniques.

TRAUMATIC WOUNDS IN GENERAL

Control of Hemorrhage

In most cases you may begin by taking off the tourniquet which some helpful soul has put on and which has served to increase the bleeding. As you know, it takes a tremendous amount of pressure to exclude arterial inflow into a limb but little pressure to occlude venous exit. Most tourniquets only serve to dam up venous flow without changing arterial inflow. In the great majority of wounds, bleeding will

promptly cease upon removal of the tourniquet and elevation.

There is very little bleeding that cannot be controlled by pressure at the site of the wound. Only rarely will one find it necessary to use the regional pressure points we all learned in anatomy to stop hemorrhage.

After removing the tourniquet, notice whether the blood is venous or arterial. If it is arterial, place your finger about ½ inch from the upper edge of the wound and make pressure both downward and proximally so as to evert the wound edge and stop the bleeding, like this:

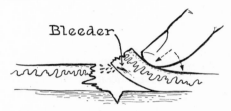

After sponging gently, reduce the downward pressure momentarily and notice where the blood spurts. In the usual case it is easy to place a clamp on the bleeding vessel if this is necessary. Never grasp about in a wound blindly. It will take less time and there will be less blood lost if you take a minute to visualize the bleeding point and clamp it.

In case an artery is bleeding under the edge of a wound, like this:

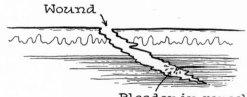

and you cannot reach it by the simple eversion procedure described, determine as accurately as you can where the blood is coming from and make an accessory incision to expose the bleeding vessel, like this:

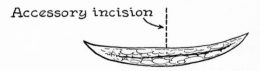

Venous bleeding may be located and stopped by the eversion method mentioned above, performed on the distal side of the wound only. Remember that it is entirely possible for an artery or a vein to back-bleed or to double back in its course so that venous blood comes from the proximal part of a wound or arterial from the distal. Control does not differ.

If venous bleeding is uncontrollable by this simple method, a firm pack in the angle of the wound is usually all that is necessary. Packs of oxidized cellulose have become deservedly popular.

Very rarely deep bleeding will be profuse and uncontrollable by the methods described. In these cases, the tourniquet or an emergency "on the spot" major surgical procedure may be necessary. One should try the tourniquet first if the wound is so located that this is possible. If not, never hesitate to perform any procedure necessary to reach and occlude a vessel that poses an immediate threat to life.

An occasional wound will be seen in which capillary hemorrhage is continuous and annoying. This may be controlled by hot, wet packs.

I cannot recall a half dozen cases in which direct pressure, either on the bleeding point or on a nearby pressure point, would not control peripheral bleeding. By all means, try the pressure method first. Control of bleeding in specific areas will be discussed in the sections devoted to those areas.

Cleansing

After hemorrhage has been stopped, the next problem is adequate cleansing of the traumatic wound. Profuse irrigation with sterile normal saline, followed by general washing with soap and water and still another irrigation, is as good as any method yet devised. If there are small particles adherent in the wound, which is frequently the case, they may be brushed away with an artist's paint brush of medium soft camel's hair. This is a good procedure to remember, for these tiny particles can be most annoying. It is probably best not to apply alcoholic solutions or the various antiseptics to the wound.

Exploration

When hemostasis and cleansing have been accomplished, wound exploration is next in order. Using a mouse-tooth forceps, pick up the edges of the wound by grasping the fat or subcutaneous tissue and lift them upward and outward so that you can see the deeper recesses.

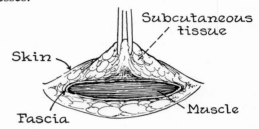

Gentle patting (not rubbing) with a small sterile surgical sponge will serve to get rid of excess fluid that prevents adequate visualization. In picking up a wound edge, do not grasp the unanesthetized skin or fascia. The structures have a great many nerve endings and are very sensitive. The subcutaneous tissues and fat, however, are only sparsely supplied with nerve endings and may usually be grasped without pain.

If there are clots remaining in the deeper portion of the wound, remove them with forceps. If these clots represent leakage from a bleeding point, you may expect more bleeding when you pull them away and you should be ready to visualize and grasp the bleeding point as it appears. Use pressure wherever possible in the control of bleeding rather than fighting the battle with hemostatic forceps. Even the smaller vessels are usually accompanied by nerve fibers and grasping them in the forceps may cause acute pain.

Be sure that you look into every nook and cranny of the wound and that you have good visualization of its true extent. Many traumatic wounds may be a great deal deeper than is apparent on casual inspection, and one should both recognize and be prepared to deal with injuries to the deeper structures.

Débridement

When control of hemorrhage, cleansing and

exploration have been accomplished, one should anesthetize the wound (see *Anesthesia* section) and prepare for any débridement that may be necessary.

The process of débridement is essentially the removing of devitalized tissue or tissues otherwise rendered useless from the wound. It is one of the difficult problems of minor surgery to know when to débride and how much tissue to remove. Depending on the nature and extent of the trauma, the process may extend from picking away a few tiny fragments of tissue up to and including excision of the whole wound. This latter process has something to recommend it in an occasional case and in all probability we utilize it too seldom.

In areas of free mobility where tissues may be shifted around almost at will, a jagged, dirty, contaminated wound may be boldly excised and closed smoothly like this:

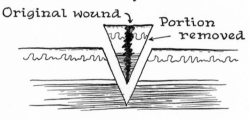

Original wound ⌐ Portion removed

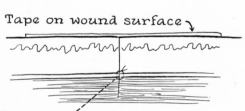

Tape on wound surface ⌐

Cotton suture in fascia

As long as tissues are not overstretched in the process of closure, healing will probably be more efficient and scarring will certainly be less if this process is followed occasionally. Several things should be kept in mind when one is making the determination as to whether or not to excise. If the tissue is not redundant and freely movable, excision may cause more difficulty in closure than it gains in making the wound smoother. Tissues should not be closed under tension if this can be at all avoided. If it would seem that excision is to be followed by closure under tension, then excision is best not practiced.

A second factor is the blood supply to the area. In areas of profuse blood supply, wound healing is much quicker and contamination seems to be insignificant, whereas in areas of poor blood supply, healing is slow at best and the slightest contamination may suddenly spring up into a rapidly spreading infection.

The decision of just what to débride in the average wound is not always easy. While there is no hard and fast rule, certain principles of physiology and pathology come heavily into play in making the decision. In the following paragraphs we will mention certain types of tissue and discuss briefly some of the factors that enter into the question of whether or not to remove them.

Skin. In general, the blood supply of the skin may be assumed to be more than adequate. It is certainly greater in some areas than in others, but one seldom sees an area of skin not sufficiently vascularized to support the healing processes.

In the jagged laceration there is always an area immediately next to the rent in the skin that seems to have lost its blood supply.

Area which loses blood supply

Whether this is due to the force applied at the time of injury, which crushes it and thereby kills the basal layers of the skin, or whether it is due to a thrombotic process of the small vessels, one is unable to say. If you will observe the healing in minor lacerations, however, you will find that this is usually present and you will also notice that it is extended if tight sutures are put in place. Check a typical jagged laceration at the end of the third day and notice the white, dead area of skin. Now look at an operative wound properly made and you will see that this area is absent or much reduced. It would stand to reason that such skin is permanently impaired at the time the physician first sees the laceration and that it serves no useful purpose.

Débridement of this area when the patient is first seen is an almost impossible problem.

To begin with, it seldom extends more than ¹⁄₁₆ inch from the edge of the wound, and until 24 to 48 hours after the laceration it is impossible to say how extensive it will be. It is, however, very probable that filling in of this area is one of the causes of more or less extensive scarring and the advocates of wound excision have a point here, for the area is removed in a typical excision.

Skin that is pale or blackened and obviously traumatized beyond any hope may be snipped away with a pair of scissors. It is, of course, wise to remember that skin has remarkable regenerative powers, and any tissue about which there is question should be left in the hope that some regeneration will take place.

It is my practice either to excise the small wound that promises a disfiguring scar or to limit skin débridement to that tissue which I am certain has no chance of regeneration.

Traumatic wounds frequently present undercut skin flaps that look something like this:

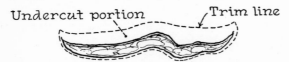

Unless these flaps are so thin as to be almost transparent they will usually reattach themselves and very little skin will be lost. Here, also, the distal margin of the undercut portion frequently has lost its blood supply so completely that it dies. If there is sufficient elasticity, it is good practice to trim the edges of the flap and the receptor area like this:

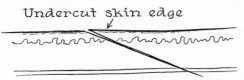

Before reattaching, be sure that the cut edges are vertical to the surface of the skin and that they fit snugly in apposition. This procedure, of course, should not be done unless tissues are mobile enough so that the flap may be anchored without tension.

Incidentally, the old technique of cutting away traumatized skin until bleeding from the deeper layers of the skin is obtained has not worked for me. In the same wound I have cut away a portion of skin until bleeding occurred, and right next to this sutured an area of skin that did not bleed. In every instance (but there have been only three or four) the undébrided skin healed more completely than would be indicated by the bleeding test. Here is what was done:

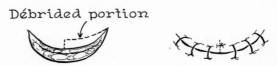

Fat. The fatty tissues may be removed almost at will. Since blood supply is not profuse, healing is not particularly rapid and persistent low-grade chronic infections extending down into the fatty tissues are not infrequently seen. It is far better to remove excess fat than to leave a tissue that is a potential troublemaker in the wound.

Fascia. Fascia should be conservatively handled and a very minimum amount removed. The tissue is seldom redundant and is most difficult to close if any but the smallest amount is excised. When possible, excision of fascia should be done in the form of an ellipse that runs parallel with the direction of fibers of the fascia itself, like this:

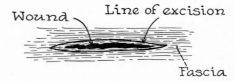

It is better to leave fascia unclosed than to close it under extreme tension.

A transverse wound of the fascial tissues should be closed gently with small suture material and should be held in place by proper positioning of the tissues so that the fascia edges have maximum slackness. As an example, take a wound of the arm that looks like this:

Observe that the edges of the fascia are nearly in apposition when the arm is flexed, but on extension the edges are pulled apart like this:

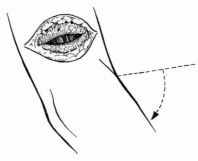

Repair should be accomplished with the arm in a position of flexion, using as little tension on the sutures as possible so that the suture line, when finished, looks like this:

Quite obviously this suture line will not hold the fascia in position if the arm is used or if it be held in extension. Position may be maintained by splinting the arm in flexion and allowing the sutures to serve only to hold the fascia in edge-to-edge apposition for proper healing.

The problem of fascial grafts has often been discussed. Since I have had no experience with these grafts any discussion would be fruitless. Many of us who do not use the fascial grafts seem to get results roughly comparable to the results of those who do, and ordinarily I would not advocate their use. This, however, is the opinion of a person who lacks experience in this technique.

Muscle. Muscle tissue is usually amply supplied with blood and unless crushed beyond repair, it reestablishes continuity quickly. The old triumvirate for establishing muscle viability—(1) color, (2) contractivity, and (3) bleeding on incision—is not entirely accurate as a means of establishing what tissue will heal and what should be removed. I have usually used the criterion of bleeding on incision to determine the muscle viability. Since the average laceration amenable to minor

surgery does not crush great amounts of muscle tissue and therefore requires removal of rather small portions, this criterion is entirely adequate. Unless the traumatized area is exceedingly large, one may cut away muscle with impunity until capillary bleeding indicates viability.

Bone. The removal of traumatized bone is determined more by contamination than by viability. Clean bone chips in all probability contain some viable cells and certainly promote healing. Grossly contaminated, crushed bone, on the other hand, is a source of infection and is probably better removed.

The periosteum is quite another matter. Every fragment that can be identified as periosteum and that seems to have even the remotest chance of living should be left in place. Even badly bruised periosteal tissue will frequently provide a focus of bone regeneration that may be of inestimable service as the wound heals.

Joint Capsules. The fibrous tissue of the joint capsules has a profuse blood supply and regeneration is remarkably quick and efficient. Unless literally shredded, this tissue will usually regenerate and form adequate protection for the joint itself.

As a general guide to the healing of tissues and, therefore, some help in determining the extent of débridement, this chart shows the areas of the body in which healing may be expected to be relatively quick, and also the areas of relatively small blood supply or areas which represent potential danger points from the standpoint of secondary infection.

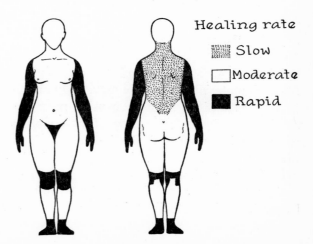

One other problem that occasionally comes up in minor surgery is the débridement or amputation of areas rendered permanently ischemic. A good example is the frostbitten toe that shows dry gangrene at first without a clear line of demarcation. I believe that the utmost of conservatism should be practiced in these cases, for in most instances self-amputation of the tissues will occur with a perfect line between living and diseased tissues, whereas any line we set up must be subject to the fallacies inherent in our own judgment. Unless there is some imperative reason for surgery, it is best in such cases to put the knife away.

Closure of Wounds

The closure of traumatic wounds is an art as old as the art of medicine itself. During recorded periods of time, countless thousands of materials have been offered as a means of coapting wound edges. Even now, the number and variety of suture materials is almost unlimited and the search goes on for better and better materials to use in wound closure.

The usual story is too many sutures of too big suture material tied too tightly. Sutures are a necessary evil, not an end unto themselves. They represent one way of holding wound edges together, and actually not a very good way. Many times they are the best material at hand to accomplish this purpose. If you will keep firmly in mind, however, that sutures are undesirable and should be used only when they *must* be used, your care of traumatic wounds will improve tremendously.

It rather appears that some sort of bonding material that attaches itself to the skin and coapts wound edges by gentle pressure will be the best answer to this problem of suturing. No such material is available now. On an experimental basis, I have been using pressure-sensitive polyethylene tape for coapting wounds with a great deal of success. It is probable that a commercial product will be available before long.

As a second choice, the tape butterfly may be used. It is made like this:

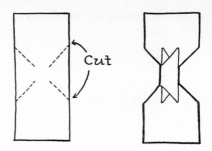

Still another possibility is the suturing together of folded edges of tape that has been applied to each side of the wound. The technique is this:

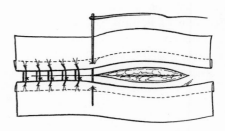

If sutures must be inserted into the tissues, I prefer plain white cotton "dime store" thread to any other material currently available. This has the advantage of economy as well as a low level of tissue reaction.

Various plastic sutures, such as Dermalon, are excellent for subcutaneous tissues. Catgut, I feel, is something that should be used as little as possible but that, in occasional instances, has values that are irreplaceable by any other suture material.

There is no objection to silk or to other material. After all, the statistical differences of results with different sutures are minute and the preference of the physician may certainly tip the scales in favor of any of those in common use.

Turning to the stitch itself, most surgery texts list a bewildering array of techniques for inserting sutures that are usually not needed to begin with. Everything from knit one and purl two to the triple-threat little Abner special for inverting everted sutures is gone into in amazing and confusing detail. The great majority of all minor surgery can be well accomplished by using three types of stitches. The first is the plain "through and through and be damned to it" stitch, which should look like this:

The second is the running lock stitch, which looks like this:

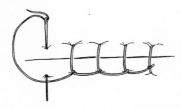

The third is the everting suture, which is done like this:

Quite frequently one will use the subcuticular suture, which is very important and too seldom used. In spite of this, it is an excellent technique for the closure of minor (or major) lacerations and leaves a highly desirable cosmetic result. To accomplish it, one uses a plastic suture such as Dermalon and bites from side to side, literally threading the wound on a string. A more complete discussion of the method is found on page 222.

Muscle. There are those who say that muscle need not be closed at all unless the muscle belly is completely severed. Although they seem to get splendid results, I have not used the technique. We usually suture any deep laceration in the muscle belly with the thought that whether or not anything is accomplished toward healing, at least we have eliminated dead space in the wound.

This is one of the few places in the body that heavy catgut such as 0 seems to be of definite use. The stitch enters the muscle belly about ½ inch above or below the site of the laceration and the needle is so inserted that it comes out at the very base of the laceration, like this:

It is then reinserted at the base of the laceration on the other side and made to emerge approximately ½ inch from the edge, so that the final line of sutures looks like this:

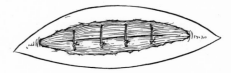

No attempt is made to tie the sutures until all are placed. The muscle is then put into position of maximal relaxation and the sutures are tied.

This technique, of course, applies only to diagonal lacerations or those at right angles to the fibers. Longitudinal or near longitudinal lacerations in muscles need not be closed at all.

Fascia. Longitudinal lacerations in fascia may be quite satisfactorily closed by a *very loose* running lock stitch using cotton suture. The final suture line should look like this:

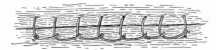

Lacerations which cut across the fascial fibers are best closed by means of individually inserted sutures doubled.

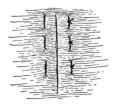

The stitches are inserted but are not tied. After all stitches are in place, maximal relaxation of the fascia is obtained and the sutures are tied *without pulling them tight*. If the physician will conceive in his own mind that the purpose of these stitches is to allow apposition of the cut edges of the fascia, not to overcome strain that may be put on the wound, his results will be much better. Avoidance of strain is secured by proper splinting.

Fat. The best way to close fat is not to.

Skin. Skin closure is one of the most important procedures in minor surgery and one that many of us frequently neglect. To begin with, one must understand that it is better not to suture if this can possibly be avoided. Various taping methods are far superior when applicable, and in a great many instances a simple pressure bandage will hold the skin in much better apposition than can be obtained with any known suture. If you will permit me to make a shocking guess, I would say that one out of every ten wounds that are sutured really need it.

If you feel that sutures are necessary, the subcuticular method is the method of choice if applicable. Use small Dermalon and tie several knots in the very end of the suture. Insert the needle through normal skin about 3 mm. from one angle of the wound so that the point emerges in the wound through the heavy subcuticular tissue. Now pick up and evert one edge of the wound immediately next to the area where the suture has emerged and place another stitch in the subcuticular tissue. It is not necessary that the needle penetrate more than approximately 1/16 inch from the edge of the wound. Grasp the tissue on the opposite side and place another stitch.

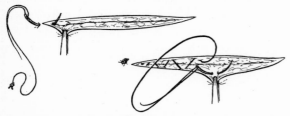

Continue on alternate sides until the distal end of the wound is reached.

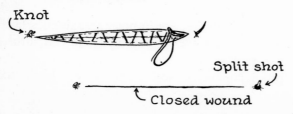

Have prepared a split shot. These may either be purchased through a surgical supply house or one may obtain a package of lead BB's and have the office girl partially split them with a pocket knife. Pick up the free end of the suture and alternately pull it taut and loosen it as you manipulate the wound edges until perfect apposition is obtained. Maintaining the same tension, place a split shot on the suture and squeeze it together so that it grasps the Dermalon firmly. As a tip, do not use a good clamp to squeeze the shot together. It won't be a good clamp very long. The best tool for the purpose is a pair of needle-nose pliers. In any of the areas of relatively good healing the sutures may be removed in 3 or 4 days; if the wound lies in an area where healing is somewhat slow, 5 to 7 days.

Should none of the techniques mentioned above be applicable, one may be forced to use the common method of suturing. Plain suturing is easy but it has one disadvantage in that it inverts skin edges. If skin sutures are necessary, the everting sutures should be applied, but one caution is quite important: When this suture is used, one should be careful to tie it rather loosely and to manipulate the skin edges so that proper apposition is obtained. When tied tightly the suture everts the edges and is in no way superior to ordinary stitching.

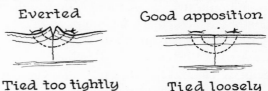

It is exasperating to remove sutures when the cut ends have been embedded in wound secretions and cannot be found. To avoid this, have the suture ends about 2 inches long and tape them to one side of the wound, like this:

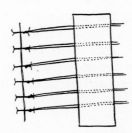

Bleeding after Closure

Only rarely do we see continued loss of blood after adequate wound closure. This does, however, sometimes happen and must be considered as a rare surgical complication. External bleeding, i.e., bleeding through the suture line, is usually due to the freeing of a thrombus from the end of a small artery.

Place a small gauze flat over the wound and apply steady pressure for 5 minutes without releasing pressure during this interval. Then remove the sponge and check whether bleeding has ceased. It may be several minutes before you can be absolutely certain that there is no further leakage.

If everything appears all right at this time, put a tight pressure dressing on the wound and caution the patient to report to you by telephone any bleeding which seeps through the dressing. To avoid being waked up half a dozen times at night, point out that discoloration of the dressing itself is not true seepage. He should only call you when blood actually drips from the dressing.

In very rare cases bleeding of this nature will sometimes be quite persistent. Should it prove so, the best course is to remove the sutures, enter the wound and explore it for the offending vessel. When found, it may be clamped securely for 8 to 10 minutes and then released to see if more bleeding occurs. If it does, time will be saved by tying the vessel.

One sees presistent oozing through the suture line much more often than active bleeding. A pressure dressing is usually all that will be needed to control this type of hemorrhage.

Internal bleeding with formation of a hematoma is a much more difficult lesion to handle properly. When a hematoma forms beneath the suture line, release one suture, if necessary, and apply pressure from the edges downward and inward like this:

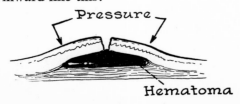

Express as much of the blood as you can. If there are clots that seem too big to pass through the opening you have devised, do not hesitate to remove another stitch. When one allows a hematoma to remain undisturbed he courts disaster from several possible sources. The extravasated blood is an excellent culture medium and may serve as such for any stray bacteria that wander into it. Hematomas are not always completely absorbed and may leave areas of fibrosis after their resolution. This fibrosis may impair function to some degree.

After the hematoma has been evacuated be sure to put a firm dressing over the wound and instruct the patient to inspect it regularly for signs of leakage or swelling.

Needle aspiration of a hematoma through the incision has been advocated and may work fairly well. I have had no experience with the procedure and so cannot say.

PERFORATING WOUNDS

These wounds are best left alone unless grossly contaminated or caused by a high-velocity missile. In the great majority of cases seen by us practitioners, the best single treatment is to omit all minor surgical procedures. Exhibit the antibiotics and give either tetanus antitoxin or a booster dose of the toxoid, whichever may be indicated.

Should you feel that enough extraneous material has been driven deep into the tissues to warrant wide incision, be sure to make the incision ample.

As an illustration, we will assume that a filthy nail has been driven deep into the tissue of the forearm. When the patient reports to the office, he states that the nail came from a grossly contaminated area and that he is afraid of infection. You concur in his opinion.

In this hypothetical case a deep cruciate incision would not be out of order.

I am sure you will agree with me that there are very few cases that need such heroic cleansing and débridement. However, should one come your way, do not hesitate to do the procedure.

Perforating wounds of this nature, even if not operated upon, should be followed carefully for at least 72 hours. Redness, tenderness and difficulty in obtaining proper function of the part involved are excellent signs of early infection. Most of these infections will respond readily to the antibiotics, but occasionally one will have to be drained surgically.

Perforating wounds by a high-velocity missile are quite another story. The tremendous impact of such a missile sends lines of force through the tissue with resulting momentary cavitation that follows the missile through the tissue, like this:

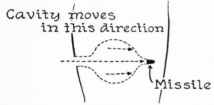

Tissues for several inches on either side of the missile tract may be severely damaged or completely killed with little outside evidence of damage.

These tracts should be opened widely and a débridement of nonviable tissue performed. Frequently this is a job for the hospital but you may have to do it in the minor surgery because of emergency circumstances.

Fortunately, in civilian life we see very few injuries by high-velocity missiles. The high-power, high-speed rifle bullet is the most common, although certain industrial injuries are very similar.

If there is question, always incise enough to look at the tract and surrounding tissue before dismissing the injury as minor.

ABRASIONS AND BRUSH BURNS

These exquisitely painful injuries should be packed for a few minutes with a surface anesthetic before procedures are undertaken. A good method is to dip a sterile 4 by 4 inch surgical sponge in 2 per cent Pontocaine and wring it out thoroughly. Then place it on the abrasion and leave it in place for at least 5 minutes—10 minutes may be better. During this time much of the pain and stinging will leave and the patient is in a much more amiable mood for definitive treatment procedures. Topical application of Cyclaine by this method holds some promise, although it has not been sufficiently explored as yet.

After anesthesia is effected, wash the abrasion with plain castile soap and water. If you are unable to remove the dirt particles by this method, use a soft brush and scrub the abraded area *gently*. This will remove all but the most persistent particles and these can frequently be picked away by using the point of a knife.

When these procedures are finished, there will probably be some oozing from the wound, which should be stopped. A hot wet pack, if available, will do this; if not, simply press a sterile surgical gauze against the wound.

After the oozing has stopped, you may turn to the problem of dressing. It has been my practice to put no dressing at all on these abrasions unless they are located in a spot where friction with other substances or tissues may occur. In this instance, one thickness of petrolatum gauze covered with a surgical sponge is all that is necessary.

The dressing should be changed the second or third day and petrolatum gauze left out of the new covering. As a matter of policy no part should be covered with petrolatum gauze for more than 24 to 36 hours at a time unless there exists an excellent reason for continuing this type of dressing. Off hand, I can think of no excellent reason.

CLOSED WOUNDS

These sound as if they should be simple, straightforward and amenable to treatment by any method. After all, a bump is just a bump and should be ignored as much as possible.

That's a good theory but unfortunately it isn't true. Some of the most serious injuries we see in minor surgery are those that show little or no external evidence of damage. You can swat a human cell and kill it just as you can swat and kill a fly. True enough, human cells are a bit better protected, but severe contusions can result in widespread areas of necrosis with consequent absorption of toxic products and fibrous repair which may diminish function. They should not be ignored.

Specific contusions will be discussed later in this section under the surgery of specific regions, but one or two general problems may well be mentioned here. The first and most important is the obvious value of splinting a contused area. Just as any other wound, the contusion will heal better if not kept actively motile. This healing process is rapid except in the most severe contusional injuries, and immobilization for only a very brief time will often be all that is needed.

The second problem is whether or not to enter surgically a severely contused area. Let me make it clear that we are speaking of the severe contusion. Minor contusions do not even come to question, for they should *not* be invaded. When a crushing injury has been severe enough to give evidence of much dead tissue, at times there may be reason for surgical invasion and débridement. Let us discuss a hypothetical example. Suppose a tree falls on a woodcutter's leg, landing in such fashion that a severe contusion is sustained. X-ray studies indicate that the bones are not broken, but the patient complains of exquisite pain. There are swelling and tenseness in the leg and a definite, progressive diminution in the pulse felt behind the internal malleolus. This grows worse so that the patient requires huge doses of morphine for pain relief and constantly importunes the doctors to "do something."

Here we have a nice problem that could be argued for months or possibly even generations by surgical experts with much right on either side. My own impression is that prompt incision of fascia to relieve tension is often greatly beneficial. Do it like this:

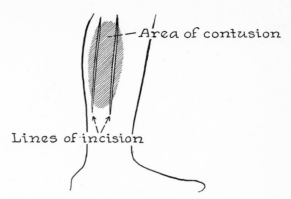

Through this incision, known hematomas can be aspirated or can be probed for with a needle. If tissue in the wound is obviously dead it may be removed, although I have never seen a case of similar injury in which I could be absolutely certain that the tissue was completely dead.

It certainly requires nice judgment to say when such a procedure should be attempted and when not. As a general rule it is best to be exceedingly conservative in performing such an operation. The operation itself is trivial, but the consequences in terms of infection can be disastrous.

BLISTERS

Going now from the sublime to the ridiculous, let's take a moment to consider the common, ordinary, household blister. The best treatment is to divert the patient's attention and let the blister strictly alone. If you are forced to open it, make a small incision at the very side, like this:

Evacuate the fluid and put a small pressure dressing on. The dressing has two utilitarian purposes. The first is to exert enough pressure to close the opening, which should not have been made at all, and the second is to hide the blister from the patient so that he will not pick off the dead skin and leave a raw, tender, weeping surface exposed. If the blister occurs at a pressure point, such as the heel where it comes in contact with the shoe, it should be protected with a felt ring, like this:

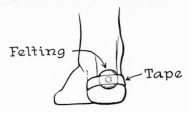

INJURIES TO NERVES

Superficial nerves are sometimes cut or bruised and are seen often in the minor surgery.

I know of absolutely no treatment that is effective for the bruised nerve. Immobilization probably speeds recovery, but even that cannot be made as a certain statement. Incised wounds of nerves, on the other hand, are amenable to immediate treatment and one may usually expect excellent results.

When a nerve is partially cut, use the smallest cotton sewing thread you have and the smallest round needle to put in a half ring of small sutures like this:

The stitches penetrate the nerve sheath only and are not put deep into the substance of the nerve. Notice, too, that they are close together but are tied loosely so that the nerve fibers are held together but not cramped together, like this:

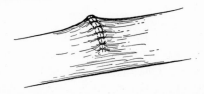

Immobilization in the position in which the least possible stretch is put on the repaired nerve should be continued for several weeks.

When a nerve is completely severed, approximation becomes even more difficult. If the severed ends are cut cleanly, reapposition

is made somewhat easier. Begin by picking up the ends, using a very small tooth forceps and grasping only the nerve sheath. Pick it up like this:

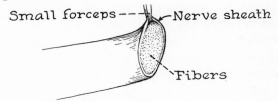

You will notice that few nerves are exactly round. There is usually some aberration in the circular shape that will allow you to tell which parts of the proximal sheath join to the particular parts of the distal sheath. It is important to get the nerves back together as exactly in position as possible.

For example, if this is a cleanly severed nerve with a tiny tag of nerve sheath, notice the place where the tag fits, and *be sure* to suture the nerve in this position:

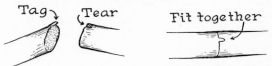

When the position is established take four stay sutures like this:

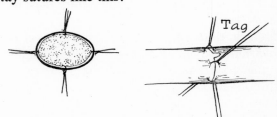

Use them to turn the nerve gently and hold it in place while the other sutures are put in. As mentioned above, try to put the stitches in the nerve sheath rather than into the substance of the nerve itself.

If the severed nerve has not only been cut but has also been severely traumatized so that it presents ragged and bruised edges, put in two "holding" stay sutures like this:

Use them to mark the proper position for apposition and to hold the nerve ends as well. Now put a sterile tongue blade in the wound and lay the nerve on it. Use a new, sterile razor blade to cut it off square like this:

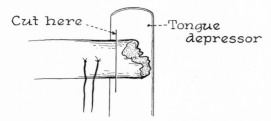

The two stay sutures, having been placed in the proper area of the arc to begin with, now show you which portions of the nerve are to be sewn in apposition, like this:

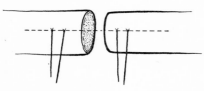

Along a straight line drawn between the two stay sutures insert one suture. Leave the ends long. Place another suture exactly opposite to this and leave the ends of it long. Now place two more stitches bisecting the arc so that the result looks like this:

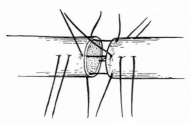

Now sew the nerve exactly as recommended before and place the extremity in a splint or cast, holding the position that allows maximum relaxation of nerve fibers. This should be maintained for 2 to 3 weeks.

After such a repair is done, be sure to warn the patient that there are a certain number of failures and that from 6 months to 2 years may elapse before maximum function returns.

If the nerve is so badly traumatized that a segment of more than 1 or 2 cm. must be removed, it is best to refer the case to a person who has special training for handling such problems. Nerve grafts are completely out of the purview of the practitioner, unless he has expert advice beforehand and consultation during and after the procedure.

INJURIES TO BLOOD VESSELS

Injuries to major vessels are, of course, better treated in the hospital. Since they are sometimes seen in the minor surgery and under such circumstances that transportation to a hospital is out of the question, the practitioner should be prepared to deal with them. Vessel anastomosis is not difficult at all. The vessel is seized in rubber-shod clamps above and below the proposed site of anastomosis like this:

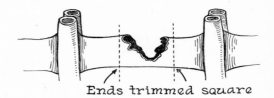

Ends trimmed square

The ends are trimmed square.

A small sharp needle is threaded with 000 silk (although I do not see why fine cotton would not work as well or better) and the vessel is sutured with many small close sutures. A running suture or interrupted sutures are permissible.

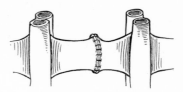

If, when first seen, one of the larger vessels has a jagged hole in it, closure of the hole is usually a waste of time. Best results are obtained if the vessel is cut smoothly across between rubber-shod clamps and anastomosed. When part of a vessel is torn away a nearby vein may be removed and sutured in place like this:

Vein graft

Of course, none of these procedures should be done in the minor surgery except in cases of emergency. When the patient can get to a hospital within a very few minutes, there is no reason even to consider such tasks. On the other hand, if you are so located that several hours must elapse before hospitalization is possible, it is sometimes much better to do the procedure on the spot than to make the loss of an extremity almost certain.

I know there are many fine surgeons who will take violent issue with this statement. It may be true that we family physicians are not very smart, but for my own part I would rather have a half-wit tie off a vessel and save my life than bleed to death on the way to the finest physician that ever lived. The same, I think, would apply to an anastomosis. I would certainly rather have a fellow not quite so bright do a poor anastomosis and save my leg than lose my leg because of delay entailed in getting to a highly qualified individual.

Here's another nickel's worth of philosophy. I think we too often forget in medicine that there are other factors involved over and above medical qualifications. Certain practical aspects of any situation crop up and may have to be taken into account. Let me give you an example. When I was a sophomore in medical school, we were rather pointedly forbidden to touch a knife or any sort of instrument to patients without a qualified physician standing by. I remember one night when I was in the emergency room watching a two month old baby die for lack of a tracheotomy. I knew perfectly well that I could do a tracheotomy and that somebody had better do one, but I was afraid of "what people would say" and of the staff physicians. So I stood by and let the baby die while we waited for the resident, who got there some 20 minutes later (it was not his fault, he got there as quickly as he could).

As long as I live I am never going to repeat that situation. If something has to be done and I can't find anyone better than I am to do it, then I am going to do it and let the chips fall where they may. There are, of course, physicians who would criticize that attitude and who will criticize you if you take such an attitude. Such physicians are not worthy of notice.

SURGICAL INFECTIONS IN GENERAL

Since the advent of the antibiotics, surgical infections are growing progressively more rare. Concurrently, their treatment is becoming easier and surer and the practitioner is progressively less frightened of the possible outcome.

One result of all this has been the question whether antibiotics should be administered routinely when minor surgery is done. There are staunch advocates on both sides of the question and, as usual, the truth probably lies some place in the middle ground. If there seems to be danger of contamination or if, in your opinion, the wound is already contaminated, by all means start immediately the administration of one of the antibiotics, preferably penicillin. The most common error is to give it in insufficient dosages and for an insufficient period of time. Routinely to "give that man a shot of penicillin" probably does more harm than good, for a single dose of 300,000 units is often not enough to protect against any type of wound contamination which may be present. If you give the drug at all, give at least three daily doses of 300,000 units or a single dose of 600,000 *or more* units of one of the long-acting products such as Bicillin.

When the wound is obviously clean and when your technique has been such that contamination is extremely doubtful, there is little or no reason for antibiotic administration.

Should a patient report with an obviously infected wound, the essential office procedures are immobilization and drainage if indicated. Excessive motility only serves to spread a surgical infection. Body defenses are at first thin and tenuous and may be broken down easily. Excessive motion of the part (and sometimes any motion of the part) will serve to aid this breakdown, which makes spread of infection more likely.

There are two indications for drainage. The most frequently seen is the formation of pus or a tendency of the wound to abscess. This is indicated by fluctuation under the palpating fingers. Incision should be made directly into the pocket of pus and not widened beyond the edges of the abscess. Do it like this: Anesthetize the skin over the area to be incised and wait 5 minutes. Now attach two towel clips to the skin on each side of the proposed incision, pull sharply upward, and incise between the two clips like this:

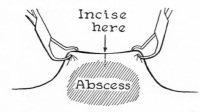

In this manner you will avoid applying pressure on the deep edges, which is excruciatingly painful.

The second kind of post-surgical infection that requires wide drainage is the rapidly spreading, burrowing infection, which tends to follow fascial planes and is usually caused by the streptococcus. Luckily for us we see very few of these infections and the few we see usually respond fairly well to the antibiotics. Only rarely is incision necessary. When it is, you should lay the tissue open with lineal incisions down to the fascia itself, like this:

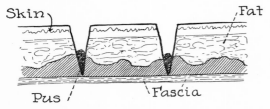

Occasionally, if infection is severe, tissue will begin to slough away near the wound edges. I have found it better to control the infection, then trim away dead and dying tissue. Remember that this is done only after the acute infection is controlled. When this procedure is complete one has a clean wound that now may be allowed to close by second intention or that may be actively treated by grafts.

Surface care of an infected wound involves frequent cleansing with plain soap and water and the application of hot, moist packs when possible. This packing should not be done continuously because of the danger of water-logging tissue with disastrous results.

After-care differs in no way from that in any traumatic wound. Closure of the wound is usually by second intention if the loss of tissue has been at all extensive. Various minor surgical procedures may have to be used to prevent an unsightly scar and to restore function as quickly as possible.

Stitch Abscess

This usually represents contamination at the time of suturing and looks like this:

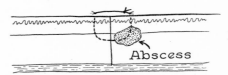

It should be drained by removal of the suture from the abscess side, like this:

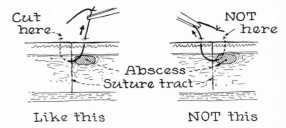

If the suture is pulled from the side opposite the abscess there is danger of spreading pus through the rest of the suture tract.

Deep stitch abscesses sometimes occur, with formation of a draining tract like this:

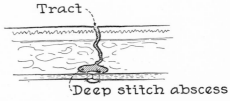

One can, if desirable, reenter the wound and remove the offending suture from the infected area. This, I believe, is a last resort to be used only after other attempts have been made to control the chronic infectious process.

These tracts sometimes heal quicker if irrigated daily or every other day with sterile, warm, isotonic saline. Use an ordinary 20 cc. syringe to which a blunt irrigating needle is attached like this:

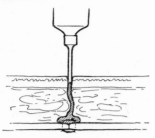

One of these irrigating needles is a handy thing around the office and may be made by taking an ordinary 15 gauge needle and filing off the point so that it is blunt.

Boils

These lesions should be treated conservatively until one is certain that pus is present. When this criterion is met, they may be drained.

Carbuncles

The carbuncle is a rapidly spreading infection of the fat and subcutaneous tissue and is prone to attack the posterior surface of the neck. Most carbuncles are moderately severe lesions with systemic toxic symptoms and acute pain. There is, in the most advanced lesions, a central core of infection with radiating "pseudopods" of cellulitis and pus formations like this:

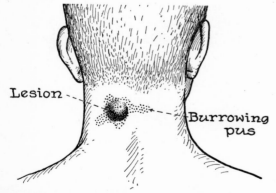

When there has been gross formation of pus, extensive surgical attack is by far the best method of treatment.

Local anesthesia is not entirely satisfactory for treatment of this lesion. We usually prefer to have the patient take a few whiffs of trichlorethylene through the Duke inhaler during the moment of first incision. Dissection of the flaps, as described later, may be done under local anesthetic. Begin by excising the central portion of the lesion like this:

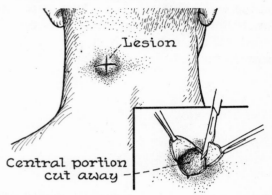

When this is complete make from three to six radial incisions, following as best you can the inflammatory process like this:

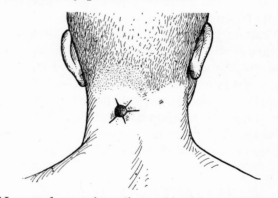

Now undercut these lines of incision like this:

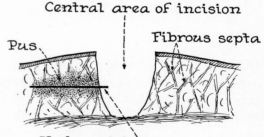

Go far enough that you are *sure* there remain no unincised pockets of pus. Active bleeding may occur in an occasional case and this should be controlled by pressure on the periphery of the wound (not in the incised area). One avoids, if at all possible, grasping and tying vessels. After any spurting bleeding has been controlled by pressure as mentioned above, then oozing is controlled by means of a hot, moist pack on which there is exerted gentle pressure. This is kept in place 5 or 6 minutes and usually suffices to control all bleeding.

Rubber or polyethylene drains may be inserted under the wound flaps and should be left in place 24 to 36 hours. A voluminous dressing of fluffy gauze is applied. If there is still some oozing of blood when you are ready to apply the first dressing, the patient may be instructed to lie face down in a comfortable position and a small sandbag may be placed across the back of the neck in such a position that it exerts mild pressure on the wound. This position should be maintained for ½ hour or more. I have never seen a case in which it was not effective in controlling this oozing bleeding.

Cellulitis

This is a spreading inflammatory process of the subcutaneous tissues that seldom is followed by formation of pus. One should use the antibiotics and conservative therapy and make no effort to perform any procedure.

Lymphangitis

This is the "blood poisoning" so greatly feared by many people. There was a day when it was a highly dangerous infection and when heroic measures were sometimes necessary to control it. With modern drugs there is seldom any indication for minor surgical procedures.

Lymphadenitis and Suppuration

The enlarged lymph node following infection in the area drained by the node needs no comment here. Surgical procedures are unnecessary unless active suppuration occurs. Unfortunately it does happen sometimes. The suppurative lymph node usually feels like biscuit dough to the palpating finger when the process is beginning. There is exquisite pain upon touch and general toxic symptoms are usually present. After 1 to 3 days, fluctuation may be suspected and make a surgical procedure necessary.

One should remember that it is not possible to feel fluctuation in the deeper lymph nodes. Enlargement is apparent, as well as general toxicity. One must, however, merely make a canny guess as to when invasion may be properly undertaken.

These nodes may be drained under local anesthesia. One bit of advice, however: *Look at the node itself* before plunging a knife into it. Dissect down and expose the node as completely as possible before the actual incision.

When the gland has been opened adequately and free drainage of pus is obtained, one should pack the cavity with gauze if it is 1 cm. or more in diameter. In any case a tissue drain should be inserted. I see no reason to use huge rubber tubing for purposes of draining when from one to three rubber bands or a crumbled up strip of plastic will do the same job with only a minimal amount of resultant scarring. The drain should be left in place for at least 24 hours and conservative therapy should be continued until healing is apparent.

Deep Abscesses

These lesions are no different than superficial abscesses from the standpoint of treatment. Incision and drainage is the important procedure.

TUMORS IN GENERAL

Sebaceous Cysts

These are retention cysts caused by blockage of a gland duct with consequent enlargement and fibrosis of the gland wall until cyst formation is complete. When seen in an infected state they should be incised and drained, with no effort being made to remove them.

When seen in the non-infected stage, removal is the best procedure. Do it this way: Begin by anesthetizing the skin and subcutaneous tissues around the cyst. Be certain that infiltration is adequate at the critical point, like this:

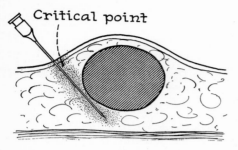

Wait at least 10 minutes for anesthesia to become effective. Now make an elliptical incision over the top of the cyst, like this:

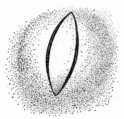

Carry dissection downward between the skin and the cyst wall until the entire circumference of the cyst is exposed, like this:

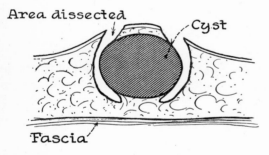

Notice that the elliptical portion of the skin is to be removed with the cyst. The incision should be designed so that the duct of the gland is removed in this elliptical portion of skin.

The cyst wall is very loosely attached to surrounding tissue and may be separated from it by gentle dissection.

The only difficult point now is dissecting underneath the cyst without rupturing it. Begin by pushing the curved dissecting scissors into the tissues under the edge of the cyst and spreading them gently like this:

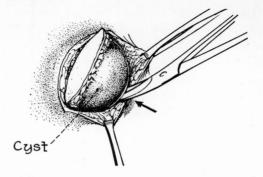

Now snip any strands of tissue attached in this immediate area. Repeat the process around the entire base of the cyst until it is held in place only by a small pedicle underneath. Now use Allis clamps on the piece of attached skin to roll the cyst slightly sidewise, like this:

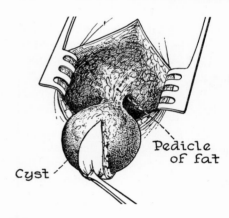

Use either scissors or the knife to cut the remaining pedicle and remove the cyst.

Should you inadvertently rupture the cyst wall during the process of dissection pick it up so that the tissues are on a stretch and continue your dissection around the outside of the wall. The line of demarcation between the cyst and surrounding structures is clear and easily identified. There should be no difficulty in removing the entire structure. Close the wound with a pressure dressing to eliminate dead space.

Dermoid Cysts

These usually appear in the area of the head and neck and are the result of inclusion of displaced dermoid cells along the line of embryonic fusion. What happens is this:

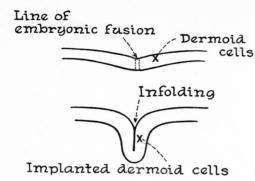

The cysts may be removed under local anesthesia but they do not dissect out as easily as the sebaceous cyst. Dermoids may send extensions along lines of fusion and require extensive dissection if all cells are to be removed. In this case it is best to remove as much as possible without creating a major anatomic disturbance, and then to use the coagulating current to destroy other groups of cells like this:

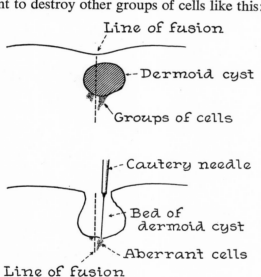

These growths may be attached to the underlying periosteum and may even dent bone. Their removal is trying in the extreme.

Warts

There are three common procedures used in the treatment of warts, any one of which is amply satisfactory, the choice being largely up to the practitioner. My own preference is to inject one drop of 5 per cent sodium morrhuate into the base of the wart, using a 26 gauge needle and a tuberculin syringe like this:

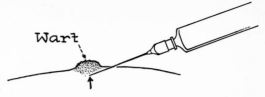

A wart may be removed by electrodesiccation after anesthesia with a drop of procaine. After blackening the surface of the wart, use a scalpel to scrape off the killed area and desiccate again, scrape again, etc., until the very base of the wart shells out. Then use a very light desiccating current to whiten the floor of the remaining cavity.

Excision under local anesthesia is good treatment except in locations where the skin may become tense, such as over a joint. In these areas it is best not to excise.

Papillomas

These are small tumors consisting of a hypertrophied area of skin attached to the underlying tissues by a small fibrous stalk containing a central artery and vein. They look like this:

The old grandmother's method of tying a thread around the base is as good a means of removal as we have been able to devise.

Keloids

In the formative stage these are best treated by means of irradiation. They should probably not be removed surgically unless follow-up irradiation can be done to prevent secondary formation. For this reason they are seldom operated on in the minor surgery.

Lipomas

Lipomas are common fatty tumors that may occur on the subcutaneous tissues anywhere on the body. They are, for practical purposes, not subject to malignant degeneration but may cause pressure symptoms and annoying disfigurations. Their removal is indicated at the desire of the patient.

Diagnosis is usually not difficult but there are two general types of lipoma, which tend to blend one into the other and may be a bit difficult to distinguish. For the sake of classification they might be called the soft and the hard type. The difference, of course, is in the amount of fibrous tissue contained in the substance of the tumor.

The soft type is most likely to be found about the neck and shoulders and may give one the impression of a fluctuant mass when first palpated. The fibrous septa are, however, attached to the deeper layers of the skin and upon pressure will dimple the skin, giving an orange peel appearance like this:

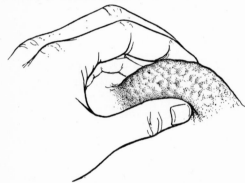

Also, there is usually an absence of tenderness or at most minor tenderness connected with the average lipoma, while the chronic abscess is painful when pressed upon.

Since the tumors usually shell out of their capsule readily, their removal is not a difficult problem. Under local anesthesia, dissect down to the tumor and explore carefully until a plane of cleavage is found. One may then shell out the tumor from its capsule with no difficulty, using blunt dissection. Remember that the blood supply to the lipoma usually enters through its base like this:

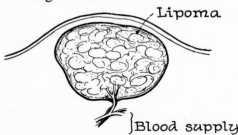

One should be prepared to deal with moderately active bleeding when the base comes free. When you can see under the tumor and delineate the vessels it is best to clamp and divide them before completing removal of the tumor.

Such an operative procedure usually leaves a wide dead space in tissues, which should be closed. I believe it is best to eliminate this dead space by utilizing pressure from outside the wound rather than by making an attempt to close it with sutures.

Fibromas

These are rounded masses of fibrous tissue which may appear any place on the human body. They may be distinguished from sebaceous cysts by noting the attachment of the sebaceous cysts to the skin; the fibroma is not so attached.

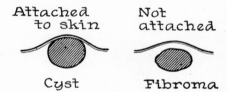

Excision is a simple procedure and should be left to the discretion of the patient.

Vascular Tumors

There are four types of vascular tumors seen frequently enough to warrant description.

Hemangioma Simplex. The simplest vascular tumor is the port-wine stain, or hemangioma simplex. This is an irregular, purplish red area not raised above the skin, most often appearing on the face and neck. Particularly characteristic is the fact that the edges are ill defined, fading into contiguous skin by degrees.

Two methods of treatment are available to the practitioner.

The first is deep excision, like this:

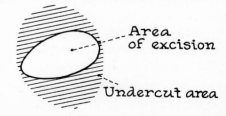

The defect may be covered either by undercutting the surrounding skin or by means of a skin graft, which will be discussed later on in this section. Occasionally high dosages of ultraviolet irradiation will give excellent results. Do it like this: Use a sheet of heavy thickness cardboard to protect all but the area to be treated. A hole is cut in the cardboard to fit the lesion. Additional protection can be gained by placing lead x-ray strips on the cardboard; this will also serve to help hold it in place.

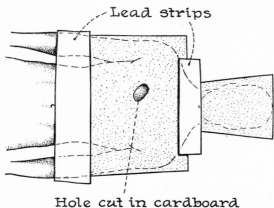

Hole cut in cardboard to fit over the lesion

Give an erythema dose of irradiation once each week over a period of several months until the lesion disappears.

This is apparently an effective treatment but one that requires very close supervision. The hemangioma simplex may be treated by roentgen irradiation in very early life. This does not fall within the pale of the practitioner. In considering referral of such cases, one should remember that these tumors gradually lose their radiosensitivity as the patient gets older. X-rays are most effective in the group under three years of age.

Plexiform Hemangioma. The second type of vascular tumor is the strawberry birthmark, or the plexiform hemangioma. The tumor is usually sharply demarcated from the surrounding skin and is slightly raised and may be lobulated. Excision is the treatment of choice for the smaller tumors, but those over 1 cm. in diameter should be first treated by injection and the response to this treatment should be determined.

Use a short 26 gauge needle to inject 5 per cent sodium morrhuate. Begin by making a procaine skin wheal in the center of the tumor like this:

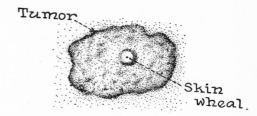

Now pass the needle for morrhuate injection underneath the skin surface into the substance of the tumor, like this:

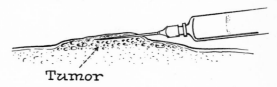

Notice that injections are made in radiating lines from the central wheal. It is particularly important that only minute quantities of the sclerosing solution be placed in the tumor area. There is a very real chance of sloughing and while this is not so disfiguring as the tumor and may often be counted as a good result, it still must be avoided if at all possible.

Cavernous Hemangioma. The cavernous hemangioma consists of large, dilated blood spaces that usually may be compressed by gentle pressure. Only the smallest of these lesions should be removed in the minor surgery. Bleeding can be a real and serious problem and equipment must be at hand to control it before excision is attempted.

The cavernous hemangioma responds very well to injections of sodium morrhuate, and this procedure may be tried before extensive surgery is scheduled. Anesthetize the skin over the hemangiomatous mass and use a small gauge needle (24 or 26) to enter one of the dilated blood spaces. Aspirate to make certain the needle is in proper position. Now inject approximately 0.5 cc. of 5 per cent sodium morrhuate and follow this with immediate and forceful compression of the lesion.

After continuing manual pressure for at least 10 minutes (this may be done by the patient), use a mechanic's waste or sponge dressing to maintain the pressure like this:

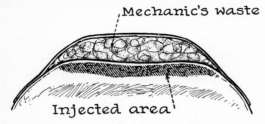

Do not remove the dressing for 24 hours.

Since there is some pain connected with this injection, it may be well to give the patient a small dose of codeine and phenobarbital preceding the actual procedure by 30 minutes or more. The stinging, burning sensation usually lasts 6 to 8 hours after injection but may be alleviated by small dosages of codeine. Don't give too much. Often as little as ⅛ grain will relieve an adult.

Glomus Tumor. This is a pinpoint-sized structure made up of arteries, veins and nerve filaments along with abnormal-appearing muscle fibers. The function is thought to be related to temperature control of the skin surface.

Rarely, for some unknown reason, this normal structure may enlarge and cause symptoms. The most frequent site of enlargement is under the nail of the fingers and toes, although it may occur on other skin surfaces. The lesion is particularly painful if located under the nail. Treatment is by excision. Recurrence is not common.

Since the tumor itself contains many nerve fibers, there may be some difficulty in gaining adequate anesthesia. Using as an example one of these tumors located under a finger nail, proceed as follows:

1. Block the digital nerves as shown in the section on anesthesia.

2. Remove the finger nail by cutting with scissors as shown. Extend the cut to the most proximal portion of nail, like this:

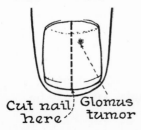

Then grasp the cut edge with a clamp and roll the nail laterally like this:

3. Now inject the entire periphery of the tumor with procaine, like this:

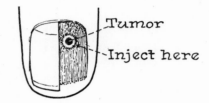

4. Wait 5 minutes.

5. Since the tumor is well encapsulated, one can shell it out of the capsule after establishing a plane of cleavage by sharp dissection like this:

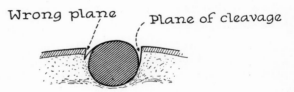

The Pigmented Nevus

This is a brownish black area of the skin, frequently raised and often showing excess growth of hair. The pigmented nevus is in itself a harmless lesion except for the fact that a certain number become malignant. The resultant malignant melanoma is, as you know, one of the most vicious and one of the most certainly fatal of all neoplasms. For this reason one may argue with some success that any pigmented nevus should be removed.

I shan't enter into that discussion, but this is essential: If a pigmented nevus shows signs of growth, extension or inflammatory reaction, it should be biopsied at once. The biopsy actually should be a bloc dissection of the lesion, done like this:

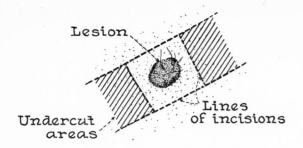

Lesion

Undercut areas

Lines of incisions

One should *never* do a partial dissection of the pigmented nevus for purposes of biopsy. It is quite true that there exists some basis for the statement that should malignant melanoma be found, even the bloc dissection will probably do no good. Nonetheless, we owe it to our patients to be as careful as possible with these potential malignancies.

BURNS

The treatment of extensive burns is completely out of the field of minor surgery. These cases should be hospitalized as soon as possible. An important point to remember is that children are more susceptible to fluid and electrolyte imbalance than adults, probably because of their smaller blood volume. A burn that would necessitate only outpatient treatment for an adult may require hospitalization if seen in a child. Burns are one of the most frequent causes of death in young children, and should be handled with great respect.

There have been literally thousands of treatments proposed for burn care. In those amenable to minor surgery I have found no treatment superior to conscientious neglect. The various ointments are of no particular service that we can tell, and extensive cleansing procedures with much débridement seem only to traumatize further an already injured area.

I treat most minor burns by exposure to the air, if possible, obtundation of pain, splinting to reduce motion, and exhibition of the antibiotics.

The antibiotics seem particularly important, since some recent work has led us to believe that infection may play an important role in the toxicity seen from burns. There are those who disagree violently with our course of procedure and I express only a personal opinion in saying that neglect is the best possible treatment.

Occasionally when exposure to the air is impossible, a simple one-layer petrolatum gauze covered by surgical flats and held in place by strips of Scotch tape is entirely adequate.

FROSTBITE

This lesion seems to parallel that of burns. Available drugs seem to have some beneficial effect on the milder cases, however. The only procedure is a negative one. Avoid warming the part so rapidly that the damaged circulation cannot keep up with tissue oxygen needs. If this rapid warming is done, there is likely to be a greater area of slough than if the part is gradually returned to normal temperature. Various time-honored procedures, such as rubbing with snow and application of various household remedies, seem to have no effect at all on the healing of the lesion.

FOREIGN BODIES

The first and one of the most important points to be settled about any foreign body is whether or not to remove it. Since the vast majority of this material is contaminated to some extent, it should be removed unless you feel that the proposed operation would be a greater hazard than the foreign body itself. In all truth, this is sometimes the case and it may be wiser in these instances to use conservative treatment with the idea of helping the defenses of the body overcome the attack of pathogenic bacteria.

Foreign bodies located in areas where they may cause active pain upon pressure, such as the heel or finger tip, will probably have to be removed for the comfort of the patient.

Locating foreign material, particularly small bits, can be a major undertaking. Certain procedures are very useful and should be kept in mind.

If the material can be visualized by use of the fluoroscope, attach a pin to the surface of the skin in the axis of the foreign body, like this:

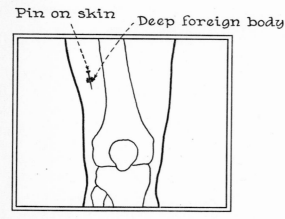

Attachment may be made with a bit of collodion. Now turn the area at right angles and repeat this procedure. The foreign body will be found, of course, at the junction of lines drawn centrad from each pin like this:

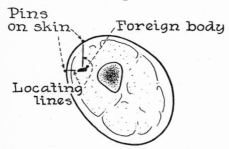

Another procedure is this: When the foreign body lies rather deep in the tissue but can be visualized by fluoroscope, anesthetize the area of skin and insert a hypodermic needle until it touches the foreign body as seen on the fluoroscope. Now place a syringe containing some Congo red dye on the needle which touches the foreign body and inject the dye as you withdraw the needle rapidly. Since the dye is absorbed rapidly, one must be prepared to make immediate incision.

The wound may be probed gently. When the probe touches the hard surface of the foreign body, one will appreciate a click, more felt than heard. The probe point is left in place and dissection is made down to it.

Since modern safety glass can be visualized by x-ray and since wood seldom penetrates as deeply as metallic or glass fragments, you will find that most deep-lying extraneous matter is amenable to location by means of the x-ray.

For small particles, direct visualization may be aided by use of the binocular loupe. Occasionally one may be able to dissect down the tract caused by such a foreign body, although this is by no means always true. It is the exception rather than the rule.

Removal of Foreign Bodies

Certain procedures are basic to removal of a foreign body once it is located. In the case of a long cylindrical foreign body, approach it at right angles to the axis of the foreign body, like this:

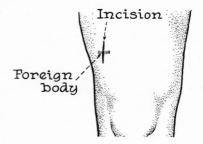

and then dissect along its course as far as may be necessary to facilitate removal.

Tiny flecks of steel may be removed with a magnet such as may be purchased at any ten-cent store. Locate the foreign body, hold the magnet wrapped in a sterile towel adjacent to it, and tease the foreign body free from the tissues with a knife. This is a much easier method for picking up tiny steel fragments than the use of forceps. One can, of course, purchase magnetic forceps which greatly facilitate the whole process.

Having gotten a grasp on the foreign body, do not tear it free if it will not come away without excessive pulling. Dissect along its course, using the point of the knife. You will usually find that it is caught in a band of fascia, which may be nicked to make removal easy.

Certain tissues offer peculiarities for which these suggestions may be of help: Foreign bodies in bone usually stick with great tenacity. A pair of sterile pliers may be used to grasp shaftlike foreign bodies embedded in bone and free them with a gentle twisting and pulling motion, like this:

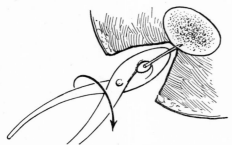

Older foreign bodies in bone may be partially encapsulated by the bone itself. A typical example is the lead shot that has been flattened out by its impact with the bone and now has a rimlike overgrowth around the edge:

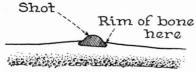

It may be necessary (if one wishes to remove the shot at all) to take a small bone chisel and chip away this overhanging shelf.

Foreign bodies in muscle are easily located by separating the muscle fibers gently like this:

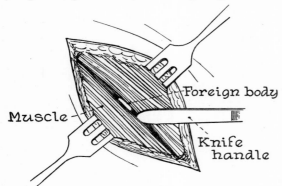

Occasionally one will see a shaftlike foreign body that lies exactly in the plane of the muscle fibers. Pick up the area containing the foreign body and twist it gently in your fingers:

One end or the other of the foreign body will usually protrude from the muscle fiber and may be picked away with the greatest of ease. This procedure should be used with caution because one may traumatize the muscle fibers if too much force is applied.

Foreign bodies in fat are usually removed if they can be located. Begin by making a narrow elliptical incision around the wound entrance, like this:

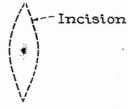

Next undercut the lateral flaps for about ¼ inch. Seize the free elliptical flap of skin in an Allis clamp but do not pull it upward.

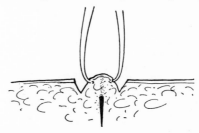

Now undercut the ellipse, running the incision deeper into the fat like this:

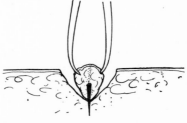

The foreign body will be contacted and may be removed along with the wound of entrance and the contaminated subcutaneous fat like this:

Metal. Only one kind of metallic foreign body seems to offer a great deal of trouble. It is the tiny chip that will fly off the edge of a hammer or the edge of a steel tool when it is struck by a hammer. The chip travels with unbelievable speed and may penetrate deeply into tissues. The tiny wound of entrance is only a rough approximation of the foreign body location, and one will usually save time if the initial procedure is localization by means of fluoroscopy.

Cylindrical foreign bodies, particularly needles, tend to move about rapidly in tissues. When one is localized by x-ray the area involved should be taken out of use by splinting unless removal can be done immediately. I have seen a needle in the heel travel as much as an inch while the patient walked back from the x-ray room. A few such experiences tend to make us wary.

Fish hooks commonly become engaged in the fingers and ears. They prove most difficult to remove. The best procedure I know of is to anesthetize the area immediately ahead of the fish hook point and push it on through so that the barb emerges like this:

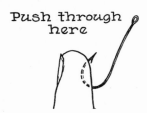

Push through here

Use a pair of wire cutters to cut off the barb and withdraw the fish hook through the original wound of entrance.

Wood. Wood foreign bodies are usually quite superficial and easy to remove, with one exception. That is the rotten wood splinter that breaks up and leaves innumerable tiny slivers along the course of the original wound, like this:

These splinters can usually be recognized at sight. In my opinion, if one recognizes such a splinter and if the first try at removal proves that a break-up is the most likely result of further attempts at removal, it is better to dissect out the splinter and remove the tract. Fortunately these are seldom deep enough to give any serious difficulty.

Glass. Modern safety glass will shatter into a million little pieces if hit hard enough. These tiny pieces of glass can literally carpet a wound. Removal of the smaller fragments from an open wound is best accomplished by brushing with a soft brush. Do not attempt to wipe them away with a gauze sponge for you will invariably transfer the glass splinters from the patient to your own fingers.

Penetrating wounds made by glass usually heal well with the foreign body in place. The only indication for removal is pain on pressure over the area, or active disturbance in function. Those splinters that need be removed may be localized by means of a fluoroscope and removed by dissection as described earlier.

Pencil Lead. The tip of a sharp lead pencil is frequently broken off in the tissues of the hand and occasionally in the soft palate by children who fall on pencils they are holding in their mouths. I have seen no bad results from this embedding of graphite. (As a matter of fact I have had some in my own hand for over thirty years.) It does make an unsightly stain. In most instances a small incision over the wound of entrance will allow the substance to be lifted out in one piece. This should probably be done.

Chronic Irritation from Foreign Bodies

We may see the formation of chronic draining sinuses after a foreign body has been embedded in the tissues. You must always remember that the most frequent foreign body is suture material. Silk is the worst offender and a large knot of catgut is the culprit of second frequency. These draining sinuses may be irrigated with isotonic saline solution and explored with a crochet hook. Quite often it will be possible to hook the offending suture, which will come away with the point of the hook and result in a complete cure. If this is impossible, incision should be done freely with adequate dissection and removal of the foreign material.

Various tumors and swellings about the body that do not seem to be adequately explained from the standpoint of usual diagnosis should be viewed with a degree of suspicion. In most instances a simple x-ray will confirm or deny the presence of a foreign body, but even with the x-ray you will occasionally get a surprise when removal is done.

INCISIONS IN GENERAL

When doing elective minor surgery, placement and method of making the incision may have much to do with the ultimate result. In this section we shall summarize the basic facts of incision and then list particular exposures that may be useful in the office minor surgery.

Certain simple surgical principles govern the making of a proper incision. The cut should, of course, be vertical to the skin surface, not at an angle.

Use the long edge, not the sharp point of the knife blade, and be sure the incision goes through the entire skin segment. An incision that penetrates only part way through the thickness of the skin cannot usually be duplicated closely enough on the second "slash" to prevent the final result from looking like this in cross section:

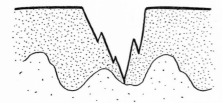

Such an incision simply delays the process of healing.

I have found it a good policy to figure out in my own mind the proper length incision for a procedure and then add on at least ½ inch. It is much better to make the incision ade-

quately long at first rather than to be forced to lengthen it after the procedure is started.

Skin Creases

One should never design an incision that crosses skin creases at right angles. Here is why: The typical straight line incision across a joint crease shows additional thickening at the "crossing" area like this when healed:

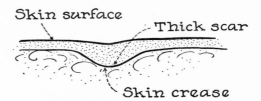

It will not bend adequately and may result in moderate to severe diminution of function. A proper incision in the same area is done like this:

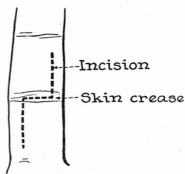

Notice in the illustrations that follow that the joint will bend around a scar that is in the same direction as the skin crease, whereas if the scar crossed a flexion crease, the scar itself would have to bend when tissues bend.

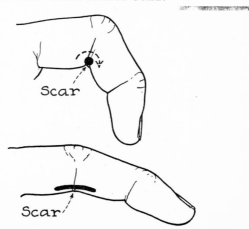

A traumatic wound that crosses a flexion crease may usually be handled like this: Make a new incision that crosses perpendicular to the wound and follows the skin crease. Undercut the wound edges near the flexion crease.

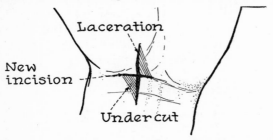

Now move the skin edges so that the laceration is changed into a modified "Z" like this:

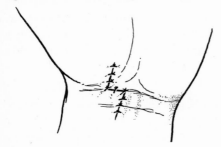

Lines of Force

There are certain lines of skin configuration on the body that are not shown by flexion creases. They are present nonetheless, and healing may be greatly facilitated by planning incisions that conform to them. To clarify that just a little bit, let's take a particular spot anterior to the pectoralis major. Notice that the skin frequently moves in the direction of the arrows, but seldom moves the other way.

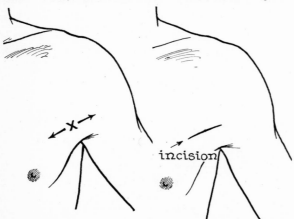

Check this on yourself. Mark a similar spot on your skin. Now move your arm about and notice how the spot moves, what tensions are put on the skin at the site of the spot. Now, to follow our example, the incision to be made in that area might be improperly made at right angles to the lines of force, in which case there would be great tension exerted upon it and it might pull open; or it could be made properly parallel to the lines of force, in which case the tension would be minimal and the incision would almost stay closed of its own accord.

There are such lines of force applicable to most body areas. If incisions are planned to accommodate to them, one may confidently expect a lessened morbidity and fewer complications. A rough diagram of these surface lines of force may be prepared like this:

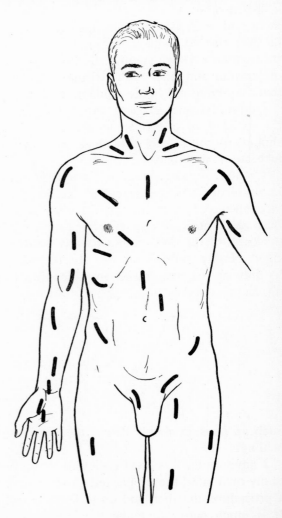

In general, you are better off to make an incision that would parallel any of the lines shown.

MINOR SURGERY OF THE SCALP

Minor surgery of the scalp is a frequent task of the practitioner. About 90 per cent of such work is confined to the closure of lacerations. It is in this procedure that many errors are made. One is the attempt to stop scalp bleeding by using hemostats, which usually is futile. Pressure will work better. Another error is overuse of stitches.

The fronto-occipital muscle and its aponeurosis is the key structure to the scalp. The muscle fibers are joined by a thick aponeurotic layer.

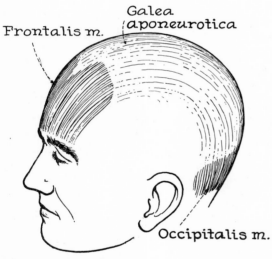

The aponeurosis is loosely attached to the underlying periosteum and movement of the scalp takes place in the plane between the aponeurosis and the periosteum. Between the galea and the skin there is a dense network of fibrous tissue septa in which literally thousands of blood vessels are enmeshed. The skin itself is thick and heavy and is replete with glands and hair follicles. Because of the fibrous septa the skin is not very freely movable upon the galea.

The arteries of importance are the temporal, posterior auricular and occipital. They course like this:

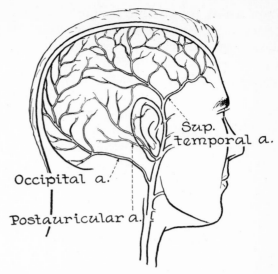

The scalp has profuse blood supply and, because of this, healing is relatively rapid and infection rare.

Lacerations

The jagged laceration from a bump on the head is one of the most common lesions seen in the minor surgery. One might classify them into deep and superficial, using relationship to galeal injury as a criterion. The first, or simple, type would be the scalp wound that does not disturb the fibers of the galea. Such a wound does not gape and it very seldom needs suturing, although it usually gets it.

The second type would be those wounds in which the galea is cut, but in the direction of its fibers. These wounds do not gape and ordinarily do not require suturing, although they, too, usually get it.

The third type would be those wounds in which the galea is cut in a direction crosswise to its fibers. These cuts require suturing and usually do better if the galea is loosely stitched with heavy cotton thread, like this:

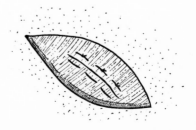

and the skin is held in apposition with sutures or tape. If one keeps clearly in mind these three types of scalp lacerations there is no reason to have difficulty with closure.

Scalp Bleeding. Because they are embedded in the connective tissue septa, vessels of the scalp do not close easily after laceration. This and their number combine to produce intense bleeding after what seems a minor laceration. Also because of their relationship to the fibrous septa it is very difficult to seize a scalp vessel in the jaws of a hemostatic forceps. If one feels that immediate application of forceps should be necessary, use the Allis clamp rather than the Kelly-type forceps. Actually I have never seen a case where it was necessary. Pressure, which compresses the vessels against the hard skull, will control any bleeding.

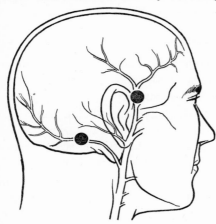

Digital compression of the arteries at the points shown above will also serve to stop scalp bleeding and one may, if occasion seems to warrant, place a rubber tube tourniquet tightly around the scalp just above the level of the ears and get effective hemostasis.

Occasionally a small vessel in the edge of a laceration seems to be inordinately stubborn about bleeding. While this is not a good routine procedure, it is perfectly permissible to catch the vessel in a stitch taken ¼ inch or more from the edge of the wound, like this:

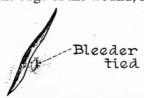

The stitch may be tied tightly for a few minutes and then released. Actually the best method of control in bleeding is simple pressure.

Cephalhematoma

This is seen most frequently in the newborn and should be ignored for a period of ten days to two weeks before active treatment should be undertaken. The reason for this is that most of these lesions absorb spontaneously. If they do not, however, it is probably better to evacuate the clot than to leave a potential source of infection. It is also possible that a bony deformity will follow, with permanent cosmetic impairment. When your judgment indicates evacuation of the cephalhematoma, inject the area to be incised with procaine and make an incision down to and through the galea in the line of its fibers.

If bleeding from cut scalp vessels is annoying, use skin clips or a suture to pull the galea up over the edge of the wound and stitch it in place like this:

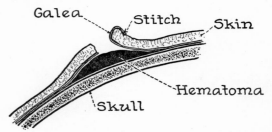

Evacuate the cavity and irrigate it with sterile isotonic saline solution. Close the galea with interrupted cotton sutures or none at all, whichever you feel is best, and tape the skin in place. An absorbent dressing is applied and left in place for 48 hours, after which the wound usually need not be covered.

Subgaleal Abscess

Very rarely we see a collection of pus form underneath the galea aponeurotica. This may be difficult to prove without aspiration, which should be done freely to confirm this suspected diagnosis. If confirmation is forthcoming, anesthetize the scalp and make a longitudinal incision (i.e., anterior-posterior) large enough to allow free drainage. Since the scalp heals with astonishing rapidity, it is probably best to insert a drain into this wound. Apply an absorbent dressing without the formality of suturing the wound at all. Be sure to see these patients daily to determine whether adequate drainage continues.

MINOR SURGERY OF THE FACE

Abrasions

These lesions of the face should be painstakingly cared for because of the possibility of scarring and disfigurement. If no foreign matter has been forced into the wound, wash it well with castile soap and water and pat gently dry with a surgical sponge. Ask the patient to repeat this procedure at home every 15 to 30 minutes, sponging away excess secretions until the wound begins to form a crust. This will usually take an hour or so. He is then to let it scrupulously alone and report to the office within 24 hours for evaluation.

In the ordinary case no dressing is needed, for the wound crust itself forms an excellent protective coating. For those who work in dust or who may contaminate the wound in some way, a sterile square of perforated polyethylene film is ample dressing. It is my impression that wounds actually do better not dressed at all and every effort should be made to care for the lesion this way.

Abrasions filled with particulate matter should be washed with soap and a soft brush after application of local anesthesia. Anesthesia may be secured by soaking a surgical sponge in one of the topical agents and placing it on the abrasion for several minutes. *Be sure* to wring excess anesthetic from the sponge before it is applied. Washing should be thorough and exacting and a sharp, pointed knife should be used to dig out particles too deeply embedded for the brush to remove. For the maximum result, all foreign matter must be removed.

Lacerations

Sharp, clean-cut lacerations of the face should be washed with soap and water and

taped together. One must use great care to make sure that the edges are as accurately approximated as possible. The jagged, undercut facial wound, on the other hand, is often best excised like this:

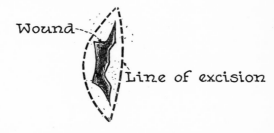

The resultant clean wound edge is held in place by tape or by subcuticular sutures. There is seldom indication for use of any suture other than subcuticular in facial wounds. Through and through sutures do nothing but add to the scarring and should not be used, with one or two exceptions as noted later.

The wound cut diagonally through the skin, even though it is exceedingly shallow, is often best excised so that edge to edge approximation may be gained like this:

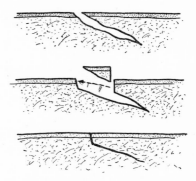

One can scarcely overstress the importance of achieving perfect or near perfect skin apposition in facial wounds. There are few such lesions that should result in anything more than a hairline scar that is scarcely discernable after several months. In spite of the fact that such results are possible, we often see botched-up jobs that look as if a shoemaker had fixed them. There are a number of special types of lacerations that must be considered, for the treatment is somewhat different in each case.

Severance of the ear. It is not unusual to see a portion or all of the ear severed, particularly in those areas where discussions are likely to be carried on with knives as well as fists. When the excised piece of ear is obtainable, it will usually reattach itself if properly placed. Clean the cut edges by irrigating profusely with isotonic saline solution. Using fine suture material, take through and through sutures which penetrate the skin *but not the cartilage* of the ear, like this:

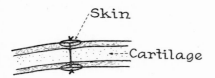

Hold the cartilage in proper apposition by placing a wadding of cotton behind and in front of the ear before bandaging. The frequent application of cool compresses to such a lesion may be of some benefit.

Injury to the Facial Nerve. The superficial branches of the facial nerve, even the larger superficial branches, are sometimes severed as they exit or cross the substance of the parotid gland here:

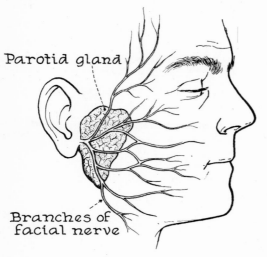

A glance at the patient or simple functional tests are all that is necessary for diagnosis. The nerve ends should be picked up and carefully reapproximated as specified on page 226. There is nothing difficult about this lesion as long as one suspects it and takes time to look for it.

Severance of Stensen's Duct. The parotid duct may be rolled beneath the finger as it

crosses the buccinator muscle to enter the mouth opposite the second molar. In deep lacerations of the cheek, it may be cut. Primary repair is so often successful that it is a worthwhile procedure. Do it this way: Find an old ureteral catheter and cut off about 4 inches from the tip. Using a cutting needle, thread a piece of heavy silk through the cut end of the piece of catheter so that it looks like this:

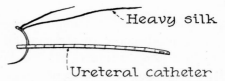

This has a utilitarian rather than a medical purpose, for it simply serves as an anchor to make sure that the catheter won't drop, fall or get lost. Now thread the catheter into the opening of the duct opposite the second molar, here:

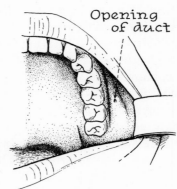

This sometimes may be considerably easier if you inject a little procaine solution into the duct (not into the tissue around the duct) 5 to 10 minutes before the procedure is to be done. Now gently advance the catheter through the duct until it appears at the base of the exterior wound, like this:

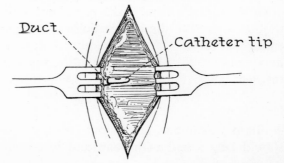

Carefully hunt out the proximal side of the duct (give the patient a little lemon juice) and thread the catheter into it so that the result looks like this:

Now use a tiny sharp needle and very small cotton sutures to sew the duct together over the catheter like this:

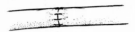

The catheter may then be trimmed so that approximately ½ inch of it protrudes through the duct inside the mouth. Never let such a patient leave your office until you are sure that saliva is draining through the catheter. Tell the patient to think hard about a lemon or give him more lemon juice and watch the opening of the catheter. If possible, the catheter should remain in place 2 or 3 days or even longer. The duct does, however, reestablish continuity quickly and in all probability you will get a good result even if the catheter comes out within 24 hours.

Wounds of the parotid itself frequently produce external salivary fistulas but these are best ignored for a period of time, since the vast majority of them close spontaneously. Undoubtedly there is an explanation why the drainage tracts from the gland itself close spontaneously and those from the parotid duct seldom, if ever, do. Unfortunately, I am not aware of the explanation.

Wounds Penetrating into the Mouth. This can be summarized in a very few words. Close the external wound as you would any other wound and do nothing at all to the internal wound. Mucous membrane will heal quickly and effectively without sutures.

Lip Wounds. This is the one exception to the rule about not using through and through sutures in facial wounds. The lip heals so quickly and so firmly (probably because of its excellent blood supply) that through and through sutures may be placed and left for 24 to 48 hours. They may be removed before any stitch scarring occurs.

In closing a lip wound one must be certain that the vermilion border is exactly approximated. After cleansing and anesthetizing, take the first stitch from the exact vermilion line on one side to the exact vermilion line on the other, like this:

The slightest deviation may (but does not always) show. With the perverse luck of medical men, you may be sure that you will get perfect results on those people who do not care and an unsightly mess on the banker's daughter who is proud of being the prettiest girl in town. The only way I know of to prevent this is to be sure to get exact apposition on every wound.

The next thing to do is to calculate exactly how many stitches will be needed to close the lip wound, divide the number by two and put in the final sum. In all seriousness, lip wounds are almost routinely overstitched. If loosely tied and properly inserted, two, or at the very most three, sutures will close the average lip wound to perfection. One other caution: Lips, of course, swell a great deal. If you tie the sutures down tight they are certain to cut. Be sure to leave them loose.

Tongue Wounds. These are best let alone unless of such great extent that a portion of the tongue falls aside owing to the laceration. Stitch it if it looks like this:

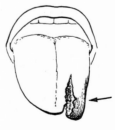

If the fragment stays in place and does not fall aside, let it alone.

The tongue can be adequately anesthetized by infiltration of procaine, but immobilization is another problem. If the laceration is far enough forward, an excellent method is to have the patient seize the tongue, using a piece of gauze as an aid to gripping it, and hold it for you while you make the repair. Use rather deep stitches of non-absorbable suture material, extending the suture into the muscle layer.

Hemorrhage

Bleeding from facial wounds is ordinarily not very serious. Occasionally when the facial artery is severed there may be an alarming loss of blood. Do not hesitate to ligate the facial artery either where it crosses the mandible or where it emerges from beneath the posterior portion of the digastric muscle as shown:

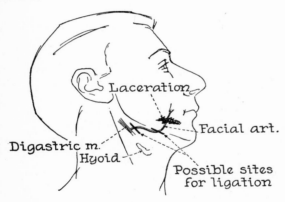

Tooth Socket Hemorrhage. Those of us in the country frequently see the episodes of bleeding following tooth extraction, but not until everything including old socks has been packed into the wound to attempt to stop it. Begin by removing the clot that is almost invariably present in the socket and irrigating it with sterile isotonic saline solution. Put one of the oxidized cellulose packs in place and have the patient hold it firmly for 5 to 10 minutes.

If bleeding still continues, I use an old country trick to stop it. I take an ordinary cork and whittle it to fit the tooth socket. Let it soak a few minutes in one of the aqueous dis-

infectants and wedge it firmly in place. It isn't very scientific but it works.

Removal of Scars

This is a worthwhile procedure in minor surgery, for it offers the patient excellent results. The simple traumatic scar may be removed by following this procedure: Anesthetize the area thoroughly and "V" out the scar by cutting around it like this:

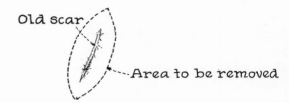

Be sure that your original incision through the skin is perpendicular to the skin surface, and begin making the "V" only after you have gone through the skin. Note that the "V" is shallow.

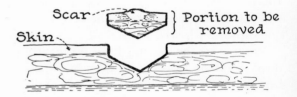

When the scar tissue has been removed, underdercut the skin edges very slightly, perhaps as little as $\frac{1}{16}$ inch or even less. Now move the edges firmly together and close the laceration with either a subcuticular stitch or surface taping. Help the patient plan painstaking after-care of the wound so that there will be no chance of infection.

The treatment of larger scars will be discussed in the section on minor plastic surgery.

In all lacerations about the face, do not forget the salutary effect of external pressure on healing. If it is possible to do so, put a pressure dressing on every facial laceration you see. This, of course, is an impossible goal, but many of them can be pressure-dressed for 24 hours or so. Certainly all scar removal procedures should be followed by pressure dressings.

Cysts

Various cysts of the facial area offer no peculiarities in treatment. They should be removed as specified in earlier sections.

One warning might be offered. In quite a few cases an infected preauricular node has been removed under the mistaken impression that it was a cyst. The node lies about here:

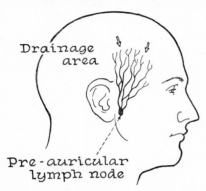

It will enlarge in the presence of any infection in its drainage area. While I suppose there is no particular objection to removing it, it does make one feel just a little bit foolish to remove a "cyst," cut it open and find out that the cyst has suddenly changed to a lymph node. Be sure to search the drainage area for signs of an infectious process before surgery.

Preauricular Sinuses

Preauricular sinuses are the result of defective closure of the first branchial cleft.

Have the patient report to the office one day before removal is contemplated and attempt to outline the cleft by probing with a flexible probe. Whether or not this seems to give an adequate delineation, inject 3 or 4 drops of ordinary methylene blue stain into the tract and leave it in place.

At operation the next day, after anesthetizing properly, make an incision like this:

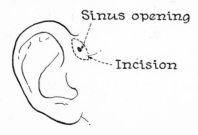

Now follow the blue stained tract by dissecting just outside it, like this:

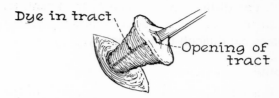

This dissection is a slow, tedious job but must be done thoroughly to prevent recurrence. When the tract has been completely removed, close the skin incision without drainage, preferably using a subcuticular suture. Apply a pressure dressing and dismiss the patient with instructions for after-care.

Mucocele

The mucocele is a retention cyst arising from one of the mucous secreting glands lining the mouth. It is most frequent on the inner surfaces of the lips.

Two methods of surgery are advocated but in my experience the most satisfactory treatment has been injection. After anesthetizing the mucous membrane over the cyst, insert an 18 gauge needle into the cystic cavity and aspirate the ropy mucous content as completely as possible. When this has been accomplished, remove the aspirating syringe and attach a tuberculin syringe containing 5 per cent sodium morrhuate. A drop or two of this solution is usually sufficient. After it has been injected, remove the needle and immediately apply firm pressure over the cyst area, catching the lip between your thumb and forefinger like this:

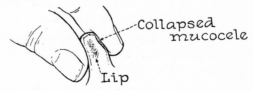

Hold it yourself for a minute or two to make sure there is no escape of fluid and then instruct the patient to hold it for 10 minutes by the clock without letting go.

There is usually minor local tenderness for a day or so. Within two weeks the cyst is reduced to a hard nodule of pinhead size or a little bigger and most of the time this disappears within six months to a year.

If one dislikes this method of treatment, an ordinary excision is perfectly acceptable but somewhat difficult to do properly.

Ranula

Practically every lesion within a foot of the mouth has been called by this name. I have neither the knowledge nor the intention to get into the argument of what a ranula is. For the sake of discussing treatment, let us call it a cyst of the floor of the mouth. Removal of these structures is possible but quite trying. They may usually be treated by aspiration and injection, as mentioned above, or by the process known as marsupialization. This is done by removing an area of the cyst roof and the membrane covering it, like this:

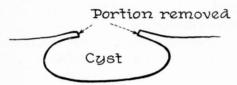

The membrane is then stitched to the edge of the cyst wall, so that a permanent large opening is formed. I have done the procedure an insufficient number of times to be able to comment on it but it does seem to work.

Surgical Infections

With one exception these are no different than infections seen elsewhere. The exception is the dangerous area of the face in which direct connection with intracranial structures is possible. Because of this, infectious processes may spread by contiguity (venous) to the cranial cavity with consequent disastrous results. The dangerous area of the face is shown here:

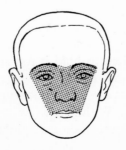

Conservatism is an absolute must for treating infections in this area. That does not mean that an obviously pointing boil with a yellow area at its summit may not be nicked for drainage. It does mean, however, that all procedures are best left out of treatment plans unless one is forced to include them.

One other infection is seen which merits standard treatment but needs comment, also. It is the common gum boil, which occurs on either upper or lower gums and is usually a sequella of dental abscess. It should be opened for drainage, using the normal procedure.

Salivary Calculi

These annoying stones are not rare in day-to-day practice and they may be treated by minor surgery. Diagnosis is usually made by noting swelling of a gland behind the stone, i.e., the stone occludes the duct and dams up secretion, causing the swelling. The swelling may enlarge at mealtime and, as gradual leakage occurs, go down between meals only to enlarge again when food stimulus is presented.

Most of the stones are radiopaque and show well on x-ray. There are two procedures of use. If the stone lies deep within the duct near the gland, one should begin dilation of the duct with the hope that the stone will pass without operative interference.

The procedure is relatively painless and may be done every other day, using material at hand for dilating. To begin with, a ureteral catheter is an excellent dilator. Larger dilators may be made out of strips of copper wire that have been filed so that the end is rounded. Not often will one have to go beyond the larger gauge wires but, if it is necessary, the next gradation is the smallest rubber urethral catheter. Dilation should be continued for at least two weeks before being given up as hopeless.

Fortunately, most of these stones are seen as they lie in the very terminal end of the duct just under the mucous membrane of the mouth, like this:

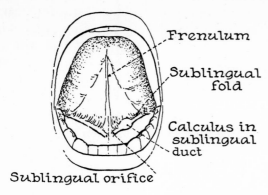

Frenulum

Sublingual fold

Calculus in sublingual duct

Sublingual orifice

After application of a topical anesthetic, one should slit the top of the mucous membrane over them and pick the stone out with small forceps.

Ear Piercing

We still see a certain number of young ladies who wish to have their ears pierced, why I cannot say. If you are trapped and must perform the procedure, do it this way: After cleansing, inject 2 or 3 drops of procaine along the proposed tract. Then thread a straight cutting needle with the largest piece of silk thread you have and pass it through the ear. Bleeding can be controlled by firm pressure. The ends of the thread are tied together leaving a large loop about 2 inches long. The young lady is instructed to wash the ear and the thread with soap and water at least three times a day and to move the thread gently back and forth through the ear until epithelization in the entire tract has taken place.

Biopsy

We see few lesions of the face large enough to warrant partial biopsy. En bloc dissection is the most satisfactory procedure. Do it this way: Select the smallest width of the lesion and make two incisions at right angles to it. Now cut across on either side of the lesion like this:

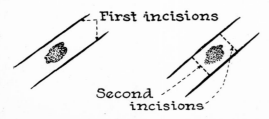

First incisions

Second incisions

Be sure to go deeply enough into the subcutaneous tissue to undermine completely the area to be biopsied. Remove it en bloc and close the wound by bringing the remaining flaps together like this:

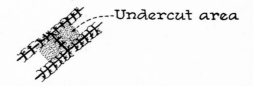

Undercut area

Use a pressure dressing to eliminate dead space in the wound.

Lesions of the lip that appear carcinomatous should be let alone by us practitioners and be referred to a cancer center for diagnosis. Lesions of the tongue, on the other hand, may be biopsied rather freely unless they are obviously malignant, in which case they should be referred. Remember that lesions of the tongue are rapidly growing and are quickly fatal, so do not temporize when one is seen. Perhaps the best technique is to take a punch biopsy under local anesthesia. Be sure to include the edge of the lesion like this:

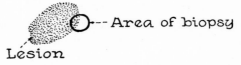

Area of biopsy

Lesion

Should you get a positive result, send the patient to a cancer center immediately.

You will perhaps ask why the difference in treatment between carcinoma of the lip and of the tongue. The reason is this: The percentage of mistakes in diagnosis of carcinoma of the lip is very low. The percentage of mistakes on tongue lesions is a great deal higher than that on lip lesions, for there are many pathologic processes that may mimic carcinoma of the tongue. Therefore, it is wise to secure a biopsy before you load your nearest cancer center with these patients, who would merely have to wait at the cancer center until a biopsy was reported.

I cannot overstress the importance of pursuing these lesions until a definitive diagnosis is made. We see occasional instances of temporization and these must not be condoned.

MINOR SURGERY OF THE NECK

Fortunately, lacerations of the neck are not common and are usually not particularly serious. The most common case we see is that of the gentleman who decides to cut his throat. He usually puts his head in such a position that the sternocleidomastoid muscles protect essential structures and all that is achieved is a slash in the external jugular vein. This, of course, causes active bleeding but it may be stopped by the gentlest of finger pressure above and below the cut. The vein is seized and tied and the cut closed in a routine manner.

The very rare deep lacerations of the neck involving such structures as the trachea, thyroid cartilage, or esophagus are not matters for treatment in the minor surgery. When one is presented with such a problem, stop the bleeding if possible and make sure that the airway is clear, but do nothing else until you have the patient hospitalized.

Strains and Sprains

Strains or sprains involve either the erector spinae muscles or the ligaments of the cervical vertebrae. The lesions can be exquisitely painful but respond to conservative therapy with occasional injections of procaine or oil-soluble anesthetics, as mentioned in the section on orthopedics. Immobilize with a cardboard collar as shown on page 205.

Cysts and Fistulas

Cysts and fistulas of the neck are usually too complicated to be placed in the field of minor surgery but diagnosis of their extent is an office procedure which has both utility and ease of performance to recommend it. Rather than giving dry rules, let's take an example. Presented with a tract opening here:

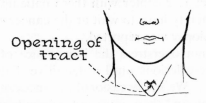

Opening of tract

begin by syringing warm, sterile isotonic saline into the tract. If there is a direct opening into the pharyngeal structures the patient will let you know immediately. If there is no such opening, continue syringing until you feel that the tract is clean and then inject some Lipiodol solution until the tract is filled. Stop up the end of the tract (with a kitchen match stick if you like) and immediately take x-rays. You can count on a relatively accurate delineation of the extent of the tract.

If operation is decided upon, have the patient come to the office the day before surgery. Once again, clean the tract and inject it with methylene blue solution which is left in place for 24 hours preceding the operation. This is very helpful when you begin to dissect out the tract itself.

MINOR SURGERY OF THE BREAST

Abscesses

There are three types of abscesses in the area of the breast which may be classified according to location. *The superficial abscess* is located between the skin and the superficial fascia, here:

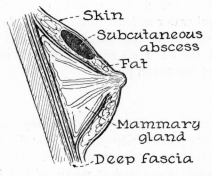

Skin
Subcutaneous abscess
Fat
Mammary gland
Deep fascia

Incision and drainage differ in no way from that of any superficial abscess except that the incision should be radical in direction with the nipple as the focus. A small drain at the lowermost portion of the wound should be used and the breast should be supported in a firm tightly fitting brassiere.

Intramammary abscess is a collection of pus below the deep fascia involving the actual mammary tissue. The breast will be red, swollen and tender. Fluctuation may be difficult to make out and in an occasional case aspiration with a large needle is required before one can be certain that purulent fluid is present. Since these lesions sometimes drain for a considerable period of time and result in more or less scarring, it is probably wise to make the incision in the crease beneath the breast if possible. If not, a small radial incision near the nipple is to be preferred to one that will show through the decolletage. Also for cosmetic reasons, it is best to avoid the upper-inner quadrant of the breast if you can do so. Upon entering the pus-filled cavity, enlarge the incision sufficiently to admit your finger and explore the entire content of the cavity like this:

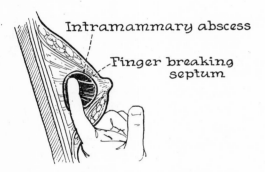

Be sure to break down all septa so that the various lobules of the abscess communicate freely with one another. If there is a lower lobule within half an inch or so of the inferior aspect of the breast, close the upper incision and make an inferior incision for drainage here:

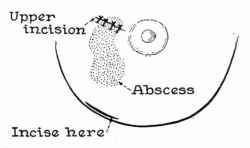

It is necessary to keep drains in place for several days and to use copious dressings. A brassiere one cup size larger than the one usu-

ally worn will make a good support for dressings.

May I interject the thought once again that women are extremely sensitive about breast scarring and deformity? All our procedures should be planned with the thought in mind of minimization of unsightly results. Women patients will be duly grateful.

Retromammary abscess is a collection of pus beneath the breast tissue, between it and the chest wall like this:

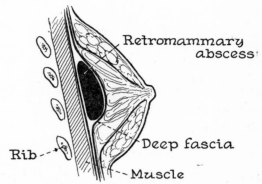

Once again, it is difficult to be certain that there is pus without making a diagnostic aspiration. In aspirating be sure to remember the three fascial planes which largely limit the extent of purulent disease. They may be represented like this:

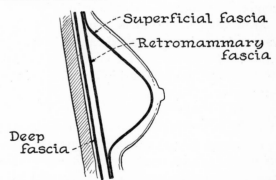

Do not push the needle through these fascial planes to the area of an abscess. You will almost certainly spread the process, i.e., if you poke into an abscess and then blithely explore with the needle, you will probably have two abscesses to deal with very shortly. Stay in one fascial plane and you are relatively safe. Upon proving the presence of retromammary pus, make an incision in the inframammary fold and use a flat flexible retractor to elevate the breast tissue out of the way like this:

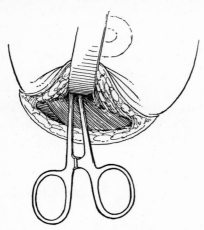

Plunge a long hemostat into the pocket of pus and insert a tissue drain. Dressing is essentially the same as mentioned above.

Contusion of the Breast

No special procedures are connected with treatment of this lesion with the exception of preventing excessive edema. This can usually be done by a tight dressing, utilizing cold packs for the first 6 to 8 hours, followed by hot packs. I cannot tell you why an edematous breast seems inordinately painful but many women have told me that the pain is intense.

Most women who incur a breast contusion want to know immediately if cancer is likely to follow. The answer, of course, is that there appears to be no relationship between a simple contusion and cancer.

The Breast Mass

We come now to one of the great arguing points of medicine. If any two doctors are in complete agreement on the diagnosis and treatment of breast mass I have yet to find them. We have all heard every opinion from the most radical to the most conservative and very few of us are sure just where we stand at any time in dealing with such a lesion. Let me be the first to say that the following discussion represents merely an opinion that has fully as many detractors as it has supporters.

The obvious signs of carcinoma are far too well known to be listed here. Rather, let us talk about the breast mass that gives every sign of *not* being carcinoma—as an example, the rounded mass that is freely movable, that feels cystic, that transilluminates cystic, that historically is cystic and has absolutely not one of the signs of malignancy.

There are those who would advocate an immediate simple mastectomy, or a tremendously complicated operative setup, or biopsy and immediate frozen section. I take the liberty of disagreeing. Ideally, such a procedure would result in a small cut in cancer mortality, but until our knowledge is more complete, the ideal is impossible of achievement. I believe the excision biopsy of a small mass that has been *carefully investigated* and shows no sign of malignancy is well justified as a minor surgical procedure.

After anesthetizing the area immediately over the cyst, make a radial incision and carry it down to the fascia. Now inject a local anesthetic underneath the fascia at these points:

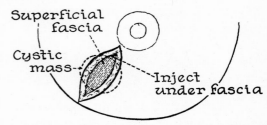

In opening the fascia be very careful not to plunge into the mass.

When the mass is seen in the wound, apply pressure on either side of it with thumb and forefinger like this:

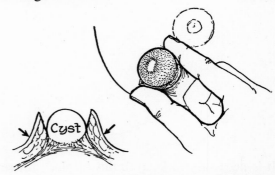

to push the mass even further into the surgical opening so that you can get a good look at it. By no means at this time put any clamps on or around the mass or touch it with any surgical instrument. If it appears to be sharply delineated from the surrounding tissue and does not look malignant, attempt by sharp dissection to find a plane of cleavage. Both fibrotic and cystic masses will usually shell out readily if one locates the proper plane. If you have a great deal of difficulty finding the plane, abandon the search, enlarge the incision and excise a pie-shaped wedge of breast tissue like this:

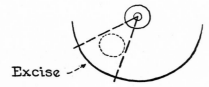

Excise

Close the wound, using the technique we have delineated before and send the tissue in for immediate pathologic study.

Should you somehow make a mistake and get in on an obvious malignancy, close the incision without disturbing the mass, hospitalize the patient and make arrangements for reopening the wound, frozen section biopsy and immediate complete mastectomy, if necessary.

I am well aware that this is not a medically perfect method but I do believe that we have to apply practical common sense to medicine along with the best scientific principles. I am sure you will agree with me that if we were to remove every breast that had a lump in it we would be doing nothing but mastectomies from morning till night.

In simple language, I believe that as long as you don't "rough up" a dubious breast mass you have not only a right but a duty to look at it and excise when your best judgment so indicates.

It occurs to me that we have discussed with somewhat horrendous detail what to do with a breast mass when you find it, but we have said very little about how to find it. This sounds as if it should be simple, but several factors come into play that sometimes make these masses tremendously difficult to locate. When a woman is lying down with one arm elevated, her breast and, of necessity, its contents are not in the same relative position that

they occupy when she is standing. It is best, therefore, when beginning the removal of a breast mass to place the patient in operative position and palpate the mass as it will be when the operation is undertaken. Various devices may then be used to mark the skin.

A method I have sometimes used is to hold the mass loosely between the thumb and forefinger while injecting the skin over it and then placing two hypodermic needles well to either side of the mass, *not* penetrating into it, like this:

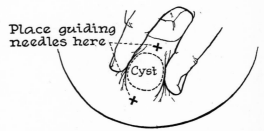

Place guiding needles here

Cyst

Anesthesia is then continued and the incision made in the usual way except that the needles serve as guide posts and will frequently lead directly to the structure we seek.

Bleeding from the Nipple

Analyses of various series of cases have shown that this is malignant about half the time, although the non-malignancies may be further divided into a half that is predominantly benign and a half that is pre-malignant. That being the case we might say that 75 per cent of bleeding from the nipple is either malignant or pre-malignant in origin.

There is, however, another point of differentiation. As age of the patient increases the statistical chance of the lesion's being malignant increases also. With these facts in mind, we might divide the cases of bleeding at the nipple into three categories:

1. The older age group past the menopause, in whom preparation should be made for mastectomy and a frozen section taken. This is a hospital procedure and has no business being done in the minor surgery.

2. The younger age group, perhaps 27 or 30 and below, in whom the chances of malignancy are slight. It is these women, too, who have the most need for functional breasts and

therefore in whom breasts should be conserved. Careful watching with local excision of any mass and minor surgical exploration of any area of tenderness should answer the problem in this age group.

3. Finally we come to the great unknown, the women between 30 and 50 who very well may have a malignancy when they present these symptoms but who have a reasonable chance of carrying a benign lesion.

I know of no good answer to the question of what to do with these women. Intraductal radiographic techniques are not accurate enough to warrant making the diagnosis on the findings from them and no other diagnostic procedure is sure enough to warrant wholesale dependence upon it.

At present our diagnostic acumen is poor, although as we progress in cellular diagnosis it will probably become possible to make a smear of cast-off cells from the milk ducts and to diagnose with a great deal more accuracy the presence or absence of a malignant lesion. Until this procedure (which has been used) is proven, these problems should probably not be explored in the field of minor surgery.

MINOR SURGERY OF THE HAND

Subungual Hematoma

This collection of blood under the fingernail is seen frequently following a bruise or blow to the digit. It is painful principally because of pressure relationships and the only effective treatment is to drain the hematoma. Place a knife point on the nail over the center of the bluish discoloration and rotate it like this:

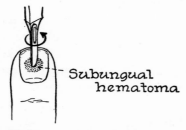

Use very little pressure, since you are using the point of the knife as a drill.

Because the subungual tissue is extremely sensitive it is well to be very cautious as you approach perforation of the nail. In most instances, blood will well up into the hole before the knife has perforated far enough to incise living tissue beneath the nail. When this blood appears it is a good idea to stop active drilling and enlarge the hole with short scraping strokes on each side.

For those of you who have a dentist friend across the hall the best possible tool for drilling the fingernail is a dental bur.

Lacerations

From the standpoint of laceration repair, the hand is one of the most important and difficult areas of the body. The functional result should be as nearly perfect as possible and cosmetic after-effects must not be ignored. Anatomically, the hand is extremely complex. In order to restore function one must, of course, restore anatomy. Surgery of the hand, therefore, presupposes as its first requisite a good working knowledge of the anatomy involved. In this discussion of lacerations, where there are peculiar anatomic points they will be mentioned.

Finger-tip Lacerations. These are common injuries and are usually shallow, with undercutting of the skin. Healing is rapid and efficient because of the ample blood supply, and infection is rare. These wounds are sutured far more often than they need to be. Washing with soap and water and closure with a piece of tape is usually an efficacious means of treatment. Actually, a firm pressure dressing may be all that is needed to secure firm apposition of wound edges.

In the case of a long spiralling cut it may sometimes be necessary to take one stitch near the midline of the cut, like this:

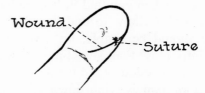

Close the rest of the lacerated area with tape or by means of external pressure. Results will be much superior if one uses the very smallest number of stitches rendered absolutely necessary by the nature of the wound.

Avulsion of Finger-tip Skin. This injury should be washed with soap and water and the avulsed area covered with a graft as described on page 275. If this is not done, exuberant granulations often form and may delay final healing.

Avulsion of the Fingernail. Usually no treatment is necessary other than cleansing and débridement. There may be several little "'strings" of tissue along the proximal nail fold and along either side.

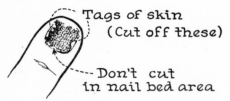

Tags of skin
(Cut off these)

Don't cut
in nail bed area

They should be snipped away with small, sharp scissors and a dressing applied. Manipulation, particularly in the area of the nail bed, simply adds to the chance of poor re-formation of the nail.

Amputation of the Finger Tip. If the separated tip can be secured, it may be sewed back in place using only stay sutures through the skin like this:

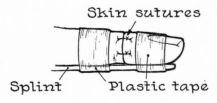

Skin sutures

Splint   Plastic tape

Splint the finger with a dorsal and a volar hairpin splint and have the patient hold it between two hot water bottles filled with ice water 30 minutes of every hour for the first 24 hours. In preparing the stump for reattachment, do not be too careful in hemostasis. Larger vessels, of course, must be tied, but a bit of oozing seems to be a salutary thing from the standpoint of the severed tip.

If the tip is lost or too much time has passed to allow a reasonable chance for reattachment, one may do a guillotine amputation and attach a graft over the finger stump like this:

Skin flap

It is, as you know, important to preserve maximum useful length of the fingers and the technique shown above is at times preferable to the formal amputation, which may shorten the finger to a greater extent.

Lacerations of the barrel of the fingers differ in no way from cuts on other body surfaces except when functionally important structures are severed.

The principal vascular supply of the fingers is this:

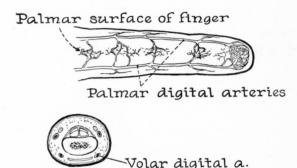

Palmar surface of finger

Palmar digital arteries

Volar digital a.

You will note that it is more than ample. Anastamoses are rich and one may tie off finger vessels with impunity.

Digital nerves are usually too small to allow adequate surgical repair. They will resume adequate function in most cases if the laceration is closed with good apposition of other anatomic parts.

Injury to the tendons in joint spaces has been discussed elsewhere.

Formal Amputation of the Finger. This may be accomplished most satisfactorily at one of these three levels:

Incisions for amputation

Do the procedure like this: First make the flaps of skin and subcutaneous tissue, being sure that they are adequately long. Notice that the palmar flap is extended distalward so that the palmar skin may be used for covering. When the flaps are made, next locate the arteries, being sure to dissect them free from their accompanying nerves and tie them. Then pick up the nerve with the point of a forceps, stretch it outward to maximum length and cut as close to the level of amputation as possible, like this:

Tendons should be cut off and anchored to the periosteum proximal to the site of amputation, like this:

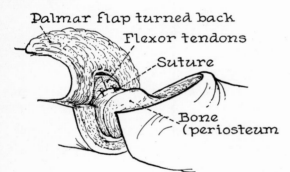

Let the tendon sheath alone. By no means pull the tendons over the end of the bone to suture them to tendons of the opposite side.

Next, sever the bone with a fine saw (if a bone saw is not available a coping saw blade that has been soaked in alcohol will do admirably.) It is not necessary to bevel the bone. Now bring the palmar flap up over the severed stump and stitch it loosely to the dorsal flap like this:

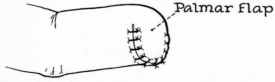

Drainage is ordinarily not necessary if the wound is sutured loosely. A splint should be worn for at least 7 days.

Palmar Lacerations. These cuts may bleed profusely when the deep or superficial volar arches are severed. The arches and their digital branches look like this:

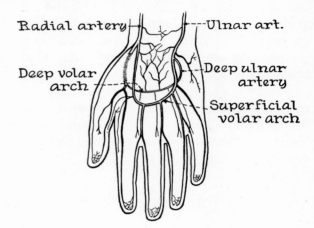

When one of these cuts is seen and is bleeding profusely, place your thumbs on the patient's wrist and exert pressure, like this:

Compression of the radial and ulnar arteries that results will effect immediate control of hemorrhage. Hold the wrist in this manner while an assistant (or the patient) washes the laceration thoroughly with soap and water. Be prepared to stop the bleeding when you release your grip.

One need have no fear of difficulty following ligation of one of the volar arches, for circulation will be little impaired. I know this sounds like a silly warning, but when one of the arches has been cut be sure to ligate both sides of the cut artery, for obvious reasons.

After bleeding has been controlled, check the function of each finger. Injuries to tendons are often seen in palmar lacerations.

If there has been no disturbance of tendinous structures, next check sensory innervation. The median nerve enters the hand here:

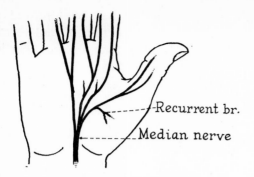

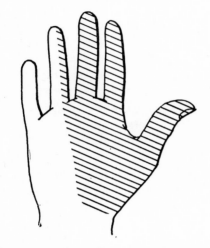

and gives sensory supply to this area:

Notice on the diagram the recurrent branches of the first common volar digital nerve, which supplies the abductor and the opponens muscles of the thumb. This nerve is often injured in lacerations of the thenar eminence like this:

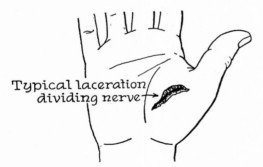

Typical laceration dividing nerve

Such injuries may result in annoying weakness in the finger-thumb grasp. The nerve is usually too small to repair accurately. When it is cut the patient should be warned about the possibility of weakness, which will exist a minimum of several months and rarely may be permanent.

Traumatic amputations extending into the palmar area are sometimes seen in the minor surgery. Any reconstructive procedures should be done in the hospital where lighting is adequate and proper instruments are at hand. When seen in the minor surgery, hemostasis should be first secured, using a tourniquet if this is necessary. Obviously dead or unsalvageable tissues may be trimmed away and the remaining viable portions of the hand treated with hot wet packs of sterile isotonic saline until arrangements can be made for hospitalization.

One should remember that débridement of the injured hand must be done very conservatively. Many structures lie just beneath the skin, and at preliminary cleansing of the wound no tissue should be removed unless one is certain that it cannot be utilized in final definitive repair.

Contusions

Of the various contusive injuries the "auto-door finger" seems the most frequent. This results when the distal phalanx is caught between the jamb and the closing door of an automobile. There is usually a crush fracture of the distal phalanx that is of no significance, and severe disruption of tissue continuity with hematoma formation.

The nail is frequently torn loose at the base, like this:

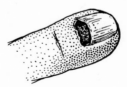

After anesthetizing by block procedure, the nail should be removed like this:

Occasionally swelling is so great and so painful that incision is indicated. If this is so, make the incision as shown:

There has been some argument that such an incision simply opens the door to osteomyelitis if bone injury is present. Before the advent of the antibiotics the contention was probably right. Now it is possibly wrong. I believe that the worst of the auto-door injuries should be incised and the antibiotics exhibited when indicated. Accessory treatment as rendered in any contusion is necessary.

Contusions in other areas of the hand are quite common but the treatment differs in no way from that recommended for the average contusion anywhere. Contusions of the dorsum may be an exception to this statement. This is seen most often as a clothes-wringer injury in which there is rupture of the dorsal veins with formation of a large hematoma, which may approach the size of a baseball.

Aspiration is not recommended. It is better to anesthetize the overlying skin and make an incision for drainage here:

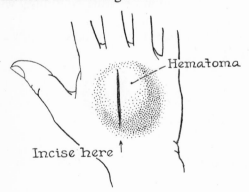

There should be complete removal of clots and fluid blood. Any hemorrhage that occurs following the procedure may easily be controlled by firm pressure.

Foreign Bodies

Splinters of glass, wood, steel wool and other substances may penetrate the soft tissues be-neath the nail. They may be removed by excising a "V"-shaped portion of nail so that the apex of the "V" nears the *proximal* portion of the foreign body like this:

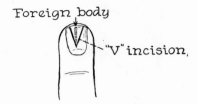

When nail removal is completed, the foreign body may be lifted out of its bed with thumb forceps.

The reason for placing the apex of the triangle near the proximal end of the foreign body is to make certain that the entire foreign body tract is open to assure adequate drainage. Subungual infection is not a frequent happening but when it does occur the pain is usually excruciating.

Foreign bodies of the soft tissues of the fingers should be removed under local anesthesia as soon as their location is demonstrated. The finger is packed with essential structures and it is difficult, if not almost impossible, for any foreign body not to impinge sooner or later upon such necessary structures.

Foreign bodies in the palm occupy a similar position. There is, however, one peculiarity that should be brought to mind in every such case. When the foreign body may be contaminated and when it penetrates the deeper palmar spaces, one should always leave an adequate drainage tract following removal. It may often be advisable to leave the entire wound made during the process of removal completely open, no sutures at all being taken. Since some scarring usually results, I prefer to close partially such wounds and insert a cellophane drain into the tissues of the foreign body tract.

Foreign bodies occasionally penetrate between the metacarpals. If they are very small and cannot be approached directly through their tract of entrance it is best to make the incision for their removal upon the dorsum of the hand.

Minor Infections of the Hand

Paronychia (or runaround) results when pathogenic organisms gain entrance between the skin surface and the fingernail. There are three common types of abscess which result, like this:

Treatment differs according to the stage of the infection when it is first seen. At the very earliest, when pus is just beginning to form at the nail border, use the back of the scalpel to lift up the tissues from the side of the nail like this:

When pus escapes, use the point of the knife to incise into the abscess cavity so that adequate drainage is established.

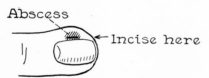

If this cannot be done at the edge of the nail, then excise the tissues over the tiny abscess like this:

When the abscess has penetrated beneath the nail, use block anesthesia and turn back a flap at the base of the nail like this:

Now pick up the nail base in forceps and lift it up from the abscess. The nail attachment will have been severed by the collection of pus, and lifting should be easy. Now cut off the nail, being sure to cut as far distalward as the pus pocket extends.

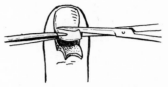

Next put a small tissue drain in place and lay the flap back in its normal position so that the result looks like this:

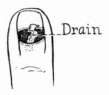

Subepithelial abscess results when bacteria are driven into the superficial layers of the skin. It is usually found on the distal volar aspect of the finger.

The abscess that forms lies between the tough dermis and the epidermal layer, like this:

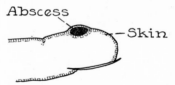

It would present no difficulty at all if it were not for the fact that pus burrows through the dermal layer to form a secondary cavity in the fatty tissues beneath the skin, like this:

Such an abscess should be opened at once. After anesthetizing the finger, unroof the superficial abscess by excising the skin above it like this:

Now apply gentle pressure on either side of the lesion. If there is a deep cavity, pus will be seen to well up through the floor of the superficial cavity. When this occurs put the point of a closed mosquito hemostat in the deep cavity and spread the blades. When drained adequately these lesions are of no significance. If not drained they may become the nidus of a severe infection.

Felon. Infections of the distal closed space in the fingers are exceedingly painful and must be treated quickly and properly if extensive damage is to be prevented. Anatomically, this distal closed space is not a closed space at all. Certain peculiarities, however, make it behave as one. In longitudinal section the space looks like this:

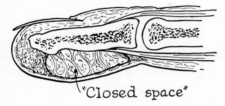

"Closed space"

Notice that the fatty tissue enmeshed in the fibrous bands is all located distal to the epiphysis of the distal phalanx. Tendinous attachments are proximal, as are the attachments of the joint capsule. Infection seldom spreads from this area toward the base of the finger except in very late stages.

The fibrous septa make impossible much swelling upon increase of tension and this, in turn, emphasizes pain. Swelling within the limited space effects partial or complete closure of the arteries, including those to the shaft of the distal phalanx. For this reason bony necrosis begins rapidly after the onset of the disease and osteomyelitis occurs with annoying frequency.

When diagnosed, the felon should be incised promptly. One may select the type of incision used according to the extent of the disease. There are three criteria to determine this extent. One is the time of existence. Since felons progress rapidly, those that have been present more than three or four days should be drained with a more extensive type of incision. Degree of pain is another reason-

ably accurate method of deciding the extent of the operation. By all means the best method is x-ray. If there is the slightest sign that would indicate a necrosis of bone (and these signs occur quite early) one should do a more extensive operation.

If you feel the moderate procedure is indicated, block the finger nerve as described on page 332 and put a tourniquet around the base of the finger. After waiting for anesthesia to become fully effective make an incision on either side of the finger like this:

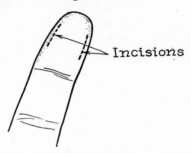

Incisions

Extend it completely through the soft tissues so that a drain may be pulled through like this:

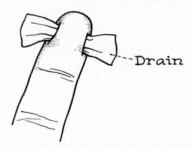

Drain

Be sure to cut as many of the fibrous septa as you can reach by extending the knife both proximally and distally from the limits of the incision like this:

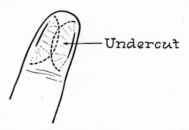

Undercut

The only advantage this more conservative incision has over the next one to be described is that it avoids a scar at the tip of the finger which may sometimes be painful for a brief period following the operation.

If you feel the infection is well advanced, do not temporize. After applying the tourniquet and anesthetizing the finger, make an incision separating all the tissues at the end of the finger like this:

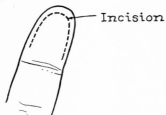

Incision

Notice that the incision is not centrally located on the finger. The bone lies near the dorsal side and the incision should parallel the volar aspect of the phalanx.

Incision

These cases sometimes come to us in the very latest stages with great necrosis of finger-tip tissues and even of bone. When such a case presents itself, make any incision necessary to allow free drainage of the entire area. If there are chips of necrotic bone in the wound, do not hesitate to remove them but be very conservative about removing questionable osseous tissue. A surprisingly large amount of it will live and resume adequate function without residual osteomyelitis. Since advent of the antibiotics not more than one of each ten or twenty thousand such cases will require amputation even though the disease may be seen in an advanced stage.

Collar-button Abscess. This term usually refers to an epidermoid abscess that has burrowed and formed a deep cavity, usually on the palmar surface of the hand in this area:

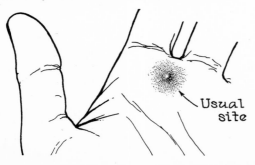

Usual site

Surprisingly enough, the deep chamber of these abscesses may extend for as much as ½ or ¾ inch without there being marked external signs. When a case presents itself showing a small superficial abscess that appears to be in the skin of the palm and yet produces profound pain, outline the area of the pain by using a kitchen match for palpation, like this:

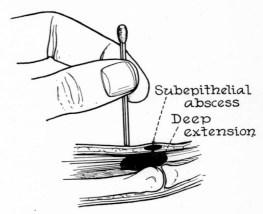

Subepithelial abscess
Deep extension

Unroof the superficial abscess exactly as described in the section on epidermoid abscess of the finger and apply gentle deep pressure to see if pus exudes from the base of the superficial cavity. If it does, follow the communicating channel with a curved mosquito forceps and, upon entering the main cavity, open the jaws of the forceps sufficiently to establish drainage. It is usually wise to put a small tissue drain into the deeper cavity, like this:

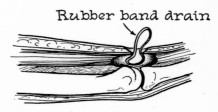

Rubber band drain

More Serious Infections of the Hand

There is a routine procedure for diagnosis that, if followed, will simplify a great deal the differentiation of serious hand infections. Such a hand will usually present a swollen dorsum. Before exploring the palm, apply firm pressure over this dorsal swelling. If it is only edema resulting from a palmar infection, pitting on pressure will be quite apparent. If, on the other hand, there is a dorsal abscess the patient will discuss it with you in no uncertain terms when you apply pressure. Now check the hand for position. With an acute palmar infection the hand usually assumes the position of rest like this:

Should there be infection of tendon sheaths, the involved fingers are usually held in flexion like this:

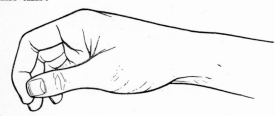

When a flexed finger is present, attempt very gently to straighten it. In the presence of tendon sheath infection the patient will complain bitterly of pain upon extension and will usually localize the pain in the region of the metacarpophalangeal joint, here:

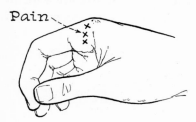

It is extremely important that these fingers not be overextended. Only a sufficient amount of motion to indicate the presence of pain should be used. Any rough handling in the early stages of the examination will cause excruciating pain and often insure that co-operation of the patient will be lost, which has the result of invalidating many of the findings. In some cases, unnecessary roughness will cause rapid extension of the infectious process.

Now look at the palmar aspect of the hand. The ulnar bursa is situated like this:

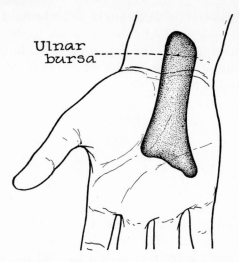

If it is involved, there will be some swelling but very seldom a loss of the concavity of the palm. The middle palmar space lies here:

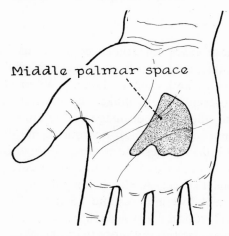

It may be infected, in which case the concavity of the palm is usually lost or, in more extensive infections, bulging of the palm appears.

The thenar space lies here:

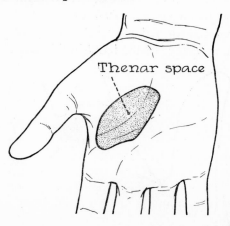

Swelling in this area is almost pathognomonic of infection of the space. There may occasionally be confusion with infection of the flexor pollicis longus sheath, which lies here:

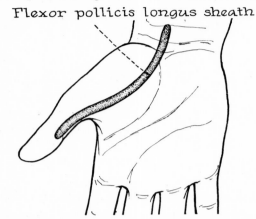

Flexor pollicis longus sheath

Flexion of the thumb may occur in involvement of the flexor sheath and of the thenar space. Attempt *gently* to straighten out the thumb. While mildly painful, this can usually be done if the thenar space is involved, but in tendon sheath infections there is extreme resistance to this extension and the patient will complain bitterly of pain if any but the gentlest attempts at movement are made.

Finally, use a kitchen match to palpate the tender areas of the hand. In a surprising number of cases, one may outline the infected area very accurately by this method. The outline itself will, of course, give a clue to diagnosis because of its relation to known anatomy.

Tenosynovitis. Tendons have a very poor blood supply. Surgical infection of the sheath may quickly obliterate even this meager supply, with resultant sloughing of the tendon substance. When this occurs it makes necessary extensive reparative surgery, which may be only moderately successful. Many times a permanent crippling injury may result.

Since the advent of the antibiotics this does not happen as often as it did previously but one must remember that the time available for treating a tendon sheath infection is very limited. If seen in the earliest stages when swelling is minimal and there is no indication of pus formation, one may safely use antibiotic therapy. Should there be the slightest ques-

tion about gross distention of the sheath, immediate incision is indicated. Do it this way:

Use field bloc anesthetic. Make no attempt to infiltrate local agents into the tissues about the tendon sheath. After anesthesia becomes effective, elevate the arm for 2 minutes and then apply a blood pressure cuff pumped at least 75 points (preferably 100) above the level of systolic blood pressure. Make an anterolateral incision along the finger or thumb involved. Incise at least three-quarters the length of the involved tendon sheath or more. When crossing skin creases, "Z" the incision like this:

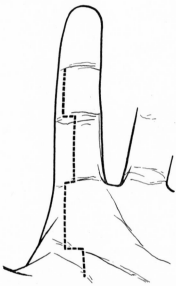

Now dissect toward the bulging tendon sheath until it protrudes into the wound like this:

Tendon sheath

Use a sharp knife or scissors to incise it, remembering that the sheath itself is very thin. Use only the tip of the knife or the very distal portion of the scissors blade to extend the incision.

After allowing the pus, which is under pressure, to drain off on its own accord, irrigate the sheath gently with warm sterile isotonic saline solution. Now release the tourniquet and clamp the vessels that bleed. Unless you have mistakenly severed one of the digital arteries, bleeding will be minor and may be completely controlled by keeping clamps in place for 2 or 3 minutes. Vessels should not be tied unless bleeding cannot be controlled otherwise.

Leave the wound open. Make no effort to insert a drain, for the fibrosis that results around the tract may do more damage than the drain will do good. Take time to instruct the patient carefully how to use constant hot packs on the hand, or, if there is a person trained in nursing available, use hot moist packs directly on the wound for a few hours after drainage.

Following such surgery antibiotics should be given. These patients recover with remarkable celerity.

Infection of the Thenar Space. Use a field block anesthetic for incision of this infection (see page 332). After anesthesia is secured, apply a blood pressure cuff and pump it up at least 75 mm. above systolic level. Make the incision on the *dorsum* of the web of the thumb near the first metacarpal, here:

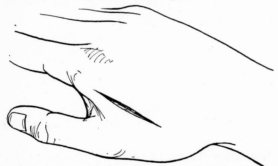

Next locate the adductor pollicis muscle, which will be seen in the incision, and push a closed hemostat gently along the anterior surface of the muscle like this:

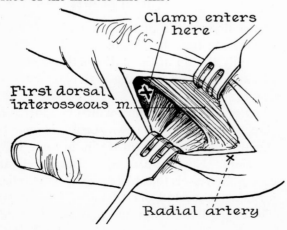

Remember the location of the radial artery and be careful to avoid it.

When purulent material is reached, spread the jaws of the clamp to insure adequate drainage space. One may insert a cellophane or a petrolatum gauze drain into the wound, but this drain should be removed in 36 hours or less.

There is seldom any bleeding of note from this incision unless one disturbs the radial artery. Simple compression will usually control blood loss. Postoperative care is similar to that of any infection.

Infection of Middle Palmar Space. These infections are best drained by incising the finger web between the middle and ring fingers or between the little and ring fingers. Most people prefer to make this incision on the palmar surface of the web, like this:

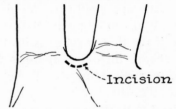

While my experience with these infections has been somewhat limited, I am inclined to incise just dorsal to the apex of the web, here:

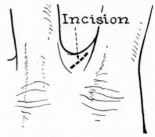

After the incision is made one then inserts a closed hemostat pointing slightly laterally from the wound so that it passes in immediate proximity to the metacarpal head and into the middle palmar space. When the pus has been evacuated and a drain inserted, the wound is dressed with absorbent gauze. It is best to put the fingers in a semi-flexed position.

An old trick that I have seen used is to dress the hand around a soft sponge-rubber ball and then ask the patient to press gently on the ball from time to time. The theory is that the expulsion of pus is hastened by this pressure. I am inclined to believe that spreading of the infection might also result and, as a consequence, have not used the procedure.

Ganglion

The argument still rages over just what a ganglion is. May I hasten to intrude my two cents' worth by saying that I don't know. It is a cystic swelling that occurs usually in proximity to joint capsules or tendon sheaths and may recur with monotonous regularity unless adequate therapy is carried out. Two office procedures are of use.

Don't overlook the grandmother's method of treatment by making the ganglion prominent and swatting it soundly with a heavy object such as a book. When thus ruptured, approximately 50 per cent of ganglia disappear completely.

This book is about the right size for ganglion smashing. For a wrist ganglion do the procedure as follows: First tell the patient what you are going to do. Then have him bend the wrist over the edge of your desk or table to make the ganglion prominent, like this:

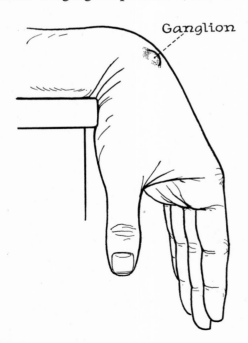

Pick up the book and hit the ganglion a sharp blow. As a word of warning, I have heard of a navicular being fractured in the process of smashing a ganglion.

If there is recurrence following this therapy, dissect out the ganglion under local anesthesia. There are only two special things to note about this procedure:

1. At the base of the ganglion excise a small block of tissue like this:

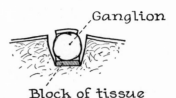

Recurrences are rare when this is done.

2. Should you unroof a joint cavity or tendon sheath in this process, make no effort to close the gap. Simply close the skin and apply a firm dressing. Splinting the part for 24 hours seems to be an advantage.

There are no common lesions of the arm that cannot be handled by methods mentioned in the general discussion on minor surgery.

MINOR SURGERY OF THE LEG AND FOOT

Varicose Veins

While there are many contributory factors in the development of varicosities, the essential pathology that we must correct is as follows: Backflow from above is prevented in superficial veins by a series of valves that look like this:

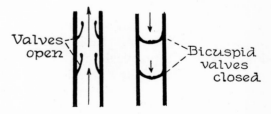

There are valves present in the veins that communicate with the deep venous system so that the protection against backflow in superficial veins sums up to this:

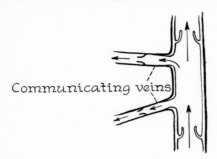

Communicating veins

When valves become incompetent for whatever reason, there is back pressure down the vein with resultant dilatation. As one might expect, the principal interference with circulation is usually at the lowermost part of the vascular system, in this case the lower leg. The direct cause of many complications is a constant stasis of blood in tissues here:

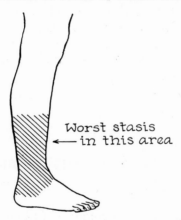

Worst stasis
← in this area

This subcutaneous stasis results in deposition of pigment in the skin and a fibrotic reaction that gradually infiltrates and replaces the normal subcutaneous fat so that the area has a firm rubbery feel rather than the normal soft pliability of healthy tissue. Circulation in such an area approaches the minimum that will support tissue life. Resistance to infectious processes is practically nil.

As a result the slightest abrasion of the skin surface frequently allows entrance of pathogenic bacteria. These organisms rapidly break down the skin and underlying tissues until the typical varicose ulcer results. Healing is slow and inadequate because of poor circulation. Occasionally local resistance will partially overcome the bacterial onslaught, with recession of the ulcer. This successful fight against invasion cannot, however, be maintained by tissues deficient in blood supply, and soon bacteria infiltrate the poor defenses and the ulcer once again enlarges. Such a picture is commonly seen by us practitioners and we frequently have the opportunity to follow it through the entire vicious cycle from the first varicosity to the crippling ulcer.

Diagnosis of varicosities is usually apparent at a glance but certain office procedures contribute much information as to their status and extent. The Schwartz test is excellent proof of venous incompetence and dilatation of veins. Place the fingers of your left hand on the varicosities of the leg and sharply tap the saphenous vein at the highest point at which it can be made out, like this:

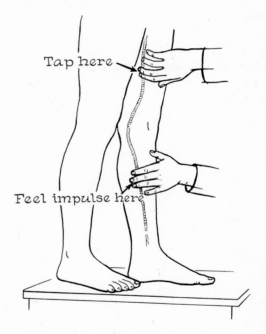

Tap here

Feel impulse here

If the vein is dilated, the impulse from the tap will travel down the column of blood and may be perceived by the fingers of the left hand. In a normal vein this is not possible.

Having established abnormality of the vein it is now imperative to elicit two further facts. The first is whether the deep veins in the leg are patent and adequate to carry all returning blood, and the second is whether the communicating veins between the superficial and deep circulation have functional valves.

As a first test use two 3 inch Ace bandages to wrap the patient's leg tightly, beginning at the base of the toes and extending to above the knee. Then ask him to walk rapidly around the block. If the deep veins are patent, he will show mild surprise and take his walk without comment. If the deep veins are not patent you may expect to see him at your office door in a minute or so with both bandages in his hand and an indignant look on his face. The Ace bandages, if properly applied, occlude the superficial circulation and exercise brings on immediate pain unless the deep circulation is adequate to carry returning blood.

Next, have the patient lie down on the examining table. Grasp his ankle and support the affected leg at a 45 degree angle for 1 minute, like this:

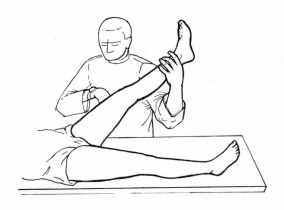

Now locate the saphenous vein high in the leg and occlude it by using a firm finger grip, like this:

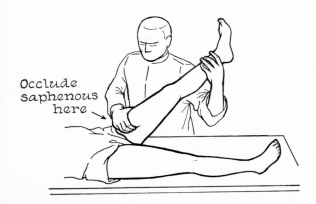

Occlude saphenous here →

Ask the patient to stand while you maintain your grip. If the veins fill promptly it is safe to assume that they must do so from the communicating veins, since you have the saphenous held shut. In such a case, simple ligation will be of no service whatever and a vein stripping procedure is the only surgery of utility.

When the saphenous remains empty after the patient arises, wait at least 30 seconds and then release your grip. If it fills promptly from above, this is ample proof that the saphenous valves themselves are incompetent and that a high ligation procedure should offer definite benefit to the patient.

There are many, many other tests designed to give information about the two saphenous systems but one seldom needs more information than that provided by the two tests mentioned above.

Injection Treatment of Varicose Veins. The usual early case of varicosities, in which deep veins are patent and communicating veins show an adequate valvular system, may be treated satisfactorily by injection. A good injection technique will result in elimination of pathology in many cases. Do it this way:

Have the patient sit on the side of the table while you prepare the site for injection. Use a 26 gauge needle attached to a 2 cc. syringe containing 1 or 2 cc. of 5 per cent sodium morrhuate. If the veins are small, one may make the injection in the sitting position. Larger veins (and most patients will be in this category) require drainage of the vein before injecting. Insert the needle into the most dependent varix with the patient seated. Then hold the syringe firmly against his leg and ask the patient to lie down on the examining table and elevate the affected leg. Be sure that you keep a firm grip on the syringe so that the needle remains in the vein.

Within 30 seconds the vein will usually collapse and the sclerosing solution may be injected. Use a very small amount—usually less than 0.5 cc.—at the first injection. Some patients show a more marked sensitivity to the drug than others. When the vein has collapsed put the required amount of solution into it slowly and maintain the elevated position of the leg for 5 to 10 seconds. Now lower the leg to the table and wrap it tightly with an elastic bandage from the toes to above the knee. Ask the patient to remain lying down for 10 to 15 minutes.

These injections are most satisfactory if done at least once weekly and may have to be continued over several months to gain maximum effect. They should not, of course, be given in the presence of any kind of irritative phenomena such as phlebitis.

Many physicians derogate this procedure, claiming that it is useless since operation may have to be done anyway. My experience has been that the procedure—wisely and conservatively used—gives excellent results. Those who criticize loudest seem either to fancy themselves as surgeons or not to know how to do the injection.

Ligation of the Great Saphenous Vein. High ligation of the saphenous vein is an easy procedure that may be done on an outpatient basis for most people. After preparing the area with soap and water, ask the patient to stand while you palpate the vein. It will be an aid to surgery if one marks the course of the vein by using an applicator dipped in Merthiolate. Now have the patient lie on the table with the leg slightly flexed and rotated outward. The important anatomic details of the area are these:

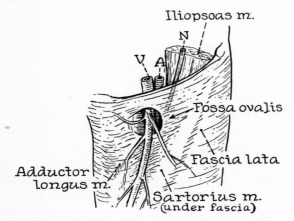

After infiltrating the skin with local anesthetic solution, make a vertical incision over the vein like this:

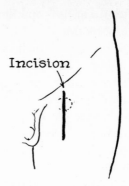

Remember that the saphenous vein lies superficial to the fascia. Dissect downward through the fat until it comes into view. If the deep fascia is seen before the vein is located, carry the dissection medially along the fascial plane. This will usually result in adequate exposure.

When the vein is exposed, do not be in a hurry to ligate it. Take a few minutes to dissect carefully up and down its course until all branches are clearly visualized. Remember that there is no normal pattern of veins at the saphenofemoral junction. Each case must be treated separately.

When this has been accomplished the field should look like this:

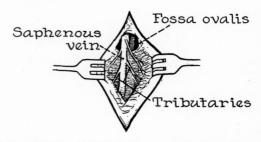

Now expose the depth of the vein where it penetrates the fossa ovalis and make a small slit in the deep fascia. Place two ligatures on the vein approximately 1 cm. apart and clamp it between the ligatures like this:

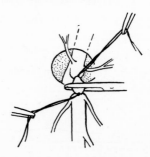

Now cut between the clamp and the distal liga-ture and take two or three through and through sutures around the clamp like this:

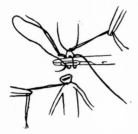

Gently remove the clamp and tie the suture so that the vein is doubly ligated on the femo-ral side. Lift up the distal end and tie the branches like this:

If you wish, you may pass a small (size 9 or 10) catheter down the distal lumen of the vein and inject sclerosing solution as you with-draw it. Carefully check all possible bleed-ing points and ligate any that seem question-able.

In closing the wound it is not necessary to take stitches in the subcutaneous fat. Fascial layers may be closed if they have been opened. The skin is loosely approximated. A firm pressure dressing should be applied and the patient instructed to sit around the house for an hour or two before attempting any activity. Since there is occasionally some pain follow-ing this operation, it may be wise to give the patient a half dozen tablets containing ¼ grain of codeine, ¼ grain of phenobarbital and 5 grains of aspirin.

Occasionally, after ligation of the great saphenous vein, the wound seems to have an inordinate amount of dead space near the base. If this happens there is a home-made type of dressing that seems to aid in healing. First, get two lengths of ½ inch copper tubing 2 or 2½ inches long. They may be boiled for sterilization. Wrap them with gauze and hold the wrapping in place with tape like this:

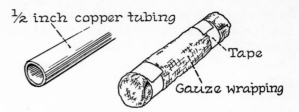

When skin closure has been completed, place the wrapped tubing about ¾ inch lateral to the wound margin and tape it in place like this:

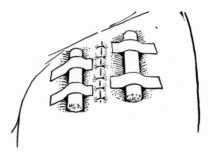

Now put a firm pressure dressing in place. The tubing helps obliterate dead spaces deep in the wound and aids in everting the skin edges, like this:

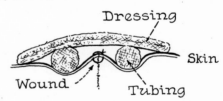

Ligation of the Small Saphenous Vein. This is best done in the popliteal space under local anesthesia. Make a transverse incision like this:

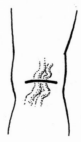

The deep fascia lies very superficially in this location and is usually reached after penetra-tion of ¼ inch or less. The veins usually lie superficial to this fascia and sometimes appear to form a groove in it. In the rare case it is necessary to open the fascia for adequate exposure. The lesser saphenous vein has fewer tributary branches than the greater but the dissection should be carefully done so that any unusual venous pattern may be accommodated.

When the vein is fully exposed, doubly ligate and remove a segment like this:

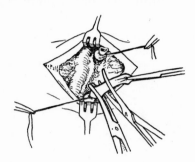

Use fine interrupted cotton sutures to close the deep fascia and the same for the skin. Apply a firm dressing and a posterior splint so that the leg is maintained in approximately 10 degrees of flexion. The patient may usually go about his affairs with no limitation other than that imposed by the splint.

Vein stripping is usually not a procedure for the office surgery.

The Isolated Varix. These may usually be treated by injection of a sclerosing agent. If they do not respond to this therapy, simple removal at their site is indicated.

Varicose Ulcers

All of us family physicians face a parade of these ulcer victims. Until the last few years this has been among the most discouraging diseases we see. Recent improvements in therapy have changed this somewhat.

Drug therapy has no place in this book but I should like to point out that there are now available compounds that materially benefit the healing process. Office procedures should begin with adequate treatment of the varicose veins. No regimen of therapy is likely to be permanently successful if the veins continue to exist. After veins are treated, support the ulcerated area by using an Unna paste boot. The formula for Unna's paste will be found on page 56. A useful technique is

to incorporate a plastic bath sponge into the dressing like this:

Since the purpose of this procedure is to maintain firm pressure on the ulcer area, one must remember that the Unna dressing is useless unless applied in such fashion that pressure is maintained. I have seen these boots carefully and well applied, only to watch the physician cut out a large area immediately over the ulcer so he "could get to the dressing." To me this is roughly equivalent to shooting a dog so you could go pet him without his running away.

Severe necrotic ulcers usually respond to bed rest, elevation and hot moist packs. These home procedures should probably be used for a few days before application of a pressure dressing in the more severe cases.

When clean granulations are achieved, a skin graft will frequently take. Unless the ulcer is larger than 2 or 3 cm. in diameter, this grafting may be done in the office with very little danger.

One "desperation measure" for epithelizing an ulcer is that of Braun. It seems to work well, although I cannot explain its advantage over other methods. One begins by carefully cleansing the ulcer. Next, an area of the thigh is prepared and a full thickness bit of skin approximately 1 by 1 cm. is removed and folded in a warm isotonic saline pack.

One then uses a small biopsy punch or the smallest Hegar dilator to bore out canals in the ulcer surface, like this:

Punch, or Hegar dilator

Skin

A tiny piece is snipped off the skin removed from the thigh and is planted in each of these canals. No effort is made to keep the implant near the surface. Then the ulcer is covered with a routine dressing.

The procedure should probably be reserved for those ulcers that do not heal after using the more usual types of therapy.

Ingrown Toenail

The ingrowing nail usually appears on the great toe. Cases may be separated roughly into two types upon the basis of whether or not infection and granulation tissue are present. The only difference in treatment is provision for excision of granulation tissue in the more severe cases.

Begin your procedure with nerve block anesthesia and wait at least 10 minutes for the anesthetic to become effective. Now push a sharp pointed scissors under the toenail, cutting as you go like this:

Cut extends to nail bed

When the base of the nail is reached, grasp the fragment to be removed with a Kelly forceps and remove by rotating it outward like this:

If there are granulations present trim them **away**. When this procedure is complete,

make a "V" incision in the tissues and close the defect with fine cotton sutures.

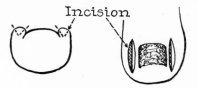

Incision

This is the object of the procedure:

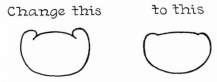

Change this   to this

If the procedure is carefully done the patient will be able to walk with only minor discomfort immediately following the surgery. Elevation and occasionally a warm soak (during which time the operative field may be washed with soap and water) will speed recovery. Stitches should be removed by the fifth to seventh day.

MINOR PLASTIC SURGERY

Full Thickness Grafts

These are not so popular as they once were but still occasionally find use in repair of a deep defect. They are usually cut approximately to size. Donor sites are legion: the abdomen, legs and arms, buttocks and, rarely, areas of the back may be used. Try to select an area that has approximately the same coloration and hair pattern as that which you will replace. In order to get an approximation of proper size, I usually use Merthiolate to sketch at the donor site an area about equal in size and configuration to that which is to be covered, like this:

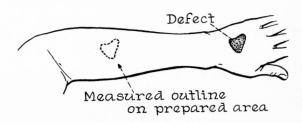

Defect

Measured outline on prepared area

After anesthetizing the donor site, make a vertical incision into and through the skin following the edge of the "pattern." Using toothed forceps, lift the donor skin gently upward and undercut it, taking only the smallest possible amount of fat along with a full thickness of skin.

The recipient site should have been prepared by gentle scrubbing until granulations, if present, are bright red and oozing slightly or until a fresh wound is clean. When the graft has been freed, it is best to make several small holes through it for purposes of drainage if it is more than 1 cm. in diameter. I use a small biopsy punch to do this. Now lay the graft in place and stitch it *loosely*. Depend upon a pressure dressing to hold it in firm apposition to the tissues, using sutures only as a means to anchor it so that it cannot "slip around." Pressure dressings should be maintained for at least 5 days.

If carefully done, well over 80 per cent of such grafts will take and one should not hesitate to use them in the minor surgery. They are best applied in cases of traumatic avulsion when first seen. The old wound with granulations usually may be handled adequately by means of pinch or split thickness grafts.

Pinch Grafts

These are most applicable to granulating wounds that have no islands of epithelium and that do not seem to warrant the split thickness grafting. After cleansing and anesthetizing the donor site, pick up the skin on a needle and snip it off with a knife or scissors, like this:

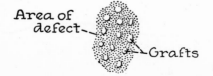

Using the needle as a means of transportation, move the graft to the recipient site and lay it gently on the granulation tissue. Repeat this until the area to be covered looks like this:

Using the utmost care not to roll or move the pinch grafts, apply a pressure dressing and leave it undisturbed for at least 5 days.

Takes are usual and rapid epithelization often follows.

Split Thickness Grafts

These are the darlings of the plastic surgeon and with good reason, for results are excellent. A granulating lesion, such as an old burn, is ideal for application of the split thickness graft. One should remember that the technique of split thickness grafting must be exacting and that only small lesions have any place in the minor surgery. In other words, when one finds out how easy it is to put on a split thickness graft, the tendency is to attempt too much. A good rule of thumb is that lesions over 3 cm. (or at most 4 cm.) in diameter should be grafted in the hospital. When large areas are to be done or when any complication exists the practitioner should have expert consultation before undertaking the procedure.

After anesthetizing the donor site, have your assistant help you by holding the skin to be removed firmly and under tension, using two tongue blades like this:

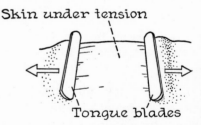

An ordinary well honed straight razor may be used to remove the skin. For a small graft the double edged safety razor blade is just as satisfactory.

All that is done is to peel off the top layer of the skin like this:

Proper thickness will vary from that of onion skin paper to that of 20 pound writing paper (ordinary stationery), depending upon the site and the individual concerned. If the graft is properly removed, the area from which it is taken should look like very white skin with numerous punctate bleeding points. By no means should any fat be visible.

Now transfer the graft to the prepared recipient site and stitch it in place like this:

It is almost impossible to get the graft the exact size of the recipient site. One usually must take a little too much skin and trim it to the proper size as it is applied. After the skin has been stitched in place, be sure to avoid rolling the edges and to perforate it for drainage like this:

Perforations

Apply a firm pressure dressing, splint the part and let it alone for 7 days. Results are usually excellent. There are, however, two items of technique which must be exacting. The first, of course, is asepsis, and the second is the avoidance of trauma. Infection will cause complete failure and excessive trauma apparently causes thrombosis of small vessels with resultant death of the applied skin.

Here is a bit of advice. Grafting is well within the province of the competent family physician, but never hesitate to ask for help. The skillful plastic surgeon can make many time-saving and technical suggestions that will prove invaluable. Unless starvation seems imminent to him he will be glad to have you handle these routine cases and reserve his efforts for those patients who must have his superior skill.

Plastic surgery is fascinating because it is not routinized like many other aspects of our art. Every case, no matter how trivial, presents a new problem and one that may be

answered several ways. A dozen books would not serve to delineate all of the procedures which may be used. Merely as a cross section to offer some ideas, here are some techniques that have been applied to our patients:

Example 1: Avulsion of a Finger Tip

Bring back a flap of skin from the thenar eminence like this:

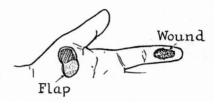

Sew the skin of the finger tip to the flap but do not sever the attachment of the flap to the thenar eminence, so that this step appears like this:

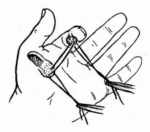

Now undercut the area of defect on the thumb and pull it together like this:

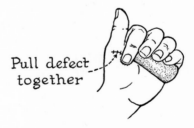

Bandage the hand in this position and leave it for 7 days. When the graft is taking well, sever the attachment to the thumb. The final results look like this:

Another trick for the avulsed finger tip is to make a "V" incision on either side of the damaged finger like this:

You will notice that you have freed two triangular areas of the skin. Sew the bases of the triangles together and lay them over the avulsed end like this:

Now close the tissues at the side of the finger like this:

Trim the graft you have made and sew it in place like this:

Example 2: Avulsion of Skin from the Back of the Hand

Raise a large flap from the upper abdomen like this:

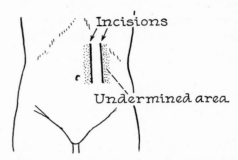

Undercut the skin on either side of the flap and sew it together like this:

Dress the suture line. Now lay the hand underneath the flap and stitch the flap to the back of the hand like this:

Leave it undisturbed for 5 days. Now sever the inferior side of the flap, trimming it to fit the abdominal wound with closure like this:

Three days later sever the upper end of the flap and again replace it in the abdominal wound.

Example 3: Avulsion of an Area of the Forehead

Have the patient put his right hand to the back of his neck so that the inner surface of the arm is close to the avulsed area, like this:

Raise a flap from the inner surface of the arm and stitch it to the forehead like this:

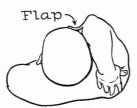

Bandage the arm in place for several days. Now sever the flap and fix the arm so that minimal scarring is present.

These should not be regarded as recommended methods for, to reiterate, each case is different. These are, however, methods that have worked. I am sure you will devise hundreds of others.

The freeing of scar tissue is another aspect of plastic surgery that is well within the reach of the practitioner in his own office. There is no possibility of giving adequate coverage to the subject in a work such as this. If you would like to do these procedures, procure a good book on minor plastic reconstruction and read it thoroughly. Most texts, unfortunately, are devoted largely to procedures far beyond the reach of us family doctors. One caution: It is easy to attempt too much as an office procedure.

Section X

INTERNAL MEDICINE

INTERNAL MEDICINE

INFECTIOUS DISEASES

Office procedures concerned with the infectious diseases are mostly diagnostic tests. There are few mechanical means of treatment needed. Minor bacteriology is within the range of every office and can be of the greatest value. I believe that all busy physicians will sooner or later begin doing the simpler bacteriologic tests. Here is how to find out for less than $10 whether or not bacteriology can be of use in your practice.

Get a cardboard box with about 2 cubic feet of space inside it. Cut off the lid. Put the box in a room in your office which stays at nearly constant temperature. Place it upside down on a shelf or table so that the space inside the box is completely enclosed by the table top and cardboard sides and bottom of the box. Buy an extension cord and a 20 watt light bulb and put the bulb in the box, like this:

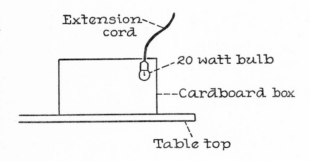

Leave it burning. Push a thermometer through the top of the box and tape it in place. After an hour or so the box will probably be too hot for proper bacterial growth. Cut a half-inch hole in the top of the box and another at the bottom margin, like this:

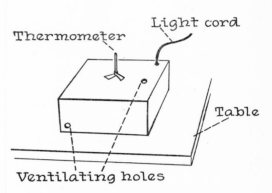

Keep adding holes until the temperature stays near 100° F. If your office gets cool at night, simply set something over the holes before you leave. This equipment is entirely satisfactory for exploring the question of whether or not bacteriology can be helpful. If you elect to do minor studies, a more adequate incubator can be built with a hot plate, a thermostat, and a homemade wooden cabinet. Commercial models may be had quite cheaply.

Petri dishes may be obtained at low cost. Plain meat extract agar medium may be purchased commercially. To make blood agar, proceed as follows:

1. Melt 100 cc. of the above agar and let cool to 45° C.

2. Add 5 cc. citrated blood.

3. Mix and pour into sterile Petri dishes.

If the medium is too hot, the blood will change color and a chocolate agar will result. Sterile technique must be followed throughout. Incubation of a test plate for 24 hours without growth is proof of sterility.

In addition to the above, Sabouraud's medium is useful for cultivation of fungi. It may be purchased commercially. Special bacteriologic techniques will be mentioned in sections on specific disease.

Brucellosis

The skin test is of some value although not positively diagnostic. Give 0.1 cc. of a 1:1000 solution of Brucellergen *intracutaneously,* like this:

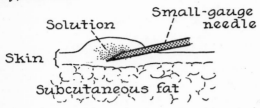

A normal saline control may be given intracutaneously in the opposite arm. Read the test in 24 and again in 48 hours.

Positive diagnosis may be gained by blood culture. This is highly technical and is usually beyond the range of the small laboratory.

Bacillary Dysentery

Do a gross and microscopic examination of the stool. Many times a typical pale pink cast (a few shades lighter than a Benadryl capsule) can be seen in certain areas of the liquid stool. Occasionally it is grossly bloody.

Microscopic preparations reveal many polys in all stages of degeneration. Red cells will be present and an occasional large macrophage which has ingested a red cell or two. The bacteria are hard to isolate without special cultural means.

Pneumonia

The only office procedure of service is smear and culture for the offending organism. This is needed only rarely. Stain the smear with Gram's stain and use a blood agar plate for culture. Check the sputum grossly. In lobar pneumonia it is usually of a rusty color; in bronchopneumonia it is frankly purulent, but bronchopneumonia may show no sputum at all for several days.

The x-ray is useful in questionable or early disease but its use in a well developed case is tantamount to an admission of incompetence.

Gonococcal Infections

The smear of discharge stained by Gram's method or with methylene blue is a necessary part of diagnosis which should not be omitted.

In cases of medicolegal importance, culture is necessary but is somewhat technical and should be left to commercial laboratories.

Meningitis

Do an immediate spinal tap. Fluid containing more than 400 or 500 cells per cubic millimeter will be grossly cloudy. Now do a cell count on the fresh fluid.

1. Draw diluting fluid for the white cell count (to which has been added a few drops of methylene blue stain) up to the mark 1 on the white cell count pipet. Then draw fresh spinal fluid up to the mark 11. Shake and fill the counting chamber. Count the cells in the four corner areas exactly as in the white count and multiply the total by 2.5, like this:

Upper left	6
Upper right	5
Lower left	7
Lower right	6

24×2.5 equals 60 cells

Now check a smear stained with Gram's stain. If no organisms are found, test for globulin. Have the druggist make a saturated aqueous solution of phenol crystals. Put 1 cc. of this in a test tube and add 1 drop of spinal fluid. In the presence of excess globulin a bluish white cloud will form.

Now test for lowered sugar content by running the spinal fluid just as you test urine for sugar. Put 5 cc. of Benedict's solution in a test tube and heat. Add 10 or even 20 drops of spinal fluid and heat again. Absence of a positive reaction usually indicates a pyogenic process.

If tuberculous meningitis enters the picture, do a tryptophan test like this: Put 2 cc. of spinal fluid in a 25 cc. test tube and add about 15 cc. of concentrated hydrochloric acid. Then add a few drops (2 or 3) of 2 per cent formaldehyde solution. Five minutes later add slowly 2 cc. of 0.06 per cent solution of sodium nitrite so that this solution forms a layer on top of the other constituents. Let stand for a minute or two. A purple ring at the junction of the two fluids is significant; a brown ring or no ring is not.

Whooping Cough

A blood culture material obtained from a nasopharyngeal swab may be of the utmost usefulness. Attach a small piece of cotton to a wire applicator and place in a test tube, like this:

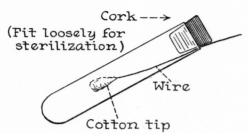

Sterilize in an autoclave or pressure cooker. I usually keep these made up but sterilize only when needed. To take the specimen, remove the wire and bend like this:

Swab the posterior nasopharynx like this:

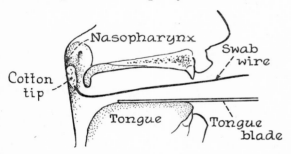

Streak the "loaded" swab over the surface of a blood agar culture plate and incubate for 24 hours.

Tuberculosis

Examine the sputum grossly in all suspected cases. This is best done by placing a sample on a glass slide and holding over a black background in adequate light. A sheet of black "drawing paper" can be purchased at any variety store.

Then stain for acid fast organisms. Take a "caseous" fleck from the sputum and smear it on a slide. Use sufficient pressure to be sure that the fleck is properly crushed and spread over the glass surface. I use a different staining routine than that usually followed. It is not necessarily superior to any other but is simply a personal preference. You may like it, too. This is it:

1. Fix by immersion in a 1 per cent aqueous solution of bichloride of mercury. This is best done in a staining dish. The slide should be left in the solution for 4 or 5 minutes.

2. Wash in tap water.

3. Immerse in a staining dish of carbofuchsin solution for 30 minutes. Heating is not necessary. The time necessary will vary with the particular batch of carbofuchsin used. Test a new batch on a known positive slide.

4. Wash in tap water.

5. Decolorize with acid alcohol (3 cc. concentrated hydrochloric acid in 97 cc. 70 per cent alcohol) until further stain does not flow from the particles as the solution circulates around them.

6. Wash in tap water.

7. Counterstain 1 minute with a solution containing equal parts of 70 per cent alcohol and saturated aqueous picric acid.

Tubercle bacilli will appear characteristically red against a faint yellow background. No other bacteria will be stained visibly and cells will not be apparent, only tubercle bacilli.

If these procedures are of no service, check the unstained sputum for elastic fibers. They look like this under low power:

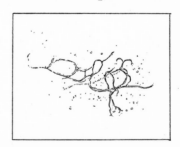

or like this under high power:

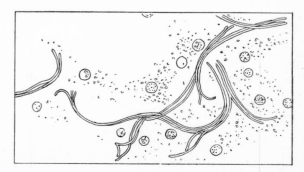

Both the patch and intradermal tests for tuberculin sensitivity are of use if properly interpreted. The patch test should be applied to the skin of the back after thorough cleansing and drying. It is not too effective in the presence of dry skin. Readings should be taken at 24 and again at 72 hours.

The Mantoux test is made by injecting intracutaneously a drop of milder purified protein derivative. Exact measurement of the injected dose, particularly in children, is easily as possible as counting the revolutions of a whirlwind. I avoid overdosage by putting in the syringe only the maximal quantity that may be injected. Gross overdosage is dangerous.

The injection is usually made on the forearm with the needle bevel like this:

Concentration of sputum is an unrewarding procedure in the average office. Aspiration of early morning stomach content is another test that is much mentioned but seldom needed. Culture, on the other hand, is of great value. Several years ago there was published an excellent hint on quick culture of tubercle bacilli.* This is it:

Secure a dozen test tubes large enough to contain a slide and make a rack for them so that they can be slanted enough to keep the liquid medium from spilling, like this:

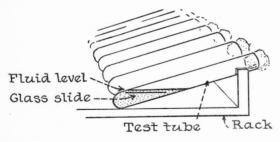

Measure an amount of liquid just sufficient to cover the surface of a slide in one of these tubes when in place on the rack as shown in

_____
* Unfortunately I have forgotten the name of the man who suggested this method. I apologize to him.

the illustration. Use a medium of Kirchner's solution of electrolyte, glycerol, and asparagin to which has been added 0.5 per cent of serum albumin. Add the determined quantity of this medium to several tubes. Do not plug these with cotton to sterilize. It is necessary to sterilize the cotton plugs separately. (Use empty test tubes.)

Prepare three thick smears of the suspected sputum and immerse in 6 per cent sulfuric acid for exactly 20 minutes. Remove the acid by immersing in sterile water several times for 2 to 3 minutes. Technique should be exacting to avoid contamination.

Slides are then immersed in the prepared tubes and placed on the rack. Routine incubation is carried out at 37° C. A standard stain is made of one of the slides at 2, 4 and 6 days. Besides acid fast staining, the characteristic "pile of sticks" appearance of the early cultures makes diagnosis easy.

We have only used this technique a few times but it seems that it will prove an excellent quick culture method.

Actinomycosis

This is not a frequent disease but it may be the genesis of a puzzling case. Office diagnosis is usually possible.

Material from draining sinuses should be collected for gross and microscopic examination. If drainage is profuse a test tube may be held at the opening and the sinus gently "milked" for a specimen. If drainage is somewhat scarce it will be necessary to curet the walls of the sinus gently with a blunt instrument to get a sample for analysis. Put the material on a glass slide and crush it with an applicator stick or with a cover glass.

Hold the slide above a black background and look for typical granules. If you fail to find them, dress the sinus with dry gauze and look in the meshes of the gauze 24 hours later.

When you find a granule, crush it on a slide and stain with Gram's stain. The filaments are gram-positive and look like this:

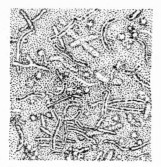

Actinomyces bovis

If there is still question, streak some of the material on Sabouraud's medium and incubate at room temperature. Sufficient growth should be present in 3 or 4 days to make diagnosis certain.

Syphilis

Most offices do not have adequate facilities for darkfield examination. Since chancres are relatively rare in practice there is little need for the average physician to purchase this expensive equipment. Spirochetes may be demonstrated with reasonable accuracy by this method:

Obtain a bottle of good grade India ink and check it by smearing on a clean slide and allowing to air dry. Examine this preparation with the oil immersion lens. Some India inks contain small vegetable filaments that look much like spirochetes. If these are found, it is easier to discard the ink and get a new bottle.

Get a drop or two of serum by gently squeezing (and scarifying the surface, if necessary). Place the serum on a slide and mix with a drop of India ink. Spread the solution to make a thin smear and allow to dry. Then examine with the oil immersion objective. Organisms will appear white against a brown or black background.

Blood tests for syphilis are best performed by commercial or health department laboratories.

Amebic Dysentery

Examine the stools grossly. In acute cases the stools usually contain more fecal matter than is found in bacillary infections. The fecal matter is mixed with blood and mucus. There is less cellular exudate in amebic disease.

Confronted with a case, do as follows: Give a saline cathartic if necessary to obtain a proper specimen. This will seldom be needed in the acute case. Have your druggist make up a 1:10,000 solution of neutral red in saline solution. Put a drop of this solution on a slide and warm by placing on the microscope light or nearby.

From a freshly passed stool select a fleck of pink (not grossly bloody) mucus and place it in the drop of stain solution. Place the slide under the microscope, heat a penny in the Bunsen flame and put it on the end of the slide. The ameba will take up the dye and become quite conspicuous. Two characteristics should serve to identify *Endamoeba histolytica*. It is actively motile, putting out pseudopodia rapidly (for an ameba) and reminding me very much of the amebae we all studied so carefully in Biology I in college. Also, *E. histolytica* ingests red blood cells. Be very hesitant to make a diagnosis unless you see the pseudopods in motion. Macrophages will ingest red blood cells and may have some resemblance to the parasite.

In cases with formed stools, examination should attempt to demonstrate cysts. Place about 3 cc. of 5 per cent Formalin in a test tube and mix a piece of stool approximately the size of a lead pencil eraser with it. If there are gross particles, the solution may be strained through a surgical sponge of 3 or 4 layers thickness.

Place a small drop of the solution on a slide and add a cover glass. Now add a drop of Lugol's solution at the edge of the cover slip. (Gram's iodine will do.) Cysts look like this:

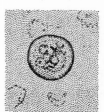 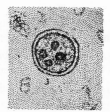

Endamoeba histolytica

Worms

Recovery of the worm in feces is a frequent means of diagnosis. Larger worms are easily found by diluting the stool with liquid and straining through coarse gauze. Pinworms are frequently seen by close inspection of the perianal skin.

For microscopic examination a piece of stool about the size of a match head should be mixed thoroughly with 1 cc. or less of isotonic saline solution and a drop of the mixture placed on a slide. Add a cover slip and cut the amount of light down by partially closing the diaphragm of the condenser. Common ova appear like this:

Taenia
saginata

Hymenolepis
nana

Necator
americanus

Ascaris
lumbricoides

Trichuris
trichiura

Pinworms are seldom diagnosed by fecal examination. The NIH cellophane swab is of some help but we use a modification of the procedure. Eggs are picked up on the sticky side of Scotch tape by pressing the tape firmly against several areas of perianal skin. A small drop of 10 per cent potassium hydroxide is placed on a glass slide and the Scotch tape (sticky side down) is firmly pressed against the slide. Ova look like this:

Enterobius vermicularis

DIGESTIVE SYSTEM

There are literally thousands of tests that may be used in the practitioner's office for detection of digestive disease. In this section we will describe only those which have been of use in our own office. Most procedures have a limited area of usefulness and can best be discussed under the heading of the disease to which they are most applicable.

Diverticulum of the Esophagus

Examine regurgitated material grossly. Absence of signs of action by gastric juices will be conspicuous. Take the pH with nitrazine paper.

Simple radiology is well within the reach of the practitioner. Begin by fluoroscopy of the neck, chest, and abdomen to rule out obvious masses or bony disease. Make two mixtures of barium, one with a single heaping tablespoon of barium to a standard glass of water, the second with 5 or 6 tablespoons to a glass. The second mixture should be as thick as whipping cream, or thicker.

The esophagus is best seen in the oblique position so that the spine does not interfere with the image. Place the patient like this:

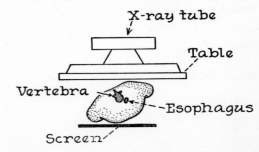

Have the patient take a mouthful of the thin mixture and hold it until you are ready to visualize. Then have him swallow. Repeat with the thick mixture.

Now place the patient in the supine oblique position and repeat, like this:

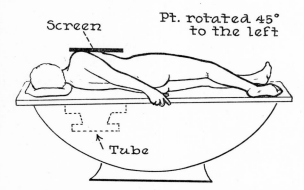

Occasionally it will be helpful to lower the head of the table slightly so that the patient swallows "uphill."

Esophageal Varices

X-ray examination will reveal most varices and is an office procedure to be done in all suspected cases. The thick mixture of barium will be best. With the patient in the oblique position ask him to take one or two swallows of the thick barium mixture. In passing the varices some of the barium will be channeled into and remain in the grooves between them, giving a typical relief pattern.

A profuse hemorrhage from known varices is an acute emergency and should be hospitalized immediately. When this is impossible and heroic treatment seems necessary, unroll an ordinary rubber condom and tie it firmly over the end of a stomach tube, like this:

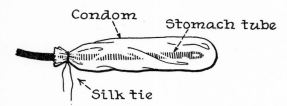

Have the patient swallow the tube and observe on the x-ray when the tip of the tube just passes the cardia. (Put a little thin barium through the tube). Like this:

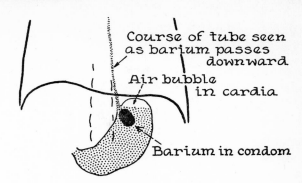

Now inflate the condom by passing air or barium through the tube under moderate pressure so that the varices are pressed upon. This is not good treatment for a minor hemorrhage. It is an heroic measure to be used in desperate circumstances only.

Carcinoma of the Stomach

The best diagnostic procedure is x-ray but, at best, this is a difficult procedure with a major margin of error. It is best left to the highly trained roentgenologist and, even so, cannot be relied upon to give a positive answer in all cases. The important point is for the practitioner to get these people to the radiologist quickly and often, until diagnosis is fully established.

In a suspect case, test the stools for occult blood. The simplest procedure is to use Hematest tablets, which are generally available. Examination of the aspirated stomach content for acid and for malignant cells is of some use but the standby remains radiology.

Peptic Ulcer

Many tests are available for peptic ulcer, but most are ignored in favor of x-ray demonstration of the crater. This is a mistake, for excellent confirmation of diagnosis is available through numerous procedures. One of the most important is the test meal. Skillful intubation is the first requisite. Do it this way:

The tube should be chilled in cold water and well lubricated with olive oil or petrolatum. It may be passed through the nose. Occasionally it will be necessary (and very much appreciated) to spray the nose and throat with 2 per cent Pontocaine. Then have the patient flex his neck slightly so that his head is thrown somewhat forward, like this:

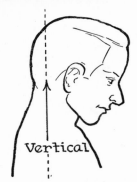

Vertical

This is the natural position for swallowing. Insert the tube straight along the floor of the nose until it bends downward.

Now ask the patient to take a mouthful of water. As he swallows, pass the tube into the nostril and along the esophagus. Have the patient keep sipping water. *Be sure* not to try to pass the tube faster than it is normally carried along by the swallowing process, for gagging will result.

If there is question about the tube entering the trachea, ask the patient to hum. It is impossible to produce a proper tone with the tube between the vocal cords.

Aspiration of typical gastric content reveals that the tube lies in the stomach.

Procedure for the test meal is as follows:

Have the patient take a tablespoonful of finely chopped spinach at bedtime the evening before the test. Appearance of the spinach in aspirated contents is rather good evidence of undue gastric retention. The patient should then take nothing by mouth until he reports for the test the following morning.

When he appears at the office he should be given two slices of toast with the crust removed, and a large glass of water. In 1 hour the tube should be passed and stomach content aspirated. Quantity of fluid obtained is of some importance. Normally between 50 and 100 cc. are found.

Now test the *p*H with nitrazine paper. Neutral or slightly alkaline fluid suggests contamination with large amounts of saliva (in the highly nervous patient), gastric cancer, or chronic gastritis. Small amounts of mucus are usually present.

Titrate for total acidity as follows: Place 10 cc. of filtered stomach contents in each of two small beakers. Add to the first 3 or 4 drops of a 1 per cent alcoholic solution of phenolphthalein. Add 0.1 N sodium hydroxide solution from a 10 cc. graduated pipet (or a buret, if available), a drop or two at a time, until the solution turns faint purple and remains so on gentle shaking. Multiply by 10 the number of cubic centimeters of 0.1 N sodium hydroxide required. This expresses degrees of acidity. Normal is 50 to 100.

Now add to the second beaker of filtered stomach contents 5 drops of Töpfer's reagent. In the presence of free hydrochloric acid the solution will immediately turn reddish pink. Titrate with 0.1 N sodium hydroxide exactly as above until the last trace of red disappears and the solution assumes a canary yellow color. Constant agitation is necessary to keep from titrating past the end point. The number of cubic centimeters of sodium hydroxide used multiplied by 10 gives total free acid. Normal range after the test meal is 30 to 60 units.

Now test for lactic acid like this: Put 5 cc. of distilled water in each of two test tubes and add 2 drops of ferric chloride solution to give a matching faint yellow tinge in each tube. Add to one tube approximately 1 cc. of filtered gastric juice. Lactic acid will give a bright yellow color instantly appreciable when compared with the control.

Dry a drop of fluid on a cover glass and stain with methylene blue. Examine under oil immersion lens. Look for numbers of large bacilli in clumps and folded chains. These are Boas-Oppler bacilli. They are indicative, but by no means diagnostic, of cancer. Other large bacilli are sometimes present but the typical arrangement and large number of Boas-Oppler bacilli are characteristic. They look like this:

If no free hydrochloric acid is found upon performance of the tests above, give 0.5 cc. of a 1:2000 dilution of histamine phosphate. Reinsert the stomach tube and aspirate the contents in 15 minutes. Test for free hydrochloric acid. If none is found, test again in 15 minutes. This should be done at least 6 times (for 1½ hours) before concluding that no free hydrochloric acid is present.

Test the stools for occult blood in any suspicious case.

Gastric radiology in the routine case is not out of reach of the conscientious practitioner who will study carefully and thoroughly and seek the advice of skilled roentgenologists frequently. A good plan for the practitioner who would do such x-ray work is as follows:

1. Obtain a good text and study it assiduously. I use as a principal reference *A Textbook of X-ray Diagnosis*, edited by S. C. Shanks and P. Kerley.

2. Have a skilled radiologist present when you do your work for at least a year.

3. No matter how skilled you may become, *always* refer questionable cases to the radiologist for recheck.

Withhold all food on the morning of the examination. Allow the patient a single glass of water upon arising. Particularly note that laxatives are not necessary preceding examination of the upper gastro-intestinal tract.

With the patient in the erect position ask that he swallow a single mouthful of barium mixture. With your hand attempt to push the barium into all parts of the stomach so as to outline the mucosal folds.

Then take a picture of any abnormality you are able to demonstrate. Next, fill the stomach with barium and note the amount taken. Average capacity will be about 12 ounces. Observe the peristaltic action, its speed, regularity, and depth of wave. Make a film of any constant abnormality. Remember that diagnosis of any lesion may rest upon its constancy as much as upon any other point. Transient shadows may mimic any lesion and frequently do. For this reason fluoroscopy alone is seldom diagnostic.

Quite often an ounce or two of secretion

will float on top of the barium into the pyloric antrum, giving a picture like this:

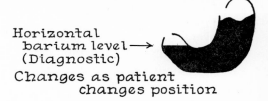

Horizontal barium level → (Diagnostic)
Changes as patient changes position

Correct it by having the patient recline on his right side for several minutes, thus allowing the juice to float upward into the fundus.

Use compression to visualize the anterior and posterior stomach walls. Proper compression should bring out such lesions as ulcers. Do this:

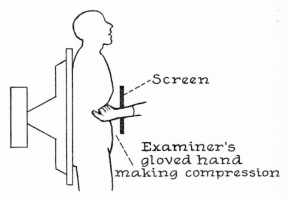

Screen

Examiner's gloved hand making compression

Now push some barium into the pylorus and through it into the duodenum. This can best be done by upward and backward hand pressure *when a peristaltic wave approaches the pylorus*. Use oblique positions and compression frequently. *Always* get a picture of any abnormality if at all possible.

After completion of the examination have the patient go home and lie down. Instruct him to eat nothing until a 6 hour film has been made. A "trace residue" at the end of 6 hours may have no significance.

This is the briefest outline of gastroduodenal radiologic procedure. The physician who wishes to learn and do this x-ray work should study exhaustively one of the standard texts.

Acute Hepatitis

Jaundice is of the hepatocellular type, i.e., there is damage to liver cells and consequent interference with the enterohepatic circulation of bile pigment. Urobilin appears in the urine. Test for it this way:

To 3 cc. of urine in a test tube add several crystals of para-dimethyl-amino-benzaldehyde. Now add several drops of concentrated hydrochloric acid to make the reaction definitely acid. If urobilinogen is present a cherry red color appears.

Bile may also appear in the urine. Shake the urine sharply. Normally the foam is white, but if bile is present the foam will be yellow.

Tests of liver function are of questionable value in any patient not sufficiently ill to be hospitalized.

Cirrhosis

Liver function tests are of value in diagnosis. The thymol turbidity test is perhaps best and can be done most easily by using the photoelectric colorimeter. Directions are furnished with each machine.

Cholelithiasis

Diagnosis of gallbladder disease is among the most difficult of all medical problems. Presence of stones does *not* mean that stones cause symptoms. With this preliminary warning we can turn to the office procedures used in demonstrating gallstones.

X-ray is by far the most important technique but expert preparation and filming are necessary if the result is to be even remotely reliable. Here is a good routine to follow:

Give the patient a mild laxative 24 hours before the examination is to be done. Drastic purgation is not indicated. The evening before reporting, have the patient eat a normal meal and take with it two eggs. Three hours later he should take 6 tablets of Priodax. Along with this he should take a half teaspoonful of baking soda in water. The soda should be repeated at bedtime and upon arising. If any hyperacidity is suspected have him set his alarm clock and take an extra dose during the night.

The morning of the examination an enema should be taken at home and 0.5 cc. of Pitressin given subcutaneously immediately upon reporting to the office. Take the necessary films with just as short a time of exposure as your machine will allow. Take time to make the patient comfortable and expose the film at the very end of expiration.

If necessary use a ball of mechanic's waste to push the gallbladder laterally away from the spine. Be sure not to compress the organ with hard pressure.

Now give the patient a glass of milk with two raw eggs beaten into it. In 10 minutes take a straight A-P and a second film with the patient rotated about 15 degrees to the right. These are sometimes better if the head of the table be lowered to 15 degrees. Still another plate should be taken in 2 hours.

In the event the gallbladder is not seen, schedule a repeat check for the next morning and give 8 tablets of Priodax. The routine used for the first preparation should be followed except for the laxative. Remember that good films are hard to get, and that study of poor films is a waste of time.

Biliary drainage may be of some diagnostic value and occasionally is of therapeutic help, although the psychic effect may outweigh actual medical benefits. Do it this way:

Have the patient sit in a straight chair and put a drape sheet over him to avoid soiling his clothes. Use one of the metal tipped plastic tubes and have the patient manipulate the tube himself. Instruct him to place it on the very back of the tongue. Now hand him a glass of water to sip as he swallows the tube. When the stomach is entered, as proved by aspiration of gastric juice, have the patient lie on his right side and remain quiet for 15 or 20 minutes. The tube should be in this position:

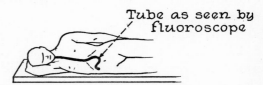

Tube as seen by fluoroscope

Position may be checked by using the fluoroscope or by aspirating a few cubic centimeters of fluid and checking the *p*H. Duodenal fluid will usually be above *p*H 5. When you are sure the tube is in the duodenum, inject slowly

10 cc. of 33⅓ per cent magnesium sulfate solution. In 5 minutes aspirate. This first solution should contain a golden yellow bile, presumably from the bile ducts.

Next instill another 20 cc. of magnesium sulfate solution and again aspirate. The darker, more viscid gallbladder bile should appear in this second specimen. Its absence indicates (but does not prove) poor function of the gallbladder.

Put the darker second bile in a separate container. Next to appear is a thin, watery, light yellow bile which is presumed to be fresh bile from the liver. A specimen of this should be saved.

Examine the second and third specimens under the microscope. Look for yellow-stained epithelial cells, crystals of cholesterol and calcium bilirubinate. Check the specimen grossly for mucus. When necessary, the gallbladder bile may be cultured.

CARDIOVASCULAR DISEASE

Examination of the Heart

Many simple and rewarding office procedures exist for estimation of the functional integrity of the heart. Most can be done with a minimum of equipment.

Electrocardiography is well within the range of the practitioner who will study and who will submit his readings to check by an expert cardiologist for a period of time before depending solely on his own skill. Levine's *Clinical Heart Disease* has an excellent chapter on cardiographic interpretation.

For routine cases the 4-lead tracing is entirely ample. In such cases, the CF lead with the chest electrode at the apex is the most useful. Complicated cases require 12-lead tracings which must be technically perfect. Write the cardiologist who will be your consultant and let him send you detailed instructions specifying exactly how he wishes these made.

Some technical points in taking the EKG are worthy of note. To begin with, make sure that all electrodes are connected to the proper lead wires whether the electrode is in place or not (some machines will not work unless they are), and that the EKG is properly grounded. Most models have ground indicators.

Never take a tracing without standardizing the machine. Some authorities recommend a standardization in every lead, and they are probably right. A properly sensitive machine should deviate 1 cm. when a current of 1 millivolt is applied, like this:

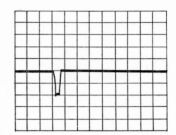

To take the actual tracing, a quiet room with no one other than the patient and the operator is best. It will probably be necessary to turn off nearby diathermy, x-ray apparatus, and fluorescent lighting unless a special room is used. An examining table is not a good place to take the EKG. No matter where it is taken, the patient must not touch metal parts.

Proper application of the electrodes is one of the most important techniques to be positive about for good results. Do it this way:

Place the arm electrodes here:

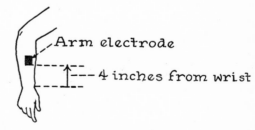

Arm electrode

4 inches from wrist

And the leg electrodes here:

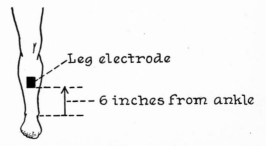

Leg electrode

6 inches from ankle

There are six standard chest positions in common use:

1. In the fourth intercostal space just to right of the sternum.

2. Same, just to the left of the sternum.

3. Over the fifth rib, the edge of the electrode ½ inch lateral to the sternal border.

4. In the fifth intercostal space in the mid-axillary line.

5. At the vertical level of 4 in the anterior axillary line.

6. At the level of 4 in the mid-axillary line.

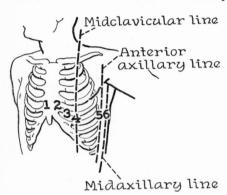

To attach the extremity electrodes put a little electrode jelly on a piece of gauze and scrub the skin vigorously until a noticeable hyperemia appears. Have the electrode firmly in place but not uncomfortably tight. Nothing is gained by undue pressure except the jagged and irregular baseline of somatic tremors. It looks like this:

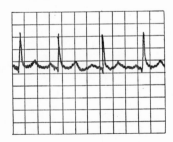

Since chest electrode contact points are relatively close together it is necessary to see that electrode jelly is applied only to the actual point of contact. It is best to prepare all areas from which leads are to be taken before the EKG is started. Cover an area of about the size of a half dollar and *be sure* the areas of jelly do not run together.

After this discussion of the electrocardiograph, it behooves me to say that this excellent machine is not needed very often in office practice. Don't get into the pernicious habit of taking an EKG on anything that is alive. In my office it is used principally for these purposes:

1. Diagnosis of rheumatic heart disease.

2. Very rarely to diagnose an arrythmia.

3. Occasionally in coronary artery disease (other than suspected occlusion—these patients are hospitalized) when diagnosis is impossible without it.

4. To reassure cardiac psychoneurotics.

The electrocardiograph is a worthy addition to the practitioner's equipment but it does not replace history and careful physical evaluation.

Function capacity of the heart is the most important determination to be made. Also, it is the most reliable index to cardiac disease. Many methods are available for determining it. The one I use is this:

Have the patient step from the floor up onto the seat of a straight chair and back down again 15 times. Check the pulse immediately before, immediately after, and 2 minutes after this exercise. You will get a good picture of functional integrity.

Another test is to ask the patient to hold his breath and time the interval during which he does not breathe.

Venous pressure may be estimated without special apparatus. Have the patient hold his arms at his sides until the veins on the backs of his hands are well filled. Then raise the arm out laterally so that the hand is on a level with the top of the heart, like this:

Observe the veins on the back of the hand for 10 seconds. If they collapse, venous pressure is near normal. Now elevate the hand 3 or 4 inches and again observe the veins. Near the end point, elevation should be an inch or less between readings. When the hand reaches the position where the veins just collapse, the venous pressure may be estimated (in centimeter of blood) by measuring the vertical distance from the top of the heart to the veins observed, like this:

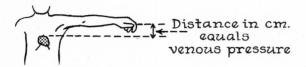

Vital capacity, measured by means of the spirometer, is a very useful test which is far too seldom applied. The instrument is cheap to purchase and upkeep is nearly nil. Performance of the test takes less than a minute. It is a measurement of the amount of air that can be expelled after the deepest possible inspiration. A normal spirometer reading practically excludes congestive failure; a progressively lower one indicates a bad prognosis.

Arm to tongue circulation time is another valuable determination. I measure it by using an injection of the B-complex vitamins as the test substance. Instruct the patient to report the taste of the material as soon as he perceives it. Then inject 2 cc. rapidly into the antecubital vein and note the number of seconds elapsed before he reports perception. Normal ranges from 10 to 15 seconds.

Cardiac x-ray can be most helpful in diagnosis. The straight P-A view exactly similar to that taken for routine chest disease is excellent for demonstration of changes in heart size. Various formulas that have been devised to establish the size of the "normal" heart are of very little use in mild or early disease because of the very wide range of normal. The experienced observer who has made a careful clinical survey of the patient can be as authoritative on heart size as any set of tables and statistics. This is not to derogate attempts to analyze statistically the heart size, but such analysis has not been perfected.

Fluoroscopy is probably the most valuable of all roentgenologic procedures in the practitioner's office. The standard positions and what they demonstrate are as follows:

In P-A fluoroscopy, i.e., with the patient's anterior chest wall next to the screen, the visualized heart borders are composed of (from above downward, beginning on the patient's right):

1. The straight, vertical edge of the superior vena cava casting a faint shadow in this location:

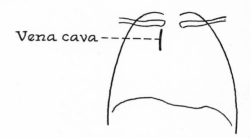

2. The slightly convex shadow of the ascending aorta, in this position:

3. The more convex shadow of the right atrium, located here:

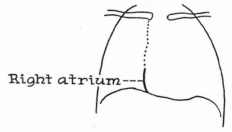

On the patient's left, from above downward, the first highly convex shadow is that of the aortic knob, or the outline of the aortic arch and beginning of the descending aorta, here:

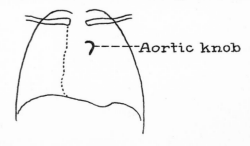

The next, slightly longer, mildly convex curve is the shadow of the trunk and left main branch of the pulmonary artery, here:

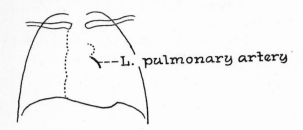

The very short straight line seen next is the left auricular appendage; and finally, there appears the left ventricular shadow:

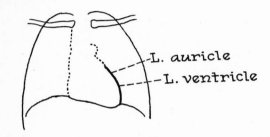

The two oblique views are of even greater usefulness and their application should be cultivated. In the view with the right surface of the chest toward the screen, the following structures are seen:

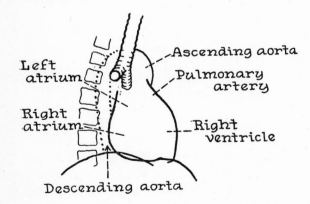

In this position, the heart is oriented like this:

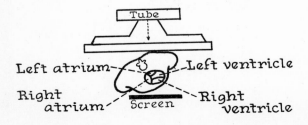

The left oblique view looks like this:

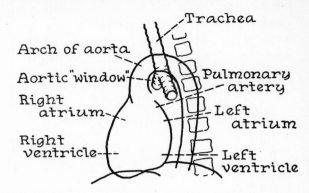

and in this position the heart is oriented like this:

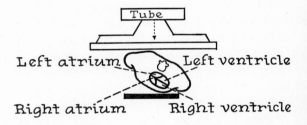

Straight lateral fluoroscopy will offer little information that cannot be gained in other ways.

There are few office procedures of great value in the treatment of cardiac disease. Establishment of proper diagnosis and the devising of a routine to cope with the pathology are strictly in the field of intellection.

Examination of the Vascular System

This is so frequently omitted or poorly done that I am going to depart from the usual course of this book and detail the office procedure for physical examination. Lesions are very common and are missed with shocking frequency.

Vascular diseases account for a significant number of the cases seen in daily practice and, unless the physician is wary, will account also for a significant number of mistakes.

Color of Extremities. If peripheral vascular disease is suspected the first step should be observation of the extremities upon change of position. Do it this way: Have the patient lie supine and elevate the legs to an angle like this:

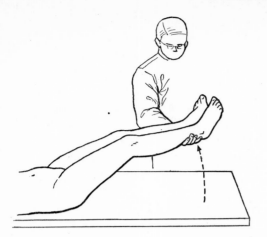

Do not have the patient maintain the position through his own effort. Brace his legs with your hand. Now observe the feet for blanching, which will be present in most cases of occlusive arterial disease. In some cases it is necessary to wait 3 or 4 minutes for this to occur.

Now have the patient sit on the examining table and lower his legs over the side, like this:

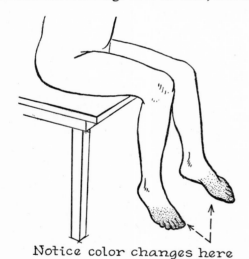

Notice color changes here

Normal color should return in a maximum of 15 seconds. When peripheral vascular disease is present the toes and feet will usually become a bright cherry red in 5 or 6 minutes. This changes to a deep cyanosis in about 10 minutes. Venous occlusive disease produces a different "dusky" cyanosis which is readily differentiated.

While these color changes are most significant, there are a very few cases in which

they are not entirely reliable. The tests should *never* be omitted if chronic vascular disease is suspected.

Estimations of surface temperature also are of utmost importance. The ventral surface of the examiner's distal phalanges is usually most sensitive to minor changes in temperature. Apply the fingers without pressure to the skin surface, like this:

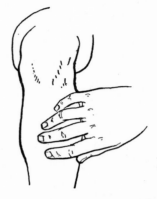

Then move the fingers from above downward, like this:

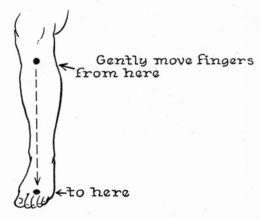

Gently move fingers from here ← to here

Be sure to check the soles of the feet in a similar manner. The palmar surface of the examiner's hand is not nearly so sensitive to minor temperature changes as are the fingertips.

Commercial devices are available for measuring surface temperature but they are more applicable to research and medical center use than to average office routines.

Determination of claudication time is of much help in studying and following peripheral arterial disease. In our office we have a hallway that can be traversed "round trip" in 45 seconds. A nurse goes with the patient and a determination is made of the number of "round trips" that can be made before onset of pain. Walking at a constant rate of speed, the time of exercise before onset of pain is measured. Repeated determinations at regular intervals give an excellent survey of progress being made.

Examination of the vascular system should be complete and must be done in a light, warm room (75° F.) with the patient completely unclothed. Notice color changes and abnormal pulsations which may be indicative of underlying pathology, then proceed to the regional check.

The Regional Examination. Beginning with the head, palpate the temporal arteries, and notice any distention of veins. Always auscultate several areas of the scalp. Notice the degree of pulsation of the arteries that may be observed near the surface. The upper neck just at the angle of the jaw is a frequent site of vascular abnormalities and should be checked. Next is the clavicular area, where aneurysms are rather common.

Arteries and veins of the shoulder girdle should be checked for dilatation, pulsation and changes in the walls. The Allen test is useful for demonstrating circulatory changes beyond the mid-forearm. Do it this way: Have the patient extend his hands toward you, palms upward. Now grasp the wrist between your fingers and thumb, with the thumb over the "good" artery, like this:

Examiner applies pressure here

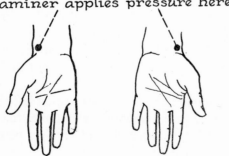

Now press firmly enough with the thumbs to occlude the "good" artery and, while maintaining pressure, have the patient close his hands and "make a fist" as tightly as possible.

The patient should hold this position for at least 15 seconds, then should relax his hands. During this operation and the ensuing inspection, the examiner should keep the "good" artery occluded.

If the "other" artery is adequate the pallor of the hands will be replaced by a reactionary rubor within a very few seconds. The test may be repeated with the examiner's thumbs occluding the opposite artery.

Next check the hands for thickening of the nails or inadequate growth. Look for small gray patches under the nails which may be glomus tumors. If one is found, press on it with the point of a pencil and see if pain is produced.

Now hyperabduct the arms, like this:

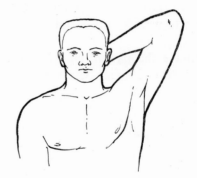

Check the pulsations of the ulnar and radial arteries. If the subclavian artery is pinched between the clavicle and the first rib, pulsations will be absent. Ask the patient to extend his arm and to turn his head forcefully away from the arm. Again check radial and ulnar pulsation. Absence should indicate further check for cervical rib. If pulsations are diminished with the head turned toward the side under study, think of the scalenus anticus syndrome.

Next, displace both shoulders downward and backward and again check the pulse at the wrist. Absence brings to mind the costoclavicular syndrome.

Now check the veins of the anus and genitalia for dilatation and thrombosis.

Turning to the lower extremity, begin by palpating Hunter's canal for its entire length. Then palpate the popliteal artery and determine the status of the short saphenous system. Next check the long saphenous system. Feel deep in the muscle bodies of the calf for the tenderness of deep thrombosis and try to elicit Homans' sign. Extend the foot gently and, when in maximum extension, further extend the great toe. Pain deep in the calf is evidence of early phlebothrombosis.

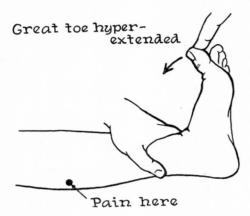

Great toe hyper-extended

Pain here

Now palpate the posterior tibial artery here:

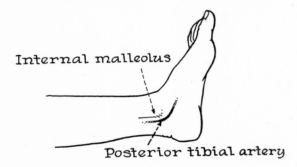

Internal malleolus

Posterior tibial artery

and the dorsalis pedis in this area:

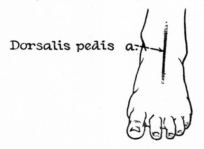

Dorsalis pedis a.

The feet and particularly the toes are the most common sites of vascular disease and should be examined with painstaking care. Look particularly at the veins on the medial side of the foot, for they are often the site of clotting.

Oscillometry. The oscillometer is a useful instrument if the readings are interpreted conservatively. In essence the instrument works like this: pulsations of the vessels are transmitted to a typical blood pressure cuff and converted into changes in air pressure. A sensitive gauge indicates these changes. Each instrument may be somewhat different and each should be checked against known circulatory changes before being put in use. Approximate normals for an average machine are as follows:

LOWER EXTREMITY		UPPER EXTREMITY	
Thigh	4–15	Upper arm	4–15
Below knee	3–12	Elbow	3–12
Above ankle	1–6	Wrist	1–8
Foot	0.2–1.0	Hand	0.2–2.0

Oscillometry should be performed in a warm room and it should be remembered that a lowered reading may be caused by temporary arterial spasm as well as by true organic disease.

The capillary fragility test is of use in many cases. We do it this way: To begin with, usual instructions are to draw two circles each 2.5 cm. in diameter about 4 cm. distal to the crease of the elbow on the volar surface of the forearm. Since a quarter is 2.5 cm. in diameter we simply trace around the edge of one, in two places like this:

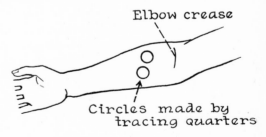

Elbow crease

Circles made by tracing quarters

Now mark any skin blemishes with a dot of ink from your pen. Put on a blood pressure cuff and raise the pressure to 50 mm. Leave the cuff in place and maintain the pressure for 15 minutes. Then remove the cuff and wait a minute or two for venous stasis to be relieved. Normally there will be 10 or fewer petechial spots in each circle. From 10 to 20 may be considered marginal; over 20 is definitely pathologic.

Count the petechiae in each circle and use

the average of the two circles as a final reading.   Counting is easier if you use a pen to dot
each hemorrhage as it is enumerated.

Regional block anesthesia is a good way to
test the ability of the arteries to dilate.   Its
most important use is in the foot.   Inject 3 cc.
of 1 per cent Cyclaine under the fascia just below the internal malleolus and behind the posterior tibial artery, like this:

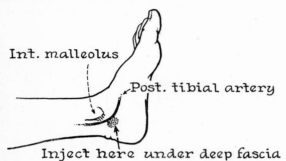

Vasodilatation is limited to the plantar surfaces
and to a portion of the dorsum of the foot.

I do not use the histamine flare test because
it is usually hard to interpret and tends to confuse the picture.

There are a great many tests published for
determining adequacy of the circulation.
Most of them are useful, good tests, but they
are seldom needed.   Vascular disease may be
diagnosed in nearly all cases by means of a
painstaking history and a careful physical
examination.

Radiology can be of much help in diagnosis.
In questionable arterial disease, the first procedure should be visualization by soft tissue
technique of any sclerotic areas in the arteries.
Our own technique is to leave all x-ray settings
the same as for osseous pictures, except the
KVP.   This is reduced 5 or 10 kilovolts as
judgment indicates.   I am not a sufficiently
good radiologist to defend this technique.   I
can only say that it works for us.

Most work will be in the lower extremities.
We usually begin with an exposure of the pelvis
and then take the entire limbs.   It is of utmost
importance to remember that the amount of
calcification present does not parallel the
amount of circulatory deficiency.   One further point of importance: you cannot visualize
the popliteal arteries on an A-P film.   Take a
lateral exposure with the knee flexed, like this:

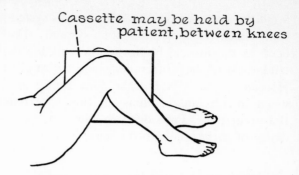

Injection of the femoral artery with Thorotrast is a relatively simple act and can give a
great deal of information.   Prepare for the
x-ray by placing two cassettes in position, like
this:

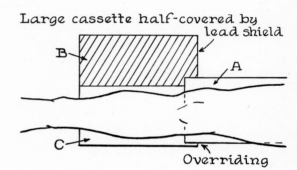

Cassette *A* overrides the larger cassette (areas
B and *C*) by 1 inch; areas *B* and *C* are covered with lead shields until *A* is exposed.

Speedy, accurate work is an absolute essential.   Prepare a 30 cc. syringe with 20 cc. of
Thorotrast solution and locate the femoral
artery here:

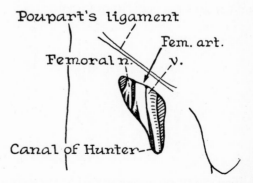

Now insert the needle (at least a 20 gauge)
sloping distally, like this:

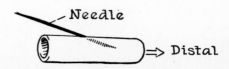

Upon entering the artery there will be several spurts of bright red blood into the barrel of the syringe. Inject approximately 15 cc. of Thorotrast rapidly and take the first exposure in the area of the knee (cassette *A* in the layout drawing) during the last 2 or 3 seconds of injection. Remove cassette *A* and, as quickly as possible, uncover area *C* of the lower cassette and take a picture of the calf and ankle.

Change the lead shield to cover area *C*, flex the patient's knee and place the plantar surface of his foot on area *B*. This last picture should be taken within 5 seconds of the first if good visualization of arteries is to be obtained.

The technique of getting these pictures quickly enough is not easy, particularly with the x-ray equipment found in the usual office. Practice in coordination between the physician and his technician will devise an acceptable technique.

Office procedures in treatment of vascular disease are mostly physiotherapeutic in nature and will be discussed in the section on physiotherapy.

DISEASES OF THE BLOOD

The Anemias

Certain basic tests may be performed in any small office to clarify problems regarding anemia. Confronted with a typical case of anemia, proceed as follows:

1. *Estimate the hemoglobin.* An increasing number of offices are being equipped with the photoelectric colorimeter. I have used one for years and would be the first to say that the instrument is an excellent investment. In doing hemoglobin estimations alone my colorimeter pays for itself many times each year, both in time saving to patients and in monetary return. It takes less than 2 minutes to make an accurate determination following the directions of the manufacturer.

2. *Determine the mean corpuscular hemoglobin concentration* (MCHC). First fill a Wintrobe hematocrit tube to the mark 0 with oxalated blood. Centrifuge at 3000 rpm for 15 to 20 minutes and read the volume of packed cells directly from the graduations on the tube. Now divide the hemoglobin concentration expressed in grams by the volume of packed red cells and multiply by 100. This is an example:

Hb. equals 14.10 $14.10 \div 40 = 0.352$
Hematocrit equals 40 $0.352 \times 100 = 35.2$
Normal value is 34 ± 2. $35.2 =$ normal
                                                           range

These two procedures will prove the presence of anemia and will serve to put the anemia in one of two great classes which have markedly differing therapy.

If the MCHC is less than 30, you are dealing with a microcytic hypochromic anemia which will usually respond to iron. This is occasionally seen in the presence of chronic blood loss and, since the gastro-intestinal tract and the female genital tract are the common sites of blood loss, a careful history about the genital tract and an occult blood study on a stool sample are rewarding procedures.

If the MCHC is greater than 36 the patient has a macrocytic anemia which will usually respond to vitamin B_{12}, folic acid, or liver. Patients with macrocytic anemias should probably be checked for changes in vibration sense and for gastric achlorhydria. To check for vibration sense, set a tuning fork in motion and apply it to both malleoli of both lower extremities. Be a little tricky and damp the fork with your finger before one or two of the four applications. Each time ask the patient if he feels the buzz. This simple test, which we have all learned, is often neglected.

Estimation of reticulocyte percentage enables one to follow the progress of treatment. Prepare a saturated solution in normal saline of brilliant cresyl blue. This should be filtered and a drop added to 5 drops of oxalated blood in a test tube. Mix and let stand for 2 minutes, then make thin smears and, if you wish, counterstain with Wright's or Giemsa's stain.   Reticulocytes look like this:

Count at least 200 cells and note the percentage of reticulated cells. Normal ranges around 2 per cent.

The above is a very casual approach to the extremely complicated subject of the anemias. It will, however, serve to differentiate and establish proper therapy for nearly 95 per cent of cases that come to the practitioner's office. Studies of peripheral blood and bone marrow are occasionally needed for accurate diagnosis of unusual cases.

Bone Marrow Studies.   Bone marrow may be secured from the sternum or from the spinous process of a lumbar vertebra. I much prefer the lumbar approach. Patients who are quite intelligent have remarked to me that sternal puncture gave them the distinct impression of a group of eager-eyed ghouls gathered with hammers to beat their chest in.   On the other hand, one can literally chew off a lumbar spinous process while carrying on an erudite conversation about fishing or politics and beget no alarm at all.

A bone marrow punch is useful but a heavy 15 or 18 gauge needle can be made to do.   Inject 1 per cent Cyclaine being certain to include the skin and periosteum.   There are few nerve endings in the intervening fat.   Put the solution here:

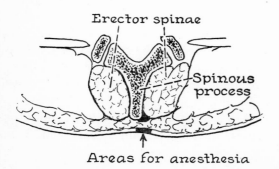

Erector spinae

Spinous process

Areas for anesthesia

Then nick the skin with a knife and insert the needle a little to one side of the midline. A firm push will usually penetrate the cortex and enter the marrow.   It is necessary to withdraw only a few drops of fluid.   Smear a drop or two on each of 3 or 4 slides and fix by immersion in methyl alcohol. This may be stained with Wright's stain, although I have found it easier to get consistently good results with Giemsa's stain.   After fixation, immerse the slides for 20 minutes in a solution of 3 cc. of stain to 30 cc. of distilled water.   Rinse and examine.   If further staining is needed, immerse the slide again until the result you wish is obtained.

Leukemia

Examination of the stained smear of peripheral blood is the only office procedure needed for diagnosis of the acute leukemias.   Chronic leukemia occasionally requires a bone marrow study as described above.   Any questionable peripheral blood and all bone marrow slides should be sent to a competent hematologist.

Purpura

Confronted with a case of purpura, enumeration of the blood platelets is the only office procedure of use except the bone marrow biopsy.   Do it this way: Use 3 per cent sodium citrate as a diluting fluid and prepare the counting chamber exactly as for a red blood count, using the red count pipet in the usual manner.   Let the chamber stand for about 10 minutes before counting, to give the platelets a chance to settle.   Count the platelets in 10 squares and multiply the total by 5000.

THE NERVOUS SYSTEM

There are few therapeutic procedures used in office care of neurologic cases.   However, the procedures of routine neurologic examination should be in the armamentarium of every practitioner. No special equipment other than the reflex hammer is needed, for everyday material common to any locality can be used.

Examination of the Cranial Nerves

Olfactory (*I*). This nerve seldom needs testing. Have the patient hold one nostril closed. Standing several feet away, dip one end of an applicator stick in oil of wintergreen (methyl salicylate linament). Turn to the patient and place the *dry* end of the applicator stick under his nostril, like this:

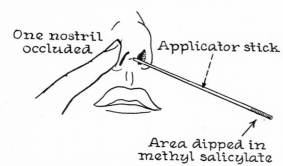

One nostril occluded
Applicator stick
Area dipped in methyl salicylate

Since wintergreen has a pungent and penetrating odor the patient may well smell it in this position. If he does not, reverse the applicator stick. I usually test the opposite nostril with a pinch of coffee on the top of a tongue blade.

Optic (*II*). Examination of the visual fields is described on pages 24 and 25 and fundic visualization on page 24.

Oculomotor (*III*). Pupillary changes are common in oculomotor disease. First check the reaction of the pupil as it changes from near to far vision. The old method of using a flashlight or ophthalmoscope moving toward the patient is not accurate. Seat the patient in such a position that you can see his pupils. Hold up one finger and ask that he look at it. Then specify an object across the room to be gazed at. Notice if the pupils change size as the gaze shifts. Next check the light reflex and the consensual reaction. When one retina is stimulated by light, both pupils should contract. Normally the constriction is almost instantaneous, but within 2 or 3 seconds there is a slight relaxation.

Extraocular movements by which nerves III, IV, and VI are further examined have been covered on page 25.

Trigeminal (*V*). Test the face for touch, pain, and temperature sensations as outlined on page 304. Next, determine the presence of the corneal reflex. When the eye is approached from the front, one gets a normal visual reflex lid closing and learns nothing of the true state of the corneal pathways. Pull on the cotton wound about a typical applicator until a tiny wisp protrudes from the end. Then have the patient look toward the nasal field of the eye to be tested and approach the cornea from the temporal side, like this:

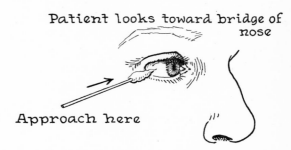

Patient looks toward bridge of nose
Approach here

The applicator must not be seen by the patient.

Test the motor portion of the nerve by asking the patient to clench his teeth and by feeling the masseters and temporals while he does so. Now have the patient open his mouth a little, put your finger along the outside of the mandible and ask him to push your finger laterally. This will give a good estimate of pterygoid function. Next have the patient open his mouth widely. Any weakness of the masseter will be obvious by deviation to the weak side.

Facial (*VII*). Ask the patient to do the following:

1. Frown (or wrinkle the forehead).
2. Wink (or close eyelids).
3. Whistle.
4. Snarl and show his teeth.

It can be very important to determine whether the interference is central or peripheral to the facial nucleus. The seventh nerve may be represented schematically like this:

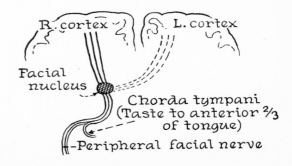

R. cortex   L. cortex
Facial nucleus
Chorda tympani
(Taste to anterior ⅔ of tongue)
Peripheral facial nerve

The upper portion of the face has motor connections with both cortices, while the lower portion derives its nerve supply principally from the opposite motor cortex. Interference below the nucleus will cause complete paralysis on the same side. Interference with the crossed tracts central to the nucleus causes weakness on the opposite side.

It may be necessary to determine approximately where in the peripheral course the nerve is blocked. In looking at the diagram you will notice that the chorda tympani carries taste fibers from the anterior two-thirds of the tongue. Rub some ordinary table salt into the edge of the tongue here:

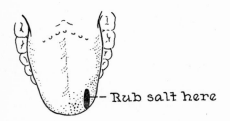

— Rub salt here

and see if the patient can taste it while the tongue is still protruded. If he can, the facial nerve is blocked beyond the point of exit of the taste fibers.

Auditory (VIII). Methods of testing cochlear function may be found on page 3. To test canal function, have the patient touch your finger in the position shown:

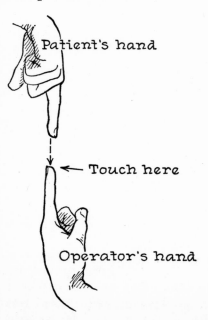

Patient's hand

← Touch here

Operator's hand

Then do the same thing in a horizontal plane. The patient should try both tests first with his eyes open, then with them closed. Consistent pass pointing to the same side is evidence of vestibular disease.

Rarely, a simplified Bárány procedure may be of some use. Prepare a basin of water at 65° F. For 2 minutes gently irrigate one ear with the patient sitting upright. Certain responses are normal. This table shows normal and abnormal response. Of course, no response at all is abnormal.

After Irrigation of the Right Ear
With head erect (vertical canals)

NORMAL	ABNORMAL
Vertigo within 2 minutes	Absence of vertigo
Nausea and, rarely, vomiting	Absence
Lateral or rotary nystagmus (left)	Response to right
Pass pointing to right	Left

With head flexed (horizontal canals)

Increased nystagmus	Absence or no increase

If the test indicates disease, consultation with a neurologist is in order.

Glossopharyngeal (IX) and Vagus (X). Have the patient open his mouth to say "ah." In case of unilateral weakness or paralysis, the soft palate and uvula will rise diagonally toward the healthy side rather than in the midline, like this:

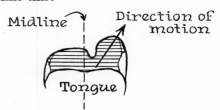

Midline   Direction of motion

Tongue

Touch the pharynx with a tongue blade. Watch the contraction of the pharyngeal muscles for signs of lateral deviation.

Accessory (XI). Have the patient shrug his shoulders while you apply moderate pressure with one of your hands on each of the patient's shoulders.

Hypoglossal (XII). Have the patient protrude his tongue. Any deviation will be toward the paralyzed side. Then ask him to protrude his cheek by pushing it out with his tongue. With your finger at the apex of the "lump" formed in the cheek, test the strength of the push.

A Summary of Peripheral Innervation

All movements of head and neck	C2, C3, C4 and XI
Shrugging of shoulders	C2, C3, C4, C5 and XI
Deltoid	C5
Supination, flexion of elbow, external rotation and abduction of humerus	C5, C6
Flexion of finger metacarpophalangeal joints	C6
Extension of all arm joints, radial deviation of wrist, pronation	C6, C7, C8
Flexion of terminal phalanges	C7, C8, T
Interossei	C8, T
Medial rotation and adduction of humerus	C5, C6, C7, **C8**, T
Adduction of **femur and** flexion of **hip**	L2, L3, L4
Extension of knee	L3, L4
Abduction of femur, medial rotation, extension of ankle and toes and eversion and inversion of foot	L4, L5, S
Flexion of foot (ability to walk on toes)	L5, S1, S2

Reflexes

Pupillary. See page 301.
Corneal. See page 301.
Biceps. Hold the patient's arm like this:

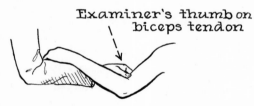

Show him how to relax the member so that the arm lies limp in your hand. Place your thumb over the biceps tendon and strike it a sharp (but not hard) blow. Flexion of the arm is a normal response.

Triceps. Hold the arm like this and strike the triceps tendon with the reflex hammer, as shown.

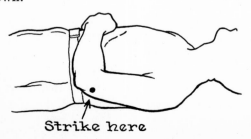

Brachioradial. Support the arm as shown and tap the radius on its subcutaneous lower third.

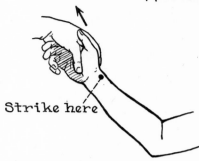

Flexion of the forearm and fingers usually results. Inversion of the reflex is flexion of the fingers with no movement of the forearm. It indicates a possible C5 lesion.

Patellar. This is best elicited by seating the patient on the edge of the examining table with his legs dangling. Make sure his legs are relaxed and then strike the patellar tendon with the reflex hammer. If there is no result, have the patient clasp his hands together and pull firmly as you strike the tendon. This will remove the "cerebral inhibition" and make the reflex stronger. If it is still not present you may assume some interference with the reflex arc.

Achilles. This is a difficult reflex to elicit precisely. The way it is usually done probably gives little information. Many satisfactory procedures are available. The one I like best is this: Have the patient get on his hands and knees on the examining table with his feet protruding over the edge, like this:

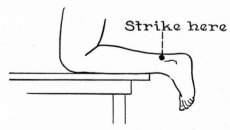

Be sure the foot is relaxed and then strike the Achilles tendon. Plantar flexion should result.

Plantar. With the foot relaxed, run an applicator stick along the plantar skin near the outer edge. Flexion of the toes should occur.

Abdominal. Scrape an applicator stick along the skin surface in these areas:

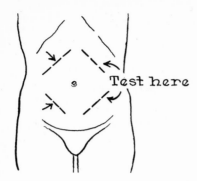

The umbilicus should deviate toward the stimulated side.

Cremasteric. Stroke the inner surface of the leg with an applicator stick. The testicle on the same side should retract.

Never assume a reflex to be absent because it is not elicited at first trial. When such absence is noted retest several times during the course of the neurologic examination.

Examination of the Sensory System

Six functions of the sensory system should be checked when indicated. They are:

Touch Sensation. Pull the cotton from a cotton-tipped applicator out into a fine wisp. Then ask the patient to say "now" when he feels a touch. Remember that different sensory areas have different innervation. Do not expect 100 per cent response in any area. Rather, expect progressively less response in areas of lesser nerve supply.

Pain. Push an ordinary straight pin crosswise through the end of an applicator stick. Ask the patient to respond to application of the test device by a single word, saying either "sharp" or "dull." Map corresponding areas on either side of the midline. Change from sharp to dull pressure irregularly.

Heat and Cold. The water in the hot and cold faucets of the average office has ample temperature difference for testing. Fill two test tubes, one with hot and one with cold water. Ask the patient to identify the touch with the tubes by saying "hot" or "cold."

General body sensory areas are as follows:

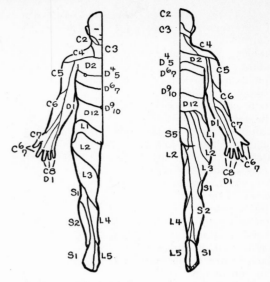

Vibratory Perception. See page 299.

Position Sense. With the patient reclining, grasp the big toe and move it up or down several times, stopping in either flexion or extension. Ask the patient whether the toe is up or down.

Stereognosis. Ask the patient to close his eyes. Hand him a pen, a coin, a match, etc., and have him identify the objects "by feel."

Examination of the Cerebellar System

Five simple tests will serve to investigate the cerebellar system sufficiently for all usual cases. In all tests one looks for degree of coordination of movement.

Gait. Test the smoothness of the patient's coordination by asking that he rise and walk rapidly around his chair without holding on to it.

Station. Ask that the patient stand erect with his feet together and his eyes closed.

Heel-Toe Test. Have the patient walk heel to toe along a straight line.

Finger-Nose Test. Have the patient close his eyes and touch his nose with each index finger.

Pronation-Supination. Ask the patient to extend his closed fists and pronate and supinate rapidly, holding the elbows in the same position. In addition to checking coordination, notice whether the arms tend to drift apart or closer while the test is performed.

There are only two diseases seen with any frequency in which office procedures are needed for diagnosis. Office treatment of minor neurologic syndromes is confined to advice, drugs, minor surgery and physiotherapy. Surgery and physiotherapy are considered in appropriate sections.

Sciatic Neuritis

Diagnostic procedures are legion and are all based on (*a*) tenderness of the nerve or (*b*) pain on stretching the nerve. Some of the more common methods of stretching are:
1. Dorsiflexion of the foot.
2. Dorsiflexion of the great toe.
3. Extension of the knee joint.
4. Flexion of the hip. (Ask the patient to bend over with his knees stiff.)

Herniated Disk

Pain is caused or enhanced by raising spinal fluid pressure. Do it by asking the patient to cough or by compressing the jugular veins, like this:

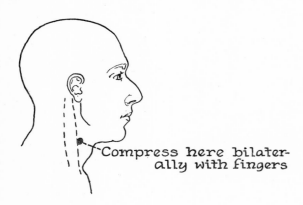

Compress here bilaterally with fingers

ENDOCRINE DISORDERS

When one performs office procedures designed to aid diagnosis and treatment of endocrine disease, certain paramount facts must be kept in mind. Perhaps the most important is to remember that we see very few endocrine disorders specific to one gland or to a single function of one gland. The majority of endocrine problems seen by the practitioner are the result of disturbance in the complex balance maintained by interplay of glandular secretions. Specific tests, therefore, are specific only in that they indicate one phase of the unbalance. They must be so interpreted.

Pituitary

Normal function of the anterior pituitary may be inferred in the presence of a positive epinephrine test. To do the test, have the patient report without breakfast (no coffee) and do an eosinophil count. This can be accomplished from an ordinary stained smear by examining 500 cells and noting the number of eosinophils. Then give 0.5 cc. of 1:1000 epinephrine subcutaneously. Four hours later, again count the eosinophils. If the test is positive there will be a drop of 50 per cent or more in the number of circulating eosinophils per 500 cells. The converse is not true; i.e., a fall of less than 50 per cent does not prove inadequate anterior pituitary function, for allergy or adrenal disease may cause such a result.

Thyroid

Mention should be made of the basal metabolic rate determination only to condemn it as a valuable test. The procedure is subject to gross technical error as performed in the average office and is not, as many doctors believe, a direct measure of thyroid function. Under hospital conditions, with preceding sedation and performed by an expert technician, the test has some limited value. Perhaps its most important use is to evaluate therapeutic trial of medication.

Blood cholesterol determination is of some help, particularly in hypothyroid cases. It can best be performed using the photoelectric colorimeter. Advanced tests such as determination of protein-bound iodine or uptake of I^{131} are not within the range of the small clinic. A painstaking history and careful physical examination remain the standby diagnostic methods of importance.

Parathyroids

Determination of calcium and phosphorus can be made wth the photoelectric colorimeter following the directions given by the manufacturer of the instrument. The Sulkowitch test is a simple means of estimating urinary excretion of calcium. To 5 cc. of urine in a test tube add 2 cc. of reagent. Note the density of the white precipitate and the time it takes to form. Grade the results from zero to four plus. Zero indicates a very low blood calcium, four plus a marked hypercalcemia. The reagent is made like this:

Oxalic acid	2.5 gm.
Ammonium oxalate	2.5 gm.
Glacial acetic acid	5.0 cc.
Distilled water q.s. ad	150 cc.

Diabetes Mellitus

A simple screening test can be performed with excellent results on those suspected of diabetes. On the day of the test, have the patient eat this breakfast:

8 oz. orange juice
1 oz. dry cereal
2 slices bread
1 egg
6 oz. milk
3 oz. cream
3 teaspoons sugar
Coffee and tea as desired.

Three hours after ingestion of this meal withdraw a sample of venous blood and determine blood sugar with the photoelectric colorimeter. A value below 130 usually excludes diabetes mellitus.

In questionable cases the oral glucose tolerance test should be performed. The patient is prepared by being given a high carbohydrate diet for several days. No food of any kind is taken on the morning of the test. Samples of blood are taken before the test and 30 minutes, 1 hour, 2 hours, and 3 hours after administration of the test substance. Immediately after the first withdrawal of blood the patient is given 100 grams of glucose in 500 cc. of water to which the juice of one lemon has been added. Typical curves resulting from this test look like this:

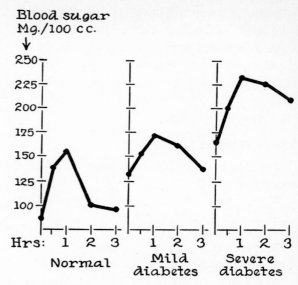

Problems of coma are best handled in the hospital, where carbon dioxide combining power can be tested as well as critical care offered.

Gonads

Testicular and ovarian problems are considered in the sections on gynecology and genitourinary procedures.

DERMATOLOGY

Office procedures in diseases of the skin are limited usually to demonstration of the offending agent and to physiotherapy, which will be discussed in a later section.

Bacteria may be identified by routine smear and culture. Fungi should be looked for by examining scrapings taken from the lesion with the back of a knife blade and mounted in 10 per cent potassium hydroxide, or cultured on Sabouraud's medium at room temperature.

In a questionable case of scabies, pick up a lesion on a needle and snip it out, like this:

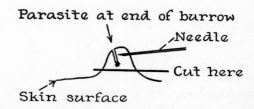

Mount the piece of tissue in 10 per cent potassium hydroxide and examine under low power. The parasite looks like this:

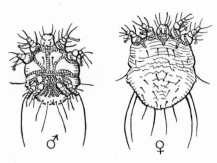

Tinea capitis may best be diagnosed by means of a Wood's light. The apparatus is cheap and the procedure highly accurate. In a dark room aim the lamp toward the affected area and examine the shaft of the hairs near the base. A pale, greenish fluorescence is diagnostic. If necessary, one can make a Wood's light by purchasing a piece of filter glass for an ordinary low-power lamp. The filter should transmit rays only in the 3300 to 3800 A range.

Demonstration of contact agents will be discussed in the next section on allergy.

ALLERGIC DISEASES

Skin testing is well within the range of the practitioner if done carefully and with intelligent interpretation. Certain basic facts are important to keep in mind. They are:

1. Commercial extracts are usually made up so that the intradermal solutions are approximately 100 times as dilute as those used for scratch testing. This compensates for the fact that intradermal tests are about 100 times more reactive than scratch tests.

2. Severe reactions are possible with either type of test. Pollens and, in intradermal testing, other inhalants, should be given on the arm where a tourniquet may be applied proximal to the test site if a reaction occurs.

3. No testing should be done without epinephrine available for immediate injection.

Many commercially prepared extracts are available. We use the following method and material:

A relatively complete set (about 150 extracts) is kept for intradermal testing with special materials ordered as needed. We use Abbott regional pollens sets for scratch testing to determine pollen allergy. These are ordered for each patient after eliciting a careful history of time of onset and duration of symptoms. Cutter Laboratories also offer excellent material. For basic screening of other allergies, we use the Abbott 44 unit scratch test kit. While more extensive fungus determinations are often needed, the Abbott "Dollar Test Kit" for fungi is useful.

Scratch Tests

The patient is stripped to the waist and asked to lie face down on the examining table. The skin of the back is cleansed with soap and water and dried thoroughly. Then numbers are written on the skin with washable ink corresponding to the number of tests to be done. These numbered test areas should be at least 2 inches apart in every direction.

A separate needle is used for each scratch. The object is not to penetrate the skin but literally to tear the surface layer open so that the extract may bathe the cells of the deeper layers. A single scratch about ⅜ inch long is made and a drop of the extract placed on it. If the test material is in sealed capillary tubes this is easy. If it is in a bottle, dip a clean toothpick in the extract and place the drop that clings to the toothpick on the scratch. Discard the toothpick and use another for the next test.

The reactions should be read in approximately 30 minutes. Unfortunately there is no agreement as to grading of reactions. Using the size of the wheal as a guide, I grade reactions about as follows:

+1   +2   +3   +4

Check scratch tests after 24 hours for delayed reactions. If the scratch tests agree with the history, it may not be necessary to continue with more advanced studies.

Intradermal Tests

Since these are potentially dangerous, I prefer to do them on the arms in daily groups of 20 or less. Do *not* do intradermal tests with substances that gave a positive scratch reaction. This is courting danger and seldom gives any positive information.

Very small gauge needles (26) should be used and they should be inserted, bevel side up, until the lumen is barely concealed by the skin. Use as little test extract as possible to make a barely perceptible "blister." Usually 0.01 cc. is entirely adequate.

Reactions are read exactly as in the scratch tests, with the exception that reactions to bacteria and fungi are quite often delayed for 24 to 48 hours and should be checked at least once 24 hours after administration of the extract.

Skin tests are about 90 per cent accurate in diagnosis of inhalant allergies, particularly pollen diseases. Accuracy in food allergy is much less, probably about 60 per cent.

Patch Tests

Patch tests are occasionally useful. The substance to be tested may be applied directly to the skin if it is not, itself, a skin irritant. Where dilutions may be necessary, olive oil or plain water may be used as a diluent. Apply the substance directly to the untreated skin and cover with a sheet of plastic 1½ inches square. Use ½ inch adhesive tape to seal the edges, like this:

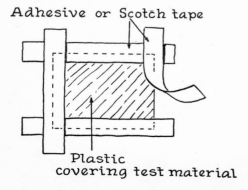

Adhesive or Scotch tape

Plastic covering test material

Read the result in 24 hours and again in 48 hours. When a control is thought necessary, simply tape a "blank" piece of cellophane moistened with olive oil (if that diluent is used) on nearby skin.

Nasal Secretion Studies

Diagnostic study of nasal secretion may be of value in cases of suspected allergic rhinitis. Have the patient blow his nose, one side at a time, on clean gauze sponges. In children who cannot cooperate, a smear may be made from material secured on a cotton tip applicator.

Use the "thin smear" technique and allow to air dry. Fix with methyl alcohol and stain with Giemsa's stain. Frequent eosinophils, particularly if clumped, are an indication of allergic disease.

Allergy to Cold

Of the physical allergies only one is of significance to the practitioner—allergy to cold. Test for it like this: First, chill a bucket or crock of water to 50° F. by adding ice or by leaving overnight in a refrigerator. Have the patient immerse one hand and a portion of the forearm in the water for 6 minutes. Then remove the hand for 6 minutes. If no systemic reaction occurs, put a tourniquet on just above the elbow and reimmerse the hand and forearm for another 6 minutes. Release the tourniquet 3 minutes after the extremity is withdrawn from the cold water and again wait 6 minutes.

If no reaction occurs, cold allergy is eliminated except that caused by breathing cold air. To test for this I usually have the patient bend over the container of cold water and breathe the cold air just above the surface for a few minutes.

Occasionally a severe reaction to immersion may take place. When this happens, dip the hand in warm water. If no relief is obtained, reapply the tourniquet and give 5 minims of 1:1000 epinephrine.

Food Allergy

Other than skin tests, which have already been mentioned, there are two procedures of much importance in the diagnosis of food allergy. First is the food diary. To prepare one, get a pad of graph paper ruled in ⅛ inch squares. Head the paper by days, like this:

	S	M	T	W	T	F	S	S	M	T	W	T
Symptoms	3	3	2	2	3	2	1	1	1	4	4	3
White bread	✓	✓	✓	✓				✓	✓	✓	✓	
Bacon		✓		✓	✓			✓				
Milk	✓	✓	✓	✓	✓	✓	✓	✓	✓	✓	✓	✓
Apple			✓							✓	✓	
Steak, beef	✓				✓	✓	✓					
Ham			✓							✓		
Sw. potato			✓							✓		
Lettuce			✓					✓				

In the first horizontal column have the patient indicate the severity of the symptoms, using the scale from 0 (no symptoms) to the figure 4 for the most severe symptoms.

Ask the patient to list the foods he eats in the column at the left and to place a check mark in the proper square each day the food is eaten, as shown. When kept accurately for 4 to 8 weeks the food diary can be of great help.

One must emphasize to the patient how very important it is that this food diary be complete and accurate. Unless every food is noted down it may serve no purpose at all.

Elimination diets are of great practical benefit. I use those of Rowe. This is quoted from his work:

Elimination Diets (Rowe)

Diet 1	Diet 2	Diet 3	Diet 4
Rice	Corn	Tapioca	Milk*
Tapioca	Rye	White potato	Tapioca
Rice biscuit	Corn pone	Breads made of soy,	Cane sugar
Rice bread	Corn-rye muffin	lima and potato	
	Rye bread	starch and tapioca	
	Ry-Krisp	flours	
Lettuce	Beets	Tomato	
Chard	Squash	Carrot	
Spinach	Asparagus	Lima beans	
Carrot	Artichoke	String beans	
Sweet potato		Peas	
Lamb	Chicken (no hens)	Beef	
	Bacon	Bacon	
Lemon			
	Pineapple	Lemon	
Grapefruit	Peach	Grapefruit	
Pears	Apricot	Peach	
	Prune	Apricot	
Cane sugar	Cane or beet sugar	Cane sugar	
Sesame oil	Mazola oil	Sesame oil	
Olive oil	Sesame oil	Soy bean oil	
Salt	Salt	Salt	
Gelatin, plain,	Gelatin, plain	Gelatin, plain or lime	
lime or lemon	or pineapple	or lemon	
Maple syrup or syrup	Karo corn syrup	Maple syrup or syrup	
made with cane	White vinegar	made with cane	* Milk should be
sugar flavored with	Royal baking powder	sugar flavored with	taken up to two or
maple	Baking soda	maple	three quarts a day.
Royal baking powder	Cream of tartar	Royal baking powder	Plain cottage cheese
Baking soda	Vanilla extract	Baking soda	and cream may be
Cream of tartar		Cream of tartar	used. Tapioca cooked
Vanilla extract		Vanilla extract	with milk and milk
Lemon extract		Lemon extract	sugar may be taken.

From Rowe, Albert H.: Elimination Diets and the Patient's Allergies. 2d ed. Philadelphia, Lea & Febiger, 1944.

Use of "Elimination Diets"

"When symptoms of probable food allergy are not controlled by diets which exclude foods to which skin reactions have occurred, or if skin reactions to foods are negative, or impossible to perform, 'elimination diets' may be used. The frequency of the negative skin reaction to foods productive of clinical allergy and the occurrence of positive reactions to foods not causative of allergic symptoms must be remembered.

"1. Diets 1 and 2 may be prescribed together or separately, modifying them by substituting similar foods for any in the diets to which skin reactions or known idiosyncrasies exist. . . .

"2. If sensitization to cereals as a group is suspected, use the cereal-free elimination diet.

"3. The selected diet must be taken for at least ten days or even three or four weeks, for in many cases reacting bodies to the causative foods disappear very slowly from the shock tissues. If relief does not occur another 'elimination diet' should be tried.

"4. Absolute adherence to the prescribed diet is imperative. Not the slightest bit of any food not specified must be taken. Restaurant and hotel food often contains slight amounts of forbidden foods, due at times to poorly cleansed cooking utensils or carelessness in cooking. No commercial breads, cookies, soups, etc., should be used unless every ingredient is known. Margarines contain 2 to 6 per cent milk solids.

"5. If body weight decreases, specified sugars, starches and oils must be increased. Prescribed fruits and vegetables assure Vitamins A, B, C and G. Adequate protein, when milk is excluded, requires meat or other protein two or three times a day. If milk is excluded longer than one month, the addition of 4 to 6 grams of dicalcium phosphate on retiring will assure mineral balance. Vitamin D must be supplemented by the use of cod liver oil, halibut oil, viosterol, sun or quartz light therapy. Until fish is added, fish oils cannot be used, and viosterol should be allowed only in an oil contained in the 'elimination diets.'

"6. With relief of symptoms for longer than former periods of freedom, other foods, one to three at a time, from the remaining 'elimination diets' are tried every four to seven days. Thereafter, other vegetables, fruits, meats, spices and nuts gradually may be added. In one to three months, milk, egg and wheat may be tried, separately, at fortnightly intervals. If the patient is allergic to any food, symptoms may occur immediately, or in days or even weeks according to the patient's tolerance. In such cases the food must again be eliminated.

"7. In the undernourished or in children, Diet 4 containing milk may be used first or milk may be tried, added to the chosen 'elimination diet' after one or two weeks. Sobee, a soya bean product, Cemac, containing beef and vegetables or almond milk, are available for infants and children who cannot tolerate denaturized cow's or goat's milk.

"*Supplemental Elimination Diets.* When Diets 1, 2 and 3 fail to relieve symptoms, then supplemental diets may be tried. Or they may be used initially if sensitizations to many different foods or to nearly all members of one or more groups of foods such as cereals, fruits, vegetables, or meats are indicated by history or skin reactions.

"In the unsolved case of possible food allergy all foods must be suspected and minimal diets be selected as follows:

"1. A choice of one or two of the following carbohydrates: Rice, corn, tapioca, sago, sweet or white potato.

"2. A choice of one or two of the following protein rich foods: Lamb, beef, chicken, soya bean, nutramigen.

"3. A choice of two or three of the following vegetables: Spinach, carrot, beet, artichoke, asparagus, pea, tomato, string bean.

"4. A choice of one or two of the following fruits: Lemon, grapefruit, pear, peach, apricot, pineapple.

"5. Mazola (corn), olive oil or sesame oil, white sugar, maple syrup or corn glucose, salt.

"6. Tea, mate (Brazilian tea) or the juice of tomato or any fruit included in the diet.

"The choice of the supplemental diet depends on the patient's history of food idiosyncrasies or any positive skin reactions, if testing is available, and on the clinical reactions to foods evident from diet trial."

Cereal-Free Elimination Diet (Rowe)

Tapioca	Carrot	Cane or beet sugar
White potato	Beet	Salt
Sweet potato	Artichoke	Sesame oil
Lima bean-potato bread	Tomato	Soy bean oil
Soy bean-lima bean bread	Squash	Sesame spread
Soy bean-potato-tapioca bread	Asparagus	Gelatin, plain
Lamb	Peas	Lime, lemon or pineapple gelatin
Beef	String bean	Maple syrup or syrup made with cane
Chicken (no hens)	Lima bean	sugar flavored with maple
Bacon	Lemon	White vinegar
Liver (calf, beef or lamb)	Grapefruit	Vanilla extract
Lettuce	Pear	Lemon extract
Spinach	Pineapple	Royal baking powder
Chard	Peach	Baking soda
	Apricot	Cream of tartar
	Prune	

Avoidance of foods that cause symptoms is the prime requisite for successful treatment. Parenteral desensitization to foods is not a very satisfactory means of treatment. I certainly do not recommend it to the practitioner unless consultation with a competent allergist be had first. Schedules for oral desensitization may be of some use in food allergies but the effect is not at all certain. A typical schedule for treatment of a milk allergy is as follows:

1. Mix 1 teaspoonful of milk with 1 quart of water. Take a teaspoonful of the mixture daily for 4 days.

2. Mix 1 tablespoonful of milk to 1 quart of water and take a teaspoonful daily for 4 days.

3. The next 4 days take 1 teaspoonful daily of a mixture of 1 teaspoonful of milk to 1 pint of water.

4. Take 1 tablespoonful of the same mixture daily for the next 4 days.

5. Mix 1 teaspoonful of milk in 1 cup of water and take 1 teaspoonful daily for 4 days.

6. Mix 1 teaspoonful of milk in ½ cup of water and take 1 teaspoonful daily for 4 days.

7. Mix 1 teaspoonful of milk in ¼ cup of water and take 1 teaspoonful daily for 4 days.

8. Mix 1 teaspoonful of milk with 2 tablespoons of water and take 1 teaspoonful daily for 4 days.

9. Mix 1 teaspoonful of milk with 1 tablespoonful of water. Take 1 teaspoonful daily for 4 days.

10. Mix equal parts of milk and water and take 1 teaspoonful daily for 4 days.

11. Take ½ teaspoonful of plain milk daily for four days.

12. One teaspoonful daily for 4 days.

13. Two teaspoonfuls daily for 4 days.

14. Three teaspoonfuls daily for 4 days.

And so on. Surprisingly enough, it works about half the time.

Inhalant Allergies

An adequate history and proper skin testing will give the true diagnosis in the majority of these cases. Accurate pollen surveys are available for every state in the United States and for most of the populous areas of the world. They are very useful and should be obtained from local or state health departments.

Treatment extracts are made up commercially by prescription. Follow the instructions of the manufacturer explicitly. I have used Abbott and Cutter prescription treatment extracts with complete success. Others are unquestionably just as good.

There are three methods of treatment for seasonal inhalants now in current use. They are:

1. *Preseasonal.* Injections are begun 60 to 90 days before the expected onset of symptoms. Injections are given twice weekly and care is taken that a maximal dose is reached just be-

fore appearance of the offending agent in the atmosphere.

2. *Co-seasonal*. This is valuable in the treatment of those persons who have had pre-seasonal treatment without relief and those who report to the physician too late for adequate preseasonal routines. Injections are begun upon the first appearance of symptoms with 1:5000 extract given in daily dosage of 0.1 cc. until relief is gained or until three injections have been given.

When relief occurs during the first three days wait until the first sign of returning symptoms and repeat the 0.1 cc. dose. Set a schedule for repetition of the original dose so that repeat injections are given *just before* reappearance of symptoms is expected.

In the event there is no relief from the first three doses, start increasing the dose by 0.1 cc. each day until relief is obtained or until a maximum dose of 1.0 cc. is reached. When relief is obtained give no more extract until symptoms return. Then give the same dose as that previously required for relief.

3. *Perennial*. Begin anytime except during the pollen season. Give doses exactly as in preseasonal treatment until 0.1 or 0.2 cc. of the 1:50 extract is reached. Give this dose every two or three weeks until 60 days before expected onset of symptoms. Then begin giving injections once weekly, increasing 0.1 cc. each time until a full 1.0 cc. dose is given. *Immediately* at the beginning of the season drop the dose down to 0.2 cc. of the 1:50 extract every two weeks. Continue at this level until the season is over. When pollen is no longer present, again give 0.1 cc. of the 1:50 extract every two or three weeks until the next season approaches.

Of the three methods, perennial treatment is probably the best, preseasonal intermediate, and co-seasonal least satisfactory.

All injections should be given into the subcutaneous fat with a small caliber needle. Always aspirate before injecting to be sure that the needle point does not lie in a small vessel.

Local reactions occur which resemble a cellulitis. They will subside spontaneously but no further treatment should be given until they are gone. Constitutional reactions, on the other hand, may be serious. They are more frequent when the patient is exposed to heat or exerts himself immediately following the injection. Most happen within 30 minutes after introduction of the extract.

When you see one of these reactions put a tourniquet on the arm immediately above the injection site and give 5 minims of 1:1000 epinephrine *intramuscularly* in the opposite arm. If relief is not quick to appear, institute measures for the treatment of shock.

Inhalants other than pollen are often best treated by avoidance. If this cannot be achieved, exposure can, at least, be much diminished. One diagnostic procedure I often use (it is a good therapeutic approach, too) is to "strip" a room in the patient's home. To do this, all furniture is removed except a bed and a plain wooden bedside table. Rugs, drapes, pictures (i.e., everything but the bed and table) are removed. The room is then scrubbed from top to bottom with Lysol water. It is not aired following this scrubbing.

The mattress and pillows are covered with plastic sheeting and only cotton bedclothes are allowed on the bed. The patient is instructed to wear only fresh washed and triple rinsed cotton pajamas and is specifically warned about cosmetics. Then she enters the room (doors and windows closed) and receives no visitors except at mealtime. The meals are served in plain dishes on a metal tray. Smoking is forbidden.

In many cases, symptoms disappear. When this happens, one item is brought back into the room each day until symptoms reappear. This makes it relatively easy to determine the offending agent.

When desensitization by injection is attempted the dosage should be similar to that for preseasonal pollen therapy. After maximum concentration is reached injections should be given every two weeks for 60 days and then every month. These monthly injections are best continued for several years.

Contact Dermatitis

There are two procedures in the diagnosis of contact dermatitis which I have found far superior to indiscriminate skin testing. The first involves a therapeutic trial. Using as an example a dermatitis of both wrists thought to be of contact origin: Have the patient continue his or her usual tasks and apply 1 per cent Cortef ointment to one wrist four times daily for two days, then examine. In a true allergy, the treated wrist will be much improved.

The second procedure is to cover one wrist (in the case we have used as an example) from the base of the phalanges to the mid point of the forearm with a snug Unna paste and gauze dressing. Contact will be eliminated and, a week later, the skin under the dressing should approach normal.

After certain diagnosis of contact dermatitis the specific agent may usually be found out by a searching history. Rarely skin tests (patch) may be needed.

Section XI

PSYCHOLOGICAL TESTING

PSYCHOLOGICAL TESTING

Minor psychiatry presupposes common sense and a sympathetic understanding of people. There are no procedures involved in most such cases. One thing, however, we physicians have neglected. There have been formulated in this country a number of useful tests which help delineate the psychological status of any individual. Almost daily we are asked questions which pertain to this field—questions such as, "Is this child of normal intelligence?" "Is this a psychoneurosis?" "Could it be my nerves?" In the past few years, physicians have become increasingly interested in this phase of medicine, but we face an impasse.

Properly, a trained psychologist or psychiatrist should administer and interpret these tests for us. There are not enough psychologists and psychiatrists in the world to begin, much less complete, this necessary testing and interpretation. With current training schedules, it is unlikely that there will be an adequate supply of these men for at least 50 years and, more likely, 100 years.

For that reason I have included a brief discussion of some of the easier tests that may be administered in the physician's office and the results to be expected. I don't particularly urge them on the family physician and yet again, to face facts, if you don't do them I don't know who will—probably those who have insufficient knowledge of people to make a reasonable interpretation.

One word of thanks before we start: My interest in these tests has been much expanded owing to the efforts of two excellent men, neither of whom is a physician. I should like to acknowledge the painstaking human studies of Mr. Al Wolfle and Mr. L. C. Beck.

These men became experts in the human problems of patients and have helped me immeasurably in the study and practice of medicine.

THE GESELL DEVELOPMENTAL SCHEDULES

This test, which was developed by a pediatrician-psychologist, is published by the Psychological Corporation.* It is designed to measure the infant's development in four areas. They are: motor behavior, adaptive behavior, language development and personal-social behavior. The tests are not difficult to administer and offer a good estimate of whether a child is retarded, normal or advanced in development. A well trained office nurse may sometimes administer the basic tests. Although this is not desirable, it may sometimes be a necessity.

Interpretation is best left in the hands of the highly trained worker but certain points are available and worth while to us practitioners. To use an example, in examining a child for adoption, administration of the test may show an apparent retardation. If no organic reason for this can be demonstrated, the child should be checked by a competent child psychiatrist or psychologist. If the child seems equal or superior to the normal (means of calculating this are given in the test manual) one may assume that an adequate mentality exists.

* Test materials for the Gesell Developmental Schedules, the Gordon Personal Profile, the Wechsler-Bellevue Tests and the Minnesota Multiphasic Personality Inventory are available from the Psychological Corporation, 522 Fifth Avenue, New York 36, N. Y.

THE GORDON PERSONAL PROFILE

This test is made up of 18 sets of four statements. In each group of four, the subject indicates the statement which is most like him and which is least like him. Answers are transformed into percentile scores. The four symbols, A-R-E-S, stand for ascendency, responsibility, emotional stability and sociability. The T score is a total score which is somewhat difficult to interpret. High T scores may signify a high self-evaluation, a genuinely high standing or an attempt to "fool the test." Low T scores, on the other hand, are almost invariably associated with poor personality adjustment.

This test takes not over 15 minutes to give and may offer some valuable information about some of the maladjustment cases which we doctors see every day in our offices. The test is of particular value in young adults. Since it is brief, simple to score and easy to interpret, it is probably worth investigation by the family physician. Here are two illustrative case histories with the profiles made on the test.

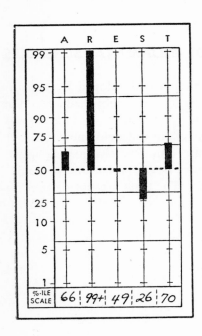

Gordon Personal Profile: Illustrative Case. Bob, a 31-year-old senior in a school of business administration, fully supported himself, his wife, and a child by working full time as an apprentice printer, but carried a 12-hour program each semester, in which he maintained a "B" average. During the war Bob obtained a job in a defense plant and soon was promoted to a supervisory position. After the war Bob decided to get college training. He indicated that he was able to hold down his job, get his studying done, and still devote time to his family by rigorously scheduling all of his time. As an aside, Bob mentioned that he had just completed building a five-room house, doing much of the work himself during week ends and holidays. (Copyright by World Book Company.)

Gordon Personal Profile: Illustrative Case. Tom, a 17-year-old high school junior, was described by the school counselor as "antisocial and a continual troublemaker." He is reported to be a member of a small gang whose members have been involved in truancy, vandalism, and attacks upon other children. Tom is from a large family. His father is a laborer on the railroad. Tom's parents have refused to cooperate with school authorities. Tom stated that his parents didn't care what he did and were "glad to have him out of the way." Tom was quite hostile during the early part of the interview but soon became confiding. He stated that the kids in school did not like him and made fun of him. He spent almost all of his time with his "buddy," who "stuck up for him." Tom appeared to be an extremely insecure boy, to have a strong need to be accepted and to find this acceptance, absent from his home and school, in his "buddy," the leader of the gang. (Copyright by World Book Company.)

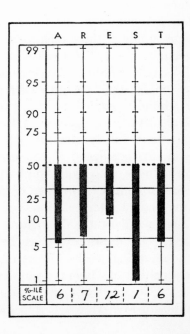

THE WECHSLER-BELLEVUE TESTS

Frequent administration or detailed interpretation of intelligence scales does not lie within the field of the family physician. There are times, however, when the testing of intelligence may be of real service in diagnosis and prognosis. The best instrument to use is the Wechsler-Bellevue Intelligence Scale.

This consists of 11 subtests and takes less than an hour to administer. The subtests are:

1. General Information. Twenty-five questions covering knowledge of everyday subjects that should be common to everyone.

2. General Comprehension. Ten items in which the subject is given a hypothetical situation and asked what action should be taken.

3. Arithmetic Reasoning. Ten arithmetic problems to be solved without pencil and paper.

4. Repetition of digits forward and backward.

5. Similarities. Twelve items requiring the patient to state in which way certain objects are alike and how they differ.

6. Vocabulary. A list of 42 words to be defined.

7. Picture Completion. Fifteen cards upon which are printed a picture with a single part missing. The subject states which part is absent.

8. Picture Arrangement. Six sets of cards; each set has a series of pictures to be arranged in proper order.

9. Object Assembly. Essentially a jig-saw puzzle.

10. Block Design. Colored blocks to be assembled into specified designs.

11. Digit Symbol. An encoding test.

Each of these tests has specific scoring methods which are listed in the instruction booklet. Final scores appear on a chart showing the extent to which the patient differs from "normal" in each of the subtests. The total score may be converted to an I.Q. by reference to tables which are provided.

Many criticisms have been leveled at the Wechsler-Bellevue but it remains the most popular instrument in general use for measuring adult intelligence. As one becomes more familiar with the test, information other than an estimate of intelligence is available from test results.

MINNESOTA MULTIPHASIC PERSONALITY INVENTORY

The Minnesota Multiphasic Personality Inventory (MMPI) is unquestionably the most complete and the best known test for psychic deviations which is available today. To me, it is also the most confusing.

The test is not hard to administer (it may be done by an intelligent associate), and it yields a profile score as shown in the examples reproduced below.*

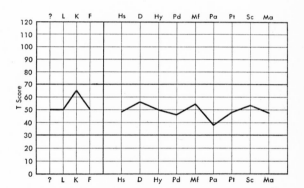

The Profile of a Normal Adult on the MMPI.

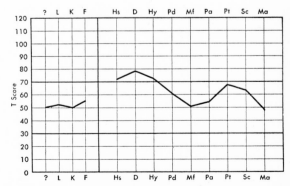

A "Typical Psychoneurotic Profile" on the MMPI.

* MMPI profiles reproduced by permission of the Ronald Press.

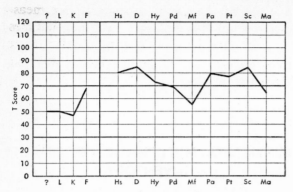

A "Typical Psychotic Profile" on the MMPI.

To give the test, the subject is furnished 550 cards with an affirmative statement printed on each one. He is asked to classify them into three groups: "true," "false" and "cannot say." The mechanical procedures for translating these classifications into scores are included in the test manual. A brief summary of scoring is this:

The Question score (?) is simply the number of items put in the "cannot say" category. The L score results from the number of probable falsehoods as measured by certain "catch" questions. It means, of course, lie score.

The K score was devised as a measure of test-taking attitude. A high K score probably indicates a strong desire to appear normal, with a defensive attitude. A low K score *may* indicate malingering or self-criticism.

The F score is intended to represent the validity of the test. A high F score probably means scoring errors, carelessness, eccentricity, or malingering. The clinical scores are: H_s, hypochrondriasis; D, depression; H_y, Hysteria; P_d, psychopathic deviate; M_f, masculinity or femininity; P_a, paranoia; P_t, psychasthenia; S_c, schizophrenia; M_a, hypomania.

Actually, interpretation of the scores on these scales is in a very confused state and certainly does not lie within the province of the family physician. The presence of two or more scores above 70 probably signifies maladjustment (but by no means proves it) and indicates the desirability of more complete psychiatric study. Where a real question exists about the status of the patient, the MMPI profile should be interpreted by an experienced psychiatrist or psychologist. In most cases the test will serve the family physician as an indicator to back up something he already suspects from his knowledge of the patient.

Neither the MMPI nor any other test replaces common sense in diagnosis and treatment. I actually have found it very valuable within my own limited ability to interpret. Depending upon the area in which you practice, you might find it worth investigating also.

PROJECTIVE TECHNIQUES

These are tests in which the patient is allowed to project his own personality into interpretation of given situations. They are, by and large, far beyond the range of knowledge of the family physician. There is one, however, that offers a good hint as to the status of the individual and which may be given a limited interpretation by any physician after a reasonable amount of study.

The test consists of a series of sentence beginnings like this:

My mind. . . . . . .
Women. . . . . . .
If I had my way. . . . . . .
What annoys me. . . . . . .

The patient is instructed to express his or her true feelings as nearly as possible in completing the sentences. Detailed scoring procedures are offered, but simple, common-sense interpretations of the answers will offer a great deal of information about the psychic status of any individual. The great drawback to the test is, of course, the fact that many times the patient will not be entirely frank.

The average person, particularly one who lives in a small town, hesitates to give frank answers to questions of psychological import. Having lived in a small town for a number of years, I can certainly agree with his viewpoint.

To overcome this, we have used in our own practice a simple little test which obviates the necessity of a written answer from the patient. We have a series of 100 questions, 30 of which are answered true by normal people and 70 of which are usually answered true in cases of psychic deviation only. We give the patient a piece of paper headed "True" and "False" and ask him to answer each question by making a tally mark under the appropriate heading. Using this means of scoring we never know which questions he answers "true" and which "false."

To check, we simply count the number of "trues." Between 20 and 40 is considered normal; between 40 and 50, a questionable psychoneurosis; and over 50, almost certain evidence of psychic deviation. The test has never been checked for reliability. Validity is proven only for our own practice, which means that it may be of no service whatever to other practitioners. On the other hand, it might be.

If you want to try to use the test, simply tear out the page containing the questions (there is nothing else on this page), give the patient a piece of scratch paper with a "true-false" heading, and have him tally his answers so that the score sheet looks like this:

True	False
₦ ₦ ₦ ₦ ₦ ₦ ₦ ₦ ₦ ₦ ₦ ₦ /// *63*	₦ ₦ ₦ ₦ ₦ ₦ ₦ // *37*

Be sure to point out that no one will ever know which questions he answers true and which ones false. If he has a "true" score of over 50, the chances are you are dealing with a psychoneurosis or, very rarely, a phychosis. This does not mean that symptoms are due to the psychoneurosis. Certainly they are made worse by it and they *might* be caused by it.

INSTRUCTIONS

You will see on this sheet 100 statements. Read each statement carefully. Then place a mark on a sheet of paper under the heading "True" if the statement is true. If the statement is false, put a mark in the column "False." No one will ever know which statements you answer true and which you answer false.

Some of the questions are a little silly—we admit that—but they are important in scoring to help us help you. Take your time to answer and remember that there are NO trick questions.

1. I have frequent headaches.
2. I have frequent dizzy spells.
3. I do not like every town I have ever seen.
4. I often see spots before my eyes.
5. Sometimes I have a choking sensation.
6. I dislike some people.
7. My heart pounds and misses an occasional beat.
8. I have difficulty breathing deeply enough.
9. I occasionally get angry with some people.
10. My stomach sometimes tightens up into a knot.
11. I have diarrhea every few weeks.
12. My legs feel weak.
13. Sometimes I am disgusted with myself.
14. I have pains in my abdomen frequently.
15. My hands and feet go to sleep often.
16. I have an occasional "bad day" when everything seems to go wrong.
17. My feet and hands are cold all the time.
18. I worry a lot.
19. Some days I feel better than others.
20. I have trouble going to sleep at night.

21. I often wake up and lie awake for some time.
22. I am a very nervous person.
23. I can tell I'm getting older.
24. I am easily upset and irritated.
25. I have had sexual relations with someone besides my husband (or wife) within the past year.
26. Some people are easier to know than others.
27. My sex life is not satisfactory.
28. I do not enjoy sex.
29. Every person has some bad habits.
30. People are against me.
31. I am often depressed.
32. I am a moody person.
33. Animal pets can be a nuisance to some people.
34. I drink a great deal.
35. I cry easily.
36. I like people to like me.
37. I wish I could go off and live by myself.
38. I do not like the people around me.
39. I would like to be wiser than I am.
40. I have no good friends.
41. I masturbate often.
42. I get angry easily.
43. I do not always do my best.
44. I always am lonely.

45. Meeting new people is hard for me.

46. Some men and women do not like to meet new people.

47. When I am nervous I have to urinate frequently.

48. I have little self-confidence.

49. I am bored sometimes.

50. Sometimes I hear voices when nobody is present.

51. I don't like people of the opposite sex.

52. I daydream more than most people.

53. Some people like to be in the Army or Navy.

54. Things seem unreal to me.

55. I daydream about sex.

56. Most people would like to be more attractive.

57. I have terrifying nightmares.

58. My conscience bothers me a great deal.

59. I sometimes wonder what will happen to me.

60. I am not a very nice person.

61. My sex organs are not very good ones compared with others.

62. My mother and/or father were mean to me.

63. Some people like flowers.

64. I am deeply religious and I think about religion a lot.

65. My hands tremble much of the time.

66. I get disgusted with people sometimes.

67. I feel all knotted up inside.

68. Simple decisions are hard for me to make.

69. I have or would like to have a pleasant hobby.

70. I would like to go to a wild sex party if I could.

71. Nobody understands me.

72. Somebody is trying to kill or mutilate me.

73. I think people should get along with one another better than they do.

74. I am too worthless to live.

75. I often dream of making love.

76. I like nice things.

77. I take a lot of medicine (at least three kinds).

78. None of the doctors seem to help me.

79. Health is important to me.

80. There is no one I can talk to about myself.

81. I have unreasonable fears (phobias).

82. I think about death often.

83. I came to the doctor for help.

84. I take sleeping pills more than once a week.

85. I have had sexual relations about which I feel guilty.

86. I have sometimes been unhappy.

87. A doctor has told me I have nervous trouble.

88. Nervous trouble runs in my family.

89. I am sometimes puzzled about which of two courses to follow.

90. I have had a nervous breakdown.

91. I am oversexed.

92. I am afraid something bad is going to happen to me.

93. Cancer is a bad disease.

94. I am undersexed.

95. I am overambitious.

96. I would like to do better than I do.

97. People do not like me.

98. My problem is sex.

99. I have been honest on this test.

100. I blush easily and often.

Section XII

ANESTHESIA

Anesthesia

The development of new techniques for local anesthesia has made possible a tremendous increase in the scope of minor surgery. There are many procedures which have been done in the hospital only because of the necessity for general anesthesia. These have now become legitimate in the field of minor surgery.

ANESTHETIC AGENTS AND THEIR TOXICITY

Procaine Hydrochloride

Procaine hydrochloride is the most frequently used of the various local anesthetic agents. It is an excellent drug for injection and will produce adequate anesthesia in almost any body tissue. The one exception to this statement is this: Procaine is not particularly effective in the presence of an inflammatory exudate when tissue pH is lowered. In such a condition, the analgesia produced is inadequate and "spotty." For this reason procaine should not be used for infiltration of grossly infected areas.

The action of the drug is short, complete analgesia being limited in most cases to ½ hour or slightly more. This action may be prolonged by adding 6 drops of 1:1000 epinephrine to each ounce of procaine solution. The action engendered is beneficial in many areas, but epinephrine should never be used when regional constriction of blood vessels may be dangerous. An example of this would be blocking the base of the finger as shown on page 332. Epinephrine should not be used in the solution employed for this purpose.

Three common solution strengths are used: 0.5 per cent will give adequate obtundation of pain for most procedures in most areas. For quicker and more intense action the 1 per cent or occasionally the 2 per cent solution may be used. Maximum dosage to be within the safe range is as follows:

2	per cent procaine	40 cc.
1	per cent procaine	90 cc.
0.5	per cent procaine	250 cc.

One should always aspirate to make certain that the needle is not in a blood vessel, for severe reactions may occur from intravenous injection. These reactions are usually amenable to treatment (if recognized!) and a method for proper therapeutic handling is found on page 328.

Pontocaine Hydrochloride

This is a long-acting local anesthetic which I have limited to surface application because of high toxicity when injected. It has, however, been used for infiltration with excellent results. In our own practice we use 0.5 per cent Pontocaine (tetracaine) for topical analgesia in the eye and 2 per cent Pontocaine for intranasal, pharyngeal and other surface anesthetic procedures. We have not used it in the urethra because of its toxic properties.

One should, of course, remember the simple point that the toxic effects of Pontocaine can only appear if it enters into the blood stream. It is absorbed with some rapidity by the intact nasopharyngeal membrane and so should be applied somewhat sparingly. A simple method to achieve the proper application is to wring out the pledget of cotton to be applied pressing the sponge against the edge of the medicine glass until the solution no longer runs down from it. This will prevent the "slopping about" of excess Pontocaine with resultant limitation of dosage.

You will recall that in the section on minor surgery we spoke of using a sponge soaked in Pontocaine as an anesthetic for brush burns or abrasions. The same wringing-out procedure should be followed when such use is contemplated. Soak the sponge in 2 per cent Pontocaine, wring it out as much as is possible and then apply it firmly to the abraded surface. Neglect of this procedure will result in an occasional severe Pontocaine reaction. While I don't know the exact figures, a clinical impression would be that Pontocaine is approximately ten times as toxic as procaine and, therefore, should be handled with a great deal of caution. There is very little danger so long as reasonable precautions are observed.

Ether

Diethyl ether is probably the most annoying anesthetic ever invented. The patient sputters and spews during the process of induction; he may crow and roar with each respiration while under the anesthetic and not infrequently is violently nauseated upon regaining consciousness. In spite of all this it is almost impossible to kill a human being with ether. The anesthetic may be administered to the point of respiratory arrest and if the mask be removed the patient usually starts breathing again, throws off the ether and comes out none the worse for his experience.

Cardiac arrhythmias are rare, lung complications frequent but not markedly serious. End results are, in general, excellent. Those of us who do anesthesia learn to have a great admiration for diethyl ether in spite of its obvious drawbacks. It is, of course, inflammable and, in certain concentrations, explosive. It should, therefore, be handled with a great deal of caution. I had a doctor friend once who used a can of ether and, without thinking, set it down on a natural gas stove when he had finished with it. Fortunately nobody was hurt but repairs to the office were extensive and expensive.

The methods of administration and general precautions in use are far too well known to need delineation here.

Vinethene

This agent is not greatly different from ether, with two exceptions. First, its action is a great deal more rapid. In the average minor surgical procedure, induction of ether anesthesia has taken from 4 to 5 minutes while loss of consciousness from the administration of Vinethene (divinyl ether) takes about 30 seconds.

Second, Vinethene is more toxic than ether and should not be used for procedures which take longer than a minute or two. Its principal uses are for induction of anesthesia which is followed up with ether, and for procedures of short duration.

The agent is extremely volatile and is best stored in the refrigerator.

Nausea and vomiting seldom follow brief use of Vinethene, which makes it a very satisfactory anesthetic for myringotomy, fracture reduction, incision and drainage and other short procedures.

Nitrous Oxide

If one has a nitrous oxide–oxygen machine, this agent is a definite asset to minor anesthetic techniques. Administered in concentrations of 80 per cent nitrous oxide and 20 per cent oxygen it is entirely safe and will produce obtundation of pain. The deep planes of anesthesia cannot be achieved with nitrous oxide in strengths of 80 per cent or less. Stronger concentrations, of course, should not be given because of the danger of asphyxia.

The anesthetic is useful by itself for producing pain relief in very short procedures. If it is to be used for more than a minute or two, some additional agent, usually a short-acting barbiturate intravenously, is necessary. The same effect can be obtained with doses of morphine or Avertin by rectum but the narcosis engendered by these drugs has a relatively long duration which is a disadvantage in minor surgery.

The principal danger in using nitrous oxide is that of asphyxiation. The anesthetist must be extremely cautious not to allow the concentration of oxygen in the inhaled gas to be less than 20 per cent. Other than this, precautions are only those that should be dictated by common sense.

Pentothal Sodium

This is the common drug used for intravenous anesthesia. It has a very limited field in the office because of dangerous toxic reactions. The 0.5 per cent concentration will produce respiratory arrest quickly.

The most potent danger, however, is not that of respiratory arrest but is due to the increase in sensitivity of the laryngeal reflexes from the drug. Severe laryngospasm may ensue from the most minimal laryngeal stimulation and may be the cause of dangerous hypoxia. For this reason the drug should not be used in procedures involving the nose, mouth or throat. Operations upon the periosteum and upon the rectum seem equally dangerous because—for some unknown reason—laryngospasm may occur with relative frequency when these structures are manipulated.

A good rule of thumb is not to use Pentothal unless one has immediately available the instruments for control of the respiratory tract in any emergency.

All this would make it seem that Pentothal is not a valuable agent. If I have given this impression I apologize, for the drug is very useful. Its dangers are often underestimated or laughed away, however, and this is a pernicious thing. I have never seen a death from Pentothal, although I have read of several, but I have seen severe respiratory embarrassment with deep cyanosis lasting several minutes before the laryngospasm could be controlled.

It is quite true that such a patient may walk out of the office looking just as well as he did when he walked in, but physiologists and pathologists have been warning us for a good many years about damage to brain cells from prolonged oxygen lack. With this to think about, Pentothal becomes less enticing. I should hate to be the one to turn an intelligent man into a jackass.

We find Pentothal particularly useful for the accomplishment of brief (5 to 10 minute) procedures on persons who are extremely nervous. Occasionally we give just enough Pentothal to induce minor drowsiness and accomplish the actual procedure by use of procaine anesthesia. By no means am I implying that the Pentothal is given in sufficient quantity to induce sleep. Approximately half the quantity necessary to produce loss of consciousness is given. The patient is usually fully awake by the time the minor operative procedure is completed. You will find this useful in those patients who have a grave dread of a procedure done under local anesthesia and who desire to "be asleep" while the operation progresses.

This same procedure may be accomplished with any barbiturate which may be given intravenously. I confess I sometimes prefer less dangerous ones than Pentothal even though they may be somewhat longer acting. Small doses of Sodium Amytal will often accomplish the same thing without such marked danger of laryngeal reaction.

Small doses of Pentothal may also be used to potentiate the action of nitrous oxide. When this is done you must remember that the action of Pentothal is cumulative and recovery time is roughly proportional to the amount given, not to the time over which it is administered. For that reason office procedures of long duration should probably not be done with the aid of Pentothal.

REACTIONS TO LOCAL ANESTHETICS

These occur when the local anesthetic drug is picked up by the blood stream and brought in contact with the central nervous system in quantity. People of course differ tremendously in their sensitivity to the drug and may show reactions of all types, ranging from a minor drop in blood pressure, with paleness and sweating, to sudden and complete cardiovascular collapse and almost immediate death.

These sudden massive reactions are usually due to accidental intravenous injections of a quantity of drug and occur so rapidly and with so much finality that treatment is not administered quickly enough for any effect. Death is the almost invariable outcome.

The slower reactions presuppose a building up of the blood level of the drug to a toxic concentration over several minutes. The quicker they occur the more likely they are to be severe. One may say with some degree of assurance that if no reaction has developed within 20 to 25 minutes of the *last* anesthetic injection, reaction is unlikely to occur.

The first thing you will notice is a tendency on the part of the patient to become unresponsive and sleepy. I have found it a good idea to chat with the patient during and immediately following the process of anesthesia and to be extremely suspicious if his attention wanders and his replies become somewhat jumbled. I suppose one must remember that the quality of conversation may have an anesthetic effect, but it is well to check anyway. You may find either an early drug reaction or an implied insult to your conversational ability.

When the patient shows signs of somnolence, check the pulse and blood pressure. A faint pulse of normal rapidity along with a dropping blood pressure are signs of drug reaction and should be treated immediately.

This reaction may gradually level off and the patient come back to normal, or it may descend into the deeper stages with alarming hypotension along with all signs of shock and respiratory difficulty, characterized by periods of apnea, shallow breathing, and an occasional long, sighing respiration. Twitching in the muscles of the extremities and of the face is very frequently seen, but the full-blown convulsion—which may occur—is not common.

When only the mental changes develop, without cardiorespiratory signs, it is usually sufficient to stop administration of the local anesthetic and give 2 or 3 minims or 1:1,000 epinephrine. This should be followed by 0.5 cc. of ⅜ grain per cubic centimeter ephedrine solution. Give this intravenously each 5 to

10 minutes until normal tension is restored. An obvious caution is, of course, not to overdo this particular therapy.

Immediately after the first injections are made, the administration of 100 per cent oxygen should be begun. Insert a pharyngeal airway and use a rebreathing bag if one is available. If not, insert a nasal catheter into the pharyngeal airway, administer oxygen through it and give artificial respiration.

If convulsions are present an intravenous barbiturate may be used to control them, either Pentothal or, preferably, Sodium Amytal given in the smallest dosage necessary to stop convulsive movements.

Another warning: If you use a great deal of local and topical anesthesia, be sure to have the material for combating a reaction on hand. It is quite true that it may be needed only once in several years, but when needed, life and death may hang in the balance. We have made it a practice to keep a small tray with the necessary material in what we call our "emergency cabinet."

The Emergency Cabinet. In the emergency room of our small clinic, which adjoins the treatment rooms, we have a cabinet which is set aside for lifesaving material. Over a period of several years, we have catalogued the things which may be needed quickly. They are put up in packs and kept in the emergency cabinet.

Nothing is allowed in this cabinet, no matter how important, unless time of its acquisition may be a major factor. For example, the drug Cedilanid may be lifesaving but it seldom is so important that one cannot take a minute to go and get it from usual stocks. On the other hand, a tracheotomy set may be needed in seconds. The tracheotomy set is in the cabinet, the Cedilanid is not.

Plasma expanders and undiluted plasma are kept in the cabinet so that one need not run all over the clinic looking for a bottle of plasma here, an intravenous set there and a sterile needle or connecting tube still another place in order to administer these fluids. If you are so located that emergencies frequently come into your clinic, you will find such a cabinet serviceable. If you establish one, be sure that it is cleaned out about every 60 days and extraneous material that always seems to accumulate kept out of it.

Hyaluronidase. This compound has been of inestimable service in two respects: First, in surface anesthesia where rapid diffusion is felt necessary it will greatly increase the speed with which the solution permeates the tissue. Second, in nerve block anesthesia, it serves as a protection for the poor anatomist. My impression is that this latter use is uncalled for and that it makes necessary the injection of greater quantities of anesthetic material than is needed when careful application is done. When one uses hyaluronidase in doing a nerve block, it is in some cases an admission that one does not know the anatomy well enough.

On the other hand, when doing a field block or when anesthetizing a single isolated area, the admixture of one ampule of hyaluronidase to each 100 cc. of local anesthetic solution will result in quicker and more diffuse anesthesia than could otherwise be possible. We use the solution containing hyaluronidase for nearly all such procedures.

TECHNIQUES OF LOCAL ANESTHESIA

Until just recently I have been led to believe that there has been tremendous advancement in the technique of local anesthesia during the past decade. We have all read of the new procedures for parasacral infiltration and for various nerve blocks. These techniques seem in all respects to be excellent ones and well worthy of the attention of the physician.

About a year and a half ago I came across a book written by Carroll W. Allen, M.D., entitled, "Local and Regional Anesthesia, with Chapters on Spinal, Epidural, Paravertebral, and Parasacral Analgesia." The book was published by W. B. Saunders Company *in 1914.* With only a few exceptions, it delineates the procedures as we use them today and it gives a complete description of some local anesthetic techniques which I had been

led to believe were brand new. It is not recommended for use but is an interesting old work that makes us blush a bit in thinking of our "recently discovered" techniques.

The Scalp

The supraorbital and the supratrochlear nerves may be blocked here:

In most people the supraorbital foramen may be palpated. If not, it may be approximately localized by noting that it lies in a vertical plane above the infraorbital foramen like this:

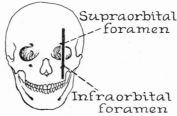

After making a skin wheal, a small needle is placed in the opening of the foramen (but does not penetrate down into it) and approximately 0.5 cc. of anesthetic solution is injected.

The needle is then partially removed and inserted medially for about ½ inch. Three cubic centimeters of the solution are injected immediately above the periosteum. The resulting area of anesthesia is this:

Deep subcutaneous infiltration across the back of the neck at the level of the external auditory meatus, like this:

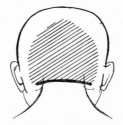

gives the area of anesthesia shown in the illustration, which may be useful in operations upon this area of the scalp.

To produce local anesthesia of the scalp the needle should be inserted into the fibrous tissue between the galeal aponeurosis and the skin, here:

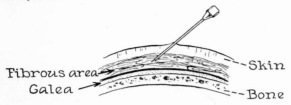

Inject enough solution to cause a bulge in the scalp about half the thickness of your finger, like this:

Scalp field blocks work beautifully but are inadequate unless there is instillation of a sufficient amount of anesthetic. The ordinary block requires 20 to 40 cc. of 0.5 per cent procaine.

The Fifth Nerve

Injection of the maxillary and the mandibular branches of the fifth nerve for anesthetic purposes may be performed using the zygoma and mandibular notch as a landmark. The mandibular branch is easiest to reach. Begin by making a skin wheal below the zygoma as near the center of the mandibular notch as you can place it. Then direct a needle straight inward until you touch the external pterygoid plate. Next withdraw the needle about ½ inch and change your aim about 15 degrees toward the back of the head, like this:

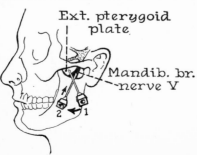

Insert the needle to the same depth as before and ask the patient about stinging and burning sensations or quick shoots of pain in the mandibular area. If these do not occur, insert the needle approximately ¼ inch deeper in the same place. Now inject 5 to 10 cc. of anesthetic solution. Be sure to wait at least 10 minutes before proceeding with any operation in the mandibular area.

The maxillary branch of the trigeminal may be injected through this same skin wheal. Two good procedures for locating this branch are these: Remember that it is just below the apex of the orbit, and that it is directly internal to a point midway along the superior border of the zygoma, here:

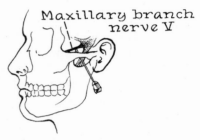

Utilizing the same skin wheal one made for the mandibular injection, point the needle slightly upward and backward so that it is aimed directly for the point just described. *Never use force to advance the needle through this area.* If the progress of the needle is stopped pull it back a few millimeters, slightly change the direction and start again. Paresthesias in the maxillary area will mark entrance of the needle into the nerve. It is worthwhile to take a minute or two to explore gently with the needle point until these paresthesias are produced, for anesthesia will be much superior if this occurs. Should this production of paresthesia seem impossible, inject 5 to 10 cc. of solution in the area nearest the predetermined point. Wait approximately 15 minutes for anesthesia to occur.

The Gasserian Ganglion

Injection of this structure is not particularly difficult. To determine the correct point of entrance of the needle upon the surface of the skin, drop a line vertically from the outer canthus of the eye. Now add a horizontal line from the mid-portion of the upper lip backward, like this:

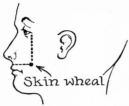

A skin wheal should be made at the juncture of these two lines. A short-bevel spinal needle from which the obturator has been removed (so that entry into a vessel will become immediately apparent) is inserted in the skin wheal. The needle takes a slightly inward direction as though along a line dropped from the forward-looking pupil to the point of insertion, like this:

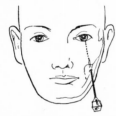

and an upward direction toward the temporomandibular articulation, like this:

When bone is reached, the needle is withdrawn and inserted slightly more posteriorly. This is repeated until the nerve trunks are entered with resulting paresthesias.

When this is accomplished, 0.5 to 1 cc. of procaine solution is injected and one waits 10 minutes for establishment of anesthesia. A brief check will indicate whether the needle is in the ganglion itself or in one of the nerves which exit from the structure. It may be necessary to advance the needle approximately ½ inch from the time the first paresthesias are encountered in order to gain entry into the body of the ganglion.

Since injection of alcohol is painful, one injects a small amount of procaine as a preliminary, then waits until anesthesia is complete or nearly complete. Then 95 per cent alcohol is injected 2 or 3 drops at a time until a total not exceeding 0.5 cc. has been placed.

The infraorbital nerves may be blocked by injecting 0.5 to 1 cc. of procaine solution into the infraorbital foramina. The resulting area of anesthesia will be approximately this:

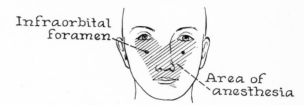

The mental foramina may be injected by penetration of the deep mucous fold between the lip and gums, here:

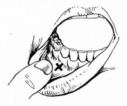

The needle may be inserted down to the foramina, which lie here:

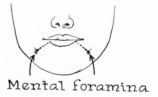

Approximately 1 cc. of procaine is injected at the side of each nerve. Resulting anesthesia covers this area:

These injections of nerves at their foramina of exit are useful when one wishes to operate on the tissues of the face without the distortion which accompanies direct injection of procaine. They are particularly valuable when one proposes a plastic procedure of some difficulty.

The Stellate Ganglion

The stellate ganglion is located here:

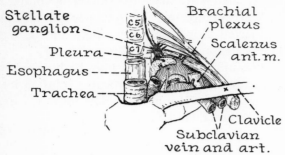

Injection may be made either through the anterior or the posterior approach. My own preference is the anterior. Do it like this: With the patient seated facing the physician, make a skin wheal 1 cm. above the mid-point of the clavicle. Then have the patient turn his head away from the side to be injected, and insert the needle in this direction, "aiming" at the body of the seventh cervical vertebra:

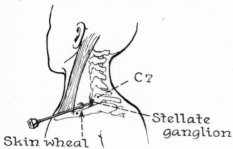

When the vertebral body is encountered, withdraw the needle ⅟₁₆ inch (if such is possible) and aspirate. If no blood is obtained, inject 10 to 20 cc. of 1 per cent procaine.

The Superficial Cervical Nerves

Infiltration of a procaine solution along the posterior border of the sternocleidomastoid muscle will effectively block the superficial cervical nerves, giving an area of anesthesia like this:

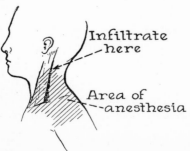

Brachial Plexus Block

Note the position of the brachial plexus and the subclavian artery:

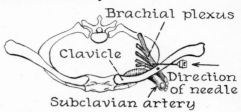

For brachial plexus block one locates the midportion of the clavicle and directs the needle medially downward toward the first rib. Paresthesias in the arm are felt when the plexus is encountered and the area is infiltrated.

Block of the Hand

Complete anesthesia of the hand may be obtained by field block done about an inch and a half above the pisiform bone. The structures that need to be injected and their approximate location are these:

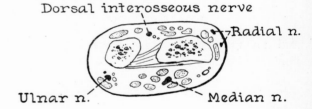

Finger Block

The nerves at the base of the finger are distributed like this in cross section:

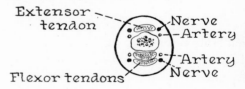

Note their location relative to the bone. Infiltration of the finger base may be done through a common wheal on the dorsum of the finger here:

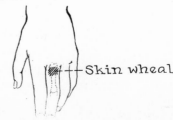

By moving the skin from side to side one may inject both nerves. If complete anesthesia of the finger is desired be sure to inject the volar cutaneous nerves as well.

Intercostal Block

The intercostal nerves run in a groove on the lower surfaces of the rib, like this:

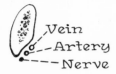

Make skin wheals over the inferior aspect of the ribs in the anterior axillary line. Aim the needle at the lowermost portion of the rib and insert it until bone is touched, like this:

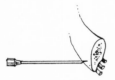

Now withdraw it slightly and re-aim in a posterior and superior direction so that the groove is entered.

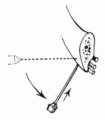

If accurate placement of the needle is accomplished, not over 1 or 2 cc. of solution need be injected through each needle.

Pudendal Block

I would call this one of the easiest and one of the most satisfactory procedures we have in local anesthesia. The area we anesthetize is this:

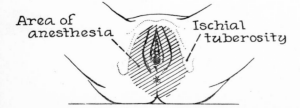

With the patient in the lithotomy position, palpate the ischial tuberosities at location shown above. Aiming at the tuberosity, insert the needle until it touches bone. Now withdraw it slightly and insert it medial to the tuberosity for approximately 2 cm., like this:

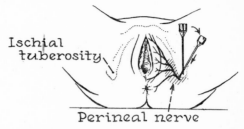

Now inject 15 to 20 cc. of procaine solution, moving the needle slightly with each 5 cc. so that the solution is spread through the shaded area shown above.

Within 15 minutes the perineal area should be completely anesthetized. Occasionally if one wishes to work far anteriorly, it is necessary to infiltrate subcutaneously to block branches of the ilioinguinal nerve, like this:

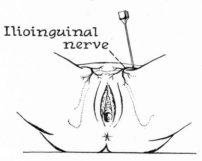

Rectal Anesthesia

Local anesthesia is so satisfactory for rectal conditions that there seldom exists an occasion for other types of pain obtundation. Begin by making a skin wheal about 1 inch lateral to the rectum on either side. Place a gloved finger of the left hand in the rectum to facilitate guidance of the needle, and infiltrate a cylindrical area around the rectum like this:

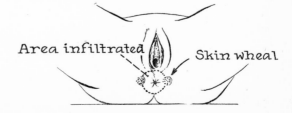

Extend the infiltration 1 to 1½ inches from the skin. Nerves to the sphincter usually enter here:

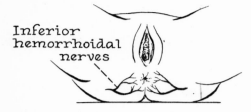

Deposit an extra amount of solution in this particular area.

The Penis

This organ may be field-blocked so that complete insensitivity to pain exists by establishing two skin wheals here:

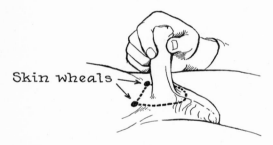

Now hold the organ in the position of erection and infiltrate around the base in a complete circle as shown above. Be sure that the infiltration is carried into the deep subcutaneous tissues. Complete anesthesia will result in approximately 15 minutes.

Perineal Anesthesia

Perineal anesthesia, using the transsacral and caudal approach, is a good procedure for more extensive office operations in the vaginal and rectal areas. Begin by locating the posterior superior spines and marking them like this:

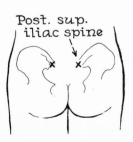

Now outline the sacrum. Next place your finger on the coccyx in the midline and move it upward until the sacral hiatus is felt, here:

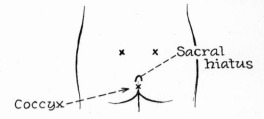

Palpate to either side of this area until the sacral cornua are found. Mark them like this:

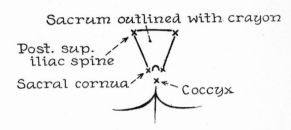

Beginning at the upper angle of the triangle measure about one fingerbreadth downward and one fingerbreadth inward and palpate for the second sacral foramen. If you can feel it, insert a 4 or 5 cm. needle through it. The needle should be pointing slightly downward. If you miss and strike bone, try a little more medially and a little more inferiorly until the foramen is entered.

Leave this needle in place and measure a little more than a fingerbreadth downward and slightly inward from it; palpate the third sacral foramen in this area:

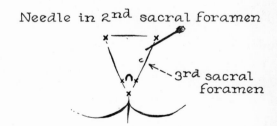

and insert the needle as above. Now palpate the sacral hiatus and insert a spinal needle through it until bone is contacted. Next withdraw the needle about ½ inch, depress the shank and allow it to slip into the sacral canal like this:

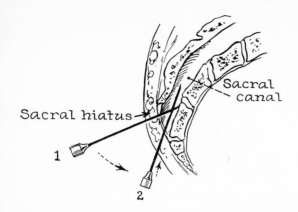

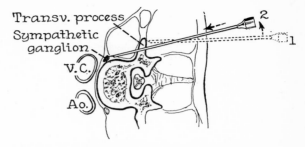

so that the needle impinges along the side of the vertebra like this:

Attach a dry syringe to the needle and aspirate. If no fluid or blood returns, put 20 cc. of 1 per cent procaine into the canal. Next inject 5 cc. of 1 per cent procaine into each of the sacral foramina in which you have inserted needles and withdraw all the needles.

The needle point should be put as close to the sympathetic chain as possible and approximately 5 cc. of 0.5 per cent procaine injected through each needle.

Paravertebral Block

Have the patient lie on his side. Draw a line connecting the spinous processes of the vertebrae and lateral lines 4 to 5 cm. on either side of the center line, like this:

Toe Block

A toe may be blocked through a wheal here:

The nerves which must be anesthetized by the solution are located here:

Now palpate the spinous processes and divide them into thirds. Draw interconnecting lines between the upper third of the spinous processes and the lateral lines, like this:

LOCAL APPLICATIONS

Lacerations

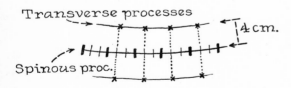

Raise the skin wheals where the lines cross. Insert a long needle perpendicularly through the skin wheals so that the transverse processes are touched. They should be at a depth of approximately 5 cm. in the average man. Withdraw the needle about an inch and go either above or below the transverse process

The clean laceration is best anesthetized through the wound edge. The needle should penetrate immediately beneath the skin edge and deposit anesthetic solution in the fatty tissue here:

For complete obtundation of pain there must be an even spread of anesthetic solution under

the skin for at least 0.75 cm. from the edge of the wound, and the angles of the wound must be blocked as well.

Infiltrated area

Cutaneous nerves do not run straight-line courses but may curve or even turn back upon themselves so that the area to be closed must be blocked completely and on both sides if pain is to be alleviated.

Those lacerations involving the fascia should have anesthetic injected along fascial planes as well as beneath the skin. Muscle tissue is somewhat insensitive and needs only the slightest of infiltration, while fascial tissues and skin need a great deal. Fat seldom needs any anesthetizing unless visible nerve trunks which may be stretched or pulled upon run through it.

Grossly dirty lacerations should not be blocked through wound edges for fear of distributing pathogenic organisms and contaminative material by means of the needle. Skin wheals should be raised and the infiltration accomplished through the skin wheals exactly as described above.

Grossly infected lacerations, i.e., old cuts that have become infected before being brought to the physician, are seldom anesthetized, for surgical procedures are not indicated on these until infection is controlled. For the rare exceptions, field block *completely outside the area of infected tissue* should be performed.

There is scarcely a location in the human body that cannot be anesthetized if one remembers the distribution of sensory nerves. I think it well worth while periodically to review the anatomy of the sensory nerves so that one may improvise to fit a particular situation which may be thrust upon a physician.

Cysts and Tumors

Various cysts and tumors may usually be removed under field block anesthesia. Make two wheals and inject an area around the cyst like this:

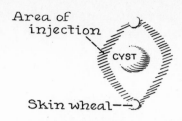

Area of injection

CYST

Skin wheal

There are only a few simple cautions to observe. Here are some "do nots."

1. Do not inject procaine into an infected area. When an abscess is to be incised, do a field block rather than attempting to block the immediate area of the abscess.

2. Do not inject procaine into a cystic tumor. Once again, field block rather than immediate injection into the area to be incised is preferred.

3. Do not inject procaine into vascular spaces. Vascular tumors should be treated with a great deal of caution and, while they may be anesthetized by injecting their immediate area, repeated aspiration is indicated to prevent injection of the anesthetic solution into the blood stream.

Bones

There are very few fractures amenable to office treatment that cannot be reduced under local anesthesia. Using the best sterile technique, insert a needle into the hematoma like this:

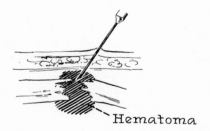

Hematoma

Aspiration of dark, bluish blood from between the bone edges or near the fracture site is evidence that entry has been made. Inject from 1 to 20 cc. of procaine, depending on the site of the fracture and the size of the hematoma. Then wait 15 minutes before proceeding.

Remember that some fractures may be intra- and extra-articular and that the hematoma between the intra- and extra-articular portions is not always so well connected that perfect diffusion will take place. In the presence of such a case, inject both intra- and extra-articular structures and the hematoma itself.

The use of purely local techniques for operations upon bones is almost doomed to failure before it starts. Field block may occasionally be mildly successful, but various regional procedures, such as brachial block, are the only truly satisfactory means of exhibiting the injection anesthetics for procedures on osseous structures.

Aspirations

To perform these procedures it is only necessary to remember which areas between the surface and the lesion to be aspirated are pain sensitive. As an example, take the knee joint. One should infiltrate the skin and the joint capsule with particular care because both of these structures are replete with sensory endings. Intervening tissues are not so important because they have few such nerve endings.

Another example would be the pleural area. One must anesthetize the skin and the pleura with particular care. The fascial layers of the intercostal muscles are more sensitive than the muscular tissue itself, and the fat, of course, is relatively important. One should deposit anesthetic as shown here in cross section:

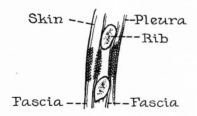

Diagnosis

Diagnostic use of a local anesthetic agent is coming increasingly to the forefront. The principle upon which this is based is quite simple. If one wishes to know which of two causes for pain is operating, it may be possible to block out the nerves or nerve endings that pick up or transmit pain of a particular type.

If pain ceases upon blockage of these nerve endings the cause is established. If not, one may be sure that the alternate cause or causes is operating. Let's illustrate that with several examples.

Suppose one wishes to know whether pain in the precordium is due to intracostal neuralgia or to coronary artery disease. Block the intercostal nerves that supply the area of pain. Be sure to block them far enough back that you have a pain-free area to test for anesthesia; the following drawing shows the areas for blocking and for testing, in relation to the area of pain. Note that the area for testing is between the block and the original area of pain.

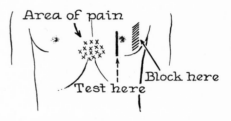

Should all pain cease upon performance of the block, it is safe to assume that intercostal neuralgia is the cause of the original discomfort. Should the pain continue unabated, one must then search for other possible causes.

Another example is the fact that pain engendered by a psychoneurosis may continue in spite of proper anesthetization of tissues. If you achieve proven anesthesia and the pain still continues you must be dealing with either (a) referred pain or (b) pain of psychic origin. One caution about this example: Pain of psychic origin may result in misinterpretation of relatively innocuous stimuli from the area in question. If you stop these stimuli, the pain will stop; therefore, if the pain stops you have proven nothing for certain. If it does not stop in spite of adequate anesthetization, you have proven that it is either referred or psychogenic.

As a third example, suppose you wished to know whether pain on the medial aspect of the knee is due to a strain of the medial ligament or to the freeing of a semilunar cartilage from its attachment. Inject the ligament, being very careful not to infiltrate in the immediate area of the cartilage. Should pain cease, the probabilities are vastly against a cartilaginous injury.

There are literally thousands of examples one could give specifying the use of local anesthetic agents for differentiation of types of pain. Space limitations won't permit even attempting to list them here, but the practitioner will be able to devise such tests as need appears for them.

Pain Relief

There are many innocuous and a few serious lesions about the body that have no immediately successful therapeutic routines that may be applied. People with these lesions cannot be quickly cured. They are, however, deserving of pain relief, which may be offered by judicious use of local anesthetic solutions, particularly those in oil.

An example is myofascial injuries, which just plain hurt until recovery begins. This pain may be well controlled by the injection of an oil-soluble anesthetic such as Intracaine into the area immediately surrounding the lesion. There are no contraindications for this procedure that I know of. The average patient will be deeply gratified to have his pain relieved.

There are some kinds of headache that turn out to be an unexplained soreness in the deep tissues of the scalp rather than true headache. These people gain exceptional relief when the sore area is injected.

Various neuritic affections may be given complete and gratifying relief by injection of procaine.

The number of lesions in which pain relief is a dominant factor are legion. Once again space makes impossible listing or even classifying this usage of anesthetic agents. One may, however, greatly improve results in his practice by keeping in mind this possibility of empiric pain relief by judicious use of local anesthetics, both the water-soluble ones and those soluble in oil.

TOPICAL ANESTHESIA

The Eye

One drop of 0.5 per cent Pontocaine may be instilled in the eye every 3 or 4 minutes for a total of three instillations. This will anesthetize the surface membranes for such procedures as minor operations upon the conjunctiva, removal of foreign bodies from the cornea and similar procedures.

Deep anesthesia of eye structures is quite easy with procaine but there is seldom or never any indication for this in office surgery.

Nose and Throat

Intranasal anesthesia may be obtained by soaking cotton pledgets in 2 per cent Pontocaine, squeezing out the excess anesthetic solution, and using a pair of bayonet forceps to place the pledgets firmly against the area to be anesthetized. When this is impossible a cotton-tipped applicator may be dipped in the 2 per cent Pontocaine solution and put in place.

Frequently it will be a help to the physician if 2 per cent ephedrine is incorporated with the Pontocaine solution for intranasal use. This will shrink mucous membranes as well as anesthetize them and give a more adequate view of the nose.

Since the nasal membranes absorb Pontocaine rather quickly and since it is rather a highly toxic agent, one should be just a little cautious about how much is applied. There is no danger at all in the ordinary conservative procedures, but repeated reanesthetizing during an hour or less may allow enough absorption for toxic reactions to occur.

The pharynx may be sprayed with 2 per cent Pontocaine at intervals of 3 or 4 minutes until anesthesia is complete. Not more than two or three applications are usually necessary.

For instillition of iodized oil to the lungs, sufficient anesthesia may usually be obtained by having the patient inhale as the Pontocaine is sprayed into the mouth.

The Urethra

We have found that there is little need for

anesthetics in urethral manipulation. If one be completely gentle, pain is trivial. There is no good intraurethral anesthetic for those cases in which pain may be moderately severe. The application of caudal anesthesia is frequently the best and most effective procedure at our command for such cases.

Abrasions

Topical anesthesia for abraded surfaces may be done with 2 per cent Pontocaine *if one is exceedingly careful*. A surgical sponge may be wet with the solution, thoroughly wrung out and placed against the lesion. If you simply slop on the anesthetic solution, the dangers of reaction are very great, whereas application as mentioned above will only rarely cause any trouble.

EMERGENCY ANESTHESIA

Occasionally we practitioners get caught in such a situation that a procedure must be done and no anesthetic is obtainable. This is particularly true of those of us who practice in rural areas. There are three procedures well worth remembering.

Pressure

Extreme pressure over nerve trunks briefly exerted will cause a partial anesthesia of distal parts. All of us may apply this simple procedure to ourselves. Say, for instance, you hit a finger with a hammer. The first and most natural thing to do is grasp the finger on either side near its base and press firmly. This force applied to the nerve trunks actually

does offer some obtundation of pain. It is not good, but it is better than nothing.

Cold

Cold will provide anesthesia of sorts. If, for example, an abscess must be drained under such circumstances that no anesthesia is available, pack it in ice for a few minutes and there will be a great lessening of pain. We have gone so far as to do an emergency amputation of a digit after ice packs for approximately one hour's duration and were able to do a reasonably workmanlike job without severe pain.

Water

Plain sterile water injected into the tissue under some pressure will in many cases get just as good anesthetic results as procaine. This is possibly due to the lytic effect on tissue cells but may be due to pressure or unknown circumstances. The fact remains, it works. Plain sterile water burns when first injected and if injected quickly under pressure, the burning is extreme. If injected very slowly to begin with and then more rapidly as pain fades, the tissues may be adequately distended with only a moderate burning sensation. This disappears within 2 or 3 minutes and the part usually becomes totally insensitive.

The anesthesia usually lasts in its complete stage for 30 minutes to an hour and the part may remain partially anesthetized for some time. This is certainly not a recommended method but it can be used to achieve complete anesthesia in an emergency. It should be limited, of course, to blocking the immediate site of entry and should never be used for regional block.

Section XIII

PHYSIOTHERAPY

PHYSIOTHERAPY

Some of the really fine advances made in medicine during the past few decades have been those in the field of physical therapy. A bit of conjecture would lead us to believe that physiotherapy is the oldest of all forms of treatment, for even subhuman species sometimes rub a contusion or seek heat or cold for injuries. Even though this may be the oldest of all forms of therapy it is proving more and more worthy of our attention as expert investigators offer better methods of application. It is my impression that the small office that intends to do the best possible work must have a physiotherapy section.

The first problem to be answered is just what apparatus and space are needed for such an installation in the office of the average practitioner. When one sees from 30 to 50 patients a day, he usually sees at least five of these who could benefit greatly from various physiotherapeutic techniques and who would be only too willing to have these techniques used were they available. For such a practice, the physiotherapy room with 3 cubicles is entirely adequate. Here is a typical floor plan:

Wall mounts for
infrared and ultraviolet

Diathermy

Waiting
room

TABLE

TABLE

The men I know who have installed such a department and used it carefully find that they soon need an extra person to devote full time to physical therapy. Unfortunately, trained technicians are rare if not unobtainable and it usually devolves upon the physician to secure the services of some interested local person and aid him to get training.

The equipment needed may be divided into two classes: One, basic equipment to allow minimal effective physiotherapy. In addition to the physiotherapy tables shown in the planning diagram, this consists of:

1. A short wave diathermy machine.

2. A small cautery unit such as the Hyfrecater, which, of course, should be in the minor surgery rather than in the physiotherapy department.

3. A reliable ultraviolet generator.

4. A small infra-red generator.

The total initial investment ranges around $1000.

Secondary equipment which should be added as soon as the physiotherapy practice allows is:

1. A microwave generator.

2. A surgical diathermy producing both cutting and coagulating current or blending the two.

From here on, one may go just as far as one would wish in securing physiotherapeutic equipment. Various special current generators are available for the hundred and one other tasks that may be done satisfactorily in the physiotherapy department. There are rhythmic constrictors for applying vascular exercises, and hydrotherapeutic units of all types. (These are not usually an asset to the small office, for hydrotherapy in the range of us practitioners can usually be done with material available in any home.) Many kinds of devices are available for the application of therapeutic exercise but this can usually be applied with material available anywhere.

To begin with, suppose we discuss just what the various apparatuses mentioned do and purport to do. Then we can give some examples about the use of physiotherapy in actual practice.

DIATHERMY

In spite of a great many claims for almost miraculous therapeutic range, the diathermy seems to have one real effect and one alone. It is to apply heat to the tissues between the electrodes. This is by no means a criticism, for proper application of heat is one of the best therapeutic methods at our command and diathermy has the extreme advantage that internal tissues may be heated just as effectively as those near the skin surface. There is no other ready means of accomplishing this.

Properly applied, the diathermy increases the use of oxygen by the tissues and increases the circulatory flow. It has a spasmolytic effect and, in accomplishing this, serves as an excellent means of pain relief. The increased metabolism engendered promotes increased speed of healing in many lesions and the increase in venous and lymphatic outflow may serve as a means to hasten elimination of toxic products.

There is little danger from the application of this through and through heating. Certain contraindications, of course, exist. They are:

1. The presence of metal in the tissues.
2. Presence of arteries incapable of dilating.
3. Inflammatory diseases of the skin.
4. Presence of possible hemorrhagic conditions.

There are other relative contraindications which will be discussed in more detail later in this section.

A common error is to expect more of the diathermy than it is designed to provide. A single application consisting of 20 or 30 minutes of deep heating is not enough to cure any lesion. It is true that the pain relief may be marked but pain will generally return. A minimum of four to six treatments at daily intervals (or more often) is needed to accomplish a complete cure and many pathologic processes require as many as 20 to 30 treatments to gain maximum benefit.

ELECTROSURGERY

There are three types of current usually used in electrosurgery. It is imperative that the practitioner know about these three current types and their effect and method of use. Such knowledge will result in far more effective utilization.

Electrodesiccation. This is a procedure involving a single electrode. The best illustration is to be found by describing the effects obtained with an apparatus common to many physician's offices, the Birtcher Hyfrecator. It is the electrodesiccator most commonly seen.

The result from electrodesiccation is dehydration and shrinkage of cells with condensation and elongation of nuclei. The desiccating current is particularly useful, for, if properly applied, there is very little degenerative change in the surrounding tissues and consequently there is minimal scar formation—much less than is seen with sharp surgical procedures. Sealing of blood vessels is adequate and hemorrhage an infrequent complication.

Electrocoagulation. Desiccation and coagulation appear to be different degrees of the same thing. The coagulating current simply has the ability to destroy larger areas more completely with a single application than does the desiccating current. For example, histologically after coagulation, the cell outline is entirely lost and the resulting tissue becomes a homogeneous structureless mass.

The cutting current is a modification using undamped oscillations. When properly applied the cutting electrode will slice through tissue with no appreciable resistance. Use of the current gives me the sensation of drawing a knife through a piece of pumpkin pie.

The effect of the current in tissues is literally to explode the cells along the actual cut, while coagulating cells a microscopic distance to either side of the cut.

Techniques

Electrodesiccation. Using the electrodesiccating current the common error is to produce too heavy and "hot" a spark with charring of tissues and poor control of the extent to which desiccation takes place. Practice on various metallic objects until you can produce a spark approximately $\frac{1}{16}$ inch in length and one which is barely visible.

An experiment devised by Clark is an excellent one to be performed by all those who would use electrodesiccation. Cover a cake of ordinary white laundry soap with a sheet of stationery. Experiment with various strengths of current until, by bringing the needle directly against the paper, you can use just enough current to dry out the soap without charring the paper. This is the proper current strength for average desiccation. Fifteen minutes spent at this process will vastly improve the average physician's use of the desiccating apparatus.

The actual operation should be done as follows: Place the part to be treated upon an insulated surface, and wash and dry it thoroughly. In many small lesions no anesthesia is needed for if the spark is kept "cool," the current itself will serve to deaden the nerve endings and reduce pain to a very minimum.

Now place the electrode a proper distance from the lesion like this:

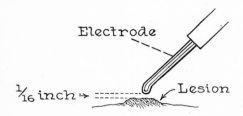

Turn on the current and move the electrode rapidly about over the lesion. After each 1 or 2 second application, break the current to al-

low dissipation of excess heat and also to avoid operator fatigue. That sounds rather silly but it requires coordinative effort on the part of the operator to cover completely a small lesion without coagulating areas of adjacent skin, and one must make allowance for the rapid fading in such coordinative ability which occurs.

For pedunculated growths, grasp the pedicle of the growth in a mosquito forceps and hold the forceps in your hand like this:

Notice that the forceps does not touch the actual skin surface on any spot. Now desiccate the growth. The current will be dispersed into your hand (painlessly) through the clamp and no tissues of the patient will be affected other than those of the tumor. Pain is reduced to an almost imperceptible degree. When a particular lesion has been completely desiccated, sparking will occur toward the edge of the tissue in this area:

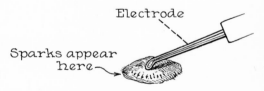

This is ample indication that complete desiccation of the lesion has occurred and that no further current need be applied. The important thing in electrodesiccation is to use the smallest possible amount of current and to avoid hot, heavy sparks. If this be done, cosmetic results are vastly improved.

Electrocoagulation. This is a two-contact technique requiring a dispersive plate and an active electrode. Practice for the technique may be secured using a piece of horse meat which may be obtained at a local packing plant. Lay the meat on the dispersive electrode and insert the coagulating electrode into it to a depth of $\frac{1}{2}$ inch or more. Turn on the current and notice that around the electrode there is blanching and ultimate escape of steam with hissing.

The tissue being coagulated becomes progressively drier and ultimately there occurs sparking around the edges, which is indication of complete coagulation. Now cut through the coagulative tract and note the sharp line of demarcation between the coagulated and uncoagulated tissue.

Repeat the experiment using approximately half the current strength and keeping it turned on twice as long. While cutting through this second tract you will notice that there is an ill defined line between normal and coagulated tissue. This is important in clinical medicine. One can do coagulation of more controlled type using a heavier current for a briefer period of time.

At actual operation, one should first be sure that the dispersive electrode is molded to the skin surface and firmly attached without pressure upon it. Severe burns may occur if this electrode is improperly attached or if it shifts during the progress of the operation. One cannot be too careful in making certain that it is properly placed and that it *stays* properly placed.

Hemostasis by electrical means is an excellent procedure in almost any minor surgery. Carefully isolate the vessel and seize it in the jaws of a clamp. Be sure to catch only the vessel and not a large amount of surrounding tissue. At the first lull in the operation, pick up the hemostat and hold it away from the other tissue and touch it firmly with the desiccating current, like this:

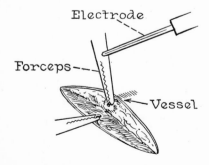

Keep the current flowing until there is some whitening of the vessel end. Then discon-

tinue application of the current and remove the hemostat. This provides good sealing of vessels and avoids burying foreign bodies such as is done with suture application.

The coagulating current is dangerous. It, of course, coagulates without choice and will damage or destroy nearby nerves and blood vessels if improperly handled. The destruction of lesions may be complete but secondary sloughs may be annoying and difficult to care for. In my own practice, I have found it best to limit the coagulating current to the sealing of blood vessels or to relatively small lesions which are not near essential structures.

The cutting current is a two-electrode technique, the dispersive electrode being applied exactly as in coagulation. Once again, a piece of horse meat laid on the dispersive electrode may be used for practice. There are three things that must be avoided:

1. The current must not be turned on until the cutting electrode is in contact with the tissue. If this is done there will be a hot, heavy spark and extensive coagulation, which is undesirable.

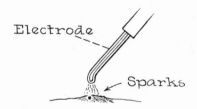

2. The electrode must not be removed before the current is turned off, for the same sparking and ultimate coagulation will occur.

3. The tip of the electrode *only* must be used. If a large area of the electrode is applied to tissue, extensive coagulation will occur. Likewise, the electrode must be kept moving while the current is on.

To summarize these in another fashion, here is a good technique for electrosurgical cutting: Place the very tip of the cutting electrode in contact with the tissues which you are to incise. Now turn on the current as you begin to move the electrode and move the electrode steadily forward until you have reached the end of the incision. As you approach the end of the incision, turn off the current and then remove the electrode from the tissues.

It takes only a few minutes' practice to become proficient at this procedure. A bit of time spent in practice will save you unnecessary complications and annoyance at actual surgery.

INFRA-RED IRRADIATION

The infra-red generator produces energy emission in the 4,000 to 40,000 Ångstrom range. This, when properly applied, will penetrate a maximum distance of 1 cm. into the tissue. Within a few minutes after exposure there is formed an erythematous area which feels hot to the patient. The erythema is due to an active vasodilation. Repeated exposure to the rays may produce a permanent pigmentation in the deeper layers of the skin.

When moderately large areas are exposed to infra-red, there is a slight lowering of blood pressure with increased respiration and increased urinary output. The circulation, and along with it the work of the heart, is somewhat increased. The ill defined entity which one might call nervous tension seems markedly lessened.

In the skin and subjacent tissues, two possible effects may be obtained. The application of intense heat is a method of counter-irritation which may offer pain relief even in deep tissues when applied to areas with the same nerve supply. It has been suggested that this pain relief is due to desensitization of sensory nerve tracts because of the increase in the number of stimuli which pass through them. Be that as it may, it does work. Mild heating, on the other hand, seems to apply a sedative effect with direct relief of pain and spasm in those areas heated.

The infra-red lamp is a worthy adjunct to any office, since the rays are adequately produced by a special bulb which may be screwed into any light socket. The expense of installing infra-red equipment is trivial. If you are interested, we have included our plan for a new installation involving both infra-red and ultraviolet at the end of the section on ultraviolet irradiation.

ULTRAVIOLET IRRADIATION

Ultraviolet has certain well established clinical uses such as its effectiveness in some cases of psoriasis, but an exact delineation of its effect is most difficult if not impossible. We know that ultraviolet irradiation will activate certain vitamin D compounds in the skin and that it will produce an erythema with blistering and severe burning in cases of overexposure. The rays are not penetrating and usually may be stopped by the thinnest of clothing or a simple sheet of paper. They do not penetrate deeply into the tissues.

Bactericidal effects have been ascribed to ultraviolet but this is true in only specified wave lengths. The generators available for the average office produce very little of the bactericidal wave lengths and may be listed as essentially useless in the direct treatment of bacterial infection. This does not mean that the rays will not kill bacteria if long enough exposure is given. It does mean that the human skin will not tolerate a bactericidal dose from the usual generator.

Without going into detail, one may say that the average physician has occasional use for ultraviolet irradiation and may find its application of occasional value. Specific uses are to be discussed later in this chapter.

I have found quite satisfactory the socket bulb for production of ultraviolet rays which may be obtained at low cost from any supply house. The bulb produces ultraviolet in the effective spectral range and the better ones are faced with a filter glass which is opaque to the very short wave lengths.

Without regard to how much information is furnished in the booklet with such apparatus, we should always calibrate each bulb individually. Do it this way: Use a piece of brown wrapping paper approximately 30 inches square. Cut five square holes ½ inch apart along the side in the wrapping paper and place it over your arm like this:

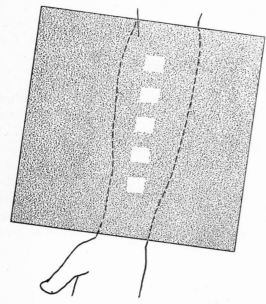

Now take a second sheet of wrapping paper and cover all five holes. Set the ultraviolet bulb 24 inches from your arm and turn it on. Take the cover sheet off all five holes and expose the arm to 2 minutes irradiation. Then cover one hole, expose another 15 seconds, cover another hole, etc., so that the final exposure pattern is this: the first opening, 2 minutes; the second opening, 2 minutes, 15 seconds; the third opening, 2 minutes, 30 seconds; the fourth opening, 2 minutes, 45 seconds; and the fifth opening, 3 minutes. The amount required to produce an erythema which has faded in 24 hours is the minimal erythema dose for the bulb.

In treating patients, one must remember several things. Blondes are nearly twice as sensitive to the rays as brunettes and men are more sensitive than women. The patient also rapidly builds tolerance and may, after a few treatments, require two to three times the original dosage to produce a transitory erythema.

Certain precautions are necessary in the use of the ultraviolet. No irradiation should be given until reaction from the preceding dose has subsided completely. The patient should never be exposed to the rays without wearing goggles to protect the eyes. Timing of treatment *must* be very exact. It is possible to produce a severe and incapacitating burn with the ultraviolet.

The treatments are absolutely contraindicated in the cachectic individual, no matter what the reason for his cachexia, and should not be used in any case of undiagnosed skin disease.

The ultraviolet light has some interesting diagnostic uses which should not be overlooked. The Wood light, which emits only ultraviolet light in the 3900 Ångstrom range, is useful in fluorescent diagnosis.

Certain dermatologic lesions fluoresce brilliantly in the Wood light and may be diagnosed by application of this method: The patient is taken into a dark room and subjected to an examination in the rays. It is particularly valuable in various fungus lesions of the scalp. Infected hairs fluoresce brilliantly, as do fungus lesions of the skin.

The ordinary crab louse also is fluorescent, as are some lesions of syphilis. I read someplace that cancers fluoresce in a Wood light. We tried it once or twice, noting that they do. This, of course, is by no means a diagnostic test for cancer, but it is an interesting sidelight.

Practical Application

In the small physiotherapy department where infra-red and ultraviolet bulbs are the particular source of these irradiations, there is one cheap and easy means for application which is worth exploring. As stated in the foregoing paragraphs, these bulbs screw into a standard light socket. An excellent means of providing the light socket is this:

Use the old-type gooseneck desk lamp. When the shade is removed this consists of a standard socket at the end of a flexible gooseneck. Remember the old fashioned telephone trellis that folded up and could be extended to bring the phone within reach? Mount the base of the gooseneck lamp on such a trellis and fasten the trellis to the wall above the treatment table, like this:

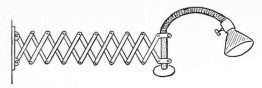

One may have any number from one to four such trellises attached to the wall. Utilizing both the extensibility of the trellis and the flexibility of the gooseneck, the lamp may be placed in almost any relationship to the patient. One may, of course, change from infrared to ultraviolet at will by simply removing one type of bulb and inserting another, although it would seem that having two of each would provide ample body coverage for any situation that might arise.

Such an installation, including the bulbs, costs less than fifty dollars.

MASSAGE

Massage is one of the most useful techniques of physiotherapy. In this country, it has been in the hands of nonmedical practitioners. European writings would indicate that continental physicians are much more interested in massage than physicians in the Americas and this is probably much to their credit. The very existence of great numbers of healers who deal principally in massage and psychotherapy should be proof that we of the profession have neglected these fields in spite of their being worth while and an advantage to the patient.

If nothing else, a well performed massage has a sedative effect and makes the patient feel better. Circulation may be stimulated and occasional muscle spasms relieved. Some types of tissue engorgement may be benefited and restricted movement made much more free.

There are a number of classifications pertaining to the proper methods of massage. Actually, one may separate the technique into three basic motions.

Stroking

To be effective this must consist of gentle stroking of the skin surfaces done slowly and rhythmically with even pressure and even time intervals between application of pressure. The stroking movement should always be from the periphery toward the central areas.

The operator should be sure that his hands exert even pressure and that they do not lose contact with the patient's skin even on the return movement.

In addition to the gentle surface stroking just described, one occasionally uses deeper stroking movements for a beneficial effect on engorged lymph channels and veins. The same technique as that described for light stroking is used, with the single exception that more pressure is applied. One absolute rule of massage is that it should never be sufficiently vigorous to cause an active pain sensation.

Kneading

This consists of grasping tissue between the forefingers and thumb or between the fingers and the heel of the hand and kneading it firmly, much as bread dough is treated. Again, one must begin at the periphery and work centrally as the kneading continues. This is a proper kneading motion:

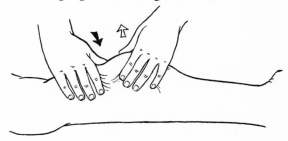

Beating

The physician should, of course, not take the name of this technique literally even though tempted to do so. The process usually consists of quick, chopping strokes rendered with the ulnar side of the hand like this:

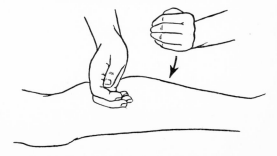

The various movements of massage first stimulate the egress of the pooled blood or lymphatic fluids with the result that arterioles dilate and fresh blood is brought into the tissue.   It is a known fact that muscle circulation is rather slow and blood may be pooled in muscle tissue for some time before fresh blood is offered and old venous blood returned to the general circulation.   Massage definitely speeds up this process.   There are reports that properly given massage will increase a muscle's capacity to work more than adequate rest, though this seems rather unusual.

Myofascial injuries of minor nature are the most frequent insult to which humanity is heir.   Fibers are constantly being torn and fibrotic attachments formed between areas in the muscle and the overlying fascia.   Trivial insults occur by the dozens.   Massage seems to aid in loosening any unusual attachment to muscular tissue and to improve circulation.

Relief of psychic tension by massage is completely unexplained but it happens.   We have all seen this in our personal experience.   The tense and irate man who goes home, has his wife massage his neck muscles and promptly goes to sleep is a perfect example.   Without making any effort to explain why, one must admit that massage is excellent treatment for tension.

Chronic inflammatory changes or engorgement following injury are often promptly and efficiently relieved by properly administered massage.

In these traumatic cases it is frequently advantageous to follow a period of heating with approximately 10 minutes of properly applied massage.   The combination seems to accomplish a great deal more than either the heat or the massage by itself.

This physiotherapeutic technique has been written up and proven since the dawn of recorded medical history.   It would seem to me that we in medicine are a bit mistaken if we do not take full advantage of it.   Most practices—even the more limited ones—are such that physiotherapy in the form of massage and adjunctive treatments could be applied with benefit both to the patient and the doctor.   I would strongly recommend these techniques to your attention.   Specific uses will be mentioned later in this chapter.

HYDROTHERAPY

The hydrotherapeutic installation of a major physiotherapy department is often the most expensive part of the entire department.   Hydrotherapy has been proven and a tremendous amount of effort has been devoted to design equipment for its proper administration.   In spite of all this, satisfactory hydrotherapeutic procedures can be done in the office or in any home that has a bathtub and sources of hot and cold water.

No effort will be made in this section to discuss the more complicated procedures.   There are, however, ways of doing the simplest techniques in such fashion that a consistent and usually better result is obtained.

Hot Packs

These must be just as hot as the patient can stand them and not too wet.   Begin by coating the skin to be packed very lightly with petrolatum.   This should be applied and "rubbed in" until only a thin coating of oil remains on the surface.

Cotton flannel material similar to that used for "summer blankets" is ideal for the actual pack.   In its absence an ordinary bath towel will do.   Dip the fabric in boiling water and wring it out with all the strength you have so that it is moist, not dripping wet.   A good means for wringing out such a pack is to place the freshly dipped pack in the center of a second bath towel.   Grasp the ends of the second towel and twist them.   Often two people, one on each end, will do a better job of drying the pack.

Wet towel

Now unfold the pack and apply it quickly to the skin. If it is hot enough the patient will object vociferously and you must lift the pack an inch or two from the skin surface and hold it for ten or twenty seconds before reapplying. Such packs should be changed every 2 or 3 minutes at first.

I know of no way to keep a pack really hot while it remains in place. To swathe the pack in plastic and apply an electric heating pad on top of it will give a sufficient caloric stimulation for many cases but does not achieve the heat one can accomplish with frequently changed packs.

Cold Packs

The local cold pack, once again, should be cold, not cool. A bath or hand towel may be wrung out after immersion in ice water and applied to the part.

If it is cold enough it should bring forth an involuntary gasp from the patient at the second of its application. This sudden deep gasping inspiration is the reason for the age-old therapeutic method of giving a sudden cold shower to the asthmatic—which, incidentally, is a trick that works well at times.

Cold packs, to be most effective in regional therapeutics, should be applied somewhat intermittently. Keep the pack on for half an hour and then remove it for ten minutes before reapplying. In the interim, one should not disturb the part being packed. Massage or the application of heat applied intermittently with cold seems to defeat the original purpose of the cold pack in some instances.

A hot water bottle filled with crushed ice is an adequate means of applying cold. However, one faces the complication that it is practically impossible to put any but the smallest chips of ice into the usual hot water bottle. A plastic bag, such as those in which some foods are dispensed, can be filled with ice cubes and tied tightly at the neck with a bit of string to form a satisfactory device for application of cold.

The Priessnitz Bandage. I have heard it said that a Priessnitz bandage will offer as much relief as a dose of morphine in certain conditions. In my own practice, this has by no means been true, but the technique has occasionally been extremely useful in relieving the pain of acute gallbladder disease. All one needs is a hand towel and a bath towel.

The hand towel is immersed in ice water and wrung out until nearly dry, after which it is literally wadded up into a ball. This ball is placed over the offending gallbladder and the bath towel wrapped around the patient like this:

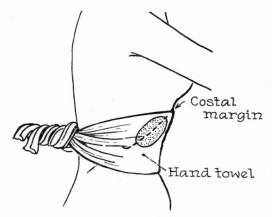

The ends of the bath towel are grasped and twisted so that pressure is applied to the ice pack and it is forced inward under the costal margin as shown. I have seldom seen a case in which some pain relief was not obtained. Many other uses for the Priessnitz bandage have been advocated but since I have not tried them I can speak with no authority at all as to their utility.

The Full Cold Pack. This is one of the best sedative measures we have for the nervous, irritable patient. It is contraindicated only in cases of debility. It may be used with equal facility in the office, home or hospital. Since it is better to observe the patient carefully during the first few minutes of the pack, I have found it advisable to have our office physiotherapy technician do the technique in the home and remain until certain the patient is responding normally. Do it like this:

Begin by covering the bed with a rubber or plastic sheet. Next place two blankets on this sheeting so that they are spread out flat, as one does in making an ordinary bed. They should not, of course, be tucked in.

Now immerse a single sheet in ice water and wring it out until it no longer drips. The sheet should be quite moist but not dripping wet. Place this sheet flat on the bed and fold the lower portion so that the border of the sheet which is toward the bottom of the bed actually lacks a foot or more of descending as far as the blankets. The bed should now look like this:

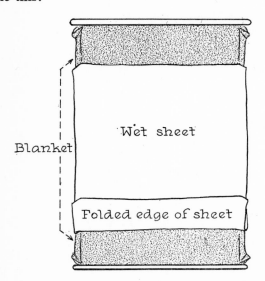

Have the patient lie on the bed on his back and instruct him to raise his arms above his head.

Now take one border of the wet sheet and place it across the patient's torso like this:

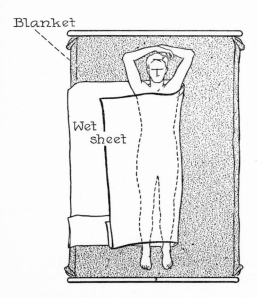

Have him place one arm by his side and double the sheet back over it like this:

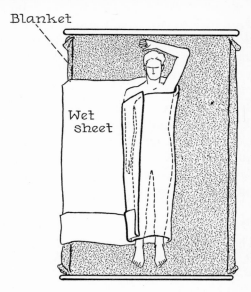

Now cross the other sheet and tuck it around the arm as shown in the preceding illustration. When you have finished the pack should look like this:

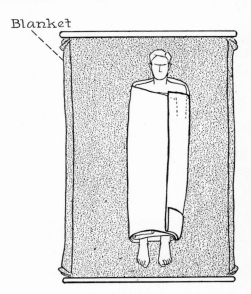

Next double the blankets over the patient so that he is well wrapped in at least two layers of blanketing.

Finally, tuck a dry bath towel around the patient's neck and cover his feet with the lower portion of the blanket so that the pack now appears like this:

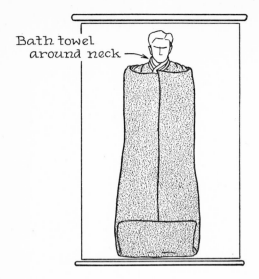

Bath towel around neck →

Should the patient complain bitterly of the cold, one may place an electric heating pad turned low or a hot water bottle filled with warm water to the feet. The pack should continue not less than half an hour and seldom more than a full hour. The average patient will be relaxed and either sleepy or asleep within a very few minutes.

Hot Soaks

These are a means of applying heat and little else. The hot soak is doubly effective because it prevents normal heat loss from the area immersed as well as actively applying heat.

There are two common errors which one must avoid in such an application. The first is too brief and too infrequent usage. To be effective the hot soak should be used at least three times daily for a minimum of twenty minutes at each session. The water should be kept at a temperature of at least 105° and in some areas 110° may be preferable. The part to be immersed may be lightly rubbed with mineral oil or petrolatum if this is desired. Ordinarily this does not seem necessary.

The second error, which is not as frequent as the first, is to overdo the process of soaking until the skin literally becomes "waterlogged." The shrunken, wrinkled, white appearance of the skin following a hot soak is normal if it disappears within a very few minutes. Should it remain, however, for a half hour or more one may generally assume that soaks are being used too long and too vehemently applied.

The great American question regarding hot soaks seems to be what to put in the water to enhance the healing value. My patients have come up with some rather unusual recommendations but the standard seems to be Epsom salts. It is entirely correct that such chemical compounds might conceivably increase the heat-holding ability of the water but it would also seem that if they are increased beyond a certain concentration they would become hydrophilic, with consequent dehydration of the superficial skin layers. I confess all of this is in the realm of theory.

I must tell you somewhat shamefacedly of a minor experiment we ran some years ago. We made a saturated solution of Epsom salt and colored it a brilliant yellowish green with ordinary food coloring. The patients were given a 4 ounce bottle of this and instructed to put all 4 ounces in the water used for hot soaks. *Every* patient on whom it was tried reported to us the almost miraculous healing effect of the soak so contaminated. Such things give a man pause. One might almost think that many of our methods are more impressive than worthy, and that possibly they cure by reason of their impressiveness.

Sitz Baths

This subject can be disposed of rapidly. It consists of sitting in a tub of hot water. One can prescribe a dozen different routines but they all seem to end this same simple way.

THERAPEUTIC EXERCISE

Within range of the practitioner there are three functions for which therapeutic exercises are prescribed. They are to increase limited motion, to add to muscle power and to increase coordination.

Increasing Limited Motion

Passive exercise, which is done by the physician or the technician without the muscular aid of the patient, and active exercise, which is performed as a result of the patient's own volition, may be used to accomplish increase of limited motion. There is no hope of listing an individual exercise for every possible limitation of motion. The exercises should be designed individually following certain basic principles.

If motion is sharply limited because of painful adherences, one should begin passive exercises first and then change to the active form. On the other hand, when motion is not painful but is limited due to adherences, one may start active motion at once.

No attempt should be made to increase the range of motion rapidly. Ordinarily, it is entirely adequate to see a 2 to 5 degree change during the one or two week period that elapses between measurements. The normal range of motion in the various joints is as follows:

Fingers. The distal interphalangeal joint should flex approximately 75 degrees while the proximal will flex normally to 110 degrees. The metacarpophalangeal joint has a total range of approximately 85 degrees.

The thumb shows an interphalangeal joint flexion of 85 degrees, while the metacarpophalangeal joint will flex approximately 75 degrees.

The wrist has a flexion-extension range of approximately 140 degrees. Abduction approaches 35 degrees, while adduction is 50 degrees.

The elbow has a flexion-extension range of approximately 135 degrees and a pronation-supination range of 180 degrees.

The shoulder joint will abduct from zero to 80 degrees. Adduction from 80 to approximately 180 degrees is possible by elevation and outward rotation of the scapula. Flexion and extension, or the swinging motion of the shoulder, ranges through 180 degrees forward to approximately 45 degrees toward the rear. Internal rotation is 80 degrees, while external rotation is only 45 degrees.

The normal hip has an abduction of 45 degrees and an adduction of 45 degrees. The flexion-extension range is approximately 120 degrees, external rotation 60 degrees and internal rotation 30 degrees.

The knee has a flexion-extension arc of 135 degrees and no other appreciable movement.

The ankle will plantar flex slightly more than 20 degrees and will dorsiflex approximately 45 degrees. Inversion and eversion of the foot are variable but usually run from 20 to 50 degrees, depending somewhat on age and occupation.

These figures are given for normal healthy adults. One must remember that we old people are somewhat "creaky in the joints" to begin with and frequently cannot go through the entire range of motion applicable to a younger person.

As mentioned above, one must always remember that exercise designed to increase motion can be grossly overdone. Be sure to set up a gradual program rather than attempting to achieve a great deal suddenly. Remember, too, that additional exercises to increase muscular strength and coordination may greatly enhance those techniques which tend to make possible a freer motion.

Increasing Muscle Power

Exercises designed to increase the power and endurance of muscle are easily designed. They consist only of contraction of the muscle against resistance. I notice in my notes the statement that muscle power is best produced against a very high resistance not often repeated, whereas endurance will come with frequent repetition of contractions against relatively low resistance. Since we need both endurance and power increase, one would think that a judicious combination of high and low resistance exercise would be most satisfactory.

Increasing Coordination

Increase of muscular coordination is simply a matter of training the nervous system. One may learn or relearn almost any function if carefully designed exercises are applied.

An example is the hemiplegic who has to learn to walk again. In many of these cases there is sufficient reestablishment of function to allow ambulation after training. The training is best accomplished by repeated sessions involving coordinative exercises. As in other exercise prescriptions, all coordinative exercises must be designed for the particular patient.

This is not difficult. Again, one must be warned: Do not try to accomplish a great deal swiftly. Begin with the simplest movements and give an adequate chance for these to be mastered before proceeding to more complex motions.

OFFICE APPLICATION

It is impossible that we should discuss with any degree of completeness the office application of therapeutic procedures. To do this would require several volumes as large as this entire book. Instead of attempting such coverage we will try to "hit the high spots," discussing the commonly seen lesions that respond well to physical methods.

The Locomotor System

Contusions. Severe contusions should be treated with cold packs if seen within the first six hours following injury. No other physiotherapeutic procedure should be done until this six hours elapses. Beginning 24 hours after the injury, local heat and occasionally massage central to but *not over* the contusion will promote rapid resolution.

Sprains and Strains. The application of cold to reduce internal hemorrhage is usually gratifying to the patient and effective. Within 12 to 24 hours one may begin application of heat, usually by means of diathermy or hot packs. As mentioned in contusions, massage proximal to the involved joint is frequently helpful and gentle passive exercise beginning about the third or fourth day is tolerated well.

Dislocations. Healing in dislocations is effectively speeded up by application of heat and massage beginning 24 to 48 hours after the original injury. Within three or four days *passive* exercises may be started. Active exercise designed to strengthen surrounding muscle groups should be given after one feels that healing is complete.

Fractures. Fracture healing can be materially speeded and results greatly enhanced by application of physiotherapy. This should begin 24 to 48 hours after reduction is completed and should consist of mild diathermy treatments and gentle massage if the part is not under a cast. Along with this, gentle passive exercises of the involved areas, except those immediately contiguous to the fracture, are useful. Within one week, passive exercises of the area of the fracture may be carried out. Even though it is surprisingly simple, recovery is often remarkably speeded by this technique.

Affections of Muscle. Muscular aches and pains are probably the second most frequent category of patients' distress. They respond well to physiotherapeutic measures. Exhibition of the diathermy, the infra-red lamp, massage or hydrotherapeutic measures used individually or in combination secures gratifying relief for people with such difficulty.

Many physicians tend to ignore these complaints in favor of what we term "real pathology," but I feel that a patient in distress is entitled to the relief that physiotherapeutic techniques can often provide.

I had no idea of the number of these minor muscular complaints until some years ago we started a physiotherapy department in our small clinic-hospital. Within a matter of three months the physiotherapy department was doing just as many or more treatments per day as I was. Many times a friend would walk in in the morning and say to me, "Doc, I've just got a bump and I'd like to go down to physiotherapy and get it treated."

Physiotherapy did no treatments unless approved by me, but this took only a few minutes to check and be sure that nothing of a major nature was wrong. The patient was then sent to physiotherapy with a prescription for a treatment or a series of treatments. As I mentioned before, the volume was astonishing.

Bursitis. In recent times, acute bursitis has responded so very well to cortisone that the place of physiotherapy has been somewhat curtailed. Even though its usefulness has diminished to some extent, it remains one of the most valuable procedures at our command. Frequent applications of the diathermy associated with active and passive exercises in the subacute and chronic stages of the disease will effect remarkable changes for the better. Reabsorption of calcified areas often takes place and relief of pain *may* be dramatic.

The Arthritides. OSTEOARTHRITIS can frequently be greatly helped by heating measures applied to the involved joints. The infra-red light, the diathermy, or hot packs applied at home are all useful in treatment.

RHEUMATOID ARTHRITIS may be helped by application of heat followed by massage of the surrounding muscle group. The release of spasm in this disease is best accomplished by mild physiotherapeutic methods. One must, however, be certain that the methods used are of sufficient mildness so that no damage is done to the inflamed joint.

TRAUMATIC ARTHRITIS. Diathermy and active exercise designed to increase motion are the standbys of treatment in this condition.

Gynecology

Abdominosacral diathermy is the best means of pelvic heating at our command. It is useful in chronic pelvic infections and in congestive states. Certain types of dysmenorrhea respond well to diathermy (see page 113). It is administered like this:

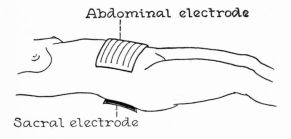

Abdominal electrode

Sacral electrode

One should keep in mind that various hemorrhagic conditions are made a great deal worse by diathermy. I remember a woman who had a ruptured tubal pregnancy with surprisingly few symptoms, and who was treated by pelvic diathermy. To change the tune of this book just a little bit from the average textbook, this error was not committed "elsewhere"—it was committed by me. Both the patient and I almost died, she from blood loss and I from the sheer shock at my own stupidity.

Rectal Disease

The cautery may be used for the treatment of minor anal fissures and ulcers as outlined in the section on proctology. Diathermy will frequently give relief from proctologic conditions, and proper application of hydrotherapy finds a prominent place in the treatment of these diseases.

I have read of a development in which a new technique of using the sinusoidal current for shrinking hemorrhoidal masses is under study. I have not tried it and, therefore, can speak with no authority at all about the procedure. In general, electrotherapeutic methods should never be used during a hemorrhoidectomy or to replace the operation. This applies also to the use of thermal heat to remove hemorrhoidal masses.

Dermatologic Conditions

The ultraviolet is helpful but by no means curative in acne vulgaris. Radiation may have to be very intense and of high dosage to produce the desired effect and one must use caution in its application.

Various fungus infections of the skin seem to clear more rapidly when ultraviolet is applied in erythema dosage. This is by no means a replacement for standard therapy but it will often speed a cure.

The course of pityriasis rosea is shortened by judicious applications of ultraviolet. If properly given, new lesions may fail to appear when the rays are used.

It has been reported that certain types of

ulcers and wounds tend to heal more quickly when ultraviolet irradiation is applied. We have not used this method enough to speak of it with assurance.

Respiratory Disorders

Chronic bronchitis is frequently benefited by daily applications of diathermy given directly through the chest. Acute pleurisy responds well to infra-red irradiation and usually to diathermy. Various chronic pulmonary diseases, such as emphysema, may improve under physiotherapeutic treatment.

The blow-bottle exercises have some ability to reexpand non-used portions of the lung. They look like this:

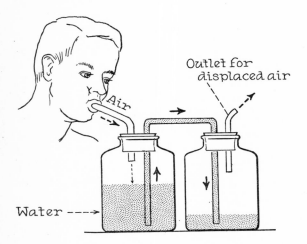

The patient blows in one of the two spouts and transfers the water from one bottle to another by means of air pressure.

Postural Correction

Poor posture is responsible for a multitude of sins and the physician is frequently asked to prescribe corrective exercises for it. The most useful are those exercises designed to strengthen the erector spinae and the shoulder girdle muscles and to stretch and strengthen the posterior hamstrings. The erector spinae and shoulder girdle may be strengthened by

having the patient face the wall and push heavily upon the wall with the elbows, like this:

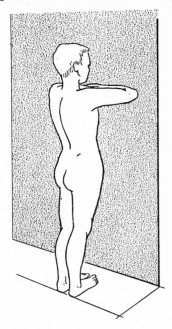

Next, have the patient stand with his back against the wall and attempt to force himself into such a position that the entire posterior surface of his body touches the wall.

The hamstrings may be strengthened by leg-raising exercises administered first to stretch them, and then by having the patient lie down under a heavy table and attempt to raise it by contracting the hamstrings like this:

Along with these exercises, the physician should prescribe proper footwear and should offer corrective exercises for any muscle imbalances observed other than those we have mentioned.

Several good texts are available on physiotherapy and one of them should be regular reading for the physician.

Section XIV

THE SMALL LABORATORY

THE SMALL LABORATORY

In this section we are going to list and tell how to do tests that might be considered absolutely essential for the small laboratory. In addition to discussing the procedure itself, we would like to devote a paragraph or two to discussing results and what they mean. This analysis of results, of course, is a matter of opinion and is open to discussion in many of its aspects. Let me make clear at first that our discussion is confined to things applicable in the family physician's practice and not to theoretical aspects of the problem.

To begin with, we are going to assume that the practitioner wishes to have a good small laboratory and that he owns or is willing to buy a microscope, a photocolorimeter and some of the simpler chemical apparatus.

BLOOD

Hemoglobin

The hemoglobin is best determined by means of the electric photocolorimeter. This is by far the most accurate means of gaining the desired reading. Most such colorimeters report hemoglobin in grams per cent (grams per 100 cc. of blood).

The normal hemoglobin level ranges from slightly below 14 to more than 18 grams. An *increase* in the amount of hemoglobin is usually significant only in that it reflects hemoconcentration or increased demand for oxygen over a period of time. For example, in moving from a lower to a higher altitude there is a consistent increase in the amount of hemoglobin, although this seldom goes out of the normal range. In various illnesses which cause a concentration of the blood, such as a severe diarrhea or severe congestive failure, one may see an apparent increase in hemoglobin which actually is not real at all. True cases of polycythemia show greatly increased hemoglobin values but are excessively rare.

Diminution in the amount of hemoglobin may be physiologic as well as an indication of pathology. An excellent example is the pregnant woman. Particularly during the last trimester of pregnancy there is a physiologic hemodilution, i.e., the fluid elements are increased without change in the total number of cells. This, of course, is reflected by a lowering in hemoglobin reading. I think you will agree with me that it may be somewhat foolish to get all excited about an anemia in pregnancy when there actually is no anemia at all—only an increase in the fluid elements of the blood.

You must keep in mind when estimating hemoglobin that it changes not only in the number of cells and the hemoglobin content of the cells *but also with the relative amount of plasma fluids*. If one does not remember this, a number of fallacious diagnoses will result.

Coagulation Time

Use a capillary tube which may be purchased in quantity from any surgical supply house. Dip one end of the tube into a drop of freshly obtained blood and notice that the tube will fill immediately with blood by capillary attraction. After the tube has been full for 2 minutes, break off a very short section and pull it away from the larger portion of the tube. Repeat this at 1 minute intervals (or less) until fibrin stretches out between the two broken tubes like this:

Ordinarily, clotting time determined by this method will be from 3 to 5 minutes in the normal individual. The only significant finding is lengthening of the coagulation time, which may be as long as several hours. Hemophilia is, of course, the cause of very long coagulation time. Various infections as well as anemias and leukemias may cause some prolongation of this coagulation time, to as much as 3 or 4 minutes beyond the normal.

Bleeding Time

Using a lancet or knife blade which has been taped to keep it from penetrating too deeply, make a small cut on the end of the finger. A small point: If you will make the cut lateral to the pressure pad, there will be no minor soreness to plague the patient during the ensuing twelve hours or so.

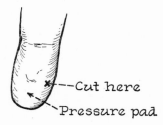

Using a piece of filter paper, blot the cut at 30 second intervals until it stops bleeding. Normal bleeding time should not exceed 3 to 5 minutes.

If the bleeding time is greatly prolonged, suspect low platelet counts or various destructive liver diseases with consequent lowered fibrinogen content of blood.

Red Blood Count

It would be an insult to the intelligence of the average physician to place in this book instructions for the counting of erythrocytes. After all, during his last two years of medical school he has served as a laboratory technician while devoting his spare time to the study of medicine. Because of this, he should be well qualified to count red blood cells or to teach the procedure to his office assistant.

Decrease in count of red blood cells is, by definition, anemia, and is an indication to seek causes. An increase in the number of red cells is somewhat rare and is frequently thought of as polycythemia vera. In very simple terms, polycythemia usually "ain't." The increase is much more likely to refer to other diseases which cause hemoconcentration.

In the actual performance of the count itself there are certain precautions that need to be taken. One may use normal saline for a diluting fluid if it is changed somewhat frequently. Hayem's fluid is made by the following formula:

Mercuric chloride	0.5 gm.
Sodium sulfate	5.0 gm.
Sodium chloride	1.0 gm.
Distilled water to make 200 cc.	

You must be sure that the filled pipette is adequately shaken so that cells are properly distributed throughout the fluid. In charging the counting chamber, it should be filled just to the borders of the platform and not allowed to "run over."

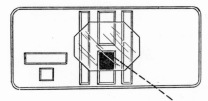

Chamber filled just to border of platform

We must realize the errors to which blood counting is subject. The error in the count itself has been variously estimated. Possibly the most frequently agreed upon error is 16 per cent. Now, this means that, accounting for no human variability, a well done count may be inaccurate 16 per cent in either direction. In a count of 5,000,000, this represents an error of 800,000 cells, without considering any human variance or error. By the time one compensates also for the deficiencies of the technician, we find that the red blood count is one of the most inefficient tests that we do.

In our own practice we are not inclined to take as significant any one count unless it is quite obviously backed up by other findings.

The Hematocrit

Prepare a series of tubes to receive blood as follows: First make a solution of 1.2 grams ammonium oxalate and 0.8 grams of potassium oxalate in 100 cc. of distilled water. Put 0.5 cc. of this mixture in each of the test tubes and evaporate the water.

When blood is drawn, put 5 cc. in one of these tubes and invert it to mix the blood and oxalate, like this:

Now use a capillary pipette to draw off 1 cc. of blood and transfer it to the Wintrobe hematocrit tube like this:

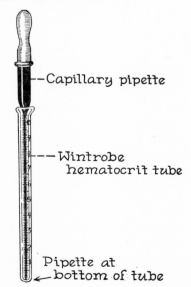

-- Capillary pipette

--- Wintrobe hematocrit tube

Pipette at bottom of tube

Fill the tube to the 10 mark. Place the tube in a centrifuge (a special holder is necessary, or one may be made from wood) and centrifuge for 10 to 15 minutes at approximately 3000 rpm. If there should be any question about cell packing being complete when the tube is removed, re-centifuge.

The reading may be taken directly from the tube. If red blood cells come to the 4.5 mark on the tube, then the red blood cell volume is 45 per cent of the total volume. Notice the light tan or gray layer immediately above the red blood cells. This represents white blood cells, which generally are packed immediately above the reds. An excellent estimation of the number of white blood cells may be obtained by measuring this buffy coat.

Repeated observation of the buffy coat by the doctor will allow him to become so accurate that the white count may largely be replaced except in a few specific instances.

The hematocrit reading is simply an estimate of hemoconcentration. In diseases where large quantities of fluid are lost the red blood cells occupy a greater portion of the total volume. For example, the fluid status of a child with severe diarrhea can be followed quite accurately by repeated determinations with the hematocrit.

Anemias, on the other hand, show lowered hematocrit readings. Because of its relative accuracy and because of the several bits of useful information obtained, I actually prefer the hematocrit to the more extensive blood counting procedures. It is easier and somewhat quicker than the complete count. Hemoglobin determination and hematocrit will give sufficiently accurate information in most cases.

As an incidental fact, notice the fluid above the packed cells. Any extreme destruction of red cells, of course, leaves free hemoglobin in the plasma which may be seen as reddish discoloration of this fluid, and jaundice may be confirmed by noting the color of this plasma, though one seldom needs the confirmation that is available through this test.

The White Count

It is, of course, superfluous to discuss the actual technique of enumerating white blood cells. One should always remember, however, that the error of the count approaches that of the red blood cell count although it is not quite so great. The method of obtaining blood and the actual diluting and counting are subject to human errors in addition to the actual inherent error of the count. At times, I feel that the hematocrit accompanied by a stained smear gives a truer picture of white blood cell status than does the formalized count. This, of course, is an impression which remains to be verified by skilled analysis in the hands of experts.

A matter of importance for us to consider is: Just what does it mean when there are variations from the normal in the various elements of the count? To begin with, too few white blood cells, i.e., a white count of 3000 or less, is probably greatly significant only when there is a marked *relative* decrease in the number of leukocytes, particularly the polymorphonuclears. For example, a count of 3200 with 30–70 distribution between lymphocytes and leukocytes most usually has no immediate clinical significance unless other findings of importance are present.

On the other hand, should one see a count of 3200 with a distribution of 40 per cent leukocytes and 60 percent lymphocytes, and should the stained smear confirm the fact that polymorphonuclears are greatly diminished or even approaching total absence, then one thinks of severe depression of the bone marrow, agranulocytosis and imminent death-dealing complications.

An increase in number of the leukocytes may be due to three causes. The first and by far the most frequent is a physiologic increase. The count taken in the afternoon or several hours following a meal high in protein may run 10,000 to 12,000 or even higher, with absolutely no significance from the standpoint of pathology. For some unknown reason, the leukocyte count even increases after a cold bath. These facts have significance in determining the reliability of the count. Particularly important is the fact that there is a normal increase in the count from low levels in the morning to relatively high levels by mid-afternoon. One should be very wary of this.

Let me give you an example. A young man comes in at three in the afternoon complaining of nagging pain in the right lower quadrant which has been present for several hours. Physical signs are negative and the history is atypical, particularly in view of the fact that the man ate a hearty dinner, including roast beef, at 12:30.

The unwary physician feels that chances of appendicitis are slight but orders a white count which is returned at 13,500 with a slightly increased relative number of polymorphonuclears. Because of this blood count, the man is promptly hospitalized and observed for 24 hours. He is dismissed as normal at the end of this time.

Such a picture is not infrequent in medicine today. The count, of course, was physiologic and the pain very probably due to some trivial effect of the large meal.

Another example which I have seen repeatedly: My group lives in the "intestinal flu" belt of America. Acute staphylococcic enteritis, intestinal flu, food poisoning, whatever you wish to call it, causes quite a few clinic visits. With this disease the colon is frequently tender to palpation and one may puzzle for a few seconds over whether or not the vermiform appendix is involved as the seat of the trouble.

I have seen, not once but many times, a reputable and otherwise intelligent physician base a diagnosis of appendicitis purely on the white count is such a case. *The white count is elevated in most infectious processes.* This includes acute enteritis, sore throat, boils, minor rectal infections, etc. I know it sounds childish to say it, but the physician should remember always that the elevated white count is not indicative of any specific disease. One must rule out infectious processes elsewhere in the body before *ANY* faith can be placed in the findings of the white blood count. That, to my mind, is the most important fact which we sometimes fail to realize about this office procedure.

Perhaps the most valuable fact used in determining whether a white count is pathologically or physiologically elevated is the relative number of lymphocytes and leukocytes. A ratio of 70–30, as you know, is normal. Eighty per cent leukocytes with 20 per cent lymphocytes is verging on the pathologic, and 90 per cent leukocytes is a nearly absolute indicator of pathology. Degree of elevation may be somewhat secondary in importance to changes in relative number.

One hears rather frequently of the overwhelming infections in which the white blood count remains normal. This is, of course, entirely proven but need give the physician little cause for worry. The patient in such a case is so obviously desperately ill that the white count is of no use in deciding whether or not grave danger is present. It simply confirms the clinical impression that the process is so severe that bodily defenses are nearly useless.

One small fact which is very handy to remember is that hemorrhage, particularly into body cavities, often causes a rapid increase in the leukocyte count to 20,000 or more. This may be useful in differentiation of obscure cases. It does not indicate an infectious process but rather the chemical irritation of extravasated blood.

Increase in number of lymphocytes is not seen very often. It is principally noticed in pertussis. Other causes are not seen often enough in the physician's office to bear major implications.

In whooping cough, the lymphocytosis begins early in the catarrhal stage and by the paroxysmal stage is usually marked enough to allow diagnosis. Counts of 15,000 to 25,000 are very common and 50,000 is not unremarkable. This procedure has the disadvantage that the case is usually diagnosed and well under treatment before the lymphocyte count tells us pertussis is present.

Study of the Stained Blood Film

This is one of the most difficult but also one of the most rewarding procedures in the small laboratory. The information gained is variegated and extremely accurate but a discussion requires so much detail that it would be entirely out of place in this book. There are many excellent reference works on the subject. One is particularly drawn to those of Wintrobe.

Blood Platelets

The platelet count is principally significant in diagnosis of hemorrhagic disease. The count is not difficult but must be done quickly to avoid clumping and disintegration of the platelets. While there is a very large error, it is not of particular importance since findings, to be significant, must deviate at least 75 per cent from normal.

There are major day by day and even hour by hour variations in the platelet numbers which are not satisfactorily explained. Because of this, the practitioner should remember always that one platelet count has very little significance. In our own work we usually have three counts on succeeding days and take the average of the three as a reasonably accurate estimation.

The diluting fluid of Guy and Leake is the only one we have used. It has been entirely satisfactory but we are in no position to compare it with other fluids because of its exclusive application. This is the formula:

Distilled water	94	cc.
Formalin, 40 per cent solution	6	cc.
Sodium oxalate	1.6	gm.
Crystal violet	0.01	gm.

The fluid is filtered immediately after being made and then is preserved in ordinary laboratory stoppered bottles. Usually it is dated and made up fresh about every 6 months, the stock on hand being disposed of.

To make a count, use a red blood cell pipette and draw the diluting fluid to the 1 mark. This, of course, can be an approximation rather than an exact technique. Next, blood is drawn into the pipette from the tip to the 0.5 mark and diluting fluid is added to the 101 or top mark. The pipette must be shaken immediately and steadily for at least 1½ or 2 minutes to make sure that the platelets are thoroughly mixed. The standard counting chamber is loaded immediately after shaking is completed and is set aside for 10 minutes to allow for settling. The actual counting is similar to that of red blood cells.

Only one thing is of real importance in the technique of platelet counting: remember that the tremendous physiologic variations plus the error of the count make a single determination unreliable. One should never base a clinical diagnosis or treatment on a single unsupported platelet count.

The Erythrocyte Sedimentation Rate

This simple laboratory procedure has some real value, particularly in the collagen diseases. There are certain facts which should be quite obvious but which sometimes may be confusing. They are these:

1. An increased sedimentation rate has absolutely no specific meaning from the standpoint of clinical entities. It is increased in the collagen diseases, in cancer, in tuberculosis, in severe infections and occasionally in other less well explained entities. One must, therefore, be relatively certain that other pathologic conditions than the one under immediate consideration are *not present* before using the sedimentation rate as a specific guide.

2. There are a number of variables in technique and in unexplained diurnal changes which make it more or less absurd to tie clinical interpretations to minor changes in the sedimentation rate.

We have used the Westergren apparatus and have no familiarity with any other and, therefore, I am unable to suggest the particular advantages and disadvantages. I am afraid I must confess to a tendency to avoid fine distinctions, for our sedimentation rates are arbitrarily divided into a normal group, less than 20 mm. per hour for either sex; a fast group ranging from 20 to 50; a very rapid group which ranges above 50 mm. per hour. Minor changes are counted insignificant and ignored completely.

BLOOD—CHEMICAL TESTS

The small laboratory can be greatly enhanced by the purchase of a photoelectric colorimeter. These machines cost about $200 and make possible relatively accurate readings on a number of tests which aid greatly in clinical medicine. Going on the assumption that such a machine will be a part of the average small laboratory I have not described any techniques for the performance of the various blood chemistries. These are amply described in the manuals accompanying the machine and the only thing we could achieve by including them here is a literal copy of such a manual.

Of the various blood chemistry tests available fewer than half a dozen are put into day to day use. Others are occasionally very valuable and laboratories should be able to perform them, but their use is not frequent enough to warrant space here. Our main problem will be discussion of just what one may infer from the result and what one may regard as fallacious.

Non-protein Nitrogen

The normal level in 25 to 30 mg. per 100 cc. of blood. When this is raised the test indicates an accumulation of waste matter in the blood stream due to one of two common causes:

1. Defective elimination, such as is found in kidney and urinary tract diseases, or

2. Excessive accumulation, such as may be found in breakdown of blood.

This latter factor is not particularly serious in most cases. It is found and then disappears in a few days following hemorrhage into a body cavity or into the gut. It is, however, an excellent trick to keep in mind for diagnosis of gastro-intestinal hemorrhage. Within a matter of 8 to 12 hours after a hemorrhage there will be a distinct elevation of the NPN and this elevation will remain for 36 to 48 hours before beginning to fall. I have several times found it of great use in elucidating an obscure diagnosis.

Blood Cholesterol

The cholesterol level ranges from 160 to 200 mg. per 100 cc. of plasma in the normal individual. In hypothyroidism the cholesterol is increased, while in hyperthyroid states a decrease is usually apparent. The value of cholesterol determinations in hyperthyroidism is somewhat questionable, but they seem quite reliable in indicating hypothyroid states.

Here is as good a place as any to mention again the BMR. This pernicious test is, in the hands of the average practitioner, an inaccurate nuisance. The psychic state of the individual is represented in the BMR findings fully as much as or more than the state of the thyroid gland.

The removal of the thyroid gland is not a cure for a psychoneurosis although it has been performed frequently on the basis of obviously fallacious BMR findings. Confronted with a supposed case of hyperthyroidism the practitioner may gain some information by performing a blood cholesterol test in the office and then sending the patient to a larger laboratory for protein bound iodine and radioactive iodine uptake studies. Then he should carefully assemble the resultant laboratory test reports on his desk, ignore them and turn to a searching history and physical examination for the diagnosis. If this history and physical examination is borne out by laboratory results, then some consideration for treatment of the thyroid gland is in order.

Blood Sugar

Blood sugar determinations have been discussed thoroughly in the section on Internal Medicine, to which the reader is referred. Please see page 306.

The Icteric Index

This is a measure indicating coloration of the plasma or serum by bile pigments. The test is quickly and simply done and will often detect mild degrees of pigmentation long before jaundice is clinically evident. The normal index is below 5. Jaundice usually becomes clinically apparent when the index is over 10 to 15.

URINE

Transparency

You will perhaps remember the old-time physician's test for transparency. One holds a bottle of the urine between his eye and a newspaper. If the newspaper can be read through the urine, it is normal. If cloudiness prevents delineation of the type there is pathology present. This is not a very good test but it can be used in the home. Here is the rest of the "home urinalysis" routine:

If the urine is cloudy, first add a teaspoon of vinegar. Amorphous phosphates are precipitated in alkaline urine, forming a white cloud or sediment that markedly diminishes transparency. They will be dissolved when the urine is made acid by the addition of vinegar. If the urine is still not transparent, heat a sample. Amorphous urates, which are precipitated in acid urine, dissolve when heat is applied.

If the cloudiness still remains, add a tablespoonful of strong lye water, which will transform pus cells into a gelatinous mass. If after these three tests the urine is still not transparent, the chances are you are dealing with blood or bacteria. In fresh urine, bacteria are seldom seen in sufficient quantity to cause loss of transparency. Blood remains.

Hydrogen Ion Concentration

The pH of the urine can be determined most satisfactorily by use of nitrazine paper. The paper is immersed and compared to a chart which is furnished with the package. Normally one expects pH between 5 and 6. Extreme deviations may be due to changes in the acid-base balance of the body or to persistent infections of the urinary tract with certain organisms. The determination is most useful in diagnosing infections of the tract and establishing proper methods of therapy.

Specific Gravity

The normal range is about 1.020. Several specimens taken at random times will vary in specific gravity according to the amount of water ingested and the water loss of the body. An entirely healthy individual may show variations from 1.003 to 1.030. It is only when the specific gravity of the urine shows a consistent change that there is clinical significance in the findings.

A high specific gravity when the urine is of normal coloration points to diabetes mellitus. High specific gravity with increased coloration of the urine, on the other hand, is usually found in febrile diseases or in acute fluid lack. In general, the higher specific gravity ranges are either not very helpful in deciding diagnosis or not gravely significant.

The fixed low specific gravity is indicative of severe change and frequently presages a fatal outcome.

Occasionally one may receive a very small sample of urine on which it is necessary to make a determination of specific gravity. Quite naturally the simplest way is to have the patient urinate a sufficient amount to perform the test. If this is impossible, make a mixture of benzol and chloroform which seems about the same specific gravity as the urine. Now place a drop of the urine in the mixture, using a long-stemmed dropper. If the drop starts to sink, add benzol and if it starts to rise upward add chloroform until the drop remains stationary in the mixture. When this is achieved, take the specific gravity of the mixture, which will be the same as that of the urine.

Chlorides

It is occasionally useful to check a patient who is theoretically on a salt-free diet by estimating the urinary chlorides. To begin with, check the urine for albumin, which interferes with the test. Excess albumin may be removed by gentle heating until a precipitate forms, followed by prompt filtration. Now add 5 cc. of urine and 3 drops of concentrated nitric acid to a test tube. Follow this by addition of 5 drops of 10 per cent silver nitrate. If the patient has a markedly diminished chloride secretion, a cloudy opalescent precipitate of silver nitrate forms in the fluid but does not settle out rapidly. In the case of a normal amount of chloride, there is a thick, heavy, curdy precipitate of silver chloride which shows a settling tendency.

Albumin

The significance of albumin in the urine is far too well known and far too extensive a subject to be discussed here. There are, however, certain points which should be mentioned for review. The best test in the practitioner's office is probably simple heating of the urine sample. Albumin forms a white precipitate if present. Unfortunately, so do some other substances if the urine be neutral or slightly alkaline. If such a precipitate is formed, add a few drops of any common acid. The albuminous precipitate will not be affected but other precipitates will promptly dissolve when this is done.

Do not overlook the fact that numerous pus cells can provide a sufficient amount of albumin and other precipitable substances to give a positive reaction. This is particularly common in female specimens, in which vaginal contamination of urine is frequent.

Sugar

The detection of sugar in the urine on any one or even two succeeding examinations *is NOT significant*. There are many known causes for sugar in the urine on a transitory basis. A blow in the head, pregnancy, drugs, anesthesia, a high carbohydrate meal. Even a difficult examination in school has been known to produce transitory gylcosuria. While each case warrants a follow-up examination and a short but carefully detailed history, I have the distinct impression that the majority of cases that we see with no symptoms or signs other than a single positive urine sugar have no relation at all to diabetes.

The actual diabetic and the occasional case of renal glycosuria are too well known to comment here.

Acetone

This compound is found in the urine only

in the presence of severe toxic disease, diabetes, and acidosis. It is most frequently of import in the severe diabetic.

One should remember that acetonuria is very common in children and may be produced much easier than in the adult. It has been said that the urine of some young children gives a positive test for acetone when the child seems entirely normal. This I have not verified but I do know that acetone in the urine is much more frequent in children than in adults. It is best detected by means of the commercial tests now on the market, which may be run in any laboratory and take only a few minutes.

Microscopic Examination

Crystals. The detection of crystals in the urine is easy and important. The following table from Todd, Sanford and Wells' "Clinical Diagnosis by Laboratory Methods" offers an adequate means of identification.

	In Acid Urine	In Alkaline Urine
Yellow crystals	Uric acid—dissolve in NaOH	Ammonium biurate—dissolve in **HCl**
Colorless crystals	Calcium oxalate—dissolve in **HCl**	Phosphate crystals—dissolve in acetic acid
Amorphous material	Urates—dissolve with heat	Amorphous phosphates—dissolve in acetic acid

Significance of urates is this: If seen immediately after voiding, the presence of urates is suggestive of a stone in the urinary tract, particularly if red blood cells are also present. You must remember that these crystals have no significance at all if seen an hour or more after voiding of the specimen. All urines will sooner or later precipitate uric acid crystals.

Calcium oxalate crystals are normally found in acid urine and have no pathologic significance.

Amorphous urates look like dust which may be slightly red in color when seen under the microscope. They have no clinical significance.

In alkaline urine one occasionally sees ammonium biurate crystals, which have no clinical significance. The amorphous phosphates are also found in alkaline urine and are without peculiar significance, as are the more usual forms of triple phosphates.

In summary, crystals may aid in establishing the *p*H of the urine, which is better done by means of nitrazine paper. The only ones that are really significant are the yellow crystals of uric acid when seen immediately after a specimen is voided.

Casts. The pathologic significance of urinary casts is well elucidated and needs no review here. There are one or two techniques for their demonstration which may be very useful. One is interested, of course, in whether or not the structures are really cylindrical casts. First notice that the casts are best seen near the cover glass edge, rather than the center. Then use a small household needle to press on the cover glass, making a motion from side to side across the long axis of the cast. Notice that it will roll when this is done, which amply confirms its cylindrical shape. If more careful delineation is necessary, place a drop of India ink at the edge of the cover glass and allow it a minute or so to diffuse throughout the microscopic field. Casts will stand out as white structures on a black background.

Pyuria. There is one minor technique which may be very useful in an occasional case of pyuria. When there exists some question as to whether the cells seen are actually degenerating leukocytes, put a drop of 0.1 normal acetic acid at the edge of the cover glass and examine the specimen again at the end of 5 minutes. After the action of the acid, the granules will no longer obscure nuclear structures and identification of the cells is positive rather than presumptive.

One should not leave the subject of pus cells in the urine without still another warning: Urinary albumin may be due to the release of proteins of degenerating white blood cells. Albuminuria in such a case is significant only in relation to the infection that is present.

Erythrocytes. Red blood cells seem to be a normal constituent of the human urine. It is only when they are increased that they have pathologic significance. Usually, of course, they are not detectable unless greatly increased, but the microscopist must remember that an occasional red blood cell such as one seen in every few fields may have no significance at all.

The laboratory may be of most assistance by using as a first procedure the three beaker test. Have the patient void successive portions of his urine into three beakers. If the first beaker contains the principal amount of the blood, the bleeding is probably in the urethra; if the last portion is the bloodiest the bleeding is probably in the bladder, and if there is a uniform mixture, the kidney or upper urinary tract is the most frequent offender.

One more tip which may be helpful at times: The urine of babies under one year old may occasionally contain a detectable number of red blood cells over a period of several examinations. This unquestionably has some pathologic significance but not nearly so much as one is first inclined to believe. The physician must be very cautious in making a diagnosis when such a case presents itself.

Kidney Function Tests

There are two of these tests which should be of great use to the practitioner: (1) the concentration and dilution test, which is exceedingly simple, and (2) the phenolsulfonphthalein test.

Concentration and Dilution Test. Begin by having the patient drink no fluid at all after 3 P.M. Have him void before going to bed and again immediately upon awakening. Ask that he not drink any fluids in the morning until his second voiding, which may usually be within an hour after awakening. This second voiding should be brought to the office in a sample bottle which the patient has been furnished.

Test it for specific gravity. If this is not above 1.020 the chances are that there is some kidney deficiency. If it is in the neighborhood of 1.010, severe limitation of kidney function may be present. After this has been determined, if you feel that a dilution test is necessary (and I see no utility at all in it), have the patient drink a glass of water every hour during the day and save the last specimen voided before going to bed. Since he will be up most of the night I would advise that he procure a good book before retiring.

The voided sample should be brought to the office the following morning and tested for specific gravity. Since there are no diseases that preclude concentration but allow dilution the test has little utility.

Phenolsulfonphthalein Test. Calculation of the output of this dye may best be done with the electric colorimeter as specified in the directions with each unit. The test itself should be conducted as follows:

Have the patient report to the office early in the morning and give him two or three glasses of water to drink immediately; then ask that he void the maximal amount possible and discard the urine. Now give exactly 1 cc. of the dye solution intramuscularly. One hour and 10 minutes after the dye solution has been administered, have the patient void, emptying the bladder completely. Treat the urine as specified in the directions which come with the photocolorimeter.

Again, at 2 hours and 10 minutes after administration of the dye, repeat the test.

Normally, over 40 per cent of the dye is eliminated during the first hour after administration and more than 60 per cent during the first two hours. Any diminution in this amount represents either kidney impairment or circulatory impairment. Since one can estimate clinically whether or not the circulatory system is grossly inefficient, the test may be counted as specific for kidney damage if there is no cardiovascular pathology.

One point is of some importance. If the urine output at 1 hour and 10 minutes is not at least 50 cc. the test result will probably not be reliable.

THE SPUTUM

Color and Consistency

Certain gross examinations of the sputum are sufficiently revealing to warrant their use by every physician. Most important is the foamy, pinkish sputum of chronic passive congestion which is usually seen in cases of heart failure. This can be identified at a glance by the doctor and is so very characteristic that its presence can often be elicited historically without actual visualization.

The red rust color of early degenerating blood cells admixed with leukocytes is quite characteristic of lobar pneumonia. Streaks of bright blood are seen most commonly in tuberculosis and bronchiectasis. Since phthisis is becoming more rare, I have the impression that most of these minor lung hemorrhages are due to bronchiectatic disease.

In evaluating one of these cases one must, of course, remember that postnasal discharge from sinus disease may be bloody and if expectorated may alarm both doctor and patient when, as a matter of fact, the blood does not come from the lungs at all.

Elastic Fibers

These are seen when doing a microscopic examination of the sputum and are characteristic although not pathognomonic of tuberculosis infection. The microscopic picture seen with the high, dry objective and $10 \times$ eyepiece is shown on page 283.

Another useful diagnostic finding with the microscope is the presence of heart-failure cells. These are leukocytes which contain brownish granules of pigment due to degeneration of blood cells. They are frequently a tip-off to an obscure case of apparent bronchial disease which is actually early heart failure. There is only one possible source of error. Sometimes these cells are confused with the carbon-containing cells which are characteristic in those who work around carbon dust. A chemical test may be easily applied to the fixed slide. Add a 10 per cent solution of potassium ferrocyanide. Leave it on the slide for 5 minutes and wash in tap water and apply a few drops of 0.1 normal hydrochloric acid. Leave this in place for about 3 minutes. If the pigment is iron-containing, such as that found in the heart-failure cells, some of the granules will assume a bright blue color. Carboniferous granules will, of course, be unchanged.

THE FECES

Animal parasites in the feces have previously been discussed beginning on page 285. Only one other test is essential to the small laboratory. This, of course, is the detection of occult blood. This detection is best done by means of Hemotest tablets which are available on the general market almost everywhere. The test is quick, efficient and accurate and obviates the necessity for long and difficult procedures and preparation which were common with other means of hemoglobin detection.

Bacteriology

The making and reading of simple stained smears should be within the purview of every small medical office. Techniques are well known to every physician and need not be enumerated. These stains are all that usually prove necessary. They are the methylene blue and the simple Gram's stain, and one of the common stains for acid-fast bacilli.

Section XV

ROENTGENOGRAPHY

ROENTGENOGRAPHY

Individual factors of technique and the processes involved in developing x-rays are matters that differ somewhat with the machine and film used.   They are not matters that can be discussed in a short chapter such as this.   Rare lesions or those that demand interpretation by a skilled roentgenologist will not be discussed. Only those entities commonly seen by the practitioner in his daily office practice will be considered.

FRACTURES

Any loss of the continuity of normally contiguous bone structure may be called a fracture.   One would think such a lesion among the easiest of all to diagnose.   As a matter of fact this is not so at all, for fracture diagnosis may confuse even the most expert interpreter of films.   These are some of the points to keep in mind:

1. Fractures may occur without rupture of the overlying periosteum but gross breaks seldom do.   This might be a fracture:

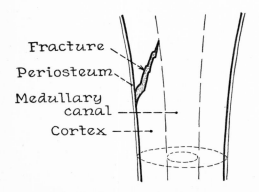

but this is more likely an artifact:

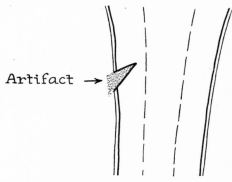

2. *Subperiosteal fractures* must not be confused with nutrient canals.   This is a fracture:

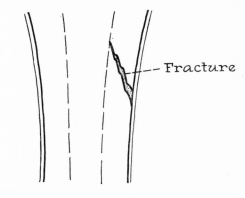

and this a nutrient canal:

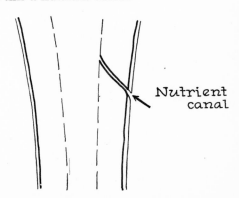

There may be cases at times in which there is confusion and in which roentgenologic evidence is not clear. These patients should be treated as if a fracture were present.

3. *Minor dehiscences* in bone are detectable only on superior x-rays. Is this a crack or an artifact?

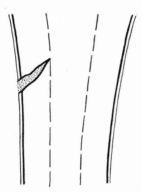

I don't know and probably would not be able to tell without a series of several more pictures. In such cases it is far wiser to be guided by physical signs than to use x-ray signs which may be spurious as a guide to treatment.

4. *Soft Tissue Injury*. I know it sounds ridiculous to mention this to physicians but x-rays are very inefficient in the diagnosis of soft tissue injury. When no bony damage is seen, it is not necessarily proven that no serious injury is present. Lesions of the soft tissues can be and often are far more serious and demanding of treatment than small fractures. *Never* accept an x-ray as final in diagnosis. This applies to any x-ray, not only those taken to demonstrate fractures.

It is particularly important that you do not pay more attention to the x-ray than to the patient. Without regard to whether pathology is shown in x-ray, if the patient has persistent symptoms, treat him as if pathology (even fracture) were present.

5. *Epiphyses*. The time of appearance and structure of the epiphyses are fairly constant but not enough so to warrant diagnosis without comparison. One should take films of both the injured area and its normal counterpart before making a diagnosis. Notice this pathology:

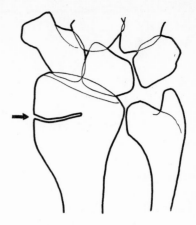

Here is the opposite wrist:

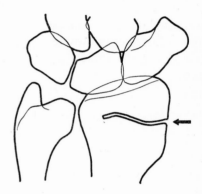

6. *Chip Fractures*. These are seldom confusing but may occasionally be mistaken for sesamoid bones. This is a normal heel:

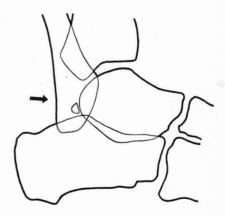

Fractures of the Upper Extremity

Fracture of the greater tuberosity of the humerus is a frequent occurrence and usually looks like this:

typical. In addition, there may be noticeable motion of the area when the arm is abducted by the patient. The calcification is seen here:

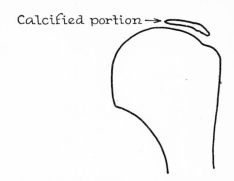

When this fracture is seen one must examine the surgical neck for a "fissure fracture" which may accompany the injury to the greater trochanter. Small fragments may separate and be drawn upward and backward. This is sometimes confused with calcification in the supraspinatous tendon. Since these fragments undergo aseptic necrosis in many cases they may become homogeneous, losing normal trabeculation, which makes diagnosis even more difficult. There is a change from this:

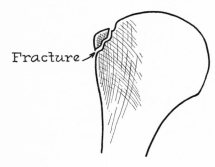

to this:

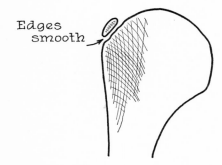

Calcification in the supraspinatous, which is probably identical with the disease we know as "calcific bursitis," is easily diagnosed by x-ray. The calcified area has a feathery appearance not typical of bone and the position is usually

When there is doubt about the diagnosis, fluoroscope the shoulder in the process of active motion (if possible) and passive motion. This will usually serve to clarify the two conditions.

After trauma to the supraspinatous tendon with avulsion of some of its fibers, there is usually a "scalloped" edge at the area of the greater tuberosity, like this:

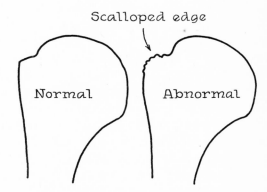

Other humeral fractures in the shoulder area are easy to identify and require no comment. Perhaps it would be wise to read a good work on epiphyseal injuries.

Clavicular fractures are not difficult. One should remember that this bone is subject to frequent greenstick fractures, particularly in children. They usually look like this:

Remember that x-rays of clavicular fractures nearly always show a "deformity" after healing. Most cases show no such appearance to inspection. If function is adequate there is no cause for alarm.

Acute dislocations of the humerus present no problem to x-ray. Standard techniques demonstrate them well. Recurrent dislocations often show a flat V deformity between the head and greater trochanter, like this:

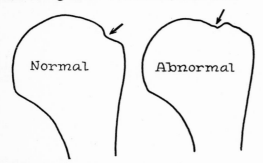

Dislocations at the acromioclavicular joint may best be diagnosed using a picture that shows both shoulder areas on a single film. If question still exists, fluoroscope the patient and press downward on the distal end of the clavicle, like this:

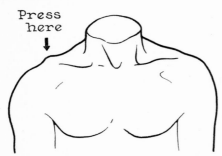

Now try the other side and compare the degree of motion that is elicited.

Fractures and dislocations about the elbow are not difficult radiologically, but a few points must be borne in mind. There is a marked difference in incidence of these fractures in relation to age. In toto, they are far more common in children.

When reviewing films of children, look especially for injury to the lateral condyle of the humerus (age 4 to 12), a supracondylar fracture (4 to 10 years), and fracture of the neck of the radius. The usual displacement of the radius is this:

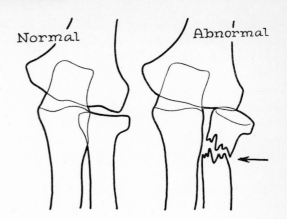

In adults look for a crack in the radius involving the articular surface, like this:

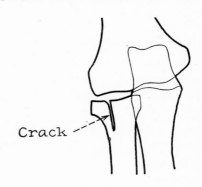

Complications following elbow injury are seen often and many may be diagnosed roentgenographically. Two basic factors contribute. First, the periosteum covering bones near the elbow joint seems less firmly attached than that near other joints. As a result it strips away from the bone at time of injury. Resultant formation of new bone is a serious complication which is seen at once on the x-ray.

Second, the fibers of the brachialis anticus are short. Because of this, they do not stretch well. Since many of these fibers are close to the joint, they may be torn at the time of injury. Such torn fibers predispose to calcification in the muscle belly which may usually be picked up on x-ray.

Fractures of the wrist and hand present no problem with the exception of those involving the navicular. To demonstrate such a fracture, place the hand in ulnar deviation palm downward on the cassette. Now raise the radial side of the hand about 1 inch. A good way to do this is to use a child's toy block placed at mid-forearm.

It is important to be able to differentiate between recent and old navicular fractures. Within 2 weeks after injury a few trabeculae are absorbed, which gives the fracture line an appearance of becoming wider. This process continues until the appearance of an elliptoid cavity is suggested at about 4 weeks. It looks like this:

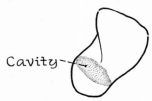

Fractures of the Lower Extremity

Fractures about the hip usually present little difficulty in diagnosis. An occasional case may prove obscure and require detailed study for diagnosis. Two mechanical procedures may be of use in establishing the presence of fracture and determining when proper reduction has been accomplished. The first is Shenton's line:

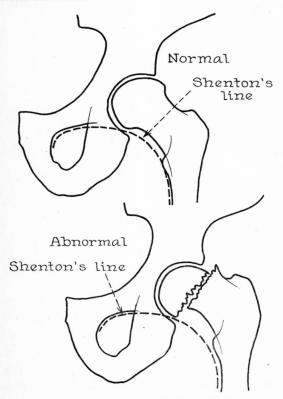

Notice the smooth curve of the line and its apposition to the bone surface on the normal picture. When a fracture is present the femoral surface no longer remains in the arc of the curve.

The second test is this: Draw a line along the mid-portion of the femoral shaft. At the level of the greater trochanter drop a perpendicular inward, like this in a normal hip:

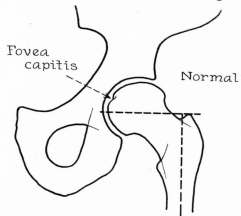

Notice that the horizontal line is at or slightly below the fovea capitis. In fracture, particularly the intertrochanteric type, the horizontal line will be above the fovea, like this:

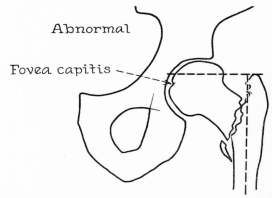

In many fractures of the hip, physical findings, if carefully established, are just as reliable as a means of diagnosis as are x-ray films. If there is doubt after films are taken, be guided in therapy by physical signs for a time. Then make further films. I have seen several patients dismissed as normal because of seemingly negative films when, in actuality, a fracture was present.

Knee injuries are not difficult, with certain exceptions. Damage to ligaments and semilunar cartilages is not shown upon x-ray. The practice of taking x-rays of every injured knee without adequate clinical examination should be avoided at all costs.

Two findings are worthy of note. The first is avulsion of a tibial spine, which looks like this:

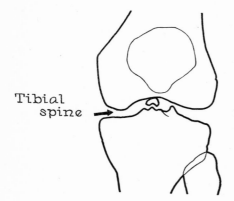

The lesion may at times be somewhat obscure and require study of carefully taken films for exact diagnosis.

The second finding is one of negative significance. Not infrequently we see a small fragment of bone that appears to have been detached from the tibial tubercle, like this:

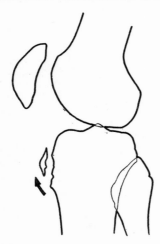

Since this is a frequent occurrence during adolescence, when it is not usually diagnosed, and since the fragment so separated seldom is absorbed, we must determine whether the injury is new or old. Look at the lower edge of the fragment. A new injury will show trabeculation of the fragment and of the tibia at the site of detachment, like this:

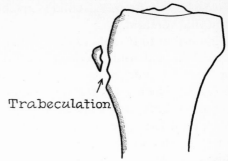

An old injury will show smooth cortical surface all around, like this:

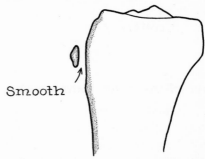

About the ankle joint the most common difficulty is failure to recognize the obvious signs of non-union in a fracture involving the medial malleolus. This is first indicated by deposition of firm, dense bone along the fracture line, like this:

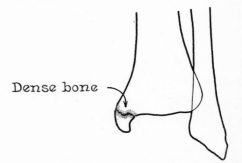

Notice the smooth opposing edges. Proper healing of the fracture looks like this:

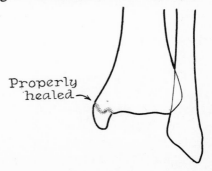

In the foot the talocalcaneal area is the principal source of difficulty. Application of Boehler's angle will do much to clarify the problem. This is the normal angle:

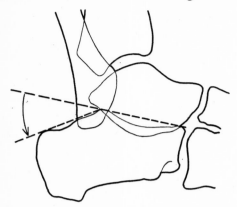

In the presence of fracture the angle may be reduced, like this:

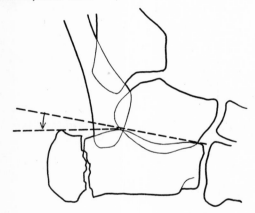

Fractures of the Skull

Fractures of the skull may be extremely difficult to detect. Before discussing the interpretation of films I must say a word about use of the office x-ray for such injuries. The acutely ill patient suspected of dangerous skull fracture has no business in x-ray either in the office or in the hospital. Not a few good people have been killed by our enthusiasm to render an exact diagnosis quickly.

Remember that a skull fracture of itself has seldom if ever been the cause of a death. It is the damage to the underlying brain that is of significance, and x-ray cannot show this damage. Put the dangerously ill patient to bed in a hospital and do not move him.

The minor concussions may be x-rayed in the office for the presence of skull fracture. This will consist of identifying fractures of the vault in most cases. The distribution of these fractures is approximately this:

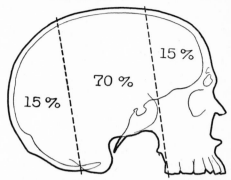

Identification is done as much by elimination as by positive factors. Suture lines show a dentate edge and are found here:

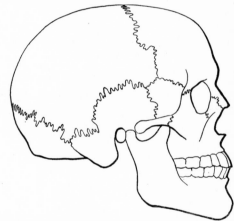

Vascular channels branch and change direction by means of smooth, sweeping curves. Fracture lines tend to change direction in angular corners. When both tables of the skull are fractured the fracture line may appear to separate into two distinct channels which roughly parallel one another for a few centimeters and then rejoin.

Fractures of the Spine

Questionable fractures of the cervical spine may require special positioning for their diagnosis. Unless the injury is one of minor degree these must be taken in the hospital.

Fractures of the transverse processes occur particularly in the lumbar area. Elimination of the psoas shadow following injury should make one suspicious of this lesion.

Fractures of the Ribs

Fractured ribs can be demonstrated by x-ray but this is totally unnecessary in the usual case. The roentgenographic technique requires exposure of several (or many) films, which adds greatly to the expense. We find that the information gained is not worth the expense except in the rare case. When displacement and soft tissue injury are suspected, x-ray assumes a much more important place.

Fractures of the Pelvis

Fractures of the pelvis usually involve the bones adjacent to the obturator foramina. On the film trace the internal edge of the foramen here:

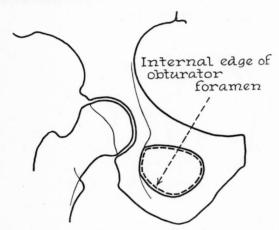

Internal edge of obturator foramen

for possible evidence of disruption. The presence of a fracture with any but the most minimal separation or displacement should make one think of the possibility of a secondary fracture like this:

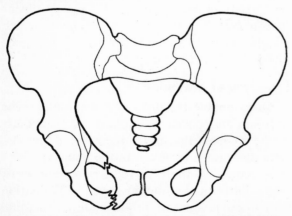

If no secondary lesion is seen, check the symphysis for possible disruption like this:

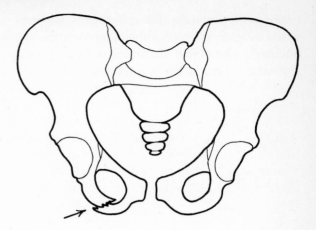

INFARCTS OF BONE

An infarct of bone—traumatic interruption of the blood supply with consequent aseptic necrosis—goes under a host of names. Some of the common ones are: Osgood-Schlatter's disease of the tibial tubercle, Kienböck's disease of the semilunar, Perthes' disease of the hip, Köhler's disease and probably osteochondritis dissecans.

Radiographically there is first a tendency toward resorption of the dead bone with formation of transparent areas where bone normally exists. Dead bone is more inclined to fragment or break up than is bone with adequate blood supply. Because of this, trabeculae may be fractured and crushed together into unusual-appearing masses of calcium-bearing tissue which is extremely difficult to revascularize. This impedes the formation of the "clear areas" mentioned above.

After revascularization has taken place, a dense matrix of new bone is laid down and the area becomes increasingly translucent to x-ray. The practitioner will do well to review a series of x-ray pictures showing this process as it actually progresses. Familiarity with it will save an occasional embarrassing mistake.

OSTEOMYELITIS

A discussion of the roentgenographic appearances of osteomyelitis in its various stages is a sufficiently broad subject to require an entire book for adequate coverage. Here we will list a few of the more important facts which may be of service in making a diagnosis. To begin with, one must realize that the x-ray has little or no utility in the diagnosis of osteomyelitis during the first 2 to 4 weeks of the disease. Only very rarely do films offer information upon which a diagnosis can be based until the disease is fully developed. This cannot be said too pointedly or too often. *Osteomyelitis in its early stages must be diagnosed clinically.*

Before attempting a description of roentgenographic evidence, a brief review of the usual course of the disease is necessary. *Staphylococcus aureus* is the most frequent infecting organism and usually spreads to the bone by the hematogenous route. Greatest incidence encompasses late childhood and early adolescence between the ages of 6 and 18. Males are more often affected.

The blood-borne infecting organism is usually arrested in the smaller vessels of bone in the metaphysis very close to the epiphyseal junction.

Pus is formed and tends to spread both toward the surface of the bone and toward the medullary cavity. The many theories as to the means by which the disease spreads need not be discussed here. The practitioner should remember that infection usually reaches the periosteal side of the bone first. Elevation of the periosteum by pus interferes with the cortical blood supply. Medullary infection may also offer such interference and there is a typical septic infarct of bone which then dies.

Since the usual infecting organism is not highly virulent and invasive, reparative processes are usually begun while the infection is still present.

The first finding by x-ray is usually seen when the infection reaches the surface of the bone. The periosteum is raised by the exudate and begins rapidly depositing new calcium, so that a linear opacity is formed running parallel with the edge of the bone but separated from it by a minute, clear area (black in the drawing) like this:

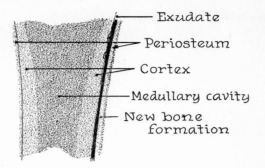

The clear area represents exudate and the newly calcified area represents formation of new bone by the periosteum.

Areas of rarefaction next appear in the shaft. There is no particular sign indicating that this rarefaction is due to infection nor is there any exact pattern which is followed. A typical picture may be diagramed, like this:

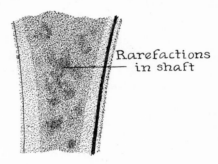

In addition to the above, the intense hyperemia that occurs during any infectious process gives the bone a fuzzy appearance. Anatomic details give me the impression of an early morning landscape seen through a fog.

As the infection passes its acute stage the hyperemia subsides and details become increasingly more visible. Cavities are easily made out and usually show more clearly defined edges.

Areas of dead bone give one the impression of somewhat greater density than surrounding normal bone and may be clearly set apart as obvious sequestra. This is what might be known, by definition only, as the subacute stage of osteomyelitis. As the disease continues to heal, there is a deposition of much new bone of firmer consistency than normal. Some bone defects remain and sequestra become even more sharply delineated. It it important to remember that these changes may be visible throughout the life of the patient. When such changes are found it indicates only that osteomyelitis has been present, not necessarily that the infection is currently active.

One thing that the practitioner must keep in mind is that this disease, like many others, has changed profoundly from the original classic descriptions owing to the advent of antibiotics. For example, if acute osteomyelitis is recognized early and treated effectively with antibiotics, *no bone changes recognizable by x-ray may take place.* In the adequately treated case, lack of x-ray evidence has no bearing whatsoever on the diagnosis. Permanent changes may be seen to a much lesser extent in early and adequately treated cases.

Osteomyelitis is somewhat infrequent but is a profitable disease to know and one to which the practitioner should devote some study. For an excellent chapter on the roentgenologic features of the disease, may I recommend the one in Volume IV of "A Textbook of X-ray Diagnosis" by Shanks and Kerley, published by W. B. Saunders Company.

THE ARTHRITIDES

This subject, as the one before, is of such magnitude that an entire book could be written on diagnosis by means of x-ray. Again, we shall attempt to hit the essential points which every practitioner must know and use if he proposes roentgenography in these cases.

May I say once more that extensive study is needed to become a competent x-ray diagnostician of the arthritides. These are beginner's facts only.

Rheumatoid Arthritis

Rheumatoid arthritis shows several characteristic signs which must be seen on the film to validate diagnosis. The first is osteoporosis. While this occurs both as a generalized and a local phenomenon, we practitioners are mainly interested in it from a local aspect. This is a picture of a normal interphalangeal joint and one with active rheumatoid arthritis.

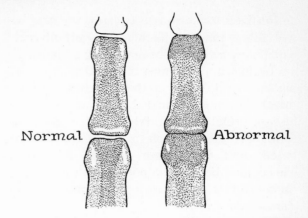

Normal   Abnormal

Notice particularly the rarefaction in the shafts of the bone on either side of the joints. Notice the tendency in this area for there to appear a uniform density rather than the normal different densities in differing areas.

Rheumatoid arthritis first shows an increase in joint space that is somewhat difficult to detect, for it is minor and a transient finding which disappears as the cartilage is destroyed. I've never done actual measurements on these joint spaces and confess freely that such widening of the joint space as I have seen was purely an impression gained from looking at the film rather than positive evidence from detailed measurement. As the disease progresses, the joint space is narrowed and finally, for all practical purposes, eliminated. This is an advanced rheumatoid arthritis in a metacarpophalangeal joint:

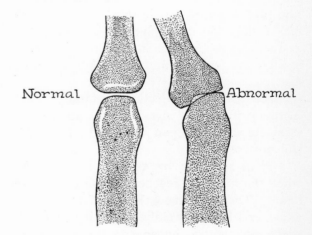

Normal   Abnormal

Finally there is bony ankylosis of the joint and a rather characteristic ulnar deviation of the fingers at the metacarpophalangeal joint.

Fusiform soft tissue swellings are seen on x-ray but are of little help because they are equally apparent to physical examination.

To me the most important point in the diagnosis of rheumatoid arthritis is the unusual rarefaction of bone near the joint surfaces.

Osteoarthritis

Osteoarthritis is seldom confused with the rheumatoid variety, although one should keep in mind that both may occur together in the same patient. Roentgenographically, one notices that the smooth curves found near joint margins gradually become more angular and that there is a deposition of new bone with spur formation.

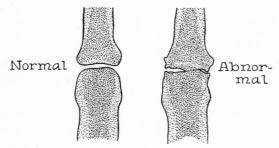

As the disease progresses the articular cartilage is destroyed and the opposing margins of the joint come closer together. The spurs formed at joint edges also draw closer together and may unite, forming a bony ridge between adjacent parts of the joint.

Small irregular areas of rarefaction may occur near the joint space, but because of their irregularity and the fact that they do not involve the entire area contiguous to joints, they should never be confused with the rarefaction of rheumatoid arthritis.

In the very late stages of the disease, spurs may break off to form loose bodies within the joint space.

THE SINUSES

Sinus roentgenography is not particularly difficult if several basic facts are kept in mind. Perhaps the most important thing is to remember *not* to compare the sinus on one side with its fellow on the other. This is standard practice in many forms of roentgenography but **can** be a serious error in attempting to diagnose sinus disease. The reason for the inadvisability of comparison is this: Any one sinus may at any time be infected and may undergo permanent change which will make it unsuitable for use as a comparative norm. An old chronic sinusitis on one side with bony change and hypertrophy of the membrane may, if used in comparison, completely mask the very slight haziness of an acutely infected sinus on the opposite side. To repeat: *Never* compare changes in sinuses bilaterally. Let **the** changes in each individual sinus speak for themselves.

The normal sinus has clear-cut, sharply defined bony walls and homogeneous air-bearing space through which the x-rays pass freely. Bony margins projected through the sinus area are seen sharply and clearly defined like this:

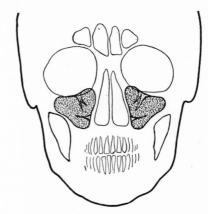

The first noticeable change is a slight haziness or opacity that tends to obscure bony details projected through the sinus, like this:

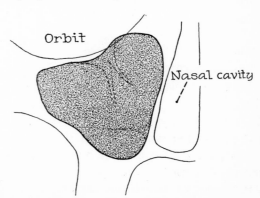

Following this period of haziness—which may be very short—there next is seen (in addition to the haziness) a slight thickening of the sinus membranes. This appears as a very fine line paralleling the bony sinus wall like this:

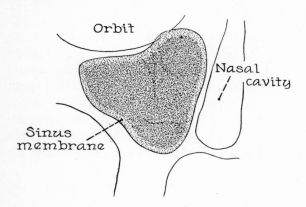

In the final stage the whole sinus becomes homogeneously cloudy and gives the impression of having been filled with an opaque substance. The best comparison I can offer is to say that it looks as if a pane of frosted glass had been placed in front of the sinus.

If the disease is allowed to progress, the bony walls lose their sharp outline and show some degree of resorption.

Chronic sinus disease shows a denser thickening of the nasal mucous membrane with a central area usually somewhat opaque but not as opaque as the membrane itself. The appearance is like this:

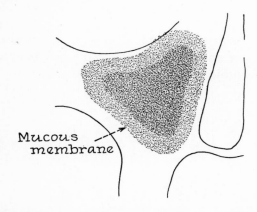

In addition, the bony walls of the sinus may show a sclerotic process which makes them appear more dense than normal.

Allergic disease of the sinuses cannot be readily differentiated by x-ray from infectious disease. There is one possible exception: The acute infection usually shows an even thickening of the mucous membrane, while the acute allergy may show concave bulges of the membrane into the sinus cavity, like this:

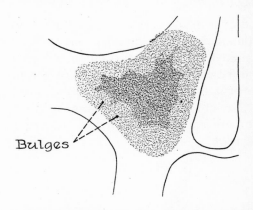

There may at times be reason to diagnose the presence or absence of fluid in these cavities. This diagnosis is in no way difficult to make. Simply tilt the head, leave it in a tilted position for five minutes and again x-ray. The fluid level will gradually assume the horizontal no matter what the position of the head.

THE SELLA TURCICA

Roentgenography of intracranial structures is far too complicated to be done by the practitioner except in the rarest instances. There are, however, occasions when information about the sella turcica can be helpful in deciding whether or not to refer a case for further studies. On that basis, we offer a brief description of roentgenography of the sella.

The normal sella may vary in antero-posterior measurement (at the upper margin) from 0.7 to 1.2 cm. and in depth from 0.5 to 1.1 cm. One may see from this variation that it is impossible to say in marginal cases whether the sella is actually enlarged or is a large normal.

The clinoid processes are located here:

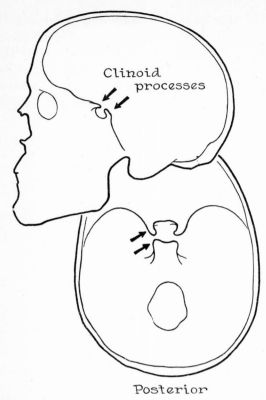

Clinoid processes

Posterior

Changes in their configuration and density are of great utility in diagnosing pathologic sellar alterations.

Of great importance is the fact that increase in intracranial pressure over a period of time will almost invariably produce changes in the sella that, while not diagnostic, certainly point to the presence of an intracranial lesion which may have a serious connotation.

When sellar enlargement is due to generalized rise in intracranial pressure, one finds an increased anteroposterior diameter without great increase in actual depth, like this:

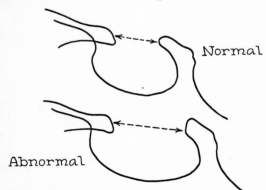

Normal

Abnormal

When, on the other hand, a pituitary growth is responsible for the enlargement, the increase is usually in both depth and anteroposterior diameter.

The earliest manifestation of increased intracranial pressure is thinning and decalcification of one or both the posterior clinoid processes, like this:

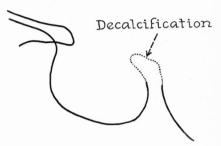

Decalcification

The anterior clinoids are not so likely to be affected. Many expert radiologists advise not to make any diagnostic pronouncements on the basis of changes in both the anterior clinoid processes. In the event that one is involved, the other being normal, one may infer the presence of an expanding lesion near the involved process.

THE HEART

Fluoroscopy of the heart is an extremely valuable office procedure which should be within the range of every practitioner. There has been some discussion of this subject in the section on Internal Medicine (see p. 293). Since there is in that section a discussion of the normal borders of the heart, I will not repeat the material here.

There are one or two aids to fluoroscopy of which one should be aware. Occasionally it is necessary to visualize the actual apex, which may be done through the gas bubble in the stomach. If the gas bubble is not large enough to allow free visualization, give the patient an effervescent drink, such as a Coca-Cola or a bottle of beer, wait 5 minutes and re-fluoroscope.

The point of opposite pulsation on the left

border of the heart must be identified accurately. As the ventricle assumes full systole, there is an expansion of the outflow tract so that the upper portion of the heart expands while the lower portion contracts as seen in the fluoroscope, which gives to the left border of the heart a rocking or walking-beam movement like this:

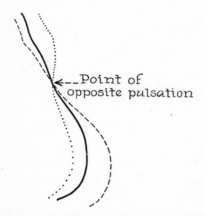

By careful visualization one may locate rather exactly this point of opposite pulsation, which will usually be about here:

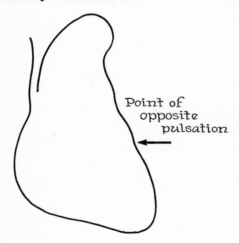

The Enlarged Heart

In discussing the enlarged heart, you will notice that I say nothing of formal measurements of heart size. Frankly, I distrust them and my impression has been borne out by many men who know far more of radiology than I. In many cases they may be quite accurate but there are too many possibilities for error. In the borderline case (the only case where measurements are needed) one will do better to base judgment on correspondence

between clinical findings and general impressions gained from x-ray than upon measurements which may be fallacious from the start.

Left ventricular enlargement in its earlier stages may show only an increased distance between the apex and the point of opposite pulsation, like this:

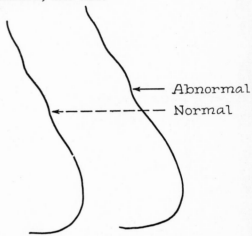

and a slight rounding of the upper portion of the left ventricle, like this:

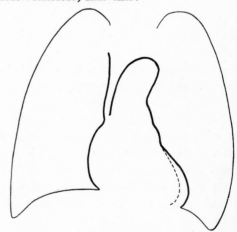

As the enlargement increases, the left side of the heart becomes globular and there is an obvious increase in the transverse diameter of the heart. The various common causes of enlargement and their x-ray signs are these:

Essential Hypertension. Aortic signs may be of more value than those available from the heart itself. These aortic signs will be discussed in the next section.

The first heart sign of consequence is usually a very minor left ventricular enlargement which occurs sooner or later in almost every case of hypertension. It has absolutely no prognostic significance, for the slight enlargement may be present for years without any other symptom. The pulmonary arteries next enlarge and the hilar areas of the lung show greatly increased vascular markings, like this:

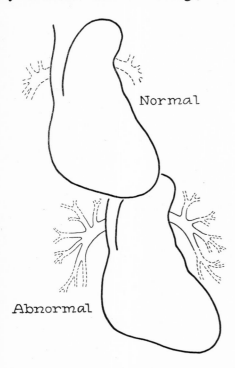

Normal

Abnormal

Such a finding indicates incipient failure in a large number of cases but it is not a 100 per cent reliable sign.

Cardiac Aneurysms. These are being recognized with increasing frequency following an acute coronary attack. The most common site is near the apex at or below the level of the diaphragm. The aneurysm may be identified on fluoroscopy by an absence of pulsation or even retraction over the aneurysmal site.

As the aneurysm ages, calcium may appear in its wall, which makes diagnosis somewhat easier.

Myocarditis

Myocarditis is seen principally in rheumatic fever and has one x-ray sign which is very valuable in diagnosis. It is the latent dilatation of Zdansky. Fluoroscope the patient in the upright position and use an ordinary ruler to measure the width of the heart shadow, like this:

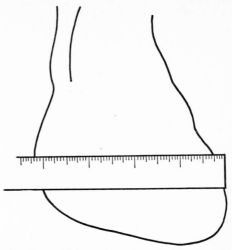

Now tilt the table so that the patient assumes a horizontal position and again fluoroscope the heart. Do not, of course, change the relative position of the screen or tube or the control factors of the x-ray while making this change in position. Notice again the relative width of the heart shadow. If it is markedly greater in one position than in the other, the latent dilatation sign is present. The amount of change apparently cannot be used to predict the amount of damage that has been done, but the sign has proven valuable in determining whether or not myocardial involvement is present.

The Aorta

The normal aortic knob is situated between the top of the second rib and the bottom of the second interspace, within this area:

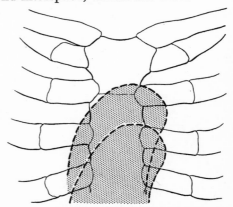

Alterations in position much greater than those shown are definite indicators of a pathologic condition. The width of the normal aorta may be established like this: On the ordinary chest film draw a line along the right border of the heart. Draw a second line along the vascular shadows like this:

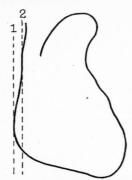

Normally the vascular shadows lie medial to the line along the right border of the heart. When they lie lateral to this line, enlargement is probable. This is not a reliable test when extraneous structures, such as tumors, push the vessel to one side.

If an aorta can be visualized at all in its descending portion, it usually shows its left border about ¼ inch lateral and parallel to the vertebral margin, like this:

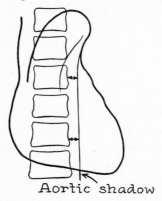

Aortic shadow

When this border shows as a convex shadow, a pathologic condition is indicated:

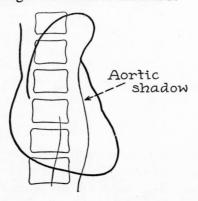

Aortic shadow

Hypertension is the most frequent cause of changes in the non-senile aorta. These changes are usually widening and elongation. In the right side of the chest the aortic shadow will usually show lateral to the edge of the heart, as mentioned above. The aortic knob on the left will be raised and will project outward into the lung field like this:

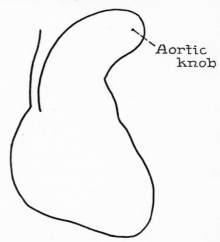

Aortic knob

When there is definite evidence of elongation of the aorta, give the patient a swallow of barium while you visualize the chest. As you know, the esophagus usually follows the course of the aorta and the barium will allow you to visualize this course accurately. In occasional cases, the changes will be as marked as this:

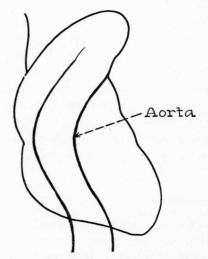

Aorta

It is wise to remember that such findings prove pathology but do not prove that the symptoms and pathology are related.

THE CHEST

The chest x-ray is becoming a standard part of the medical examination, and this is basically good so long as it does not substitute for medical skill on the part of the physician. Since few of us learn much of x-ray in medical school the practitioner should begin by having his interpretation of every film checked by a competent radiologist.

Fluoroscopic examination of the chest is probably the most valuable x-ray procedure available to the practitioner. The information gained is of great utility and the technique is easy to master in its simpler aspects. Begin by examination of the entire chest while the patient breathes normally. Notice the relative aeration of the various portions of the lung. Then ask the patient to sniff and notice whether the diaphragm moves freely and equally on either side.

Next instruct the patient to inhale and exhale deeply and once again check aeration of the lungs. Now, if there is any reason to do so, close the diaphragm down to a half inch horizontal slit and compare air entrance on either side of the chest by moving the slit up and down and asking the patient to take a deep breath each time you stop.

If there appears to be an area of density in the lungs, rotate the patient about his own axis while you observe apparent motion of the area. After very little practice, you will find yourself adept at judging the relative depth of the lesion from its movement.

The oblique and lateral positions are useful and should be used.

One very valuable trick in chest fluoroscopy I learned from a fine country practitioner, the elder Doctor Claude Bloss. The lobular structures of the lungs approximately parallel the ribs in their distribution. If you will have the patient take a step forward, then bend his shoulders backward to the table surface so that the ribs assume an approximately horizontal position, then fluoroscope, you will gain a great deal of practical information as to the location of various lesions. Do it like this:

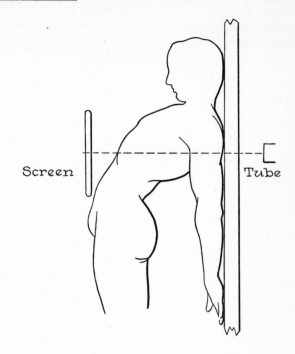

Screen   Tube

Pleurisy

Pleural thickening on the x-ray is, of course, familiar to us all. By no means, however, is it an early occurrence. It is probably best seen on the chest film taken tangentially to the area where physical signs and symptoms are most manifest, like this:

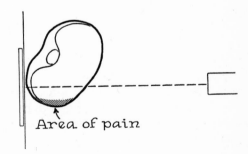

Area of pain

Pleurisy can be more accurately diagnosed by means of the fluoroscope. Look first for limitations of motion. Keep in mind that there may be little difference in the appearance of an old lesion and the new one except that motion is often much greater than would be expected in the old lesion, whereas in the new, active pleurisy is practically not seen without severe restriction of motion. Notice that normal lung markings usually change their relative positions with regard to ribs like this:

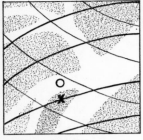 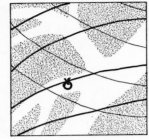

Expiration   Inspiration

In pleurisy they remain constant like this:

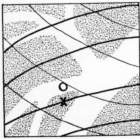 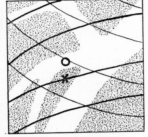

Expiration   Inspiration

Pneumonia

Differentiation of the pneumonias is definitely in the field of the experts. Even then, the technique is subject to surprising inaccuracies and final diagnosis should rest with the procedures of the bacteriology, fungus, or virus laboratory. Certain points are of interest. One, of course, is that consolidation clearly definable on the x-ray does not always occur with the inception of the illness. As much as 24 hours may elapse between onset of febrile symptoms and clear-cut pulmonary consolidation. Since we are using the x-ray much more frequently than in former years and since antibiotics tend to call an immediate halt to the progress of the disease, many of the "negative chests" we see in early febrile illnesses, particularly of children, may be actual cases of pneumonia examined before positive generalized consolidation and cured by antibiotics before actual full-scale development of the disease. An x-ray showing in-

creased hilar markings may be, but by no means necessarily is, a picture of early lobar pneumonia.

There may occasionally be confusion between an area of atelectasis and an area of pneumonic consolidation. You can tell the difference by adding approximately 15 KVP to the setting of your machine and again x-raying the chest. In this over-penetrated film, vascular markings will be seen in an area of pneumonia but are usually absent in atelectasis.

In the process of resolution there is a gradual diminution in opacity. The area that was involved, however, shows irregular cross striation with a series of fine lines, more marked near the periphery of the affected lobe, which are probably engorged lymphatics. These usually disappear within one to two weeks, leaving no signs of the previous pathologic process.

Bronchopneumonia is easy to diagnose if you keep one basic fact in mind. The principal structure involved is the lobule, which varies in size from 2 to 10 mm. With the surrounding zone of hyperemia which occurs, this casts an x-ray shadow varying from 0.5 to 2 cm. in diameter and roughly rounded in form. Any number of these lobules may be involved in bronchopneumonia but involvement tends to limit itself to one or more general areas.

The most common area is at the base of the lungs near the midline in a roughly triangular area with the base at the diaphragm and the apex at the hilus. By no means are all cases of bronchopneumonia seen in this area. Disease of the upper lobe which may closely simulate tuberculosis is a not infrequent occurrence, particularly in children.

Bronchiectasis

There is a great deal of discussion about the exact etiology of bronchiectasis and its proper classification. Since the arguments that are bound to arise in such a discussion are not as yet clarified, it would seem unlikely that any classification now proposed would turn out to be completely right; therefore, I shall confine this discussion to the primary signs upon x-ray of bronchiectasis of *all* types without discussion of the proposed individual classes. The first sign usually seen is an increased striation extending usually into the lower portions of the inferior lobes and originating at or just below the hilus, like this:

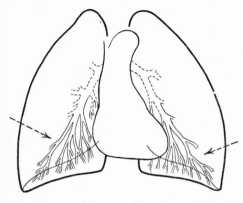

During an acute attack when the dilated bronchi are filled with pus, they may cast individual tubelike shadows that extend to and even below the leaves of the diaphragm in posterior lung tissue. They look like this:

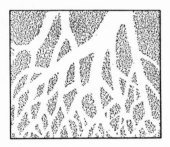

Such a picture, when accompanied by proper clinical findings and history, should be a positive indication for the performance of bronchography. Begin by anesthetizing the pharynx and trachea. Have the patient inspire strongly while you spray a solution of 2 per cent Pontocaine into the pharynx. Usually four to six deep breaths will suffice if the deep oropharynx is gently swabbed in addition. After this procedure has been completed, wait about 3 to 5 minutes and then drop iodized

oil, drop by drop, down either lateral groove in the pharynx like this:

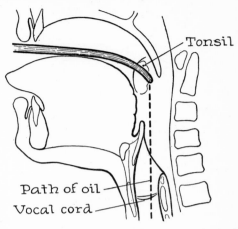

Have the patient lean slightly toward the side in which you wish the oil to gather. Ten cubic centimeters is an ample amount for one lung.

After the acquisition of some degree of skill you can easily carry out bronchography without local anesthesia and this is, of course, the method of choice.

Atelectasis

Massive collapse of the lung is seldom seen in the office because of its dramatic symptomatology. Minor atelectases are relatively common and usually quite easily identified by either film or fluoroscopy. There is increased density of the atelectatic area, varying from the most minor degrees of partial collapse, with barely discernible opacity, to complete collapse with solid homogeneous density throughout the involved area. If vascular markings are visible at all they will seem to be crowded together in comparison to the rest of the normal lung. There will be a zone of compensatory emphysema surrounding the atelectatic area and any adjacent interlobar fissures will be seen to be pulled in toward the collapsed portion.

Emphysema

The x-ray diagnosis of emphysema is an easy one to make. First look at the chest cavity as a whole. It will be increased in both transverse and A-P diameters. Now, notice the chest cage. It looks like this:

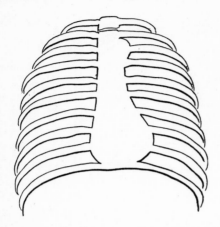

The ribs lie a great deal more horizontally than in the normal individual and the diaphragm seems lower than normal. Notice that the heart shadow looks small and narrow and particularly that air is visible beneath the heart in the P-A film.

Notice that the diaphragm is one or more interspaces lower than normal (usually one) and that the central portion has lost much of its doming and tends to be flat. There is, too, an increased translucency of the lungs with absence or great lightening of the usual peripheral markings and a relative increase in density of hilar markings.

Tuberculosis

The roentgenographic diagnosis of tuberculosis is in itself almost a specialty. For that very reason, it would be impossible to even scratch the surface of the information available in a volume such as this. Rather than attempting any discussion of the subject, I should like to mention the four most common types of early lesions as seen in adults, and their general appearance. When you see such a lesion, be sure to check the patient's sputum and to send a film to an expert roentgenologist for interpretation and advice.

1. A small segment of atelectasis with the base usually lying near the periphery and seldom wider than 2 cm. at the base is a common finding in early pulmonary tuberculosis. The segment is usually homogeneous and dense and, varying with the projection, may appear triangular (which is its actual shape) when viewed from its side and rectangular or square when viewed on end. Such a focus should call for immediate sputum studies.

2. *Assmann's Foci.* These are round, sharply defined homogeneous densities, usually found in the apices and varying in size from 0.5 to 3 cm. They may occur singly or in groups of as many as three or four. These foci are not very dense and must be looked for carefully on properly made films if diagnosis is to be accurate.

3. Small round foci varying from 1 to 5 mm. in diameter are frequently seen in groups, most often in the apices. They should be looked for especially in the peripheral portions of the lung and usually appear like this:

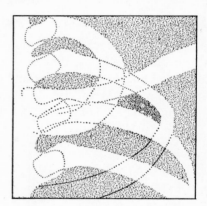

4. Soft, round lesions similar to those described in the paragraph above in the vicinity of what appear to be calcified previous lesions are most suspicious of activity. Such a picture might look like this:

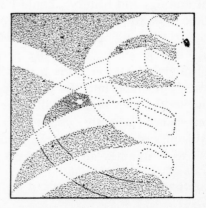

In more extensive disease the tuberculous "fan" is present. It consists of streaks passing out from the hilus to the area of the tuberculous lesion like this:

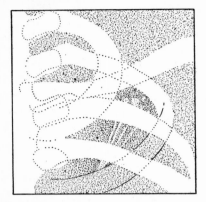

Hilar glands may also be enlarged.

I cannot repeat too often: In the presence of a suspicious lesion always confirm your impression either by finding a positive sputum or, in the absence of such findings, having your films read by an expert roentgenologist.

THE ABDOMEN

Herein lies one of the great questions in the field of radiology. Should the practitioner participate in abdominal radiology, which is difficult and requires both training and experience? My answer would be similar to the one I would give to most such problems in medicine. The answer is an unqualified "No" if the practitioner is not willing to devote himself to study, if he is not willing to benefit from friendly and helpful advice from experts in the field and if he is not willing to have his results consistently checked by those who know more about the work than he.

On the other hand, there is certainly no reason why any man of average intelligence cannot become a competent abdominal radiologist after some years of study (even the limited amount of study allowed in the busy program of the practitioner). The important thing, I think, is not to overestimate one's own capabilities and not to base the handling of patients on one's own roentgenologic interpretations until one has been checked a sufficient number of times to gain full confidence. Even after a half dozen years of constant radiologic experience, any case that offers the slightest obscurity should not be passed upon without the help of consultation with a well qualified radiologist.

By all means, learn all the radiology you can and do cautiously what you can, seeking often the advice and counsel of experts. One of the objections to medicine today is that it is an assembly line technique, involving a number of semiskilled workmen, each one of whom does a single job indifferently well. Some people would even go so far as to say that there are no doctors any more—just mechanics—which is, of course, wrong. We can all do our part in helping to overcome this by trying to learn as much as we can and doing as much as we can faithfully and well, thinking a bit more of working to help the patient and a bit less of the obvious loss of profit involved in taking the time to learn.

Cardiospasm

The principal difficulty in the diagnosis of cardiospasm is to eliminate more serious lesions such as carcinoma of the esophagus. Upon the administration of barium to a patient with cardiospasm, it is found that the barium is held up in its passage down the esophagus by a constricted band at approximately the diaphragmatic level. Normal esophageal peristalsis is not seen but unusual waves of contraction appear in its place, giving the esophagus occasionally a crenelated appearance. When the section in spasm is very short, one may be able to differentiate it from carcinoma by noticing its extreme flexibility and change of outline upon deep expiration and inspiration and upon change of position of the stomach. It may look like this:

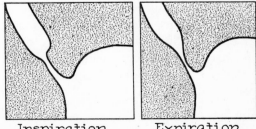

Inspiration   Expiration

Carcinoma shows mucosal irregularity in the stenosed portion, which is not seen in cardiospasm.   The two lesions look like this:

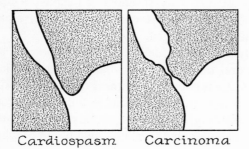

Cardiospasm   Carcinoma

If there is any question at all, the patient should be sent at once to an expert roentgenologist for further study.

The Stomach

The technique for performing barium examinations of the stomach has been briefly described on page 289.   Here, then, we will discuss the more prominent signs of certain common lesions.   By no means is this brief discussion sufficient for the seriousness of the problem but it will form a basis for review and a point of departure for more extensive reading.

Gastric Ulcer.   Gastric ulcer is the least common of the gastric-duodenal group, occurring approximately once to each four cases of duodenal ulceration.   It is usually found on the lesser curvature of the stomach or in the prepyloric area, practically never on the greater curvature.   It is, in fact, so rare on the greater curvature that a lesion so located is presumed to be cancer until positively proven not to be.

When a swallow or two of barium is first used to outline the mucosal pattern in the stomach, a bit of barium may enter the ulcer crater which usually will show then a typical spot of barium surrounded by a clear zone (which represents edematous mucosa at the ulcer edge).   Surrounding this there may be malformation of the rugae with radiation from the ulcer crater as spokes from the hub of a wheel.   This pattern is usually more pronounced in chronic ulceration.   In general, the appearance is like this:

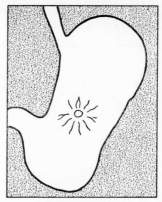

The crater in such an ulcer usually appears deceptively deep.

Pyloric ulcers have a somewhat different appearance because of the extensive musculature involved.   Deep craters are seldom formed and mucosal edema is very limited in extent and very frequently not appreciable at all.   In the pyloric area, then, one looks principally for a small niche or slit filled with barium and for obvious deformities of the canal without the grosser signs of ulcer that are seen elsewhere in the stomach.

Most important of the indirect signs indicating gastric ulcer is severe gastrospasm with hourglass or "B" form contracture like this:

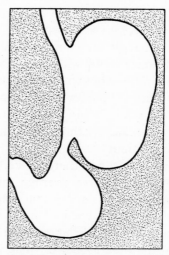

The contracture usually occurs at the level of or very slightly below an ulcer on the lesser curvature. Careful observation will allow one to determine that a contracture is all at the expense of the greater curvature, none occurring along the lesser curvature. It is particularly important to notice the difference between such contractures in the presence of ulcer and in the various malignant changes. The very basic description of the "B" form in ulcer and the "X" form in malignancy is in itself an excellent means of differentiation. The contracture in ulcer is nearly always in the middle third of the stomach and the upper portion may pouch downward so that there exists a dependent portion of the stomach below the outlet canal. Reexamination in several weeks after intensive use of the antispasmodics may be well worth while.

The presence of a 6 hour barium residue is some indication of functional or organic stenosis of the pylorus. Twelve hour residue is almost certain evidence of this. Using fluoroscopy, it is usually possible to demonstrate the presence of pyloric stenosis like this:

When the stomach becomes partially filled with barium there will begin a forceful hyperperistalsis consisting of deep and wide waves almost equal along both the greater and lesser curvatures. These peculiar waves seem to be an absolute characteristic of pyloric obstruction. Only a minor amount of barium is seen to enter the duodenum, considering the force applied from this peristaltic action.

Healing peptic ulcer shows filling up of the ulcer crater by granulation tissue from below and lessening of edema at the edge. In profile the ulcer changes from this:

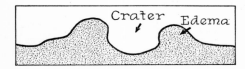

to this:

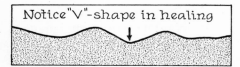

and finally to this:

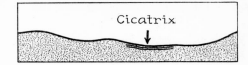

Gastric Carcinoma. Carcinoma of the stomach is one of the most difficult of all x-ray diagnoses to make. The practitioner should never pass final judgment on a lesion that he believes to be carcinoma. This is not to say that such lesions should not be examined for or should not be studied by the practitioner, but *without exception ALL cases* in which carcinoma is suspected should be referred to the radiologist for evaluation. It may at times be impossible to make diagnosis from one, two or even three radiologic examinations and one should not hesitate to urge repetition as often as necessary until final diagnosis is made.

The scirrhous growth is perhaps the most common and its characteristic is contracture of the lumen. It would be impossible to catalog all the possible defects that might result from luminal contractures, but there are certain characteristics that are very important. First, they are aperistaltic. The normal peristaltic wave of the stomach fades out completely as it impinges upon the carcinomatous area and recurs as the wave impulse reaches normal tissue once again.

These deformities remain relatively constant in shape. They do not have a boardlike rigidity but they are much more resistent to motion than typical gastric tissues. This may be quite apparent when pressure is applied over the barium-filled stomach. These defects usually present a relatively smooth or wavy outline in contradistinction to the spiky effect of intraluminal growths.

The mucosal patterns are altered by scirrhous infiltration but show no characteristic pattern. The normal mucosal relief appears to the edge of the lesion but it is there broken up into a totally disorganized and irregular pattern.

By far the most common site for such lesions is in the prepyloric area and a respectable number give the napkin-ring constricture appearance, which looks like this:

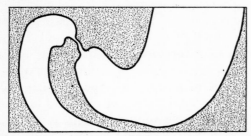

When the lesion is higher up, one frequently notices the characteristic "gaping pylorus of cancer." Apparently this is due to the lack of hydrochloric acid in the stomach. One notices the barium pass immediately through the stomach and flow quickly through the open pylorus and into the duodenum, a phenomenon which is common to all cases of low gastric acidity.

Scirrhous constrictures of the stomach are commonly of the "X" type, like this:

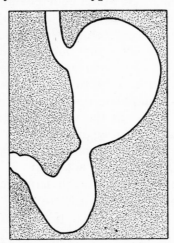

rather than the "B" type, which is seen in ulcer. In prepyloric constrictions the only evidence may be a long and irregular pyloric canal, the irregularity being much more marked than in stenotic varieties.

The medullary carcinoma is identified by the characteristic filling defect which occurs when tumor masses project into the lumen of the stomach. The signs mentioned for the scirrhous carcinoma are equally present in this type, to which the filling defect is added. The

filling defect often shows jagged edges like this:

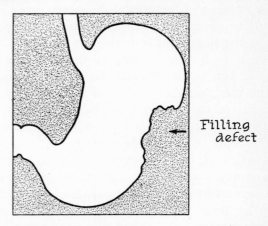

Diagnosis of this type of lesion is made relatively certain by several reexaminations at proper intervals, noting the constancy of the defect.

CARCINOMATOUS ULCER. There is a rule of thumb that any ulcer greater than 2.5 cm. in diameter shall be considered malignant until proven otherwise. While this rule is subject to many mistakes, according to the literature, the mistakes are on the conservative side and the rule remains valuable. In my own practice I can recall this having been wrong once. Kirkland's meniscus sign is of some value in malignant ulcers situated near the lesser curvature. It looks like this:

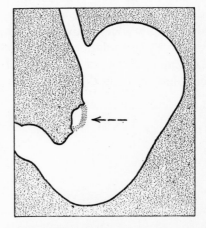

It is not an infallible sign of malignancy but at least points in the direction of malignant change. A therapeutic trial with repeated x-rays at appropriate intervals may be advisable in certain cases suspected of malignancy.

However, probably the best thing to do if an ulcer seems to stand the slightest chance of being malignant is to secure expert consultation at once and join your consultant in following the lesion until its nature is proved.

Duodenal Ulcer. Demonstration of ulcerous lesions in the duodenal cap is somewhat more difficult than the equivalent demonstration of stomach ulcers. Since one scarcely need worry about the presence of malignancy, the exact location and nature of the lesion is of more academic importance than the signs indicating its presence or absence.

The typical mucosal signs spoken of in gastric ulcer are equally prevalent in duodenal ulcer, but one must be a bit more careful in making certain that the signs are constant. The duodenal bulb is quite capable through normal peristaltic action of mimicking temporarily (for a few moments) typical ulcer patterns. Careful examination to make sure that the mucosal patterns are constant is a procedure worthy of use.

Edema, spasm, and permanent scarring will all produce deformities of the duodenal bulb. If seen in close profile, edema produces a gentle rounding like this:

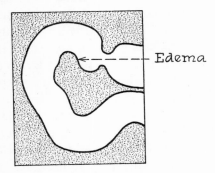

spasm a deeper but still rounded niche like this:

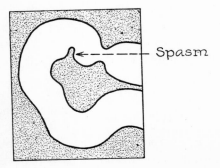

while scarring may take any form at all. Scarring, however, usually produces deformity of the entire bulb and remains relatively constant in a series of pictures taken some weeks or months apart.

In the stomach itself there may occur a hyperperistalsis in the presence of active duodenal ulcer along with increase in the thickness of gastric rugae along the greater curvature. These are by no means pathognomonic signs but do indicate the presence of irritation somewhere in the upper gastro-intestinal tract and should be a warning to look carefully for possible ulcerous processes.

Intestinal Obstructions

The widely distended arches of gut in a typical case of intestinal obstruction are easily diagnosed by means of x-ray. It is, however, important that one be able to distinguish different areas of the gut when distended so that an estimation of the location of the obstruction can be made. This sketch gives an idea of typical appearance.

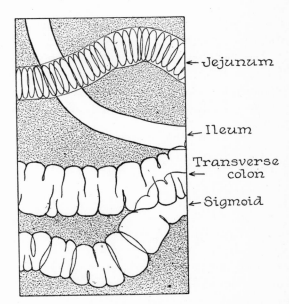

An erect picture of the paralytic ileus patient is diagnostic, the gas-filled coils of intestine rising through the top of the abdominal cavity, while the lower portion is occupied by a homogeneous opacity caused by free fluid in it.

The Colon

The technique for the barium enema is a rather exacting one and must be fulfilled accurately if best results are to be obtained. To begin with, the entire colon must be emptied without resort to irritating laxatives or fluids if one is to get proper delineation of structures in their normal form. Perhaps the best means of doing this is the repeated use of enemata of normal saline solution given until the return is clear.

The barium mixture for the enema should be inserted through a rectal tube while fluoroscopy is in progress. By injecting a small amount at a time one can visualize specific structures and also avoid discomfort to the patient. After examination of the colon fully distended with barium, one should then have the patient evacuate once or twice and reexamine, both by means of fluoroscopy and with films. One may now use the sigmoidoscope to fill the colon with air and recheck by means of fluoroscopy. In a significant number of cases too much barium will remain in the colon and the patient should be allowed to evacuate the air-barium mixture, after which still another insertion of air is made.

The irritable colon usually shows a relatively spastic, smooth-contoured descending segment in which haustrations, if visible at all, are very shallow. This is a typical appearance:

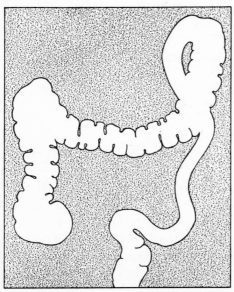

The irregular narrowing of the large bowel in cases of carcinoma is so entirely typical that it needs no discussion here. These are two such cases:

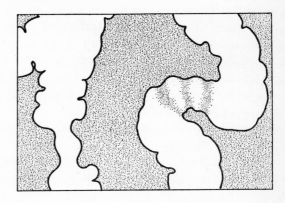

The Gallbladder

Methods for examining the gallbladder have been discussed on page 290. Here I should like to take a few paragraphs to discuss the validity of the method. It is quite true that a gallbladder that fills poorly, showing a faint shadow, and empties slowly has probably been the victim of disease. There is a great deal of argument pro and con but I believe that this is by no means an indication for surgery. X-rays of the gallbladder will show when the organ has been damaged, will show any obvious filling defects and will give some indication as to the extent of damage. By no means should they be used as a criterion for opening the peritoneal cavity.

I have seen several patients whose gallbladders refused to fill for me, and who were sent to an expert radiologist who reported no concentration of the dye in the gallbladder. If one is to believe the current textbooks, these people should have been operated on immediately for gallbladder disease. Instead, they were x-rayed again in one year and, if my memory serves me correctly, all but one showed complete normal filling of the gallbladder.

By no means is this intended to discredit cholecystography, for it is a fine test and one that we should certainly use. It is not, however, the complete answer for gallbladder diagnosis, as some would have us believe.

The Urinary Tract

Visualization of the kidneys and ureters by means of intravenously injected dye is a valuable procedure which is not difficult to do in the office. Usually Diodrast or Neo-Iopax are the drugs of choice for these injections and should be given slowly into the antecubital vein after a sensitivity test with diluted solution has been made intracutaneously.

Begin by having the patient take an enema at home before reporting to the office. Then give him a 0.5 cc. of Pitressin as soon as he reports and ask him to take a walk for 10 to 15 minutes. To accomplish one's own ends it is sometimes profitable to point out the advantages of solitude during this walk. When the patient returns and a preliminary film indicates that most of the gas has been expelled from the intestinal tract, injection of the dye is made. Compression of the ureters with soft felt pads like this:

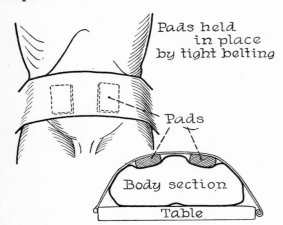

seems to have some advantage, as does 5 degree Trendelenburg position.

Films should be taken at 5, 15 and 25 minutes. Before each film is taken the ureteral compression should be released for at least 1 minute. The amount of dye and, therefore, the translucency in each kidney pelvis is roughly equivalent to kidney function. One may, therefore, assess with some accuracy the presence or absence of kidney disease from the intravenous pyelogram. You must, however, always remember that all glomeruli may not work at one time and unquestionably one kidney may have more glomerular units in function than the other, which would tend to give a denser shadow. Minor changes, then, should be confirmed by a repeat test, rather than being taken as gospel because of a single result.

◆ ◆ ◆

That finishes this book. As you know, the book is the principal means we in medicine use to pass our own ignorance down to succeeding generations. I rather hope this one will not be too great an offender. If you know a better way to do some of the things I have mentioned I would consider it a personal favor if you would write and tell me your method.

Again, I hope this work will be of real service to you.

PAUL WILLIAMSON, M.D.

INDEX